Julia Wedgwood,
The Unexpected Victorian

Julia Wedgwood, The Unexpected Victorian

The Life and Writing of a Remarkable Female Intellectual

Sue Brown

ANTHEM PRESS

Anthem Press
An imprint of Wimbledon Publishing Company
www.anthempress.com

This edition first published in UK and USA 2023
by ANTHEM PRESS
75–76 Blackfriars Road, London SE1 8HA, UK
or PO Box 9779, London SW19 7ZG, UK
and
244 Madison Ave #116, New York, NY 10016, USA

First published in the UK and USA by Anthem Press in 2022

Copyright © Sue Brown 2023

The author asserts the moral right to be identified as the author of this work.

All rights reserved. Without limiting the rights under copyright reserved above,
no part of this publication may be reproduced, stored or introduced into
a retrieval system, or transmitted, in any form or by any means
(electronic, mechanical, photocopying, recording or otherwise),
without the prior written permission of both the copyright
owner and the above publisher of this book.

British Library Cataloguing-in-Publication Data
A catalogue record for this book is available from the British Library.

Library of Congress Control Number: 2022950946

ISBN-13: 978-1-83998-859-2 (Pbk)
ISBN-10: 1-83998-859-2 (Pbk)

Cover image: Reproduced from B and H Wedgwood
"The Wedgwood Circle 1730-1897" (1980)

This title is also available as an ebook

CONTENTS

List of Illustrations	vii
Introduction: 'The Formidable Snowie'	1

Part I The Education of Julia Wedgwood

Chapter One	A Brilliant Child	7
Chapter Two	Mentors, Friends and Pioneers	27
Chapter Three	Waiting	47
Chapter Four	The Young Novelist	61

Part II Great Men and Female Friends

Chapter Five	The Promise of Darwinism	81
Chapter Six	'The Era of My Life'	99
Chapter Seven	A Woman's World	123
Chapter Eight	The Responsibilities of the Poet	139

Part III Becoming a Woman of Letters

Chapter Nine	Finding a Voice	157
Chapter Ten	A Forgotten Feminist	173
Chapter Eleven	Doubt and the Fallibility of Idols	195
Chapter Twelve	Domestic Contentment	211
Chapter Thirteen	Coming to Terms with Darwin and His Legacy	227

Part IV The 'Thoughtful Woman Par Excellence'

Chapter Fourteen	The Message of Julia Wedgwood	251
Chapter Fifteen	'The Old Order Changeth'	271
Chapter Sixteen	'A Satisfied Guest'	291

Acknowledgements 309
Notes 313
Bibliography 349
Index 365

ILLUSTRATIONS

1	Maer Hall	8
2	The infant Snow in her dancing frock	10
3	Snow's first letter	11
4	Snow and Mack as children	14
5	Silhouette of the young Fanny Wedgwood	16
6	Rachel Martineau's school in Liverpool	29
7	James Martineau in 1847	32
8	Frederick Denison Maurice	39
9	Francis Newman	43
10	Water colour of Milton Bryan	53
11	Victorian hearing devices	57
12	Mrs Gaskell in the early 1860s	58
13	Hensleigh Wedgwood	73
14	Fanny Wedgwood	77
15	Cartoon of Charles Darwin	85
16	Robert Browning in 1864	100
17	1 Cumberland Place, Regent's Park, London	103
18	Julia Wedgwood as a young woman	107
19	Water colour of the view across Regent's Park	116
20	Thomas Erskine of Linlathen	127
21	Emily Gurney	129
22	Harriet Martineau	159
23	Richard Holt Hutton	171
24	George Eliot in 1872	206
25	Effie Wedgwood	214
26	Water colour of sitting room at 1 Cumberland Place	216

27	Hope Wedgwood	218
28	31 Queen Anne Street and 56 George Street, London	222
29	Emma Darwin in old age	242
30	Water colour of the Grange, Cambridge	244
31	Julia Wedgwood at work	252
32	Hensleigh Wedgwood in the sitting room of Julia's home	273
33	Water colour of Idlerocks	275
34	Julia Wedgwood's water colour of 'Youth and Age'	292
35	The young E. M. Forster	294
36	Hope and Effie Wedgwood	306

INTRODUCTION:
'THE FORMIDABLE SNOWIE'

I first came across Julia Wedgwood in the selection of Browning's work and letters edited by Adam Roberts.[1] Her surname was, of course, familiar. I assumed that she was some comfortably off lady who happened to know Browning socially and was intimate enough with him to offer her thoughts on his work. But as I read on through their letters, I discovered someone quite different: clearly very intelligent and at ease with a surprising range of literary references from Homer to Shakespeare, Shelley to Newman, but also quirky and unpredictable. Sometimes her sentences were complex and confusing: at others she came up with striking aphorisms. Though her criticisms of Browning's work were remarkably fearless, she could be self-deprecatory too. Browning's reactions to her criticisms suggested he set great store by them. 'I take all your blame far better than other folks' praise', he wrote to her after she said that *The Ring and the Book* showed what he had lost as a poet through the death of his wife. He also valued her as a person. 'I lost something peculiar in you, which I shall not see replaced,' he told her when their friendship ended.[2] Roberts published more of Browning's correspondence with her than with anyone else, apart, of course, from Elizabeth Barrett. Who was this 'Dear Friend'? And what exactly was their relationship?

Turning to the Wedgwood family history written by Barbara and Hensleigh Wedgwood, I found a more orthodox figure: a woman keenly interested in the history of her family, brave and gifted, dutiful and only partly fulfilled – in other words, yet another example of the stereotypical middle-class Victorian spinster author. Following up on the hundreds of her letters in the Wedgwood Archive at Barlaston, the variety of her connections surprised me: not only Browning but her uncle, Charles Darwin, Harriet Martineau, Elizabeth Gaskell, Carlyle, Ruskin, George Eliot, F. D. Maurice, most of the leading feminists, and, in her later years, E. M. Forster. Reading these letters I was also struck by the contradictory elements in her character. She could be morose but funny, acerbic as well as compassionate, both needy and generous and high-minded yet commonsensical.

When her correspondence with Browning was published in a slackly edited collection in 1935, most of the reviewers dismissed her, wondering what on earth Browning could have seen in this sententious spinster with her firm ideas of the poet's responsibilities. The only reviewer who had known her, E. M. Forster, offered a very different image. He leapt to her defence, resisting any notion that she was the 'bleak' 'portentous female' her critics had assumed. 'She was not like that at all,' he protested, 'she was polite and cordial, extremely modest about her work and [what might most have surprised them] decidedly gay.' Above all, she had 'fine qualities of the heart as well as the head and they ought to be recorded'.[3]

Julia had known Morgan Forster since he was a baby, wryly describing him at the age of 15 months as this 'dainty little waxwork doll' who was 'very fond of kissing'. She kept an eye on the fatherless child as he grew up, worrying about the 'oppressive' effect of the adoring circle of widowed and single women who surrounded him, especially his great aunt, Marianne Thornton, an able, energetic woman whose influence was almost entirely confined within her family.[4] She sensed early on (or so she later said) that he was destined for a literary career. In his rather aimless years in London after university, she co-opted him to assist her in the revision of what she saw as her major work, *The Moral Ideal*. Forster thoroughly enjoyed 'devilling' for her while for Julia he was her connection with the younger generation she wanted to reach through her writings. The relationship was not all one way, however. When he emerged as a novelist, Julia felt a strong sense of responsibility to pass on to him what she had learned from her own writing career. She invited him for tea soon after his first novel, *Where Angels Fear to Tread*, was published, characteristically feeling emboldened to 'peck fearlessly' by the fact that his reviews had mostly been favourable.

Her main concern was that his novel lacked a consistent tone. To make her point she went back to a conversation at Mrs Gaskell's in the 1850s with Catherine Winkworth, Charlotte Bronte's friend, about the ambivalent ending of *Villette*. Winkworth had assumed from the melancholy tone of the novel that Paul Emmanuel would not return. Bronte confirmed that her friend had spotted what the reviewers failed to see. She had written it in the way she did to spare her father who liked happy endings. If this was drawing Forster into a distinguished literary tradition that Julia had known first-hand, her next comment came closer to the contemporary concerns of Bloomsbury: she wanted more sexual passion in his novel. 'Impropriety should be worthwhile,' she told him, suggesting something Forster was more at ease with in life than his novels. She also urged him to fall in love before he wrote another novel. To her amusement he assured her that he already had 'with Hamlet'.[5] This was hardly the conversation that Julia's critics in the 1930s would have expected in their eagerness to expose the dreary repressiveness of their Victorian forebears.

As Forster knew, however, Julia could attract widely divergent views in her own lifetime and after. When he wrote his biography of Marianne Thornton, he included a letter from her dismissing 'Snow' (her family nickname) as 'a dreadful bore' discussing 'fate and free will, the plurality of worlds, objective and subjective influences, till she drives me wild'. (Talking about religion was never Thornton's favourite subject.) But Forster also slipped in a letter from Maimie Aylward, the widow of one of Thornton's favourite nephews, advising a friend to 'look out for Snow Wedgwood. She may prove an angel in the dark.'[6]

The disagreements continue. Two of Darwin's biographers, Adrian Desmond and Desmond Moore, conclude that he saw his niece as 'an opinionated bore', while another, Janet Browne, says he treated her like a surrogate child.[7] Jenny Uglow has written more than once about her anger at reading Julia's criticisms of Mrs Gaskell and reacted by describing her as manipulative, self-dramatizing and callous as well as dismissing her 'dark, spiky' handwriting (not something I noticed). José Harris, on the other hand, sees her as a major figure second only to George Eliot in her ability to deal with 'masculine' subjects.[8]

Julia Wedgwood does not fit easily into ready-made categories either as a person or as a writer. In both she was impulsive. As Forster remembered, she was always encouraging her coachman to drive faster.[9] She took the initiative in starting – and ending – the brief but intense relationship with Browning that some thought might have ended in marriage. In her work she chose the subjects that interested her, venturing without hesitation into the reserved territory of the late-Victorian Man of Letters. In response to her father's objections, she abandoned a successful early career as a romantic novelist but then, in spite of his continuing reservations, turned to writing about the origins of language, Greek Classical thought, Darwinism, Augustinian theology, English mysticism, Lucretius, Virgil, Philo and Origen, German Biblical criticism, contemporary novels and much more. She had a far less acute sense than most of her contemporaries of gender difference and what was and was not permissible for the female writer. Temperamentally, she had always felt different. Modest though she was in many ways, she refused to conceal her gifts or downplay her unusual learning whatever the discomfort this caused in her family.

A key part of her sense of being different came from her deafness, an inherited weakness exacerbated by an attack of viral meningitis in her teens. This limited her social interactions. Like Harriet Martineau, who knew and admired Julia from the time she and Malthus dandled her on their knees as a baby, most of her conversations took place through an ear trumpet (though Browning with his loud, high-pitched voice was probably an exception). As a result, though she collaborated with Barbara Bodichon, Emily Davies, Josephine Butler, Emily Shirreff, Elizabeth Garrett Anderson and many other leading feminists, she did not join networks like the Kensington Society or the Langham Place group. Nor, unlike her great friend, Frances Power Cobbe, did she campaign in public. She made her mark instead through articles and letters in upmarket periodicals including the *Spectator* and *Contemporary Review*, a pamphlet for the London National Society for Women's Suffrage and the key essay in an important collection Butler edited in 1869 *Woman's Work and Woman's Culture*. When Cobbe retired to Wales in 1891, the *Glasgow Herald* picked out Julia as the one who had taken her place as 'the thoughtful woman *par excellence*' (italics added).[10]

Unlike Cobbe and, indeed, Martineau, Julia never thought of writing her autobiography and resisted when friends pressed her to publish her lengthy correspondence with her closest woman friend, Emily Gurney. But she went to some trouble to compile a fine volume of family history for her niece and arranged her own papers with care, destroying some letters, annotating others and tucking away revealing snippets in obscure piles. Because of her deafness, letter writing was particularly important to her.

As her friend Harold Herford wrote, 'She moved in this medium with spontaneous zest,' finding in it 'a kind of liberation'.[11] She dashed her letters off sitting up in bed after her early morning devotions as she waited for her maid to bring up the hot water; in pencil, in crowded trains where deafness protected her from interruption; in station waiting rooms with a glass of brandy and water to fortify her; after church on dull Sunday afternoons when staying with elderly relatives; or as she sat at her desk in the Reading Room of the British Museum waiting for her books to be delivered.

Her letters contain a mix of keen social observation, anguished confessional self-examination and gentle self-mockery, intellectual speculation, natural description and religious philosophizing. They can be funny too. She scribbles out accounts of her encounters with Darwin, Eliot, Carlyle, Gaskell, Maurice and many others, though never, except in the earliest days of their friendship, with Browning. She writes of her severe depressions, paralyzing migraines and religious doubts, but also about the marriages, engagements, friendships and fallings-out in her extensive family circle with some acerbic comments on the vanities of great men and even less charitable accounts of their wives. And she tries out some of the ideas that would underlie her two major books *The Moral Ideal* and *The Message of Israel*. Even those in the family who found her work challenging enjoyed her letters.

Julia had firm views on writing biography. In the furore over the posthumous publication of Carlyle's intimate 'Confessions', she wrote in the *Spectator*: 'There are few lives in which the endeavor to tell all that can be told will result in a true picture of the character portrayed [...] the intimate recesses of a life may be left in shadow, without any injury to the picture of that portion with which alone the public has any concern.'[12] Now the 'intimate recesses' have become at least as interesting as the public spaces, as have the connections between the two. As Barbara Caine has written, feminist biography seeks to discover not just what its subjects did but also 'how they felt about their private and familial life – [and] what it cost them to follow their own path'.[13] Because so much of Julia's public and private writing survives, making that connection is much easier in her case than in many others, and it is perhaps surprising that this has not previously been attempted.

E. M. Forster nicely combined the mix of regard and affection he always felt for Julia Wedgwood in his description of her as 'the formidable Snowie'.[14] This biography sets out to explore 'the fine qualities of the heart as well as the head' that he celebrated and wanted to see preserved.

Part I

The Education of Julia Wedgwood

Chapter One

A BRILLIANT CHILD

Julia Wedgwood was the great granddaughter of the famous potter Josiah Wedgwood, a man she did not come to appreciate fully until late in her life. As a writer she was more drawn to the romantic reputation of her Scottish maternal grandfather, Sir James Mackintosh, who died shortly before she was born. Just as her mother enjoyed being described as his daughter, so Julia, in turn, delighted in being identified as his granddaughter. Mackintosh, who came of modest Highland stock, made his early way in London as a lawyer before becoming famous in 1791 for his *Vindiciae Gallicae*, a moderate defence of the early stages of the French Revolution. He went on to serve as a Recorder in Bombay but was happier back in England, where the East India Company appointed him to lecture on law and politics alongside Thomas Malthus. From 1818 until his death, he served as an MP for Knaresborough, a seat in the gift of the Duke of Devonshire. His parliamentary eloquence earned him the title of 'The Whig Cicero', but with the Whigs out of office until 1830, he had a long wait for the secure, well-paid government place he needed to enable him to complete his planned masterpiece, the 'History of Great Britain from the Revolution of 1688 to the French Revolution in 1793'. Though everyone thought him a genius, Mackintosh's achievements never quite equalled his reputation. As a talker, however, he was unmatched. Charles Darwin remembered him as 'the best conversar' he ever knew, often though his fondness for conversation at breakfast held him back from getting down to work.[1]

They first met at Maer Hall in the village of Maer in Staffordshire, the home of Josiah Wedgwood's second son, Jos, who had been landed with the job of managing the family business. Jos's wife, Bessie, was Mackintosh's sister-in-law through his marriage to Kitty Allen, Bessie's sister. Disentangling the family trees of the Wedgwoods, Darwins and Allens is an arduous task as they intermarried so frequently. Just as Darwin married his cousin, Emma Wedgwood, so too his sister, Caroline, married Emma's oldest brother, Josiah, while another of her brothers, Harry, married a Wedgwood cousin, Jessie. Rev. Charles Langton, though outside the family, went one better, marrying first Emma's older sister, Charlotte Wedgwood, and after her death, Darwin's sister, Catherine, while both Jos and his elder brother, John, chose one of the nine brilliant Allen sisters, as did Mackintosh for his second marriage. Maer Hall was the place where the Wedgwoods, Darwins and Allens got together in the summer and at holiday times. Though they delighted in their own company, they also welcomed neighbours like the Tollets and the Caldwells, including the prolific novelist, Ann Marsh, who would later take a particular interest in the young Julia.

Maer, or 'Bliss Hall' as Darwin called it,[2] was where Julia's father, Hensleigh, fell in love with Mackintosh's favourite child, Fanny, in 1827. Their courtship was protracted. Though a graduate of Trinity College, Cambridge, with a first in maths and a college fellowship,

Figure 1 Maer Hall, Staffordshire, and behind it the church where Charles and Emma Darwin were married

Hensleigh was slow to establish himself as a lawyer in London.[3] Nor did Fanny want to give up her freedom. She went with her father on his research trips for his 'History'; she presided at his dinner table where William Wilberforce was a frequent guest; she sat in the Ventilator, the tiny space reserved for ladies above the House of Commons chamber, listening to debates; and, whenever she could, she attended the opera, sometimes in the company of Emma Wedgwood. Maria Edgeworth found her 'one of the best informed and most unaffected girls I ever knew'.[4] Some in the family, like her half-sister, Mary Rich, thought Fanny could do better than Hensleigh Wedgwood and tried to keep him away. He persisted, offering to make a home for Sir James, whose unhappy second wife had died in May 1830; his son, Robert; and the widowed Rich, if only Mackintosh could procure a job for him that enabled him to marry Fanny. In the autumn of 1831, having used up most of his political credit securing places for himself, his son and his son-in-law, Mackintosh finally got a police magistracy at Bow Street for Hensleigh. He and Fanny married on 2 January 1832.

The early months of their marriage were dominated by the excitements of the final stages of the Great Reform Bill. At one of the many Whig dinners, Mackintosh choked on a chicken bone. A botched operation led to his slow decline. He died on 30 May, just five days before the Reform Act was passed, leaving only £863 to be shared amongst his five children. His books, however, proved more valuable and eventually sold for £1,800. The task of sorting them fell to Fanny, about whom Mackintosh wrote with typical grandiosity in his will: 'My most deserving children will not be surprised or displeased at a preference for my dear Daughter Frances which has lasted for twenty six years.'[5] While his only son inherited his Cicero, Fanny was given the two books he most cherished, Milton and

Francis Bacon, who would also be precious to Julia. She was conceived as the newly-weds nursed the dying Mackintosh. Whatever her doubts about marrying, Fanny was grateful for her husband's 'unwearying and tender care and affection' at this painful time.[6] After Mackintosh's death, they moved from Langham Place back to Clapham. Mary Rich went with them.

Frances Julia Wedgwood was born on 3 February 1833 at Lark Hill Lane in Clapham. Frances, her mother's name, she never used. There were already two Franceses or Fannys in the Wedgwood family and a third, Hensleigh's sister, had recently died. Julia was the name she would choose as a writer. Her intimates, however, always called her 'Snow', supposedly because she had been born in a violent snowstorm. The true explanation was more romantic. On the day of her birth, her father had found an early clump of snowdrops in the garden and brought them to put beside her on her mother's pillow. Both Hensleigh and his sister Emma were soon describing the baby as 'Snowdrop'.[7]

Though not quite the first of the new generation – her cousin, Godfrey, the eldest child of Hensleigh's brother Frank and his wife, Fanny, preceded her by two weeks – Snow attracted attention from the beginning. Her mother described her to her mother-in-law, 'She is a very tiny little thing [...] but words cannot tell how lovely I think her [...] [her eyes] are a dark blue, & so bright that I was a long time making out the colour & her hair (what there is of it) a bright golden colour with her head very like Hensleigh's shape.' Hensleigh, conforming to the views of his class and time, insisted that his wife feed her baby: 'he pretends he shall not care half so much otherwise for our Snowdrop'.[8] (A book he later published on metaphysics managed to include a surprising number of descriptions of breastfeeding.) They showed her off to friends like Ras Darwin, Charles Darwin's older brother and Hensleigh's college contemporary, Harriet Martineau and Thomas Malthus bringing the 5-months-old child down after dinner. Martineau set her on her feet and pretended to get her dancing; Malthus, much kinder in person than in his theories, affectionately stroked her cheeks.[9]

Snow was precocious. At the age of 1, she was standing and walking and looking longingly at the piano Bessie and Jos had sent as a gift.[10] Hensleigh's eldest sister, Elizabeth, who took a particular interest in the infant, began a book of her sayings and doings. Though the green leather-bound volume of 'Snowiana' has not survived, several of the letters about Snow intended for it do. Here, for example, Elizabeth writes to her mother about the 2-year-old who constantly interrupts her letter-writing 'romancing on, and acting, and speechifying. [...] I have just made out "a large wind blew the little wind down" with a very important shake of the head'. Fanny's great friend, Marianne Thornton, had given Snow a pink silk frock, and she twirled happily in front of the delighted adults: 'she dances so gracefully and unconsciously of all our looking and laughing'.[11]

The act of writing always fascinated Snow. Until she learnt to manage it herself, she competed for the attention of grown-ups absorbed in the act. Her mother was obliged to abandon a letter to Emma Wedgwood to lift Snow up: 'I had her sitting on my lap quite still with her eyes staring open – luckily the moon was shining which soothed her immediately and she began in a rapture crying out – the Moon how bright – so high – Bro [her younger brother] can't reach it – Mum can't each it – Ras [Darwin] can't each' shaking her head mournfully every time.' (Tellingly, her father does not appear in this litany of

Figure 2 Snow in her dancing frock possibly drawn by Ras Darwin. Fanny Wedgwood Album in the possession of Janet and Alan Wedgwood.

the important people in her life.) Her 'sentences are wonderfully filled up now with all the prepositions & conjunctions', Fanny noted when Snow was just 2. 'I could tell many clever things if she wd let me have time to write but she won't & is very panicy.'[12] Two years later she commandeered another letter her mother was writing to Emma and turned it into what was probably her first. In carefully joined-up writing, begun in pen and ink and

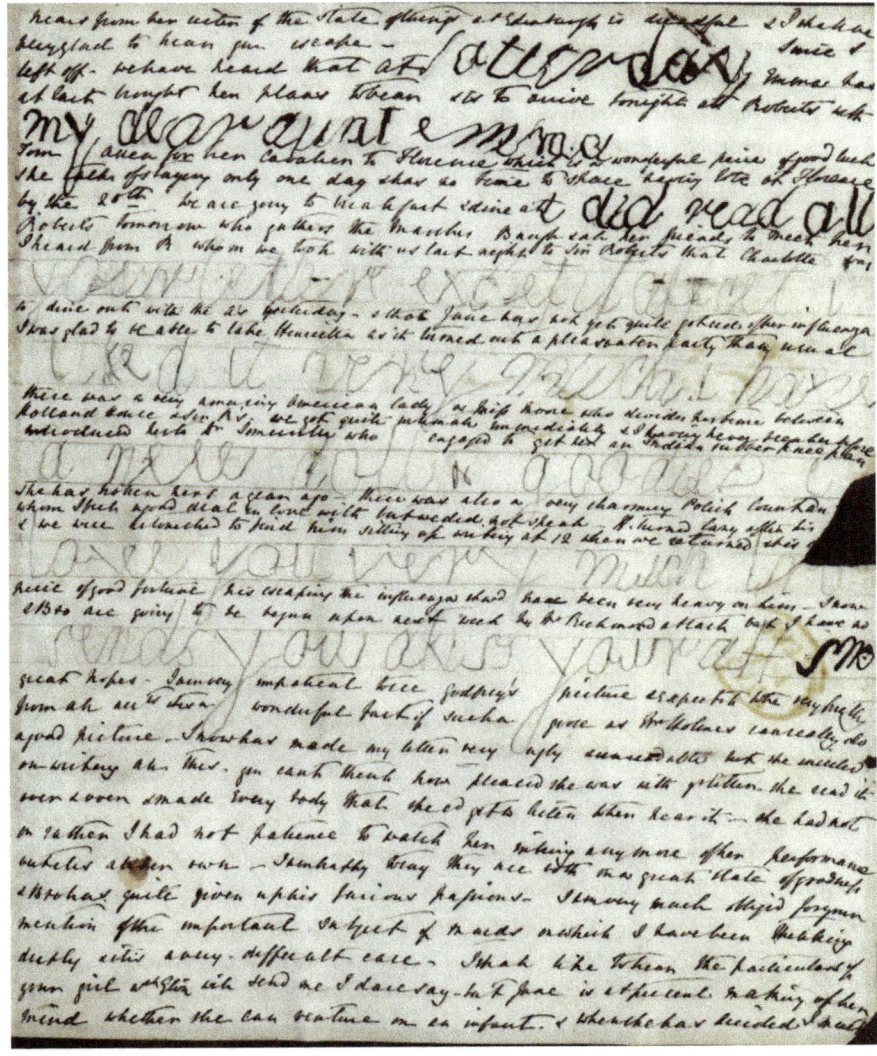

Figure 3 Snow's first letter, inserted into one from Fanny Wedgwood to Emma Wedgwood, 28 January 1837. Courtesy of the V&A Wedgwood Collection.

continued in pencil, she says the conventional things an affectionate niece should say to a favourite aunt but rarely manages at the age of 3.[13]

When she was 6, she dictated a poem to her mother as she was getting ready for bed:

In the month of May
When the fields look gay,
Nothing seemed to have sorrow;
Oh, wait till tomorrow
When there will come a wintry day

That will drive away this joyful May.
We, like the flowers, fade away
For we are made of dust and clay.
And then there comes a wintry blast
Which drives them away with the wind and the past.
But for the saints there's another May
Which is a longer happier day,
Where they never say good-night,
Always peace and never fight,
With crowns of glory on their heads
There they never rest on their beds.

Aunt Elizabeth thought these 'more than mere parrot verses of a child with a good memory' and liked the implied protest in the last line against going to bed.[14] Now, apart from its length and facility, it is the poem's gloomy religiosity and fearful sense of transience that are most striking, evidence of the anxious morbidity Snow absorbed from her children's books of religious instruction.[15]

She could be worldly too. Her great-aunt Fanny Allen watched her having her hair curled at Maer when she was 2. She asked her what Mary Rich might say about this vanity. Snow 'acted with her hands out and strong emphasis, "Oh! Snigs Snogs, how elegant you are!"'[16] A year later she entranced the still unmarried Darwin, clambering up on his knees at a tea party to flirt with him.[17] From the age of 4 she was attending 'balls' and children's parties, getting so excited that her mother took Anne Marsh's advice and kept her at home in the winter of 1839.[18]

At Maer, Elizabeth wrote fondly of her gifted niece: 'her curious, romantic drawings – her sensitive nature – she is forever talking to herself and making up stories which are as good as the stories of most grown-ups – so trusting and affectionate – something in Snow's thoughtful manner which promises an exceptional woman – Snow's a most entertaining child, always smiling and happy'.[19]

In her self-absorption and delight in the attentions of her admirers, she can come across as an only child. In practice, she was quickly obliged to share her parents' love. Their second child, a son, was born when she was 15 months old, with five more children, one of whom died, following in regular succession up to 1844, giving her two more brothers, Erny and Alfred, and two sisters, Effie and Hope, the last child who was 11 years younger. The extended Victorian family presented lots of opportunities for grouping, especially in pairs, and for defensive and offensive alliances amongst siblings. Snow paired off with the brother nearest to her in age. Born in May 1834 and christened James Mackintosh in honour of his grandfather, he soon acquired the nicknames 'Mack' or 'Bro'. As young children they were inseparable, helping their father in the garden, entertaining friends and commenting solemnly on the absence of 'Mum' from the breakfast table when Fanny was off on one of her many visits.[20]

Mack was a typical young Wedgwood: boisterous, good-humoured, self-confident and, as the eldest son, the apple of his mother's eye. Though his arrival undermined Snow's pre-eminence as the first born, she accepted from an early age that he would dominate.

More gifted than Mack, she was not resentful. Instead, she clung to him, running in and out of his sickroom when he was ill or in floods of tears at the end of a day when they had fallen out. She begged for a kiss from him before she went to bed. 'Is your face wet with tears?' he asked with the caution of a true Wedgwood before gingerly complying.[21]

Mack's arrival reminded Harriet Martineau of her own relationship with her younger brother, James, 'who has certainly filled the largest space in the life of my affections of any person whatever'. 'I was truly happy to hear yesterday of the birth of your boy,' she wrote to Fanny '& particularly that it is a boy. I have reason to know the blessedness and friendship between a sister and brother so nearly of an age.'[22] Ultimately, her relationship with her brother would end in a bitter public break-up and mutual estrangement. Snow and Mack's closeness subsided more gradually as he moved out into the world. Nor did Snow feel Elizabeth Barrett's compulsion to dominate the nursery as the eldest child. That came later. Instead she copied rather than competed with her brother. Ras Darwin, who studied the Hensleigh Wedgwood children as closely as anyone, was concerned. 'Mind and cure Snow of imitating Bro,' he warned Fanny, 'or she will become just like him and be ruined.'[23]

She tried to imitate her mother too. When Fanny's third child arrived, a sickly infant who would soon die, Mack happily looked in to 'grin' at mother and baby. Snow kept her distance, absorbed in following what she saw her mother and the nurse do as she bathed and cared for her doll but avoided acknowledging her new brother. When Fanny asked her and Mack to suggest names for the baby, she came up with 'Louisa' and 'Dalia'.[24] Did she resent the arrival of another boy or long for a sister she could take under her wing? Or was the inappropriate name her protest against the disruption of the happy but sufficient quartet that already existed with Mack and her parents?

Her reaction to the naming of Miles is an early indication of a mystification about gender that persisted throughout her life. Even in her 70s she still puzzled over it, finding it hard to put her finger on the innately distinguishing qualities between men and women.[25] The portrait of Snow and Bro commissioned from James Holmes by Fanny and Hensleigh, after George Richmond said he was too busy, shows two graceful young children full of smiles and dimples, both with long curls and in frilly frocks and satin pumps. Of the two, Bro looks the more feminine. Whatever appearances suggested, however, it was clear from their father's attitude and mother's devotion that the weight of family expectation rested on Mack, not Snow.

As her preoccupation with her surrogate baby when her mother was nursing Miles suggests, Snow was not only a needy child but also keen to be needed herself. But Fanny had many calls on her time. Hensleigh was often ill and required nursing, as did their close friend Ras Darwin. Her children too had more than their fair share of childhood illnesses. And Fanny was also keen to maintain the place she had had as Sir James Mackintosh's daughter in the London literary and political world. She was a guest at Samuel Rogers's select breakfasts for the literati, she attended Thomas Carlyle's lectures and became a good friend of both Thomas and Jane, and she and Hensleigh hosted regular dinner parties. They attracted not only the Carlyles and distant cousins like Sydney Smith and Anne Marsh but also literary lions like Richard Monckton Milnes and Macaulay or Mazzini, the émigré Italian leader. Fanny also helped organize charity bazaars, making

Figure 4 Snow and Bro painted as children by James Holmes

the familiar progression from the anti-slavery cause to Italian unification and women's higher education.

Julia wrote that her mother 'had a great dread of emotion which increased with time'.[26] That may have been true, at least by comparison with Julia's own supercharged intensity. What struck most people, however, was Fanny's solicitude for the sick and elderly and her tenderness as a nurse. All Victorian families were prone to bouts of illness: their consequences in incapacitation or unexpected deaths could be catastrophic. Fanny was always the first to respond when one of the great aunts or her own children fell sick. In 1836 Snow and Mack as well as the baby had whooping cough. Miles died of it. A year later at Maer they were both ill again, with Fanny spending sleepless nights at their bedsides. At Christmas 1843 Snow had measles, and 10 years later the Darwin children caught mumps from their Hensleigh Wedgwood cousins.[27] Julia's illnesses in her teens were yet more serious.

Fanny's reputation in the family for nursing skills made her indispensable to the Darwins in the greatest crisis of their married life. In April 1851 their daughter, Annie, fell dangerously ill in Malvern. The heavily pregnant Emma could not join her and her father. In her place, Fanny cared for the child through her last hours, comforted her distraught father and made the funeral arrangements he could not face. 'We are under deep obligations to Fanny never to be forgotten,' Darwin wrote to his wife.[28]

Widely though she spread her energies and absent though she often was, Fanny was not a negligent mother. When she was away, she wrote regularly to 'Snigs', describing the places and people she was visiting and trying to amuse her with accounts of pet dogs. Snow treasured these miniature letters. Nor could she bear to feel at odds with her mother. She kept and dated to 1841, when she was 8 years old, a sad little peace offering written in best copper plate and decorated with lively drawings of a cabman and a girl putting on a pair of skates:

> My dear Mamma,
>
> You cannot think how sorry I was this morning to make you so unhappy. I do not think anything made me naughty but pride. I have prayed to God to forgive me & and I think you will see I am really sorry. Oh! Mamma you do not know how unhappy I was to see you unhappy all today I know I have been cross for 2 or 3 days I cannot help disliking my lessons but I will try to do them well Goodbye—

Contrite and unusually self-aware for an 8-year-old, Snow's strong sense of justice, a quality her mother always appreciated, required her not just to apologize for her bad temper but also to explain it.[29]

Julia would later accept that she had wanted more from her mother than she could offer.[30] For her part, Fanny was sometimes uneasy with her daughter's brilliance and passion but did her best over her education, first making enquiries about governesses when Snow was 3. Lucy Bennett was brought into the nursery a year later.[31] As in most middle-class homes, however, Fanny accepted that it was her responsibility to teach her children to read. She brought her children up on the same stories she had known as a child, just as Julia would later use them when teaching an orphaned boy in the workhouse: Maria Edgeworth's tales in *The Parent's Assistant*.[32] Carefully graded for children of different ages and abilities, these offered lively narratives in familiar settings with clear moral outcomes, often arbitrated by the local community or some older person standing apart to set the world to rights.

Though she generally kept to the family estate in Ireland, Edgeworth had been keen to get to know Sir James Mackintosh and travelled to London to stay with him and his family in the winter of 1821. His brilliant but exhausting conversation took the edge off her enthusiasm. Nor did she feel completely at ease when staying with Jos and Bessie Wedgwood. She had no reservations, however, about Fanny: 'not handsome nor ugly – with a sweet voice and admirable conversation'. In 1841 Fanny was able to introduce the old lady to her own daughter. The famous author 'addressed me', Julia remembered 50 years later, 'with a lively cordiality. […] [I] felt much honoured by the notice'.[33]

Maria Edgeworth was only one of several leading women writers Julia knew as a girl. Mary Somerville was a regular guest of her parents, as was Ann Marsh, who, Julia recalled, 'was always especially kind to me'.[34] The first to encourage her creative abilities, however, was Harriet Martineau. Martineau got to know the Hensleigh Wedgwoods on one of her first visits to London and remained friends with them for the rest of her life. When she was 7, Snow followed her mother's example and wrote her own letter to Martineau, who was then living the life of an invalid in Tynemouth. She got an immediate response with a nice little tale in the Edgeworth manner about a poor lady who

Figure 5 Silhouette of the young Fanny Wedgwood chosen by Julia Wedgwood for inclusion in the Family History she compiled. Courtesy of V&A Wedgwood/Mosley Collection.

collected and sold seaweed. 'So the woman got the money she wanted, and the rich people got to know about the sea-weeds; and everybody was pleased' was its cheerful moral.[35]

In September, Martineau asked Snow and Mack to help her as she prepared some stories for children by telling her what they liked best in Maria Edgeworth and why. Another edifying tale followed, this time about the kindness of her servant, Jane. Though the language was simple, the letter was long. It is not difficult to imagine the pride with which the 7-year-old would have opened the envelope addressed by one of the best-known writers in England to 'Miss F J Wedgwood'. She wrote back often, accepting the responsibility her new friend laid on her to report the family's news when her mother was 'ill or busy'.[36]

In 1849 Snow was able to visit Martineau in her new home in Ambleside, where, after an apparently miraculous recovery in her health that she attributed to mesmerism, she had built an attractive house, 'The Knoll', and ran a happy, energetic female household. She also cultivated her neighbours, who included the Wordsworths. Martineau took Ras, Fanny and the children to meet them at Rydal Mount, giving Snow her only encounter with a poet whose work she idolized. His crusty sense of self in old age, however, impressed her less than her meeting with his demented sister, Dorothy, whose invalid carriage stood ready for her at the gate. 'I looked into those "wild eyes"', Julia recalled 60 years later, 'which kept all their life and light, though the mind had grown dim. There was no dimness in her interest when she heard my name. "From whom are you sprung?" she enquired eagerly.' Hensleigh's name meant nothing to her, however: it was his uncle, Tom Wedgwood, Coleridge's great friend, who had died over 40 forty years earlier and was scarcely even a name to Snow who Dorothy Wordsworth remembered.[37]

These vivid encounters with writers – Elizabeth Gaskell would soon become another friend – gave Snow an early sense that writing was a natural occupation for a woman.

She was not a quiescent child in the nursery. Impressed by her mother's Mackintosh principles, she harangued her bemused governess with the pronouncement that 'Mamma says Liberty is the price of Justice' doing her best to argue a complex case.[38] At the age of 11 she could write a very decent letter in French[39] and was later taught Italian by 'Miss Rossetti', possibly Christina, but more probably her older sister. ('She has a sort of ugliness I don't mind' was Julia's verdict.)[40] Alongside languages were her favourite subjects, history and English literature, as well as geography and mathematics. Like most middle-class girls, she was also taught drawing and sketching. All three sisters would become far more expert than the usual amateur lady water colourist and sometimes decorated their letters to each other with detailed pen and ink sketches of the places where they were staying. Of the three, Julia produced the finest results. There was music, too, particularly for Effie, who liked to show off her bright singing voice.

Though Hensleigh would later play a role in supporting university education for women, he had a limited view of innate female abilities. Watching children at play at Maer in his bachelor days, he mused on 'how soon the difference of sexes' appeared in them with the boys 'full of spirits talking and running about all day long' but the girl 'such a quiet little thing'. As his sister, Emma, commented after his death, for all his gentleness, Hensleigh 'never had a taste for children'. Many of the most talented women of his time, including Hannah More, Anna Barbauld, Anna Seward, Octavia Hill and Maria Edgeworth, had been taught by their fathers. Hensleigh was untypical of the Wedgwoods in not playing a part in this. The great Josiah had gone out of his way to secure a good education for his daughters, including Sukie, Charles Darwin's mother. His father, Jos, played a major role in helping his father's great nieces, the Byerly sisters, establish and maintain one of the most successful girls' boarding schools in the country.[41] He also sent his daughters, Fanny and Emma, to school in London for a couple of years before they travelled on the Ccontinent. Intermittent though this education was, Emma emerged from it more than able to understand from the earliest days the radical drift of her husband's scientific theorizing.

Hensleigh, by contrast, was a distanced presence in Snow's childhood, far less involved in his children's lives than his cousin Charles Darwin would be in his. Darwin's work and experiments spread all over the house and garden, with his children recruited to help him however they could: Hensleigh kept to his study, emerging only to go to work, host a dinner party or attend church and his various committees. When he got a day off work and Fanny insisted he use it to make calls, he went unwillingly: 'he is so busy now with languages and metaphysics that it was rather hard to make him spend the holiday so' she conceded just three years into their marriage as Hensleigh struggled with *The Developement* [sic] *of Human Understanding*, an inconclusive book whose publication in 1838 went largely unnoticed.[42] By then he had already precipitated a major crisis in his marriage.

In December 1837 he abandoned the police magistracy his father-in-law had procured for him, on a point of principle about swearing oaths.[43] Fanny, Snow, Bro and the new baby, Erny, were despatched to Maer, while Hensleigh looked for a new post in London and pursued a campaign against oath-taking. In retrospect, Julia would see this as the most principled and characteristic action of his life.[44] That is not how it seemed at the time to Fanny, who dreaded being obliged to live in the Potteries.[45] Nor did she share her husband's concerns about oath-taking.

Julia would later describe her as a 'Deist', a polite way of suggesting that religion was never a fundamental concern for her. But Fanny went to church regularly with her husband and enjoyed a good preacher like Frederick Denison Maurice or her favourite, the great Unitarian teacher James Martineau, who was appointed joint minister at the Little Portland Street Chapel in 1858. Though Wedgwoods tended to join the Church of England as they moved up in society and Hensleigh sent two of his sons to Rugby under the headship of the Broad Church Thomas Arnold, he was happiest with independent preachers like Alexander Scott or Martineau. By temperament he remained a Unitarian.

Unitarians were clearer about what they did not believe than what they did. They rejected Christ's place in the Trinity but disagreed over whether he was simply an outstanding moral exemplar or a man with divine authority. Miracles were proof of divine intervention. The Bible, however, though a key source of religious authority, was not divinely inspired. They rejected the idea of original sin and the Calvinist idea of an elect predetermined for salvation and went along for a time with Joseph Priestley's materialist determinism. His emphasis on rational thought, however, slowly gave way to Martineau's growing recognition of the place of emotion in religion and the role of individual conscience. Both, however, agreed on the vital importance of science as a way of understanding God's purposes for mankind. If Unitarianism sometimes seemed more a state of mind than a collection of fixed beliefs, it was not lax or passive. Its followers believed in the perfectibility of man, were concerned about the environment in which he grew up and were keen promoters of education for both boys and girls. The fact that so many outstanding Victorian women had started out as Unitarians was no accident.

Despite his education at Rugby and Cambridge, Hensleigh's stance on oath-taking demonstrated his continuing sympathy with Dissent. Even before he was married when his income was uncertain he had given up his Cambridge fellowship with its £70 a year on a point of principle worrying that he had subscribed to the Thirty Nine Articles as required for his fellowship without sufficient thought. He told Fanny what he had done only after the event. Giving up his magistracy, however, had much more serious consequences for him in his new role as a family man. Dissenters had always disliked swearing oaths. As a police magistrate, Hensleigh had put up with administering oaths to others but drew the line in 1837 when he was obliged to swear them himself 42 times as proof of his allegiance to his new sovereign, Queen Victoria.[46] If a promise of loyalty was not sufficient without the sanction of an oath, what remained of honesty and truthfulness in day-to-day living, he asked himself. 'I think it very possible', he explained to his father, 'that it may be lawful for a man to make a judicial oath, but I feel that it is not lawful for me & there is no use in letting £800 a year persuade one's conscience.'[47] (Nor, apparently, his obligation to provide for his wife and children.)

The family was divided in its reactions. Fanny Allen and Elizabeth Wedgwood strongly approved, Jos acquiesced, but Charles Darwin had his doubts, while Fanny dreaded the prospect of having to abandon metropolitan life. Hensleigh diverted his energies into getting up a petition for the creation of a non-jurors' register in a campaign for an alternative to oath-taking that would not succeed for another 50 years. His stance, however, had won him admiration in reforming circles. A few months later, Lord John Russell secured him the post of Registrar of London Cabs. At £500 a year it was less well paid than his magistracy but did not strain his conscience. The relaxed hours and undemanding nature of the work allowed him time to pursue his etymological studies, take on some lucrative directorships and keep up with intellectual life in the capital. Periodically, his health broke down, and the children would be packed off to their grandparents at Maer or the Darwins' house at Down. They were also kept out of the way when Fanny was confined, returning home to find yet another brother or sister with their mother absorbed in nursing her new baby or, as in 1844, absent convalescing after a particularly difficult confinement. With so many demands on her time, Fanny encouraged others to play a major role in bringing up her children. Three very different people, Emma Wedgwood, Ras Darwin and Mary Rich, filled the void for Snow.

Fanny and Emma, Hensleigh's younger sister, had been good friends before either of them married and became particularly close after the sudden death of Emma's sister, Fanny, in 1832. Emma would take almost as much interest in her brother's children as she would in her own. She first met Snow when she was just a month old. 'She is a nice, pretty little thing and one gets very fond of it,' she told her Aunt Jessie.[48] Four years later she got to know Snow and Mack much better when they spent six months at Maer after Hensleigh abandoned his magistracy. Both children fell seriously ill, and with Fanny going up and down to London, Emma kept watch over their convalescence. 'Snow is going on very well. She is come downstairs and sits very gravely by the fire cutting out paper or reading and Bro offering her the proper attentions,' she reported to her fiancé Charles Darwin.[49]

Hensleigh and Fanny played a key role in Charles and Emma Darwin's early days together. Darwin was startled by the unexpected sight soon after his return to England of

Hensleigh walking down the street with a bandbox in one hand and Snow tugging at the other.[50] It made him realize just how far his friends' lives had moved on during his long absence on the *Beagle*. Even so, he took his time to get round to marriage. His first priority was to secure his collections and begin to make his name amongst fellow scientists and geologists. But holed up in dingy lodgings at 36 Great Marlborough Street, a few doors away from his brother at 43, he could not help but think of the advantages of having 'a nice soft wife on a sofa with good fire, & books & music perhaps'.[51] He had known Emma most of his life but not taken much notice of her. Indeed, when a rumour reached him on his voyage that Ras was about to marry her, he predicted that he would quickly become 'heartily sick of her'.[52] A dinner party at the Hensleigh Wedgwoods in June 1837, however, set Emma in a new light as she relaxed in their company.

True scientist that he was, Charles went to Maer a year later to have a closer look at Emma on home territory. He liked what he saw and finally plucked up courage to propose to her there in November 1838. Having been accepted, he collapsed in a nervous heap while Emma, still in a daze, went off to teach Sunday school. Fanny, who immediately guessed what had happened, organized a midnight celebration with Charles and Emma.[53]

Successfully establishing them in London became one of her projects. When Darwin rented a house close to the British Museum, she advised him on dyeing its strident canary yellow curtains. She also recommended a cook though Emma, consciously playing the country mouse to Fanny's town mouse, found her too overbearing and quickly replaced her with 'a countrified woman'. The Darwins' first dinner party was for Fanny, Hensleigh and Ras, with everyone in high spirits over the news about Hensleigh's appointment as Registrar of London Cabs.[54]

Soon after, Hensleigh and Fanny moved to a house just four doors down on Gower Street. But metropolitan life was too fatiguing for both Charles and Emma. By 1842 they were looking for a home outside London. They found a rather unpromising house with lots of garden beyond the Bromley suburbs in the village of Downe. Down House would take the place of Maer Hall for visiting Darwins and Wedgwoods. Sent there frequently as a child, Snow would often invite herself as she grew up. 'I am always so very happy here as you know,' she wrote to her sister Effie, 'it is a place which suits me in every respect – most of all in its dear inhabitants.' But like the young George Eliot sitting ostentatiously alone at a children's party and explaining, 'I like to talk to grown-up people,' Julia, too, 'used to feel the [Darwin] children rather an interruption to the converse with their father'.[55] Even so she welcomed the relaxed way of living at Down House in contrast to the orderly, but often empty Hensleigh Wedgwood establishment in London.

Henrietta Litchfield, the Darwins' third child, wrote of her mother that she had an unusually 'large-minded, unfussy way of taking life'. 'She lived with her children and grandchildren in every detail of their lives. But she was never a doting mother. She knew what we were and never imagined we were perfect or interesting to the outside world.'[56] Emma's keen eye for the individuality of children made her the ideal aunt for Snow, attentive, tolerant and calming. In 1842 she had particularly enjoyed watching Snow, Mack and Erny's reactions to a 'most dreadful blood and thunder' pantomime she attended with them at 'the Tottenham theatre, very low' as she confessed to her sister, Elizabeth. While 'poor Erny' hid his face in her lap, the 9-year-old Snow puzzled over the morality of it all: 'Whether they were really killed? [...] whether the wicked Squire was really a bad man? [...] whether the waxwork woman was nice or not.'[57]

That autumn, Hensleigh's health had broken down again. Though the Darwins had only moved to Down House on 14 September, where Emma's third child, a girl called Mary, was born on 23 September and died less than a month later, they agreed to take Snow, Bro and Erny while Fanny remained in London. On a wintry day in November, Emma felt confident enough in the good sense of the children to allow them to go for a walk in Cudham Wood. Only the new 13-year-old nursemaid, Bessy Harding, accompanied them. They quickly got lost in the tangle of undergrowth and narrow paths deep in snow. Emma waited hours for their return before spotting Snow and 'Doddy' (William Darwin) in the distance: 'she brought him home from more than a mile off, dragging him along up to their ankles in mud. She kept him from being frightened or crying and from crying herself, and behaved like a little heroine. [...] I was easy as soon as I saw Snow.' Safely back at Down, she told Uncle Charles where she thought the others were. He and his manservant, Joseph Parslow, rescued them from a farmhouse where they had taken refuge and carried them home. Young Bessy was laid up for weeks with the strain of their misadventure, but Snow, as Emma reassured Fanny, was soon 'happily curled up in a corner reading and occasionally joining in a romp with the little ones'. The 9-year-old had done her duty. Aunt Elizabeth was, predictably, full of praise for Snow's 'steadiness of mind'.[58]

As important to Snow as Aunt Emma was her father's cousin, Erasmus Alvey Darwin, born almost five years before his brother Charles and always known in the family as 'Ras'. Ras was the major intellectual influence on the young Darwin, who would throughout his life anxiously await his older brother's reactions to his work.[59] Charles never doubted that Ras was at least his intellectual equal and admired his wider range of cultural interests. But Ras never had his brother's drive. Cushioned by his private income from his father, he chose to lead a more limited, valetudinarian life mostly devoting himself to his friends but making a useful mark in his few involvements in the public sphere as with Bedford College and the London Library. For a time when Charles was abroad, he had escorted Emma around London. They shared a love of music, and Ras was an attentive escort. The aunts did not approve, however, and Emma herself was always wary of Ras's free-thinking on religion. It is possible that he made a half-hearted proposal in April 1833.[60] If so, Emma had quickly refused him, and for a time they saw less of each other. There was even more unhappy talk in the family and concern about scandal in the papers over Ras's very obvious devotion to Fanny after her marriage. Ras and Hensleigh had been at Cambridge together and, in their early bachelor days in London, enjoyed rowing up the Thames, going to the zoo and holidaying on the Isle of Wight.

The suggestion that Ras and Fanny had a 50-year-long affair is almost as hard to clear from the record as the idea that Julia got her nickname because she was born in a snow-storm. Neither is accurate.[61] After his death, Julia and her sisters, who had all adored Ras, read through his letters to their mother and even had some of them typed up. They found nothing amiss. Affectionate though they were, there is nothing in them about passion. Ras lacked the energy and, possibly, the inclination for a sustained affair. Lean and lanky, he liked to lie on his sofa smoking or taking snuff, a habit he shared with Fanny, while he read from his well-stocked library. But Ras was not as malleable as this might suggest and was an effective, interventionist committee man at the London Library and the new College for Women in Bedford Square.

He also enjoyed squiring strong, independent-minded women around town. Harriet Martineau was delighted to have him as her escort on her triumphal visit to literary London in 1835. The sharp-tongued Jane Carlyle, stuck in noisy, inconvenient Chelsea with her dyspeptic, gloomy genius of a husband, was another he took for a regular airing in his phaeton. She forgave him his preference for cats over dogs, while he allowed her to borrow risqué French novels from the London Library under his name. As Ras himself remarked, 'There is no lack of desolate females in the world': taking care of them was his self-appointed mission.[62] But it was Fanny, a far-from-desolate female, who spent most time with him. Neither Carlyle nor Hensleigh saw him as a threat. The attentions he paid their wives freed them to get on with their own pursuits.

Ras ran errands for Fanny, packing up her corsets to send off to country houses where she was staying, puzzling over the difference between cambric and muslin and getting in a muddle over whose library books were whose. He liked to present himself as an ineffectual bachelor constantly battling with the minor challenges of life like noisy builders next door or struggling with the complexities of Bradshaw's railway timetables. When Fanny was in London, he complained that her restless energy exhausted him, but when she was away, he missed the bustle and sank back on his sofa anxious for news of her and her children.[63]

For the children, Ras was a much-loved bonus in their lives, while he could enjoy all the vicarious pleasures of marriage without the bother of it. He lived by proxy: he was happy to see his brother feted for work to which he had contributed; he admired Fanny's energetic engagement with the world, something he could not match; and, above all, he had the best of family life without having to take responsibility for its trials.

Children fascinated Ras, especially little girls. He drew magical pictures for them and invented fantasy worlds; he remembered to get the ice creams on family outings and observed them even more closely than Emma Darwin, spotting their needs and worrying about them with a concern their parents sometimes failed to show. He had known 'Miss Snow' from the beginning and happily prolonged his summer holiday at Maer in 1833 to stay with Fanny, her baby, and Emma Wedgwood, 'all his favourites around him', as his sister, Caroline, informed Charles Darwin. As Snow started to write letters to her mother, Fanny would pass them on to a delighted Ras. One was the 'most interesting thing I have read this week. [...] The female talent of character drawing is com[ing] out very strongly,' he commented on one of the 8-year-old's productions. When Fanny took the 9-year-old Snow off to stay with Harriet Martineau in Ambleside, however, Ras fretted. 'It would have done her a world of good to have staid in town with me.' He fussed over her education and was the first to notice that Holmes had made one side of Snow's face too large in his joint portrait of her with Bro. He insisted on a correction being made.[64]

Ras was most watchful when Snow entered her painful teens. He helped her out at awkward family dinner parties when her parents were away and advised her on how to manage the household; he encouraged her to try out a new apparatus to assist her hearing and defended her from family criticism when her first novel was published. In later years, with Julia absorbed in her own very different circle of friends, he would give more of his time to her sisters. Hope, the youngest of the Hensleigh Wedgwood children, became his 'little wifey', just as Fanny was always 'Missus'.

No two people could be more different than Ras Darwin and Mary Rich, the one fussy, retiring and sceptical but with a fine mind, the other warm and colourful but rigid in her views on faith and conduct. They did not like each other. Ras always called her 'Mrs Rich' behind her back as if reluctant to acknowledge her family connection with those he described to Fanny as 'our children'. Just as Ras was a surrogate father to Snow, however, Aunt Rich was in many ways her surrogate mother and closer in temperament. Of all the key figures in her childhood, she was the most influential. She meant 'all the world to me', as a child Julia later remembered: 'in her best days she had most power of love'.[65]

Mary Rich had a glamorous past. The eldest child of Sir James Mackintosh, she had caught the eye in India of a dashing, gifted, ambitious young member of the East India Company, Claudius Rich. They married when she was 18 and he 20 and moved to Baghdad, where he had been appointed the Company's agent. His taste for extravagance went hand in hand with his skill as a linguist and discriminating appreciation of Arab culture. He surveyed archaeological sites, collected rare inscriptions and fine manuscripts and took Mary with him (often disguised as a boy) on his adventurous travels. His sudden death from cholera when Mary was in Bombay awaiting his arrival there for a new posting was a catastrophe for her. She always believed that their love for each other was far beyond the ordinary. 'We may be laughed at for a silly couple,' she had written to her sister, 'but we glory in it, as it proves to us our love is superior to what is generally felt, and what few people are capable of feeling.' On her return to England, her father secured a pension for her from the Company. With that and the £7,500 the British Museum paid for Rich's collection, his widow set out to wait for her eventual reunion with her husband. Religion became her new passion in her 50 years of waiting.

Victorian aunts came with the implicit stamp of parental approval. They could advise on 'behaviour, dress and expected standards' as well as 'guide, warn, and teach by example without maternal emotional baggage'.[66] Living with the Hensleigh Wedgwoods, secure in the best front parlour, Aunt Rich was an interventionist presence, advising Fanny on her recovery from a difficult pregnancy (not something of which she had experience herself), criticizing Snow's childish writings and setting out her religious views with authority in letters to her half-sister.[67]

With no children of her own, she devoted lots of time to Snow's upbringing. She arranged outings to see the illuminations for the Coronation or to watch the celebrations of the young Queen's marriage. She encouraged the romantic in her and went to great pains to strengthen her appreciation of her Scottish heritage, taking her to her grandfather's birthplace and fostering her relationships with her Erskine cousins. Most important of all, she would introduce her to the man who would have the single greatest impact on her, Thomas Erskine of Linlathen. She also told her impressionable niece tales of her exotic early days in the East 'like something out of the Arabian nights'. On special occasions she would open up her treasures, showing the child one of Claudius's snuff boxes, the padlock and key of his travelling trunk, his ball and powder case or some of the beautiful robes he had worn in Baghdad. She had colourful stories to tell as well about her early days crossing deserts, shivering in mountain huts, braving fever in peasant hovels or making supper for a hundred of her husband's sepoys.[68]

For a time Rich followed her father's favourite preacher, Edward Irving. She relished his histrionic eloquence and ability to recreate the expectation of the first Christians, nurturing an apocalyptic fever in his congregation by encouraging 'speaking in tongues'. But as its activities became increasingly scandalous and the fashionable were scared away, Rich turned to Irving's assistant, Alexander Scott. Both Scott and Irving were stripped of their licenses to preach in the Scottish Church, but while Irving drifted back to Scotland and died prematurely in 1834, Scott set up his own congregation and quickly developed a reputation as one of the most thoughtful and compelling of the independent preachers. Rich moved to Woolwich in 1838 to be near him and his wife, Ann. For Hensleigh, too, Scott became not just a friend but also the family pastor. Scott's independence tempered Rich's Calvinism. So too did her growing attraction to Thomas Erskine, who had no time for the idea of a punitive God or for an elect predestined to salvation. Julia would fall under Erskine's spell at a later, more critical stage in her life. As a child, however, she absorbed her step-aunt's confidence in the existence of another world where all would meet again, an assurance that would always be fundamental to her faith. The thought of the life to come was not entirely comfortable, however, for a young child brought up on the prospect of the Last Judgement.

As Valerie Sanders has suggested, 'Religion occupied a more prominent place in a Victorian child's anxious inner life than sex.'[69] Later, Julia shuddered at the grim Manicheanism of the faith she learnt from her step-aunt. There was the insistence that 'God chastiseth those who he loveth', a pronouncement about the meaning of suffering that took on particular significance as Snow's hearing began to deteriorate. There was the bareness of the Old Testament with its remote, punitive God and brutal stories of fraternal conflict like Cain's murder of his brother Abel and the bitter rivalry of Jacob and Esau. 'The Old Testament', she recalled many years later, 'presented to my mind nothing but painful problems, and anything that tended to upset the idea of its ultimate authority […] was welcome.'[70]

Milton aroused even more anxiety. Like Emma Wedgwood, Harriet Martineau and many other girls in the nineteenth century, Snow read *Paradise Lost* as a child. Martineau adored it: 'I sent myself to sleep by repeating it: and when my curtains were drawn back in the morning, descriptions of heavenly light rushed into my memory.'[71] Julia's temperament was less robust. With her, the darker archetypes prevailed and were intensified by the resonance of Milton's language by comparison with the plainness of Genesis. Satan, original sin, the fall of Man, the expulsion of Adam and Eve from Paradise and the reality of Hell seized her imagination. Years later she could still not forgive Milton for 'infusing a mythological spirit into English theology' and 'exposing the meagerness of the narrative in Genesis'.[72] There were sexist stereotypes, too, which she was able to discount only years later when she mocked Milton's account of 'Eve being sent away like the ladies from a modern dinner table so that Adam and the Angel may talk more freely'. Even more insulting was the suggestion that woman could only communicate with God through the intermediary of a man: 'He for God only, she for God in him' was a line that 'must raise a protest in all women and most men.' As a child, however, the shadow of Miltonic theology, reflected in the religious books for children she read, left her 'struggling and wounded, and I was always reaching out for warmth and light elsewhere'.[73]

Charlotte Yonge shared Snow's night-time terrors as a child lying awake at night fancying that wolves were leering at her or she was being smothered like one of the Princes in the Tower. She pulled hairs out of the mattress to distract herself from the fear of being asleep when the end of the world arrived.[74] Julia too 'always went to bed as a child elaborately expecting the Judgment Day, remembering that passage about its coming like a thief in the night, and not feeling sure about my own account in the reckoning', as she later told Browning. By then she could make light of being burdened with huge moral issues no child could handle and saw how darkly they had coloured her anxiety: 'that kind of anticipation', she wrote, 'is an unfortunate element in a child's life, and it is the natural form which is taken in a child's mind by what are true grown-up motives and beliefs'.[75]

Emma Darwin's quiet faith makes a nice contrast with Rich's insistence on religion as drama. Her nightly prayer after the death of her sister had a sober composure: 'Merciful God, as my uncertain life may soon be ended and I must appear before thee to give an account of my life, prepare me I beseech thee for the hour of death and for the day of judgment.' When Rich introduced her to one of the speakers in tongues, she was unimpressed by the histrionics but very concerned by how 'worn and depressed' the young girl looked.[76] As a child, however, Snow was more drawn to the drama of Aunt Rich's religion.

The differences between Snow's childhood protectors foreshadowed the later complex coexistence in Julia of the high intelligence and playfulness she knew with Ras Darwin, the good sense of Aunt Emma and the emotional intensity of Mary Rich. All three, however, came with her mother's blessing, and when Snow looked around for her own friends, she often chose those of her mother's generation, taking the initiative in writing to Harriet Martineau, ingratiating herself with Jane Carlyle and Ellen Tollett, Emma Darwin's closest friend from Staffordshire and, as a teenager, going to stay with Fanny's friend, Elizabeth Gaskell. Nor did she shy away from older members of the family. One of her proudest childhood memories was of sitting next to her taciturn grandfather, Jos Wedgwood, at the whist table. Another who did not deter her was Great Aunt Sarah Elizabeth, the last of Josiah's surviving children, terrified though most of her cousins were by this 'somewhat forbidding' old lady. She was impressed too by her parents' distinguished friends. Macaulay talked to her about Milton and held out a chair for her; Jane Carlyle wanted her to keep in touch; and Sir John Herschel, the distinguished astronomer and mathematician, invited her to his children's parties on Gower Street.[77]

In all, Julia would have 62 cousins. Though she and Emma Darwin could be wry in private about Wedgwood limitations, the sense of family solidarity was strong. C. V. Wedgwood, the fine historian two generations after Julia, wrote that to be a Wedgwood was 'like being at a large school. There are traditions and relationships that you are expected to know by instinct. [...] Somehow you do get to know – the network of cousins assumes coherence, you get the hang of it, and then all is well.' The intricacies of her family tree intrigued Julia. She also absorbed the characteristic Wedgwood respect for older generations. For 'little things' having two generations of elders to consider was, she wrote, an 'inestimable advantage'.[78]

She and her sisters made regular tours round the family circuit. There were cousins Godfrey, Amy and Cicely, Uncle Frank and Aunt Fanny Frank's children at their estate at Etruria, and at Seabridge, Louisa, the daughter of Uncle Harry and Aunt Jessie. Very different though Snow and Louisa were, they would go through many of the same teenage rites of passage. Leith Hill Place in Surrey, the home of Hensleigh's eldest brother, John, was another frequent place for holidays despite the growing eccentricity of cousins Sophie and Lucy. And Julia had her own siblings for company: 'Bro', Erny, a cheerful, good-looking child, always struggling with his schoolwork but a natural at cards; Effie, who was 6 years younger, lively and self-possessed; Tim, the dullest of the children but good-natured; and Hope, the youngest, who idolized Effie.

Snow's childhood was a happy one, or so she always said. Though George Eliot warned that childhood could only ever be happy in retrospect, the contemporary evidence supports Snow's later memory of 'the joy and wonder of childhood, a new opening world'.[79] A close circle of admiring friends and family surrounded her, she was not yet fighting for dominance over her sisters and there were all the excitements of discovering new books, learning to draw and sketch and pursue her studies. It was said of Charlotte Yonge that, for all her fame as a writer, at 50 she was still, in essence, the girl she had been at 15. Julia, too, remained, in many ways a child well into middle age, highly intelligent, imaginative, demanding and needy, but also a born performer, sociable, observant and affectionate. As a child, her gifts had enchanted her admirers: as she grew older and more formidable, they could repel and alienate some as unbecoming in a woman. From the start, however, as Ras Darwin spotted, it was clear that she was a born writer. Here, she is at Etruria at the age of 13 listening to an old family retainer reminiscing about her parents:

> I feel in a humour to write on for hours tonight [she wrote to her mother]. All is very quiet the only sounds being three pens, viz Aunt Fanny's Uncle F[rank]'s and mine. [...] Mrs Jones has been sitting over the fire for two hours talking with us all about Maer. [...] Papa was very dull when Uncle H[arry] went to school and used to console himself by reading Pilgrim's Progress to her. Uncle Frank aspired higher – he used to read Campagnes de Gaul – but she said 'That was a very romantic sort of book – we couldn't make out all the grand words in it, and yr uncle used to run downstairs into the drawing room & I used to sit waiting for him, to have them explained! [...] Her admiration was much excited by some buff & white plaid frocks which you and Uncle R[obert] wore on yr return from India. "Our children was always very nice, you know, and very clean but not so nice as them frocks!" [...] "It all feels like a dream now" she said as she was going. I could not help thinking of the time when I shd look back on so many whom I had known passed away from the earth & how little important all my affairs.'[80]

Snow's fascination with a past she loved to imagine is more striking than the conventionally morbid turn into which her unfinished letter descends. That it has survived at all is a tribute to the pleasure it gave her mother – and, no doubt, Ras Darwin.

Chapter Two

MENTORS, FRIENDS AND PIONEERS

In 1843 Mack was sent away to school. For Snow this was almost as crucial a break as for Mack. He lost the close companionship of home but found a wider circle of friends as well as the expected toughening up of school. She, at the age of 10, was now largely alone in her studies since her sister, Effie, was only 4. George Eliot found the separation from her brother, Isaac, traumatic: 'School parted us,' she remembered 40 years later.[1] Harriet Martineau was another stuck-at-home sister feeling wretched when her brother James was away at school and college.[2] She was agog to know how Snow was reacting to Bro's absence at school:

> Is Snow's heart very anxious for him? I know what that is O! what I suffered for Jas when he went to the grammar school at Norwich! I trust […] that she will not have to endure what most sisters have to go through from the school boy shame at sisters.[3]

Snow was readier than either George Eliot or Harriet Martineau to accept that a more important vocation was opening for her brother. Mack, Erny and cousin Godfrey would all write to her from school: Mack rather stiffly as he tried to show off, Godfrey conscientiously and Erny struggling to find things to say but glad of a pretext for not doing his prep. Snow's first novel *Framleigh Hall* depicts boys' public schools as necessary but painful places designed to test their courage and masculine spirit and enable them to develop new friendships. But her need to quiz Mack when her publisher wanted her to include more scenes of school life in her novel suggests that he had given her little sense of what life was like at Rugby School in the aftermath of Thomas Arnold's transforming headmastership. The texture of schoolboys' lives as described in *Tom Brown's Schooldays* came as a revelation when she read it two years later.[4]

Her isolation after Mack went away to school brought with it a kind of liberation. It was well understood in the nineteenth-century nursery that girls, even if older, could not be seen to outstrip boys at their studies. Charlotte Yonge who also had a younger brother, whose birth was 'the greatest event of my life', dealt with this in her 1856 novel *The Daisy Chain*, imagining, or perhaps remembering, a scene in which her heroine Ethel is told by her brother, Norman, to stop trying to keep up with him and give up her Latin and Greek 'or you would get into a regular learned lady, and be good for nothing'.[5] Clever though she is, Edith abandons her classical studies (with the evident approval of her creator) and devotes herself to charitable work and family affairs. Only in the dysfunctional royal family was the gifted Victoria encouraged by her father to discomfit her younger, slower brother, Bertie. Unlike the Princess, Snow had no one to compete with once Mark and

Ernie had gone to school. Her mother, with Ras at her elbow, did not try to hold her back despite Hensleigh's downplaying of his oldest child's abilities. When Harriet Martineau asked to see some of Snow's sketches, he felt obliged to apologize that though the female figures were done 'with grace', the male ones were 'sad sticks'. She disagreed: both of them were 'curious and romantic'.[6]

Schooling at home could not meet Snow's needs for long. She needed more than the rote learning of elementary subjects under the supervision of a governess. Nor can it have been easy to manage the family schoolroom with the boys away, given the age gap between Snow and her sisters and her own precocity. Ras Darwin called round on the Wedgwoods' splendid new home in Chester Terrace at Regent's Park in 1846, 'that cynosure of neighbouring eyes & only despised by its vagrant Mistress who ought to come back'. He found 'only poor Snow, ennuied out of her very life, Mama being gone away made the house so dull and the children all so good and quiet that life was become a burthen to her'.[7] Almost certainly Ras encouraged Fanny to think of something more challenging for her.

Fanny's own schooling had been haphazard, but her father's liking for the company of bright women and way of including her in his research and writing gave her an education that set her at ease with brilliant men. Like Richard Edgeworth, Sir James made a point of reading aloud to his daughters on the evenings he was at home. 'You could not have valued and appreciated him as you now do as well as loved him unless he had so highly cultivated your understanding,' Maria Edgeworth wrote to Fanny after his death, 'nor would you now enjoy and give the intellectual enjoyment which you do.'[8]

Fanny would become one of the pioneers of higher education for women, closely involved in the early years of both Queen's and Bedford Colleges, and later active in the Ladies Educational Association, which organized courses for women at University College in the 1870s.[9] While some might have seen her lack of an active strategy for marrying off her three daughters as the sign of a negligent mother, no one could criticize her for neglecting their education. Snow, the only one to attend boarding school, had outstanding teachers there and at college; Effie and Hope attended the preparatory class at Queen's College that opened in 1849, were given private maths tuition by Dorothea Beale and later enrolled at Queen's before switching to Bedford College, where they studied Latin for three years from 1860 to 1862. Effie went on being 'improved' at her parents' expense well into her 20s with art lessons in Paris and voice training in Germany. In choosing a school for Snow in 1846, Fanny made a careful, well-informed choice picking out one of the best and most expensive in the country, Rachel Martineau's establishment in Liverpool. Like several other leading boarding schools for girls, it was Unitarian in its ethos though not exclusively in its intake.

Unitarianism produced many of the great nineteenth-century women writers, thinkers, administrators and reformers. Harriet Martineau, Elizabeth Gaskell, Florence Nightingale, Mary Somerville, Mary Carpenter, Anna Swanwick, Harriet Taylor (J. S. Mill's wife), Octavia Hill and Elizabeth Reid, the founder of Bedford College, were all brought up as Unitarians, while Frances Power Cobbe also gravitated towards them once she had thrown off her father's conventional Anglicanism. Free of the prevailing gendered expectations about female capabilities, Unitarianism offered a much broader education

Figure 6 Rachel Martineau's school in Liverpool.

than was available in most girls' schools, which focused on developing the attributes that might attract a mate and equipping girls for marriage and motherhood. The curriculum in Unitarian girls' schools was broad. Alongside gentle arts like music, dancing and drawing were history, logic, mathematics and the natural sciences, and Latin.

Rachel Martineau's school with its emphasis on healthy living, exercise and a varied curriculum, all offered in a reassuringly intimate atmosphere, exemplified the Unitarian ideal of female education as well as the 'domestic model' which characterized the best girls' schools.[10] Despite her rather scratchy relationship with her older sister, Harriet Martineau had been singing the school's praises to her friends Fanny Wedgwood and Julia Smith for some time.[11] Snow was enrolled alongside Julia Smith's two nieces, Blanche (who would later marry A. H. Clough) and Bertha, and their cousin, Alice Bonham Carter, who would become one of her most supportive friends.

Rachel Martineau had been obliged to fend for herself after the failure of her father's business and premature death in 1826. She took the most obvious way forward apart from marriage for an able, well-educated girl and became a governess. Her ambition, however, was to open her own school. In 1837 she used her savings to start one in Liverpool, where a number of Unitarian girls' schools had already been successfully established.[12] This also enabled her to provide a home for her demanding, elderly mother, whose presence contributed to the school's ethos as a safe home from home for middle-class girls living away from their families for the first time in their lives. Yet more critical to its success was the presence in Liverpool of her brother, the great Unitarian preacher and teacher James Martineau. He would always be the school's principal attraction.

Its prospectus promised a domestic setting for 'ten young ladies' 'in an airy location' and 'the usual elementary studies' as well as French, which Rachel probably taught herself having briefly worked in Paris, and music, dancing, drawing and singing, for some of which she engaged James Herrmann, 'the leader of the Liverpool concerts' (forerunner of the Royal Liverpool Philharmonic Society).[13] While the basic curriculum centred on girls' appropriate fare of reading, writing, mental arithmetic, geography, history and botany, the extras on offer ventured firmly into boys' educational territory: Latin, German and mathematics as well as Italian. James Martineau taught most of these 'hard' subjects together with New Testament studies.[14]

Going to boarding school was a formative time for any girl, a chance to establish herself away from her own home and explore a new kind of collective life. For Julia her year at Rachel Martineau's school was one of the richest of her life. She made friends she would continue to see when she later went to Bedford College, she was excited by her independence, she began to learn in a more structured way and, above all, she encountered the inspirational teacher who, for the first time, gave her a sense of the excitements of learning and taught her to think for herself. At Rachel Martineau's school, she was a star, not only the great granddaughter of the famous potter but also the granddaughter of Sir James Mackintosh, whom James Martineau had met and much admired in his youth.[15] She was aware of her status. Reminiscing about their school days, the more timid Alice Bonham Carter told Julia how awed she had felt by her fearless way of taking on the formidable Mrs Martineau.[16] Her experience of handling older generations of Wedgwoods, Darwins and Allens served her well in Liverpool.

Harriet Martineau, who had worried that the delectable young Snow with 'the large eyes', susceptible temperament and 'little hands fumbling' at her white fur collar, might get lost in the persona of the schoolgirl, found her unusually demure at her dancing class in Liverpool, looking 'desperately solemn when going through her evolutions. My sister told me,' Harriet reported to Fanny, 'I could no more judge of the ten faces by that hour than at church, – they were so intent on their business, and the intentness looks so droll in contrast with their frolicsome movements!' Though Rachel said with satisfaction that her year's intake were 'all [underlined 3 times] good',[17] behind her back the girls were not always so biddable and had the usual complaints about boarding school life. Both Julia and Meta Gaskell who attended seven years later remembered that the dinners were 'awful'.[18]

Even so, Elizabeth Gaskell had never had any doubt that Rachel Martineau's school was the right place for her most gifted child, Meta, while she sent her more placid, older daughter, Marianne, to Mrs Laylor's less-demanding school in London.[19] Though she never warmed to James Martineau, reacting against his unrelenting seriousness and lack of small talk, Gaskell respected his gifts as a teacher.[20] She and her husband encouraged him to repeat a course of lectures for young women he had earlier given in Liverpool in Manchester in 1846. They had a profound impact on his audience. Though Julia would move on to other idols like Frederick Denison Maurice and Thomas Erskine, she acknowledged that her greatest single intellectual debt was to Martineau. 'He opened the doors of learning to me,' she told Harold Herford years later. At the age of 13 she was keen to go through them.[21]

After a false start as an engineer, James had enrolled at Manchester College (then confusingly based in York), studying science, philosophy, the Classics and theology in preparation for a career as a Unitarian minister. Despite invitations from a number of congregations, he turned first to teaching filling in for a year at Lant Carpenter's school in Bristol, where both he and Harriet had been pupils. Teaching and preaching went hand in hand for much of Martineau's career, as they did for many Dissenting ministers. Of the two, teaching attracted his most sustained effort. In 1828 he was made junior minister at Eustace Street Presbyterian Meeting House in Dublin working with Rev. Joseph Hutton, the grandfather of Richard Holt Hutton, who would play a major role in his and Julia's careers. In 1832 he moved to Liverpool to be the junior minister at Paradise Street Chapel, where he quickly built up a reputation as a persuasive preacher and sophisticated advocate of Unitarianism.

Cautiously but surely in his very long career, Martineau moved Unitarianism on from Priestley's rationalism, freeing it from doctrinal insistence and introducing a reliance on the role of inner conviction that he first learnt from Coleridge and later developed through study in Germany. True moral power, Martineau preached in 1841, came not from will and reason but from love.[22] This was heady stuff for Unitarians. Some in Martineau's congregation accused him of self-aggrandizement when he sought to express his Romantic spiritual aesthetic in a soaring Gothic church on Hope Street that replaced the bare eighteenth-century octagonal meetinghouse at Paradise Street. When Julia first encountered him, he was embroiled in a disagreement with his congregation that would eventually lead him to take a year's leave from Liverpool to study theology in Dresden and Berlin in the company of Richard Hutton. Before that he conducted a remarkably busy life, teaching and preaching in both Liverpool and Manchester. Pastoral work he largely left to others: his reserved, authoritative presence meant that it was not his bent.

Much of his time was devoted to teaching, beginning in the home where he taught his seven children on Hartleyan principles with lessons adapted to the age and ability of each child. He also gave morning talks before Sunday service and taught in the afternoon Sunday school and during the week lectured on chemistry and astronomy at the Liverpool Mechanics Institute and led Bible study classes for young men before they went to work. In addition to that, he spent one or two days a week at Manchester New College as the Professor of Mental and Moral Philosophy and Logic. Nor did he confine his teaching to young men. The series of lectures on moral philosophy, logic and theology he delivered to an audience of young women in Liverpool in 1838 changed the life of the 18-year-old Anna Swanwick, whose parents had stopped her education at age 13 because she already knew as much as they thought appropriate for a girl. Their impact when he repeated them in Manchester in 1846 was just as profound on Catherine and Susanna Winkworth, who would, like Swanwick, become fine translators.

Martineau's gift for teaching very bright but haphazardly educated young women drew on his experience at his sister's school, where he managed to fit in two four-hour sessions a week. His classes there were less about handing down knowledge than about teaching his pupils to ask the right questions. Julia remembered him encouraging them to discuss whether it was appropriate for women to study mathematics, the difference between induction and deduction, the morality of the Marian persecutions and 'the significance of a law of nature'. Subjective answers were discouraged, but 'even his apparent coolness', Julia remembered, could not damp down the enthusiastic admiration of his

Figure 7 James Martineau in 1847 painted by Charles Agar. Courtesy of Harris Manchester College, Oxford University.

teenage female scholars. Together they read Lingard's *History of England* and Herschel's *Astronomy*. He made them seem as exciting as fiction.[23]

Eleanor, the future wife of A. V. Dicey and the youngest of the three Bonham Carter sisters who attended Rachel Martineau's school, filled her letters home with gushing accounts of James Martineau. 'I do so wish I could do my Latin better for him I am sure it is a great trial of his patience,' she wrote. 'Mr M is delicious, so sweet, you should have seen him say Good night to me the other night, how he ran half way up stairs & almost tumbled down & with such a sweet dear face.'[24] Julia's letters from school do not survive. It is unlikely she experienced the same schoolgirl crush. She remembered Martineau not for his charisma but for his ability to bring apparently abstruse subjects to life. Here was a brilliant man who did not talk down to his girl pupils but was patient and, as they sensed beneath the austere façade, kind. Many years later she recalled a particular moment:

I remember the very pattern of the oil-cloth at the long table and him at its head, leaning forward with the earnest gaze that might have been bent on a set of learned and mature men instead of a few school-girls and I hear the deep, rather hollow voice that seemed, though perfectly distant, not to bring all its sounds from the lips, but as it were to express a thought as much as an utterance.[25]

Several of his female pupils described his impact in very similar terms. A contemporary of Anna Swanwick's wrote: 'My mind seemed to be suddenly opened. I saw things I had never before imagined.' Catherine Winkworth, who had returned from a period of study in Germany with her head confusingly full of Goethe and German Romantic philosophy, acknowledged Martineau as the man who rescued her from her mental 'chaos': 'his teaching had fixed for her the intellectual foundations of faith'.[26] Julia remembered his understanding of teaching as an iterative process between teacher and pupil.

She stayed in touch with him for the rest of her life and wrote a warm and thoughtful appreciation of him shortly after his death in 1900. Her starting point was a recent conversation she had had with him about the nature of teaching. Martineau had been mulling over a criticism J. S. Mill had made that his published lectures showed that he had diverged from common positions the two of them had earlier shared. He accepted the criticism but attributed his change of view to the teaching process itself: in 'giving out one's convictions to other minds one is insensibly led to new views of their truth'. Mill might have been a better thinker had he too undergone the 'testing and transforming influence of teaching'. Martineau's understanding of teaching as an active exchange explained the sense Julia had had 'of a living, growing spirit in his lessons to us'.[27] He showed them what questions they might ask but purposefully did not always answer them. He preferred to sow seeds in their minds that might not germinate for several years.

The lesson that Julia remembered most vividly and reflected on for longest was one in which Martineau had laid side by side a primrose and a cowslip and asked the girls to identify what they had in common and how they differed. Having identified them as similar but separate species, he then asked them to consider why different species existed. His answer was not, it seemed to Julia, definitive: ' "To that question," he concluded, "we can give no answer except the will of the Creator." ' In recalling his words, which she claimed to remember precisely nearly sixty years later, Julia drew two rather different conclusions. In one reminiscence she suggested that Martineau was pointing his class towards a Kantian recognition of the limits of human knowledge and the fact that empirical observation could never offer a complete explanation of the natural world. He was, she wrote, implying no more than 'a provisional state of mind, merely asserting that the universe owes its origin to Divine will, and coupling it with a boundary line where secondary causes [as currently perceived by human beings] seem to fail us'. But in another account of the lesson, she drew a rather different conclusion: 'I took from his words an impression which all succeeding years deepened – the belief that those who clearly and definitely grasp any theory are thereby the better prepared to accept its opposite, if that be brought home to them by effective reasoning.'[28] Her reflections on Martineau's teaching laid the foundations both for her approach to Darwinism and for her lifelong fondness for dialectics.

Martineau's Sunday sermons were as impressive as his classroom teaching. Rachel rented two pews for herself and her pupils at her brother's chapel, and the girls were encouraged to write down summaries of his sermons. This cannot have been an easy task given Martineau's deliberately impromptu, inspirational style. One listener remembered him as 'the Tennyson of preachers [...] with the same lyric intensity: the same ascent into a realm where thought and emotion were transferred into each other'. His way of talking as if he were simply thinking aloud was remarkably effective. For Richard Hutton, hearing Martineau preach was the real 'beginning of his life'.[29]

Julia absorbed from his sermons a sense that the spiritual life could encompass both the intellect and the emotions. But the emotion Martineau imported was far from the anxious religious foreboding of her childhood under Mary Rich's influence. He talked instead about 'an absolute reliance upon internal convictions' which sat alongside the more familiar Unitarian concern with 'the truths of religion and morals'. Listening to Martineau, Julia lost her childhood fears of eternal damnation.[30] As formative was the feeling he gave her for the Classical world. While Priestley had decried the 'malign influence of Greek thought' and held it responsible for 'Christianity's unhappy descent into mystery and obfuscation', Martineau cherished the Classics with 'half-guilty' delight. He could not disguise the fact that 'often Greek and Roman history stirred the tides within me more than the images of the Galilean apostles'. He was 'surprised into passionate admiration by the story of Socrates', as Julia would be and found 'unspeakable religious depth in Plato, and even in Cicero and Seneca'.[31] Julia's love of the Classics lay at the core of her most important book, *The Moral Ideal*, just as Martineau's hints of a historicist approach to the composition of the Bible informed her study of Biblical criticism *The Message of Israel*.[32]

She was at Rachel Martineau's school for only a year. There was nothing particularly unusual about this. Middle-class girls like George Eliot, Harriet Martineau and Emma and Fanny Wedgwood tended to pop in and out of boarding schools. In Julia's case her parents would have been aware of moves afoot in London to provide more advanced teaching for young women. Perhaps, too, with three daughters to educate as well as three sons at public schools, Hensleigh baulked at paying another year of Rachel Martineau's expensive fees (80 guineas for basics with up to 42 guineas on top for extras). Probably the most decisive factor was the prospect of James Martineau's absence from Liverpool. Though he did not in the end go to Germany with his family till 1848, he had originally planned to escape his fractious congregation in 1847, and this may well have persuaded the Hensleigh Wedgwoods to bring their daughter back to London.

Perhaps Julia was homesick too. Though Harriet Martineau visited her and Jane Carlyle arranged for a cousin in Liverpool to keep an eye on her, there is no record of her parents seeing her at school. Julia did not complain but may have had mixed feelings. At the end of the family summer holiday in Tenby in 1846, she was so excited at the thought of going back that she made herself ill. But when Harriet Martineau saw her in Liverpool, she had to listen to 'much childish outpouring' as Snow opened her heart to her mother's friend.[33]

Life for the 14-year-old back in London may have seemed dull by comparison, but there were compensations for being at home. This was, she remembered, the time when the Hensleigh Wedgwood family was happiest.[34] The intellectual isolation of her bright, but only partly educated daughter, however, was a daily reminder to Fanny and Ras Darwin of the patchiness of educational opportunities for girls and a stimulus to improve things.

Most of the prime movers in the drive to establish higher education for young women in London were part of the Hensleigh Wedgwood circle: Elizabeth Jesser Reid, Alexander Scott and Frank Newman on the Dissenting wing and F. D. Maurice and Charles Kingsley on the Anglican. Fanny was closely involved from the beginning, becoming one of the first Lady Visitors at Queen's College, which opened its doors in 1848, and then at the College for Women in Bedford Square (or Bedford College as it would become) in 1849.

Julia was in the first enrolments at both. Temperamentally, she, like her mother, would be more drawn to Bedford College with its more testing syllabus and demanding teachers. Emotionally, however, she would remain for the next 20 years under the spell of Maurice, the leading light at Queen's, and her next great mentor. Under his influence she moved from Unitarianism to Anglicanism, following his own spiritual journey.

Maurice was the son of a Unitarian minister. As the only boy in a family of seven children, he had a keen sense of the importance of education for girls and taught his sisters himself. Intending to practice law, he studied at Trinity College, Cambridge, where he became a leading member of the Apostles alongside his closest friend John Sterling, Arthur Hallam and Tennyson, who occasionally attended. Though he was placed in the first class, his refusal to subscribe to the Thirty Nine Articles debarred him from taking his degree. Despite this, he had, like all undergraduates, attended obligatory morning chapel in College, where he grew to love the Anglican liturgy.

From Cambridge he went to London writing for the *Westminster Review*, briefly part-owning and editing *The Athenaeum* and, in the company of Sterling, moving in reforming circles. A family crisis had led his mother and sisters to reject Unitarianism. Maurice was slower to abandon his father's faith but began to look for a more intensely spiritual religion. In 1830 he enrolled at Oxford to study theology in preparation for ordination in the Church of England. Now he subscribed willingly to the Thirty Nine Articles, defending their imposition as an honest test of acceptance of the historic dogma taught at the ancient universities. For all the appeal of an established national church, however, Maurice retained many Unitarian friends and was always a great admirer of James Martineau, an admiration Martineau returned.

In 1836 he was appointed chaplain at Guy's Hospital, where he made his mark not only through lectures on moral philosophy to the medical students but also through bedside Bible study classes for patients. In 1840 he was also made Professor of English Literature and History at King's College and on the strength of his defence of Anglicanism in *The Kingdom of Christ*, published in 1842, chosen to be its first Professor of Theology in 1846. That same year he moved from Guy's to become chaplain at Lincoln's Inn Chapel, where he quickly acquired a devoted following.

Alexander Scott first got to know Maurice during his time at Guy's Hospital and they quickly became friends. By the time Scott moved from Woolwich to Gloucester Crescent near Regent's Park in 1846, he had become the leading independent minister in London as well as a respected public lecturer. He rented his own premises at the Marylebone Literary Institute, preaching on Sunday evenings and lecturing during the week on literature, history and philosophy. Maurice came to hear him as did Thackeray; Carlyle; John Sterling; Coleridge's daughter, Sara; and the Hensleigh Wedgwoods, Mary Rich and Julia. In 1848 he was appointed Professor of English Language and Literature at the non-sectarian University College, where Hensleigh served as a trustee. At the Scotts' weekly soirées, Maurice got to know Thomas Carlyle, 'the best growler of the day'.[35] He was more impressed, however, by a very different Scotsman, Thomas Erskine, whom Scott invited him to meet at Erskine's home in Linlathen in 1847.[36]

In 1831 a friend had lent Maurice Erskine's recently published *The Brazen Serpent*. Reading it helped resolve some of the tensions surrounding his family's recoil from Unitarianism. 'It has been an unspeakable comfort to me,' he wrote to his sister: 'a light has fallen through him on the Scriptures'.[37] Erskine's theology was distinctive but undogmatic. He abhorred Calvinism and the idea of eternal damnation. For him God was not a judge holding mankind on probation or requiring atonement for original sin but an educator lovingly making his children aware of Himself. Nor was eternal life some future condition but rather a quality that could be apprehended now as part of the reality of increased communion with God.[38] Erskine's thinking liberated Maurice's theology. He also delighted in the man when they met. He was, he wrote, 'so gentle and truthful and loving: the best man I think I ever knew'.[39] Erskine's effect on Julia would be equally profound.

Maurice's openness to men outside the mainstream like Scott and Erskine gave him a persistent air of unorthodoxy. His social activism also contributed to suspicions about his unsoundness. However misleadingly, his actions in 1848 had made him appear a dangerous radical at an anxious time of social unrest in England and revolution in Europe. In this year he not only established the first college for women in England but also founded the Christian Socialist movement in response to the Chartist demonstrations in April. His colleagues were an eclectic mix: Alexander Scott, Charles Kingsley, Thomas Hughes, John Ludlow and Edward Neale. 'Co-operative', however, was a more accurate description than 'Socialist' for their initiative to help working men help themselves through education and association in craft groupings that sold their products to middle-class subscribers. The educational element of Christian Socialism proved more durable than the economic. The cooperative workshops rarely paid for themselves, but the London Working Men's College founded in 1854 survived well into the twentieth century, as did its counterpart the London Working Women's College established a decade later. Julia would be closely associated with both.

The appearance of Christian Socialism was more subversive than its reality. Though Maurice believed in educating the working classes, he saw their improvement as a good in itself not as an engine for social mobility. He resisted for as long as he could the idea that working men should have a say in the running of their College. Women, too, were kept out of the governance of Queen's College for 25 years. Similarly, though his idea of a college for women broke new ground, its ambitions were limited.

Queen's College had its origins in the Governesses Benevolent Institution founded in 1843, which offered temporary accommodation for governesses between engagements and acted as a clearing house for potential employees and employers. A training college for women teachers and governesses had opened at Whitelands in South London in 1843. Marianne Thornton thought it 'perfect'. 'There seems such a desire to make them really humble unpretending Village Teachers, making them clean and cook and iron (not wash) that they mayn't fancy themselves fine ladies because they teach them Geography and History and so on.'⁴⁰ Others, including her friend, Fanny, had higher ambitions for women's further education.

A course of lectures for governesses was organized at King's in 1847. Once Maurice got involved, the idea of setting up a separate college for women moved ahead quickly. Nor would it be confined to governesses. The quality of its professors, some of whom already held chairs at King's, attracted a wider range of aspiring young women, while its affiliation to the Church of England and the gentility of its Lady Visitors promised respectability.

Maurice set out his aims for the new college in an inaugural lecture at the Hanover Rooms on 29 March 1848. Limited though they now appear, his audience, which included Fanny, Hensleigh and Julia, found them inspirational. He began by disassociating the new venture from Princess Ida's Amazonian, man-hating college, which his old friend, Tennyson, had memorably created but then satirized in *The Princess* published the previous year. 'I never think of the poem', Julia wrote 50 years later, 'without hearing again in those deep, serious, slightly tremulous tones [Maurice's] allusion to possible sneers against a project which would, he warned his hearers, be considered 'as equally extravagant, if not equally imaginative, with that lately set forth by our great poet in his picture of another college for women'.⁴¹

Maurice brought to his prospectus for women's education a Hartleyan concern for the associations of the learning process together with the Platonism he had absorbed at Cambridge from his tutor, Julius Hare. He drew on the distinction he liked to make between Aristotle, who merely collected pieces of information, and Plato, who intuited underlying principles. 'Study', he proclaimed, 'is not worth much if it is not about the roots of things.' Students would be encouraged to make connections between subjects. Drawing and music, for example, were ways of 'looking below the surface of things for the meaning which they express' and finding 'the sense of an order and a harmony in the heart of things'. Similarly, mathematics was on the syllabus not to teach girls how to do household accounts but as an intellectual discipline. Latin, too, controversial though its inclusion was, would put girls on the road to mastery of the English language. In English literature girls should express their own reactions rather than learning chunks of literature by heart. Nor should they show off. Just as Maurice believed in cooperation amongst workingmen, so at Queen's College he looked to girls to learn together. There would be no prizes, and brilliance would be discouraged. The difference between the ethos of the men's colleges at Oxford and Cambridge and the new college for women could not have been clearer.

Maurice attracted some distinguished colleagues to lecture on their own subjects. Charles Kingsley was Professor of English Language and Composition for a couple of years, Samuel Clark taught Latin and William Sterndale Bennett, 'the English Mendelssohn', was responsible for music with William Hullah. Not all the teaching was at this elevated level, however. With girls admitted from the age of 12 and no entry qualifications, class teaching could be mundane. Julia, for example, remembered an inspiring lecture from Professor Cock on arithmetic which 'opened a door leading to a palace […] even to glance in and follow in imagination those stately corridors has made the whole intellectual life a different thing for me'. As she confessed, however, she barely 'crossed the threshold' in the classes that followed. Dorothea Beale, who arrived at Queen's with the benefit of an education in Paris, dismissed them as 'elementary'.[42]

Maurice's classes were a different matter. Some of his students at King's found him hard-going: at Queen's, in contrast, 'he inspired an enthusiasm which is difficult to describe […] and […] to exaggerate'.[43] Schoolgirl hearts fluttered at the obvious signs of melancholy in their teacher's face. They would have known that he was recently widowed but not perhaps that he had also lost, in quick succession, his favourite sister and his closest friend, John Sterling. While James Martineau opened up new intellectual horizons for young female minds, Maurice engaged their imaginative sympathies. Caroline Fox remembered a lecture in 1849 'so full and solemn that it left us all trembling with emotion'. Camilla Crudance described his professorial style: 'The roll being read, he leaned his head on his hand, and gave his lectures without notes, gently rubbing his forehead all the while as though to press out the ideas that came to him.' Like Martineau, Maurice did not seek to impose interpretations: 'anything like second hand opinions of books which one had not read, was in his eyes a breach of honesty'. In one English class he read the death of Falstaff. '"I shall not say anything about it," he quietly intoned, "because I want you to think it over for yourself."'[44] This was the kind of active learning, founded on female intuition and sympathy, two qualities Maurice prized, that few at Queen's had previously experienced and none ever forgot.

Maurice was innovative as a teacher but conservative on governance. Queen's College embodied a man's view of a becoming education for women and neither sought nor admitted women's own views on how it should develop. The Lady Visitors appointed to chaperone girls in the classroom were primarily there to guarantee the respectability of the new institution. They included 'the stately and beautiful' Lady Stanley of Alderley, Lady Monteagle, Lady Caroline Stirling and 'Mrs Hensleigh Wedgwood, the daughter of Sir James Mackintosh, so clever and kind, whom everybody liked', as Dorothea Beale remembered.[45] Increasingly, they complained about their exclusion from College management. The College's lack of ambition and the male domination of its governance contrasted with the harder-edged Bedford College that opened in 1849.

Though this offered a more promising outlet for Fanny's energies, she and her two younger daughters remained involved with Queen's. Effie, then aged 10, was one of the first pupils in the preparatory class started in 1849 and lucky enough to be taught by Dorothea Beale.[46] Despite her developing commitments at Bedford College, Fanny stayed as a Lady Visitor at Queen's and was chosen to sit on the Committee of Education in 1873 when the Lady Visitors finally established their claim to be represented on it.

Bedford College, with its more speculative, challenging and unorthodox roster of teachers, was a more natural intellectual home for Julia. Her move there did not, however, break her links with Maurice, who remained a close family friend. On Sunday afternoons she and her parents went to hear him preach at Lincoln's Inn Chapel enjoying his adventurous theology and impressed by the fervour of his devotions. They also attended his Christian Socialist Bible study groups, and under Maurice's influence, Julia would also begin a lifetime's habit of workhouse visiting on Sunday afternoons. She rarely derived any satisfaction from it, complaining about the 'torpidity' of some of the inmates and looking forward to a restorative tea with friends after each visit. Leslie Stephen was

Prof. Maurice.

Figure 8 Frederick Denison Maurice in the 1850s, a major influence on Julia's life and thought. Courtesy of the National Portrait Gallery.

outspokenly dismissive of the anti-intellectualism of Maurice's reverence for the wisdom of 'the bed-ridden woman'. Julia tried harder to share Maurice's confidence in the truths that could be learnt at the bedsides of 'men and women overladen with appalling misery' without ever quite experiencing her own epiphanies in the workhouse.[47]

Maurice, Julia wrote, 'was one of the persons I have most loved' and 'the most truly humble man I ever knew'. Simply writing his name down in a letter 60 years after she first knew him gave her intense pleasure.[48] Through him she also met two of her closest friends, Julia and Hester Sterling, the orphaned daughters of John Sterling. Maurice, whose first wife, Anna Barton, was Sterling's sister-in-law, had been appointed their guardian on Sterling's premature death in 1844 at the age of 38.

Maurice laboured under an intense feeling of guilt and sin for much of his adult life. He felt responsible for some of the early tensions and splits in his family over religion; he believed he might have softened his first wife's sufferings before her early death in 1845; and he blamed himself for not preventing John Sterling's steady loss of faith. His sense of failure was exacerbated by the fact that though Sterling entrusted his two daughters to his guardianship, he arranged for his oldest son, Edward, to be brought up by Frank Newman, the brother of the future cardinal and a man Maurice deeply distrusted. Both made unconventional spiritual journeys, but while Maurice found a safe harbour early on in the Church of England, Newman continued his spiritual quest. He moved from Evangelicanism to the Baptists and on to Theism if not, as many thought, agnosticism, before James Martineau finally drew him into Unitarianism. One of the most brilliant intellects of the Victorian age and an authoritative writer on an extraordinarily wide range of topics, the unpredictability of Frank Newman's personal odyssey left him more marginalized in the academic discourse of his times than his gifts merited.

His close involvement in the moves to establish the non-sectarian Bedford College undermined any chance of associating it with Queen's College. Both Ann and Alexander Scott approached Maurice about cooperating. But Maurice was adamant: he would have nothing to do with an institution that included Frank Newman.[49] Elizabeth Jesser Reid, the founder of Bedford College, may well have been relieved. She and her friends now had a freer hand to establish the sort of College she wanted and engage a varied team of professors, including Newman.

Mrs Reid was the daughter of a Unitarian iron monger. A brief marriage to a London doctor, John Reid, left her a wealthy widow living with her unmarried sister in the family home at York Terrace, Regent's Park, close to the Hensleigh Wedgwoods. Like Fanny, she was an active anti-slavery campaigner and advocate of the Italian cause as well as a life-long friend of Harriet Martineau. Mrs Reid believed in education as a moral good and saw no reason why women should be excluded from its higher reaches. Generous to a fault, idealistic and romantic but not always cool-headed and practical, she gave most of her money and energy to the establishment of a college for women that would, at least in part, be run by women.

Encouraged by a small but like-minded circle of men and women with the Hensleigh Wedgwoods at its centre, she set up a course of lectures in her own sitting room over the winter of 1848–49 at which professors, mostly from University College, spoke to a largely female audience, offering a taster of what the new College might provide. By June 1849 a General Committee, chaired by Hensleigh, had been set up, and when Mrs Reid provided £1,500 to help establish the new venture, three trustees were appointed: Hensleigh, Ras Darwin and Thomas Farrer, a young barrister.

Influential though Hensleigh was in the early stages and useful in strengthening the new College's links with University College, Frank Newman played a more decisive role. He served as a secretary to the Board and drew up a constitution for the new College. This still left women in a minority on the governing Council but gave them a more active role than at Queen's. Lady Visitors were also given clearly defined duties and much was made of their existence in the College prospectus. They included Mary Rich and Fanny Wedgwood and close friends like Julia Smith and Ann Scott, as well as Anne Procter, Anna Jameson, Jane Martineau and Anna Swanwick and her mother. Not only were they to sit in on classes 'to uphold decorum and silence' and make sure that teaching rooms were properly ventilated, but they were also expected to act 'as friends to whom [Young Ladies] may come for advice'.[50]

Hensleigh remained a member of Bedford College until his death in 1891 but soon withdrew from active oversight. Fanny, by contrast, was a member of Council for 20 years. Despite Ras Darwin's occasional irritation at the amount of her time taken up by the

College, she threw herself into its affairs. Even Ras had to admit that she was blossoming under the new challenge. Julia Smith, he told her, 'is going about declaring the world has not yet found out what an astonishing woman you are [...] and I am anxious to come and see with my own eyes whether there is any truth in the account'.[51] Perhaps it was primarily in the hope of seeing more of her that, once Hensleigh had withdrawn, Ras took over as Chair of the Council in 1850, a post he maintained until 1869 when he became the College's Visitor. Ras's involvement with Bedford College was the most sustained of his limited public life. Though he did not share Mrs Reid's Unitarian beliefs, he was like her keenly committed to education for women and unlike her able to see and defuse difficulties. He also had the tact that Mrs Reid lacked. 'Mrs Reid's rudeness to our two parsons was beyond her usual scale,' he complained to Fanny after one fraught Council in 1850.[52]

Avowedly non-sectarian, like University College, Bedford College found room in its academic and managerial staff for a range of religious opinions. Lady Romilly, a liberal-minded churchwoman and the daughter of the principal at King's College, was one of its prominent Lady Visitors but so, too, was Ann Scott. William Sterndale Bennet, who taught at Queen's College, was also on the staff at Bedford and moves were made to appoint two professors from King's (though the Principal there refused to release them). And then there was Frank Newman, whose brilliant *Phases of Faith, or Passages from the History of My Creed* published in 1850, made him increasingly hard to categorize.

The early years of Bedford College, when Julia was a student, were not easy. Enrolments declined, professors complained about poor pay, the syllabus was not well organized with students free to pick and choose their subjects and drop in and out of College terms. The College soon lost two of its ablest professors, Alexander Scott, who left to head the new Owen's College in Manchester (the nucleus of the future University) in 1850, and Frank Newman, who resigned in 1851. Nonetheless, it attracted a rich crop of students in the early 1850s including Anna Swanwick, already a successful writer, Marianne Evans (George Eliot), beginning to be known in literary London for her work on the *Westminster Review* as well as her messy private life, Julia Smith's legitimate nieces, Blanche and Bertha, who had been at school with Julia in Liverpool, and her illegitimate niece, Barbara Leigh Smith. Alice and Eleanor Bonham Carter also attended, as did Dickens's most gifted daughter, Katey.

The curriculum on offer was broad and serious. It included Latin, maths and German and, in its first year, a course of lectures on political economy given by Frank Newman and attended by Julia and possibly her mother.[53] The most popular course in the first year, however, was the series of lectures on moral philosophy given by Alexander Scott.

College registers also show Fanny attending lectures on geography and astronomy given by Rev. Thomas Wilson. She was probably there to keep an eye on the lecturer who was seen as theologically unreliable. When the College tried to sack him, Newman offered his resignation too. The Council narrowly came down against him (with Ras and Fanny on opposing sides), and the College lost its most brilliant but troublesome star. With its future in doubt, Mrs Reid withdrew for two years as Ras steadied the ship. A subscription was opened, a preparatory school set up, some scholarships endowed by Mrs Reid and the College kept going.

Frank Newman's resignation from the academic body at Bedford College did not mean his disappearance from London. He remained at University College until 1862 and was a regular guest of the Hensleigh Wedgwoods throughout the 1850s. He and Hensleigh were both men of scruple and integrity, though low on practical sense; both were passionately interested in etymology where Newman's expertise took him into obscure areas of the ancient world which fascinated Hensleigh; both loved conversation on abstract subjects and moral problems; both were essentially speculative, open to new ideas and critical of authority and, in their later years, inclined to crankiness. With his wispy moustache, long, lank hair, battered clothing, awkwardness with women and total lack of humour, Newman lacked Maurice's charm. For Julia, however, one of the greatest pleasures of her teenage years was listening to Newman and her father in animated talk at the dinner table. 'There was conversation in those days around our table and I had ears to hear it,' she wistfully wrote 60 years later. In compiling the Family Album of letters from distinguished correspondents of the Wedgwoods, she included more from Frank Newman than anyone else, recalling 'the atmosphere of ardent hope and keen desire which surrounded us in the years after 1848'. 'As I look back,' she told Alfred Benn, 'all the intellectual interest of that time [1850] for me seems to centre in him.'[54]

Julia, like some of the other gifted female writers of her time, including the Winkworth sisters and Anna Swanwick, was lucky to study under the best teachers of her age outside the established universities: Martineau, Maurice, Scott and Frank Newman. All of them taught a remarkably broad range of subjects, but none could compare as a polymath with Newman and none were as innately gifted. Four years younger than his more famous brother, Frank romped through his studies at Oxford in a way John Henry could not match. He was only the second man (after Robert Peel) to win a congratulatory first in both Classics and Maths, and at the age of just 21 was made a fellow of Balliol, the most academic of the Oxford Colleges. Like his brother he began as an Evangelical. Both abandoned their early faith but then moved in very different directions. While John Henry looked increasingly for the validation of external authority in religion, Frank became increasingly sceptical even of Biblical authority. He gave up his fellowship; went on a quixotic journey to Iraq, which nearly killed him as he distributed pamphlets and sought, unsuccessfully, to convert the Muslims of Mosul and Baghdad; married a gentle, pietistic member of the Plymouth Brethren, whose religious practices and poor health would limit his career prospects; and was obliged to take up academic appointments in nonconformist colleges at Bristol and then Manchester New College.

Throughout it all he remained an intensely moral man of absolute, if pedantic, integrity. Elizabeth Gaskell 'reverenced' him; James Martineau loyally stood up for him through all the twists and turns of his spiritual odyssey; whilst for the young George Eliot he was 'our blessed St Francis'.[55] He was always a keen proponent of the Italian cause and in later life, like Julia, an anti-vivisectionist. For Julia, however, his commitment to vegetarianism, teetotalism and anti-imperialism went too far. 'His enthusiasms were sharpened to shrillness,' his 'sweeps of intellectual movement from West to East [became] something incalculable and unhelpful.' As a professor, however, and despite his awkwardness with young women – his instruction to one not to blush when he spoke to her was inevitably counterproductive and made Julia squirm – 'a dearer and more interesting teacher could not be'.

Figure 9 Francis Newman in the 1850s, the third of Julia Wedgwood's outstanding teachers. Courtesy of the National Portrait Gallery.

'There was no fumbling, no groping after his thoughts, they came forth clothed in definite, appropriate language free from doubt […] he listened & he answered,' she wrote.[56] Anna Swanwick, a generation older than Julia, sat in on his classes as a Lady Visitor. She was brave enough to tell him privately that he had made a mistake in one of his calculations. He rewarded her with the offer of private tuition in Greek and differential calculus, decidedly adventurous subjects for women. She made good use of the first, becoming a noted translator of Aeschylus.

The Bedford College register shows Julia attending a range of courses. As well as Newman's lectures on political economy, she also went to his classes in logic and studied elocution in 1850 alongside Latin in the Michaelmas and Lent terms. But though Godfrey heard in the spring of 1852 that it was all 'work! work!! work!!!'[57] for Julia, the end of that Easter term was her last at the Ladies College.

The odd mix of subjects she followed and the way the names of her friends and contemporaries come in and out of the register illustrate the College's lack of rigour in its early days. Eleanor Bonham Carter, for instance, showed up for just one term in Easter 1850 to study English literature, with her sister, Alice, opting for moral philosophy, while Barbara Leigh Smith devoted a term to natural sciences. Nor were there any exams to test what they had learnt. For many years both Queen's and Bedford rejected the possibility of involving their students in London University examinations. Having later seen at first hand the galvanizing impact of preparing young women for Cambridge University examinations in the early days at Girton, Julia came to think of their absence from her own education as a major weakness: 'The power of testing knowledge was not in my youth open to women, and no stimulus to learning can do for the mind what is effected by the examination, teaching us to *know what we do know*.'[58]

Passing exams implied acquiring qualifications, but qualifications to do what? Inevitably, there was confusion of purpose at Bedford College. Unlike Queen's, it did not primarily aim to fit its students for the life of a governess, but nor was it specifically preparing women for any other profession, since there were few openings. Those who were already starting to make their way in the literary world, like Marian Evans and Anna Swanwick, welcomed the opportunity to follow some of the only regular courses available to women under reputable university professors. For others, like Julia, the usefulness of what she had learnt was less obvious.

Though Fanny was a believer in higher education for girls, the rest of the Wedgwoods took a more nuanced view. Uncle Frank was quite impressed with what he saw of Effie and Hope after their years at Queen's when he came to stay at Cumberland Terrace in 1854: 'a girl's college', he suggested to his son Clement, 'is a very convenient and agreeable way of getting a girl educated'. When it came to his own daughters, however, he sent them to a finishing school in Paris. Similarly, when the question of whether Effie and Hope should go on to Bedford College arose, their cheerfully un-intellectual brother Erny, who had been to Rugby and Cambridge, was strongly in favour of Grosvenor College – 'so much more aristocratic', he suggested to Julia. Godfrey, too, though always in awe of Snow's intellectual gifts, could not take what went on at Bedford College entirely seriously. When he first heard a garbled account of the row over Wilson, he imagined his cousin 'advancing at the head of a phalanx of fair maids dictionnaire à la main, and taking some unfortunate master by storm'.[59] This heavy-handed reference to Princess Ida and her companions did not amuse Julia or encourage her to believe that even sympathetic associates saw much point to her education at the Ladies College. Fifty years later she still recalled the 'witless laughter' roused by the mention of it. 'It seems incredible that such stupidity should have the power to sting, but it is true.'[60]

In the spring of 1852, when she was just 19, Julia finished her formal education, such as it was. Perhaps she had grown tired of the piecemeal syllabus or, as in Liverpool five years earlier, lost interest when her favourite teachers, Scott and Newman, dropped out. She may too have found the varying abilities and levels of commitment of her fellow students trying. Her serious illness in the autumn of 1852 and consequent deterioration in her hearing almost certainly confirmed her decision to leave. Had she chosen, she might have gone back to Queen's to try and keep up with Dorothea Beale in her Greek class there. As it was, she had to teach herself Greek in the mid-1850s and, as she always regretted, never mastered it though she liked to include chunks of Greek in the original in her work.

In his earliest article on female education, Maurice had described as 'the happiest incident in the condition of women that they are exempt from the necessity of being prepared for professional avocations'. If this implied that women could more easily enjoy learning for its own sake than men, Maurice qualified the thought in his Inaugural. First, he warned his hearers that 'those who had no dream' of becoming governesses 'might be forced by some reverse of fortune to think of it next year'. Even so, he suggested, the name College implied 'a general' not a 'professional' culture. Queen's would not be about imparting information but rather about 'the apprehension of principles'. Women, he argued in a burst of Hartleyan eloquence, had a special right to this kind of knowledge. 'They have to watch already the first utterances of infancy, the first dawnings of intelligence, how thoughts spring into acts, how acts pass into habits.' Queen's, in short, would provide the sort of education that made girls into good mothers. For all her belief in education for women as a good in itself, Mrs Reid, too, fell back on a similar argument as enrolments at her College fell in the early 1850s: 'if they could but see and feel, as I do, that we shall never have better Men till we have better Mothers, they would come flocking about us'.[61]

None of this helped Julia sort out what use she might make of her haphazard but unusually advanced education if she failed to marry and become a mother. Painful years of waiting lay in store before she discovered her vocation as a writer.

Chapter Three
WAITING

Thinking back to her college education 50 years later, Julia wrote that the difference between the sexes then was as great as the difference between rich and poor.

> Individual zeal might in either case overcome common disadvantage, and the distinction of such exceptional achievement, stamped like all exceptional achievement with the impress of strong individual character, was perhaps more striking than anything with which we can compare it today; but ordinary women were then shut out from the intellectual opportunities open to ordinary men, and even extraordinary women were thus excluded from the employments and dignities accessible to ordinary men. They were obliged to look for their opening towards interesting or important activity and often their actual maintenance, through the portal of marriage, and this event was the centre of all their interest.[1]

Given the surplus of women in the population, however, a lively point of concern amongst male commentators in the 1850s and 1860s, marriage was not available to all.[2] 'Women', Julia crisply wrote in 1869, 'spend the best part of their lives in preparing for an event which may never happen,' 'the time thus spent is not only wasted and unsatisfactory, but unreal.'[3]

Living through this limbo of uncertainty at the end of an incomplete college education that opened intellectual doors but offered no obvious way through them, Julia struggled. Aimlessness never suited her. 'I do not believe', she later wrote, perhaps comparing herself with the feckless but reasonably successful Erny, 'the idlest youth who just saves his degree at College, wastes more of his undergraduate years than an energetic girl of the corresponding period of her life.'[4] She concluded quite early on that she was unlikely to marry. This left her with a life-long sense of incompleteness but not the willingness to fall back on a shadowy life of spinster friends like Alice Bonham-Carter, attending to demanding elderly parents and relatives, supporting married siblings or friends and working unobtrusively for good causes. Julia had always had a sense of mission that grew in response to two serious bouts of illness in the early 1850s. It took time and some false starts before she found her way to a successful career as a writer and thinker. Tensions with her family were often acute during this period of frustration.

The signs of what was to come were apparent at her 'coming out', such as it was, when she was 17. This important staging post in the life of well-bred girls marked both their readiness for adult company and their availability for marriage and offered opportunities to meet potential partners. Julia's 'coming out' was organized in Scotland rather than London and not by her mother but Aunt Rich, who escorted Snow and her cousin Fanny Erskine to their 'coming out' ball in Inverness.

Fanny, the daughter of Rich's sister, Maitland, and William Erskine, was a regular guest at the Hensleigh Wedgwood's home. Her letters, which Julia kept for many years before entrusting them to her daughter, Ida, are a curious mix of light-headed gossip, high religious sentiment and warm affection. Though less systematically educated, Fanny sent Julia painstaking, if not always coherent, accounts of the public lectures she attended, including Scott's attempts to balance Kant, Schelling and Fichte with eighteenth-century British philosophy. At other times, they attended together, both scribbling furiously. Julia remembered herself as often 'discontented & ungracious' in her friendship with Fanny but 'grateful for her affection & forbearance (forbearance which even then I perceived)'.[5]

Fanny was rather in awe of Snow's 'full gallop' to Queen's College '& should not object to popping in upon you to improve my education by dipping into some of your profound Studies [...] it is very difficult to do anything at all regularly, when school days are over'. She sent Snow a pen portrait of the two of them by the fireside: Fanny relaxed with her feet on the fender, unlike the 18-year-old Snow, 'fain to dive into a note-book or laugh over Carlyle'. But for all her admiration for Snow's cleverness, Fanny was wary of her speculations and anxious to draw her back to orthodox piety: 'Oh may we be found watching & praying, loving and full of Hope, at whatever hour our summons hence may come!' she ended her letter of New Year greetings in 1849.[6] Snow bridled at the religiosity. 'I thought her views narrow & dreary, & turned aside to my own thoughts which merged over a wider surface than hers but lacked their deep root.'[7] For all Snow's coltishness over Fanny's attempts to share her Evangelical convictions, however, their affection remained. Fanny sometimes signed her letters 'Your ever loving Madre'. Julia remembered her as 'the romance of my youth'.[8] She was the ideal companion for a coming out.

Julia did her best to get into the spirit of the evening. She pinned up her hair and dressed it with pearls and danced energetically when she was invited, relieved that this was more of a Highland fling than a London ball. But though she was glad not to be under her mother's critical eye, she was keen to consult her on points of etiquette. Ought she to pay 'my gentleman' for her supper ticket or the glasses of champagne he got her? 'Aunt Rich says it wd. be a direct insult, but she has such magnificent ideas.' By her second 'ball', a week later, the excitement was already beginning to pall. No longer the graceful little girl whose dancing had enchanted Marianne Thornton, she felt clumsy on the dance floor as the pearls fell from her hair during a lively reel. While Fanny Erskine never lacked a partner, Julia was glad to sit out some of the dances. The company too began to irritate. She got cross being among 'ignorant heathens' constantly asking who Maurice or Kingsley were. As she told her mother, she would far rather be discussing Kingsley's novel about Chartism *Alton Locke* at Maurice's study group.

Her comments on it show that her critical tastes were developing:

> It is intensely interesting, and very painful. – it will just suit you [...] it will be discussed at your Sunday evenings for the next six months and will furnish Mr Furnival with weapons against Mr Newman – The opening I think beautiful – not the least constrained or highflown, but as it gets on it is a little spoilt by imitation of Carlyle and 'scented aristocrats in your painted halls.' – 'Yes, shriek in your Belgravian retreat ye flunkies!' – etc ad libitum – but I still think it

very interesting. – I know it is Kingsley for if it were possible to mistake the style I recognize a long description which Mr Froude gave me of the novel he was then writing.[9]

This, rather than country dances and the awkwardness of accepting drinks from escorts she did not care for, was the world in which the teenage Julia felt at ease.

As her comments suggest, she had no need to 'come out' in their world. She was already at ease in the sort of company that would prove most congenial to her, whether at her parents' dinner table or in the circle of friends and colleagues that revolved around Maurice and, later, the Working Mens' College set up in 1854. E. M. Forster described the ethos of the Hensleigh Wedgwoods as 'an atmosphere which was worldly yet moral, intellectual yet public-spirited. [...] They were in the swim, breasting the slow Victorian waters with determined stroke.'[10] Fanny attracted big names to their dinner parties, including the Carlyles, Ruskin, Harriet Martineau and, later, Matthew Arnold and Browning. Hensleigh particularly enjoyed the company of unorthodox thinkers like Frank Newman, Alexander Scott and Charles Darwin though their conversation worried Julia. While Frank Newman sat 'at the centre of a warmly admiring group', her parents 'inadequately realized his heresy'.[11] This was the intellectual ambience in which, as Randal Keynes has described, Charles Darwin began to question his Christian faith.[12] Hensleigh, by contrast, held to his moorings.

In 1848 he published his own contribution to the ongoing debate on free will and determinism, necessarianism, natural theology and the inner voice of conscience. *On the Developement [sic] of Human Understanding*, published by a Gower Street bookseller, was both ambitious and obscure. He took on Locke as well as Euclid but lost himself in donnish distinctions and incomplete conclusions. The most confident chapter was his last about the development of moral awareness which anticipated some of the debates he would have with his brother-in-law when Darwin was writing *The Descent of Man*. Hensleigh's moral compass was steady: the undoubted fact of a conscience in man was, he suggested, proof of God's existence.

Fanny, like her father, was more interested in politics than religion but enjoyed attending Maurice's services at Lincoln's Inn Chapel. Julia tried to recall their impact 40 years later.

> That tremulous voice returns upon the ear [...] the pathetic monotone, weighted with a profound conviction. [...] The preacher passed from a statement of difficulties [...] to a new world in which these difficulties were out of sight and forgotten, the transition being made during an invasion of glowing and poetic mist, which found everything clear, and left everything clear.[13]

Fanny admired without being entirely convinced: Maurice's social activism appealed to her more than his theology. Julia came under the spell of both.

She remained in Maurice's orbit long after she had left Queen's College. As her letter to her mother from Scotland mentioned, both of them regularly attended the weekly Bible study meetings he organized in his home. These focused less on the Bible text than on its relevance to contemporary problems. They attracted a varied, though carefully selected attendance, including such different people as Frederick Furnival, the man whose noisy energy always repelled Julia; Fenton Hort, the brilliant young Cambridge academic she would get to know better a few years after; and Octavia Hill, whose charitable work Julia supported in her later years. The group was both a fertile source of ideas for the new Christian Socialism and a forum for what would become its most lasting achievement, the creation of the London Working Men's College. By 1853 the study sessions had expanded into a series of public lectures at the Hall of Association with speakers such as Rev. Llewelyn Davies, Charles Kingsley and the musicologist George Grove. Maurice also gave talks at Willis's Rooms to raise funds for the new college. It opened the following year. Julia would know many of those involved, including Furnival; Lowes Cato Dickinson, who became a lifelong friend; Richard Litchfield, who flirtatiously invited her to join the College men on one of their regular Sunday country walks;[14] Arthur Munby, who taught Latin at the College; the Lushington twins, Vernon and Godfrey; and John Ruskin, who, with Dante Gabriel Rossetti, taught for a time in the art department. Remarkably, given Maurice's continuing role as the hesitant but central authority in key decisions about the College, few of them held conventional religious beliefs.

Julia vividly recalled one evening when she and her mother took their houseguest, Florence Nightingale, to the study group. Wrapped in a red cloak, she made an immediate impression on the inarticulate workingman who tried to address her.[15] This probably happened in the early 1850s when Nightingale was beginning to find her mission. Like Julia, she too had been full of undirected energy in her early womanhood and longed for 'some great thing to sweep away this loathsome life'. 'I had three paths among which to choose – I might have been a married woman, a literary woman, or a Hospital Sister.'[16] Nightingale got the opportunity to be all three though she rejected the first. Julia would have only the second. As she struggled to find it, she, like the young Florence Nightingale, took out her frustrations on her family.

For all its idealization in contemporary sermons, novels and biographies, and, indeed, in Julia's later writings, the extended Victorian family was often a scene of intense emotion as siblings fought for control, influence, affection and possession in a painful process of self-definition.[17] Of the six Hensleigh Wedgwood children, the boys were more passive than the girls. Mack, like his father, was self-contained; Ernie happy-go-lucky; and Alfred, known as 'Tim', too dim and tractable to cause tensions in his younger days. The fiercest struggles arose between the three sisters. Julia was often at the heart of them, demanding but not finding an unquestioning love and trying, but failing, to establish herself at the centre of family life.

The first role she essayed was common to many families: as the oldest sister she tried to mentor her two younger sisters. Hope, 'My dear little Dot', was given a mini lecture on the sort of 'interesting facts' she should include in her letters, though the list – 'whether you have a garden, whether you are near the sea, whether you bathe, what time you are down in the morning, how many of you sleep together' – was not inspired. Effie was ticked off as too young to read *Persuasion*, 'the worst sort of good novel you could read' and steered instead to Scott's *Ivanhoe*.[18] But neither Effie nor Hope wanted instruction from Snow. For that they could always turn to their mother or Ras Darwin.

Nor did another key relationship in the Victorian family, the one between the eldest sister and brother, provide Snow with its usual satisfactions once she and Mack had outgrown childhood. Mack had his father's temperament. When he was abroad, he wrote his sister long letters full of careful observation, rather like Hensleigh's early letters. Clearly, he wanted to keep up with his clever sister, but there is little warmth in them. Nor did he do what other brothers often did and introduce her to friends he had made at Cambridge as possible suitors. Like other Wedgwoods, he preferred his own kith and kin and travelled abroad either with Godfrey or with his mother. In London he was happiest in the company of his books.

The children were, in any case, rarely all at home together. The girls spent at least a third of the year on separate visits to family and friends choreographed by Fanny. 'If one begins to speculate on all your plans,' Ras wrote gloomily in 1858, 'one gets lost in a hopeless entanglement of children and all the old ladies you are bringing into play.'[19] She sent on clothes, prompted Hensleigh to provide the money they needed, organized accompanying servants and generally weighed the claims of old and young, family and friends. Though she was in great demand herself, she did not always accompany her daughters or, having deposited them, took off on her own visits or returned to London to be with Hensleigh and Ras, attend her committees, go to lectures and meet friends at dinners and parties. Meanwhile, her daughters were left to repay family obligations, particularly to elderly relatives, spend time with their cousins, enlarge their social circle and be seen and, perhaps, admired.

For her time, Fanny allowed them a remarkable degree of independence, leaving them to the care of their maids, like the indispensable Clarke, who spent many hours with Julia in station waiting rooms as she caught up on her correspondence. Though she expected them to help out at charity bazaars for the Italian cause, an activity Julia came to loathe,[20] Fanny did not want a clutch of dependent daughters accompanying her on her calls or keeping her company at home in the way many unmarried girls did as they waited for marriage. She looked to them to be as independent as she had been as a young woman. Her own freedom was the price she exacted for theirs. Effie thrived on it: Julia was resentful. In 1865 she complained to Effie that their mother was at a 'Negro emancipation meeting', 'her 3rd committee this week. She is like the wicked woman in Dickens' novel' (presumably Mrs Jellaby, whose children starved as she devoted herself to relieving hunger in Africa). Even Hope objected when Fanny announced 'the alarming intelligence that she has got 60 calls to make – I shouldn't mind so much if I was not sure that at least half were unnecessary'.[21]

The sisters went to stay with Wedgwood uncles and their families at Woking, Leith Hill Place and Barlaston and with the Darwins and Aunt Elizabeth, who had moved to be close to them in Downe, as well as the redoubtable Susan Darwin at Shrewsbury. For Julia there were also visits to her mother's friends, like Harriet Martineau and Elizabeth Gaskell, and to friends of her own generation, like Alice Bonham Carter at Ravensbourne or Julia and Hester Sterling, Maurice's wards, in Falmouth.

Increasingly, she was at Milton Bryan, where Mary Rich set up home with its owner, the widowed Lady Inglis. She and Sir Robert, a reactionary Tory, had generously taken on the seven Thornton orphans after the sudden death of their father, the banker John Thornton. E. M. Forster described Milton Bryan as 'a resort for ageing ladies, who pottered about the gardens and the little village, and drove through the quiet lanes'.[22] Though much younger than her hostesses, Julia often retreated there when at loose ends.

Life at Milton Bryan was peaceful and well-regulated, with household prayers, afternoon naps, walks round the vegetable garden, sketching and reading aloud in the evenings. The Evangelical Mary Inglis was, for all her willingness to put out a few novels in deference to the tastes of younger visitors, a strict Sabatarian. Julia remembered anxious Sunday conversations during the Indian Mutiny in 1857 about what might be happening. The previous day's *Times* that would have answered some of their questions lay tightly rolled and out of bounds on a side table as they talked.[23] Despite the constraints, Julia looked forward to these visits: 'It is always a pleasure to me', she wrote forlornly to Aunt Rich in December 1854, 'to be with anybody to whom one can imagine oneself any sort of amusement or use in any way – one goes to see so many people to whom one gives not the slightest pleasure and from whom one receives none.'[24] This was unduly self-deprecating. Fanny Allen, stone deaf but fiercely intelligent and keenly interested in the world, was always pleased to welcome her great nieces for summer holidays in Tenby.

Most years the family went on jaunts abroad. They were rarely a success: wallets got lost, rendezvous were missed and Hensleigh usually fell ill or fretted about getting back to his dictionaries in London. With Fanny eager to see everything, they sometimes went their separate ways for a while, as in 1873 when he stayed in Lucerne while she crossed the Alps into Italy.

Snow travelled with her parents only three times. Her first journey in 1845 with the 7-year-old Erny delighted her as they went from Boulogne to Paris and on to Chêne, the home of Great Aunt Jessie Allen's husband, the historian J. C. Sismondi. They continued to Switzerland and Northern Italy and back to Grindelwald, where Snow and her mother concocted a joint letter to Effie, who had stayed behind in London with the two younger children. 'Mr Wedgwood', Fanny reported, 'was not very well,' and they were thinking of coming home early, 'which Snow thinks very foolish'. Snow sketched herself wearing 'a large broad Swiss hat that looks so queer'. One day she went for a walk down the mountainside, seeing 'lots of little low speckled houses. [...] When you are at the top it looks like a great flock of brownish sheep feeding'.[25] She would store up memories of the scenery for use in one of her novels.

The next journey was less adventurous. In 1854 the family travelled to Paris with Aunt Rich and Alexander and Ann Scott to buy outfits for Fanny Erskine's marriage to Hensleigh's fellow trustee at Bedford College, Thomas Henry Farrer. Snow was one of the first to be invited to be a bridesmaid.[26]

Her last foreign family holiday in Switzerland in 1857 was a disaster. Hensleigh was plagued by boils, there were rows over whether Effie and Hope should go on to Italy and Julia got separated from the rest in Vevey, where she spent hours sketching and writing with only Tim to keep an eye on her. Expected letters fixing a meeting point with the rest of the family never arrived, leading to an anxious time before all was resolved. Ras Darwin confided his worries about this latest unhappy holiday to Carlyle, who passed them on to his wife: 'Wedgwoods have had to <u>leave</u> their daughter in Switzerland (<u>couldn't</u> stand traveling).'[27] Julia never went abroad with both her parents again.

Ras was always anxious when the Hensleigh Wedgwoods were abroad. Lying tired and melancholy on his sofa, he imagined Fanny on her

Figure 10 Milton Bryan, watercolour painted by Julia Wedgwood. Courtesy of V&A Wedgwood/Mosley Collection.

first morning, when you had exhausted all the resources of the place before 11 o'clock, bought all the guides, the pictures at the top of note paper, some soap and a few other trifles, & then sat down to consider what upon earth you could do for the rest of the time. What do you do? For I know you cannot sit like a wise man, thinking of the vanity of human wishes.[28]

Even Fanny sometimes nearly gave up: 'When all goes well I enjoy traveling,' she told Effie, 'yet I often feel that receiving my letters is what gives me more pleasure than anything else.'[29] She persisted all the same. In spring 1855 she and Hensleigh took an unusually long tour through France, Switzerland, Italy and Germany, where they dropped Effie off for a stay in Bonn to improve her German and take singing lessons, before going on to Prague and Vienna. With Ernest and Alfred still at school, Hope was despatched with her governess, Sophia Sennett, to stay with Aunt Elizabeth.

This left Julia and Mack alone in the grand new Wedgwood home at 17 Cumberland Terrace overlooking Regent's Park. She seized on her first opportunity to practice household management. As Ras reported in a half-hearted attempt to persuade Fanny to cut short her travels:

Snow seems very happy and goes about like Mrs Schwabe [the wife of the prominent Manchester industrialist] with a packet of stamped envelopes and writes notes in the intervals of business. She is as full of housekeeping as a bride and it evidently is a very interesting subject. You will have to resign the keys of office to her she will get it up so thoroughly.[30]

Julia took on her new responsibilities with characteristic seriousness but only partial success. Beatrice Webb, the daughter of a secure upper-middle-class household, once wrote that the 'true distinction of the upper middle class [was] the habit of giving orders'.[31] If so, Julia was not typical of her class. She worried that the servants were cheating her, and when Mack complained about the state of his room, she went to dust it herself. After some sleepless nights fretting over 'small, but important things', she wrote anxiously, 'I feel as if I never cd. manage a household of my own, but it wd. be easier in some ways if it were quite my own.'[32] Her greatest trial was the Sunday evening Wedgwood dinners. With Sir Robert Inglis having recently died, Aunt Rich stayed away to keep his widow company, leaving it to Julia to both watch the servants and keep the conversation going. Cousin John (Uncle Harry's son) only said 'Yes, No or Oh!', Aunt Moll droned on inaudibly, Mack was 'funereal' and the scandalous Aunt Turnbull proved 'the only person who will put her shoulder to the wheel without which the whole vehicle wd. soon come to a stand-still'. Ras, who arrived unexpectedly, 'like an angel of light upon our flatness' saw Snow struggling and offered to take over the dinners 'to my great delight [...] Robert P[arker, Ras's nephew] is the dullest man I ever saw'.[33]

Despite her trials and her increasingly outspoken criticism of her mother for staying abroad too long, Julia welcomed the chance to spend more time with Mack. She wrote up an account of a long heart-to-heart they had with the fervour of a romantic novelist:

> I felt as if I had never appreciated him before, nor known the depth of his heart. I must tell you one thing he said – speaking of his difficulty of expression 'I do long sometimes to tell you that I love you all as much as possible, but I have no power of expressing those sorts of things.' He said he hoped I should never think him cold again.[34]

This was the closest Julia and Mack came to regaining their old intimacy. As the old Wedgwood constraint re-emerged and Mack's health began to decline, she would go back to this treasured conversation. The characters of Mack and his cousin Godfrey together inspired the most convincing fictional male she ever created, Edward, a man of integrity and deep emotion, but tight-lipped restraint. Creating this character was a consolation for the way she had missed out on the emotional satisfactions of the close brother–sister relationship that sustained a remarkable number of eminent Victorians, including Mathew Arnold, A. H. Clough, Disraeli, Macaulay, John Henry Newman and Browning.[35]

Increasingly, Effie, not she, emerged as the true centre of the Hensleigh Wedgwood family. Self-confident and clever, she was very much her mother's daughter. She gloried in her golden hair and bright singing voice. Young men flocked round her though, like her mother, she was happy to bide her time before surrendering her freedom. Hope, who attended classes with her at Queen's College School and Bedford College, adored her, and of all Fanny's children, except perhaps Mack, Effie was closest to her mother. They had the same energy, charm, adventurousness and pleasure in being admired, and they shared confidences kept from others. Effie, with her 'perfect love and confidence', was always Fanny's 'own dearest child'.[36] Family life was happiest when she was at home. As Julia wrote to her just before Effie set off for her six months in Germany in the spring of 1855: 'I can't tell you sometimes how I hate the independent life we all lead of one another & wish we cd. fuse into each other more. I am sure you are the most fusible one of us – what should we do without you?'[37]

Snow reacted to the emergence of Effie as she had to Mack's pre-eminence as a child. She tried to ingratiate herself, creating tensions with her sister for the satisfaction of resolving them. Looking back on her life from the serenity of her later years, she remembered with a shudder the way she had courted emotion as a young woman.[38] Casting around in 1855 for some purpose in her aimless life, she sought to establish a special claim on Effie, 'my dearest child'.[39] Effie tried to respond, but now Snow drew back, keen to establish her separateness and painful vocation in life. As Leonora Davidoff has suggested: 'a feeling of being singular could at least be a way of forging a more individual identity' in the crowded Victorian home.[40] Julia cultivated it. Portentously, she told Effie in 1855 that she had been marked out for a life of suffering: association with her could only dampen Effie's bright spirit. 'My youth is past,' she informed her sister, at the age of just 22.[41] Effie did not persist.

Strains amongst siblings were not unusual in middle-class households as they competed for status and acceptance. Florence Nightingale's sister, Parthenope, came close to madness as she struggled unavailingly to keep control of her younger sister before unexpectedly finding emotional stability and a fulfilling life in marriage to an elderly suitor Florence had rejected. Elizabeth Gaskell encouraged the match: it is good to 'be loved and sympathized with' and to be another's 'principal object', she told Parthenope.[42] Julia would take much longer to satisfy her need both for a shared love and for pre-eminence. Meanwhile, she continued her sometimes dispiriting round of visits to friends and family.

One place where she was usually happy was Manchester. Here she could choose between staying with the Scotts or their friends the Salis Schwabes or with her mother's new friend, Elizabeth Gaskell. The Schwabes took her to their North Wales holiday home at Glyn Garth. 'I never saw so large a house with such a poor library but nobody troubles it much, small as it is,' she commented.[43] Books were much more in evidence at the Scotts' home. In 1852 she and Aunt Rich planned a long visit to Manchester, staying first with Ann and Alexander Scott and then the Gaskells at Plymouth Grove. Elizabeth went to her usual trouble in preparing for Julia's first stay, inviting 'Katie W[inkworth] to help me entertain them'. But in the event, Rich had to go on her own for just an evening, where she enchanted the Gaskell girls as she ran through her repertoire of stories about her younger days.[44] Julia remained at the Scotts. She had fallen seriously ill and could not be moved.

So ill was she that Fanny and Hensleigh were summoned from London and unsuccessful attempts were made to engage the in-demand Sir Henry Holland to care for her.[45] A local doctor diagnosed rheumatic fever, a potentially fatal infection at the time. Her parents stayed till it was clear she would recover, leaving Mary Rich and Ann Scott to nurse her. Godfrey wrote to cheer her up with a description of the Duke of Wellington's impressive funeral; her sisters in London passed on the best wishes of friends at Queen's College; and Fanny Erskine wrote affectionately but did not pass up the opportunity to moralize: 'You are having a severe lesson of patience taught you.'[46]

Second-guessing the diagnoses of Victorian doctors is a thankless task. When Julia suffered another similar attack two years later, the doctors made the vague diagnosis of 'bilious fever', while Fanny referred to a recurrence of 'rheumatic fever'.[47] More probably, both illnesses were viral meningitis, the residue of an attack of measles at Christmas 1843. The symptoms were the same: a skin rash, vomiting and diarrhoea, high temperature and severe headaches. With careful nursing they were treatable but left unpleasant after effects in increased sensitivity to light, painful teeth, nervous irritability and loss of hearing.

Julia's predisposition to deafness, her unhappy inheritance from her grandmother, Kitty, and the Allen great aunts had already been exacerbated by childhood illnesses. After her illness in 1852, her hearing got worse. In March 1854 Ras persuaded her to try wearing a set of 'ears' at parties. Possibly they were what was marketed as Aurolen phones, a pair of cups, one for each ear, connected by a band over the head that could be concealed by careful hair styling.[48] Parisian makers had the best reputation for devices of this kind, and it may be that these were acquired on the family trip to Paris in 1854. Ras's reassurance to Fanny and, no doubt, Julia, that they were 'very inconspicuous as seen in front', was tactfully silent about the rear view. She tried them out at an evening party at the Spottiswoodes but found them confusing. In time she would learn to use an ear trumpet that could be folded up and carried in her reticule though it remained an embarrassment for her as a young woman.

Harriet Martineau, who, like Julia, began suffering serious hearing loss in her late teens, offered robust but compassionate advice in her 'Letter to the Deaf' on the need to avoid false shame by discussing deafness openly with friends and family. Julia took longer to come to terms with her disability. Nor did she agree with Martineau that there was more to gain 'in têtes-à-tetes [through an ear trumpet] than is given to people who hear general conversation'.[49] She missed the lively interchanges at her parents' dinner parties. She was mortified when her friend, Julia Sterling, stopped her from going to a dinner where Maurice had promised to introduce her to Charles Kingsley because her deafness would be too stressful for her – and them.[50] Her mother did her best to give her the gist of conversations at the dinner table but sometimes found that 'she could not manage that Snowie got much'.[51] Others were less sympathetic. Marianne Thornton complained about her way of putting her trumpet across her dinner plate 'till I can't get a mouthful into my mouth'.[52] In later years, Julia would try and count the advantages of her deafness, valuing the extra time it allowed her for reading and relying on 'her private springs'.[53] As a young woman, however, her struggle to hear was a frustrating source of misunderstandings and self-loathing.

Deafness and the aftermath of her bouts of meningitis changed Julia. Much of the lightness, good humour and affectionate self-mockery in her letters disappears from the mid-1850s, not to return till the poise of her later years. But, like John Henry Newman, she also emerged from serious illness with a keen sense of mission.

Though some saw deafness as an impediment to marriage, the experience of three of her deaf Allen great aunts showed that this was not necessarily the case. Fanny never married; Kitty married unhappily, but the cheerful Jessie was famously contented in her marriage to Sismondi. For Julia, her loss of hearing was not the only factor in her early recognition that she was unlikely to marry. As important were her passion for learning, her insistence on truth-telling, her physical awkwardness and a fundamental sense of being

Figure 11 Victorian hearing devices. Courtesy of the Wellcome Foundation.

different. If she was not to be married, or become the emotional focus of her family, she must find another way of fulfilling her mission.

She continued her studies, undirected though they sometimes were. She taught herself Greek and continued to read widely when the time left from meeting Wedgwood social obligations allowed. Striking the right balance was not easy. A few years later, she would write feelingly about the distractions and pressures that kept a young middle-class woman away from sustained study:

> How can [a girl of 18] sit reading history in her own room, when her conscience and her inclination whisper in concert that she may be wanted to settle a plan with her parents, or entertain a visitor? [...] A guest is coming, or a guest is going; or it is a beautiful day, and the girls ought to go out; the books will remain, and the sunshine will not. And the daughter does not discover for some time, that, even if the books will remain, the power of using them is, under these constant interruptions, more evanescent than the sunshine.[54]

Clearly, she was describing her own experience. Her stay with Elizabeth Gaskell in 1855 changed everything.

Gaskell had long wanted to entertain her in Manchester. 'I wish she would write to me herself and tell me how she is, and what she is doing,' she wrote to Mary Rich in March 1853. 'I should give a letter from her a great greeting and consider it as a sort of pledge that sometime or other she would pay the long-projected visit.'[55] At last, in October 1855, it was arranged. 'Mrs Gaskell will be a great delight to me,' Julia wrote to Effie. 'She is one of those people whose society is a great happiness to me, much more than I should have expected from her books.'[56]

In Shrewsbury on her way to the northwest, she took stock of her life in a long letter to Effie. 'I have got into an uncomfortable, discontented state with everything – I think it is from long idleness, not that I have not been doing things, but no regular work.'[57] She described the ennui that overtook unmarried young girls acutely in an article in 1869: 'She may try to read history, or teach poor children, or cultivate a musical talent; but for a certain interval all is vague, and difficult. The question "Is this to go on?" takes the edge off every pursuit, and drains off interest to a possible future which has no continuity with the

Figure 12 Mrs Gaskell in the early 1860s. Courtesy of the National Portrait Gallery.

present.'[58] At the Gaskells' home, by contrast, there was no time for idleness. When Julia wrote again to Effie a couple of weeks later, she was in very different spirits:

I enjoy being here extremely […] the house is so comfortable and well-arranged. I have a charming room the size of Mama's or larger – sofa writing table etc all so comfortable. […] I like all the family arrangements, there is never any bustle and never any dawdling, which makes the beau ideal of domestic occupation. – everybody is occupied, the rooms are always tidy and one never sees any tidying.[59]

The contrast between the purposeful order of Plymouth Grove and the emptiness of Cumberland Terrace could not have been greater. Elizabeth Gaskell was engaged in the most difficult writing assignment she ever faced: everyone was co-opted to help with the biography of Charlotte Bronte she had been asked to write by Bronte's father. Julia's involvement moved her life in a new direction.

The years of aimless waiting were about to end.

Chapter Four

THE YOUNG NOVELIST

Elizabeth Gaskell was distantly related to the Wedgwoods and always took an interest in the family.[1] The cascade of marriages precipitated by Fanny and Hensleigh's union in 1832 particularly delighted her.[2] She was about to marry herself, but while she was 21 and her groom, Rev. William Gaskell, just 5 years older, Fanny was 31 when she married and 3 years older than Hensleigh. Respecting their difference in age, Elizabeth would always refer to Fanny as 'Mrs Wedgwood' and saw her as her metropolitan role model, taking her advice on who to call on and copying her way of leaving visiting cards. Elizabeth's trips to London, where she regularly stayed with Fanny and Hensleigh, offered a welcome break from her duties as the wife of a Unitarian minister in Manchester. Her husband had been appointed an assistant minister at the Cross Street Chapel (in preference to James Martineau) shortly before their marriage. Elizabeth played her part conscientiously, teaching in the Sunday School and sharing his concern to improve the lot of the poor through education and self-help, but avoiding the smoke and stink of the city by settling in comfortable houses on the outskirts of Manchester, where she could tend her garden and manage a few farm animals. Four of her six children survived, Marianne, Meta, Flossie and Julia. Both of her sons died early.

Her first novel, *Mary Barton*, was written in the aftermath of her younger son's death. Its unsympathetic portrait of the northern millocracy outraged her husband's congregation. Elizabeth escaped the outcry by going to London.[3] Both she and Fanny were keen for their daughters to get to know one another. In the summer of 1849, Snow joined the Gaskells on a holiday in Skelwith in the Lake District; in 1852 the Wedgwoods and Gaskells were together at Silverdale after Meta had stayed for several weeks in London. Elizabeth had joined them there for a 'very pleasant' dinner to celebrate Snow's 18th birthday.[4] Ras Darwin and his sisters, Susan and Catherine, were there, as were Effie and Hope, Lady Alderson, one of the Visitors at Queen's College and, rather oddly, A. H. Clough, then spending a miserable time as the reluctant Principal of the new University Hall, and Frederick Furnival. If this was Fanny's attempt at match-making for her eldest daughter, it was not well considered. More probably she was taking pity on two intelligent but awkward young men.

Despite their friendship, Fanny and Elizabeth were very different mothers. While Fanny allowed her children remarkable freedom, Elizabeth actively managed her daughters' lives and friendships. She was delighted when Hope and Flossy began a correspondence[5] and keen for Snow to find a special friend amongst her daughters. She picked out for her not Marianne, who was closest in age, but Meta, who was 4 years younger but the daughter in whom Elizabeth took the greatest interest. Meta was affectionate and outgoing, clever and hard-working. Snow readily succumbed: 'it is the compound of a very lively imagination with great unconsciousness that makes her so charming' as well as 'her caressing ways'. They shared a love of music and a passion for sketching, working side-by-side in Shrewsbury in October 1856: 'I never had a companion who suited me better than she, but a great taste in common is an immense bond.'[6] Soon after, Meta was the first to learn Snow's big secret, a secret that grew out of her stay at Plymouth Grove in November 1855.

Everyone there had been involved in Elizabeth Gaskell's latest project. 'She is going to write the life of Miss Bronte, who wrote Jane Eyre, & is busy copying her letters. She gave me a bundle to copy, they take an immense amount of time. I have been about 2 hours at them today & shall set to again as soon as I have dispatched you,' Julia excitedly told Effie. Five days later she planned to copy for a whole day to help get the work finished.[7] Invited by Rev. Patrick Bronte to write a biography of his daughter, Charlotte, who had died just seven months earlier, Gaskell had set about the task energetically, visiting those who had known her and seeking out letters from Charlotte to her friends. All had to be copied before being returned to their recipients.

They fascinated Julia. She wrote to Effie,

> Yesterday in my copying, I got to such a warm eloge on all this party, (in which I most heartily joined). Mrs Gaskell read it aloud, and Mr G was so much amused at Miss Bronte's saying that the family consisted of 4 little girls all more or less pretty and intelligent, he asked if "less" was not dashed under.[8]

Here was the good-humoured, paternal affection Snow missed in her own home, proof that erudition need not be at odds with domestic relaxation. William Gaskell was more than a match intellectually for Hensleigh Wedgwood with whom he shared a passion for etymology, but though both spent many hours in their studies, the minister, unlike his London friend, could emerge ready for some easy banter with his daughters. Though Snow recounted this incident to her sister, she saved up her choicest literary gossip for her mother:

> [Mrs Gaskell] showed me a letter from Miss Nussey giving an account of Ann Bronte's last hours – it was a very touching one though expressed in the stiff evangelical phraseology of that school, – her death was a great contrast to her sister's – calm and resigned.

She also reported on a long talk about the Brontes when she and the Gaskells spent an evening with the Winkworth sisters. Kate Winkworth had met Charlotte Bronte in Manchester and bravely accompanied Elizabeth Gaskell when she first went to Haworth to talk to Patrick Bronte and his recalcitrant son-in-law, Rev. Arthur Nicholls, about the proposed biography:

> She is such a nice little creature, I had much interesting conversation with her about Miss Bronte, who seems to have taken a fancy to her. She sd. she (Miss B) was quite disappointed at Mrs G's thinking that Paul [Emmanuel in *Villette*] came back she sd. she had th[ough]t she would have understood it. She had left it that way because her father cd not bear melancholy endings so that he might understand it differently Miss Winkworth said to her she thought one felt through the

book that Lucy Snowe cd. never have had a great happiness. – Miss B. sd 'well that is the most sensible thing I have yet heard about it, no review has seen that'.

Fifty years later, Julia would recall this conversation about the significance of consistent tone in a novel when she set out to advise the young E. M. Forster at the start of his career as a novelist.

Kate Winkworth had another nice story about John Ruskin's doting mother that Snow knew would amuse her mother:

> When [old Mrs Ruskin] was showing Mrs Shaen the pictures [John Ruskin's celebrated collection of Turners] she talked a good deal about her son. & when they had seen them Mrs S sd. some polite speech about hoping she had not detained her too long. Mrs R. drew herself up very stiffly & sd 'I th[ough]t you wished to hear about my son. I am sorry I have been tedious' – it is a sort of speech that makes me like the person who made it.[9]

Kate Winkworth could recount an incident well but could not match Elizabeth Gaskell's talents as a storyteller. When the day's copying was done, she would enchant Snow with memories of her uncle Harry Wedgwood's visits as an undergraduate at Cambridge and the jokes he would tell. She had a funny story too about Julia's least favourite Christian Socialist:

> Mrs Gaskell told us an anecdote of Mr Furnival which amused me much. – that Mr Ludlow had met a boy crying on the stairs of the Sunday school where he teaches, & on asking him what was the matter it turned out that little F. had turned him out of his class for saying he was just like a Weasel '& he is just like one'. – I think it is the best simile that has yet been found for the little man.[10]

As Kate and Susannah Winkworth wrote of Elizabeth, her 'playful geniality [...] drew out the best side of everyone. [...] When you were with her, you felt as if you had twice the life that you had at ordinary times [...] you were less conscious of her power than of her charm'.[11]

Julia spent a month in Manchester in the autumn of 1855, moving on to stay with Kate and Susanna Winkworth before going back to the Scotts, where she had been so ill in 1852. Scott was not having an easy time. Like Julia, he suffered from incapacitating headaches, carrying a huge teaching load at Owen's College on top of his lectures to Salis Schwabe's factory workers and embroiled in controversy over how far his non-sectarian institution should teach theology. Some students were bored by his passion for *Beowulf*, Bede and Middle English: others found his lectures life-changing. Carlyle thought him a man of 'extraordinary mental powers', Thomas Erskine the most impressive man he knew, but as Julia recorded in her Family History Album, he left remarkably little mark.[12] She talked to him more than anyone else about her literary work. As she wrote to her mother in 1855, when the idea of writing a novel was first shaping itself in her mind: 'there is nobody like him, – or at least equal to him, with such wide sympathy, such fine sensibility, such vivid imagination & humour – who has besides so much thought'. She was rather less kind about his cheerful, chatty wife, Ann, comparing her with Miss Bates in *Emma*. But she could also see her virtues. As she told Ellen Tollet, Ann Scott was three people in one: 'a very deep & noble spirit' with an intense faith; 'a very bustling, fussy housewife, careful & troubled about many things'; and 'the most wonderful gossip that ever was'.[13]

The highlight of her month in Manchester in late 1855, however, was her time with the Gaskells. Elizabeth captivated her. 'I was so very sorry to part from Mrs Gaskell again,' she told her mother. 'She took a very affectionate leave of me. – I don't think she is exactly warm hearted, I shd never expect her to think much about the absent, but as far as she goes I feel so sure of her, & the share of affection she gives is so entirely one's own, though it may not be ardent.'[14] And she had seen her at work. Talking about Charlotte Bronte, copying her letters and reflecting on her life as a writer, Julia began to sense her own vocation. She would write a novel.

She wrote in secret and at great speed in the spring of 1856, sending her manuscript to Hurst & Blackett in May. Margaret Oliphant, who, like Fanny Trollope, Anne Marsh and Elizabeth Gaskell, published some of her less important work with them, concluded that Henry Blackett was neither a 'genius' nor 'exactly what you understand as a gentleman'. George Eliot was more outspoken, decrying their list as 'trash' and shuddering at their energetic but formulaic efforts to promote it. But Blackett and his partner, Daniel Hurst, knew their market, turning out a steady stream of three-volume novels designed to appeal to the female subscribers at Mudie's lending library. For Julia, who believed that her novel would appeal only to women readers, they were an obvious firm to approach though success was far from guaranteed.[15] Julia had an anxious wait through the summer before hearing that they were prepared to publish at their own expense if she expanded her novel into the usual three-decker.[16]

By then she had already begun a second novel. She shared its opening chapters with Meta in Shrewsbury. 'She was so flattering about what I showed her that it quite raised my spirits, as I really think a great deal of her judgement,' Snow told Effie on 24 October, five days after she had heard from Hurst & Blackett about her first. But she was concerned that she could no longer keep the secret of her authorship from her family. 'I really don't know how I shall manage receiving Hurst & Blackett's letters without creating suspicion. However I am going to risk it.'[17] Soon she was consulting Mack about the school scenes that her publishers wanted expanded and trying to take account of his and Effie's comments on her manuscript. Her declared aim of keeping the publication of her novel from her family was not, as she knew at heart, realistic. Hurst & Blackett were happy with anodyne pen names. Julia's chosen pseudonym 'WJ' was more transparent than it needed to be.

Part of her was still keen to be seen as the clever child showing off to the world: the other half dreaded the emotional exhibitionism. Above all, she did not want her mother to see *Framleigh Hall*, as it became when her publishers insisted on a more glamorous title than her original choice of *The White Feather*. It said too much about what she saw as the deficiencies of Wedgwood family life, while the character of Isabella contained a degree of self-revelation that she knew her mother would dislike.

In the 1850s, novel-writing by single women could still bear a shameful taint. An article by John Ludlow in 1853 in the *North British Review*, which Alexander Scott edited, had suggested that married women made much better novelists than single ones. While

Elizabeth Gaskell was wholesome and womanly, Charlotte Bronte was dismissed as harsh and rough. For single women writing novels was no more than an outlet for 'morbid' frustration. They would do far better to devote their energies to charitable work. Unlike Gaskell, however, Julia could never have written a 'condition of England' novel: despite her Christian Socialist connections, she lacked instinctive sympathy with the poor. Instead, she wrote about the narrow emotional range she knew and did what she could to square her sense of mission by trying to write a book with a moral. She chose as her theme 'a strong principle by degrees triumphing over a weak nature' but concluded after the publication of *Framleigh Hall* that 'somehow in the writing it is so overlaid with morbidity that the impression is that of defeat rather than of conquest. [...] You will be glad to hear I never mean to have any morbid hero or heroine again.'[18] As usual, she was a perceptive critic of her own work.

Framleigh Hall tells the story of Maurice Delamere, a timid but truthful boy whose stern father, Sir Arthur, is determined that he follow family tradition and join the army. As a child, Maurice is taunted for his effeminacy by Mortimer Granville, a friend of his loutish brother, Hugh. Both his sense of honour and a mistaken reticence leave him looking dishonest and untrustworthy, and he is packed off to Eton as a punishment. There the bullying intensifies until he is almost blinded by a stone thrown at him by Granville, who is expelled. Both, however, join the army, as does Maurice's best friend, Will Hayes, who is killed when Granville, who might have saved him, fails to rescue his comrade at arms. Though Maurice runs away when first under fire, he recovers to fight valiantly. Much of the plot revolves around his guilt over his initial cowardice and unease over his subsequent inflated reputation for bravery.

Back in England, Maurice falls in love with Eugenia, who is already secretly engaged to Mortimer. Mortimer's mother, Lady Granville, schemes unsuccessfully to get Maurice to marry her own plain but generous-hearted daughter, Isabella, who becomes passionately attached to him. Maurice and Eugenia eventually marry after Framleigh Hall, the family seat, has burnt down. He restores his reputation by braving the fire to rescue Granville, who, conveniently, dies of his injuries, having first begged Maurice's forgiveness. The ending is equivocal as the hero looks forward to married life with perplexity, and Isabella to a lifetime's selfless devotion to Maurice and Eugenia.

While the plot is sometimes awkwardly contrived, Maurice himself is far from the usual hero of the 1850s novel. Julia went out of her way to emphasize his feminine characteristics: his diffidence, sensitivity and lack of aggression. The dilemma he faces is also unusual: how to recover from an act of cowardice and prove his true honour and integrity. F. D. Maurice's son, Edmond, by then a colonial governor in Canada, wrote to Julia 20 years later: 'I have always felt so grateful to you for making a coward your hero in Framleigh Hall – I think you are the only novelist I know of who had the courage or the charity to do so.'[19]

The most deeply felt character in *Framleigh Hall* is Isabella, whose love for Maurice is unrequited though he values her selflessness. At one point he feels obliged to propose to her but then draws back, repelled by her 'extreme unattractiveness'. 'Isabella's plainness was not a kind that people forgot as they got to know her better.' In return, Isabella self-sacrificingly spares Maurice his ordeal by revealing that Eugenia is in love with him, so propelling him towards her and condemning herself to a life of unsatisfied passion. Just as Julia drew on Effie for the character of Eugenia, who starts out brittle, heartless and surrounded by admirers but, under Maurice's influence, becomes warm-hearted, malleable and sincere, so she put herself into Isabella. Her protracted descriptions of Isabella's feelings tend to unbalance the novel. The conclusion of *Framleigh Hall* is a high-flown tribute to the power of love for those whose hopes are frustrated:

> Truly love has various shapes to the hearts visited by it. To some it is a cooling spring – to others a fiery furnace; to some, a wand of support – to others, a scourge. It had turned Eugenia's life to a flowery paradise – Isabella's to a barren waste.
>
> But in whatever shape, it is the real good of life. Returned or neglected, or even given to an unworthy object it is never really wasted. It may give nothing but pain, but that pain is the exercise of the most god-like part of our nature, and not to be exchanged for any happiness in which that divine impulse has no part.

Both Eugenia and Isabella had 'loved much, and each, therefore, knew the life of the soul'.[20]

Much in *Framleigh Hall* is immature. The narrative tension drops away in volume 2, which Julia herself found 'dreary', while volume 3 teeters into melodrama in part because of her publisher's insistence that Mortimer, not Maurice, should die. Nor could Julia write a battle scene or, more crucially at this stage, a love scene. When her lovers need to converse, they discuss the relative merits of Walter Scott's and Maria Edgeworth's novels, talk about Milton or even the rights of women. Similarly, schoolboys at Eton relax by chatting about Latin poetic scansion. Julia's villain, however, is more original than he seems since, although *Framleigh Hall* was published in 1858, a year after *Tom Brown's Schooldays*, Mortimer was conceived before Flashman made his infamous debut.

Julia was 'absorbed' and 'enchanted' by Thomas Hughes's novel when she read it.[21] It gave her a sense of what she had missed: the energizing world of school where boys found their independent selves, confronted moral issues and dealt with day-to-day questions of conduct and choice of interest in a community of constant social interaction. They fought, too – and then, like Tom Brown and Slugger, shook hands. Above all, they started to become young men. And in Arthur, the friend picked out for Tom by his headmaster, Julia found a youth of strong religious feeling who, like her, believes that he has been narrowly saved from death for a purpose. By contrast, Maurice in *Framleigh Hall* is a principle masquerading as a character. He remains a victim at school: the enmity between him and Granville cannot be dissolved in a gentlemanly bout of fisticuffs. It is poisonous and persistent, as is Maurice's own weakness and apparent lack of virility.

But there are good things too in *Framleigh Hall*. Like Harriet Martineau, who reread Jane Austen in preparation for writing her first novel *Deerbrook*, Julia also took Austen as one of her models, conscious that the Wedgwoods would measure her work against their favourite author. Sir Arthur, Maurice's father, is a convincing character, despite Julia's fear that the *Athenaeum* would find him 'a bad imitation of Sir Thomas Bertram in Mansfield Park'. And though she told Effie, 'I cannot write about people as Miss Austen does. [...] My people, if they are anything at all, are more intense,' Julia did have a minor gift for social comedy.[22] Here is Sir Arthur at his most irritated with his uncharacteristically defiant wife:

> He made the most formal enquiries as to her appetite etc; asked her whether no dish on the table suited her taste, suggested some which were not there, proposed her retiring if she felt ill, and, in short, went the round of those ingeniously disguised reproaches, with which most people are familiar, on a similar occasion.[23]

Julia is perceptive too about the dynamics of upper-middle-class life. At the height of the melodrama in volume 3 when Mortimer has been put to bed with a burst blood vessel and Eugenia is in hysterics, the rest of the company assemble for dinner:

> It is a fortunate arrangement that there is a fixed pole in the day, as it were, round which all the most absorbing customs and agitations must resolve. It is sometimes a very good thing for people to have to meet on an ordinary commonplace ground, and discuss everyday topics, while their minds are occupied with much more exciting ones.[24]

But familiar frustrations also emerge, which in part explain Julia's anxiety about her mother's reactions. At one point, Maurice complains to Eugenia about his family's coldness in similar words to those Julia had used with Effie: 'I have sometimes felt so tired of our cold, rigid politeness to each other. I have half wished we were uncivilized enough to speak out our minds to each other, and know the worst.'[25] One of the morals of *Framleigh Hall* is the way in which reticence and inhibition, though honourably maintained, can lead to dangerous misunderstandings.

The novel is revealing in other ways too. Julia's descriptions of nature and the changing seasons are evidence of someone who had looked long and hard at scenery and landscape in preparation for sketching it. Her depictions of servants, on the other hand, with a housemaid screaming 'in the vehement manner peculiar to her race' are patronizing and unsympathetic. As her brother, Erny, a slow but careful reader, pointed out, her aristocratic characters all had 'lofty names', 'then directly you have to bring in a poor person you call [them] King, Hayes or Robinson'.[26] Above all, there is a poignancy about her use of accidentally overheard conversation as a way of moving her story forward. This was, of course, a familiar plot device in Victorian fiction: in *Framleigh Hall* it is sadly overused, a measure of the extent to which Julia now felt excluded from the world of high romance and drama that she depicts.

She did her revisions in the autumn of 1856, mostly at Alice Carter's home in Bromley, where she was eventually obliged to confess her secret as a way of getting a fire in her bedroom. She went through the usual elation and despondency of the first-time author. She was pleased that Effie found Maurice 'interesting' but on copying it out for the third time found it 'very dull', 'so weak and demeaning'. 'Oh dear! I have given myself to be made a pincushion of,' she lamented to Effie. Though the publishers did not want her manuscript till the following spring, she was desperate to get it off her hands by Christmas. Hardest of all to write was Mortimer's deathbed conversion. Julia hated writing (and reading) about evil. 'I have one thoroughly bad character which very much dissatisfies me, but I cannot improve it,' she told Effie.[27]

Inevitably, her secret was leaking out: Meta Gaskell gave advice about dealing with publishers, reassuring her that her mother was in the habit of covering her proofs with corrections; Hugh Carter shouted into her ear trumpet, 'Are you writing a book Miss Wedgwood?' and Hope, who had been rummaging through Julia's drawers, wanted to know what all the 'White Feather' stuff was about.[28] Effie told Hope and, inevitably, Hope told her mother. Julia comforted herself with the delusion that so long as Fanny did not know the novel's title, she would not read it and soon forget the whole sorry business. But though she promised herself the treat of some 'dry, stiff reading' once she had despatched her rewrite, in 1857 she turned not to German philosophy but to completing her second novel.[29] This time she took her parents into her confidence. Fanny contentedly reported to Effie in August 1857, 'Snow is quite well and writes much in her own room.'[30] Her father's reaction was less happy.

Framleigh Hall and *An Old Debt* were published within a few months of each other. For her second novel, Julia won acceptance from Gaskell's main publisher, Smith, Elder, who had discovered Charlotte Bronte and knew how to look after their authors. Their announcement of *An Old Debt* written by 'Florence Dawson' appeared in a long list of novels by well-established writers, including Harriet Martineau, Gaskell and the Brontes.

Framleigh Hall was well reviewed and went into a second edition in six months, but Julia was more concerned with the reactions of family and friends. She was pleased that Erny, not a natural reader, had persisted to the end and thought it 'wonderful'. Uncle Harry, too, liked the 'good writing', and Aunt Rich conceded, to Julia's relief, that there was not too much of herself in it.[31] Both Ras Darwin and Fanny knew better. Initially, Fanny joined in the excitement over her eldest daughter's publishing debut: 'Eras went to order his copy at his boookseller's Baire grave and classical who was so surprised at his ordering a novel, "very odd someone else ordered it" & on looking in his book – he read out it was R A Mackintosh [her brother] so 4 copies we know are sold incl. Cath[erine Darwin]'s fm Mudies or bought making 5.' Her private reaction to the novel, however, was what Julia had feared. While Ras took his time over it and thought it 'quite a wonderful book', Fanny finished it quickly with 'unabated interest [...] but I still hate Isabella so much – there is something very real about her character Eugenia is original I think & very pretty Altogether I feel a great relief now that I have read it.' But she avoided going to Clapham, where she knew that Marianne Thornton and her friends would want to talk of little else and she was still cross about her daughter's secretiveness.[32] Snow's letter to her mother defending herself has not survived, but Ras's reaction to it has: 'Poor Snowie, her letter is quite pathetic,' he wrote to Fanny, 'and I almost take her side that you ought not to read her confession for that I suppose it amounts to, to you who have the key.'[33]

Was self-revelation an inevitable part of novel-writing? In *An Old Debt*, Julia established a more authoritative authorial tone. Though it drew on the same preoccupations – love and self-denial, misunderstanding and personal honour, self-knowledge, duty and death – Julia was determined to avoid the mawkishness of *Framleigh Hall*. *An Old Debt* is both more professional and more conventional than its predecessor; the plot is tighter and the dialogue crisper. Mrs Scudamore, the heroine's stepmother, is another convincing comic character, drawing on Julia's travails with outspoken elderly relatives. Its main characters, Ellen and Edward, are fully drawn. Ellen begins as a handsome, free-spirited, rebellious teenager who has still not fully absorbed the impact of her father's death. She learns compassion and self-knowledge through her encounters with her guardian, Lord Conyngsford, restrained but susceptible, and the noble self-sacrifice of Edward, on whom the sins of his father are visited. Edward embodies the integrity, high standards and reserve of the best of the Wedgwoods. Julia stresses his manliness, but that does not exclude a night of anguish on a mountainside in Switzerland as he realizes that he cannot declare his love to Ellen without breaking his bond of honour and obligation to Lord Conyngsford (who has meanwhile become Ellen's improbable fiancée). The tale is well-paced, there are some nice descriptions of Swiss scenery, and, at only two volumes, *An Old Debt* does not, like the extended *Framleigh Hall*, risk outstaying its welcome.

In retrospect it became almost too painful for Julia to read[34] because of her depiction of Ellen's relationship with her brother, Fred. Fred is gentle and tolerant, and as with Maurice in *Framleigh Hall*, Julia insists on his effeminacy. Her first depiction of the pair reads like a re-imagining of the childhood double portrait with Mack. Few Victorian novelists would have attempted to engage the reader's sympathy for their heroine by first showing her reading Plato for amusement as her brother plays with a King Charles spaniel: 'he was very lovely, and she very handsome'. Fred, an invalid, is sent with Ellen and Mrs Scudamore to Switzerland to recuperate. Edward, a family dependent, accompanies them as Fred's tutor. As they travel together, Ellen becomes increasingly jealous of Fred's closeness to Edward, 'such an affection as Jonathan may have felt for David'. Ellen and Edward fight for control of Fred. Edward wins, and in so doing, gains Ellen's love: 'she could feel no interest in any man who had not first proved himself her superior in strength'. When Edward, who has a double first from Oxford, agrees to tutor Ellen and Fred together, she proves much cleverer than her brother, spotting literary parallels with the text from Cicero they are studying and launching into metaphysics. Mrs Scudamore is appalled. She 'did not see the use of such masculine studies in a woman. They were not going to take degrees or pass examinations she hoped. A woman's business was to make herself agreeable, and what did Greek and Latin help her in that? Only to make her very conceited and pedantic.'[35]

Poignantly, when the wise and gentle Fred is close to death, his one regret is that, because of his poor health, he has been educated at home. Now he will never go to university. 'I should have made lots of friends and got on and lived really like a man. All those years I ought just as well have been a girl – exactly. If I could but have gone to Oxford.'[36] As Julia implies, the qualification for getting into the ancient universities is good health and gender – not ability.

Was there a wider 'sub-text of dissent, which is not quite repressed' in her novel, a dissent that Julia scarcely acknowledged even to herself?[37] Writing novels not only enabled women to enter worlds like the public schools and ancient universities from which they were excluded but also allowed them to reorder their existence, putting brothers in subordinate positions as with Fred or even killing them off. Julia was not the only female Victorian novelist to transgress the gender boundary. Elizabeth Gaskell would create a brother and sister in *North and South* where Frederick is a 'much prettier' baby than

Margaret and Margaret will come to regret her inability to speak out as a man may. Eliza Lynn Linton fictionalized her own life by turning herself into the hero of *The Autobiography of Christopher Kirkland*. Julia was quick to spot the deception.[38]

Her creation of insistently effeminate male characters in both her novels, however, was unusual. In part, as her father suspected, it was a technical failing. Inventing characters did not come easily to her and so she invested some of her male characters with her own emotions. But it was also a statement of her belief that the distinctions between men and women were far less certain than her society assumed with its differing expectations of the lives they should lead. She confessed to Browning, as indeed Elizabeth Barrett had, that people did not find her feminine, though this was more an assessment of her willingness to take the initiative and her passion for ideas than a description of her temperament. As he had with Elizabeth, Browning gallantly promised to play the feminine part.[39] But while Browning was not disconcerted by this transgression of the usual boundaries, Julia's father reacted strongly against her failure to make clear-cut distinctions between the emotional worlds of her male and female characters. This was unsettling territory. Did he sense in Julia's creation of strong, clever women and effeminate men an unacknowledged desire for revenge on a world that offered little opportunity for the full expression of her ability and personality?

In *An Old Debt*, her double portrait of the brilliant older sister and sensitive, younger, invalid brother who dies at the end of the novel was painfully high risk, given that by then Mack had already started his own steady decline.[40] He, with his Wedgwood self-containment, was, in fact, far from the vulnerable, dependent Fred of the novel. The only thing that excited him was Liberal politics and the wistful hope that he might join Garibaldi in his Sicilian campaign.[41] But though there is more of Mack in the noble but restrained Edward than in Fred, Julia's decision to kill off her younger brother in *An Old Debt* made the book impossibly uncomfortable for her to read after his death. However conflicted her feelings towards the brother who had usurped her place of pre-eminence in childhood, there is no doubting her envy of the warmth of male comradeship. In the novel, Edward dies shortly before Fred, who is then reconciled to his own impending death: 'He told me just now [Ellen says to Lord Conyngsford] that he had hoped to have Edward with him to the last, but now it would be from the first, and that was better. They two will be together, and we must wait and comfort each other.'[42]

Most of the reviews were favourable, though she probably remembered the criticism in the *Athenaeum* better than the praise in the *Saturday Review*. The *Saturday* was developing a reputation for smartness, and Julia had dreaded what it might say,[43] but its reviewer found: 'an energy and vitality about this work, which distinguish it from the common herd of novels. Its terse vigour sometimes recalls Miss Bronte, but in some respects Miss Florence Dawson is decidedly superior to the author of Jane Eyre. Her strength is free alike from hardness and morbidness, and her passion for reality is not narrowed into realism.'[44] Erny was sure this praise must go to his sister's head. 'Mercy on us!' wrote Julia to Effie. 'What a turnable head he must attribute to me.'[45] It was, however, some consolation for the *Athenaeum*'s review. As *Framleigh Hall* and *An Old Debt* were published within months of each other, the one anonymously and the other under a pseudonym, reviewers did not make a connection between them. While the *Athenaeum* gave *Framleigh Hall* a very enthusiastic review (dismissed by Julia as 'rather absurd' though Hurst & Blackett were quick to use it in their publicity),[46] it took a very different view of *An Old Debt*. The reviewer, possibly Geraldine Jewsbury, described it as 'an extremely disagreeable and painful book to read – it breathes of morbid self-contemplation, and of emotions churned up out of self-concerned imagination, and has no connexion with the world without'. But the conclusion gave Julia yet more to think about: 'The author shows much promise, possesses excellent ability, but she fails in real knowledge of men and women, in experience of real life. [...] The author has it in her power to do so much, that we cannot judge her by any standard below what she herself suggests.'[47]

Nonetheless, *An Old Debt* justified Smith, Elder's commercial judgement. By the end of Julia's life, it had gone into six editions. On the whole, her family and friends preferred it to *Framleigh Hall*. In Tenby, the home of the Allen great aunts, she briefly became a celebrity, finding herself sought out by a Mrs Dyster, who cornered her with a long story of her broken romance 'as you are a novel writer'. Julia shied away. She was not 'anxious to get the reputation of a seeker after sentimental histories'.[48] Sophia Sennett, the young artist championed by Ruskin, who taught the Hensleigh Wedgwood children drawing, reported excitedly: 'Everyone was very cross if they couldn't get their second volumes immediately. Everybody thinks it an immense improvement on Framleigh Hall, & so do I too.'[49]

Julia Sterling agreed. She had sat up all night reading it, her eyes full of tears: 'how thoroughly good and healthy it seems to me', she wrote, conscious of Julia's sensitivity to the charge of morbidity and self-indulgence in *Framleigh Hall*. Meta, too, sent a fan letter: 'My admiration for Ed[war]d exceeds Effie's [...] if you knew how real the characters were to me, you wd see how little I can <u>conceive</u> of there being an author to the book'. Cousin Godfrey had not only read the book aloud to the family, including his father Uncle Frank, who 'unusually' had insisted on hearing every word, but had also read it 'nearly all again to myself'. But though he 'admire[d] Edward very much', 'passions that drive a man to bury his face in the damp grass all night are far beyond my ken'. Ellen, on the other hand, was 'a girl after my own heart – whimsical, changeable, impulsive, full of warm feeling'. All that Godfrey missed were 'the society scenes' from *Framleigh Hall*. He hoped Julia would include some of those in her next novel.[50]

No one's praise meant more to Julia than cousin Godfrey's. Yet by the time his letter reached her, she had already put aside her third novel. Julia Sterling, as always, wrote sympathetically: she would not press her to write another. She had enjoyed *An Old Debt* so much that a follow-up could only disappoint.[51] Perhaps so. W. R. Greg, in a perceptive but not uncritical notice of *Framleigh Hall*, which he reviewed alongside Elizabeth Gaskell's *Ruth*, wrote that it was 'evidently the production of a lady, and of a young lady, who has read and thought more than she has seen and felt; but of whose powers, when they have been developed and enriched by the experience of life and a wide and varied knowledge of the world, we are inclined to augur very highly'.[52] In her second novel, Julia did, indeed, draw on her Continental travels and 'rheumatic fever' in Manchester. But increasing deafness and a morbid sense that she was already more than half way through life's journey limited the reserves of experience on which she could expect to draw in future novels.

All her doubts about the temptations for the novelist of self-indulgence, emotional extravagance and subversive role-play were highlighted by a letter from her father about

An Old Debt. It is one of only three letters from him that she kept. It has no date or place but was probably written when the novel was at proof stage. It may well reflect what Hensleigh felt he needed to write but could not say to his daughter:

> My dear Snow,
>
> I am sorry you take such an uncomfortable scheme of novel, it quite gives me a pain in the stomach. It is a radically false position in which you place Edward and one in which it is very difficult to sympathise with him It is a man in a woman's place & the feelings you describe are more those of a woman than a man. You must be content to leave my softening down of the scene where Lord Conyngford catches them. It would not have done as it stood & I should like to have altered the exclamation 'do not leave me desolate'
>
> Pray write something more chearful [*sic*] the next time –
> Your affecte father
> H Wedgwood
>
> You should try to make the interest of your story centre in the heroine instead of the hero.[53]

Hensleigh's letter to his daughter, just as she was emerging as a professional writer, was breathtaking in its insensitivity. Nor had he read the novel carefully. Clearly, he had his own idea of what 'lady novelists' should be writing, something along the lines of what he saw as the light social comedy of Jane Austen or the elegant sentiment of Maria Edgeworth and Anne Marsh, rather than the emotional incontinence of Julia's people. The character for whom he seems to have had most sympathy is Lord Conyngford, who has something of his own tight-lipped integrity. Surprisingly, he passes over Julia's deliberate feminization of Fred, perhaps because it is so overt, fastening instead on Edward's supposed lack of virility. It is possible that Julia added the adjective 'manly' to her descriptions of Edward at proof stage in response to her father's criticism. Unlike the loutish Hugh, dastardly Mortimer, cowardly Maurice and weakling Fred, however, Edward is the only rounded male character she succeeded in creating, just as Ellen is, indeed, the central character in the novel. Was it Edward's closeness to Fred that made Hensleigh shudder? Underlying his letter is an instinctive distaste for his daughter's vocation as a romantic novelist as well as a failure to recognize her ability. In the summer of 1857, she bravely wrote back resisting his advice.[54] But Hensleigh's disdainful criticism had exacerbated her own insecurities. She abandoned her promising career as a novelist almost as soon as it had begun. As she wrote to Effie in 1860 about their parents: 'I know so well the flat effect of not being encouraged by them.'[55]

However great her disappointment, Julia accepted her father's authority, in part, perhaps, because his reservations about her writing mirrored her own. Her sense of her limitations as a novelist would be reinforced the following year with the emergence of a new novelist, the author of *Adam Bede*, who could not only create convincing characters and situations but also convey moral themes with a grandeur and accuracy that Julia came to think were unrivalled even by her previous favourite woman author, Elizabeth Barrett Browning. But though Hensleigh's disdain might have pushed his daughter into a frustrated authorial silence, inadvertently it diverted her from a false start as a writer. The

Figure 13 Hensleigh Wedgwood drawn by Edmund de Clifford. Courtesy of Anthony Wedgwood.

critic's life of the mind, as she would discover, drew on her keen intelligence and had fewer pitfalls than the novelist's world of emotion where she was at her most vulnerable.

One of the lessons that Julia was particularly keen to impress on E. M. Forster in 1906 was that he should fall in love before writing another novel.[56] Was she drawing on her own experience? Did Ras's suggestion to Fanny that *Framleigh Hall* was a 'confession' suggest that both knew what underlay her lengthy description of Isabella's frustrated love for Maurice? If so, Julia took great care to cover her tracks when sorting through the family correspondence many years later. There are a few deliberate incisions from her letters to Effie in the 1850s as well as her admission that she threw away some letters from 1859 about her grievances against her mother but no surviving references to any named suitors.[57] Her brother Erny liked to tease her about the men she admired, including 'Thurstan' (possibly the Holland cousin who would, eventually, marry Marianne Gaskell) and, of course, cousin Godfrey. 'The Duchess' (Aunt Turnbull?) annoyed her by suggesting that she would have accepted one of Effie's discarded suitors, a man both sisters called 'the tin can', while Julia herself told Effie about putting away an unwanted pair of candlesticks, 'an unromantic present' from an unnamed admirer.[58]

Though there is little else to go on in identifying Julia's early suitors or the objects of her own love, it is difficult to think she imagined Isabella's romantic agonies. As she told Effie when she was struggling with Mortimer's deathbed conversion, 'I have not invented any thing till now, the incidents all seemed real, but this new end must be all made up in my own head.'[59] Her attitude to marriage fluctuated. When she went on holiday to France in the summer of 1856 with Uncle Harry and cousins Louisa and Caroline, she was amused when the femme de chamber at their Rouen hotel put out an extra pillow on her bed, assuming that her uncle (35 years older) was her husband. But she was uncomfortable when the Darwins teased her about her marriage prospects; cross when Great Aunt Fanny tried to find suitors for her in Wales; and angry when the servants speculated good-naturedly about her and her sisters' chances of finding husbands.[60]

When it came to the scene of Maurice's proposal to Eugenia in *Framleigh Hall*, she fell back on coy evasion: 'He soothed her with tender words – Heaven forbid that their sweet folly should be chronicled. Most of us have heard or spoken them once in our lives, and can easily supply them from memory.'[61] The artificiality of the language suggests that more probably Julia could not. But however limited her own experience, as a young woman she longed for marriage just as much as she feared it. 'How near is the thing one desires to lose, and the thing one cannot bear the thought of losing,' she wrote to her friend Emily Gurney from Switzerland in 1884, thinking back to her holiday there 30 years before. 'Is the impulse that craves always to substitute we for I a growing consciousness of the first'. The veiled language suggests not only a fear of male sexuality but concern about losing her emotional identity in the tyranny of 'wegotism' of which she was often a caustic observer. The longing for 'a complementary existence', however, never left her. It was, she wrote in 1886, something she had 'never known, & I think specially needed'.[62]

Increasingly at odds with the young men she knew and ill at ease with her own physicality, Julia lived vicariously through the emotions of others, taking a passionate interest in the courtship, engagement and marriage of her friends. None took a heavier toll on those around her than Meta Gaskell's engagement to Captain Charles Hill in August 1857. Hill had attached himself to Elizabeth, Marianne and Meta Gaskell and Catherine Winkworth on their journey home from Rome, where Elizabeth had fled to avoid the fall-out from her controversial biography of Charlotte Bronte. A month after their return to England, Meta agreed to marry the glamorous widower, an officer in the Madras Engineers, with two young children.

Julia, who was probably the first outside the family to hear of the engagement, was enthralled though Effie sensed from the start that something was not quite right. As Gaskell and her daughter picked up suggestions that Hill was untrustworthy over money, Meta steeled herself to break with him. Intensely involved though she was, Julia became disillusioned, sensing that Effie was replacing her as Meta's confidante. She was particularly exercised by a 'silly' letter from Meta 'saying "for me" only' that told her less than she already knew from Effie, who had learnt the full story from her mother who had visited the Gaskells.[63]

Jenny Uglow, Mrs Gaskell's brilliant biographer, has berated Julia for her 'extreme over-reaction', oscillating between 'violent affection' and 'equally violent rejection' in her feelings for Meta.⁶⁴ In Julia's defence, it should be said that the behaviour of both Meta and her mother exacerbated her insecurities. Though Meta insisted, 'I will not be thrown off – Snow – you shan't do it – I shall stick to you,' Julia no longer trusted her.⁶⁵ Going through life only half hearing what was said and yet more fearful of what was said out of earshot, her growing sense of missing the whole picture of other people's lives could turn small breaches of trust into big emotional dramas. Meta too could create dramatic tests of loyalty as her later friendship with Effie would show.

Others too found something oppressive in Elizabeth Gaskell's intense involvement in her daughter's relationship and questioned the sincerity of both. Harriet Martineau had already warned Julia to be wary of Gaskell's warmth after her experience with her over the Bronte biography:

> [She] came over on purpose, you know, to consult with me, and see and hear what I could give her. She covered us all with kisses and wept when she went away, and asked, as the greatest favour, that she might write occasionally, to tell me how she went on. She never wrote a line, nor even sent me a copy.⁶⁶

Ellen Tollet was also critical of the way Gaskell was exploiting her growing popularity in literary London. As Meta turned towards Effie, Julia tried to protect herself. Though she could never be entirely impervious to the charm of both mother and daughter, she preferred to see them separately and in Manchester.

> I wish I could never see or hear Mrs Gaskell except in her own house, – here she is so charming. […] She has so much of the hospitable impulse, which is a very pleasant quality but at the same time may mislead one as to people's enjoyment of one's company. […] I never feel quite safe with mother or daughter […] with those impressionable, sympathetic natures one is never sure of finding what one left, & this makes it dangerous to 'let loose one's affections on them'.

She had the same mixed feelings after a 'most agreeable evening' at the Gaskells in 1862: 'I felt very much all their charm, conquering my virtuous disgust, undignified for an elderly woman to be carried away by the society of young men [as some said she was by the attentions of Charles Eliot Norton] but not really so contemptible.' Nonetheless, when a new puppy had gone scampering about making friends with other dogs, she described it as 'Gaskellising all over the common'.⁶⁷

As Julia recognized, she had, once again, been edged out by her younger sister. In time she would find a new friend, someone 'so very charming she very much reminds me of Meta'.⁶⁸ In the meantime, she had not only lost her closest confidante but also been stalled in her literary career. Writing many years later about Samuel Taylor Coleridge, Julia sympathized with his waning powers as a result of opium addiction: 'that most grievous bereavement, perhaps, which befalls a human being, when that spring of literary production which is the source of almost the keenest delight that man can know, dries up under some baleful influence and leaves life empty'.⁶⁹

By the end of the decade, she, too, was close to breakdown⁷⁰ and embroiled in family rows about her mother's failure to stand up to some curmudgeonly behaviour by Susan

Darwin in Shrewsbury. Fanny's references to 'Snowie' in family letters are always affectionate: she sympathized with her migraines and depressions; she nursed her tenderly when she was ill; she liked to pass on news of her literary successes and was always interested in her accounts of family and friends. But she also kept her at more of an emotional distance than Effie, conscious that, instinctively, she did not understand her eldest child. Nonetheless, she tried to straighten things out:

> My dearest child,
> It is not that I need agree with everything you say or feel, for as you know I feel differently on many things – but I know that you say them to me because you think them right & true, & that is what I long for you to do & thank you for with all my heart […] [but] you feel too keenly and morbidly anything like outward failure of duty or respect to me […] [and] you lessen your just influence over Effie by so overstraining your authority […] though I know it pains you to hear the truth how much your standard is higher & deeper than mine I think I do feel it in my heart & therefore value & accept all your affection more than words can speak.[71]

This compassionate letter was not enough for Snow. She complained to Effie that though her mother talked of openness, 'she only wishes to wish it. […] I only wish to consider her happiness, yet I certainly do not add to it. […] I suppose the only way wd be to have no troubles or difficulties, which is not an aim I feel capable of reaching'.[72] Julia Sterling, watching the upset from a distance, suggested to Effie: 'her mind as well as her temperament is a very peculiar one […] things may exist together in her wh. cd. not in other people […] she is in some things very like a child, tho' so clever'.[73] Fanny liked these comments:

> Some things she says are very true about Snowie's nature, & how much it wd. surprise her I was thinking partly of the childish nature she speaks of – I always feel so strongly also – that if A <u>could</u> hear what B had said to C all painful feelings must be at an end. It seems sometimes so hard in the world that <u>truth cannot</u> appear.[74]

But truth reached Julia only in part through her ear trumpet.

Writing remained her resort. In April she went to Worcester to see the cathedral, getting into a long conversation on the train with the Mother Superior of the convent at Stone: 'I felt a sort of curious half-envy for her, she was so hedged in her faith, – no indecisions or fluctuations in her.' She was grateful for the kindness of railway porters too: 'if I ever write a novel called the Attractive Man my hero should be a railway porter'. Best of all was the journey home, 'as I cd scribble incessantly, & as long as I can do that nothing does me any harm'.[75] For all her father's discouragement, Julia was unstoppable. By the end of the decade, she had set out on a new track – non-fiction. Her mother may have facilitated the switch.

At some stage in the 1850s, she wrote to F. D. Maurice, seeking his help in furthering her daughter's writing career. Maurice readily promised to do what he could, saying, 'I know very few persons indeed with the same depth & subtlety of mind or whose character interests me as much as hers.' When Julia read his letter in the 1890s, she dated it to '1850 I think or earlier', assuming it was written at the time she was finishing her college

Figure 14 Fanny Wedgwood as a young woman. Done in pastel by George Richmond.

education.[76] Maurice's own datings of letters are not always reliable, but if his 'Wd Dec 9' can be trusted, his was written in 1857. (The only other possibility is 1846, which is, obviously, too early.) Perhaps Fanny reacted to her husband's block on Julia's career as a novelist by going behind his back to enlist Maurice's support in a turn to non-fiction.

Maurice had influence with *The Leader*, which had been founded in 1850 with backing from several Christian Socialists keen to attract a new audience of radical artisans. Over the decade it steadily moved upmarket, acquiring a reputation for smartness and thoughtful comment on the arts. George Eliot began her journalistic life on it. In 1863, a group including John Ludlow and Thomas Hughes established another literary journal, *The Reader*, aimed at an educated, liberal audience. Julia's reticence about her apprentice work makes it almost impossible to identify her contributions to either periodical. But when Browning asked to see her writings in 1864, she reluctantly sent him some articles from *The Leader* (and possibly *The Reader* too) dismissing them as 'slight attempts' on 'objects of criticism which were worthless in most cases, poor things'.[77] Whatever their intrinsic value, they had got her in training for reviewing a far-from-'worthless' book: Uncle Charles's *On the Origin of Species*.

Part II

Great Men and Female Friends

Chapter Five

THE PROMISE OF DARWINISM

Julia's review of *On the Origin of Species* published in two parts in *Macmillan's Magazine* in June 1860 and July 1861 was her first attempt at a 'masculine' subject. She carried it off well, earning generous praise from Darwin as one of the few who had fully understood his book. Her article was an early example of a defence of the new theory of evolution by natural selection written from an avowedly religious point of view. It also proved far-sighted in its foreshadowing of the basis on which the Idealist school would learn to live with Darwinism 30 years later. The fact that the review was written by a woman made it even more remarkable.

Julia's initial reaction to her uncle's great work was one of intense intellectual excitement. Later, she would be disillusioned. As churchmen, initially hostile to Darwin's views, began to find ways of accommodating themselves to Darwinism, Julia travelled in the opposite direction, appalled by what she saw as a growing divergence between science and religion and, even more, by the claims of the scientists to a separate, even superior knowledge. The most vocal of them, Thomas Henry Huxley, marked out some of the battle lines for the coming conflict early in 1860 in an article in *Macmillan's Magazine*. Julia's two articles, which she called 'The Boundaries of Science', were, in part, a response to him.

Macmillan's Magazine, which began in 1859, had its roots in Christian Socialism. David Masson, its first editor, was recommended by the Christian Socialists Thomas Hughes and John Ludlow, while its proprietor, Alexander Macmillan, had first come under the spell of Maurice when an undergraduate at Cambridge. The magazine quickly established itself in the new market for reasonably priced monthly publications designed to appeal to middle-class readers. It both promoted existing Macmillan authors like Charles Kingsley and Thomas Hughes, and discovered new ones like Julia, who would go on to publish two books with the firm. Both Masson and Macmillan were keen to introduce female authors. Christina Rossetti would first publish some of her poems in *Macmillan's Magazine*, including 'Up Hill', one of Julia's favourites. Frances Power Cobbe, Barbara Bodichon, Octavia Hill, Millicent Garrett Fawcett and her sister, Elizabeth Garrett Anderson, and Arabella Buckley would also write for the magazine. They usually published under their own names since Macmillan, who had initially planned to call his new magazine 'The Round Table', was keen to get away from the authoritative but undifferentiated 'We' of older periodicals like the *Quarterly* and *Edinburgh Review*.[1] He also shared Maurice's concerns that anonymity tempted reviewers into factionalism.

Though troubled by *On the Origin of Species*, Macmillan recognized its importance from the outset and was anxious to stimulate a wide debate. As he wrote to his friend Tennyson in 1859, 'Darwin's book is […] remarkable certainly. I thought of "Nature red in tooth & claw" as I was glancing over it. I wish someone would bring out the other side. But surely the scientific men ought on no account to be hindered from what they find as facts.'[2] Huxley quickly stepped forward to champion the case for allowing 'the scientific men' a space in which to get on with their work. Finding those who could 'bring out the other side' proved harder. The last thing Masson and Macmillan expected was a woman. Julia submitted her piece anonymously, possibly through Maurice, whose recommendation would ensure that it was read carefully. Both Masson and Macmillan were struck by the author's ability, though Macmillan wanted 'him' to sharpen up his argument. They eventually published it anonymously, perhaps a mark of Julia's own uncertainty as a novice, but also of her editors' doubts over whether the public would take seriously an article on one of the most contentious subjects of the day written by a woman with no other apparent qualification for the task than her family connection with the author of *On the Origin of Species*.[3]

Julia showed part II of her Dialogue to her father before publication, knowing that Hensleigh had long been involved in the development of Darwin's thinking on evolution.[4] Darwin had written a first sketch of his theory at Maer in 1842, expanding his outline in the winter of 1843–44. He was well aware of its immense implications and conscious that he would not get a fair hearing for his ideas until he had accumulated much more supporting evidence. In the meantime he took the precaution of asking Emma and Hensleigh to ensure that his outline was published if he died before his work was finished.[5] He then turned to a 10-year study of barnacles, which gave him a reputation as a biologist to add to his existing standing as a geologist and provided him with examples of species development and transitional forms. Once that was done, he went back to his earlier ideas about evolution and transmutation. He had intended a very long book but was obliged to publish a shorter though still substantial one in 1859 after Alfred Wallace, a scientist and professional collector based in Borneo, had written to him setting out his own very similar conclusions on species variation as a result of the fight for scarce resources.

Darwin prepared the ground skilfully for a favourable reception of *On the Origin of Species*. He cultivated younger scientists, like Huxley and the botanist J. D. Hooker, who would become his closest collaborator. He also tried to attract established figures like Sir Charles Lyell, the leading geologist, and Asa Gray, the distinguished American botanist, with insights into his theory not just of evolution but also of its more unsettling mechanism, natural selection.

Lyell's *Principles of Geology*, published in three volumes between 1830 and 1833, had familiarized scientific readers with the idea that the earth was very much older than accounts of its origin in the Bible suggested. His views reached a much wider audience through Robert Chambers's sensational bestseller *Vestiges of the Natural History of Creation*, first published anonymously in 1844 and frequently reissued. This presented evolution and species mutability in a reassuring way as part of a process of steady improvement working under a natural law ordained by God.[6] Despite the growing respectability of ideas on evolution, Darwin trod carefully in 1859, deliberately not going further beyond Lyell and Chambers than he needed. But though he kept away from theology and the question of man's place in the natural world, he could not conceal the fact that his theory had far-reaching implications for both. All species, including humans, he argued, had descended from a common indeterminate ancestor. They had varied and become more distinct according to their success in the fight to survive and reproduce themselves.

Darwin adopted various stratagems to make his theories palatable. He chose an agreeably modest, persuasive style, dealing with potential objections as he went along. Though undermining Paley's version of natural theology with its emphasis on organs of perfection like the eye, Darwin still succeeded in presenting his theory in a way that made it acceptable to those who, like Julia, had been brought up in the British tradition of natural theology. He prefaced his work with quotations from Francis Bacon and Rev. William Whewell and, in later editions, added a third from Bishop Butler. He summarized his discoveries in eight 'Laws', an approach which those schooled in natural theology found congenial since laws implied the existence of a law maker. He also adopted some of the optimism of natural theology, giving the long struggle for survival a generally progressive outcome. 'As natural selection works solely by and for the good of each being, all corporeal and mutual endowments will tend to progress towards perfection,' he wrote. Above all, in the famous final two sentences of his book, he described the original act of creation as the work of an external influence, called in his second edition 'the Creator':

> Thus, from the war of nature, from famine and death, the most exalted object which we are capable of conceiving, namely, the production of the higher animals, directly follows. There is grandeur in this view of life, with its several powers, having been originally breathed [by the Creator] into a few forms or into one; and that, whilst this planet has gone cycling on according to the fixed law of gravity, from so simple a beginning endless forms most beautiful and most wonderful have been, and are being, evolved.[7]

This overlay of natural theology in part reflected the transitional stage Darwin had reached in his own thinking – he would later describe himself as a Theist when he wrote *The Origin of Species*.[8] But the gaps he deliberately left in his exposition enabled his readers to fill them in from their own philosophical predisposition – as Julia certainly would.

Some of the more independently minded were immediately impressed by *Origin*. 'What a book it is! [...] The range and mass of knowledge take away one's breath,' Harriet Martineau enthused.[9] Edmund Gosse wrote of his father, Philip, a respected marine biologist and member of the Plymouth Brethren: 'every instinct in his intelligence went out at first to greet the new light'.[10] Unitarians, too, conscious of their obligation to find in the scientific exploration of nature the evidence of God's intentions, approached Darwin's theory with open minds. Darwin was well aware of the value of their support and worked hard to bring Asa Gray, Professor of Botany at Unitarian Harvard, round to his theory.[11] Though Gray never fully accepted the mechanism of natural selection, Darwin was happy to publicize his recognition that 'Natural Selection was not inconsistent with Natural Theology'. He had his articles on Darwinism in the *Atlantic Monthly* reprinted as a pamphlet, advertising it in successive editions of *Origin*. William Gaskell was another receptive Unitarian. In 1864, he wrote, 'The more we come to know of [God's] working, the more clearly we shall see how marvelous it is, and the more profoundly be led to adore.'[12]

Charles Kingsley, a liberal Anglican, was just as excited. He wrote to Darwin that *Origin* 'awes me. If you be right I must give up much that I have believed.'[13] His children's story *Water Babies* published in instalments in *Macmillan's Magazine* in 1863 softened the bleakness of Darwinian theory. In it Mother Nature sits with hands folded: 'I am not going to trouble myself to make things. I sit here and make them make themselves.' And the Giant who appears at the end is Darwin himself, obsessive and with more brains than heart, but genial, honest and kind.[14]

Though other thoughtful clergymen set out to come to terms with Darwin's theory, many were hostile.[15] High Anglicans, Low Church men and vocal Nonconformists led by the Methodists decried *Origin*. Generalist writers in the upmarket reviews and the periodical press concentrated on the theological implications of a theory that described a universe developing mechanistically without clear moral purpose or supernatural intervention except at the point of first creation. Not only that, but Darwin had implied man's kinship with apes, which left open the question of whether man possessed a soul and with it the promise of an afterlife. The popular press focused on Darwin's 'ape theory', with Darwin portrayed in its cartoons with heavy prehensile forehead, a tail and yet more hair than the original possessed. In a good mood, Darwin would make light of this, writing to Julia from Torquay in July 1861 that he was 'admiring the beautiful scenery more than could be reasonably expected of an acknowledged descendant of an Ape'.[16]

The debate produced one of its liveliest clashes at the British Association meeting at Oxford in 1860, when Huxley and Hooker took on the august Bishop of Oxford, Samuel Wilberforce. Wilberforce was far from expert on the details of Darwin's theory. He was, however, concerned by its implications: if man was not God's special creation, the whole superstructure of theology collapsed. Unwisely, he allowed himself to be provoked into asking Huxley on which side he was descended from an ape. Both Huxley and Hooker dismissed the question with contempt.[17]

Julia was well aware of the concerns of orthodox churchmen. As with her later review of Darwin's *The Descent of Man*, however, she created her own space in a crowded polemical area, focusing on two issues that particularly interested her: the relationship between scientific and religious truth, and what the struggle for survival said about God's purposes for the world. Both would be central to the reconciliation between Darwinism and theology in the later years of the century.

Huxley himself was never entirely convinced by Darwin's theory of natural selection. He was, however, determined to defend the scientist's right to pursue his investigations wherever deduction from the facts led. He set out his claims in uncompromising fashion in his article in *Macmillan's Magazine* in 1860. He also explained Darwin's theory in stark terms. That geological time extended far back beyond Biblical time was now, he said, widely accepted, as was the fossil evidence for a multiplicity of species, some of which had become extinct. But while the work of pigeon fanciers and dog breeders showed how species could be modified, no one had previously explained the cause of variations that occurred in the natural world without man's intervention. Darwin had provided the answer: 'that which takes the place of the breeder and selector in nature is Death'. In his 'remarkable chapter' on the 'Struggle for Existence', 'Mr Darwin draws attention to the marvelous destruction of life which is constantly going on in nature [...] the weakest goes to the wall, and death is the penalty inflicted on all laggards and strugglers.' This, Huxley argued, rather than questions of man's relationship to the apes, was at the centre of Darwin's theory, which should not be caricatured 'to enlist the prejudices of the ignorant,

Figure 15 Cartoon of Charles Darwin in 'The Hornet'. Courtesy of the National Portrait Gallery.

or the uncharitableness of the bigoted'. The best that the public could do was to stand back and allow time for 'the painstaking, truth-loving investigation by skilled naturalists' of Darwin's thesis.[18]

Huxley's concern to reserve a space in which the scientists could pursue their work free from the distraction of an ill-informed theological debate was not shared by Julia. From the start she was far readier than Huxley to accept the idea of evolution through natural selection and, as a Christian, impatient to consider its theological significance. The title of her article 'The Boundaries of Science' implied a riposte to Huxley.

For Julia, science was a world full of wonder. Like many middle-class Victorian young ladies, she loved botanizing, peering through microscopes, looking at the stars or finding unusual specimens in rock pools by the sea that she could send home for her father to identify.[19] She shared his passion for collecting and classifying objects and looking for underlying patterns in the natural world. Though she was less intimately involved than her father in the development of Uncle Charles's thinking on evolution, Julia knew something of it before the publication of *Origin* and was familiar with all the evidence of scientific experimentation in the house, gardens, greenhouses and dovecotes at Down. She shared the family interest when strange-smelling packages of specimens arrived from around the world and approved of the regular hours Darwin kept in his study. When she came to write about *The Origin of Species*, she did so with respect not only for the family connection but also for her uncle's scientific vocation. By then, as she later remembered, she had had time to absorb her initial shock. When he first outlined his theory of natural selection to her in the 1850s, her immediate reaction was of 'extreme repugnance to this idea & the sense of loss in giving up the belief in Creation'.[20] Her Unitarian grounding, however, encouraged her to consider how Darwin's new conception of the way in which the world had developed might be reconciled with her own religious convictions.

Julia had been formed in a world that still relied on Francis Bacon's description in *Advancement of Learning* of the 'two books' that provided evidence of God's existence: the Bible and the natural world. Both, Bacon suggested, contained 'signs to be discovered and then, little by little, made to speak'. Paley's natural theology took this further, while Sir John Herschel, Hensleigh's friend and the pre-eminent scientist of his day, stressed the interdependence of science and religion within the unity of all knowledge. For him, however, science, which identified secondary causes, was subordinate to religion, which dealt with the revelation of first causes.

Julia grew up with a profound respect for the British scientific tradition. For her, the discoveries of the Newtonian scientific revolution were an extension of theology, proof of the working of God in the divine ordering of the vast universe. But she also brought to her reading of *Origin* an overlay of the German Romantic idealism she first absorbed from James Martineau and Maurice. As with them, her early training in Unitarian necessarianism was tempered by a Kantian recognition of the limits to human knowledge and perception, which reinforced her consciousness of a spiritual reality beyond the reach of scientific effort. On this she and her uncle would increasingly diverge. She persuaded a reluctant Charles Darwin to read some Kant but was disappointed when he handed it back telling her that it said nothing to him. (Frances Power Cobbe would later have better luck.)[21] Though she became increasingly disillusioned with what she saw as Darwin's refusal to consider the theological implications of his discoveries, the two of them always saw eye to eye in one respect: both believed in the unity of creation. Julia was never troubled by her biological closeness to the apes: accepting the myriad linkages and resemblances between the animal and human kingdoms was easier for her than abandoning her childhood investment in Milton's evocation of a primal Eden and man's subsequent fall.

Her keen awareness of evil as an active force in the world made the amount of destruction in nature that Uncle Charles had uncovered less shocking for Julia than it was for him. Her intellect responded to his unfolding of the slow evolution of the natural world and the mechanism that explained the continuing development and variation of species: her imagination was captured by the spectre of the evil that had produced the imperfect but progressive development of mankind. 'What a book a Devil's Chaplain might write on the clumsy, wasteful, blundering, low & horribly cruel works of nature,' Darwin wrote to Hooker when he was working on his chapter on 'The Struggle for Existence' in 1856.[22] The harshness of Darwin's world did not deter Julia. Nor was she troubled by the long vistas of time incorporated into his theory. For her, as she reflected on the teachings of Maurice and Thomas Erskine, the vast reaches of the world's history were only a prelude to the more recent epoch when God had revealed himself through the incarnation of his son.

Julia set out her reactions to *Origin* in the form of a dialogue between Philocalus (lover of beauty), a conservative but thoughtful exponent of religious orthodoxy, and the more venturesome Philalathus (lover of truth), a doctor who, in effect, speaks both for Darwin and for Julia. The dialogue form fit nicely with the ethos of informed debate Macmillan wanted to foster, as Maurice may have told her. It was also a recognized vehicle for philosophical discourse. Hume used it in his *Dialogue Concerning Natural Religion*, where one of his interlocutors was called 'Philo', while Asa Gray had also recently published a dialogue on Darwinism in the *American Journal of Science and Arts*.[23]

The first part of the Dialogue published in June 1860 is essentially concerned with the obligations of the scientist. Philocalus responds to Darwin's new theory rather as Julia had when he first explained it to her: natural selection had turned 'the pure stream where we have been accustomed to find the reflection of heaven, into a turbid current where we can perceive nothing but the dark hues of earth'. The world had become a monstrous place where progress depended on selfishness. But Philalathus warns him not to confuse 'the tools of the builder' with the architect's plans, deploying an apt quote from Bacon: 'the wisdom of God [is] more admirable when nature intendeth one thing, and Providence draweth forth another'. Science has its limitations. The scientist works by deduction from the facts: he cannot be expected to consider the metaphysical implications of his work. To do so would be like asking him to use a microscope and a telescope simultaneously. Science and spiritual truth will eventually come together even though the point of convergence is now too far off to be discerned. In the meantime, 'the researches of the man of science must not be cramped by fears of trespassing on the entangled boundary of a neighbouring domain'.

This defence of the scientist's freedom to work without concern for the wider implications of his discoveries was a welcome tribute to the integrity of her uncle's work though it was not unqualified. Philocalus raises an objection that would come to be Julia's: 'it is exactly that habit of mind, that readiness to find the spiritual in the material, that seems to me wanting in scientific men'. Philalathus retorts, 'The window is their work. What lies beyond is without the boundaries of science.'[24] As Huxley and others increasingly maintained that there was nothing beyond the window and Darwin worked up naturalistic explanations of man's religious feeling and developing moral sense, Julia's disillusion would mount.

The second, more extensive part of her Dialogue was published in July 1861. It began by considering a current controversy that was then arousing even more discussion than *Origin*, the publication in 1860 of a collection called *Essays and Reviews* by seven leading Anglicans, including Benjamin Jowett and Frederick Temple. Their aim was to encourage a more enlightened response to the gap that was opening up between Christian doctrines and the beliefs of educated men. Miracles and prophecy, the traditional signs of revelation, were not, they argued, proofs in themselves: poetry, myth and legend, as in the Old Testament, could all offer religious truth. This careful plea for a more informed, historicist approach to Bible criticism was ahead of its time. Jowett's suggestion, 'interpret the Scripture like any other book', became particularly notorious, as did Baden Powell's questioning of some of the Bible accounts of miracles.[25]

Maurice, who gave a cautious welcome to Darwin's thesis, remained true to his Unitarian inheritance in his reluctance to discount the stories of Balaam's ass speaking to him or Jonah being swallowed by a whale, happier though he was preaching about the much larger miracles of divine creation or the incarnation. Julia's Philalathus follows suit, brushing aside Philocalus's objection that Darwin's theory 'is a contraction of the miraculous'. 'There is more power evinced in creation in proportion as the miraculous is restricted to a smaller area,' Philalathus maintains. Nothing can detract from the original miracle of Creation. The scientist can describe the tree and its roots, but he cannot account for the origin of the seed. 'The principle of natural selection is the answer to the question, How were these forms perfected? It throws no light on the question, Whence do they originally spring?'

This was Julia taking her stand on the same ground as Kingsley, Temple and William Carpenter, the Unitarian physiologist. An essential but more difficult area she then confronted was the one that had troubled Darwin in 1856, theodicy. How could the mechanism of natural selection, which, as Huxley had pointed out, relied on death and brutal competition, be seen as compatible with the working of a benevolent God? Though she no longer thought of Genesis as a literal account of the creation of the world, Julia clung to its imaginative truth: 'In the beginning God created the Heavens and the earth.' Evil was an integral part of His world. The evil that Darwin had described might, she suggested, be the instrument of God's purposes for man. In the first place, 'the very want of adjustment between man and his dwelling-place' on earth was God's reminder of the more perfect home to come, while the imperfection of man as seen in the evolutionary process showed that he was destined for completion only in the afterlife.[26]

Beyond that, Darwinian evolution enhanced man's worth by demonstrating the high price that had been paid for his emergence. 'Can we imagine a fitter home for man during this season of probation than one that bears this lesson inscribed at every turn – that failure, and suffering, and strife, and even death, are but the steps by which he has been raised to the height at which he finds himself.' The 28-year-old Julia spoke from her own frustrated experience in the conclusion to her Dialogue:

> In the ebb of hope which comes to most of us when the morning freshness is past, when our path is cumbered with the rubbish of abandoned and incomplete work, and the blunted tool drops from the nerveless hand, and we sink into the numbing apathy of failure, what a depth of meaning do we find in such a view of creation as this – of such mighty changes accomplished through such faint and dim gradations, such innumerable failures for one success.

The 'one success' was man: the proof of his success was the incarnation when 'the costly vesture of humanity' had 'been found worthy to clothe the Son of God'.[27]

Darwin was full of praise for Julia's article. 'I think that you understand my book perfectly, and that I find a very rare event with my critics. Your article will strike and interest many reflecting minds.'[28] Perfect understanding did not mean complete agreement as he went on to say, but nor was Darwin's letter an empty compliment. He maintained a huge correspondence with a wide range of scientists and thinkers designed to further his studies, protect his reputation and out-manoeuvre his critics, but was not obliged to send anything other than an affectionate note acknowledging an unsigned article by an apprentice author who happened to be his niece. Darwin took seriously those of Julia's concerns that reflected his own. He welcomed her defence of his integrity. He also paid her the compliment of identifying what he saw as the substance of the disagreement between them and pointing her towards a scientist whose views would prove more sympathetic, Asa Gray.

Darwin and Gray had been corresponding for some time over whether species variation was accidental or providential. Though Gray had come to accept the mechanism of natural selection, he was never convinced that Darwin had explained its cause. The gaps in his theory (gaps that would later be filled by genetic science) left room, as Gray saw it, for the working of God as an active presence in the evolutionary process. Nor was Gray willing to abandon his conviction that man's responsiveness to the divine differentiated him from the rest of creation.[29] In referring her to Gray, Darwin was introducing Julia to a man she would come to revere as disenchantment with her uncle grew.

In 1860 Darwin had still not quite made up his mind on whether species variation was exclusively accidental and so was still willing to debate the issue. He was much more averse to entering a discussion about the function of evil. 'The ideas in the last page [of your article] have several times vaguely crossed my mind,' he told Julia. 'Owing to several correspondents I have been led lately to think over some of the chief points discussed by you. But the result with me has been rather a maze.' The suggestion that it was all too difficult increasingly became Darwin's defence. Julia's sense at this time that suffering had a purpose in fact mirrored his own thinking when he first began to develop his thoughts on natural selection. In 1842 he too had speculated on whether laws 'leading to death, famine, rapine & the concealed war of nature' might be justified because they produced 'the highest good, which we can conceive, the creation of the higher animals'.[30] Twenty years later he was less willing to get into the subject. Julia could never quite shake her conviction that Darwin's shying away from it sprang from a resistance to his own lingering sympathy with religion.[31]

Deep affection for her uncle and aunt, reverence for Charles Darwin's occupation as a scientist and family pride in his growing international reputation all contributed to Julia's continuing confidence that his theories had not only scientific but also theological significance. As late as the mid-1870s she could still predict to a close friend that the longed-for revival of a national religious life that had grown tired and formulaic might come from the new science: 'the Parable of Nature' would offer a new revelation 'to the unmoral part of our being'. Though she admitted that it might seem 'a far-fetched idea', the theory of evolution by natural selection remained for her an optimistic parable. It was, she wrote, at a time of deep depression in December 1872, 'so very consolatory in this phase of dreariness [...] it gives one a sort of patience with the disproportion of means and ends in one's own small world to be taught to see this very disproportion on a scale which assures us that it can only be seeming'. The apparent randomness of Darwin's world would, as she saw it, be absorbed in an overall unity: 'the desire for unity and the need of finding our place as parts of an orderly whole belongs to the deepest part of our nature'.[32]

The success of Julia's review of *Origin* encouraged Alexander Macmillan and David Masson to look to her for reviews on related subjects. In 1862 she wrote about the current controversy on the origins of language, a subject of passionate interest to her father; in 1863 she reviewed Charles Lyell's long-awaited *Geological Evidences of the Antiquity of Man*, and in 1866 she was invited to write the introduction to a collection of lectures Alexander Scott had selected for publication shortly before his untimely death. These were all weighty assignments on subjects thought of as beyond a woman's range.[33] By taking them on, Julia not only established herself as a non-fiction writer but also became her father's apologist.

Virginia Woolf famously wrote that the best response for Victorian children to patriarchal oppression was to 'cheat the father, to deceive the father, and then to fly from the father'.[34] As both Frances Power Cobbe and George Eliot discovered, 'flying from the father' was not easy. Julia tried the opposite course, seeking to expunge the shame of her brief career as a novelist and regain her father's approval by writing about the things he thought important. Her starting point was her brave but accurate recognition that, for all his erudition and standing among his colleagues, and despite his disparagement of her abilities, she was a better writer than her father. His controversial views on the origin of language would, she concluded, get a wider hearing when she, rather than he, explained them. Julia later wrote of him in her album of family history, 'My father had no facility of expression and never wrote for the general reader.' She went even further in a tribute to him published in the *Bedford College Magazine* a few years later, suggesting that it was his 'lack of readiness in finding words' that first drew his 'attention to the relation between language and thought'.[35]

The relationship between language and thought was at the heart of the vexed debate in the early 1860s over how speech had originated. Julia wrote two articles on the subject. The first was published in *Macmillan's Magazine* in 1862. The second more substantial piece, which has not previously been attributed to her, appeared in the *Westminster Review* in 1865. Both underwent the exhaustive scrutiny of her father, much though Julia tried to avoid it. 'Beg Papa not to bother himself with my note,' she wrote to Effie about her first article. She would ask Alexander Scott 'to look it over, if it would do him any harm'.[36] But though Fanny and Hensleigh were on holiday in Switzerland, everything, including a new packet of family letters, was put to one side to enable them to concentrate on Julia's draft.

Fanny thought it 'most capital – only much too short'. Papa got out his blue pencil and began 'correcting' it.³⁷

Securing his approval for the *Westminster Review* article was even more tortuous.

'To-day I made Papa let me read him all my contributions & pass it through the sieve of his mind,' she reported to Effie, 'and a deal wd not go thro'. Oh dear how he did clear his throat & make such painful efforts to find words. I felt quite cruel, but twas the only way of being any use to him. I got so tired of saying – 'then you don't think that relevant'. – Then you can accept that? – However I think I can do something with the small portion which he did not reject, which will be of use to him.³⁸

Being 'of use' to her father was the penance Julia paid for her unseemly career as a novelist.

Hensleigh had always been fascinated by words and became a dedicated collector of rare dictionaries. He spent hours in his study, browsing through them as he accumulated the material for his massive *Dictionary of Etymology* published in 1857. He was a founder member of the Philological Society of London in 1842, delighting in its gentlemanly, antiquarian atmosphere, which Hans Arsleff, the historian of British philology, has decried as parochial and amateur by comparison with the university-based German school of philology. Hensleigh's tireless defence of the derivations in his *Dictionary* was closely linked to the theory that he and most of his colleagues in the Philological Society shared of language as 'mimetic' or imitative in origin.³⁹

This naturalistic explanation traced the origins of human speech back to the time when man first imitated the sounds of nature around him as a way of communicating with his fellows or instinctively exclaimed in response to emotions of pain, pleasure, fear or animosity. Support for the theory came from a variety of examples designed to show that even apparently unlike words were derived from common originals that were often onomatopoeic. Not surprisingly, Darwin was attracted by Hensleigh's views and incorporated one of his favourite examples, 'bishop' and 'evèque', in *On the Origin of Species* as an analogue for the way seemingly different species could be descended from a common ancestor.

What might have seemed an obscure theoretical debate emerged into the glare of publicity in 1861 when Max Müller, the Taylorian Professor of Modern European Languages at Oxford University, gave a series of lectures at the Royal Institute on the Origins of Language. They attracted huge interest. Queen Victoria attended, as did Tennyson, Faraday and J. S. Mill. *The London Illustrated News* and *Macmillan's Magazine* carried reports of some of the lectures. A second series in 1863 attracted an even bigger audience.⁴⁰

Müller took a very different view from Hensleigh and the London Philological Society. For him man's power of speech was a sign of his distinctness from the rest of Creation. As he forcefully maintained to his gratified audience: 'Man speaks, and no brute has ever uttered a word. Language is our Rubicon, and no brute will ever dare cross it. This is our matter of fact answer to those who speak of development.'⁴¹ Müller, a product of the German idealist school and a noted Sanskrit scholar, had a Romantic explanation for man's unique ability to speak. 'Language and thought are inseparable. [...] The word is the thought incarnate.' In his view, speech originated in roots, the smallest units into which words could be deconstructed. These resonated in a man's mind at the moment a thought was conceived. Many of these roots had now been lost, but though Müller admitted that some words might have begun in imitation, he decried the onomatopoeic view of the origin of language as the 'Bow Wow' theory and the advocates of exclamation as the 'Pooh Pooh' school. In turn, his opponents dismissed Müller's views as the 'Ding Dong' theory. This was the sort of rhetoric an educated but inexpert public could follow and enjoy. And, unlike Darwin, Lyell and the British philologists, Müller made people feel better about themselves.

The debate over the origin of human speech became an integral part of the thoughtful public's attempt to reassess man's place in the natural order initiated by *On the Origin of Species*. Those who resisted Darwin's naturalism clung to the signs of man's distinctness from the rest of creation. The most obvious was his power of speech, another was his faculty for abstract thought. Müller's theory appeared to bring both together and also implied divine intervention to bestow these faculties on man alone. Some of Darwin's collaborators, though not Darwin himself, found themselves wrong-footed by the debate. As a trained linguist, Müller acknowledged that though different in structure, Sanskrit, Latin and Greek were all descended from some lost prototype language. This had a reassuring sound to moderate Darwinians like Asa Gray, who saw parallels with Darwinian theory. An alarmed Darwin sent him a copy of Julia's 1862 article in *Macmillan's Magazine* to try and keep him straight.[42] Lyell, whose uniformitarianism appealed to most British philologists, was another attracted to Müller's belief in the divine spark in man. He set out his ideas on language in a separate chapter in *The Geological Evidences of the Antiquity of Man*, where he excluded the purely naturalistic explanation of man's ability to speak: 'voice alone can never enable brute intelligence to acquire language'.[43]

Julia too might have been expected to share Müller's idealism. In time she would praise his editions of Sanskrit sacred texts and must have known that his friends included several of the men she admired including Charles Kingsley, Arthur Stanley and Benjamin Jowett. Darwin, however, worked hard to keep Hensleigh and, through him, Julia onside. But though he told Müller when they met in 1874 that he had taken all 'his facts and opinions [on the origin of language] chiefly from his friend, Mr Wedgwood', this was not quite true. Darwin had his own interest in promoting the naturalistic view of the origin of language. As he also explained to Müller, starting from a belief in man's evolution from the lower animals, he was 'almost forced to believe a priori that articulate language had developed from inarticulate cries'.[44] In *Descent of Man* published in 1871, he worked up his own theory of co-evolution, suggesting that as man's capacity for speech developed, so did his mental powers, helping to ensure his survival in a world of otherwise physically more powerful species. This, in turn, led to the development of his faculty of abstract reasoning and of a moral sense that relied not on instinct alone but on the consideration of a common good. The conclusion took Hensleigh further than he was willing to go but did not lessen his attachment to the mimetic theory.

In mounting a case to which she was not naturally inclined, Julia needed quick wits in finding her way, under her father's watchful eye, through the minefields of philological argument. Though she owed something to what she saw as Darwin's scientific method, her greater debt was to Lyell, whose emphasis on tracing the steady accretions of the past from the evidence of the present had an obvious appeal to philologists. In her attack on Müller, she adopted a more pugnacious style than in her later work and in her article for the *Westminster Review* even framed her critique in the unsympathetic format of Comteian analysis. Privately, she decried Comte and his methods as 'utterly over-rated', while in August 1871, she attempted to rebut Comtism's deceptive claims to superiority over Christianity in the *Spectator*.[45] Professionally, however, in 1866 she recognized that she needed to appeal to the Comtean sympathies of her editors at the *Westminster Review*. That she could manage this was a sign of her growing journalistic expertise.

Her first article in *Macmillan's Magazine* gave a straightforward account of the naturalistic theory of the development of language. While Müller's success in interesting the public in philology was welcomed, his suggestion that 'man in his most primitive and perfect state [...] possessed [...] the faculty of giving more articulate expression to the rational conceptions of his own mind' was criticized as too vague. It was also, Julia argued, poor science since, as Lyell had shown, science worked by 'observing those effects which are working now, and tracing the chain of cause and effect of which they form one link as far backwards as we can'. No one disputed that there were examples of onomatopoeic words that could be traced far back or that the words for father and mother in every language were an 'imitation of the simplest sounds that can be formed by the lips of a child'. Similarly, when two foreigners without a common language needed to communicate, they would use onomatopoeia. The Englishman in China hoping that the meat on his plate was duck would say 'Quack quack?' to which the waiter would respectfully reply 'Bow Wow'. But while Müller could offer no evidence for his alternative theory of the origin of language, Julia could give examples of several etymological derivations, which, when traced back through German, Icelandic or Sanskrit, were clearly onomatopoeic in origin. In her conclusion she introduced an implied reference to the debate over 'the missing link' in Darwinian biology, of which his critics made much. Though the 'portion of language that could be traced back to its mimetic origins' was 'a small fraction of the whole', the fact that it existed proved that 'the working of this principle is limited by our ignorance, and not by its own nature'. Her article ended with a confident assertion:

> The study of language, we doubt not, is destined to achieve an analogous triumph over the weakness of our imagination, teaching us, in the imperfect accents of the child or the savage, to recognize the working of that principle which has perfected for us the instrument of thought.[46]

The anonymously published *Westminster Review* article was much more substantial and by far the longest she had yet published. Much of it went over the arguments she had earlier used to demonstrate how little evidence there was for Müller's theory by comparison with the 'mimetic theory'. The most interesting part of her complex article comes towards the end where she attempts to undermine the imaginative appeal of Müller's theory and writes about the objections to the exclusive naturalism of the mimetic theory.

The latter, she suggested, was 'perplexing from its very simplicity'; Müller's theory, however, was no more than 'a fine name for our ignorance'. Unlike the mimetic theory it failed to join the present with the past. His arguments attracted credence, however, because they appealed to an idealistic strain in man's sense of himself. 'We may suppose etymology to be a mere human work [...] but we cling unconsciously in ourselves, to the belief that there is something more than this in <u>roots</u> – that they reflect some inherent connexion between sound and sense'. By comparison, the onomatopoeic explanation was distasteful: 'We cannot go back in thought to a period when our ancestors communicated with each other by mimetic cries and gestures without going back a little farther, and ask ourselves whether such creatures could, properly speaking, be called human.'

The problem could not be avoided in the new Darwinian world, despite the fact that 'the conception of humanity [...] slowly emerging from a state scarcely distinguished from the brutes conflicts with our belief on other subjects'. The mimetic theory of the origin of language like Lyell's work on primitive human sites in his *Geological Evidences*

> lead[s] us far away from the Golden Age. We smile at the extravagance of the earlier theologians of the Church of England in their pictures of the primitive state of man [...] – at that strange glow which [...] turned Adam to a paragon of wisdom, and created a vision of excellence which exceeded anything that we could make the goal of humanity; but we cling to the illusion all the same.

Müller's theory was no more than 'a softened form of the Golden Age', a reflection of Platonic idealism. But facts were facts. Though they might not always fit together like the pieces of a child's jigsaw, they must be allowed to find their place.

No one could predict where the ultimate truth would be found. 'Perhaps', she concluded, revealing some of the strains of acting as her father's apologist, 'the truth is less unlike the first instinctive feeling of childhood than the negative criticism of youth, and mature thought, enriched by the knowledge of the ages, may yet return to that simpler view from which it started, and learn, in some sense that is still impossible to us, to recognize the force of the universe as *One*'.[47] The contorted language, with its underlying hope of a return to innocence, was evidence of the struggle involved in coming to terms with the new science. What mattered, Julia would always maintain, was not to shirk the challenge of trying.

A review that Julia had been asked to write for *Macmillan's Magazine* in 1863 of Sir Charles Lyell's *Geological Evidences of the Antiquity of Man* had already accustomed her to the dreariness of primitive man's existence. Lyell had been a major influence on Darwin's intellectual development. His *Principles of Geology*, which he had with him on the voyage of the *Beagle*, described a world in constant flux with the small accretions of the actions of nature steadily building up over unimaginable expanses of time. This enabled Darwin to look with a fresh eye on the mountain ranges, coral atolls and stratifications he saw in Central America.[48] Lyell rejected catastrophism, the view that the world was shaped by sudden interventions like the Great Flood described in the Bible. The gradualism of Lyell's 'uniformitarianism' gave Darwin a perspective within which he could develop his own ideas on the evolution of species.

Lyell, a dominant power in mid-nineteenth century science, helped Darwin at various critical points in his career. Of all the men in his scientific circle, his was the endorsement that Darwin most wanted to secure. But the Unitarian Lyell was deterred by the bleakness of Darwin's universe and failure to see any innate distinction between man and the rest of creation. Though Darwin had high hopes that he would use his *Geological Evidences* to endorse natural selection, Lyell lined up with Asa Gray in favour of Special Design, cautiously concluding that 'a profound mystery remains over how the huge gulf between man and beast might be bridged'. 'Oh!' wrote a disappointed Darwin in the margin of his copy.[49]

Julia had the advantage of a 'most agreeable evening" with Uncle Charles talking about Lyell's book as she prepared her review.[50] That may be why she decided to avoid the debate over design, choosing instead to concentrate on what Lyell had written about the pre-history of man, where, as she said, she looked only at 'the scientific view of man'. Her lengthy descriptions of the evidence for dating peat bogs in Denmark, analysing ancient rubbish dumps in the Baltic and identifying long-lost houses on stilts in Lake Geneva were, nonetheless, evidence of the arduous adaptations forced on believers by the discoveries of nineteenth-century science. Primitive life as Lyell described it was far from the world of Eden. As she concluded, 'a certain repugnance to the notion of man's antiquity, as here presented [...] does not appear to us altogether unnatural. There is something dreary in the indefinite lengthening of a savage and blood-stained past.' The only 'consolation' in all this bleakness was the thought of a very different after-life: 'in heaven', Julia bravely maintained as she turned away from Lyell's depressing world, 'there is lined up a pattern for him who wishes to behold it'.[51]

In 1865 Julia got the opportunity to write for Macmillans on a subject that she was much more at ease with than Darwinian biology, mimetic language theory or Lyellian geology. She was invited to contribute the introduction to a collection of lectures that Alexander Scott had prepared for publication shortly before his early death in January 1866 in Switzerland, where he was convalescing from the strains of trying to run Owen's College. Later she would describe the book as 'the only publication remaining to testify to one of the finest minds I ever knew' but dismissed it as 'quite inadequate for that purpose'.[52] She would also suggest in her introduction that Archdeacon Hare would have been a far better choice, had he lived, to introduce Scott's work. Both Hare and Alexander Macmillan had been huge admirers of Scott. The fact that Macmillan chose Julia to present their collection of his work was a mark of his confidence in her.[53] This was her first, not entirely successful venture into a genre she would later master of matching the subjects of her profiles to the temper of their times. She relished the chance of drawing attention to Scott's idealistic view of the role of science in the pre-Darwinian age.

Class antagonisms in the 1840s, she wrote, were much sharper than in her own day when 'it would hardly be just to say of even an average Englishman of our day, that he is indifferent to the claims of those beneath him; whatever may be the fault of the present generation of the upper and middle classes, a reluctance to communicate its own culture to the poor cannot be reckoned among them'. How to reach out to the artisanal classes remained a challenge, however. Their absorption in mechanical operations allowed no scope for the exercise of free will and left them susceptible to determinist doctrines like necessarianism, Calvinism and pantheism. Christian Socialism had helped to re-channel the energies of workingmen from Chartism into self-improvement and co-operation. With the church's hold on the imagination of thoughtful workingmen now in decline, however, they had turned to 'Professor Huxley's lay sermons at St Martin's Hall' where science was 'satisfying the yearning for intellectual space and sublimity'. If the church 'failed to draw living water for the intellectual wills and spirit of careworn men on a Sunday', 'the men of physical science' would monopolize their attention.[54]

Scott's concept of science was, like Julia's, very different from Huxley's. 'Perhaps the most striking idea [in his lecture on Socialism] is the certainty that every scientific method will guide the learner towards the invisible world. Those who value science, Mr Scott saw, can be shown that they confess the presence of something invisible and mysterious – that what eye hath not seen nor ear heard, may yet be the subject of knowledge.' There is, she asserted, 'a spiritual element in the material world'. Scott had captured it in his metaphor of science as a Jacob's Ladder with its foot on the earth but God at the summit and angels moving between. Describing this mystical conception of science, Julia looked back fondly to a simpler time while still clinging to her hope that it could help explain the Darwinian world.

In writing about the new discoveries in science, Julia began to establish herself as a non-fiction writer and develop her own style. She could be both magisterial and intimate, fond of metaphor and sometimes mystical, but also, as she showed in her demolition of Max Müller, outspoken and crisp. Close at hand she had a fierce critic, her youngest sister, Hope. An offhand letter from her to Emma Darwin survives only in mutilated form:

> I am very glad you have taken to acting as censor over her articles. She knows we don't read them so all our criticisms are read with unbelief. [...] She is dreadfully allusive & her metaphors & similes are apt to be so tedious. One doesn't want every fact illustrated. She is also getting to use hyphens to a dangerous extent.[55]

The details in Hope's criticism belie her claim that she never read her sister's articles. And Julia was ready to acknowledge her sister's reservations. In the second of her Dialogues on *Origin*, she introduces a wry echo of them: 'I wish you would not involve a meaning, which seems to me sufficiently obscure, in metaphors, which render it still more so,' Philocalus complains.[56] But Julia always paid more attention to her critics than supporters, like her mother or Alice Bonham Carter, whose praise she tended to discount. Someone whose opinion she might particularly have valued was her brother Mack. Her emergence as a writer, however, coincided with a painful period in her life as his health steadily worsened.

In 1862 he had been obliged to take leave from his post at the Colonial Office to go to Algeria with cousin Godfrey in search of the sunshine that the doctors recommended as a cure for his undiagnosed ills. He returned no better in early 1864. Fanny, who may have been in denial, insisted on taking Effie and Hope off for a spring holiday in Italy, leaving Julia to take care of her father and brother. She took her responsibilities seriously, boiling her father's breakfast egg herself for his required three minutes, not trusting the task to the servants and nursing Mack.[57] At the beginning of April the doctors finally diagnosed that Mack's cancer had spread from the bowel to his lungs and was terminal.

Emma Darwin would always blame Fanny for being away on her 'unfortunate journey' at this time. Julia, incredibly enough as Emma saw it, told her that her mother had already been reconciled to Mack's death when she left for Italy.[58] This odd misconception perhaps helps to explain the extraordinarily high-minded, proprietary letter Julia sent her sisters after the doctors' diagnosis. Their brother, she wrote, needed 'great quiet' as he approached the end of his journey while she 'dreaded' giving up nursing him. 'To me', she loftily wrote, implicitly comparing herself with her mother, 'this world seems such a small part of our experience that death is not the terrible thing to me that it is to some people'.[59] If this was designed to dissuade her mother from abandoning her holiday, it missed its mark. Fanny immediately returned from Rome, and as Julia would quickly discover, her deafness was a hindrance in the sickroom.[60]

When Mack's end came suddenly in the afternoon of Friday, 24 June, only Effie and her father were with him. There were no words of farewell or any of the religious consolations that eased Victorian deathbeds. 'His breathing had ceased before I got there,' Julia told Ellen Tollett. 'I shall never forget the first look of his face'. 'Perhaps it is as well to look at the empty garment, that one may realize "he is not here, he is risen"'.[61] But these were standard pieties designed for an old friend. Mack's death shook Julia to the core, calling into question her deepest beliefs and the convictions that had sustained her and underlain her initial reactions to Darwin's work. Now her certainties about the afterlife wavered. She revealed her anguish to the two men on whom she had come to rely during Mack's illness: Maurice and Robert Browning.

For all his pastoral skills, Julia found Maurice wanting. At a time of crisis, his confidence no longer convinced her. 'I have all my life, from my earliest infancy,' she wrote to him,

> had the most ardent desire to believe in the unseen world, [but] I feel more & more it is with me only a <u>hope</u> not a belief [...] now that I am brought face to face with Death this comes upon me more than ever, that I do not actually believe in God as I believe in the existence of my human father.

Maurice knew when not to press. On the day of Mack's death, he wrote much more simply about 'a spirit quietly going as I think & believe to acquire a greater light & knowledge'. Though Julia told him that his was the only letter she could bear to read that night, she still wavered. Belief in the afterlife would always be her supreme test of faith. 'Ah for you,' she replied, 'how different it is, for one who <u>possesses the Future</u>. Mine is a more trembling hope, I have heard the voice sink into silence & cannot say <u>I know</u> that I shall hear it again! Oh how shall I bear life with the doubt.'[62]

She turned from her old idol to a new one, a man who had, like Maurice, lost a much loved wife but was more receptive to doubt: Robert Browning, the most famous widower in London. The day after Mack's death, she wrote to him with astonishing abandon, inviting him to see her through the darkest time of her life. 'I prefer the scorn which falls on those who say too much, to the price which may have to be paid by those who say too little.' The chivalrous Browning did not scorn her. He replied the same day: 'whenever I may be of the slightest good to you, it will be my pride and privilege when you count on me'.[63]

Chapter Six

'THE ERA OF MY LIFE'

Despite his wife's declining health, Elizabeth's gentle death in his arms in the middle of the night on 29 June 1861 had come as a complete shock to Browning. He knew he could not remain in Florence and brought his son, Pen, back to England to be educated. But for all of the uncertainty of life without Elizabeth he saw himself as irrevocably connected to her. 'My life is fixed and sure now,' he wrote to his sister, Sarianna. 'I shall live over the remainder in her direct influence, endeavouring to complete mine, miserably imperfect now, but so as to take the good she was meant to give me.' And to Euphrasia Flower, a friend of his youth, he predicted: 'I shall grow, still, I hope – but my root is taken and remains.'[1] Just how far he was still rooted in Elizabeth, both as a man and as a poet, was a question that would trouble him over the nearly thirty years that he survived her.

He signed a lease on a new home in Maida Vale, London, in May 1862. He went for long walks on the dreary Paddington side of Regent's Canal and, initially, avoided all company except that of Isa Blagden, his and Elizabeth's friend from Florence who loyally stayed in London for a time, and Arabella Barrett, Elizabeth's sister. His principal concern, apart from getting Pen settled, was to see into publication the volume of Elizabeth's *Last Poems*, which came out in March 1862, followed a year later by her essay *The Greek Christian Poets and the English Poets*.

As a young man in London, Browning had been an active diner-out, noisy, opinionated and desperate to prove himself. Now, though hostesses were keen to have him at their dinner tables, he hesitated. In February 1862 he joined the Athenaeum, the best place in London for meeting his intellectual peers. A year later he began to accept a few invitations but told his old friend in Rome, William Story, that he got very little pleasure from them.[2] In company he put on his party face with a loud, good-natured stream of vivid talk and amusing anecdote. Some found this boisterous presence hard to square with their romantic idea of the poet who had carried off the sickly Elizabeth Barrett to the sunshine of Italy and written a handful of often-quoted lyrics and accessible narrative poems.

Fanny got to know Browning soon after he ventured back into society. She was so excited by the encounter that she called Julia up to her room next morning to tell her about it. 'We are getting very clerical,' Julia reported to Effie on 12 February 1863, 'M[am]a dining out with a Bishop one night, & I with an Archdeacon the next! She sd. he [presumably Connop Thirlwall, Bishop of St David's, a man not known for his social graces] was as dull as his own history of Greece, but she liked Browning, who sat by her, very much – only he is a fearfully jolly widower.'[3] Fanny was keen to keep up the connection. A couple of months later, at loose ends after one of her committee meetings, she dropped in on 'the great Browning who lives by that lake with the island that we drive by sometimes in summer'.[4]

Figure 16 Robert Browning in December 1864, a less kempt presence than he later became. Courtesy of the Armstrong–Browning Library, Baylor University, Texas.

Julia was the next to meet him in July 1863, at one of the Salis Schwabe's evening parties, to which Aunt Rich chaperoned her with her cousin, Louisa, and Hilary Bonham Carter. She sent Effie a breathless, but not uncritical, account:

> I had Browning to myself for the chief part of the evening. He was perhaps a little too loud and rollicking. I got into a very comfortable corner between him, Mr [Monckton] Milnes and

Mad[ame] Mohl [the Brownings' great friend in Paris] [...] it was all very loud & jovial, & I did wish once or twice that some music wd. strike up.[5]

Doubtless, Julia took her ear trumpet to the party. But with Browning, she did not need it.[6] He had grown up with his father's deaf half-brother, Uncle Reuben, and learnt to pitch his voice at the right level and volume to make himself heard. So habitual had this become that one of his greatest anxieties after his first meeting with Elizabeth was that he had spoken too loud.[7]

Whatever Elizabeth thought then, Julia would have welcomed her ability to hear Browning. She also enjoyed the literary gossip. Algernon Swinburne was then still looking for a publisher for his first major collection. Milnes had encouraged him to approach Chapman Hall, who sought Browning's opinion. He said some guarded but agreeable things about the man but gave a more ambivalent verdict on the work: 'moral mistakes, redeemed by much intellectual ability'. Chapman Hall decided not to risk publishing. (Edward Moxon, who did, was quickly obliged to withdraw his edition in the face of a storm of protest over Swinburne's sensuous pantheism.)

> The great subject was this Mr Swinburne's poems. Milnes was attacking Browning for attacking them, & Browning defended himself very indignantly from the charge of having dissuaded the publisher from accepting them. in which story he sd. there was not a word of truth. [...] I thought it wd have been better taste of Mr B. not to have said so much against the unhappy poems – he said they were a third-rate imitation of Byron, the sort of effusion which if a man believed he wd jump over Waterloo Bridge, & then went on with a very fierce contempt against them, – which he said the author wd attribute to the jealousy of a 'brother bard'.[8]

She was happier taking the opportunity to sort out a disagreement she had been having with her cousin Claude about Browning's poem 'The Lost Leader', published soon after the once youthful radical Wordsworth had dismayed some of his admirers by accepting a Civil List pension and the Poet Laureateship. Claude spotted the connection, but Julia 'could not the least see the applicability'. Now she plucked up courage to ask the author. 'He said he shd. be very sorry for anyone to take that as his opinion of Wordsworth, but it had been suggested by him, as a dramatic expression of the feeling excited by his desertion of the democratic party.'

In time, Browning would talk more to Julia about his poetry than to any woman apart from Elizabeth and, later, Alexandra Orr. With others he avoided explaining his poems, complaining, a little unfairly, that their meaning was clear enough when they were read aloud. Wisely, Julia held back at their first meeting. 'I shd. much have liked to have propounded a few more of his poems for explanation, but I think if there is a loathful experience (to use your favourite word) it wd be having to expound one's own works, so I spared him.'

He took an immediate liking to this sympathetic, intelligent young woman. He observed the proprieties, however, when making clear that he would like to see her again. 'He was so particularly civil, wanting to know what time he shd find Mama at home, then, when I sd. she was out of town hoping we shd see something of each other in October when he comes back to town. I never saw such an un-lionish lion,' wrote Julia.[9]

This was the first and the last time she referred to Browning in her many letters to Effie. When she started seeing him in the autumn, she quickly became possessive. Both pride in her new friendship and fear of its loss made her secretive. At Mrs Schwabe's party she had been desperate to conceal her clumsiness: 'I was in your green silk & hardly ventured to move, having also Hope's great hoop, so I trembled for the tables in that little room – & wd not even cross it to get a cup of T tho' dying with thirst.' She compared herself to Hilary Bonham Carter, 'so handsome – in a new semi-high silk, very good taste – just the lady of a certain age', assuming that it was she who had caught the poet's eye. Others too would later make the same assumption to Browning's irritation.[10] Julia was also mistaken in assuming that her lack of interest in Italian politics would have put him off. 'Of course you are enthusiastic on the subject,' he had suggested. Her confession of 'stolidity' and weariness at having to do duty at charitable bazaars would have endeared her to Browning, who had always had reservations about the intensity of Elizabeth's devotion to the Italian cause.[11]

Fanny Wedgwood was never going to let this 'lion' slip through her hands. In November 1863 she gave a dinner party for him. Though a severe headache left him feeling out of sorts, Browning forced himself to go. But he could not sit out the meal and withdrew to the next-door room. Julia, who knew all about debilitating migraines, went to minister to him, holding an ice pack against his forehead as she looked into his eyes. For Browning this brought back memories of Elizabeth's way of holding his head in her hands and soothing his headaches away. The resemblance between Julia and his dead wife was uncanny.[12]

Both were small and dark; both were highly intelligent and resented the superior education their brothers had received; both could read Latin and Greek; and, though Julia was only at the start of her career, both were writers. They shared too a sharp eye for social comedy as well as deep religious convictions. Over the winter of 1863, Browning discovered a yet more compelling resemblance. In compiling a volume of Elizabeth's *Last Poems* the previous year, he had included several that had been written before he knew her. The most poignant was 'De Profundis', written immediately after her oldest brother's death in a boating accident. Like Mack, he was nicknamed 'Bro'. Elizabeth's acute feelings of loss and guilt over his death precipitated a breakdown and months of isolation and depression. Sensing that Julia too was about to lose a brother, Browning was keen to offer her the support he had been unable to give to the young Elizabeth.

Fanny invited him to dinner again in December. He was not free but promised to call soon. 'I am counting upon seeing you often, indeed,' he assured her.[13] In February he wrote letters of introduction to some of his best friends in Italy for her, 'a very charming and accomplished Lady, the daughter of Sir James Mackintosh', to use on a holiday in Italy with Effie and Hope.[14] No doubt there were meaningful glances among the servants when he continued to call during Fanny's absence abroad. On her mother's return, Julia anxiously staked out her prior claim to Browning's attention, writing twice to let him know when she would be at home and inviting him to change his usual Sunday visiting day so she would not miss him. Unusual though this was, Browning responded warmly: 'if I can ever be found capable of the least use to you, it will make me glad and grateful indeed'. He pointed out that his door-to-door journey from Paddington to Cumberland Place took only 20 minutes. He did not say what must have struck him as he emerged

Figure 17 1 Cumberland Place, where Browning called on Julia Wedgwood.

from the Regent's Park station that he was then half-way between Elizabeth's old home on Wimpole Street and Julia's at 1 Cumberland Place.[15]

Julia knew she had acted unconventionally in writing to Browning and tried to defend her forwardness. She welcomed his sympathy, she explained, as someone who had lived through a far greater loss even than her own impending one. Beyond that: 'You were an old friend to me long before I saw you.'[16] Again, like Elizabeth, Julia had first got to know and admire Browning through his work. Now, during the testing time when she nursed Mack alone, she began to know him as a man, discovering a very different person from the 'rollicking' diner-out she had first met.

Neither Julia nor Browning left any account of their regular meetings. The letters they exchanged when they were apart, however, do survive. Hers after Mack's death are extraordinarily uninhibited and often morbid and self-abasing. But despite her grief over her brother, her intelligence and occasional wit did not desert her when she wrote to Browning. He too had his self-deceptions. While she insisted that she wanted no more than a spiritual friendship to help her through her time of mourning, he denied that he was trying to recreate what he had lost in Elizabeth. His language, however, contained a remarkable number of echoes of his courtship correspondence. Like Elizabeth, Julia also tried at the outset to lay down the rules for their relationship. Browning knew from his own experience that these could be broken but, intrigued though he was by the pathos of Julia's situation, he was never quite certain how far he wished to go. Meanwhile he took great pleasure in their conversations, and though he described himself as a 'born, bred and bigoted hater of letter writing',[17] he sent Julia the liveliest and most revealing of all his letters since his courtship of Elizabeth.

When Julia wrote to him the day after Mack's death, she claimed the privilege of grief to propose that he should be her 'Barnabas'[18] until she had recovered from her loss. She also implicitly apologized for her forwardness by making clear that she had no long-term expectations of him: 'I am shielded [against that] by the deliberate decision of my mature life.' This was not to be a physical relationship. 'I can only speak as spirit to spirit. [...] I know that the strangeness would strike anyone else, but I believe that it will seem quite natural to you. I believe that you, from the first, have consciously supplied that place which has for some time been empty to me!'[19] Bold though she knew her letter to be, Julia had not miscalculated what she could expect from Browning. Her honesty and vulnerability appealed to his natural chivalry. He replied the same evening, hand delivering his letter the next day. He brushed aside her suggestion that their closeness could only be temporary and offered the best assurances he could manage about the probability of an afterlife.

> My dear friend,
>
> You know that I feel for you from my heart. [...] If I have any interest or insight – if I can rightly retain and rightly reason upon the rare flashes of momentary conviction that come and go in the habitual dusk and doubt of one's life – (and this in spite of a temper perhaps offensively and exaggeratedly inclined to dispute authoritarian tradition, and all concessions to the mere desires of the mind) – if the result of all this can no more be disputed as <u>something</u> – or even, as <u>much</u> – than pretended to be <u>everything</u>, then I dare believe that you and I shall recover what we have lost: I am not given to hope, nor self-flattery: and my belief is a very composite and unconventional one. [...] I tell you conscientiously how it is with me.

This was as far as Browning was ever prepared to go on the afterlife (until the bombastic assertions of the epilogue to his last collection, written to console his family in his last days). Immortality was a hope, not a certainty. His qualifications suited Julia far better than Maurice's confident assertions: 'I prize the intense conviction of the minds which can rest in [authoritative forms of traditional belief],' she wrote back, 'but I prize more – at least, I find more possibility of approach towards – those minds which can retain the hope of the future amid the complex suggestions of intellectual doubt, & the distrust of that mere <u>wish</u> which forms so large a part of the faith of most people.'[20]

Browning was more straightforward about their own relations: 'I do understand you, and know that you understand me. Be assured that your friendship has always been precious to me. And that while I live it will be most precious. [...] Simply I value your friendship for me, as you shall know, if you will but wait. [...] God bless you, dear friend! Yours affectionately ever, Robert Browning.'[21] The talk of waiting contained a distinct echo of what he had said just a month after he first met Elizabeth: 'Wait and know me better, as you will one long day at the end.'[22] Was he once again precipitately anticipating a permanent relationship? Julia's constant expectation of failure made her pull back:

> I dread myself, for I know there is in me an exacting spirit that dries up all the love & kindness which it needs so terribly [...] if, as I think in spite of your words, there is something fugitive in [our friendship] if I fear that the mere accident (as I feel it for all its influence on my feelings for you) of your being a man and my being a woman is inimical to its long existence in this

personal form, you must remember that what I had before I knew you, perhaps the larger part of your mind, I should still have after our intercourse had ceased.[23]

But though she tried to prepare her defences against Browning – and herself – she reveled in his letter. She showed it to her mother, confessing that she, not he, had taken the initiative.[24] Fanny was startled but not dismayed by her daughter's impulsiveness. Unlike Hensleigh, she did not raise any objections. She would have been delighted to have Browning as a son-in-law if only Julia could carry it off.

It was impossible for any man, let alone one as eligible as Browning, to pay regular calls on a young spinster without arousing speculation among the servants. They opened the door for him, took his hat and coat and showed him into the sitting room where Julia was waiting. Julia hated to have her marriage prospects gossiped about by the servants. Browning, too, as he recreated himself in London was aware of the busy talk about his marital prospects. 'I thought myself too plainly a sort of tombstone to be scribbled over when so many blank walls spread on every side,' he wrote before telling Julia of the silly speculation he had caused by sitting at dinner next to some woman who had insisted on it. But if Julia thought she had her defences prepared, so did Browning: 'I can only remind you that […] the veriest weathercock may rust and hardly turn again, – and that I see a plain line to the end of my life on which I shall walk, unless an accident stop all walking – I shall not diverge at least'. But another metaphor was more ambivalent. Julia had opened her picture gallery to him: 'let me tell you I like pictures and do not stand before them merely from a wish to wipe the dust from their frames'.[25]

Mack's funeral was on 29 June 1864, the third anniversary of Elizabeth's death. In a letter to Julia two days before, Browning returned to the theme of the afterlife, stating his belief in it as firmly as he dared: not to entertain the hope of it would be 'a crime against humanity, while the other is consistent with wisdom and benevolence – and therefore the likelier hypothesis'.[26] He sent her a note of sympathy on the day of the funeral and called the next afternoon, talking to her about Elizabeth as she listened eagerly. 'I have thought so much of your Past since yesterday,' she wrote to him. 'I felt after you were gone that one might defy the adage […] & call some men happy before their death. […] Do you remember she quotes that to add "and no man unhappy" – & I think that is the truest version of it. What a senseless question to put, do you remember!'[27] Her reverence for Elizabeth and for the Brownings' marriage was an essential element of her growing feelings towards him.

A week later, she was in low spirits when Browning called. She explained why in a letter the next day.[28] Her father was objecting to their friendship. Overprotective as ever, Hensleigh was probably more aware than either his daughter or Browning of the extent to which he was being talked about. Both were members of the Athenaeum as too was the gossipy John Forster. Hensleigh, doubtful of his daughter's ability to carry off a successful relationship with a man like Browning, was threatening to bar the door to the poet, or so Julia told him. She had given her parents a letter asking him to stay away, leaving it to them to deliver it if they saw fit. Julia reveled in the drama, envisaging that he might evade her parents' prohibition and come to her surreptitiously. 'Do not come to me shrinkingly,' she implored in the sort of language Isabella might have used in

Framleigh Hall. Was she aware that the frisson of paternal disapproval might have stirred old memories in Browning?

He asked to see her work. Reluctantly, she sent him some of her articles, writing with her usual modesty, 'They are not very strong, poor things. I wish they could gain some vigour from a short stay with you!'[29] He had to press her again before she would send him a copy of *An Old Debt*. Her comments on it were shrewd and honest.

> I was looking over it, & the greater part appears to me tawdry, where it was done from without, the fragment that was done from within has a certain value I think, – but part of it [presumably the death of Freddie] has been translated with such terrible irony into my own life, as you will see, that I cannot judge it.

He brought her some of Pen's things, perhaps envisaging a future relationship for her with his son. He would have enjoyed her comments: 'they have interested me greatly. [...] In all his delight in actual objects he reminds me of his mother.'[30] And more than once, Browning asked for her photo. This could have been no more than a token of friendship, but it was also a recognized stage in courtship. Initially, Julia ignored his request.

When a photo of her as a young woman was published in 1937, along with most of her letters to Browning, one of the reviewers unkindly suggested, 'It does not encourage romantic imaginings.' Betty Miller was also unflattering, picking out what she describes as Julia's 'large insensitive ear' in a cruel reference to her deafness. Her contemporaries were little kinder. Her distant cousin, Eliza Wedgwood commented after her death that Snow 'was ugly beyond the usual Wedgwood plainness'.[31] Taken in profile, the photo shows a formidable forehead reminiscent of Uncle Charles's famously simian brow. The eager, intelligent eyes have been less often noticed than the half-open mouth, characteristic of someone struggling to hear. Despite her disclaimer to Browning, 'I am not feminine,' to which he gallantly replied that he would play the part of the woman,[32] she is nicely turned out with lace to bind her hair, a locket at her neck and pretty crochet work decorating her dress. Sitting across from such a face, when animated by conversation, Browning did not find it nearly as unappealing as some of his biographers. It was not just lack of confidence, however, which held Julia back from giving Browning her photo. Not only was she unhappy about her looks, she was also fearful of his virile presence. She had insisted from the start that the friendship was to be asexual. Good humouredly, but a little awkwardly, Browning agreed to comply: 'I am unused to this way of direct transfusion of souls.'[33]

In place of a photo, she sent him a devastatingly uninhibited self-portrait full of neediness and despair. She wrote of her longing for death in the absence of her brother and her deep insecurity:

> With me, all the relations of life are unfortunate, & I do not feel that it just so happens because the beloved and honoured ones with whom I share them are what they are – but because of something in me which grates against all the material bonds of life [...] my love is inseparably entangled with fear, the two chords vibrate together. [...] I want to have no more disappointment. I want to live in tents. [...] Fate [...] will have to change all her treatment of me, if she leaves me you.

JULIA WEDGWOOD

Figure 18 Julia Wedgwood at the time Browning knew her.

This extravagant self-dramatizing would have frightened off all but the wisest of suitors were it not for the characteristic dash of self-awareness: 'Shall you be tired if you have many of these letters from me? – I think you will be tested. I rather think you are an impatient personage, and that it will be good for you to read many effusions from such a tiresome person as yours, FJW.'[34]

Browning professed to be flattered by her openness. 'You make me very happy,' he wrote by return of post, 'and could not do it in any other way. You know I understand you

[...] besides what else you are, you are truthful and generous, with the courage proper to these.' Nor would he fail her.

> I shall last [...] without needing to be better than my fellows, I am lifted by past experiences above the temptation to be false and selfish and vain in such a relation as ours – do I want to wear you like a ring round my neck-tie, as the fashion is? – I am older than to care to look fine so [...] I entertain no doubt or fear of the future with us two.

But he drew back a little from Julia's passionate intensity, deploying the conventional defence of the 21-year age gap between them:

> Don't cut, in that royal way, your palm-tree to the heart, that the poor traveler you delight to honour may have a draft of palm wine, 'after which' says Xenophon, 'the whole tree withers'. A better than I, God knows, should have the whole palm tree in season. There, that's said. Meantime, grow and be happy, and let me sit under the branches to my day's end, come what will.

His awkwardness showed in his conclusion: 'Forgive me all that is stupid in all this, which I dare not re-read and only mind the main truth that I am ever yours, R.B.'[35]

Julia moved on to Milton Bryan to stay with Aunt Rich and 'Milady' Inglis. As usual, she had mixed feelings about its atmosphere.

> I always feel muzzled here, & overflow in pen-and-ink, to the oppression of my friends, who however are not obliged to flow back again. Strait is the gate, and narrow is the way, is impressed on one's soul at every step, & I feel as if my hoop, tho' not a very large one, wd. hardly get through. – Well, narrow is the spirit that cannot bear with narrowness!

This reads rather as one imagines Julia talked, lightly and quizzically. She had taken Browning's hint about avoiding the excesses of her earlier letter and also, as he would have expected given their shared fondness for allusions, picked up on his reference to Xenophon:

> Love – I wanted to put that everywhere, to fill every cup to the brim with it, & it was singularly annoying and inconvenient to others to find them all so full. [...] What you charge me not to do for you, I have been trying to do for everybody (Xenophon's palm wine) and my ten Thousand did not want my wine very often.

Her apparent equanimity concealed much that had been happening at Milton Bryan as Mary Rich began her offensive against Julia's friendship with Browning. First she claimed that he did not look like a poet. 'I thought it hard to be called to account for your looks!' Julia told Browning. But she had also implied that he might see her niece as 'a pear left basking over a wall', implying that she was ripe for the picking. Once again, Julia recoiled from the idea that others might anticipate a conventional romantic conclusion to their relationship. Her claim that her deafness made her indifferent to gossip, however, was the opposite of the truth as would soon become clear, while her aunt's insistent evocation of her own lost love could only encourage Julia to make invidious comparisons. 'My

Aunt today speaking of her past happiness [...] described it in the words of Lady Rachel Russell "it wanted nothing of Heaven but immortality". With whom were my thoughts then?'[36] How could Julia compete with the fabled perfection of the romance between Mary and Claude Rich, let alone Browning's love for Elizabeth? When he wrote asking for a little palm wine to cheer him up, he could not help telling Julia that 'palm-wine is not proof spirit, of which I am not without the experience of certain thimble-fulls'. Now Julia increased her references to Browning's 'grey hairs' even promising to write a posthumous commentary on his works – 'and as you are so old', she clumsily teased him, she would not have long to wait. 'Reading it will probably be yr. occupation in Purgatory.'[37]

As they approached separation during the holiday season, Browning was keen to leave the record straight. He assured her of 'the pure truth that you are most dear to me, and will ever be so'. He compared himself to a dried-up insect kept in a pill box that

> had the sea to swim in once: I can't get that again, but any globule of your palm-wine will set me free within its circumference, to legs' content; and it is far more likely that you will decide 'Enough of kicking and capering – back to your box now!' – than that I shall object [...] to partially recovering the use of my precious limbs.[38]

As he polished off his correspondence in the library of the Athenaeum before he left for France, he could not resist slipping in another quick note to Julia:

> Goodbye, dearest friend,
>
> I go to-morrow, stay, as I very likely have told you, some two months, and see you prominently on the white cliffs as a landmark for return. We won't teaze each other with any more 'last words', but take the good of understanding each other without further labour and pains: I will not be older than you like, nor you younger than I want. I daresay nothing but good will come of it all to you and me …
>
> I have been reading your admirable articles in the 'Reader', – admirable, I mean every letter of the word.
>
> So, 'I stretch out my hand for bread' – had you any fancy of the possible attitude in the future of
>
> Yours ever affectionately,
> R.B?[39]

Had Fanny seen this letter, she would have been delighted by the apparent progress of her daughter's 'courtship'.

Browning and Julia would not see each other again for over four months. Without the oxygen of regular meetings, their correspondence changed. For us, if not for Julia, it becomes much more enjoyable. Stimulated by memories of their conversations, Browning sent her some of his best letters. She responded in kind, with literary gossip, thoughts about what she was reading and reflections on Elizabeth's poetry and character. In the intimacy of private letters, safe from the insinuations of others, they romped agreeably together as Julia proved her ability to interact with one of the keenest intellects of her day. Browning filled up every inch of his small pages, careful not to increase the postage she would have to pay, his letters crackling with holiday energy. Hers were more melancholy, but her literary insights could still surprise. As Bonamy Dobrée commented, she 'had ideas to put together, and could do so charmingly'. 'She was the very correspondent for Browning.'[40]

Initially, Julia was melancholic. On her return from a stay with Julia Sterling in Cornwall, she sat in a deserted 1 Cumberland Place, going over the old sore of Mack's failure to offer words of comfort when he was dying, thinking of the wide expanse of water and the white birds 'flapping' above it, which separated her from Browning, and peering at small creatures in the dusty schoolroom. 'Perhaps one of these dry insects will come & fly near me now,' she wrote, picking up on his earlier description of himself. Everything reminded her of Browning. 'How strangely you haunt me!' She had met a young schoolmaster from Rugby who insisted on talking about his poems; she had relaxed with a sentimental novel, 'the sort of thing you could not look at if the tortures of the Inquisition were brought to bear upon you', and found it full of quotations from his and Elizabeth's works; she had gone into a Cornish farmhouse and happened on a picture of her. She read and re-read the volume of Elizabeth's *Last Poems* he had given her, thinking of Elizabeth as 'my companion till my head gets strong enough to walk up-hill again'. Her two favourites were the saddest, 'Confessions' and 'De Profundis', written, though she did not then know it, after the death of Elizabeth's 'Bro'. The coincidence would have struck Browning, as would Julia's comment: 'I care perhaps too exclusively for herself in her poems, those which are merely artistic have less interest for me, out of all proportion to their real merit.'[41] The immediacy of Elizabeth's poetic diction and the sense of harmony between woman and poet were what had first attracted him to Elizabeth.

But Browning was in holiday mood and keen to encourage Julia to forget her morbidity. He picked up her reference to white birds over the Channel to give her a fine description of 'a great white-breasted hawk I saw sunning himself on a ledge with his wings ready'. This became a metaphor for the spirits of Elizabeth and Mack watching over Robert and Julia: 'If you wish another spirit to keep close by you while you go up higher, offences must come, and the wings get in the way of each other: how easily that must be seen by the bird that gets first to the height!' Knowing how much Julia reverenced his marriage, however, he hastily corrected himself. 'Of course I was fortunate through the peculiarity of the relation: in that closeness there could be no misunderstanding.' Now he relied on an eventual reunion with his dead wife,

> when the dark cloth is suddenly twitched from your face, and fancying yourself lost in the dark, you find yourself at home. 'The world has no perdition, if some loss' – This is no chatter or cant with me, I can tell you. [...] When you can <u>mean</u> with Dante 'Thus I believe, thus I affirm, thus I am certain it is, and that from this life, I shall pass to another better, there, where that Lady lives, of whom my soul was enamoured.'[42]

These were the words Browning had inscribed in Elizabeth's Greek New Testament when he unpacked their things back in London, setting up her empty chair and small writing desk next to his own in his study in Warwick Crescent and hanging her portrait on the wall. He would not repeat them to anyone else until he came to write 'La Saisiaz' in 1878, his long, hopeful but ultimately inconclusive reflection on mortality and the afterlife.

Julia was always willing to think unconventionally: now she questioned Browning's apparent certainty. Perhaps, she wrote, echoing the ideas which had got Maurice into so much trouble, 'immortality' was simply a sensation, a feeling available to a few but a delusion for 'others who merely live on a second-hand investment of their hopes and convictions of others [...] to be immortal is to know it, & then I am sure I am not'. 'I saw my stars in the early dawn,' she continued, remembering the religious fervour of her childhood, '& perhaps I shall see them again in the twilight.' Now she looked to find them reflected in a deep well but saw nothing. For Browning a child's unquestioning readiness to accept religious dogma was little better than 'practical atheism'. Only as its unthinking assumptions were thrown off did 'the shape of a conceived possibility of a life beyond' occur: 'it is because one cannot so live on now, under the present conditions, in virtue of the very desire to live in a conceivable absolute freedom and fullness of life, – that I hope this is to be one day'. Browning had articulated Julia's abiding sense of the incompleteness of life on earth. She responded with a vivid account of her childhood fear that she would not be ready for the Last Judgement, agreeing that children suffered under the weight of religious beliefs imposed on them by the grown-ups.[43]

For the most part, however, they ranged across the literary world and discussed the politics of family relationships. Like everyone else in London, Julia was reading Tennyson. She had more reservations than most. At first sight, she found the dedication of his latest collection to his wife 'Dear, near and true' 'very fragrant and delicate' but, on second reading, liked it less: 'there is a little too much about himself in it and not enough about his wife'. It reminded her of 'so many little unpleasantnesses [I know] of him' but perhaps, she judiciously suggested, that was too much 'like judging the tree by the caterpillars that drop off it'. Browning defended his old friend and even Julia Margaret Cameron, 'the poisoned cup-bearer' as Julia dubbed her. ('How glad I am you have not a Mrs Cameron! It is amusing to see how that species of woman ignores the wife.') Not 'poison' but 'a tray of brandied lollipops,' Browning suggested, 'what harm does she do Alfred? [...] there will always be a buzzing of silliness about such a person. Depend on it, nobody has done him the least harm at any time: nobody has more fully found out at the beginning what he was born to do, – nor done it more perfectly.'[44]

A brief reminder from Julia of an earlier conversation about the ending of Tennyson's 'Enoch Arden' stimulated Browning to try his own sardonic re-write. While Julia thought it would have been 'more heroic' for the long-lost sailor not to reveal himself to his wife, Browning turned the poem into one of his own dark dramas with Enoch, far from enjoying the costly funeral Tennyson envisaged, consigned to a pauper's grave as his unwitting family cast complacent glances over it. Julia was 'much amused' but enjoyed most Tennyson's 'delicious' 'Lincolnshire Farmer', finding it much more realistic and sincere than most of his work.[45] Browning agreed with her when he came to read it and subsequently wrote (with more flattery than honesty) to Tennyson, ' "Enoch" continues the perfect thing I thought it at first reading, but the "Farmer", taking me unaware, astonished me more.'[46]

Julia and Browning wrote not only about others' work but also about his own. She had been reading Homer: 'I wonder what the charm is of <u>unfeelingness</u> wherever it is not unnatural. One feels it in such different things, in a young animal, & in those old stories […] I don't mean there is no pathos, but […] the want of any care for humanity […] has a curious sort of satisfaction in it'. This sense of the moral impartiality of the Greeks was something she would later develop in one of her best articles. It led them on to discuss Helen of Troy. Browning had thought of writing a poem about her derived from Euripides's fancy that the true Helen was 'living sadly and saintly' in Egypt rather than Troy and later mourned by her husband for the world's misconception of her character through the doings of her eidolon (the false spirit in Troy).[47] 'I hope there will be another poem […] when I see you again.' Julia eagerly replied. 'You know you promised me an early instalment of it.' She doubted, however, whether Biarritz, where Browning then was, would be 'propitious' for writing poetry: it 'sounds a horribly commonplace & fashionable retreat for you'.[48]

In their meetings before he left for France, Browning had told Julia he was planning an important new work. He replied two weeks later from Paris: 'I have got the whole of that poem, you enquire about, well in my head, shall write the Twelve books of it in six months, and then take breath again.'[49] This was the start of *The Ring and the Book*. Its composition would, in fact, require four years of very hard work. It would also prove very different from the poem Julia imagined.

Another topic that absorbed them was family. Browning was aware of Julia's sense of isolation. He sympathized with her over the way her family had not developed as she had.

> [But] they may grow just as you grow, only – here's the fault – you none of you profit by each other's growth, it is not in your direction, but for somebody else to profit by – much as with a cluster of fruits on a common twig: each may bulge out round and red enough in the sun's eye, but the place where all the clustered knobs touch, where each continues to be known to the other, that is as hard & green, and insipid as ever, and if peach can only judge of fellow-peach by that place of junction and communion, the result's generally poor enough.[50]

She seized on this analysis of the strains in her family writing about the advantage of 'a peach which has succeeded in elongating its own stalk sufficiently to detach itself from that parent cluster'. Hilary Bonham Carter was a good example, as was the subject of her most recent sculpture, Florence Nightingale. Here indeed was 'one of those detached peaches – better so on the whole […] but meantime not without heavy loss', wrote Julia thinking of the impossible demands that Nightingale made on her family and closest associates.[51]

They were less of the same mind about John Henry Newman's newly published *Apologia pro Vita Sua*. She found his certainties about Hell and Purgatory far more congenial than the scepticism of the *Saturday Review* or the easy-going assumptions of the Broad Church community:

> Leave out that part of it [Hell Fire and Purgatory] which nobody really imagines or believes, & the conviction of unsounded depths below us seems to me not only truer, but a better guide in life than that general comfortable feeling that after all there's not so much difference between one course of action and another, or one character or another.[52]

Browning's roots lay too deep in Dissent for him to share her sympathy with Newman. He was also in mourning after the death of his old friend, Walter Savage Landor. 'He has written passages not exceeded in beauty and subtlety by any literature that I am acquainted with.' But these were things they could discuss when they met. Julia too eagerly awaited his return: 'I am to be seen at C.P. and my company is particularly edifying about 1 o'clock on Sundays,' she reminded him.[53]

The prospect of seeing her was one of the few things Browning could look forward to in London. 'Write and hold out a light, if I am ever to swim across the dark strait from Boulogne to the Abydos of Warwick Crescent, which invites me very little otherwise,' he instructed her in language reminiscent of his early courtship letters to Elizabeth.[54]

First Julia had to visit Milton Bryan again where Aunt Rich resumed her campaign against Browning. By now it had a harder edge. Was she motivated by jealousy and the fear that her own romantic passion would be cast in the shade by her niece's? Certainly she had strong views about the unacceptability of new partnerships for the widowed, given the complications that would ensue when everyone reassembled in the afterlife. She reacted too against her niece's disregard for social propriety in taking the initiative with Browning. Perhaps she was protecting Snow, knowing her passionate, self-destructive nature. Whatever her motives, she now passed on some hurtful gossip she claimed to have been told by those in the know – that Browning regarded her as a 'gêne' (a nuisance or an embarrassment). Julia was devastated. When she eventually told Browning five years later, he was incredulous that she could have believed such a slur. At the time, however, the comment amplified all her insecurities. She immediately changed her travel plans. Instead of returning to London to see Browning, she arranged to go and stay with the Scotts in Manchester.

She suggested that while she was away, he might call on her mother, as, indeed, he did. The stratagem was transparent. If Browning could be re-established as a family friend rather than a possible suitor, gossip would stop. She could not, however, stop writing to him. In letters she had the Browning she most wanted, free of his troubling physical presence. But the tone of hers became more brittle, and she increased the references both to Elizabeth and to her morbid fears for Pen. Initially, however, she gave no hint of the unsettling dramas at Milton Bryan. 'I am spending such a tranquil visit here,' she told him, 'with two old ladies & two cats our time seems chiefly spent in prayers and meals and the day is half gone, before one can do anything else. We have a bit of youth to contemplate in the kitten, but I almost supply that to these ladies.' She wrote again, briefly, a week later repeating the plea to visit her mother. Her conclusion was deliberately nonchalant: 'Whether I care for your letters I believe you know pretty well, but I daresay you will be busier now you are returned to London, & I hardly expect to have them often.'[55] He replied immediately reassuring her about Pen's health and giving her an amusing rundown of his modest life-long tally of sore throats and fevers, linked as they often were to hectic bouts of creativity. One episode he particularly remembered: 'I could not get sleep for the pain, and my wife took my head in her two little hands, in broad daylight, and I went to sleep at once, and woke better.'[56]

Thinking about Elizabeth, Julia was easily tempted into morbidity. 'I sometimes wonder that all conventional expression has arranged itself on the theory that one is glad to stay as long as possible in this world. But those hands that hold the aching head are strong links here, till they become strong and painfully stretched links in another direction.' Just as Mack had been relieved on his deathbed by the thought that he would not outlive his mother, so Julia was sure that Browning was 'better able to endure' than Elizabeth would have been. 'Forgive me that my own thoughts lead me so much to your sacred place. I know that you are always there – but one likes to be there alone.' 'I am not going to let another day go by,' Browning replied, 'without […] saying this particularly that you are never in my way in the "sacred place" you speak of, and, so far as you go, I like walking with you. Nobody else goes many inches over the threshold of it.'[57]

In Manchester, Julia found Elizabeth's *Sonnets from the Portuguese* in an old copy of *Blackwood's Magazine*: 'they are wonderfully beautiful. […] Generally the life & the art are two things, at least, it seems to me an exception when they are so much one as they were with her'. Her perceptiveness evoked one of Browning's most touching and precise memories of Elizabeth:

> Yes, that was a strange, heavy crown, – that wreath of Sonnets, – put on me one morning unawares, three years after it had been twined, – all this delay, because I happened early to say something against putting one's loves into verse: then again, I said something else on the other side, one evening at Lucca, – and next morning she said hesitatingly 'Do you know I once wrote some poems about you?' – and then – 'There they are, if you care to see them,' – and there was the little book I have here – with the last Sonnet dated two days before our marriage. How I see the gesture and hear the tones – and, for the matter of that, see the window at which I was standing, with the tall mimosa in front, and little church court to the right.[58]

Obsessed by the woman she had never met but knew well through her work, Julia had 'a curious realistic dream in which I met you both at a theatre, & the double image seemed so much more natural than the single.' 'You know that God can make up to her for even this short loss of you, if indeed the loss is not merely yours, & she is not much closer to you than she ever was – as I think.'[59]

While Julia wanted to corral Browning in his resonant, romantic past, he was more anxious to see her in the flesh. She returned to London sooner than expected but did not tell him. Instead, she prepared for the final break. She drafted two letters asking him not to call on her again. She was anxious not to hurt him and took on herself all the responsibility for precipitately initiating the relationship and now ending it. She was, she said, acting out of deference to the concerns of 'those very near to me who think there was grave indiscretion in what I did'. They 'had put it before me in a way that whether or not it convinces my judgement, unquestionably influences my will'.[60] But she was not yet at the point where she could bear to forego her friendship with Browning. She put her letter aside.

In late November, almost four months since they were together in the same room, the two met again and continued to do so until Christmas. Browning was now established back in London. *Dramatis Personae*, which had come out in May 1864, was generally far more respectfully reviewed than his previous great collection, *Men and Women*, which had been a critical failure in 1855. His publishers too were planning a three-volume collection of his works to complement the four-volume edition of Elizabeth's *Poems* he was seeing through the press. He was fizzing with London literary gossip and full of his new long poem, which would have 'an Italian heroine'. Julia was keen for him to make progress on it.⁶¹

A heavy cold obliged him to cancel his planned visit on Christmas Day. Julia happily spent the evening in his company browsing through the copy of *Dramatis Personae* he had sent her as a Christmas present. 'Rabbi Ben Ezra' ('My times be in Thy hand! / Perfect the cup as planned! / Let age approve of youth, and death complete the same!') could 'almost convert one to grow old cheerfully', she wrote to him that night (as, indeed, she later would). There was no need to comment on 'Prospice', Browning's account of braving the perils of death to find peace with Elizabeth: it encapsulated much that they had talked about over the previous months ('the fiend voices that rave, / shall dwindle, shall blend, / Shall change, shall become first a peace out of pain, / Then a light, then thy breast, / O though soul of my soul! I Shall clasp thee again, / And with God be the rest!').

Instead, she directed her critical powers to 'James Lee's Wife'. Surely, such proletarian people could not have such a complex view of life. 'Those are not the feelings of people who are earning their bread,' she opined from her rentier pinnacle. Though Browning rarely admitted defects in his poems to anyone but Elizabeth, he took the blame for having misleadingly described them as a humble couple.

> I meant them for just the opposite – people newly married, trying to realize a dream of being sufficient to each other, in a foreign land (where you can try such an experiment) and finding it break up, – the man being tired <u>first</u>, – and tired precisely <u>of</u> the love: – but I have expressed it all insufficiently, and will break the chain of poems up, one day, and leave so many separate little round rings to roll each way, if it can [as, indeed, he did after Julia's criticism].⁶²

Once again, though his description of 'James Lee's Wife' might have suggested otherwise, Julia refused to pick up even the faintest hint that Browning's marriage had not been the ideal union of souls she imagined.

When she put him off with another flimsy excuse the next Sunday, Browning walked over to gaze at 1 Cumberland Place through the railings. 'Yours hungrily and thirstily ever,' he signed off a note to her.⁶³

At the beginning of February she cancelled again on the cursory pretext that she was 'going to a distant church'.⁶⁴ Pen then came down with measles. This gave her another couple of weeks' respite from Browning's physical presence. Worrying about the premature deaths of gifted young men, she proved as anxious as Elizabeth had been about the impact of the critics on Keats. '(Please don't tell me the Q[uarterly Review] never killed Keats, I hate having all the old legends disturbed) – so whether we love, or whether we hate we kill all the same,' she gloomily concluded, as she steeled herself to destroy the most precious friendship she had ever known.

Without their regular meetings, their correspondence lost some of its liveliness. They sparred over Lord Houghton. Browning, like many others, thought him two-faced. Julia had 'a weakness' for him: he was 'content to be 2nd rate himself, which very few people are'.⁶⁵ Her question about Keats, however, stimulated one of his most energetic letters: 'What you said about Keats is truer than as you say it: because I believe Keats did have death accelerated, if not induced, by that criticism.' He had heard from Joseph

Figure 19 Julia Wedgwood's water colour of the view across Regent's Park towards St Marylebone Church, where the Brownings were married. Courtesy of V&A Wedgwood/Mosley Collection.

Severn, Keats's last companion, about the intensity of the poet's final sufferings. Julia tried to read some Keats but found 'all the gods and goddesses unendurable'. Thoughts of Keats's early death revived her old superstition that Pen was destined to die young. She had been so concerned about his measles that she had called on Adelaide Procter, one of Browning's regular hostesses, to find out how he was. 'All this year', she wrote, thinking of her mother's grief over Mack, 'I have been feeling as if there was no other sorrow in the world, but that of a parent for a child.'[66]

Now with Pen recovering and no longer infectious, Browning was ready to resume his calls. Despite the transparency of Julia's attempts to put him off in the winter of 1864–65, her letter of 1 March came as a shock.

> I have been intending to write to you for several days, dear friend, to say – what I do not say willingly – that it would be better that we did not meet again just now, at least that you did not come here. [...] I have reason to know that my pleasure in your company has had an interpretation put upon it that I ought not to allow. I have no doubt the fault has been mine, in uncautiously allowing it to be known that I made an object of your visits. You will feel at once that it is a mistake which must be set right by deeds, not words. I am reflecting on myself, not upon you. You have only accepted a position into which I invited you. [...] It is no use asking myself how far such an opinion would affect me if I had no one to consider but myself, for there are others to consider. [...] They know that I am the author of all that is peculiar in our

intercourse, but I cannot explain this to those who impute to me anticipations irreconcilable with that fact. I have no reason to think your attitude is misinterpreted, but perhaps all the more for this I ought to be careful to correct the view they have of mine.

Though she would no longer see him, she had the consolation of being able to read his work.

> I rejoice to think how much I shall still be able to enter into your mind [...] – if you can still let me see what you promised it will be an even greater pleasure to me than it would have been while I was in the habit of seeing you. Dear friend, I spin out my letter in reluctance to say goodbye, but it must be said – you know all that it means from me, all you have been to me & how my thoughts will twine round you and yours. – & yet you know too [she bravely concluded] that I am not giving up more than I can afford.

He had helped her through the 'darkest' time of her life. What she now wanted, she said, was his 'sympathy' rather than 'acquiescence' and 'the support of your longer experience and more matured judgement' in reassuring her that she was doing the right thing.[67]

Julia's letter, which drew on her earlier drafts was sensitive and dignified but showed in its contradictions how far she inwardly rebelled against the conventional requirements of others, obliged though she felt to go along with them.

Commenting on the affair with his connoisseur's eye for the dramas that erupt when passion and convention coincide, E. M. Forster wrote: 'Browning is frightfully nice, as men often are after a snub, but he feels a fool and their correspondence dies.'[68] As a gentleman, Browning had no choice but to accept Julia's decision. He generously offered her the reassurance she wanted:

> My dear friend, this comes to me as no surprise: I thought from the beginning it was too good to last, and felt as one does in a garden one has entered by an open door, – people fancy you mean to steal flowers. I consider you are altogether right in deciding so – and certainly you are right in being sure that I understand you.

Even if he no longer called, his view of her would not change. 'What I know, I know & shall always know, and after this world, I hope, when completion ought to be. As to the past, it was only incomplete thro' my wife's absence: she never had any woman-friend so entirely fit for her as you would have been, – I have told you so sometimes.' It had always been for Julia to decide how far he was allowed into her garden though he pointed out that 'two persons who suddenly unclasp arms and start off in opposite directions look terribly intimate'. He would, of course, send her his poem on which he was working 'unintermittingly' and the new edition of his works when it was published. He concluded with an amusing example of his misrepresentation in an American illustration of him composing *Dramatis Personae*, 'profoundly melancholy, close shaven, with close-clipped hair, black above a vast brow and lanthorn jaws, a face like Tasso's'. So much for the opinion of 'other people', he concluded his letter.[69]

For all the generosity, poise and apparent good humour of Browning's letter, he was more deeply hurt by the break than he admitted. She too concealed the extent of her loss, even wondering if they might meet just once more. But there was relief too 'for I know how near I had come to all misconceptions & distrust – rather of myself than you. [...] I think you very clever to understand such a person as I am.' Now she echoed his sense of the incompleteness of their relations in the absence of Elizabeth. 'Some parts of our intercourse have been almost the best of life to me – specially when you have spoken of your wife – & these do not pass away. Oh, if she had been here when we met.'[70]

She constructed a private shrine in her room, hanging his photo alongside Elizabeth's above her bookshelf, where the four green volumes of her works and the three blue ones of his sat side-by-side 'that they may be as close together as the two writers have always been in my mind – and always will be, throughout the large part of my life in which my thoughts are busy with you'.[71] Here was the place where she would always be most at ease with the Brownings.

There have been several very different interpretations of this 'broken friendship' between Julia Wedgwood and Robert Browning. He never discussed it with anyone and Julia only rarely and, even then, usually in code. Julia Sterling, her solicitous but sentimental friend in whom she did confide at the time of the break, put her own slant on it when she congratulated Julia on her dignity in concealing the fact that she had fallen in love with Browning, a love that he did not return.[72] The tradition in the Wedgwood family, however, was that Browning was far keener on Julia than she on him and had eventually to be called to heel.[73] Maisie Ward, with her insights into the mores of late-Victorian society, concluded that if Julia had played her cards better, she would have become the second Mrs Browning. Betty Miller suggested that the friendship derived its piquancy from Browning's neurosis about his dead wife but concluded that, having escaped from the artistic captivity of his marriage, he was not about to abandon his freedom. Ian Finlayson, a more recent biographer, saw the correspondence as 'enigmatic in many respects and susceptible to all manner of interpretations'. Pamela Neville-Sington had a simpler explanation. As Browning made clear at an early stage, he was not in love with Julia. She was obliged to break off the relationship as she recognized the inequality in their emotional commitment.[74]

Most of these interpretations present the relationship between Julia and Browning as a failed courtship. That was also how her mother saw it: 'you hear the disap[pointmen]t about Mr B——', she confided in Effie, 'it was rather what I expected & am very sorry for Snow, it will be so diff[icul]t for her to get another chance'.[75] But part of Julia thought of it more as a failed friendship. Perhaps the most telling comment on her relationship with Browning was something she wrote herself in 1870 about the difficulties of friendship between men and women. 'Friendship between men and women is for average specimens of both, impossible,' she suggested in her contribution to *Woman's Work and Woman's Culture* that she might have expected Browning to see.

> Instances of such friendship [...] in their power of encircling life [...] make so much impression upon us, that we are apt to forget they belong only to the exceptions of humanity [...] it needs exceptional force of character for a woman to hold at bay the idea of marriage whenever it is possible. To welcome it is easy, to determine against it is easy, but to leave it out of sight – the only basis for friendship – is, to the average girl, whose future is a blank but for this prospect, impossible.'[76]

She had taken the initiative in the friendship with Browning believing that she was 'exceptional'. By the end of it she was obliged to consider that she might, after all, be only an 'average girl'. She was also conscious of having misled Browning. At the outset of the relationship she had assured him that she did not have any romantic expectations and that the fact of their gender difference was incidental to their friendship. But as she became aware of the assumptions of others and began to share them, she realized that she was breaking her deal with Browning. As she told him, 'I am reflecting on myself, not upon you.' Now she 'distrusted' herself and was obliged to end a relationship she had begun on false terms. That, at least, was how she rationalized her behaviour. But her concern to behave honourably was only part of her motivation.

The possibility of marriage to Browning troubled Julia. All her most successful emotional relationships were with women: Emily Gurney, whom she got to know shortly after the break with Browning, and later, Marian Hughes and Kathleen Jervois. Even her feeling for Browning was bound up with her reverence for Elizabeth. Though she believed she needed the closeness of coupledom, her feelings about marriage were complicated. Her eulogy of the extraordinary celibate marriage forced on Lawrence Oliphant and his first wife, Margaret, which, she wrote, redeemed him from the pressures of 'animal impulse' suggests a fear of male sexuality. Had Browning tried to kiss her? Did Julia recoil? Emily Gurney wrote to her with an unmistakable shudder in 1869 about Julia's 'duty in putting a stop to that intercourse as it was'.[77]

Communicating with Browning by letter was an intimate but less disconcerting exchange than coping with his tousled, noisy, affectionate presence in the sitting room, a presence in his first years back in London less neat and groomed than in his last two decades. Deafness compounded her awkwardness. In telling Browning at the outset that she had already determined to avoid marriage, she was retreating behind the cover of her disability. Her vision of marriage remained both demanding and unrealistic. Wedded life was 'supernatural' compared to the 'natural' life of the celibate.[78]

In retreating into the 'natural' rather than the 'supernatural' life, Julia may also have absorbed her Aunt's attitude towards second marriages. They were not unknown in her circle. James Mackintosh had remarried within a year of the death of his first wife. So too would Julia's uncle by marriage, Rev. Charles Langton. Closer to home was Maurice's difficult second marriage. Nearest of all would be the marriages of her sisters who both became second wives, causing particular upset to Rich.

Julia raised the question of second marriages with Browning in August 1863, pondering over the pressures on cousin Godfrey to remarry after the death of his wife in childbirth:

> I cannot help shrinking in imagination from the time which for a young man is natural & so I suppose right when the absorbing grief shall yield to the more material want of a new companion. It is so disappointing to see it, it seems to me like a sort of abdication of the rights of immortality, all my relations who want that everybody should be comfortable are always anticipating it, and it always jars on me so painfully.

'He is rather bound up with you in my mind,' she told Browning.[79] The prospect of taking Elizabeth's place was daunting.

Her concerns over second marriage were only one example of the way that social convention constricted relations between men and women. One of the reasons that her female friendships were more satisfying was the lack of rules governing them. With Browning, unlike Emily Gurney, Julia remained more vulnerable than she had realized to conventional expectations of how she should behave as well as the fear of being talked about behind her back.

Browning, who was familiar with the freer ways of his women friends in Florence, was not perturbed by her momentary forwardness. He liked her honesty and enjoyed her ability to respond to him intellectually. The shared eroticism of mourning drew them together. He warmed to Julia's genuine appreciation of his wife's work and character. Her attempt to associate herself in his mind with Elizabeth might have seemed a deliberate ploy were it not for her lack of calculation in relationships. The resemblances between them were, in any case, real. Julia's construction of a spiritual ménage à trois in which the three of them could conduct a sacra conversazione appealed to him imaginatively. Apart from his wife, Julia was the cleverest woman he would ever know. Though she lacked Elizabeth's entrancing wit and lightness of touch and was never on the same level as a writer, she could match his critical insights, not showing off her learning and intelligence but responding to his out of sheer pleasure. Like Elizabeth, when Browning first knew her, Julia was absorbed in thoughts of death, loss and guilt, but also like Elizabeth, she could be sharp about the problems women faced in an unequal world.

For Julia there was also the intense excitement of intimate friendship with a poet. However great her respect for Uncle Charles as a scientist, her reverence for Browning as a poet was of a different order. As she told Emily Gurney in 1870, he 'mirrored the infinite' becoming 'a manifestation of God'.[80] In reassuring him that she would still have the essence of him when their friendship ceased, she was not falling back on an easy compliment. Julia would continue to read and reflect on his work for the rest of her life.

For his part, Browning was reluctant to recognize the extent to which he was trying to restore comfortingly familiar emotional furniture. He protested rather too insistently that he was not seeking to recreate through his friendship with Julia what he had lost in Elizabeth. Consciously, or unconsciously, in his letters to Julia, he evoked some of the phraseology and even more of the imagery of his earlier letters to Elizabeth. One example was the frequent avowals of both Julia and Browning about how well they understood each other. But with Browning and Elizabeth, these assertions were part of a genuine and deeply touching process of mutual exploration and self-definition. After a time, the correspondence between Julia and Browning became more poised and static, and the 'occasions when, every week at least' he 'could inhale' Julia's company and conversation[81] just a part of Browning's reassuring routine, satisfying in themselves rather than full of potential, as the emotional intensity Julia had initially injected turned into affectionate trust and the pleasure of talking together.

The familiar imagery continued, however. Just as Browning wrote to Julia in the summer of 1864 about Helen, the exiled eidolon in Egypt, so, as a young man, he had imagined the eidolon of Elizabeth sitting in his study in Camberwell. He had also 'held up a light' to Elizabeth in the same way as he asked Julia to do when he gloomily contemplated his return to London after his holidays. The image of the palm tree that Browning promised Julia he would sit under to the end of his life was one first used by Elizabeth, who told him in December 1845 that she had been living in the desert but was now 'among palm trees'. Browning returned it gratefully a few days later, telling her, 'you are my palm branch'. And Elizabeth incorporated it in one of her 'Sonnets From the Portuguese'.[82] Most evocative of all was the image of the gallery. Browning wrote to Elizabeth in January 1846 about a dream he had had of meeting her on stairs and passages and in 'galleries, (ah those indeed!)'. Similarly, he described the private space Julia had opened to him as her picture gallery and told her of his pleasure in contemplating the pictures there.[83] It was fitting that the last time they set eyes on each other was at the Burlington House Gallery shortly before he died.

Even if Julia had not fallen victim to conventional mores in 1865 and called off their friendship in a panic, it seems unlikely that she and Browning would have married. He was too ambivalent about what it meant to be Elizabeth's widower and she too insecure. Emily Gurney, who knew Julia well, told her frankly, 'it wd. have been too constant a strain upon you if yr. life had flowed side by side with that impetuous torrent – tho' you wd. gladly have lost yourself in it.'[84] Browning's emotional investment in the friendship was never as great as Julia's, but he had trusted her not to 'throw up his glass heart' and 'catch it again with the pavement underneath'.[85] Her apparently sudden and largely unexplained decision to stop seeing him left him wary and newly conscious of how much more complicated relations between unattached men and women were in London than in Florence.

Both Julia and Browning now avoided accidental meetings. She twice turned back in the street when she saw him coming: he fled from a dinner party at the Spottiswoods when told that their friends 'the Wedgwoods' would be looking in later.[86] Though they never spoke to each other again, they remained in each other's thoughts. Unusually for him, Browning kept all her letters, while for Julia he would always be 'My Dearest Friend' though like Mary Rich, who never spoke the name of her dead husband, Julia avoided Browning's name. Meanwhile, their lives moved in different directions as they would discover when they got back in touch three years later.

Chapter Seven

A WOMAN'S WORLD

Until her later years, Julia was as impetuous in beginning friendships as she was in ending them. Within months of the break with Browning, she was launched on the most satisfying relationship of her life, her friendship with Emily Gurney. This time she had the full approval of her family. Nor did the conventional restrictions and expectations that had undermined her intimacy with Browning apply. With Emily, Julia could behave entirely as she wished: she reveled in morbid self-disclosure, showed off her brilliance and generally took the lead knowing she could always rely on unquestioning love. Their friendship had a special grace because Thomas Erskine, a man they both revered, had initiated it at Linlathen, the place where Julia was always happiest.

However bravely she had assured Browning that in stopping his calls she was not giving up more than she could bear, the breach between them revived the depression she had felt after Mack's death and her doubts about the afterlife. A guilty Aunt Rich steered her towards Erskine for reassurance.

Rich was distantly related to Erskine through the marriage of her sister, Maitland, to William Erskine. She first met him in Edinburgh in 1828 when both she and Thomas Erskine were devotees of Edward Irving. When Alexander Scott broke with Irving, she followed Erskine's advice to stick with Scott. In 1838 she introduced Hensleigh to Erskine, who found him 'a delightful man, full of truth of heart to God and man and well endowed intellectually'.[1] Fanny was never as impressed with Erskine as her stepsister. Behind his back she called him 'St Thomas' and never challenged Marianne Thornton's brusque complaint that he was 'affected and dictatorial'.[2] As Julia's friendship with Erskine became increasingly central to her life, her parents tolerated rather than encouraged it. Rich, by contrast, shared her niece's devotion to him as did Maurice, who first met Erskine at the Hensleigh Wedgwoods.

Julia had been 17 when Rich first took her to Linlathen. After that she saw Erskine on his occasional visits to London, cheered by his continuing interest in her. Erskine was delighted by *An Old Debt* and read it aloud to his sisters. 'I like the theology of it very much. [...] There is an elevating demand for veracity in Snow's book which to my taste is very good & infectious,' he wrote to Rich.[3] By then he had been obliged to stop writing about theology. His rejection of Calvinism had aligned him with other radical thinkers in Scotland including McLeod Campbell, who was tried for heresy by the Church of Scotland. Erskine too was asked to stop taking communion at his local church.

He withdrew to his estate, conducting services twice a day on Sundays for his household and any others who chose to come. From the late summer of 1847 he organized annual house parties, inviting like-minded friends to join him in these spiritual retreats. They included the Carlyles, Charles Kingsley, Benjamin Jowett, Dean Stanley and his wife, Lady Augusta, Queen Victoria's indispensable Lady-in-Waiting, Maurice and Scott. He also corresponded with a wide circle of devotees, mixing thoughts on public affairs, where he shared the assumptions of his class, being anti-Irish but pro-Italian, with spiritual advice for those who were troubled.

When Julia wrote to him about her doubts and depression in May 1865, two months after the rupture with Browning, his response was immediate and comforting:

> Beloved Snow, I have read over your sorrowful letter more than once with deep sympathy. I wish I could say anything that might help you. At all events I know you are in the hands of <u>One</u> who can help you, & who not only sees these dark gropings in you, but who in a certain sense put them there.

Gently and at length, Erskine set out his view of God as a loving father, patiently educating his children in 'a goodness continually to be received through sympathy'. 'My whole being is a contradiction,' he assured her, 'if there be not a spiritual world and if I do not belong to it.'

> If I believe in God, in a Being who made me and fashioned me, and knows my wants and capacities and necessities [...] I yet can trust, yea, be assured, that all will be well, that He can draw light out of darkness, and make crooked things straight. Without such a thought of God, the consciousness of being embarked in an unending existence out of which we cannot extricate ourselves, would be a horror insupportable.

A second letter set out another of his central concerns with man's conscience as 'the central point of contact' through which God guided him: 'Is my inner sense and my consciousness less to be trusted than my outward senses? Have I firmer reason to believe in an outward world than in an inward? I think not. I believe in the reality of goodness and rightness, at least as much as I do in the reality of earth and water.' This reliance on the validity of inner conviction would sustain Julia through the doubts and depressions of her middle years.[4]

The undogmatic simplicity of Erskine's piety appealed to her. In contrast to the apparently haphazard world of cruelty her Uncle Charles had uncovered, Erskine's brand of optimistic natural theology was consoling. 'The beauty and order of the material world seem to me to contain an assurance that in the higher region of creation, in the moral world, a similar order will yet take place, and must take place.'[5] They corresponded over the summer, and he invited her to join his September house party. The experience transformed Julia.

Linlathen, which she would visit most summers until Erskine's death in 1870 and occasionally after it, became the place where she could be herself, cherished and admired as nowhere else and at ease in the atmosphere of pious tranquillity and reverence for its gracious host. 'Something emerged in me then,' she recalled 25 years later, 'that has never found any atmosphere since [...] I seemed to come upon a "moi" that went to sleep again.'[6]

The house itself was, she remembered, unremarkable. Tall and built of grey stone, it stood tightly enclosed by high, dense trees 'warding off an alien world'. The surrounding countryside held no particular interest: a stream polluted by the effluent from a nearby dye works ran through the grounds towards the sea a mile away. There were none of the usual attractions that brought the English to Scotland at the end of the London season. 'There was no sport, no gaiety, very few neighbours, the drives were mainly to Dundee and Broughty Ferry, "an expedition" was a thing unknown.' There were morning and evening prayers for the household and guests and ample meals prepared by Erskine's two devoted sisters, David Patterson, a widow, and Christian Stirling. The *Times* was ironed and laid out on the library table each day but not always opened. Erskine preferred reminiscing about his famous Scottish ancestors as his friends sat beneath the family portraits in the dining room or recalling his travels in Europe as he pointed to his fine collection of Old Masters in the drawing room or the library with its 'creamy vellum' wallpaper and 'mellow russet leather' chairs.[7] Though Julia sometimes regretted the lack of interest Erskine and his friends took in the world's affairs, she loved the 'refinement and high breeding' she found at Linlathen. She was not the only one who found the return to ordinary life a jolt. 'To return from [Linlathen] to common doings and every-day talk was like descending from the mount of vision to the dusty highway,' wrote another regular.[8]

By 1865 many of the 77-year-old Erskine's contemporaries had died. Getting to know a lively, responsive young woman was a consolation. 'There are not many,' he wrote to her, 'from whom I anticipate the same kind of sympathy [...] it is a great reason for thankfulness to find in a younger generation those who may in some measure fill the places that have become vacant.' Now deaf in one ear and dimly sighted, he took Julia on slow walks round his garden or on occasional drives to Broughty Ferry, patiently answering her many questions and explaining his own appealing theology.[9] Though optimistic, it was never trite. Erskine's God was a loving father with infinite patience and a plan for the redemption of all, no matter how long it took in this world and the next. Suffering was part of His plan. The central event of Christianity was the incarnation of God in Christ with the crucifixion not an act of atonement but the ultimate demonstration of God's love for mankind through the sufferings He allowed His own son to endure.

Julia was a sympathetic listener. Like Erskine she knew the Bible intimately and loved the rubric of the Book of Common Prayer, and both admired the English mystic William Law. 'I felt as if I had found a great treasure,' Erskine wrote at the end of his life recalling his first encounter with Law's work. 'He regarded Christianity not as a system of doctrines imposed on us by God, of which we could know nothing except from the Scriptures, but as the eternally true and natural religion to which all our spiritual faculties are adapted.' Julia expanded this thought in a long article she wrote for the *Contemporary Review* in 1877 on 'William Law, the English Mystic'. Law, she wrote, went against the intellectual currents of his day in suggesting 'not only that the divine spark lay hid in every human creature, but that in every human creature it was to be kindled'. He bore 'witness to the realities that wordly good sense hides as daylight hides the stars'.[10]

The metaphor she used here was one she had learnt from Erskine. His fondness for analogies drawn from the natural world was frequently reflected in her own later writings. Stopping in his hesitant walks, he would quietly point out that though the stars were not visible at mid-day they were still present or suggest that the clouds veiling the sun were like the obstacles to man's apprehension of God. The 'scenery of life', however, was no more than 'the furniture of an inn' where man stayed for a while on his long journey to eternity.[11]

Erskine was reassuringly unconcerned by some of the things that had unsettled Julia. Darwinism impinged on his thinking only as an illustration of the long vistas of time through which God worked out his plans. As he wrote to a friend in 1863, 'He who waited so long for the formation of a piece of old red sandstone will surely wait with much long-suffering for the perfecting of the human spirit.' Nor was he troubled by Biblical criticism. The literal word of the Bible interested him far less than the meaning behind the text. His certainty about the existence of a moral order in the world particularly appealed to Julia: 'He said, "to my feeling Christianity itself has more analogy with natural science than with history. It is a revelation of laws that are independent of facts. There must be a centre of gravity in the moral world, which when once found we shall be right, like the planets, not only as to that centre, but to everything else." '[12] She sent her aunt long letters from Linlathen describing Erskine's thinking while her memory of their conversations was still fresh.

The letters she sent to Effie were rather different. Sometimes she worried that she might muddle up the envelopes 'as they do in novels'.[13] The appeal of Linlathen to Julia lay not only in its delicate spiritual atmosphere but also in its select social tone, something she liked to convey to her sister. On her first stay she coincided with Benjamin Jowett and Arthur Locker, the journalist brother of Frederick Locker Lampson. Locker amused her with his calculations of literary earnings though not by his habitual lateness for breakfast and prayers. She also met two regular members of the circle, whom she already knew a little, Caroline Batten and her daughter, Emily, the wife of the newly elected MP for Southampton, Russell Gurney. The widowed Mrs Batten was a link to Julia's early days in Clapham. Her father, John Venn, had been rector there from 1792 to his death in 1813 and ministered to the developing Clapham Sect. One of her sisters married Sir James Stephen, which left Emily Gurney cousin to James Fitzjames Stephen (who she admired) and Leslie Stephen (who neither she nor Julia much liked).

Despite her distaste for Evangelicanism, Julia was drawn to Mrs Batten. They went for walks together, admiring the gleam of the setting sun slanting on a field of stacked corn sheaves and 'sharing such a wonderful sense of the beauty of the earth being a veil that was almost being drawn aside'. At Linlathen, Erskine created some of the apocalyptic expectancy that Mary Rich had relished in her Irvingite days. With her room close by, Mrs Batten came to collect Julia for prayers, knowing that she would not hear the gong. As always, Julia warmed to the protective kindness of a woman of her mother's generation. Erskine saw what was going on and shrewdly realized that she was making the wrong choice. Emily rather than her mother was the one best placed to cultivate a friendship with Julia.[14]

Julia would always envy the closeness of Emily Gurney and her mother. In part, it was born of circumstance. Rev. William Batten, a housemaster at Harrow, had died when Emily was a child while her only surviving sister, Florence, also died in her teens. Not surprisingly, Mrs Batten clung to her daughter. When Emily finally gave way to the attentions of a much older man, Russell Gurney, in 1852 she admired his 'air of savoir faire' but could never quite forgive him for taking away her child. She accompanied them on their

Figure 20 Thomas Erskine of Linlathen in his prime. Courtesy of National Portrait Gallery.

honeymoon. Gurney had been a contemporary of Hensleigh Wedgwood at Cambridge but went on to a more successful career at the Bar becoming a QC in 1845 and Recorder of the City of London in 1856. In 1865 he entered Parliament for the first time, quickly becoming a spokesman for the Low Church interest as well as a leading advocate of women's causes.

He was soon picked out as the sort of conscientious, fair-minded lawyer governments liked to have on royal commissions and committees of inquiry. When Julia first got to know the Gurneys, they were already planning to leave at the end of the year for Jamaica, where he was to be one of a three-man team looking into accusations that Governor Eyre had suppressed an uprising in the plantations with unnecessary brutality. The commission bravely found against Eyre, who was dismissed from his post, giving rise to one of the great Victorian causes célèbres, pitting Mill, Darwin, Lyell, Leslie Stephen, Thomas Hughes and John Bright against Eyre's defenders, Carlyle, Ruskin, Tennyson, Charles Kingsley and Dickens. Similar splits would arise over the American Civil War.[15] Once again Gurney was involved in the aftermath as a member of the commission which sat in Washington to determine claims for damages against the British government for the depredations to Northern shipping caused by the *Alabama* and other UK-built ships which had operated in the Confederate interest.

As Julia soon discovered, Emily was a founder member of the Kensington Society, the group set up by Adelaide Manning in 1865 to debate issues of particular concern to women. Julia already knew several of its leading lights like Barbara Bodichon (née Leigh Smith), Anna Swanwick, Dorothy Beale and Emily Davies and would get to know Frances Power Cobbe and Elizabeth Garrett. She shared other friends with Emily, including the Thorntons and Forsters as well as the Diceys and the Rossetti sisters but liked to think of the Gurneys as, socially, a cut above the Wedgwoods. Untainted by any factory connection, they traced their descent from judges, clergymen and masters in the great public schools. Living close to royalty at 3 Kensington Palace Gardens, Emily was also required to attend at Court from time to time. But she was just as happy when visiting old ladies in workhouses. Julia admired her un-showy way with charity work, finding it a refreshing change from what she thought of as the stiff, self-congratulatory philanthropy of the Wedgwoods.[16]

Emily's warmth, sincerity and deep faith soon held Julia in thrall. Her letters to Effie from Linlathen are full of her excited discovery of the Battens. When she was in bed with an incapacitating migraine, Emily had come to find her, holding her in her arms and comforting her. She reminded Julia of Meta Gaskell. 'I'm afraid too I must say there's the same very pleasant odour of approbation about her which the stern Wedgwood blood so avoids & which I do so like. I think our people are too afraid of flattery.'[17]

She pursued Emily and her mother with the same determination with which she had initially sought out Browning even though her experience with the Gaskells made her wary. 'I am sure Mrs Gurney will commit some grievous sin, she is so very enchanting.' Her fears were quickly put to rest. Emily Gurney was 'like Meta at her very best [...] all [...] her grace of mind & more than all her intellect, and so much improved by being tacked to a sensible woman of the world instead of a Mrs G'.[18]

After initial calls on Mrs Batten and Emily at Palace Gardens, Julia was invited to join the Gurneys in Brighton. Here, she consciously played the 'littery lady', arriving and leaving in some disarray with her papers flying about her as she discoursed on famous friends like Carlyle and Maurice. Emily was flattered by Julia's interest in her. In later years she would describe Snow as the 'casket of treasure' unexpectedly given to her at Linlathen, while Julia would always be grateful to Emily for discovering in her 'the lark within the songless egg'.[19]

Emily's faith was more venturesome than her mother's. Even as a child she had resented the fact that a Clapham Sect Christmas Day was no more than another Sunday.

Figure 21 Emily, Mrs Russell Gurney in 1861, Julia Wedgwood's ever-reliable friend. Courtesy of the National Portrait Gallery.

She envied her friends who were allowed to amuse themselves without falling foul of the Ten Commandments.[20] Now with Julia as her mentor she could begin to think outside the confines of her mother's Evangelicanism and her husband's dutiful Low Church sympathies. They sat together for hours on the sofa in her sitting room, their arms round each other beneath Emily's water colour copy of Luca Signorelli's 'Angels Crowning Saints', talking and 'wondering' about spiritual matters.[21] Snow appealed to her imagination in a way that her judicious husband could not. She also brought out the maternal in the childless Emily, who was 10 years older than Julia.

Julia was only too happy to take the role of the seer. Her visit to Linlathen had given her a new awareness of her mission: 'the sense of Eternity [...] came like a sudden tide [...] & flooded all life with new meaning [...] all around me was suddenly revealed as mere hyroglyphics [*sic*] [...] the energy which had been spent on endurance might be turned to deciphering something of meaning'.²² Linlathen had satisfied her need to be again the brilliant, original child basking in the adulation of the grown-ups.

Julia never kept a private journal. The confidences she might have entrusted to it were given instead to her friend. As she herself commented many years later when she re-read their correspondence, it contained on her side 'a revelation as complete as possible, & perhaps more complete than it is wise, for one human spirit to make to another. I am penetrated afresh by the wonderful love which was not alienated by confidences as monotonous and depressing' as these.²³

By the time she met Emily, Julia's relations with her family had reached an impasse. She was irked as she had always been by her mother's restless engagement outside the family, and though she had reached an accommodation with her father, she had long doubted whether he even noticed when she was at home.²⁴ Her most difficult relationship remained that with her sisters as they rejected her heavy tutelage. It was a sign of the importance of her new friendship with Emily Gurney that as soon as she returned home from her first visit to Kensington Palace Gardens, she attempted to redefine her relationship with her sister:

> My Effy I am sometimes afraid my great love for you should oppress you, & that you should think I expect to be something like Hope to you – but never do think it for a moment. [...] I wish no earthly thing so much as your happiness. [...] I could now bear to see that that would be helped by my occasional absence or remoteness without a shade of pain or offence.²⁵

The prospect that her sister might find a different outlet for her love was a relief for Effie.

The few letters from Hope to Effie that survive from the 1860s revolve around two subjects: Hope's desperation to be with Effie and her frequent irritation with Julia. She schemed obsessively to ensure that she and Effie coincided in London and that the constant stream of family and friends invited to Cumberland Place was checked so that 'we can cadoodle each other in our bedroom where they don't intrude'.²⁶ When Effie went to study in Paris in 1865, Hope, her 'widow', was desolate and resentful of 'Saint Snow's' attempts to ration her letters to her absent sister to one a day. 'She is so unwise,' Hope protested. 'She kept saying all thro' "Oh if you could but see what is in my mind" & I had to assure her 20 times that I didn't & couldn't see it & so on we went round & round till I felt I must send her away or I should go into hysterics.' Hope complained, too, about Julia's way of prioritizing her work: 'she is wonderfully difficult to manage considering both her goodness & her cleverness'.²⁷ With Effie away, Julia's presence was all the more irksome. Hope worked off her frustration in long walks round St John's Wood.

Everyone welcomed Julia's new friendship with Emily Gurney. For Fanny it provided an opportunity to renew acquaintance with Caroline Batten; for Hensleigh a becoming relationship for his daughter with the wife of one of London's most respected lawyers; and for Effie and Hope a respite from their sister's neediness. Nor were there any of the usual agonizing dramas in Julia's new relationship. The only tension came from Emily's dutiful travels with her husband to Jamaica and America and, later, a holiday in Egypt. When they set off for the Caribbean at the end of 1865, Julia promised to write regularly. Emily was grateful. 'I want very much one of your refreshing awakening letters,' she wrote from King's House in Spanish Town the following February, 'I am in danger of letting my brain get very soft in this heat.'[28]

The intellectual disparity between them is clear from the correspondence. While Emily sent some rather strained descriptions of tropical scenery and complained that 'the blacks are mostly silly naughty children', Julia speculated in a 'very Buckle-ish' way on the impact of climate on race. 'There must be some reason why no tropical people has had a history – (or have they? As soon as I have propounded my theory I invariably find my facts are rather shaky),' she wrote. Less conventionally, she was also willing to consider the adverse impact of colonialism, not just on the conquered but also on the conquerors. The worst effect, she ventured, of 'living in constant contact with an inferior race' was 'the blunting of the sense of equal rights'. She thought particularly of relations between 'the Anglo-Australians' and Aborigines: 'I wonder how far any inequality of race really modifies the duty of governors to the governed, – how far we ought to assume inferiority and how far assuming it is the means of perpetuating it.'[29] Though her sense of solidarity with her class and country remained, the findings of the Eyre commission upset her: 'I would rather have discovered that the Negroes had behaved badly than we.'[30]

As Emily readily admitted, keeping up with Julia could be a struggle, though one she was happy to attempt. Snow was her tonic 'against the comfortable deadening sleepy atmosphere of middle age'. In her final bequest to her of the Signorelli 'Angels', she praised 'my faithful wonderful friend [...] so patient with my stupidity'.[31] As this recognized, the closeness of the friendship did not depend on intellectual equality. It was as important for Snow to teach as it was for Emily to be taught. The reciprocity in the friendship came from its balancing of different needs, together with the freedom both enjoyed to reveal themselves without constraint. Emily's character was far more straightforward than Julia's: she was gentle and generous, pious and sometimes sentimental, charming, cultured and impressionable but true. And she wanted more spiritual and intellectual excitement than either her mother or husband offered.

For her part, Julia needed an understanding confidante but also an unquestioning love which would not be alienated by even her most self-abasing reflections. There were indeed times when Emily was alarmed by the extent of Snow's self-loathing. 'I am a terrible Parasite,' Snow wrote early in their friendship when Browning was still much on her mind, 'and cling dreadfully close sometimes, so that I am always afraid of stifling my tree. What comes to me through others is exceptionally large, the harsh tuning within makes me the more appreciate a melody that I never get near enough to hear.' This was a confession not only of the impact of her deafness but also of her emotional isolation. Drawn as she was to the external world as a respite from her own internal discord, Julia found much of her socializing unrewarding. 'One wonders why there is so much waste in life – why one piles the fire so often and cannot find a match. [...] I feel society specially perplexing for I am sure the net result in the way of enjoyment is wonderfully small in proportion to all that is expended upon it.'[32] Tête-à-têtes with Emily were quite different. Remembering one 'very sweet reunion', she chose a telling metaphor: 'it did not seem to have any of the tiresome <u>waste</u> in it which I feel with so many friends after a long absence. I mean that fringe of meaningless talk like the loose sand above high water mark that one has to plod through with some people.'³³

Both acknowledged a strong maternal element in the friendship. Julia wrote to Emily: 'I have a sort of feeling to you as to a mother – the same sort of trust that nothing will be taken amiss.' Similarly, Emily observed to Snow: 'It is so odd when you are away I feel as if you were twenty years older than I am, & when I look at your face you seem my infant.'³⁴ When Julia confided in her in April 1869 over what looked like a final breach with Browning (whose identity she did not divulge even to Emily), Emily was quick to console:

> To let me have any part in what has so moved your inmost being does indeed make me feel a kind of pride in yr love – but it does not lower you, tho' I feel it lifts me up – Yet, I have too a kind of 'Motherly' sensation in my upward-looking love to you – a longing to take you in my arms & to rock you & shelter you.

As well as the physical comfort, Snow enjoyed the psychological reassurance that a child gets from its mother, as a metaphor she used to describe their friendship suggests:

> No one can deliver me as you, others bring fresh keys and open new doors, but you take a lamp into the dusty cupboard where I thought my enemy was hid and show me that after all it is empty, or at least that the enemy is only some frightened creature that has taken refuge there & is not an enemy at all.³⁵

Both Julia and Emily were quick to see a connection between maternal and divine love, a connection that would colour the development of Julia's distinctively feminist theology. When she grieved over the Gurneys' impending departure for a holiday in Egypt in 1875, Emily consoled her by transferring her friend from her own arms into God's: 'My dearest I was going to say my arms are around you, but no they are not wide enough to embrace you or strong enough to uplift you but here and now it seems so natural to say take her into Thy own wide stretching comforting life giving embrace.' For Julia, maternal love not only surpassed paternal love but was also, in its completeness and experience of suffering, the closest approximation to God's love: 'the love that begins in pain [sends] its roots so far below the love that begins in pleasure', she wrote to Emily in 1870. And again in the same year: 'Ah that wonderful maternal love! – which cannot help taking as the type of God's love so much more than the father's [...] a love that is wholly independent of return [...] if we could believe that the severity of God is the severity of a mother, how different all pain would be to endure.'³⁶ Twenty years later she would develop these ideas more fully in the aftermath of her mother's death.

Julia's and Emily's language to each other now sounds extravagant. 'My own belovedest' was Julia's favourite; 'Darling Snow [...] I strain to thee with needy love, Thine, Emily' was her response, or 'Sweet it was to feel thy head and little ear close to mine last eveg Yr E.' With its aura of maternal feeling, intense shared religiosity, possessiveness and passionate language, it is tempting to place the friendship some way along the spectrum of same-sex feeling that Adrienne Rich, Martha Vicinus and others have detected in several Victorian female friendships.

That is not how Julia and Emily saw it. Theirs was an example of one of those profound Victorian female relationships which, though highly emotional, was not sexual; one, where, as Martha Vicinus has suggested, 'women strove to achieve a passionately spiritual intimacy that subsumed the erotic'.[37] Its vitality sprang from the fact that there were few rules to govern it. As Julia had learnt with Browning, male–female relations were full of gendered expectations about conduct and roles. Female friendships, by contrast, were free of imposed norms and unusually liberating.[38] Julia and Emily Gurney could be themselves, take the initiative, speculate on theology (normally seen as a male preserve), exchange thoughts on social issues and mutual friends, recommend books to each other, lead and be led and, above all, give and receive unqualified love and support. Nor, for all the extreme exposure of self, particularly on Julia's part, did the friendship require the same surrender of self as marriage. Here there was no need for what she would call the 'compounding' necessary to the marital bond.[39]

Julia was quite worldly enough to be aware of the existence of 'Sapphic' relationships in her social circle. Some, like Frances Power Cobbe's 'marriage' to the Welsh sculptress, Mary Lloyd, were quite open. Julia was curious rather than disapproving, anxious only that Cobbe's general bustle and forceful personality should not overshadow the talents of her 'spouse'.[40] She was more wary, however, of the homo-erotic feelings that swirled around in early feminist circles. Bessie Parke's obsession with Barbara Bodichon was tolerated, but Matilda Hay's passions proved too destructive and she was relieved of her duties as editor of the *English Woman's Journal*. Julia was particularly dismissive of what she called female 'crushes'. 'Unrequited attachments,' she wrote crisply to Effie in 1869, 'are worse among women than between women & men cos there's no end of 'em.'. 'Catherine's' passion for Meta Gaskell was a case in point. (Could this possibly be Catherine Winkworth?)[41] By comparison, Julia and Emily's friendship, for all its emotional charge, always fell within the boundaries of what was acceptable and, indeed, approved of in upper- middle- class society. 'My Em,', Julia wrote in 1872, 'what a wonderful boon it is to be able to love another human being as much as I love you. And to be at liberty to utter that feeling without fear or shame.'[42] Indeed, so little shame was there in the correspondence and, as Emily saw it, so much of value, that she hoped Julia would agree to its publication.

The three bound volumes Emily assembled in 1876, together with another of later uncollected letters, offer an unusually full account of Victorian female friendship. Emily, shaped by the tradition of Evangelical self-examination, suggested that publication would help those confronting the same spiritual difficulties that they had faced. Briefly, Julia was tempted. The literary critic in her was always alert enough, however, for her to sense that, as with Erskine's letters, their tone might seem too monotonous. But she could not bring herself to destroy them, not only because they were a record of a precious friendship but also because she hoped that they contained enough insight to be of use to those she described as her 'Sisters in Spirit' who might chance to read them. Carefully she went through them, adding some annotations to help the reader (but never including Browning's name), cutting bits out to save family susceptibilities and, not always successfully, gluing down pages she did not want others to read.

Some of what may have been her most interesting letters do not survive. When the Gurneys were abroad, as in 1865 in Jamaica, the winters of 1871 and 1872 in Washington and in 1875 in Egypt, Julia wrote at length to her distant friend, numbering her letters as she did so. Only a handful of those sent to Washington survive. Julia sympathized with Emily's long exile amongst the 'vulgarity and humdrum' of Americans. Initially, too, Emily quailed before the interminable stream of Senators' wives coming to call. But she developed a soft spot for President Lincoln and liked to repeat his witticisms. (When told that the sun never set on the British Empire, he quipped 'that's because God doesn't trust those fellows when His back's turned'.)[43] And Russell got professional advice from 'a wise man there who would tell him who to ask to meet who'. Julia was ahead of her time in sensing that this sounded like 'an excellent profession'. Perhaps she and a friend could set up in London 'an Office for the confidential amelioration of Society, in these days of superfluous women it wd. be a boon to find such a female line of bizness'.[44]

Julia was delighted when the Gurneys lent her their 'Cottage' at Woolhampton, near Reading, during their absence. This gave her her first opportunity to practice household management as she judiciously invited friends and family to stay. Her father particularly liked it, priding himself on finding the perfect spot from which Snow could sketch her new home. With Effie and Hope, however, there were predictable rows over the terms on which they were allowed to use it.

The Gurneys' venture to Egypt in the winter of 1875 with their nieces turned into tragedy when one of the boats in which they were travelling down the Nile overturned and sank. Two of them drowned and were buried in the sands beside the river. A telegram reporting the accident was published in the *Daily News* before Julia was aware of it. Hensleigh showed his mettle, sending Erny to make enquiries at Kensington Palace Gardens and writing to Julia when confirmation arrived that the Gurneys themselves were safe.[45] Her first thoughts were about how intolerable life would have been if Emily had drowned.[46]

In the early days of their friendship, Emily had looked to Julia to be her spiritual guide, nervous though she sometimes was of her unorthodox speculations. After Mrs Batten's death in 1870, however, it was Julia who held her friend back. Emily longed for contact with her dead mother and tested her out on the possibility of Spiritualism. Julia was indulgent but cautious when Emily described her dreams as 'visions' of her mother's comforting presence. By the mid-1870s, however, the balance of tutelage had changed as Julia faced her own crisis of faith after Erskine's death. Now Emily's simple piety became her mainstay. They went together to the great religious revival meetings at Broadlands, the home of Emily's friends, Lord and Lady Cowper-Temple. Emily was carried away on a surge of new enthusiasm: Julia never quite surrendered her doubts, but was consoled.

Religious observance and charitable work increasingly absorbed Emily Gurney's energies after her husband's death in 1876, with her only self-indulgence her annual visits to Bayreuth. In the earlier years of their friendship, however, she had put Julia in touch with a world of feminist activism that she might otherwise have kept apart from as her sisters did. Emily was a key supporter of Emily Davies's efforts to establish a women's college at Cambridge, in which Julia would also become closely involved. Russell Gurney, too, was one of the most active and reliable advocates of women's causes both in and out of Parliament. He led the move to repeal the Married Women's Property Act in 1872 and campaigned for the admission of women to the medical profession; he presented what was known as the 'householders' petition' for female enfranchisement in Parliament in 1867; and he advised women campaigners on parliamentary tactics, chaired public meetings about their issues and regularly attended the conferences of the Social Sciences Association at which both men and women spoke. He was, as he liked to say, 'The Friend of Women'.[47]

Julia gave him less credit than he deserved for his advocacy of what was still very much a minority cause. She claimed that he only took it up to please his wife and rarely listened to what any other woman said. This was not how Cobbe or Emily Davies saw him, but Julia would be less directly involved than them in the day-to-day organizing of parliamentary campaigns and public events. After his death from overwork in 1876, she tried hard to be fair to him but her heart was not in it. He was, she wrote, 'an able lawyer, a patriotic public servant & a deeply religious man but rather a loving than a sympathetic husband'.[48] In struggling to enumerate his virtues, she did not list his championship of women's causes.

From time to time, she would put herself out to engage him in an evening's conversation on political issues but generally preferred to see Emily when he was out. When she mentioned him to Effie, he became 'the old fellow', and she berated herself to Jane Gourlay for her 'want of something I should like to feel to [Emily's] husband'. 'I have such a profound respect for him – but he gives me a sense of high walls all round and no vista anywhere. [...] I sometimes think I should have compounded for a man not so good with more movement & stir about him – but they seem so perfectly one it is waste of feeling to pity them.' Grudgingly, she admitted to Effie that the Gurneys' marriage was just about the happiest she knew.[49]

It was certainly a decorous coupling. Emily was 29 when she married and he 48. For all his professional standing, respectable family connections, private rectitude and devotion to her, Emily took her time before accepting Russell Gurney. There were to be no children, and it may be that the marriage was asexual. Early on in their friendship, Emily appeared to confess that Julia was her compensation for the lack of emotional excitement in her marriage:

> This day 14 years ago I had a misgiving as I sat with Russell after we were engaged, that tho' I should not be unhappy or rather tho' I should have no cause for unhappiness – yet that there shd be no richness no infinitude in my happiness – but I <u>have</u> found it an overflowing cup – Snow dearest Snow – & you who are so much worthier! But 'Good measure, pressed down and running over' dearest Snow you give it into my bosom in return for a poor word.[50]

The confused syntax suggests the awkwardness of the confession, which was never repeated. Her grief on Gurney's death was profound. Julia did what she could to share it mourning over what Emily had lost and she had never known.

For both Emily and Julia, women were incomplete without marriage. 'To feel <u>oneself completed</u>,' she wrote to Henrietta Darwin when she was about to marry in 1871, 'is so different from having to join on to others. I think one only half knows oneself till one's experienced that complementary intercourse.'[51] An important part of Emily's attraction for Julia lay in the fact that she was married, giving her a perspective she missed as she made her rounds of elderly maiden aunts and widows. 'The best life,' she wrote to Emily, 'is the union of male and female element in it. [...] I feel so constantly that we dwell too exclusively in the <u>women's world</u>, – and see only one half in consequence'. Much of Emily's unfailing kindness was devoted to bolstering Snow's sense of self-worth despite her spinsterdom and countering her view of herself as a second-class being. She did not always succeed. 'I am but half a person,' Snow wrote to Emily in a fit of self-mortification in 1874, 'and seek this integration from each and all of my beloved ones in turn. [...] There is none who needs my wealth to fill up anything, and so there is none who can make the response of which that need is but the other hemisphere.'[52] Her sense of inadequacy would reach a new pitch when both her sisters married. She also recognized the way that marriage could change the friendships she had enjoyed with men. She had been quite close to Richard Litchfield before his sudden engagement to her cousin Henrietta Darwin in 1872. She mused to Emily Gurney about their new relationship: 'such a sisterly friendship is apt to get broken in all the jolting which it must undergo in the transition from a necessity to a very dispensable luxury to a man'. She would keep the 'broken bits' of their friendship 'in a large drawer full of such relics: some of which ought perhaps to be thrown away'.[53]

Marriage was always for Julia the ideal state: her concept of it was highly romantic and dauntingly demanding. 'It is, from a spiritual point of view, no mere accident that this union, in its perfection, passes on to the creation of new life, that is the clue [...] to its deepest meaning.' Marriage required compromises and a surrender of self she longed to make but, in practice, could not face even if suitable candidates had been available. In their absence she observed the marriages of others with an acute eye. In general, she found that marriage was in an unsatisfactory state. Men, she complained, did not value it as they should:

> It is not <u>unhappy</u> marriages I fear, it is the comfortable marriages that have not the element of true love in them but enough of mutual liking to satisfy a selfishness a deux and leave to the world a set of small satisfied beings that have never known aspiration. [...] I hardly see how small people can be good otherwise than single, it would need heavier virtue to care more that your husband should speak the truth than your sons go to a good school.[54]

Julia's vicarious excitement at the marriages of friends was intense. Was Henrietta Darwin marrying Richard Litchfield too quickly, and were they sufficiently in love? Would Eleanor Bonham Carter be overwhelmed by Albert Dicey's brilliance and volubility? And did Emily Rendel know enough about young Clement Wedgwood to ally herself with him for life? He was, she wrote to Emily,

> a nice lad – but I rather wonder at anyone marrying him or should wonder if I did not know that marriages take place daily. Perhaps it is rather arrogant to be astonished at one mind finding its nexus [...] with another, when all that one knows of that other is the mere front parlour and dining hall so to speak – and even if one feels sure from the size of the house that there can't be vast suites of apartments to explore behind still one never knows what may lie hid in the tiniest attic even.

Astonished though she claimed to be at others' willingness to leap into the intimacy of marriage with men they scarcely knew, Julia ruefully acknowledged her essential ignorance: 'One learns very early in the day, that what married people see in each other is not the same as others in kind and more in degree, but something that comes in no other way at all.'[55] Reluctantly, too, she accepted the inevitability of exclusiveness in marriage: 'the exclusiveness which in every other relation we discover to be the sign of poverty & feebleness in the Love, seems here a test of its purity'.[56]

Despite her private insecurities about her single state in her public writings in the 1860s and 1870s, Julia became for a time, like her friend Frances Power Cobbe, an advocate of the claims of unmarried women. In 1867, when Henry Fox Bourne invited her to contribute an essay on married women's disabilities to a collection he was planning, she turned him down. As she explained to Effie, 'I feel inclined to write back & say if they let me write on the position of old maids I might have a good deal to say. [...] I suppose everyone has got tired of hearing about single women & want to hear about the plural.'[57]

A few months later, however, she was given an opportunity to say what she wanted in a review in the *Westminster* of a collection of essays, *Social Reform in England*, by the French commentator Lucien de Portes. She attacked him with brio, particularly criticizing his support for the popular nostrum of the enforced emigration of surplus women. Above all, she rejected as 'the most unfortunate illusion of our day' his suggestion that a woman has 'a sort of adjective existence, needing the substantive corelation of the other sex to give her completeness'. 'We shall err ignominiously', she wrote, 'if we [...] make [young women] feel that the pursuit of independent circumstances of their own is, per se, unwomanly.' Some people (and here she included men as well as women) stayed single because 'they had no choice', some because they 'would not imperil their own personal comfort', but others, amongst whom she included her idol, Charles Lamb, 'have chosen solitude because it appeared to them the strait gate that leads to life'. Her conclusion was rather braver than her thoughts in private letters:

> There is no fear that marriage will ever meet with insufficient honour. It is the happiest state, and will always, therefore, be the commonest. Let those who are called upon to enter it do so thankfully, but let them remember that there may be a higher life than even that of conjugal joy – a life which few are called to share, but all to revere.[58]

This was bold talk. Cobbe would write yet more eloquently about the emotional support women were able to offer in their friendships. Both were reacting against the claim in a notorious article published in 1859 in the *Saturday Review*, 'Queen Bee vs Worker Bee', which had concluded: 'married life is a woman's profession and to this life her training, that of dependence, is modelled. Of course by not getting a husband or by losing him she may find she is without resources [...] all that can be said of her is she has failed in her business.'[59] Julia, like Cobbe, found other 'business' to pursue. She chose for herself 'a higher life' not without sometimes painfully regretting what she was missing but consoled by the unfailing support of her married friend, Emily Gurney.

When in London, she had settled to regular habits of reading and writing. Much of her work was done early in the morning before the servants were up, a habit she would maintain into old age, often settling to her books before it got light.⁶⁰ She then moved on to the Round Reading Room at the British Museum. Two rows of desks at 'the British', as she called it, were reserved for 'Ladies Only', and at one time or another, she might find there other female writers and readers like Caroline Stephen, Adelaide Procter, Cristina Rossetti, Emily Shirreff, Dinah Mullock, Mathilde Blind, Sophia Jex Blake and Arabella Buckley. One she probably did not meet there was George Eliot. Though Eliot got her reader's card on 14 November 1861, she went as little as possible, generally sending George Henry Lewes ahead to choose and order her books. For her the Reading Room was too public and egalitarian. She preferred to work at home or the London Library. But her domestic set-up organized around her creative needs was very different from Julia's. For Julia the attraction of the Reading Room was the freedom it gave her from the many distractions of trying to work at home. She happily filled in the waiting time 'while slaves are tediously hunting for books [...] for me' by catching up on her correspondence.⁶¹

Like her mother, she was also an enthusiastic member of the London Library. As Erny wrote to her in 1872: 'I also enclose a note from the London Library, with a very heavy and learned list of books which I observe the Secy says he is "happy to say are at your service." I suppose his happiness consists in getting rid of such works.' But if Erny was no scholar, Julia could sometimes find avid readers in unexpected places. She emerged from the Library one day in February 1864 to find her cabman anxious to talk about books. When she offered to lend him some, he asked for *On the Origin of Species*, Buckle's *History of Civilisation* and Milton's *Political Letters*. 'Uncle Harry', she told Effie, 'thought I would do better to give him a pound of bacon.'⁶² But Uncle Harry, like most of the Wedgwoods, was as suspicious of ambitious auto-didacts as he was of young women who spent their time in libraries. Julia remained undeterred by her singularity within the family.

Chapter Eight
THE RESPONSIBILITIES OF THE POET

For all the new emotional satisfactions in her life, Julia was far from forgetting Robert Browning. Her mother, too, had not given up hope that the courtship might be resumed. In May 1867, without consulting her daughter, she invited him to dinner. Browning replied not to Fanny but to Julia, making little attempt to conceal his continuing anger and hurt over her earlier decision to end his calls.

> The truth is best said. I underwent great pain from the sudden interruption of our intercourse three years ago: not having the least notion of why that interruption must needs be, then or now, I shrink – altogether for my own sake – from beginning again, without apparent reason, what may be stopped once more as abruptly and as painfully without reason one whit more apparent.

But though he refused to come to Cumberland Place, he was keen to show her the long poem he expected to finish later that year. Julia's reply was graceful and affectionate: she was sorry not to see him but excited to hear about his new work. Privately, she was far more disappointed than she admitted to Browning about his decision to stay away. Aunt Rich was quick to offer sympathy.[1]

Julia would have to wait more than a year before Browning was able to send her advance copies of *The Ring and the Book*, and as he admitted, by the time he got them to her, it was too late to make substantial revisions to his text in the light of her comments. Nonetheless, he was keen to know what she thought of it. Julia looked forward expectantly to seeing his new long poem: 'I so long that this shall be your best gift to the world.' She was even more excited by the chance to re-engage with Browning himself. 'I only look for you in your work, and find so much of you, that all judgment is quenched as absolutely as when after long exile in some barbarous land one should hear English spoken once more.'[2] The question of how far Browning's poetic voice was Browning himself, rather than an attempt to animate a wide range of characters, would become one of the major points at issue between them. Julia knew Browning's personal voice more intimately than most of his readers. Now she found it almost everywhere in the *Ring and the Book*: its energy, cleverness and dark imagination both exhilarated and repelled her.

Working for at least three hours every morning for four years and, in the later months, many more, Browning had been absorbed in what he believed would be 'something remarkable'. Despite the ridicule his first long poem *Sordello* had attracted, he had always aspired to write another. 'I do hope [it] will strike you and all good lovers of mine,' he wrote to Isa Blagden.[3] Except for his great friend and supporter, Joseph Milsand, who read the first two books in the spring of 1868, Browning would not show it to anyone, working alone 'without an eye over my shoulder to read, much less, whisper in my ear to counsel and criticize'.[4] He missed Elizabeth's eye for mistakes in his script. As he later told Julia,

> It has been a particularly weary business to write this whole work by my dear self – I who used always to be helped by an amanuensis, – for, I cannot clearly see what is done, or undone, so long as it is thro' the medium of my own handwriting […] yet I have had to do all this scribbling, and how much more that you will never see.[5]

It was a measure of Browning's confidence both in his own creation and in Julia's critical intelligence that, once his poem was printed, he showed it in advance only to her. He wanted, he said, not just her sympathy but also her honesty.[6] By then he was not short of female support. As well as the many hostesses with literary tastes keen to have him at their tables, there was his sister, Sarianna, who came to live with him after the death of their father in June 1866 and Isa Blagden, Elizabeth's closest friend in Florence to whom he wrote monthly. He kept her in regular touch with his progress on his 'Italian murder thing' and was grateful to her for tracking down an important manuscript account of the Guido Francescini legal case. When it came to it, however, he did not send her a copy of his new poem. Though she made her living from writing, he did not rate her work at the level of Julia's. Nor could she provide the sympathetic but critical eye he had relied on from his wife. For an approximation of that, he re-engaged with Julia.

His new publishers, Smith, Elder, decided to issue *The Ring and the Book* in four monthly instalments of three books each. Julia received the first two parts at Linlathen early in November 1868 and the third and fourth a few days before their publication in the following January and February. 'I am your eager listener always,' she assured Browning as the first volumes arrived, anxious though she was that he might expect too much of her. 'How vain is the attempt to criticize when I hear your voice in my ear again.'[7] She opened the first volumes in high excitement, reading them with great care over the next 10 days – and was both fascinated and appalled.

In the more than three years since they had last met, Browning's and Julia's lives had moved in different directions. He had quickly become a leading member of cultured London society. *Dramatis Personae*, published in 1864, began his rise to critical acclaim. Younger artists welcomed his originality and willingness to tackle the great issues of the day: Darwinism, Bible criticism, religious doubt, materialism and individualism. Here was an invigorating contrast to the dreaminess of mid-career Tennyson. Oxford gave him a rare honorary MA, and Balliol, the most prestigious of its colleges, made him an Honorary Fellow. His sister's, Sarianna's, arrival in London ensured that he had a well-run house as well as shrewd but devoted company. Pen remained a worry, as he often would be, but was now on his way to getting into Oxford, where he would spend his (father's) money as freely as the rest of the aristocratic hearties at Christ Church and study as little but excel at rowing. Above all, in the time when he and Julia were out of contact, Browning had re-found the poetic energy that had deserted him in his last years in Italy. *The Ring and the Book* was one of the most ambitious undertakings in English poetry since *Paradise Lost*.

Julia's life too had become more stable, but also narrower. She was establishing herself as a reviewer and essayist and working on her first full book, a biography of John Wesley. Her friendship with Emily Gurney brought emotional satisfaction, while her acceptance at Thomas Erskine's Linlathen had given her new confidence. By 1868 when his health was failing, Julia insisted on going to nurse him there. Nothing could have been further from its otherwordly fragrance than the brutal, noisy duplicity of Rome in the late seventeenth century. She responded to Browning's depiction of it with a mixture of excitement and recoil. Here once again was the voice of the Browning she had known: 'a very imperfect soul, full of vanity, impatience, arrogance, not without cruelty even' but still 'mirror[ing] the infinite'.[8]

Browning's *The Ring and the Book* grew out of a collection of papers bought for a lira ('eight pence just') in the San Lorenzo Market in Florence in 1860, about the trial and execution of Count Guido Franceschini in Rome in 1698. Guido, with four accomplices, had murdered his young wife, Pompilia (as Browning named her), and her parents, Pietro and Violante Comparini. His justification was that the pregnant Pompilia had been having an affair with a handsome young priest, Giuseppe Caponsacchi, who had carried her off from the marital home in Arezzo, and that her parents had defrauded him. First, they passed off the child of a prostitute as their daughter, in hopes of securing a family inheritance, and then refused to pay the dowry they had promised him in return for aligning themselves with Guido's noble family. The courts condemned Franceschini, but because he held minor orders he had the right to appeal to the Pope for clemency. Against popular expectations, Innocent confirmed the sentence and Guido was beheaded in the Piazza del Populo.

Browning tells the story from many different points of view: those in Rome who are for Guido, those against and those who see both sides of the case; the lawyers who defend and prosecute him; Caponsacchi, Pompilia and the Pope. Guido gets two, very different, books to himself: the first a suave defence of his brutality, the second a howl of outrage on his last night. By presenting the story from many different points of view, Browning engages the reader as an active participant, weighing the evidence and meting out sympathy and abhorrence in response to an accumulation of the various facets of a story of brutality and deception, tempered by chivalry, purity and wisdom.

Browning had talked to Julia about his 'long poem' even before he returned from his holiday in France in 1864 with its structure already clear in his mind. As she wrote to him before she saw *The Ring and the Book*, 'I know the outline of the story (you told me) but one has a poor judgement of the necklace from the thread.' This suggests that she understood the dramatic method Browning would be using but expected his poem to focus on his 'Italian heroine', already vaguely identified in her mind with Elizabeth.[9] Italy was never a country of much interest to Julia – her mother's preoccupation with it took the edge off her curiosity, and she had not yet travelled there. The brilliance of Browning's depiction of Italian society, character and intellect, perhaps his greatest achievement in *The Ring and the Book*, did not elicit the admiration from her it deserved. Her interest was in the moral dimension of his work, and here she found the voice she wanted to hear rarely but the one that troubled her all too often.

Their renewed correspondence began in the old tone of affectionate friendship and gentle teasing. Julia was anxious that his new work should be well reviewed knowing how much Browning had been affected by adverse criticism earlier in his career. She worried, however, that his own estimate of his work might differ from the public's ('concave and convex are so wonderfully unlike in the world of Art'). Browning brought her up-to-date with family news and even, rather wryly, suggested that they might meet again, away from prying eyes at Cumberland Place: 'My sister keeps house here, & people come to see her sometimes, – women-people: is the notion that I might see you, so – a birth of this memorable Gun-powder-treason-&-plot-day – [he was writing on 5 November] fraught with fire & brimstone?'[10]

It was unfortunate that the first six books of *The Ring and the Book* were all that Julia had seen when she first reacted. They lacked some of the leavening she would later welcome in 'Pompilia' and 'The Pope' (Books VII and X). Though prefaced by a disclaimer that her opinion could not be worth what he had claimed, she set about her critique of the first half of *The Ring and the Book* with the confidence she was now bringing to periodical reviewing as well as her passion for truth telling. She approved the design of the poem and was not put off by the amount of surface detail but objected to his choice of subject. His fascination with evil was, she told him, a falling off from his calling as a poet. 'I look upon the Poet as essentially the supernatural man, & I complain of him, when he only mirrors our weakness'. As in her review of *On the Origin of Species*, she quoted from Francis Bacon to make her point. The 'office of poetry' was 'to satisfy the mind' by some shadow of a higher justice than any exhibited in actual life, 'the soul being so much greater than the world'. For her, the focus of Browning's story should have been on Pompilia's redemptive power over Caponsacchi, not on the surrounding villainy.

> The picture of a fribble turned to a man [...] by his first contact with a pure spirit [...] & that rarely felt, still more rarely conceived emotion [...] when a woman leans upon a man's disinterested tenderness & finds a love that ends with itself – all these things, surely, form the core of what you have to say? So much fringe of blackness as brings out this we accept willingly. [...] But surely surely we have more of this than that small white figure can bear.'

Even Caponsacchi, with his taste for irony, was too darkly drawn. 'An intense pure love does not distance indignation – far from it'. To underline her point she quoted back at him something he had told her about Elizabeth: 'Do you remember once saying to me that your Wife was quite wanting in – I am not sure of the exact words, but the sense was, the scientific interest in evil? – I think you said the physiology of wrong. I feel as if that interest were in you unduly predominant.'

She moved on into yet more perilous territory, explaining her disappointment with *The Ring and the Book* as indignation at his refusal to be the idealistic poet and great moral teacher he could be. He was qualified not only by his poetic gifts but also by his precious personal history. 'Do you know what an exceptional case yours has been?' So many marriages were based on incompatibility. Married love was as much 'the discipline as the refreshment of life' with partners 'whose presence is a continual scourge to our taste. [...] Or we deliberately choose companions – perfectly satisfactory to a part of our nature perhaps – but utterly unresponsive to so much, that the joint life seems a starved poor mutilated thing'. But with the Brownings shared tastes, mutual reverence and intellectual sympathies had all run together. 'Did you not thereby contract this debt to us to give some intellectual translation of your experience, and make us feel that love is the principal thing in this world, & the world beyond.' Here was the morality of Linlathen, as Julia wrote late at night after a testing day tending to the frail Erskine.[11] For all Browning's attempts to persuade her otherwise, at heart she would not shift from her initial conviction that in his choice of subject and obvious relish in developing it, Browning had betrayed his wife.

Narrow, conventional and sentimental though Julia's reactions appear, Browning, at least initially, was not disposed to undervalue them. Nor, before the reviews came out, could he discount her suggestion that others might share her opinion. 'Perhaps I am merely indicating my own intellectual limitations,' she admitted, 'yet if that is all, they are still the limitations, I think, of a fair specimen of the class you address.'[12] The poetic persona she wished to impose on him was what much of the late-Victorian public came to value in the man Henry James called 'a Philosophical and Religious Teacher'. Browning was more widely admired as the chivalrous young man who had rescued the sofa-bound Elizabeth, written a few accessible poems and made confident assertions that good would prevail than as the demanding, virtuosic dramatic poet he was at heart.

Browning too struggled with his poetic identity. As he started work on his new poem he had written to Isa Blagden about his sense of Elizabeth as his continuing poetic inspiration: 'I feel such comfort and delight in doing the best I can with my one object of life, – poetry – [...] it shows me I have taken the root I did take, well. I hope [...] that the flower of it will be put into Her hand somehow.'[13] He returned to the thought at the end of Book I, claiming Elizabeth as his inspiration for *The Ring and the Book* and asking for her blessing on it. His description of his 'lyric love, half angel and half bird' recalled his description to Julia in the summer of 1864 of the 'great white-breasted hawk' perched protectively above him and ready to fly higher.[14] But in all of their increasingly fractious debate about what he owed to Elizabeth, neither Browning nor Julia referred to this invocation, much admired though it was. Its hollowness would not have withstood Julia's critical scrutiny, while Browning knew that he could not have written *The Ring and the Book* when his wife was alive. Julia's insistent comments, criticized by Maisie Ward as of 'an unconscious sublime impertinence', were, in fact, painfully pertinent.[15]

Betty Miller suggested that Browning sought Julia's opinion on *The Ring and the Book* as the best proxy he could find for what would have been Elizabeth's distaste. The masochist in him welcomed the chastisement he would get for his four years' absorption in establishing his creative freedom from his wife.[16] Certainly, Browning rather grimly begged Julia 'to lay [the rod] on again & spare not!' before he sent her the third instalment of his poem.[17] But it is unlikely that he wanted the eventual estrangement that came from her inability to admire his work. At least initially he enjoyed the challenge of trying to prove her wrong.

He began, good-humouredly enough, by telling her: 'I value your criticism, over and above its being an utterance of yours, beyond what words are likely to make you believe.' And he immediately admitted her main charge: 'I think you do correctly indicate a fault in my nature, – not perhaps a fault in this particular work, artistically regarded: I believe I do unduly like the study of morbidness of the soul, – and I will try and get over that taste in future works.' 'The curious depth below depth of depravity here – in this chance lump taken as a sample of the soil – might well have warned another from spreading it out, – but I thought that, since I could do it, and even liked to do it, my affair it was rather than another's,' he explained, glossing over the fact that he had offered his story to at least three other writers who had all declined to take it up.[18]

His defence lay in his realism. 'Before I die, I hope to purely invent something,' he wrote, echoing his old promise to Elizabeth that one day he would write 'R.B. A Poem'.[19] 'Here my pride was concerned to invent nothing.' Julia knew Browning well enough to doubt that from the beginning. In all her reading of *The Ring and the Book*, she was both fascinated and repelled by the resemblances she found between Guido's and Browning's voices. Even as she saw this as an artistic failure, she could not help 'always enjoying' the instances where the two voices sounded the same. But Browning wanted her to agree that he was depicting the world, not as it ought to be, but as it was: 'this is God's world, as he made it for reasons of his own, and [...] to change its conditions is not to account for them – as you will presently find me try to do'. Though the story was villainous, it also contained 'the incidental evolution of good' for Caponsacchi, Pompilia and Pope Innocent. He warned her of what was to come, confident that whatever her concern for the disproportionate amount of wickedness he had described, she would find a moral too in 'the Pope's Judgment (longest book in the poem)' as he inaccurately described it. The 'coarseness' of Guido and many other of his Italian characters he defended as 'quintessentially Italian': 'all great (conventionally great) Italians are coarse – showing their power in obliging you to accept their cynicism'.[20]

One of Julia's criticisms did hit home, however. She had complained that Guido's references to Justinian and the Pandects were pure Browning. He was wearily familiar with this criticism of his failings as a ventriloquist. Eliza Flower, John Ruskin and, later, Henry James, all complained that too many of Browning's characters spoke in his, rather than their own, voice. Though he now defended his presentation of Guido to Julia, he did not dismiss her criticism: 'What are the other escapes from dramatical propriety into my own peculiar self – do tell me that!' he anxiously enquired. 'Continue to help me. [...] Write to me again; your letters will be absolutely alone in the delight they give me.'[21]

Julia took him at his word. Stopping with her friends the Backhouses in Richmond on her way home, but still enveloped in the world of Linlathen, her second letter was even more uncompromising. Part of her outspoken repugnance to so much of *The Ring and the Book* sprang from her own intense awareness of the existence of evil. As she confessed to Browning, 'I shared your interest in morbid anatomy.' But though she was prepared to accept the existence of suffering in the natural world and tried to confront the reality of evil in her theology, she looked to the poet to offer relief. His task was to go beyond depicting the finite by revealing the infinite. She suggested to Browning that artistically the most promising area was the delineation of the boundary between good and evil. Later she would see this as one of the supreme achievements of *Middlemarch*. Guido, however, was villainous throughout. Erskine had taught her to find in all God's children an openness to the educative power of His love. Now she, who had struggled to write a deathbed conversion for Mortimer in *Framleigh Hall*, looked to Browning to provide one for his villain: 'oh be merciful to us in Guido's last display! Shame & pain & humiliation need the irradiation of hope to be endurable as objects of contemplation, you have no right to associate them in our minds with hopeless sordid wickedness.' Once again, her objection was pertinent. The record did, indeed, suggest that Guido had made a final confession and sought forgiveness. But though this is reported in the final book, there is scarcely a hint of penitence in the brilliantly defiant second monologue Browning imagined for him.

The rest of her letter showed how far apart she and Browning had grown since they last met as Julia resumed her responsibilities as the guardian of the spiritual home she had constructed for herself and the Brownings. 'It was not only in a critical spirit that I complained to myself as I read,' she frankly told Browning, 'for I felt as if I were reading what you had lost in your wife. The sense of good seemed dimmed.' She returned to her idealization of his duty as a poet.

> Oh yes, dear Friend, do give us something purely from yourself. Give her a monument more durable than that at Florence – give us something that all who read may recognize as the utterance of one who has been taught supremely to believe in goodness by the close neighbourhood of a beautiful soul. I look yet to recognize the sunshine of her presence in the ripe fruit of your mind.[22]

Not surprisingly, Browning was nettled. This debate over his poetic mission bore on the tension that underlay all his work between his aspiration to become a subjective poet and his inclination towards being an objective one. In an *Essay on Shelley*, published in 1852 but quickly withdrawn and not reprinted till 1881, he defined the difference between the two. The 'objective' poet reproduced 'things external' and 'the doings of men' which were readily understood by his audience. The 'subjective' poet worked not with 'reference to the many below' but 'to the One above him, the supreme intelligence which apprehends all things in their absolute truth', leaving behind 'the noisy, complex, yet imperfect exhibitions of nature in the manifold experience of man around him, which serve only to obstruct and suppress the working of his brain'. For the subjective, unlike the objective, poet, poetry and personality were one, 'being indeed the very radiance and aroma of his personality, projected from it but not separate'.

Though he was writing about Shelley, Browning clearly had his wife in mind too. But he could only aspire to Elizabeth's achievement as a subjective poet. And was his aspiration to write 'R.B. A Poem' sincere? He had thrown his energies over the past four years into depicting 'the noisy, complex, yet imperfect exhibitions of nature' in seventeenth-century Italy, discovering that this was how, as a poet, he might be himself. Could he honestly claim a common root with the subjective poetry of his wife, when the objective flower that grew from it was so different? Only Julia had the temerity to point out his self-deception. Earlier he had allowed her to tell him what he was thinking about Elizabeth; now he drew the line when she tried to tell him what Elizabeth was thinking of him. He, not Julia, owned the memory and legacy of Elizabeth. What he was to do with it was a matter for his own perplexity, not Julia's dictates. He defended his poem more grimly.

'The worst is,' he told her, 'I think myself dreadfully in the right, all the while, in everything: apart, of course, from my own incapacities of whatever kind, I think this *is* the world as it is & will be – here at least'. Guido would not be redeemed, though he hoped she would find 'poor Pompilia' 'prettily done'. But for all his irritation he assured her that 'I take all your blame far better than other folk's praise'. Was that because it reminded him of Elizabeth? 'By the way,' he told Julia in a crucial concession that would embolden her further, 'my wife would have subscribed to every one of your bad opinions of the book; she never took the least interest in the story so much as to wish to inspect the papers. It seems better so to me – but is it better?'[23] He went on to show how closely he followed the development of Darwin's thought on sexual selection, which had not yet achieved the prominence it later won through *The Descent of Man*. 'So, the naturalists say that all female beauties are weaknesses & defects except to the male creature, and all real beauty is in him, if he could but see! Only he can't'. Were Julia and Elizabeth right in their very different sense of what was beautiful and he wrong? Contending against a headache on a dreary winter afternoon in Warwick Crescent, Browning tussled with the guilt of recognizing his new-found freedom as a poet.[24]

Julia sensed the need to mend fences. She relished his admission that her reactions were those Elizabeth would have had. ('It is a historical fragment in your letter that gave me most lively pleasure.') And Pompilia entranced her, 'that dainty lovely pathetic little picture is an exquisite pleasure to me'. How well he understood 'the woman's nature!' Pompilia is variously described in *The Ring and the Book* as 'a flower' or 'a rose'. Julia chose to give her the source of her own nickname and call her, more appropriately, 'a lovely Snowdrop growing out of that dunghill'. She also spotted a defective sentence. Browning was grateful. But then she was obliged to turn from Pompilia to two characters Browning had already warned her she would not like: the loquacious, unscrupulous lawyers, Hyacinthus de Archangelis and Johannes-Baptiste Bottinius. Nor did she. How could Browning give so much time to such worthless characters? 'You lead us through your picture gallery and your stable yard at exactly the same pace.'[25]

Humorously, but defensively, Browning had allowed at the outset for the possibility that his work would not be well received, addressing his readers in Book I as the 'British Public, ye who like me not, / "God love you" – whom I yet have labored for.'[26] To his and Julia's surprise, most of the initial reviews were favourable. Though the *Saturday Review* bemoaned 'the intrinsic disagreeableness' (of the theme) 'which acts rather as a hindrance to the expression of lofty and noble sentiments', it concluded that Browning's work needed to be judged by a higher standard than others' and praised 'the originality, the compass, and the solidity of Mr Browning's genius'. The *Fortnightly* was enthusiastic from the start: 'The theme [...] lies in that department to which English taste, narrow and rigid, usually expresses its repugnance by labeling it as morbid anatomy,' but 'Mr Browning is never morbid. [...] Of all contemporary poets he is the most healthy, life-like, and human in his style and colour.' If that must have seemed like coals of fire on Julia's head, so too were the thoughts of Mercure Conway, the American Unitarian minister at South Chapel, Finsbury, in the *Atlantic Monthly*: 'the world of forms, the city of bodies, represents to [Browning] the scattered rags of this mysterious humanity; and his art is not to change them into any moral monotony, but to cultivate and guard them in their various vitality and meaning, and report their dramatic interplay'.[27] This read almost as a paraphrase of Browning's own defence to Julia.

As she began to see that she had failed to grasp Browning's purpose, his confidence was growing. He became more impatient with her persistent criticisms. If they had still been meeting face to face, the gulf might have been bridged. Four years earlier he had told her,

'You fit into all the angles of my nature.'[28] Now when they no longer talked, their angularities collided. Julia appealed to him to sort out her confusion. 'I have a wonderful sense that you can drop some grain into these muddy thoughts, that will make them clear – clearer than they are to myself.' But Browning would be irritated by her comment on Pompilia: 'I can not venture to tell you all that Pompilia seems to me. I felt as if it was only half yours. But indeed I do not divide the other influence from your own.'[29] Tactlessly put it may have been, but it was not off the mark. Alexandra Orr, who later took on the task of explaining Browning to his readers after long conversations with the poet, wrote many years later, 'Mrs Browning's spiritual presence [...] entered largely into the conception of Pompilia.'[30] Now Browning crossly complained to Julia: 'It is a shame, that when there is anything you contrive to like in it, you cry out, "It's not yours, you know – only half yours," and so on: then comes an ugliness, and "Ah, there you are at home, – there I see you at work!" – you comment.' But he was beginning to be wary of her flattery too and peevish about the earlier rupture in their friendship: 'I think, on the whole, it is probable we shall never meet again, face to face. Depend on it, I keep what I gained, and shall never part with an atom of it. It was foolish of whoever or whatever deprived me of what would have done good to me, & harm to nobody.'[31]

On 12 February he sent her the final instalment of *The Ring and the Book* comprising the Pope's monologue, explaining why he would refuse Guido clemency, Guido's second monologue and Book XII which described his execution, the sermon of an Augustinian brother, Fra Celestine, about good coming out of evil, and Browning's final dedication to Elizabeth. 'Here', he testily told Julia, 'is my last trial of your patience.' She was sensible enough to read and comment on the Pope before she turned to Guido. In Innocent she found everything she had wanted. Here, at last, Browning was fulfilling his poetic vocation: 'I feel as if there were more of that which seems to me your special message to us in the Pope's speech than in anything else you have written. [...] I know that sense of everything falling into its place which it gave me – & I hardly feel with anything but Beethoven's music.' Innocent restored her hope

> that this poor little Planet is a good inn for our souls to rest in, before they start on the long journey – [...] that sense of the wealth and glory of this life, & its insignificance, – I can only hurry from one to the other, but you, in some rare flashes, show me them together. This miserable incompleteness, the straining of the growing plant against the tiny pot, which in prosaic hours seems hopeless misfit and mistake by that light turns into a promise.

She (mis)quoted Shelley to underline her sense of Browning as at heart an idealistic poet: 'All harmony, all medicine are mine.' Surely, for all his depiction of a world 'in which things foul and hideous have their place', he agreed with her. 'You do feel that your work is the deliverance of captives, & the opening of the eyes of the blind.'[32] As she would put it more simply in a letter to Emily Gurney, Browning was, when he chose, 'a manifestation of God'.[33]

But then she turned the page to find more of the repulsive Guido. She felt so strongly about him not only because she sensed Browning's own voice in his but also because he offended against her views on social status and her respect for the Classical education that she had had to struggle to put together. For her it was inconceivable that an aristocrat who could quote Greek and Latin could also be a 'mere brute, hacking Pompilia to pieces'. 'I do not feel that doubleness so much in any other figure. [...] This has not struck anyone else, so I suppose I'm wrong, but still I can't help saying what I think about it.' Given the positive critical reaction to *The Ring and the Book*, Julia no longer needed to fear the impact on Browning of a hostile reception. This made her yet more outspoken. They had reached an impasse. 'Yes, I suppose your first summary of my criticism was true – I cannot sympathise in your choice of a subject. Surely, I must be wrong here, you cannot have spent all these years on a mistake.'[34]

For Browning, who had confessed to Isa that he would need to 'wash his hands clean for a minute' before he saw Elizabeth again 'as I trust to do', Julia's bewilderment articulated his own unease.[35] As a young man he had warned Elizabeth that 'for every poor speck of a Vesuvius or a Stromboli in my microcosm there are huge layers of ice and pits of cold black water'.[36] This was not an aspect of his nature that Elizabeth wanted to recognize. Nor did Julia. But confronted with the evidence of *The Ring and the Book*, the work that Elizabeth was spared from seeing, she had no choice. The duality in Browning's artistic nature, the co-existence of the poet who could write convincing monologues for both Pope Innocent and Count Guido, disturbed her just as much as the masculine presence of the poet who illuminated the infinite but revelled in the finite.

She was not the only friend to conclude that Browning had demeaned his art by choosing such a shabby little shocker as the subject of his most ambitious work. Carlyle commented that it was an Old Bailey story that could have been told in 10 lines: it was obvious that Pompilia and Caponsacchi were having an affair. (Though the record bore this out, Browning never conceded it.) But Browning angrily showed the old sage the door when he enquired, 'What had happened to the eternal verities' in the poem.[37] Though Julia was wearing out his patience with a similar complaint, he was prepared to give her a much fuller answer than Carlyle ever got.

His story, he argued, was true.

> How do you account for the 'mere brutal hacking Pompilia to pieces' in a nobleman thirty years the intimate of Cardinals: is this the case of a drunken operative that kicks his wife to death because she has no money for more gin? [...] We differ apparently in our conception of what gross wickedness can be affected by our cultivated minds, – I believe the gross*est*, – all the more, by way of reaction from the enforced habit of self-denial which is the condition of men's receiving culture. Guido tried the over refined way for four years, and in his rage at its unsuccess, let the natural man break out.

He could allow Julia to avert her eyes: what disappointed him was her failure to detect in his work the indirect 'utterance of congenial feeling' which, he said, emerged all the more clearly because he had not insisted on it. Now as he admitted defeat, he no longer concealed his anger: 'I will try and please you better another time: yes, I have given four full years to this "mistake" – but, what did I do with my fourteen years in Italy? I must go on, busy myself now, and rub my dry stick-like self into a blaze in this cold evening of life. And whatever I write,' he concluded through gritted teeth, 'I will always send you, and you will always like to see it, will always speak your mind about it, and will always be exactly in the relation that you are now to R.B.'[38]

Unwisely, Julia persisted. 'Tant pis pour les faits, if they are not artistic,' she replied. He should 'give us some relief from [Fate's] coarse picture gallery by your truer representations'.[39] Sensing Browning's wish to close down the correspondence, she now anxiously tried to straighten out the record of their friendship. For some time she had been confiding in Emily Gurney though referring to Browning only as 'the Friend I have talked to you so much about' (a description she would later annotate in the margin of her letters 'My Dearest Friend'). She confessed to Emily that her letter of 5 March was likely to frighten him away with its pathos. 'I implored him to spare me the pain of thinking I had given him pain. [...] Yet I am glad I made that appeal. I think we ought not to let each other be cruel.'[40] Now Browning found himself in an unwanted exchange about mutual standing with Julia denying that they could ever be on an equal footing.

It mirrored his courtship correspondence with Elizabeth. The issue of equality was, as Daniel Karlin has shown, an essential element of Browning's successful attempt to build up Elizabeth's confidence for the escape to Italy by showing her that he, not she, was the one who most needed support.[41] With Julia, the discussion was more arid, not least because Browning, once again, refused to accept his superiority. Nor would he have it that only she had suffered from their earlier breach: 'in some ambiguous way I am motioned to step up to some pretty pedestal whence I am to observe you somewhere below – which I decline doing'. But he coupled his refusal with an ironic account of a royal tea party to which he, Carlyle, George Grote and Sir Charles Lyell had been invited: 'provided the Queen don't send for the Siamese Twins, the Beautiful Circassian Lady, and Miss Saurin as her next quartette-party, I am in a way to rise', he noted. 'I wish I could see you again,' he wistfully wrote, telling her of his failure to visit the house of an old acquaintance who had dropped dead the next day.[42]

Julia became more candid about what she had lost by ending their 'friendship': it had been 'the era of my life'. 'My friendship with you was – is – the great blessing of my life, but it was impossible to me to carry on that outward indulgence of it after it had been implied to me He feels it a gêne."' Browning was taken aback. He had assumed, taking his cue from her letter of 8 July 1864, that she had stopped his calls because of parental opposition. 'I enjoyed seeing you much, – there is a fact, – and acquiesced in giving up that enjoyment for any cause that seemed sufficient to you, – there is another: and if you, of your very own self could, however, fantastically, assure me, "Oh, but it was all done to relieve you from a gêne!" – well, I shall say – "You know better!"' He would always send her his work. 'I dare think you do feel as kindly to me as you say: ask yourself whether you can disbelieve me when I repeat that my trust in that, is one of my most precious possessions [...] yours affectionately now then and ever, R.B.'[43]

This was a generous goodbye, but Julia could still not let go. She went back to explaining and defending her earlier decision. There was a strong hint of Aunt Rich's influence (though she did not name her) and an honest confession of the emotional inequality in their earlier friendship. Now, she claimed, she could be philosophical about their 'separation'. 'What I feel about you does not occupy a large part of the surface of my mind – no feeling can which is not in any way linked with action. But nothing else casts its roots as deep, or comes so near the region where I am alone with God – & it is a satisfaction to me that you know this.' She had shown part of her draft to Emily Gurney, who suggested she soften its tone of finality. She tried her own graceful but forlorn way of trying to maintain contact by offering to serve as his copyist: 'Perhaps you would be afraid of any interpolating moral sentiments? – & it might be a danger.'[44] Browning, who was about to go on holiday, did not reply.

As she admitted to Browning once the correspondence on *The Ring and the Book* had ended, 'It feels flat & dismal to have no more fuel for my critical fire.'[45] A year later, after a long silence from Browning, she made an ill-judged attempt to revive their correspondence, recognizing that she had been too frank in expressing her distaste for *The Ring and the Book*.

She wanted, she told Browning, 'to pass on the impression made by Pompilia on a beautiful soul, among my friends' (doubtless, Emily Gurney). Her exaggerated praise ('its effect was a beautiful sunset [...] no music even was so pure & aspiring [...] the character shone before her eyes like an upward flame') was the sort of sentimental gush Browning disliked. He had always preferred Julia's more acerbic tinge. 'I should be disconcerted and uneasy,' he replied, 'were it your [opinion] also; I don't want you in that attitude.' But it was Julia's final sentences that riled him the most as she again reverted to the familiar theme he had always avoided tackling head-on: 'I look for something from you that I can fully enter into. You know you owe us an adequate translation of what your wife was to you.'[46]

Just as her suggestion that he had been wasting his time on *The Ring and the Book* had finally provoked him in February 1869 to wonder aloud about his lost years in Italy, so now he finally confronted the issue of his personal and poetic debt to Elizabeth.

> But why or how do I owe you – or whomsoever is included in 'us' 'any adequate translation of what my wife was to me?' – except in saying, as I devoutly do on other occasions than sitting at meals, 'For these and all other mercies God be praised!' Let us show forth that praise 'not in our lips but in our lives'.

This was not, as both of them knew, a complete answer to Julia's demand, nor to her complaint that it was ungrateful to come back from Eden to tell us 'only that Human beings are devilish'. But Julia had said the unsayable. Gently, but this time very firmly, Browning closed down the correspondence: 'Come – let us go back to the quiet place, where we "do not forget each other" – Good bye, dear friend; it was very pleasant to hear your voice in the dark – though I see no face since years now. RB.'[47]

Three weeks later in his delayed monthly letter to Isa, he wrote wistfully in a possibly indirect reference to Julia: 'Whom does one care to teaze that one does not also care to kiss? [...] It is a bad sign that I teaze nobody now, nor let them teaze me in the rare cases when they are able.'[48] He had grown more wary in his dealings with women, having narrowly escaped in the summer of 1869 being trapped into marriage by the phenomenally wealthy and very determined Lady Ashburton. She appears in a variety of unflattering guises in some of his later, grotesque poetry, as he took his revenge.

By contrast, he stayed silent about Julia. But there are faint traces in his work of his emotional response to her. It is hard, for example, not to think that he had her a little in mind, when he told Sir Frederick Pollock that writing *The Ring and the Book* had felt 'like bawling into a deaf man's trumpet, and then being asked not to speak so loud, but more distinctly'.⁴⁹ His next long poem, *Balaustion's Adventure*, written quickly in 1871, might also be read as an indirect answer to Julia's insistence that he tell the world what his wife had meant to him since many saw resemblances to Elizabeth in the character of Balaustion and the poem introduces a re-working of Euripides's *Alcestis* about a wife who offers to give up her own life to save her husband's. But if Julia was looking for a more 'subjective' account of life with Elizabeth, the other side perhaps of those *Sonnets from the Portuguese* she adored, she got a dusty answer in his poem 'House' published in 1876. 'Shall I sonnet-sing you about myself? / Do I live in a house you would like to see? / [...] Invite the world, as my betters have done? / Take notice: this building remains on view, / Its suites of reception every one, / Its private apartments and bedroom too; / For a ticket, apply to the Publisher / No: thanking the public, I must decline.'

Browning had, briefly, admitted Julia across the threshold into his private world of grief, longing, frustration and obligation, where both delighted to talk about Elizabeth. He was wary of the misuse biographers might make of letters and regularly destroyed them apart from the correspondence with Elizabeth, which he could not bring himself to re-read until 1887. But he also kept all of Julia's letters. He tried to explain to her in March 1869 that he had not seen her as some kind of dim reflection of his dead wife but valued her for herself. The opacity of his prose does not quite convince.

> I think I <u>have</u> things thoroughly and effectually and, in a sense, sufficingly, – it would be all the worse could I say to myself 'These half-experiences may be expected to recur or, if the missing <u>halves</u> follow, <u>that</u> may do as well, and be novel besides.' But the acquiescence in absolute loss should remove all misconception or scruple as to what proves, when it subsequently presents itself, – gain, – new and unexpected.⁵⁰

A last hint of the emotional association he made between Julia and Elizabeth came in 1889, the year of his death, when he undertook a revision of *The Ring and the Book*, smoothing out awkward lines, improving the syntax and pointing up his meaning. In the closing lines where he compares the power of the visual arts with music and with the written word, he changed the original, 'So, note by note, bring music from your mind, / Deeper than ever the Andante dived' to 'Deeper than ever e'en Beethoven dived.' Elizabeth's passion for Beethoven may well have been in his mind but so too might Julia's praise for his portrait of the Pope as comparable in its effect only with Beethoven.⁵¹

Like Aunt Rich, romantically refusing to let the name of Claudius Rich pass her lips, Julia kept silent about Browning. She might refer to him alongside Tennyson or Meredith as a poet whose work she knew, and later taught. She even tried to interest Emily Gurney in *The Inn Album*, one of Browning's darkest and most repugnant late poems. 'I do not know whether such things should be written,' she wrote to her, 'yet I cannot imagine anyone reading this without feeling evil more hideous.' 'Surely that is a fit aim for a teacher,' she concluded trying hard to draw the moral she had failed to find in *The Ring and the Book*.⁵²

In devoting much of the 1870s and early 1880s to her own magnum opus, *The Moral Ideal*, however, she turned to a different and more welcome aspect of Browning as the poet of aspiration. The book was dedicated to him in the guise of 'An Old Friend'. In her lengthy dedication, she claimed his sympathy as of right as well as 'some criticism tinged with the desire to approve', a fair summation of what Browning had hoped from her in showing her his major work. 'You will look in vain,' she continued, 'for a suggestion or an idea not already familiar to you.' Her assertion that 'if you can care for what I have written, sooner or later one or two others will feel its meaning' was as bold as it was vulnerable and eerily reminiscent of Elizabeth Barrett's dedication of her 1844 collection of poems to her father: 'it is my fancy [...] to conjure your beloved image between myself and the public, so as to be sure of one smile'. There is no record of what Browning thought of Julia's best-known book if, indeed, he ever read it. It was not in his well-stocked library at his death.

In 1887, having not seen each other for over twenty years, they happened to coincide at the crowded private view of the Royal Academy exhibition at Burlington House. She was conscious of someone looking intently at her. When she turned to see who it was, she found Browning – and fled. 'O [...] such a gaze! I mean that <u>read so much in me</u>,' she wrote to Emily with all the tremulous excitement of a schoolgirl. Once again, his physical presence unnerved her.

> The look stirred much that I would forget, oh very much! But the sense of the Eternal was there too. [...] I trust I may meet that glance no more until we meet elsewhere. Something there was sweet to me in that look, some fears were laid to rest. [...] So much was stirred that is unseasonable so much that may wake elsewhere, but now should lie in its winter sleep & indeed for the most part it does. [...] It is unwithered with me and yet perhaps to him it was nothing.[53]

At the time that Browning had finally ended their friendship, she wrote to Emily about her unnamed friend: 'I have felt more sure of God in my moment's glimpse into a deep soul, than in all the rest of life [...] it mirrored the infinite to me, it made me feel how life might be all flooded with wonderful joy in a moment, how supernaturally one might be raised above the din and dust of earth – and all things harsh and painful be shut out by a miraculous influence.'[54] Julia's friendship with Browning, brief, but intense, was the high point of her life.

While she may well have had regrets about succumbing to Rich's pressure to break it off and about the outspokenness of her criticisms of *The Ring and the Book*, her overriding sense was one of gratitude. Through her years of depression and disappointment, ill-health and hard work, the Brownings' poems remained an inexhaustible resource, as she dreamed of a union with them both in a place where misunderstandings and disability, insecurity and physical inhibition played no part.

As the friendship with Browning ended, Julia began a new one with a woman he much admired and always respectfully referred to as 'Mrs Lewes', George Eliot. Ironically, Julia's distaste for *The Ring and the Book* but intense admiration for Eliot's long poem *The Spanish Gypsy*, published at the same time, first brought them together. Yet more ironically, Eliot passed on to Browning a tactfully selected extract from a letter from Julia in an attempt to cheer him.[55]

George Eliot's switch to verse surprised her public. Though early reviews were respectful, more considered critiques pointed to faults in versification, lack of dramatic power and the improbability of the plot of *The Spanish Gypsy*. It tells the story of a young gypsy princess, Fedalma, who loves and is loved by a Spanish nobleman, Don Silva. Her stern father, the patriot Zara, calls her away to rejoin her race. Silva follows her, but after his three companions and uncle are murdered by the gypsies, he stabs Zara. Fedalma becomes leader of her people, forgiving Silva before she sails away with them to Africa. Julia was one of the few who found the combination of sentiment and grand ideas irresistible, attracted as she was to the idea that love might become subordinate to national feeling.

Barbara Bodichon, having heard her enthusing about the work and knowing that Eliot was feeling bruised by her critics, encouraged Julia to write a fan letter.[56] She readily agreed, comparing her admiration for *The Spanish Gypsy* with her reservations about *The Ring and the Book*. 'I never felt in anything else (or only in Browning's poetry)', she wrote, 'that same complete fusion of passionate feeling and complex intellectual ideas.' But in *The Spanish Gypsy* unlike *The Ring and the Book*, 'one gets the white light of the purest heroism without any blackness of villainy.' Eliot had shown how 'the most exquisite joy can be less attractive than the misery which we share with our own'.[57]

Julia's assessment of the relative merits of Eliot's and Browning's poems was little shared then or now. Octavia Hill showed a surer literary judgement: 'We are reading the Spanish Gypsy,' she wrote to a friend. 'To me it seems full of wonderful passages of fresh fact [...] but the whole is disjointed; the story improbable. [...] Now Browning, with all his dramatic power, & turning it upon such various (& often such low) people [...] has definite grasp of some positive good.'[58] Julia's literary judgements were not usually so perverse. Underlying her hostility to *The Ring and the Book* lay her unresolved unease over the robust reality of Browning the man and her idealization of his poetic vocation.

George Eliot still managed to extract from Julia's letter a few words to pass on to Browning. She had, she wrote, received a letter 'from a very rare young woman, whose words were all alive with sincere meaning', referring to 'the whole works of the poet from whom I have sucked most – Robert Browning'. 'Perhaps the assurance of having fed a valuable young life may come just in time to neutralise the effect of some nonsense you have lately endured.'[59] Browning might well have guessed the identity of her unnamed correspondent. The description of the 'very rare young woman' was an unwitting echo of what he himself had told Julia just two months earlier: 'I lost something particular in you, which I shall not see replaced.'[60] Nor would he.

Part III

Becoming a Woman of Letters

Chapter Nine
FINDING A VOICE

The rediscovery of the variety of women's non-fiction writing in the Victorian age is a fairly recent phenomenon. Some, like George Eliot, graduated from non-fiction to fiction: others like Margaret Oliphant kept their hand in both. Most concentrated on specific areas of interest like art history or devotional literature, natural science or translation. Their emergence has led Deirdre David to see the woman intellectual as 'an increasingly powerful social figure' in this period and Benjamin Dabby to detect in the nineteenth century a specific tradition of women writing as public moralists.[1]

Julia's ambition exceeded that of most women writers. For all her passionate love of art, she avoided art history. Nor did she attempt detailed narrative history. When she wrote about religion, this was not as a guide to private devotion but an attempt to get to grips with the big questions of theology. Similarly, she looked at Classical thought and literature not for their pre-echoes of Christianity as Augusta Webster and Anna Swanwick did, but on their own terms as a key element in world history. Her chosen subjects in her mature years were those of the newly emerging 'man of letters': moral philosophy, theology, the Classics, world history and literature. The fact that women were largely excluded from this preserve did not deter her.

Her closest model amongst her contemporaries was Frances Power Cobbe. Cobbe was not only a brilliant journalist and a committed campaigner but also a fine, reflective writer on Kant, Darwinism and her own brand of Theism, which owed much to American Transcendentalism. While lacking Cobbe's quickness and ready wit, Julia's tone was more elevated and her range even broader. When Cobbe retreated to Wales in the early 1890s, the *Glasgow Herald* installed Julia in her place, describing her as now 'the Thoughtful Woman par excellence'.[2] By then she had published the first of her two big books, *The Moral Ideal*, and was working on her second, *The Message of Israel*.

In choosing a bigger canvas than her female contemporaries, Julia was aware of the hostile reaction she courted. She summarized the condescension of the *Saturday Review* towards women writers in a letter to Browning, wryly noting 'their stock remark on all women's productions', 'it is gratifying to reflect that so much labour etc cannot but have produced valuable results to the writer, however etc'.[3] But Julia was tone-deaf to its gendered expectations. She also had the good luck to find an editor at the *Spectator*, Richard Hutton, who saw no limits to what women might do as writers. He, more than any of her female literary contemporaries, became her role model. As a result she developed an ability to handle 'masculine subjects', which, as José Harris has suggested, was seen in her own time as second only to George Eliot's.[4] In tackling them, however, she consciously adopted a recognizably female voice.

Margaret Oliphant's thoughtful but often hostile comments about George Eliot show how difficult it was to pull off this combination. Oliphant described Eliot's style as 'less defensible in point of sex than the books of any other woman who has ever written'. Its hallmarks were the 'absence of timidity' and the fact that 'her scientific illustrations and indications of a scholarship [were] more easy and assured than a woman's ordinary furtive classical allusions'.[5] Like Eliot, Julia was never 'furtive' or 'timid'. In finding a rather different voice, however, she rejected the woman who might have seemed her most obvious role model, Harriet Martineau.

Martineau had shown that a woman 'could write about anything'.[6] But though Julia also chose her own subjects, she defined herself as a writer in part by reacting against her childhood friend. 'I always feel now', she wrote to Ellen Tollett in 1871, 'that a certain sort of man speaks of Woman with that curious goddess in the background of their minds as a type, and I feel rebellious against our representative.'[7] She admired some of Martineau's work, like her travel writing, her novel about Toussaint l'Ouverture and her biographical sketches,[8] but there was much she did not like, particularly her outspoken advocacy of Comtism.

Julia's disagreement with Martineau (though there was never an open breach between them) was as much about tone as substance. Martineau was too combative, too ready to air private grievances in public and altogether too strenuous and triumphalist. 'For about twenty years,' Julia wrote in 1878, 'I felt at the sight of her hand-writing a sort of shrinking as if I should see a snail crawling over something precious – always an ugly mark was left on some character one wanted to admire.' Beyond that, Martineau not only dismissed the idea that was most precious to Julia, the prospect of an afterlife, but did so with 'delight'. Like the Winkworth sisters, Julia was repelled by her 'strong sense of relief and freedom at escaping from belief in God and a future life'.[9]

Martineau had been conscious at the outset of her career that she lacked obvious role models, describing herself to Lord Brougham in 1832 as 'a solitary authoress who [...] had no pioneer in her literary path'.[10] She deliberately constructed a 'genderless ideal of writing' that enabled her to comment on whatever subject she chose.[11] Julia worked out a different authorial style, which the aging Martineau, nonetheless, admired.[12] Like Cobbe, she developed a feminine voice. While Cobbe chose wit, eye-catching headlines and the frequent restatement of female solidarity, Julia's style was resonant and authoritative, poetic and full of metaphor, occasionally humorous and always intelligent, but sometimes cluttered. Her biography of John Wesley published in 1870 was the testing ground for this careful construction.

As with her first novel, it had a difficult birth. The subject was not one she chose. On the strength of her introduction to Alexander Scott's *Discourses*, Macmillan invited her to contribute a volume on Wesley to their 'Sunday Library' series, which, as Julia described it, consisted of books of 300 small pages in 'rather large' type.[13] 'I began with being much interested in the subject & intensely wishing to write about it,' she told her cousin, Henrietta Darwin.[14] She was at home in the eighteenth century and Wesley's career raised questions about the nature of religious experience that interested her. But she could not wear the straitjacket of Macmillan's preferred format. Nor did she want to write another pious life of Wesley, relying on the findings of others. Though Wesley's character did not

Figure 22 Harriet Martineau, the gifted woman who could write about anything, that Julia Wedgwood rejected as a role model. Courtesy of the National Portrait Gallery.

interest her, his ideas did. As she got into her subject, the background quickly expanded. When she submitted her draft to Macmillan in spring 1868, they rejected it as outside the scope of their series.

Uncle Charles generously invited his own publisher, John Murray, to take a look. 'I have not seen the M.S.,' he wrote, 'but I know Miss Wedgwood to be a remarkably clever woman & I know that she has bestowed much labour on the work, & has consulted during many months, all sorts of authorities in the British Museum.' The note by Julia that he enclosed would not have attracted any publisher. Summarizing Macmillan's reaction, she wrote that her manuscript 'was regarded as wanting in simplicity, & implying too much culture in those addressed [...] too full of allusion, not distinctly explained'.[15] After a respectable interval, Murray sent the rejection Julia expected. Macmillan, however, having taken another look, decided to publish it independently of their series if Julia would take out 1,200 of her hand-written pages. Quite how much she did cut is unclear though the last quarter of the book shows signs of hasty rearrangement. By September 1869 she was impatient to get it finished, 'such is my loathing for it'. But she was quite ready to stand up to her publishers. If they did not like her revised text, she would withdraw it and come back to it in a few years' time. The book was finally published in 1870. Julia was vexed by the number of misprints in the published text, but wrote to her mother with a resigned shrug, 'I dare say it does not matter so much as one thinks.' She was becoming a hardened author. Though she was 'tired of dwelling so long among such very narrow people as all these early Evangelicals were', working on the book had given her a passion for writing and taught her what she could and could not do.[16]

Her first venture into the non-fiction book world, unlike that into romantic fiction, was conducted with the full knowledge of her family and friends. Alice Bonham-Carter copied out corrections and even offered to contribute to the costs of a private publication, a fallback Julia rejected. Hope cast a critical eye over the manuscript, and her mother read at least part of it, since Julia kept in one sentence she had intended to cut simply because Fanny liked it.[17] Hensleigh's reactions are not recorded.

Julia was entering a contentious field, split between the biographies, memoirs and letters published by the Wesleyans and what had long been regarded as an English classic, *The Life of Wesley* by Robert Southey. Praised for its charm and literary skill, it was deeply disliked by the Methodist community. Julia too was critical: 'I am afresh struck with the extreme poverty of Southey's picture,' she told Mary Rich in October 1869.[18] As a first-time author, however, she had the good sense not to attack Southey in print. Instead, she relied on the marginal comments on the biography made by his brother-in-law, Coleridge, and published by his son. Coleridge described the biography as 'the book more often in my hands than any other in my ragged book-regiment' and his notes as a conversation with it.[19]

Neither Julia nor, perhaps, her publishers were aware that a major new biography of Wesley was about to appear. Volume 1 of Rev. Luke Tyerman's monumental *The Life and Times of the Rev John Wesley M.A., Founder of the Methodists* was published at the same time as her book and contained a mass of new material, the result of 20 years' study in the archives. Its tone was defiantly triumphant. Wesley, Tyerman wrote, was 'one of the most remarkable men that ever lived' and Methodism 'the greatest fact in the history of the church of Christ'.[20] Julia would have rejected both claims out of hand but benefitted from the interest aroused by simultaneous publication of two very different biographies of Wesley.

John Wesley and the Evangelical Reaction of the Eighteenth Century was the only full-length biography she attempted until her last years, when her sisters prevailed on her to write the life of her great-grandfather, Josiah Wedgwood. Her book on Wesley is less affectionate. She presents him as a man of great longevity and extraordinary energy, disciplined, hardworking, calm, strong-willed and intellectually gifted, but above all impersonal. In her sense of Wesley as 'a very external man',[21] she took her cue from one of Coleridge's notes as well as her reading of Wesley's 'Journals', which were then only available in truncated form. His passing concern over his mother's illness she described as the only example of 'personal feeling' in his life, while his lack of interest in natural beauty was a significant shortcoming. Wesley, she suggested, was impressive but monotonous like a range of barren mountains. She defends him, however, from Southey's charge of ambition and careerism. Arrogant he may sometimes have been, but his leadership of the Methodists was, she argues, forced on him by others, while his 'imperturbability' and logical intellect made him an effective controversialist.[22]

Her sense that Wesley lacked feeling complicated the task of explaining his conversion and the overpowering emotional impact of his preaching. Her analysis of the second is more convincing than the first. She suggests that it was Wesley's own coldness, a failing he thought of as a sin, that led him to see the convulsions he aroused in his hearers as evidence of divine grace at work and to overestimate their lasting impact. She was less comfortable with Wesley's account of his conversion on 24 May 1738, when at 'about a quarter to nine [in] the evening [...] as someone was reading Luther's preface to the Epistle to the Romans [...] I felt my heart strangely warmed. I felt I did trust in Christ alone for salvation [...] and then testified openly to all there what I first felt in my heart.' Julia's comment is tart: 'It was characteristic of the man [...] that he should at once utter the inmost feelings of his soul, and that this transaction of his inmost being should take place, as it were, in public.'[23] Though Julia cherished her own occasional moments of 'epiphany', the idea of 'conversion' as a sudden transformational inrush of religious feeling was alien to her spirituality. She offered an essentially rational explanation of this totemic moment in Methodist history. Wesley had simply reacted against the ideal of the 'golden mean' that pervaded the literature of his day.

This analysis fitted her presentation of Wesley as a man of his age. In her preface she wrote that her book was 'not to be regarded as a biography [...] the object of representation is not the vicissitude of a particular life, but that element in the life which impressed itself on the life of a nation'. 'We have only to do with the man as he represented a great religious movement,' she later reminded her readers, dismissing the arduous quarter of a million miles Wesley travelled around the country as having no more than a 'mingled character of restlessness and monotony'.[24] Similarly, the richness of the Wesleyan Hymnal, Methodism's most abiding legacy, is barely mentioned. Wesley's instrumentality and the extent to which he operated against the dominant forces of his time are her main concern.

Julia had been educated to see history as a story of oppositions, King versus people, liberty against repression, conservatism leading to reform. Methodism, she suggests, was a reaction against a moribund Church, a degraded populace and an upper class whose morals lay only on the surface. This was familiar liberal historical analysis. Her defence of the Calvinist belief in a small élite chosen by God was more original. 'Of the attractions of the doctrine,' she wrote, 'one is the noblest and one the least noble of all the instincts of humanity. It fills the soul with a sense of entire dependence upon God and it gives it a spiritual platform from whence it may look down upon all besides themselves and a favoured few.' Insofar as it left the initiative with God rather than man, however, it was not, she suggested, a 'superfluous utterance'.[25]

Though Julia was most at home when analysing religious controversy, there are lively pages describing the impact of Wesley's and Whitefield's preaching on their vast open-air congregations. She did not dismiss the phenomena of miners with tears streaking their coal-blackened cheeks as they listened to Wesley preach or agitated women calmed by his presence. Was it, she asks, 'imposture, more or less unconscious hysteria, and all the intermediate shades of self-deception and malady'? Given her own ambivalent feelings about mass demonstrations of religious enthusiasm, her conclusion was more scrupulous than Southey's.

> What remains, then, when the large element of nervous irritations, unconscious acting, and that strange love of producing a sensation so remarkable in uneducated persons, are subtracted? [...] there was something in the personal influence of Wesley (for it certainly does not remain in his sermons) which had the power of impressing on a dull and lethargic world such a sense of the horror of evil, its mysterious closeness to the human soul, and the need of a miracle for the separation of the two, as no-one, perhaps, could suddenly receive without some violent physical effect.[26]

Despite this even-handedness, Julia's own sympathies are clear. She defines a church as 'an association of persons who have sufficient religious sympathy to worship together'. This liberal definition would not have been recognized by most Anglicans or any Roman Catholics though a Unitarian or Quaker might have welcomed it, as did the religious movement which most appealed to Julia, the Moravians. Their piety was a strong early influence on Wesley though he later separated from them over doctrine. The Moravians, Julia points out, were 'noted by Coleridge as fulfilling, with trifling exceptions, his ideal of a Church'. She, too, was attracted to these 'monks of Protestantism'.[27]

She gives a vivid description of Wesley's visit to their community at Herrenhut, describing the regular rows of small, uniform houses, the careful separation of the sexes even in burial and the regularity of their 16 hours of manual labour a day. 'The general impression is of a quiet, childlike, joyous religion, devoid of all gloom, and of all awe.' She regretted the absence of mysticism but was full of praise for one aspect of their communal life: 'marriage was held by them in particular honour; and, little as the arrangements above mentioned would appear to further conjugal happiness, the tranquil and harmonious life seems to have been uninterrupted by any unhappy marriages'.[28]

Here was Julia's characteristic voice in the 1870s: assured, perceptive, scrupulous but not bland, patrician rather than upper class, and feminine. She was also developing the hallmark of her style that would delight Richard Hutton, the apophthegms or trenchant observations that critics liked to extract in their reviews. 'Amusements', she wrote, are 'the clearest index to the moral state of any class or nation'; imperturbable good temper, as with Wesley, could be just as trying for others as bad; the bourgeoisie was much further off from the aristocracy than the lower classes; anti-Catholicism in England was not doctrinal but nationalistic: 'It is not any opinion about justification by faith; it is the sturdy John Bull hatred to a foreign authority that stirs up such a strong fiery indignation against any papal claim.' She was shrewd too about the nature of religious controversy: 'They had got to that pitch which indeed is very soon reached in religious controversy, where argument had done what little it can do, and those who attempt to carry it further merely repeat the same words with increasing irritation.' (She would have hoped Maurice would read that.) The electrifying impact of George Whitefield's sermons puzzled her: 'Sermons containing all their essential doctrine have been heard many times in the English pulpit without depriving one hearer of his customary nap.'[29]

For all the travails over its publication, *John Wesley and the Evangelical Reaction of the Eighteenth Century* was a confident performance. Biography, she would later write, required 'laborious passivity' in 'the effort to record and interpret complex facts'.[30] As Darwin had pointed out to Murray, she had put in the hours at the British Museum Reading Room, searching out a wide range of sources, listed in no particular order at the front of her book. They included not only memoirs and biographies but also contemporary journals, letters, poetry, sermons and pamphlets as well as periodicals and newspapers. The result, if not always well-organized and hampered by its one-dimensional portrait of Wesley, is intelligent, fresh and, mostly, very readable.

Characteristically, Julia said nothing to friends and family about the critical reaction to her book, which was generally very enthusiastic. Even her old enemy, the *Saturday Review*, was complimentary, praising her 'great fairness and discrimination' as well as 'her literary skill'. It could not, however, resist the suggestion that women should not trouble their heads over the niceties of theological disputes: 'Theologians may smile at the lady's logic, which enables her to settle so neatly the knotty dogmas respecting Pre-Destination and Free Will.' The well-established Methodist periodical the *London Quarterly Review*, however, devoted a long review to her book, regretting only that it was not much longer, a comment that may have caused Julia a sad smile. *The Pall Mall Gazette*, unusually, devoted almost a full page to its review of a biography that 'is excellently adapted to spread an interest in the subject among intelligent readers and shows throughout not only considerable literary power but a thoroughly liberal and comprehensive spirit'. *The Westminster Review* scoffed at Wesley but applauded Julia's 'very sensible comments on the violent physical manifestations' resulting from his preaching. The *Athenaeum* offered unqualified praise (and a quote Macmillans could use in their publicity): 'In style and intellectual power, in breadth of view and clearness of insight, Miss Wedgwood's book far surpasses all rivals.'[31]

Julia's *John Wesley* has long been superseded by biographical studies in the twentieth century but retains its place as an important early study of Methodist history and was recently re-issued in America as one of a 14-volume edition of 'classic texts' about John Wesley. The most authoritative tribute paid to it was Lecky's in his much admired six-volume *History of England in the Eighteenth Century*, where he praised Tyerman's industry but then continued: 'I must also mention Miss Wedgwood's remarkably able study on Wesley which throws light on many sides of the religious history of the eighteenth century.'[32]

Little guessing that her approval was unwanted, Harriet Martineau praised the book generously:

> I wish you would write biography for the rest of your days (as I have been saying to my sister Rachel.) Large and noble subjects, I mean, of course, – Sagacity, dispassionateness, power of justice, power of analysis, power of appreciation, and remarkable power of expression in

capital style, – these are your characteristics, it seems to me, – and these are what I take to be the chief requisites of a biographer.'[33]

Was Martineau right to describe Julia as a born biographer? Though this was a recognized area for women writers, Julia only attempted it once again in book form. She did, however, produce a long series of profiles of famous contemporaries and other historical figures, starting with Erskine in 1870 and continuing into her last decade. Most of these appeared in the *Contemporary Review* with a few others in the *Spectator*, to which she regularly contributed from 1871. Like all other pieces in the *Spectator*, her contributions there were anonymous. By contrast, all but two of her articles in the *Contemporary* (her posthumous tributes to George Eliot and Thomas Carlyle) were signed, enabling her to build up a distinctive presence. Alongside these profiles, she wrote about the Classical world, English mysticism, sixteenth-century radical history, Shakespeare and Scott, and feminist theology. When the *Contemporary* finally ventured into regular fiction reviewing in the mid-1880s in an attempt to broaden its largely male readership, it relied on Julia with her recognizable voice and reassuring moral stance to guide its subscribers through this new field. From 1883 to 1886 she contributed six-monthly surveys of recent fiction.[34]

Though Julia recognized that fiction had now become the most influential literary form, biography remained 'the most instructive and delightful'. It enabled the reader 'to taste some of the pleasures alike of friendship and of fame, with absolutely none of the disadvantages of either'. Her sense of its didactic function underlay all her profiles. Exaggerated praise was, she wrote in an article on biography in the *Spectator* in 1882, as misleading, and unfair to the dead, as unwarranted criticism. And while it was important to tell the truth, this should not necessarily be the whole truth. Like many others she was outraged by Froude's publication of Carlyle's guilt-ridden, lachrymose *Reminiscences* just three weeks after his death. 'We do not reveal a man when we give to the public what his mature, deliberate judgment would have withheld.' Carlyle's 'wailings for his wife' were 'the repetitious jottings' of an 'enfeebled' mind.[35] The desire to include everything, however unrevealing or unworthy, was further evidence of the scientific spirit whose encroachment she regretted. Above all, she sought to make a balanced assessment of her subjects. When many of her profiles were collected and published in 1909 under the title *Nineteenth Century Teachers*, the *Spectator* complained about their 'lack of characterization' but was full of praise for her description of the intellectual background to her chosen subjects, especially when dealing with religion: 'much of the collection is memorable in an unusual degree. [...] She is at her best when dealing with authors who tempt her to religious disquisition.'[36] This was a rare tribute to a woman writer trespassing on male territory.

As her private letters show, Julia had strong views on the character of her friends and family. In presenting famous contemporaries to the public, however, her concern was with the interplay between them and their times rather than the personal details that enlivened Anne Thackeray Ritchie's very different and apparently artless pen portraits of friends like Browning and Tennyson. Julia's nice description of Ruskin as a young man was unusual: 'the general impression [...] was somewhat pallid, somewhat ineffective. There was nothing in the unsubstantial, but not ungraceful figure, the acquiline face, the pale tone of colouring, the slight lisp, to suggest a prophet [...] there was no glamour about

Mr Ruskin.'[37] But though she knew Carlyle well enough to drop round on him without an invitation, she confines her personal remarks about him to mentions of his 'roughness' and 'scorn' and the fact that he was a poor listener.

What interested Julia was the way her subjects had responded to the great events of her age. For her the turning points had been the aftermath of the French Revolution, the failed revolutions of 1848, the Oxford Movement and the drift towards Rome, the publication of *On the Origin of Species*, the extension of democracy through the Reform Acts of 1832, 1867 and 1884 and the growing divergence between science and religion. 'Our time', she wrote, 'has turned to Science, and poetry seems somehow to belong to the past [...] the present is rich in other directions – material progress, inventions, "knowledge of things we see", and the Invisible has grown dim, like the stars just above the electric light.' The response of her subjects to this change was for Julia a marker of their effectiveness. Maurice had failed to accept the challenge with sufficient seriousness. Unusually, Charles Kingsley had believed in both the inner and the outer world with 'a taste for science' that was 'rarely compatible with a keen love of beauty'. But though his was 'a healing influence', it was ultimately ineffectual. The growth of doubt and then agnosticism, which she defined as 'doubt emptied of Faith, and turning its face towards Denial',[38] had exposed the genialities of the Broad Church as an inadequate response.

Julia would always be a keen analyst of the divisions in the Church of England. She was sympathetic towards the High Church tendency as seen in the Oxford Movement, regretted the ineffectiveness of the Broad Church and was always critical of the Evangelical Low Church. Her portrait of the Clapham Sect in her profile of Fitzjames Stephen is affectionate, paying tribute to the bravery of the childless Sir Robert and Lady Inglis in taking on the nine Thornton orphans after the death of Henry Thornton as well as the earnestness with which the Sect fought 'a holy war against the age-long crime of humanity', slavery. It was, however, 'startling to think of the contrast between what Evangelicanism *did*, and what it *taught*. It raised the wretched; it freed the slave; it penetrated the dungeon of the criminal; it took thought for all that were desolate and oppressed; and it preached a Creator, who, we may say broadly, had no sympathy with any of these things.'[39] The Broad Church, by contrast, whose founder, she saw as Coleridge, was born of a less rigorous but more generous spirit than Calvinism. 'Forty years ago, that school of liberal theology which accepts both the traditions of antiquity and also the alliance of modern speculation, had the effervescence resulting from any combination of previously hostile elements of thought.' But that effervescence had now fallen flat and the Broad Church had become 'trite'. The High Church remained distinct because of its attachment to the sacraments, the Low Church because of its insistence on conversion, but the 'Broad Church believes what every Christian believes'. This, Julia concluded, was 'a bond that does not bind'.[40]

Evangelicanism was a more persistent influence. Both Carlyle and Fitzjames Stephen owed more to the Calvinism of their parents than they recognized, despite the fact that they had rejected it. Carlyle was a secular Calvinist in his way of distinguishing the select from the mass of mankind. Similarly, Fitzjames Stephens's absolutism was a relic of his upbringing. 'In the rough, vigorous, somewhat contemptuous lawyer [...] scornful of emotion, critical of tradition, sceptical towards all spiritual pretension, we detect the hidden

Evangelical, half-feeling for a lost creed, half-defensive against a rejected superstition, but always consciously reminiscent of a form of faith long discarded.'[41]

The recognition that goodness and greatness were rarely found together was a more painful conclusion for Julia to draw. The sunny life and genial disposition of Dean Stanley did not lend him any lasting influence, while Carlyle, though a genius, was far from heroic. The most striking case was that of Coleridge, a genius whose influence would prove immense but far from a good man. Coleridge was 'a teacher and a seer such as the world has not often known in its whole history'. How then to explain his failed marriage, the frequency with which he tested the kindness of forbearing friends (who, though Julia omitted to say, included her grandfather Jos Wedgwood), his indiscipline and opium addiction? The key to his life was 'that experience of struggle with evil which teaches the meaning of reality as in this world nothing else does'. 'He was driven to ask more earnestly [...] than any of his generation, the questions which centre in the very idea of human choice.[42]

Julia's sympathy for Coleridge's imperfect life was matched by her 'reverence' for Carlyle. His belief in the sacredness of work had, she thought, influenced a generation of leisured aristocrats to become more actively involved in the world. Though his biography of Frederick the Great was 'the most repulsive thing he ever wrote' and Julia had reservations about his worship of great men, she welcomed his willingness to 'point out clearly and emphatically the dangers of Democracy'. By contrast, Kingsley's early engagement with Christian Socialism had led him into the mistake of 'confound[ing] sympathy or pity with a political creed'. Ruskin had travelled to the yet further shores of Socialism but she forgave him much because he had taught her and her generation how to see. 'Where we saw a vague blur he gave a definite form and distinct colour.'[43]

Julia's chosen gallery of representative figures of her age had some notable absentees including Darwin, Browning, Harriet Martineau and Elizabeth Gaskell, with all of whom she was too emotionally involved to be able to write objectively. Some of her subjects, like Kingsley, Maurice and Stanley, had held to their faith: others, like Carlyle and Fitzjames Stephens, had abandoned it. In general, she was more sympathetic to the doubters than to the faithful. Her criticisms of Kingsley's failure to recognize the challenge of science, Dean Stanley's affable conventionality and Maurice's dogmatism were outspoken. Julia looked for, but never found, the spiritual leader who would have responded to the full range of the religious, political and social challenges of her age with the same effectiveness with which the opposing forces had made doubt respectable and advanced the dominant claims of scientific truth. The two she might have turned to, James Martineau and John Henry Newman, were too far from the mainstream of British public life to fill the vacuum.

Had Julia not believed that fiction had become the most influential of all literary forms, she might not have been willing to devote so much time to reviewing it in the mid-1880s. She accepted, however, that by then it attracted the widest readership and best reflected the spirit of the age. For our fathers 'it was the diversion of an idle hour [...] to us it is the vehicle of almost all thought for which a large audience is desired'. The novelist had taken over from 'the preacher, the essayist, and the biographer'. As a result, she did not take her new responsibilities lightly. Nor, as she regularly reminded novelists, should they underestimate their responsibility to their readers.

Julia's duty was to guide her regular readers in their reactions to books whose critical fate was often settled by the time she reviewed them. She was also keen to advise novelists on the exercise of their craft. Her tastes were mostly conventional, but she could sometimes surprise as with her praise for Zola's *The Ladies Paradise* set in a large Parisian department store. Although the book was only 'just decent', it was also 'profoundly moral if rightly understood'. Zola, she wrote, was asking the right questions about the consequences of 'the vast culte of luxury' and 'why we set the visible above the invisible' (a comment that might have irked her Wedgwood cousins in the Potteries).[44] In general, however, she stayed with the mainstream. She forgave Wilkie Collins for his waning powers in his later years, welcomed Anthony Trollope as 'an old friend' but branded him primarily a women's author, was always indulgent to Charlotte Yonge, described Margaret Oliphant as a 'wonderful writer' but, like many others, regretted her 'intemperate production' and harshly criticized Vernon Lee.

Two aspects of fiction that particularly interested her were its depictions of work and of marriage. Her fascination with Zola's description of the working environment in a department store was matched by her interest in Mrs Humphry Ward's depiction of the world of the bookseller, David Grieve, surprised though she was that 'a lady in her position can have learnt so much of the circumstances' of the trade.[45] She was less tolerant, however, of the 'marriage of tepid affection and diverse aim' to which the author consigned her hero. 'If marriage is to be no more than this, licence will be victorious in the future as it has been in the past.' She was even more outspoken in her review of W. E. Norris's *Adrian Vidal*: a disappointing marriage was 'one of the colossal sorrows of life. It is true that it has been the experience of many who are not conscious of having known any colossal sorrow.' By showing marriage at its best, novelists could alert their readers to what they were missing. 'Love, however gained, is something holy [...] is one of the most elevating lessons a writer of fiction can teach, and it can be taught by him alone.'[46]

Characteristically, this lofty pronouncement sat alongside more practical criticisms. Fictionalized biographies, let alone autobiographies, rarely worked. Eliza Lynn Linton's *The Autobiography of Christopher Kirkland* produced 'a disagreeable intellectual squint' since the author was clearly describing her own experiences. Similarly, attempts to portray genius in fiction did not succeed. Wisely, 'Miss Austen' had never attempted 'a hero, a genius or a saint'. Though more common, portraits of artistic life were almost as futile. Was their increasing frequency an indication of the 'individualizing influence of modern democracy' and the attempt to associate individuality with 'creative power'?[47]

Even more significant than the fragmentation of the old social order was the influence of science on fiction. On the whole, Julia did not see it as helpful. Even George Eliot had succumbed to the new requirement for 'a *vraisemblance* of surroundings, a wealth of detail, a variety and definiteness of character', while Darwin's influence could be seen in the lengthy explanations novelists felt obliged to offer about the origins and circumstances of their characters. Julia dismissed this as 'photographic fiction'. She was concerned too about the effect of the loss of consensus around religious belief. The unspoken certainties of Thackeray's day had fractured, giving way to 'a profound sense of blank and emptiness, a gaze of longing turned back to the past, a weary sigh, a feeling of the littleness of life'. Contemporary fiction emphasized 'whatever is perplexing, disappointing, and bitter'.[48]

An important exception to this was Robert Louis Stevenson's *Dr Jekyll and Mr Hyde*. Her review of it was much the most enthusiastic of all those she wrote for the *Contemporary*. This, she wrote, was 'a shilling story, which the reader devours in an hour, but to which he may return again and again to study a profound allegory and admire a model of style'. The book was a 'perfectly original' investigation of 'the meaning of the word *self*' and one of 'those rare fictions which make one understand the value of temperance in art'.[49] 'Temperance in art' was for Julia the supreme virtue. She attacked its absence from Henry James's *The Bostonians* vigorously.

Julia was never likely to warm to the story of how a charismatic young orator is taken up by a dedicated, wealthy, middle-aged feminist in Boston but eventually abandons a promising public-speaking career in the service of the cause to run off with an impoverished Southern gentleman. Her objections went beyond the plot, however, amounting rather to a charge of literary bad manners. James, she wrote, was 'a clever and brilliant writer whose wit and shrewdness force us to listen with pleasure to an adulteration of familiar truth with vulgar prejudice and a narrative written on a plan that seems to us nothing less than execrable'. So much for the plot: James's narrative technique was even more annoying.

> He is such good company that we sit helpless while he insults our deepest convictions, and listen with irritation to what we term, with a sense of inadequate virulence, the interruption of a perpetual *aside*. To be told not only what his *dramatis personae* express but what they thought and kept to themselves, what they felt inclined to express and why they refrained [...] seems to us a violation of every conceivable rule of literary good breeding and affects us [...] with no less sense of fatigue [...] than such an experience would in life.

James's 'perpetual stippling, his touching and retouching of every line' made him 'the greatest sinner [...] that literature can produce' in 'the *feminization*' of the age about which he himself had complained. William James, Henry's brother, was more succinct: 'Say it out, for God's sake & have done with it.'[50]

As Julia's admiration for *Dr Jekyll and Mr Hyde* showed, she was well able to move beyond the early and mid-nineteenth-century fiction she liked best. But James, like George Meredith, another novelist to whom she did not warm, did not repay her trouble. After her combative review of *The Bostonians* in August 1886, she ended her stint as a reviewer in the *Contemporary*. Perhaps her editor, Percy Bunting, a founder member of the National Vigilance Association in 1885, regretted his decision to give so much prominence to fiction reviewing.[51] Perhaps, too, Julia no longer had the time to read a regular crop of new novels when she was trying to complete *The Moral Ideal*.

After its publication she briefly returned to the subject in two later articles in the *Contemporary Review*. The first, 'Fiction and Faith', published in 1892, largely concentrated on Mrs Humphrey Ward's work: the second, 'Ethics and Literature', published in 1897, drew invidious comparisons between the moral impartiality of George Meredith and Robert Louis Stevenson and the ability of Shakespeare and the great Greek dramatists to engage their listeners in huge moral dilemmas, despite their presentation in apparently 'non-moral' ways. Contemporary fiction, Julia wrote, missed that imaginative sympathy. Nor could its 'lack of reticence' compensate. 'Girls in the schoolroom are ready to discuss matters which their mothers shrank from recognizing, and their grandmothers did not understand.' Though the new freedom in fiction reflected the times, its impact would be transient. What 'was not possible yesterday, will not be audacious tomorrow', she accurately predicted. Meanwhile, the new passion for 'scientific accuracy in the elaborate detail of fiction' distanced the reader.[52]

Meredith's impartiality was very different from that of the Greeks or Shakespeare. Shakespeare had drawn more convincing evil than good characters. In Iago and the Macbeths, he had led his audiences to understand and even sympathize with actions and emotions they could never condone in daily life. The Greeks had gone even further. Orestes murders his mother in retaliation for her murder of his father and is then pursued by the Furies seeking vengeance on him. Following the drama the audience experiences 'that balance of alternate sympathy, so utterly unlike the languor of an equal sympathy'. 'Greek sympathy is elastic, dramatic, reversible, to an extent impossible to modern feeling,' she wrote in 1897, developing a theme she would later expound to undergraduates at Newnham College to the delight of Jane Harrison.[53]

Among British novelists, Julia's idol would always remain Walter Scott. Like many Victorians she saw him as the only writer fit to be placed in the company of Shakespeare. She admired his 'manliness' and 'sense of life and stir'. Scott was that rarity, 'a modest man of genius'. His power came from the tension between his imaginative attachment to lost causes, like the stability of feudal society, medieval chivalry or the Stuart monarchy, and his intellectual commitment to the very different post-1688 constitution, eighteenth-century enlightenment and opposition to the French Revolution. His 'dramatic sympathies array themselves on the side which judgment condemns [...] the double feeling supplies the place of impartiality, and art has the mellowing atmosphere it needs'. Like her grandfather, James Mackintosh, to whom he had been close in his last years, Scott knew the emotional pull of a lost cause. Their early hopes for the French Revolution had crumbled away, leaving only 'an anxious, perhaps an exaggerated, desire to keep justice unwarped by sympathy'.[54]

Alongside her lifelong affection for Scott was Julia's idol, Shakespeare. She shared 'the late Victorian infatuation' with him, describing him as 'the greatest genius who ever lived'.[55] Many women wrote about him usually focusing on his female characters.[56] Julia tried a different angle in her two pieces on *Midsummer Night's Dream* and *Julius Caesar* in the *Contemporary Review*. In the first she dismissed the quartet of lovers as much less interesting than the 'clodhoppers' and fairies, but was particularly interested in Duke Theseus's defence of the inadequacies of the tradesmen players. Shakespeare's 'sympathy with the members of his special craft' was, she suggested, 'a window, whence he looks on life as a whole, and sees in its hurry, its transiency, its strange misfit of capacity to claim, of knowledge to impulse, a repetition of the experience of the player'.[57]

Her piece on *Julius Caesar* was more fanciful. It reproduced a lecture she gave in 1893 to the St Andrew's Club for Women, one of several informal women's groups devoted to the study of Shakespeare. She started from what she shrewdly saw as Shakespeare's focus on Julius Caesar's physical debility (including deafness in one ear). This was, she suggested, 'a brilliant revelation as to the meaning of history'. By comparing the weakness of Caesar when alive with the potency of his reputation after death, Shakespeare was implicitly drawing a comparison with his near-contemporary, Christ. This was to read a good deal too much into Shakespeare's Caesar. In its confident sweep and determination to be different, however, it went well beyond most female commentary on Shakespeare even as it fell below the crisp intelligence of her early work in the *Spectator* at the beginning of the 1870s.

Just as Harriet Martineau learnt her journalistic trade from W. J. Fox, the editor of the *Monthly Repository*, and Margaret Oliphant from John Blackwood at *Blackwood's Edinburgh Magazine*,[58] so too did Julia from Richard Hutton, the joint editor with Meredith Townsend of the *Spectator*. Owen Chadwick has described it as 'the most revealing guide to the progress of the English mind' in the last three decades of the nineteenth century. Others were less kind. The *Saturday Review* decried its readers as 'sheltered in leafy rectories and in sunny villas of rich nonconformists from the headlong decisions and rowdy activity of the world', while another rival, the *Academy*, dismissed them as 'gentle souls, fond of flowers and birds [...] middle-aged and declining gracefully to a future existence for which they were fully prepared'. Julia was well aware that its readership was 'rather a_ public, than the_ public'. And though Virginia Woolf would later describe Hutton's voice as 'a plague of locusts', Julia set out to learn from his style as well as his substance.[59] A *Saturday Review* critic had told her that he could not get on with the *Spectator* because it was 'so just'. 'Nothing [...] is less dull than justice,' she retorted.[60] Serious, widely read, intelligent and judicious, Hutton was probably the most influential editor of his day. His reviews were the only ones George Eliot paid attention to, while his principled break with Gladstone over Home Rule was the defection Gladstone most regretted.[61] 'So well did Julia learn from Hutton that E. M. Forster remembered that 'her writings were said to be indistinguishable from his.'[62] Whatever Virginia Woolf thought, Forster meant this as a compliment.

Julia had much in common with Hutton. Both came from Unitarian families, both fell under the spell of Maurice and both ended up as High Church Anglicans. Like Hutton, Julia also moved from Liberalism to Unionism. Their literary tastes were similar too: a passion for Walter Scott, deep interest in George Eliot and qualified admiration for Browning's 'keen, cold, dramatic intellect'.[63] In later life, both would become ardent anti-vivisectionists, their concern fed by their experience of suffering in their own lives. Nor, unlike Julia's more fallible idols, did Hutton shirk the challenge Darwinian science posed to earlier religious certainties. Their only fundamental disagreement was on female suffrage, where Julia readily forgave his opposition given his support for higher education for women and readiness to entrust his female contributors with issues most editors would have judged them incapable of handling.

The first of their many public debates happened in May 1870 when Julia wrote to the *Spectator* arguing the case for enfranchising single women on the same terms as men. Frances Power Cobbe wrote in to support her, but Hutton could not agree with them: 'careworn widows and spinsters of the working class have enough to do to earn their own livelihood without thinking of politics'.[64]

The following spring when Julia wanted to write a review of Darwin's *The Descent of Man*, she approached Hutton. Though he had already published two reviews of the book, he readily accepted a third from Julia. Its 'cleverness' caught the eye of Darwin, who

Figure 23 Richard Holt Hutton, the great Victorian editor, hard at work.

was, at the time, unaware of its authorship.[65] It also encouraged Hutton to invite her to review two collections by Rev. James McCosh, the Scottish clergyman who was president of what became Princeton University and one of the earliest in America to argue that the Darwinian world was still recognizably the handiwork of a divine designer. The first of these reviews dealt with a series of lectures McCosh had given on Comtism, and the second with his thoughts on how science and religion might be reconciled. She dismissed both more impatiently than they deserved.[66] But for Julia, compromise on the issues they raised was dangerous: the appeal of both Comtism and the new attempt to distinguish the supernatural from the natural world needed to be recognized if they were to be successfully overcome. Rhetoric, however comforting, was not up to the task. Intellectual discrimination was required. 'The Christian orator', she wrote, 'need not be debarred more than any other from the use of rhetoric but we would not have him give us his rhetoric as logic, and as long as chairs are founded to establish the evidences of Christianity and none are founded to dispute them, this is what he is almost certain to do.'[67]

Though Julia would resist the appeal of Comtism in her teatime chats with George Eliot and George Henry Lewes,[68] she set out its claims forcefully in the *Spectator*. It presented itself as a science in a way that proved particularly attractive to those without a scientific training; it set love above reason; and it distinguished itself from the factionalism of Christianity by preaching universalism. Unlike Christianity, it looked forward rather than backward. Its allure should not be discounted. Only as Christians identified those things 'however venerable and precious' that needed to be 'shaken' could they ensure 'that the things which cannot be shaken may remain'.[69]

Her concern in her second review was to counter the growing tendency to put religion in the realm of feeling and science in that of knowledge and treat the supernatural and the natural worlds as entirely separate. The loss of the idea of special creation had, she suggested, destroyed what had previously been 'the common territory of theology and science', but now 'the everyday crowd' proved too willing to accept a facile distinction between a science that cast the life of the soul as 'superstition' and a theology that branded intellectual life as 'infidelity'. She returned to one of Christ's sayings: 'To those that are without these things are done in parables.' Only in this way would 'we [...] come to appreciate that the laws of the Supernatural are exhibited as unquestionably as the laws of the Natural in the phenomenon of every-day practical life'.[70]

Julia's review of a volume of Newman's early writings took her argument a stage further. She, like Hutton, admired his 'perfect style', where 'every word is relevant' as well as 'the rigidly logical character of his mind'. Logic, however, could only take the believer so far. Greater intellectual discrimination was needed. Reliance on 'an infallible church or an infallible book' relieved the believer of the responsibility to test 'what <u>seems</u>' against 'what <u>is</u>'.[71]

Julia's apparent confidence in the power of patient intellectual effort to hold together the external world of observation and the internal world of sensation would come under pressure in the 1870s as her religious doubts and private despair accumulated. Her trust in Hutton remained, not least because he was never prone to discount the doubts of friends like A. H. Clough or dismiss loss of faith as a moral failing. She admired his writings too, defending his complex style after his death:

> The endeavor to strain away from criticism every word that is untrue in itself, and then again every word that, being true in itself, is yet misleading in its general connotation, as so many true words are – this is an endeavor which the exigencies of periodical writing almost inevitably associate with an involved style. [...] I never found his meaning obscure [...] and his careful parentheses were to me a characteristic expression of his anxious candour.[72]

As Julia knew she was defending her own style as much as Hutton's. If her later work lost some of its early freshness its high seriousness owed much to her long and fruitful interplay with Richard Hutton.

Chapter Ten

A FORGOTTEN FEMINIST

Initially, the neglect of Julia Wedgwood's role in the first wave of Victorian feminism seems surprising.[1] She wrote the key article in an important collection of essays on women's issues edited by Josephine Butler in 1869. She campaigned for Elizabeth Garrett Anderson's election to the new London Schools Board in 1870 and also spent two terms as an informal tutor to the first intake of what became Girton College. She signed the big petition calling for female enfranchisement in 1884 and wrote a series of articles as well as an outspoken pamphlet pressing the case. She was not, however, a member of the two most influential women's networks, the Langham Place Group and the Kensington Society. Nor was she involved in the successful campaigns to amend the legislation on married womens' property and the Contagious Diseases Acts. Her feminism was less passionate than Josephine Butler's, less far-reaching and practical than Barbara Bodichon's and less organized and determined than Emily Davies's. But though it does not fall into well-established categories, it was an important part of both her private and public personae in her middle years. She was also more influential than her current absence from the record suggests.

Her family did not share her outspokenness on women's issues. For all her energetic campaigning for good causes and connection with Anna Swanwick and Elizabeth Bostock, Fanny never joined their discussions in the Kensington Society. Nor did she sign suffrage petitions. Similarly, she only got involved in the committee Emily Davies set up to establish a new women's college in Cambridge as a way of protecting the interests of Bedford College. Effie and Hope also kept away from women's causes. Julia, by contrast, contributed what she could.

Her feminism was distinctive. She was as ready to attack unhelpful female attitudes as male obfuscation and misogyny; she was less interested in the political effects of securing the vote for women than in its social implications; she avoided talk of equal rights; and she addressed herself as much to men as to women, conscious that with an exclusively male Parliament, change could come only when men had been persuaded that this was in everyone's interests. Most of her writings reflect the preoccupations of her upper-middle-class milieu. As her sense of frustration mounted in the 1870s, however, her sympathies broadened and her tone became more combative.

The leading feminists tended to come from professional or gentry backgrounds though Cobbe threw hers over to make a more precarious living from her writing. All, however, were aware that the disabilities women faced were not exclusive to their own class, and Butler and Cobbe, in particular, highlighted the many abuses affecting working-class women. Initially, Julia concentrated on the concerns of the sort of women she knew best. She presented women's exclusion from the vote as of totemic rather than practical political significance. Removing that impediment would open the way to what she prized the most, a more natural relationship between the sexes and a society in which men and women could be friends and collaborators rather than seeing each other exclusively as actual or potential marriage partners. The harshness of the criticism she attracted for proposing even this changed her approach. Her language became more direct, her insistence greater, her condemnation of male attitudes more dismissive, until in 1884 she, like Cobbe, recognized defeat and turned to other issues.

Fifteen years earlier the prospects for enfranchising at least some women had looked promising. Though John Stuart Mill had failed to carry an amendment to the 1867 Reform Bill that would have given women the vote in national elections on the same terms as men, progress was being made. Female householders gained the vote in municipal elections in 1869. A year later, W. E. Forster's Education Act gave women the right not only to vote in elections to the new school boards but also to stand for election themselves. Motions for female enfranchisement were regularly brought before Parliament in the 1870s and attracted respectable minority votes.[2]

The publisher, Alexander Macmillan, alert to the change, proposed a book of essays on women's issues in 1868. He asked Josephine Butler to edit it. She was the wife of Rev. George Butler, a former Oxford don who was by then serving as headmaster of Liverpool College. The tragic death of her youngest daughter had already deepened Josephine Butler's social conscience. She assuaged her own pain by trying to ameliorate that of others, becoming the most charismatic as well as the most fearless of the Victorian feminists. Though she campaigned for female suffrage, womens' higher education and the amendment of laws on married women's property, her most passionate involvement was with practical and legislative initiatives aimed at improving the lot of prostitutes and exposing the misogynistic double standards that widely applied in society. As well as campaigning on public platforms, sometimes in perilous situations, she was also a prolific writer. Her first pamphlet on 'The Education and Employment of Women' was published by Alexander Macmillan early in 1868. He was impressed by its success. In June he suggested to her that 'a few of the ablest & most thoughtful ladies who have interested themselves in the elevation of their sisters [might] write a volume of Essays rather in the fashion which has been common of late'. He invited her to edit it. Butler's experience with Macmillan over her pamphlet from which he took a 50 per cent share of the profits had not been happy. Nor did the condescending tone of his letter appeal: though he was sympathetic to women's causes, he did not support female suffrage. *Macmillan's Magazine* was, however, more open to women's writing than most. He promised Butler a free hand over the choice of subjects in her collection and offered to 'venture the names of two more ladies who might write'.[3] Julia was probably one of them.

Emily Davies was also planning a volume of essays on women's issues and wrote to a friend, Anna Richardson, outlining possible topics and contributors. They included Mrs Butler's husband, George; Albert Rutson, who had just edited a collection of *Essays on Reform*; Barbara Bodichon on Comtism; James Bryce on the Quaker system; Mrs Manning on Celibacy; F. T. Palgrave on 'Culture as Applying to Women'; Susanna Winkworth on 'If Women's Brains Are Cultivated, Will the Next Generation Be Idiots?' and, in an equally improbable matching of author and subject, Julia on 'Women's Part in Public

Affairs'.[4] For a time Davies and Butler talked of collaborating with each, editing their own volume but agreeing not to poach the other's writers and subjects. 'Her contributors will be lively young Radicals, mine, grave ancient women and men' able to adopt a Burkeian 'disposition to preserve and an ability to improve,' Davies wrote. But she grew increasingly mistrustful of Butler ('I have found her not strictly truthful') and abandoned her project.[5] The only name carried forward from her list to Butler's was Julia's. Since she was neither a 'young Radical' nor a 'grave ancient woman', this was a mark of her growing standing as an author.

Butler, who had been keen to have an equal number of male and female contributors, lost heart when many of the men she approached turned her down. A visit to London revived her. 'I continued to feel rather indifferent to [the book],' she confessed to Bryce in February 1869,

> until I met in London several persons whom I spoke to about writing. When I said 'I should prefer not to give you your subject precisely but that you should write what is burning in your heart, & what you long to say' these people said at once 'O if I may do that, then I will write for you' [...] the longing for work [twice underlined] among the daughters of the great is as touching as it is among my poor [...] tramps.[6]

Julia may well have been one of these 'daughters of the great'. The opportunity to write what was 'burning in her heart' was hard to resist.

At Mill's suggestion, Butler recruited Cobbe to counter the 'devilish' nonsense of the Comtists. She also collected a good group of younger feminists. Sophia Jex Blake wrote incisively about the need to admit qualified women as doctors, particularly as women preferred to have doctors of their own sex. Elizabeth Wolstoneholme, one of the most active of the Langham Place Group and radical in both her public and private life, wrote well about the need for grammar schools for girls in all large towns, while Jessie Boucherett turned the heated argument about 'surplus' women upside down. It was men, not women, she suggested, who should be obliged to emigrate to make room in the labour market for women. The male contributors were less lively. Nor did they avoid familiar stereotypes about women's domestic aptitudes and particular fitness for handiwork and crafts.

The two most substantial contributions were Butler's introduction and Julia's essay on female suffrage. Butler operated on a big canvas, laying on her brushstrokes with energy and eloquence as she argued the case for the benefits which would follow for both men and women as well as the institution of marriage if women were able to lead freer and fairer lives. She urged 'thoughtful women of the better classes' to speak up on behalf of 'the millions of their less favoured countrywomen' and press for their 'liberty to work and live in honesty and self-reliance'. She also exposed 'the old-fashioned Lady-Bountiful way of dispensing alms and patronage' and the ladies 'living at ease and ignorant of the facts of life' who were often the severest critics of attempts to change women's status. Nor could she resist a reference to prostitution ('Think of this, you mothers who are living at ease, in your pleasant drawing-rooms, with your tender darlings around you!'). She capped off her passionate article with an onslaught against St Paul's views on women's subordinate role.[7]

By comparison with her editor, Julia sketched in water colour. Although her essay was ostensibly about the suffrage, she concentrated rather on the frustrations of intelligent, middle-class young women leading unstructured lives but constricted by social convention. But 'the personal is political'. Though Julia argued only a moderate case for the extension of the franchise to women, and suggested that its political consequences would be slight, her essay has a twentieth-century feminist feel to it. Instead of developing a theoretical case, she wrote first-hand about women with no obvious career path, cramped by their exclusion from the world of power and responsibility and about the artificiality of relations between the sexes.

The title of her piece, 'Female Suffrage, Considered Chiefly with Regard to Its Indirect Results', reflected this. Julia's concern was with the impact of enfranchisement on the status of women rather than its political consequences. She dealt with the case for female suffrage in a single paragraph at the beginning of her essay, arguing along familiar lines that representative government should reflect: 'the views, opinions, desires, even prejudices of the governed, in as far as the latter have, by possession of a certain amount of property, given a pledge that they have something at stake in the matter'. How then could 'half of the community' who satisfied this test be excluded from the franchise? Though she conceded that giving the vote to women might marginally strengthen 'whatever is unreasoning in Conservatism', its practical consequences would be small. It mattered because of 'what it implies' rather than 'what it is'. Enfranchisement would transform their status by putting them on 'a platform whence the ground slopes away without interruption to that which is common with men'. It would broaden their horizons, open up new employment opportunities, encourage them to look beyond their current obsession with the particulars of family life, and make them more interesting wives and discerning mothers. Above all, women would become involved in 'a wide, enduring, common life'.

Though Julia deliberately maintained an un-combative tone, she could not avoid pointing to some of the inequalities from which women suffered. Young men operated within a structured education system of school and university, while young women struggled to continue studying after the age of 18, under pressure from well-meaning but shortsighted mothers to put family duty and social obligation first. Similarly, men decided to marry as and when they chose without any special preparation for it, whilst young women were brought up to see marriage as their sole vocation in life: 'Those who think the office of wife and mother the highest, will be the most anxious to cut off every temptation for any one to enter upon it whose motive is dearth of other interests.' The social pressures on young women to marry introduced expectations that made ordinary friendships between men and women impossible for all but 'exceptional' people and impoverished marriage itself through the artificiality of the relations that preceded it. Women's lives were 'unreal'. At the age when men were settling to their careers, a young woman lived in suspense, uncertain about whether or not she would marry.

> That women spend the best part of their lives in preparing for an event which may never happen – an event for which the very worst is to hanker after it, while the very best is to be strenuously occupied with something different, is the result, not of God's decision that one form of life should be happier than another, but of man's invention that it should be deemed more womanly.

What might women do if liberated to operate in a wider sphere? Mill would argue in *The Subjection of Women* that centuries of male oppression had so constricted women's lives that it was impossible to know their true potential. Julia was more cautious. Though never comfortable with gender stereotyping, she came close to conceding the distinctions John Ruskin had made in his now notorious 'Of Queen's Gardens' but left open the question of whether these were innate or the result of conditioning. Women excelled at insight and sympathy; men at judgement and a feeling for justice, born of that sense of proportion which women, confined within their domestic sphere, were unable to develop. This fitted men to take the lead on 'imperial' policy, but women had more first-hand experience of education. They also had an eye for detail and a feeling for how things worked. If women's knowledge of education and the administration of the Poor Law could be turned to practical effect by giving them power and the associated responsibility for making choices, both their lives and that of the nation would be enriched. Giving women the vote was not a question of rights but of expediency.

Finally, she turned to some of the objections to female suffrage. Her answers were cautious. First was the question of where it might end. Might enfranchised women demand to stand as MPs, claim entrance to Oxford and Cambridge or seek admission to the legal as well as the medical professions? Natural selection, she suggested, would sort out what women could and could not do. They might well prove effective as doctors but were unlikely to succeed in confrontational professions like the law or politics. Nor should fear of what might follow become the pretext for denying the necessary first step. Admitting women to 'higher culture and wider responsibilities' would 'make marriage nobler and more complete [...] enrich and strengthen the mother's influence, and give single life dignity and strength'.[8] Few of Julia's readers would have missed the implied reference to one of Browning's best-known aphorisms in her conclusion: 'If we aimed only at what we could reach, we should reach nothing.'[9]

She took pains over her article, showing it in draft to Julia Stirling and soliciting Hope's critical scrutiny. 'I care so much it should be well written,' she told Effie, 'more almost than for anything I shall ever write again for I feel the truth is so wrought up in literary merit.'[10] Much of what she wrote came from her own experience. She took it for granted that young women would want to study but pointed to the difficulty of doing so in an unstructured atmosphere. She underlined the need for women to acquire knowledge and understanding through engagement in the external world and pointed to the lack of satisfactory female role models except in the literary world. Like Butler she attacked the condescension of upper-class philanthropic women and their smug satisfaction with 'words of gratitude however shallow' as well as the impulsive nature of their charity, which encouraged dependence. But she was also outspoken about the handful of women who had already forced their way to prominence, criticizing 'the extravagance of some among women's advocates' and disowning 'the women who are warped and strained by the effort of holding their own against the aggression of the world's hostility or suspicion'. She probably had both Harriet Martineau and Florence Nightingale in mind here. 'Most mothers, however high in the social scale, would be glad to see a daughter occupy a position in the front rank of literature [...] but they would be anything but glad, probably, to see her manager of a hospital.' This had become more common but 'at what a loss of moral loveliness in the scars that bear token of the conflict!'[11]

Though her tone was gentler, Julia also implicitly criticized her mother, offering a lively double portrait of the two of them, with 'Snow' anxious to get down to her books and Fanny thinking up schemes to keep her daughters entertained and meet the family's many social obligations:

> How does a girl pass those precious years of her life, from eighteen to four-and-twenty? Emancipated from Schoolroom inferiority, and moving for the first time among her elders as an equal, she enters the enchanting grown-up world, with all its responsibilities – so, at least, she delights to think – and is eager to take up the full burden of the important duties which her imagination creates out of every small conventional opportunity. All invitations to gossip become social claims; she hears it said that she should help her mother; and all that is best in her nature throws its weight into the same scale with frivolous tastes and thinly-disguised self-indulgences. [...] The mother [...] is anxious, on the one hand, that her daughter should make the most of every chance of pleasure [...] and on the other she regards studying as something that can be taken up at any time, and may therefore be actually laid aside.[12]

As a portrait of Fanny Wedgwood, a pioneer of women's higher education, this was harsh but mostly accurate. More striking was Julia's silence about the dispiriting effect of fathers with narrow expectations of their daughters' abilities. But she was anxious to conciliate male readers. The modesty of her strategy was highlighted by Mill's *On the Subjection of Women*, which came out when *Woman's Work and Woman's Culture* was still in the press.

As Butler recognized, Mill's book took some of the wind out of the sails of her collection. She was at pains to explain in her introduction that all her contributors had completed their essays before seeing it. Inevitably, it attracted more interest than the uneven volume she had put together though both were widely reviewed.

Julia was brought up to share her father's distaste for the godlessness of Mill's utilitarianism, but both were impressed by his *Principles of Political Economy* and Julia gratefully followed up Uncle Charles's recommendation that she read Mill's *Logic*.[13] Now she seized avidly on *The Subjection of Women* deliberately travelling the long way round on the Circle Line underground to give herself more time to read it. Her reactions were very mixed. 'It made me so angry', she wrote to Effie, 'to have to read what I consider important truth (& indeed a good deal's like my Essay) mixed up with such extravagance & I think even folly.' Her friend, Juliet Hawkshaw, liked it even less, describing it as 'a very raw book'.[14]

On reflection, Julia came to see that she and Mill had been looking at 'very different facts'.[15] While she had written about the frustrations of young middle-class women, Mill took a larger perspective, arguing that the present subordination of women was the result of centuries of male oppression (originating in women's inferior physical strength), now bolstered by inequitable laws and distorted social conventions. The subjection of women was, Mill claimed, the last surviving example of slavery. Women had a right to equality:

> the principle which regulates the existing social relations between the two sexes – the legal subordination of one sex to the other – is wrong in itself, and was one of the chief human

hindrances to human improvement, [...] it ought to be replaced by a principle of perfect equality, admitting no power or privilege on the one side, nor disability on the other.

This was a far more radical claim than Julia would ever venture. Similarly, while she wrote about the way mothers unwittingly held back their daughters, Mill targeted male chauvinism supported, as he saw it, by laws that reinforced a one-sided domination in marriage and social expectations that encouraged mean-minded male attitudes. Mill was far more aware than Julia would ever be of the way that the law on male ownership of women's property, earnings and children encouraged abusive working-class unions, but he was equally critical of middle-class husbands and fathers. 'If the family in its best form is, as it is often said to be, a school of sympathy, tenderness, and loving forgetfulness of self, it is still oftener, as respects its chief, a school of wilfullness, over-bearingness, unbounded self-indulgence, and a double-dyed and idealized selfishness.' However self-absorbed Julia found her father, she would not describe him in those terms.

To the disappointment of some of the early feminists, Mill's focus lay primarily with married women. Apart from the odd reference to the 'wasted lives' of spinsters, he largely avoided the situation of single women. But his championship of companionate marriage was in line with Julia's own high ideals:

> When each of two persons, instead of being a nothing, is a something; when they are attached to one another, and are not too unlike to begin with; the constant partaking in the same things, assisted by their sympathy, draws out the latent capacities of each for being interested in the things which were at first interesting only to the other.

In marriage, each should 'enjoy the luxury of looking up to the other'. Only equality of this kind would produce 'the moral regeneration of mankind'.[16]

Julia had said something similar about marriage in her article but was far from accepting Mill's claim that women existed in a form of slavery. From her own comfortable perspective, it was hard to see women as 'victims' rather than people unwittingly conniving in the artificiality of their limited lives. As she and Juliet Hawkshaw agreed, 'Nobody reading that book would suppose marriage to be a voluntary association.' She came back to the point many years later, writing to Alfred Benn in 1910 that Mill had been wrong to say that women were subservient to men because that was what men wanted. Women chose their subservience.[17] This may have been true in her circles but overlooked the harsher social pressures on women who lacked Julia's economic independence.

In her article in the *Westminster Review* published in January 1869, she had defined Mill and the *Saturday Review* as standing at opposite poles on women's issues.[18] Now she waited anxiously to see what the *Saturday* would say about her essay. Charles Kingsley tried to forestall a hostile reaction with a sympathetic piece in *Macmillan's*. Reviewing the collection alongside Mill's book, he suggested that Mill's argument about the basic equality of the sexes would soon become commonplace. He picked out Butler's introduction and Julia's article as evidence in their different ways of 'the temper, as well as the intellectual calibre of the ladies who are foremost in this movement' for women's rights. A man who read them on their merits should 'ask himself [...] whether women who can so think and write have not a right to speak, and a right to be heard when they speak of a subject with which they must be better acquainted than men – women's capacities and women's needs'.[19]

But the *Saturday Review* had already answered that question. Allowing women to have the vote and enter the professions would force them into an unequal rivalry with men: 'the better they succeeded the more masculine they would become [...] the inevitable result would be to create a kind of third sex, lacking alike the grace of woman and the vigour of man'. (Clearly, they did not foresee the phenomenon of Margaret Thatcher.) Nor was there any practical need to give the vote to women: married women would vote with their husbands, while nine-tenths of single women would do as their priests told them. Much of the reviewer's distaste was directed against Butler and her dismissal of Pauline doctrines sanctioned by the church over the centuries. Cobbe, too, was quickly dismissed as 'a well-known [...] writer and philanthropist, though of somewhat eccentric views', Sophia Jex Blake's conclusion that male and female medical students might train together without embarrassment was thought 'exceedingly doubtful', while Julia's article was cherry-picked to support the reviewer's prejudices. 'Her explicit admission, from which some of the other writers seem to shrink, that the changes they are set upon "would tend to blur the edge of contrast between the sexes", is worth noting.' Apart from that, 'she pleads the cause of "Female Suffrage" temperately, but very inconclusively.'[20]

Julia felt let down by the *Saturday Review*'s refusal to engage in the argument. 'I am disappointed at their not attacking me more vehemently,' she wrote to Effie, 'and I think their description of my article the most loathful I ever read – ie that it is "temperate but inconclusive" can you fancy anything duller?'[21] Like other pioneering feminists, however, she would learn to dismiss 'the Saturday Review twaddlers'.[22] The review in the *Times* hurt her much more. It devoted almost a whole page to demolishing *Woman's Work and Woman's Culture*, attacking its female contributors (the men received more respectful attention) as fantasists and pseudo-philosophers with little sense of the real world who spoke only for themselves. The introduction was dismissed as 'a piercing wail'. Wolstonehome's suggestion that funds should be equally divided between male and female educational institutions was 'preposterous'. Similarly, Boucherett was ridiculed: 'Platonic dreams of a new status of the [female] sex are a waste of time.' Julia's essay attracted the fiercest criticism. What particularly riled the reviewer was her suggestion that, ultimately, men and women might meet on common ground and, above all, her claim that young women's lives were too exclusively dominated by the thought of marriage. The first, the *Times* suggested, in a deliberate distortion of what Julia had written, implied the extraordinary spectacle of women competing to become Lord Chancellor or 'Commander of the Forces'. The second flew in the face of what 'the mass of men and women' knew: 'it is very easy to talk of "hankering after husbands", and otherwise place that genuine interest which sets towards marriage, motherhood, and domesticity in a mean and ridiculous light'. 'These lady essayists,' the *Times* concluded, 'are too much in the sneering vein, but they will not succeed in making even their own sex ashamed of their natures, reason as they may they cannot turn women into men any more than they can turn men into women.'[23]

Julia rarely complained about bad reviews.[24] This one, however, got under her skin. 'I hope I shall never hear who wrote that article in the Times,' she wrote to Ellen Tollett.[25] She knew that it would be widely read and was shocked by its dishonesty. Aunt Elizabeth had been disturbed by it hoping that the *Times* had been 'unjust' to her niece. 'I have been cast down by The Times,' Julia wrote to Emily Gurney, 'or rather perturbed by it, wondering what effect it would have upon the conventional and narrow minded portion of my friends which, though not large is precious to me. How few men would in other ways do one so great an injury as to put a paragraph in the Times saying untruly one had sneered at conjugal love.'[26] She was still feeling disconcerted when the *Times* reviewed Mill's *Subjection of Women*.

> After reading it I solemnly assure myself that I must make up my mind to be disappointed or in some way shocked or ruffled by everything that a man says on the subject. Either they tell us that we are angels, like Kingsley, or they look upon us merely as possible wives, like this writer. [...] I am coming sorrowfully to think what I used to think unjust and even fanciful, that men do like women's interest to centre in them.[27]

Dispirited by her inability to get her views taken seriously, however much care she took to present them in 'womanly' fashion, she turned for a while from writing to doing.

The Municipal Elections Reform Act in 1869 and Forster's 1870 Education Act created new opportunities for female political involvement. Both Elizabeth Garrett and Emily Davies stood for election to the London Education Board, less out of an interest in elementary education than from a determination to test whether women could be elected to public office. Garrett had struggled to join the medical profession. Though a quirk in the rules had enabled her to qualify as an apothecary in England, she had been obliged to go to Paris to become a doctor in 1870. By then she had already established a Dispensary for Women and Children in St Pancras, ministering to a largely working-class clientele. This was one of her power bases in her election campaign though the area for which she stood also included Hampstead, Marylebone and Paddington.

She canvassed with energy and enthusiasm and a real flair for organization, recruiting a distinguished election committee and a network of women to knock on doors and distribute literature. She was also an effective public speaker. Davies found campaigning more of a trial but persevered. 'It cannot be worse than those terrible drawing-rooms about the College at Mrs Russell Gurney's which I did survive,' she wrote to a friend.[28] She chose Greenwich as her constituency.

Though Julia was closer to Davies than Garrett, Garrett's constituency was on more familiar territory. She came up to town to do her bit. Emily Gurney congratulated her on her dedication in an unappetizing task: 'I do think it very desirable to have a woman on the Board not only for what she can do there but as Miss D[avies] says for drawing room women to take a part in public matters – but to go on canvassing for this amongst the ignorant is so hideously revolting.'[29] Deafness spared Julia too much direct contact with the voters: she shared her friend's distaste for 'this loathsome business'.

> It has given me a curious feeling of how I should hate to be a barrister. Never to live in the serene region of reason, but always in the murky fog of persuasion – always to be thinking of what part of truth will be acceptable to a vulgar mind, or indeed any mind, instead of bending one's whole energies to discern what truth is.[30]

The backroom organizing was more rewarding. She was off to Garrett's headquarters at 8:30 in the morning, finding her

> in her dressing gown, having been up till 3 last night arranging the letters to be written, & ready to set me to them directly. [...] I sat convoking assemblies all morning, she wants subcommittees for every parish & to undertake to forward circulars & addresses to every home [...] she is very businesslike & pleasant to work with. I came home to dinner & brought some of the letters to finish & have just shut up the last Envelope (4PM) & now I am going back to her to draw up Schedules and what not when she comes in & till then am to study the map of the wards & parishes.[31]

Garrett's confidence was infectious. 'She has an immense belief in herself,' Julia wrote to Effie. 'I do not mean that she is vain – but everything she says implies that she knows she has a right to one's service, as I think she has. While women have gone on writing & clamouring she has <u>done</u> something, & I feel it quite enough to justify confidence.'[32]

Both Elizabeth Garrett and Emily Davies headed the polls in their districts, with Garrett securing 47,858 votes, way ahead of Thomas Huxley's 13,494. Even the *Saturday Review* was impressed, discovering that women could enlarge their sphere without losing their femininity.[33] Settling to the day-to-day work of the Education Board proved less exhilarating. Having made their point, both retired from the London School Board in 1873.

Julia never canvassed again in an election. As she had discovered, rubbing shoulders with voters fell outside her comfort zone. Helping Davies in her new educational project was much more congenial. Unlike Julia, Davies had not had a college education. The inadequacy of her schooling, largely at home while her brothers went off to Cambridge, was a key factor in her campaign to secure university education for women. Again, unlike Julia, she was neither a scholar nor an intellectual, a fact which led her to downplay the difficulties of expecting haphazardly educated girls to compete with men on the same terms at university level. But she had a point to prove that Julia shared: women were not innately intellectually inferior to men. Davies was also a good strategist. Her first step was to secure the admission of girls to the local examinations originally introduced in 1857 and 1858 to set a standard for boys as they left school. She then ensured that girls' schools were included in the remit of the 1866 Royal Commission inquiry into the state of secondary education. And in 1867 she began exploring the possibility of establishing a residential college at which women would prepare for the same university examinations as men.

She set up a council of influential people, chaired by the Bishop of St David's and including Russell Gurney, F. D. Maurice, Lady Eastlake, Anna Swanwick and G. O. Trevelyan. The real work was done by an Executive Committee made up of the mix of people Davies judged most likely to prove effective: titled ladies, distinguished men and those of both sexes with relevant experience. Dr Alford, the Dean of Canterbury, presided. The members included Lady Goldsmid and Lady Stanley of Alderley; John Seeley from Cambridge and James Bryce from Oxford; Charlotte Manning, who had been President of the Kensington Society; Fanny Metcalfe, a headmistress; and Emily Gurney, who topped her proposed list of members. Gurney was anxious to distinguish the new venture from existing ones. 'I find', she wrote to Davies, 'when I mention the scheme the general superficial idea is that Queen's and Bedford Colleges supply what is wanted.' They were better described as 'Attempts': their weakness was their lack of final examinations and the undemanding qualifications they offered.[34]

Davies was already a Lady Visitor at Bedford College and may have hoped to draw on the best of its experience when she invited Elizabeth Bostock and Julia's mother to join her committee. They proved uncomfortable recruits, putting up a rearguard defence of their own institution.

> Mrs Wedgewood [sic] asked whether we thought young women would like to go from home to College. Miss Bostock's point was that whatever there is a demand for, Bedford College is ready to give, & we were rather embarrassed in replying, as it was awkward to insist that the people we expect to get have either never heard of Bedford College or despise it & won't think of going near it.[35]

Davies vented her irritation to Garrett: 'Miss Bostock was troublesome & objected to everything, while Mrs Wedgewood [sic] hesitated about everything, which does not speak well for women.'[36] But Fanny attended the big public meeting at the Architectural Gallery on 28 March 1868, designed to attract support for the new college. Bostock too had 'come round' by the end of the year.[37]

Davies was an effective committee woman. She kept good records; she knew how to make alliances and work around opposition; she never lost sight of her final objective and rarely compromised. Her committee faced difficult problems. How were they to attract young women away from their families for a period of concentrated study? Where should the college be sited? What syllabus should it follow? Would women be allowed to take the same examinations as men? And, most difficult of all, where would the money for the new venture be found?

Initially, Julia shared her mother's scepticism about whether girls would be willing to abandon a London season or leave home to study.[38] The location of the college was also a vexed issue. Cambridge University had always been marginally more sympathetic to Davies's ambitions than London, which envisaged less demanding examinations for women, and Oxford, which dismissed her approaches. At Cambridge there were also a few dons who were willing to teach and examine women. Barbara Bodichon, whose generous gift of £1,000 got the new project going, saw it as the natural home for the college. But Julia and Emily Gurney, as well as Maurice, agreed with Davies on the risk of distraction in Cambridge as a result of unwanted encounters with male students ('the chaffy sort of life', as Julia called it).[39] If parents were to be persuaded to release their daughters, there could be no hint of impropriety in the new institution.

With very little consultation with her committee, Davies signed a three-year lease on Benslow House in the village of Hitchin. It was half-way between Cambridge and London and close enough, she hoped, to attract dons living in both places. As important was the presence of the local clergyman F. J. A. Hort. Both Julia and Davies knew him through his involvement in Christian Socialism and the Working Men's College. Though their theological paths later diverged, Fenton Hort remained devoted to Maurice from his first encounters with him as an undergraduate. He was also one of the first Anglican clergymen to find ways of reconciling Darwin's theories with his own theology.[40] Later he would become a regular dinner guest of the Hensleigh Wedgwoods. An outstanding textual scholar, he shared Hensleigh's interest in philology and would, with his Cambridge colleague, B. F. Westcott, become the driving force behind the production of the Revised Version of the New Testament, published in 1881. In 1870, however, he was marking time as a conscientious but unhappy parish priest at Hitchin, awaiting his recall in 1872 to Cambridge, where he was eventually elected Lady Margaret Professor of Divinity, the highest paid of all the Cambridge chairs.[41] Julia, who got to know him well at Hitchin, was always delighted to sit next to him at dinner. He was, she told Emily Gurney in 1876, 'much the most interesting man I now know'.[42]

In 1870, however, J. R. Seeley, the recently appointed Regius Professor of Modern History at Cambridge, looked like the more prestigious catch for Davies. Like Hort he had been inspired by F. D. Maurice as an undergraduate going on to teach Classics at the London Working Men's College as well as University College, London. Though he never publicly admitted it, his authorship of the sensational best-seller *Ecce Homo* first published in 1865 was an open secret in the literary and social circles in which Julia moved.[43] Its attempt to rediscover the historical Jesus from the Gospel records and focus on his human character and teachings rather than any supernatural powers was designed to persuade even agnostics of the contemporary relevance of Christ's universalism and message of love for all humanity. There was enough of F. D. Maurice in Seeley's book to appeal to Julia, despite its deliberate avoidance of any doctrinal apparatus. She gave a copy of it to her friend, Emily Gurney, early in 1866 as something for her to read during her exile in Jamaica.[44] At Hitchin, however, she saw little of Seeley, who quickly fell out with Davies over the curriculum. Cambridge had recently introduced two new degrees in Moral Philosophy and Natural Sciences that he preferred to the old-fashioned Tripos in Classics or Mathematics. Davies insisted on sticking with the tried and tested, anxious to avoid any suggestion that women were unable to prove themselves in the studies their fathers and brothers had followed. Her decision took little account of how prepared her students would be: mathematics was a notoriously weak area of female education, and few girls learned Greek. Seeley dropped out of teaching at Hitchin after a term.

Although in poor health, Charlotte Manning, the President of the Kensington Society, was persuaded to become the first Mistress assisted by her stepdaughter, Adelaide. The College opened its doors to five students in October 1869, with a sixth, Rachel Cook, joining early in 1870. Davies had hoped for 15–20 in the first year, but the demands of the entrance examination and parents' concerns about releasing their daughters held numbers down. Anna Lloyd, a 33-year old Quaker, was admitted only on the understanding that she would not sit the Tripos.

Conditions at Benslow House were Spartan: the food was poor and leisure activities initially confined to country walks and a weekly singing class.[45] The tuition was variable, with both Hort and Seeley straying from the syllabus, though E. C. Clark's patient thoroughness in teaching the Classics was an asset. Davies insisted that her girls should sit not only the same examinations as men but also to the same timescale. This put pressure on them to read and study systematically often for the first time in their lives. The immediate challenge was 'The Little Go', the University's qualifying examination, which was taken in the fifth term and required knowledge not just of Latin but also of Greek as well as

Mathematics and the tenets of the Established Church. Someone, most probably Emily Gurney, suggested that Julia go to Hitchin to help.[46] Alice Bonham-Carter, who would play an important role at Newnham, the rather different women's college established closer to the centre of Cambridge in 1871, also encouraged her to get involved.[47] Emily Shirreff, who succeeded Charlotte Manning at the beginning of 1870, was glad to have Julia's company and though Davies worried that her deafness might prove a handicap, she was pleased to have her 'noble character and keen interest in study' associated with the new enterprise.[48] Julia, who was then laboriously reworking her biography of John Wesley, doubted she could spare the time but agreed to go for a month. She stayed for two terms, enjoying the company and pleased to be doing something useful at a painful time in her life as she learned to accept the final breach with Browning and experienced some of Erskine's distressing last days.

'At first I felt it dreary to be plumped in among a set of people I did not know,' she wrote to Effie, 'but wonderfully soon I came to feel quite at home here. [...] I read about 5 hours a day with the girls, & tho' it is true I can arrange my hours as I like, I don't like to see quite nothing of them in a friendly way.' She tried to keep up Shirreff's spirits too 'so that a good deal of time slides into company'. There were compensations for the time lost on her own work: 'it is very rare that there is a decided <u>anxiety</u> to learn in any one, & it is only in a tiny picked assembly like this that I could look for it'. 'Pray give our compliments to all Fellows,' she gleefully instructed her sister, who was staying in Oxford, '& tell them that their days are numbered, but we wish them well.'[49]

She spoke more bravely than she felt. Comparing Anna Lloyd, who was only 4 years younger, and Louisa Lumsden, who was 8 years younger, she approved of Lloyd's desire to study for study's sake but worried that Lumsden was aiming at qualifying for a career that did not yet exist for women. Lloyd, Julia wrote to Emily Gurney, was not 'at all angelic [...] but very satisfactory and sensible, and (what I am so glad of) studying merely to enrich her life and not to work up her learning for any particular aim. I don't mean that I am sorry that there are students with ulterior aims but I like to think that study can be its own reward.'[50] George Eliot took a similar view: 'the Hitchin experiment' required 'girls or young women whose natures are large and rich enough not to be used up in their efforts after knowledge'.[51]

Lumsden, however, was already showing early signs of her life-long frustration with the restricted opportunities available to clever women. Alongside Rachel Cook, who would marry the great campaigning editor of the *Manchester Guardian*, C. P. Scott, she was one of the ablest of her year and a natural leader. She stood up to Davies, sensing that she was more interested in proving a point about women's innate abilities than encouraging their individual development. Lumsden came from a Scottish aristocratic family and had been well, if not systematically, educated but now lacked a sense of direction. She would end up with a DBE and an Hon DLitt but had a bumpy career in the academic world, baulked by Davies in her ambition to become Mistress of Girton, bored by teaching and at loggerheads with various management committees, including the one which eventually forced her out of her final position as Principal of the Women's Hall of Residence at St Andrew's University. Julia, who enjoyed having Lumsden to stay in London, foresaw the problems she would face:

> I am afraid that the question of education is less separable than I had thought from the question of professions. Miss Lumsden will be a thoroughly unhappy woman unless she gets into some position which is not tenable now for a woman, though I hope it very soon may be. I mean some kind of teaching which is on a level with an Oxford tutor's position. She is I think quite fitted for it by nature – but of course the work of fitting oneself to hold a position that is not yet carried [*sic*] is one that inevitably stirs up a great deal of anxiety.

Though this was an anxiety Julia had never had to face, she understood the frustrations of the Hitchin pioneers.

> Of course one must expect that those who are seeking something beyond the average accessible woman's life shd. pass through a phase of dissatisfaction, and there is a good deal of that here, – or at least what there is is very prominent. 'What is to come of it all? – are we unfitting ourselves for the work of life? – shall we find a groove?' They cannot help sometimes asking those questions.[52]

Julia had asked the same questions in the early 1850s and painfully found her own answers. Unlike her charges at Hitchin, she had been largely alone, isolated within her family and without the sense of female solidarity that sustained the new generation at Hitchin. Her greatest value there was as a role model, the living answer to the first question put down for discussion in the Kensington Society: 'Is it possible for women to be learned & yet perfectly womanly?'[53] Julia was proof that a woman could write about big subjects without losing her charm. She brought with her glimpses of the exciting London literary world and humanized the austere college atmosphere. Davies was full of praise: 'Miss Wedgwood is very useful & enjoys her work extremely. The students also enjoy reading with her & she is delightful to have there. Everybody likes her.'[54]

Sarah Woodhead, the youngest and perhaps the most brilliant of all the students, who would be the first to attempt the Cambridge Tripos, was less impressed with Julia's gifts as a teacher. They read the book of Herodotus set for the 'Little Go' together. Woodhead reported to Davies in March:

> Miss Wedgwood is not quite so much help to me now as she was at first which I suppose is quite natural. She seems to have given her attention rather to seeing the sense of passages easily than to making out the construction and it is in the latter that I need most help now. It is very pleasant reading with her but I am afraid she does not save much time.[55]

The fact that Julia was self-taught in Greek left its mark. Like other women of her time with a knowledge of the Classics, she lacked the grounding every schoolboy got in the basics. For her, meaning was always more interesting than grammatical construction. As Sarah Woodhead knew, however, the Little Go was tailored to testing schoolboy knowledge, not feminine insight.[56] Similarly, Emily Gibson remembered: 'I do not know that her classical training was any great assistance, but she was an interesting and delightful personality, and enriched the life of our little community.'[57]

Julia made her most memorable contribution to life at Hitchin when she went off syllabus. Browning was the girls' favourite poet. One of their first initiatives was to set up an informal club 'The College Five', where they read his poems aloud, starting with 'Abt Vogler'. By March, Emily Gibson had moved on to 'Paracelsus', 'one of the grandest things Browning has written', but struggled with 'Sordello'. 'I should be very sorry to be subjected to an examination on the facts of Sordello's life, either inner or outer,' she not unreasonably confessed to Davies.[58] Julia's reading in February of Browning's 'Easter Day' may well have inspired this pursuit of recondite Browning. 'I felt as if the veil of the world's show was slipping aside as I read it,' she told Emily, using her favourite analogy for a moment of exultation in sympathetic company.[59] The Hitchin girls would have been awed to learn just how close Julia had been to the poet: it is very unlikely she dropped any hint.

Hitchin, for all its privations, became a place of sacred memory for those who had been there. As Louisa Lumsden later recalled: "'Twas here I mused, 'twas here I read, / Here learned the worth of friendship, here / Felt the world widen round.'[60] Its ethos of female solidarity consoled Julia when she returned from a miserable final visit to see the dying Erskine in the spring of 1870. When she went back to London in the summer, she missed the shared pleasure in study and the sense of playing her part in a young, determined female community. Whatever the shortcomings in the teaching of Classics there, all five students who presented themselves for the 'Little Go' in December 1870 passed, an achievement celebrated in *Punch* with surprised merriment.

Shirreff resigned after two terms, feeling that she could no longer play second fiddle to Davies, who continued to control all the key aspects of life at Hitchin from London. Julia approved the appointment of a submissive successor, Davies's old friend the widowed Annie Austen: 'She is a gentle and soft reflex of Miss D which I think is what is wanted there. I do not think she will exercise any influence, any more than a gentle nature cannot help exercising, but you know I think it is better so, while the girls are what they are.'[61] As doubts grew over Davies's uncompromising regime at Hitchin, Julia and Emily Gurney continued to support her, despite the reservations of Bodichon and Shirreff. Julia lost patience when Shirreff poured out her grievances: 'I did get a little angry with her speaking of Miss D. being bespattered with praise by Mrs Manning.'[62] Although she was present, she also kept silent when Davies took offence at some student amateur dramatics in which Rachel Cooke and Louisa Lumsden appeared in men's costumes. Only Barbara Bodichon had the tact to forestall the threatened student walk-out.

Six years after her time at Hitchin, Julia again tried teaching Classics to young women. Her efforts at the College for Working Women that Frances Martin had set up in 1874 as 'a living monument to F. D. Maurice' were a failure.[63] She began her Latin class with three students but had lost them all by the third term. Subsequent attempts to revive the class under male Oxbridge graduates fared little better in contrast with the Working Men's College, where Arthur Munby attracted respectable numbers to the courses he ran for several years. Julia tried a class on Shakespeare but again could not hold her audience. Her father was not surprised: he blamed her teaching for giving her 'so many headaches'. But though Julia described her task as 'full of enjoyment',[64] she was far less at ease with working-class women, hoping to better themselves than aspirant middle-class girls at Hitchin. Learning for its own sake was a luxury that students at the College for

Working Women could ill afford. Julia and her mother, however, always supported the College generously.[65]

Campaigning for Elizabeth Garrett and nurturing the abilities of a brave new generation of university women left their mark on Julia's writings. She became less tolerant both of patronizing male attitudes and of the reactionary views of 'drawing room ladies'. A new assertiveness appeared as she dropped the cloak of 'womanliness' which had failed to protect her from the taunts of the *Saturday Review* and the sneers and misrepresentations of the *Times*. In 1870 she was gently dismissive of the tone of the Franchise Bill opponents: 'I was so amused at Lord Elcho's wishing not to deprive any lady of her just rights. It sounded so dinner table-ish.'[66] Six years later she was much more impatient: the description of women in the House of Commons by the Tory Edward Knatchbull-Hugessen as 'the silver lining, which gilds the cloud of man's existence' was simply 'childish'.[67] She recognized beneath this male rhetoric a proprietorial approach to the adjudication of women's claims that increasingly annoyed her.

The substance of the debate could be just as infuriating. 'I have been made so fiercely indignant by the treatment of the Bill in the Lds,' she wrote to Emily Gurney about debates on changes to the Married Women's Property Act in 1870. 'It is not so much even as justice to women that I feel it, it is that men who are counted by units shall regard a question like this as it concerns <u>them</u>, while the men who are counted by thousands are even individually more interested in the result.'[68]

The existence of the Married Women's Property Act bedevilled debates on extending the franchise to women. Under it, married women did not have a separate legal identity and could not (with small exceptions) control their own property. As a result, a property-based test of eligibility for the vote would exclude them, creating, so the opponents of female enfranchisement claimed, invidious distinctions between married and single women. Julia joined the debate with a letter to the *Spectator* in May 1870 in support of Jacob Bright's Bill, giving the vote to single women meeting the same property qualification as men. Clearly, she suggested, the best outcome would be to repeal the Married Women's Property Act and admit all women on the same basis, but that would take time. In the meantime, single women were being unfairly treated. They faced far greater difficulties than men in running small businesses, opening shops and managing farms. Bright's Bill would ensure that these 'exceptional women' were 'admitted to share in the rights and responsibilities of average men'. 'We cannot think', she defiantly wrote, 'that nature has appointed that every woman should have a husband to care for her, and those who are forced to perform a man's work ought surely to enjoy a man's advantages, whatever they may be.'[69]

Cobbe jumped in to support Julia, praising her 'very great lucidity' and drawing attention to her 'singularly suggestive essay' in Butler's collection the previous year. Those who were not represented, Cobbe argued, remained disregarded. But Hutton, the editor, disagreed: the head of household test was not a test of political ability but of 'moral respectability'. Single women did not have the time to think about politics.[70]

This sort of female stereotyping played a major part in debates on the suffrage in the run-up to the 1884 Reform Act. Julia tackled an important aspect of it in an article in the *Contemporary Review* in 1872. Her arguments meshed with her private concern over the impoverished state of national religious life. They also highlighted some of her differences from other leading feminists like Cobbe and Butler. Barbara Caine has suggested that 'a concern about women's social and moral duties, about their need to preserve a moral order and create social harmony [...] gives Victorian feminism its distinctive character'.[71] At this stage, Julia was more concerned with the damaging effects of attributing moral status exclusively to women and confining religion to the domestic sphere where women reigned supreme. Women, she suggested, clung to a feminised Christianity centred on a meek and mild Jesus. The result was 'a moral code [...] permeated with hypocrisy [...] we pass our lives with those we love best without ever seeking a common contemplation of the unseen and eternal world [...] the world which is thus unvisited becomes unreal for both parties – for men, practically ceasing to exist; for women becoming the refuge of all the sentimentality of their nature'. A shared sense of spiritual truth would revitalize both public life and marriage itself. In contrast to Mill's 'companionate marriage', Julia proposed an ideal of 'moral' marriage. Unlike Mill's model, 'moral marriage' would not be confined to 'the cultivated and leisurely': it was just as appropriate for 'the ignorant and hardworking'.[72]

As in 1870, she accepted that the vote could be given only to women 'who are not men's actual or probable wives' but argued as she had in her 1869 article that what mattered was its symbolic significance. 'We desire it more for what it would make us than what it would give us.' 'It would be a step towards a kind of union between average men and women such as is now seen only between the most exceptionally gifted specimens of the race.'

Alongside this, Julia also increasingly defended female autonomy: 'The theory that one set of persons [men] can decide for another [women] what their sphere is, belongs to that feudal world of which the last traces are rapidly passing away among us.'[73] Though opponents of female suffrage might find the growing 'tone of bitterness' 'ludicrously out of place', there was 'no question that it exists'. Four years later, she made no attempt to soften that bitterness, arguing an uncompromising case for the vote in a pamphlet for the London National Society for Women's Suffrage. This time she addressed herself directly to single women.

The debate over female suffrage had, she wrote, exhausted itself. The arguments were over-familiar and the claims women were making frequently caricatured by male opponents. All that women sought was 'citizenship' on an equal basis with men. Their continuing disabilities cast a 'slur' on them. The argument over 'separate spheres' became irrelevant when one in every three women was unmarried and had to earn her living. Women who worked paid their rates and taxes as men did and were, indeed, much closer to working men than the 'drawing room ladies' whose hostility to the franchise was often evoked in Parliament. 'Lower down in the social scale, you would find a very different kind of view of the subject,' she wrote about the Married Women's Property Act, 'than that taken in drawing rooms' where 'most gentlemen' knew women as 'social equals'. But Julia was not writing for women (like herself) whose wealth was protected by private trusts but on behalf of 'the shop keeper, the schoolmistress, the lodging-house keeper, the writer in magazines, the painter of second-rate pictures – all the commonplace women [...] who earn their bread'. Even when women did work, they were denied the recognition that went with it. She cited the case of a woman farmer who had won the Royal Agricultural

Society's prize for the best-managed farm in the Midlands but was unable to accept it because the Society did not admit women members.

Turning to the misrepresentations of women's opinions, she dismissed the familiar canard (which had particular resonance in the Irish context) that enfranchised women would prove unduly susceptible to clerical influence. 'Women are as little under the influence of feminine men [as she dubbed the priests] as men are under the influence of masculine women'. And once again she derided the idea that men should decide what was best for women. 'That is our own concern.'

She also discarded her old cloak of 'womanliness':

> As for the graces and refinements of life, we believe that they will survive when women lose the shelter accorded to weakness and cease to be debarred from the independence conceded to strength. But supposing we are mistaken in this: supposing that we must purchase the greater good by the lesser, we would say – let these things go. It would be a pity that ladies should lead less graceful lives in drawing rooms, but it would be worthwhile, if it led to other women leading less miserable lives elsewhere.

Her conclusion returned to the argument that had always underlain her advocacy of female suffrage: the importance of the vote lay in its indirect rather than its direct effect. 'All other measures for the benefit of women would find a new atmosphere and a new soil to grow in when once women were made citizens [...] till that time comes all such measures [to remove female disabilities] will form part of a mere patchwork.' 'What we demand,' she concluded, 'is justice', implicitly reminding her readers that she was not only a Wedgwood who knew about drawing room attitudes but also the granddaughter of Sir James Mackintosh.[74]

To those like Uncle Charles who complained about the obscurity of Julia's writings, her 1876 pamphlet was proof that she could say what she wanted plainly enough when she was not aiming to replicate the complex style of periodical contributors. She read her pamphlet aloud to the Darwins. 'It a good deal converted W[ilia]m & me,' Emma wrote to her daughter, describing an evening when Snow had been 'agreeable and entertaining'.[75]

Expectations ran high when Gladstone returned to power in 1880 with a big majority. In October 1883 the National Liberal Federation, the body representing local party associations, passed a resolution in favour of female suffrage. The following year he introduced a Bill intended to settle the suffrage question for the foreseeable future. It extended the vote to all male householders over the age of 21, so bringing in agricultural labourers alongside the urban workingmen who had been enfranchised in the 1867 Reform Act. Female campaigners sensed that their time had come and organized a letter setting out their case:

> We respectfully represent that the claim of duly qualified women for admission within the pale of the constitution is fully as pressing as that of the agricultural labourer, and that the body of electors who would thereby be added to the constituencies, would be at least equal in general and political intelligence to the great body of agricultural and other labourers who are to be enfranchised by the Government Bill. [...] The continued exclusion of so large a proportion of

the property, industry and intelligence of the country from all representation in the legislature is injurious to those excluded and to the community at large.

Seventy-eight prominent women, headed by the Countess of Portsmouth, signed the letter. They included not just those of the older generation like Anna Swanwick and Anne Clough but also younger campaigners like Millicent Garrett Fawcett, the sister of Elizabeth Garrett and wife of one of Gladstone's cabinet ministers, and Edith Simcox, a skilled union organizer, as well as Butler, Cobbe, Bodichon, Garrett and Davies. There were some surprising names too like Florence Nightingale, not known for her promotion of women's causes, and Mrs Humphrey Ward, later a vehement opponent of female suffrage. Julia was among this group of 'ladies who stand high in literary, philanthropic and educational circles'.[76]

They asked to meet the Prime Minister but were told he was indisposed, suffering from the strain of carrying through a measure likely to face strong opposition in the Tory-dominated Lords. Like her mother, Julia was fascinated by Gladstone. When he came to have tea with the Darwins in 1875, she waited impatiently to hear how it went. Darwin had been surprised by Gladstone's gentle manner and interest in his conversation though he had avoided answering the Prime Minister's question about whether the future belonged to America. 'He said he was struck [...] with something in Gladstone's mind', Julia noted, 'that was quite remarkably opposite to the scientific temperament – he did not say this at all arrogantly & I was not tempted to tell him that this was what gave the character its greatest interest to my mind.'[77]

In introducing his Reform Bill in 1884, Gladstone warned his party against trying to extend its scope. In 1866 he had failed to carry a Reform Bill and then seen Disraeli get the credit for the more radical measure put through Parliament the following year. In 1884 he faced determined Tory opposition led from the Upper House by Lord Salisbury and moved cautiously. When William Woodall introduced an amendment on 10 June to extend the vote to women on the same terms as men, the Prime Minister stepped in to claim that this would 'overweight' his Bill: if the amendment were carried, he would withdraw the legislation altogether. A total of 104 Liberal MPs pledged to support female enfranchisement voted in the majority that defeated Woodall's amendment by 271 votes to 135. 'Gladstone,' wrote the romantic Tory Frances Power Cobbe, 'has been our ruin'.[78]

Though Gladstone avoided taking a public stand on the substance of the debate until late in his career, he had always opposed female suffrage. Nor were his views untypical amongst thoughtful Liberals. Hutton, Bryce, Morley and Dicey, all men Julia admired, shared them. Their reservations show why arguments about equity and expediency made so little headway. Victorian Liberalism revered 'manliness' and a sense that men had inherited from the days of ancient Greece a heroic obligation to engage in the public sphere. The householder was seen as essentially male (Gladstone even referred to 'paternity' as one of his characteristics): independent, self-reliant, stable and respectable, the outward face of his harmonious household. Politics was a strenuous masculine calling, and as Gladstone saw it, women needed protection from 'the stormy sea of politics'.[79] Their involvement, he wrote in 1892, would 'unwittingly trespass upon the delicacy, the purity, the refinement, the elevation of her own nature, which are the present sources of [women's] power'.[80] Yet more unpalatable to early feminists than this enforced closeting in virtuous domestic security was the moral status accorded to the new male voter. In pressing to extend the urban householder qualification to the counties, Gladstone sidestepped earlier debates on the need to represent property or particular classes or interests, or link taxation to representation, or reward those who met educational tests. Instead, he focused on the moral fitness of the new voters to be regarded as 'capable citizens'. They included minor tradesmen, skilled artisans, miners and what Gladstone called 'the peasantry'. The independent women running their own businesses or managing farms that Julia had described in her 1876 pamphlet fell outside this definition of capable citizenship.

The rhetoric of 1884 was even more disheartening than the reality of women's continuing exclusion from national political life that would continue for the rest of Julia's life. As Cobbe pointed out in the title of one of her articles, only 'Criminals, Idiots, Women and Minors' were excluded on principle from the parliamentary franchise.[81]

Julia was disillusioned. She never again wrote directly about securing the vote for women. Like several other Liberal feminists, she broke with Gladstone over his adoption of Irish Home Rule in 1886 and in her later years became increasingly conservative supporting Joseph Chamberlain, a determined opponent of female suffrage. When Davies sought her support in 1910 for a circular letter in favour of the first Conciliation Bill, which would have extended the vote to some women on the basis of a property qualification, Julia did not sign fearing that this extension of the franchise was the precursor to universal suffrage. 'I wish I cd hope to convince you how large a part of my deep regret in this step arises from the breach in memories of common endeavour – poor and futile as these were on the part of yours very sincerely F Julia Wedgwood,' she sadly concluded her letter.[82]

Her advocacy of female suffrage had relied on the power of reasoned argument to establish the case for rectifying an injustice. She underestimated the opposition, which was not confined to drawing room ladies and men in clubs and misread the equivocations of Liberal politicians.[83] Cobbe, with her journalist's instinct and wider knowledge of the world, was shrewder: 'It is Sentiment we have to contend against, not Reason; Feeling and prepossession, not intellectual Conviction.'[84] The suggestion that however able, responsible and independent women might be, they could not become citizens because of their sex ran counter to Julia's belief in the importance of intelligence, moral sense and justice. Establishing more natural relations between men and women, the prize that she believed would be the most important indirect result of enfranchising women, became a private goal. In her later years it brought her to the fringes of Bloomsbury.

In many ways Julia was untypical of Victorian feminism. Though she attacked the views of drawing room ladies and spoke up for hardworking single women, class assumptions circumscribed her approach. Her discomfort when canvassing for Elizabeth Garrett Anderson, her failure as a teacher at the Working Women's College and her insensitive reference to 'commonplace women' in her 1876 pamphlet all show her ill at ease with a very different social class from her own. So, too, her concern with the social advantages that would follow from female enfranchisement reflected the preoccupations of her own circle, not the claims of economic necessity. Nor, unlike Cobbe, did she celebrate the virtues of womanhood or generally write about the satisfactions of spinsterhood. She could be just as critical of women as of men. She pilloried not only the unimaginative opinions of 'drawing room Ladies' but also the sentimentality of pious women and the self-serving nature of much female philanthropy. She was even more critical of female icons like Harriet Martineau and Florence Nightingale, who had, she believed, been coarsened by their fight for prominence. Her principal concern was less with the unrewarding lives of many spinsters than the failings of marriage and the deterioration of relations between the sexes so long as women suffered under the 'slur' of their exclusion from the nation's political life. And though she had no time for sentimental descriptions of women's vocation in the domestic sphere, she respected the protective instincts towards her sex of men like Hutton and Dicey as well as the reservations about female suffrage of women like Octavia Hill. She also deplored hostility towards the opposite sex. The fact that Barbara Bodichon was not 'anti-Man' was, as Julia saw it, a great mark in her favour.[85]

Ray Strachey suggested in her history of the women's movement in the nineteenth and early twentieth centuries that, as a Wedgwood, Julia, like the daughters of some other well-known upper-middle-class families, had a relatively easy time.[86] Strachey was right that women like Julia could largely create the life they wanted. Unlike the hyper-productive Margaret Oliphant or Eliza Meteyard, she did not need to work for a living. She was also able to establish her own household. But her life was not as easy as it might seem two generations later. In presenting herself unapologetically as an intellectual, she had to face down the objections of her father and friends of her mother's generation like Marianne Thornton. The implication that her attachment to women's issues was no more than an indulgence is also misleading. On top of the frustration of discovering that reasonable arguments moderately expressed could be dismissed as besides the point, the sense of exclusion was real. So was Julia's sense of injustice. For her, the argument was not over equality but equity: it was about 'simply not <u>preventing</u> a qualified elector voting on account of sex'.[87]

Like Cobbe she turned away from the rights of women to campaigning for the rights of animals. What a male Parliament refused to accord to women as a spur to their fuller development they would have to find for themselves.

Chapter Eleven
DOUBT AND THE FALLIBILITY OF IDOLS

For all the confidence of her early articles in the *Spectator* about confronting the challenges to religion through intellectual rigour, Julia was beset by doubt in the 1870s. The disparity between her reassuring public voice and her private despair troubled her. 'I have used good words and sometimes have struck out high thoughts in collision with other minds,' she wrote to Emily Gurney in 1871, 'but when it comes to endurance [...] there is no strength in me [...] there is in me a perpetual thirst and craving which repels others and makes any word I have said of the peace of God hypocrisy.' The 1870s were a time of 'strange, dreadful misery [...] the problem of [my wretchedness] was unremitting [...] I saw nothing around me but evil [...] it seemed put there by an omnipotent power'. 'Sometimes', as she confessed to Jane Gourlay, the rather dour Scottish teacher she had got to know at Linlathen, 'an icy despair comes instead of patience when I try to wait for [spiritual assurance]. And then the plausible rational views of all my acquaintances press upon me like a choking vapour. I feel how like all this is to there being no God.'[1]

She felt too that her idols had failed her. Had she been less prone to 'idolatry',[2] this might not have mattered so much. Mack had died without any word of consolation, her friendship with Browning was broken, Erskine had turned away from her in his last unhappy months, Mary Rich was a burden on everyone at the end of her life, Maurice became over-fond of religious controversy and even her new friendship with the charismatic George Eliot came up against its inevitable limits after a couple of years. Though her deep affection for Aunt Emma remained, she also became increasingly disillusioned by Darwin's refusal to see his discoveries as part of the 'religious education' she believed them to be. Plagued by migraines and increasing deafness and left isolated by the marriages of both her sisters, Julia was profoundly depressed. Only Richard Hutton remained a reliable guide alongside the constant and solicitous Emily Gurney. By the end of the decade, however, she had created her own unorthodox but satisfying domestic establishment and mastered many of her doubts as she worked up the resonant assertions of *The Moral Ideal*. The painful process of discovering her new 'rootedness' in the world contributed to Julia's readiness to acknowledge the validity of honest doubt.[3]

'Those who would end with certainties must begin with doubts' was one of her favourite Francis Bacon maxims.[4] One of her keenest criticisms of the new assertiveness of the scientists was their readiness to confuse genuine doubt with denial. In this they failed to apply the standard they used in their own work of 'continuous attention and suspended judgment' when facing uncertainties. She was equally dismissive of those who found in tepid religious observance a 'convenient shelter for that indifference to everything spiritual which those who have never either doubted or believed like to dignify with the name of doubt'. True doubt as Julia experienced it in the 1870s was active, agonizing and necessary. Faced with the challenge of Biblical criticism and Darwinian theory, 'many awakened to the discovery that, if it were no longer possible to believe in God, it was quite easy to forget Him, and that while belief was arduous, distracting, incomplete, oblivion might be absolute'.[5] 'Oblivion' was never an option for Julia.

The apparent disjunction between faith and conduct distressed her. 'If Christianity is to regain its hold on the world,' she wrote to Gourlay, 'scientific men must see that there is some connection between what Christians do and what they believe.'[6] She looked around her own circle and found few signs of this 'connection'. Richard Litchfield was 'pure', 'generous' and 'unselfish' but had turned away from God.[7] Her childhood idol, Mary Rich, by contrast, proclaimed her faith vehemently but behaved intolerably. 'What is the blight of Christianity', she wondered, 'that this is its mature fruit [...] half a century [...] in a sincere endeavor to follow the will of God & the character be left what I see.' Rich had become a whited sepulchre, her religion no more than 'a sort of covert for one's sin to lie hid in'.[8] She could not help contrasting her behaviour with that of Lady Inglis, locked into her narrow Evangelical faith but selfless in her care for visitors.

Inglis died in October 1872. Under the terms of Sir Robert's will, Milton Bryan passed to Marianne, the eldest of his Thornton wards, leaving Rich homeless. As her status declined, her snobbery increased. When Marianne Thornton tried to soften the blow by offering her some of Inglis's silver, she protested that only one salt spoon was included, and a silver-plated one at that. House-hunting with Fanny, she refused to consider a property on their street because a brass plate on the door implied a professional presence. The family was appalled by the prospect that Mary Rich, 'this trumpery old woman', might have to stay with them. Her death at Hopedene in 1876 was a relief.[9] Twenty years later, Julia was able to remember her more fondly: 'She was noble, magnanimous, vivid, dignified, not original. [...] She is one of those to whom I most look forward to re-union [...] the last years of her life [...] do not intercept with its fog and frost my gloss of gratitude and undying love.' In the 1870s, by contrast, she had been yet another incubus as Julia struggled. At her bleakest she even lumped her with the aging Erskine. Both were 'majestic beings [...] who hold one's heart with a grip quite independent of their merits [...] all the more they seem to torture one with a deep sense of the terrible deep rootedness of evil beyond what religion can get at'.[10]

In Wales she had a more bracing role model. Still living in Tenby and stone-deaf, Great Aunt Fanny Allen never compromised on her principles or altered her habits. She 'has her whole nature still at her disposal', Julia told Gourlay in 1875 just a few months before she died at the age of 94. Well into her 80s, she stood for a couple of hours each morning reading the *Times* and went for regular walks. Accepting their deafness, the two spent long periods together in silence. Fanny remained as unsentimental and independent-minded as when she first met Coleridge as a girl and took him on in discussion. Now she waited, rather impatiently, for death. She returned from one walk telling Julia that she and a little Persephone had been picking wild flowers. Sadly, Pluto had not come to scoop them up. Julia came to admire her stoicism: 'I am making a mental list of almost everything she does to copy when I am old – the only exception being that I will never pretend to hear when I don't.'[11] But Fanny Allen's harshness sometimes grated. She was contemptuous of Erskine's 'short cut to religion by manufacturing religious feeling' and reluctant to abolish 'the dread of Hell'.[12] For Julia, in contrast, the appeal of his theology was its generosity. Erskine spoke about love as a far more potent force than the fear of eternal punishment.

Yet even he had proved fallible in his last years. Senility and physical ailments made him irritable, contrary, depressed and fearful rather than exultant about the approach of the afterlife on which his attention had been fixed for so long. Friends had suggested he publish a final collection of his theological reflections. Julia was keen to help. In the autumn of 1866 she attempted to bring his thoughts into some coherence at Linlathen but concluded he had little new to say. He too was now unsure of himself, constantly rewriting or surreptitiously tearing up her careful copy. When she went back for four months in 1868, the situation was worse.[13] In his last months he wrote begging her not to come. 'I could not speak to you,' he said, conscious that he could no longer raise his voice to penetrate her deafness. 'I know that I could not bear it.' She went all the same for a few days in spring 1870. It was not a happy visit. She longed for his life to end, but was devastated when it did. 'Oh how large a part of all the activity of my heart & mind is left now without an object,' she wrote.[14]

Several of Erskine's friends as well as Richard Hutton urged her to write an appreciation of him. Despite some qualms, she undertook it as an attempt to recover her sense of him in his prime. Her article appeared in the *Contemporary Review* within a month of his death. She reminded her readers of the originality of his early work. Now, when his rejection of eternal damnation was far more widely shared, the simplicity of his language and sincerity of his belief could be accepted with more sympathy. She highlighted his lack of interest in Biblical criticism: his concern was not with the evidence for incidents recorded in the Bible but with their meaning. In this, Julia suggested, he was more like a scientist than a historian, looking for the universal laws that underlay inner experience and explained man's attraction to God. Goodness could not be willed but grew from the recognition of man's filial relationship to God and the reality of divine love. 'This once perceived, everything else fell into its right place [...] our efforts were based on a knowledge of the laws of the unseen world, and ceased to be futile.' His influence was, Julia suggested, rather like Coleridge's. 'Not a few' 'among the thinkers of his day', she wrote, without specifying distinguished men like Stanley, Jowett and Maurice, had come under his influence: 'it was by a kind of manifestation of the invisible world that he laid hold of those who came near him'.

She was not entirely uncritical, however, accepting her responsibility to 'give all the shadows too'. Thomas Erskine was too other-worldly. He took little interest in day-to-day affairs. Now 'one who long endured an uncongenial climate is recalled to a region after which he has long panted and where he feels himself at home'.[15] For herself, however, in the years after his death, she resisted the temptation: 'I feel far more than I ever did before that we are meant to live in the unseen,' she wrote to Ellen Tollet in 1874. 'I yet feel also that we want to multiply and enlarge our relations with the visible world, & that to have gone out of this world without having taken root in it will be to go out unprepared for whatever is to come after.'[16]

She knew that Erskine's death had left her more vulnerable. She had delighted in being called 'Beloved Snow' or even 'Well Beloved Governess'. If her parents had died, she would readily have gone to live with him. Just as she had needed Erskine, so, she persuaded herself, he had needed her. 'I am full of dread for myself,' she confided in Emily Gurney. 'A wonderful longing has been satisfied in these years, now how shall I escape all kinds of wrong effort to satisfy that craving?' Though she occasionally went back to Linlathen and hosted reunions of the circle in London, her feeling of loss did not diminish. At the time of his death, she told Jane Gourlay, 'I feel as if my life were suddenly left empty – this is an exaggeration.' 'No it was not,' she firmly wrote in the margin when she re-read her letter 20 years later.[17]

As when Mack was dying, she turned to Maurice. Without the prospect of further reunions with 'the Saint' at Linlathen, 'this summer is […] a very desolate one to me', she wrote to him in May 1870. She missed 'the feeling I had grown used to with him that in some way he leant upon me, that I could watch over him, and wait upon him – in short that he wanted me'. He had left her £100 as 'a token of affectionate remembrance'. 'Will you not let me associate you with him in this remembrance?' Perhaps the Maurices could use it for a holiday abroad. 'Do not answer this in a hurry,' she begged the man who was known for keeping on top of his huge correspondence through quick, sometimes illegible replies.[18]

Maurice did not reject Julia's appeal. The legacy paid for a break for the three of them in Clifton, and Julia regularly stayed with them in Cambridge, where Maurice held the Chair of Moral Philosophy from 1868 until his death in 1872. But Maurice could not replace Erskine. Though he was, Julia wrote, 'the best man I ever knew', he was 'not to me a great Teacher'. Maurice's theological certainties were very different from Erskine's mystical confidence. As she complained to Aunt Rich, 'What I feel the want of in him is of sympathy with the spirit of search'. Nor did they have the same emotional bond. After one argumentative session – 'a manifesto from me and a sermon from him' 'not very interesting because he never listens' – she and Maurice made up. 'We kissed each other tenderly afterwards which was not a sign of much for his wife was complaining that it happened when any woman came to see him!' Julia wryly noted.[19] The extent of her intellectual debt to him was something she discovered only in her later years. From James Martineau, she had learnt a Kantian sense of the limits of human knowledge, but through Maurice she came to appreciate Kant's distinction between the 'sensual' and 'the logical intellectual region'.[20] Holding the two in balance became key to her understanding of faith. Others detected his influence in her major works of the 1880s and 1890s, and she herself would come to recognize that ideas of his that had originally seemed 'far-fetched' or not worth saying were more rewarding than she had first thought. His suggestion that the material wealth of the Great Exhibition was worth less than a single human spirit had seemed trite when she first heard it. Fifty years later, it had 'almost the force of a prophecy'.[21] Above all, his insistence on an underlying unity between God and man and within the family and nation influenced her growing receptiveness to idealism.

Maurice died on Easter Sunday 1872, exhausted by his many responsibilities and self-denying life. For all the forcefulness of his polemics, he kept an unassuming simplicity to the end, exacting a promise from his wife the day before he died that she would explain to his barber why he had been unable to keep his appointment with him on Monday morning.[22] His death produced an upsurge of national sorrow that some said had not been experienced since the death of the Duke of Wellington in 1852.²³ His funeral at what Julia dismissed as that 'unpretending commonplace Cemetery' at Highgate attracted a massive attendance. She was unable to get into the chapel but did manage 'with great difficulty' to get close to the grave.

The heavy solemnity of the typical Victorian funeral oppressed her: 'that terrible array of mourning coaches & the bearers staggering under the pall'. She was probably remembering Maurice's own denial of bodily resurrection in her longing for 'a pyre & the flame that shd make an end of the worn out garments the wearer needs no more'. Westminster Abbey, which had been offered but refused, might, she thought, have done better at sorting out 'we crowd of heterogeneous mourners'. Prominent amongst them were the students of the Working Men's College, walking four-by-four behind the coffin. The normally austere James Martineau was seen sobbing like a child. In the hush, as the coffin was lowered, Julia heard 'the sudden song of a thrush'. It gave her 'a suggestion of hope & brightness I cannot describe'. Though Maurice's loss was 'nothing to me in comparison with Mr Erskine's death [...] the world seems wonderfully empty without him'.²⁴

Maurice's insistence that there should be no biography of him was not a request his son could honour. The long-expected *Life and Letters of Frederick Dennison Maurice* did not appear till 12 years after his death, however. This allowed Julia time to arrange her thoughts. The piece she wrote for the *British Quarterly Review* in 1884 was one of her most carefully judged. Unusually, it gave a strong sense of Maurice's physical as well as intellectual presence. She recalled 'the glad triumphant accents in which he repeated the Creed' and the welcome he gave to his friends. 'Who that ever knew it has forgotten his greeting – that eager stooping movement, that outstretched hand, that sweet smile, that fullness of unaffected sympathy in the inquiries after all whose welfare was a matter of particular interest to the person whose hand he grasped?' But after the initial greeting came awkwardness as he struggled to find things to say. Julia attributed this not to shyness or reserve but to the fact that he dwelt in 'the universal' rather than 'the particular'. It made him reluctant to act as a spiritual mentor to individuals, a disinclination that came from his 'wonderful humility' and fear of being awarded a specious authority. Though he was averse to judging the failings of others, however, he was vehement in condemning opposing theological views.

Julia wrote with insight about Maurice's theology as, at heart, a reaction against the Unitarianism in which he had grown up and the distinction she saw in it between 'God's goodness and man's goodness'. She refuted the prevalent view of him as the leader of the Broad Church. His greatest sympathy, she claimed, was, like her own, with the High Church tendency and its attachment to Sacramentalism. Julia was less interested in Maurice's doctrinal originality, however, than in his approach to the three subjects of greatest concern to herself in 1884: the meaning of suffering, the nature of the afterlife and the challenge of Darwinism.

Maurice had as keen a sense of the reality of evil as Julia. One of her gifted contemporaries, Susanna Winkworth, who suffered from similar bouts of depression and a sense of alienation from God, wrote that she had found particular consolation in his assurance that 'joy is a gift which many of God's dearest children may be left without in this life'.²⁵ Julia was more reluctant to accept this bleak conclusion. She did, however, find some consolation in

Maurice's understanding of pain 'as a *teacher*'. 'He regarded sickness as the shadow and type of sin, and yet in some sense a spiritual privilege.' 'Illness,' she wrote drawing on her own unhappier times, 'is a source of such varied misery, and of misery sometimes so little obviously connected with any physical cause, that the invalid does indeed at times find himself in contact with an evil influence.' But, as Maurice suggested, illness could also be seen in the same way as in the prayers for the visitation of the sick, as 'the hand not of an evil spirit, but of a Father, chastening His children that they might be partakers of His holiness'.

She was less happy with his view of the afterlife. For Julia, as for most idealists, the association between theodicy and the existence of an afterlife was critical. For her, the afterlife was a place of completion and perfection and, poignantly enough given her deafness, a sphere of unfettered communication with loved ones. The Unitarian writer Anna Swanwick shared her expectations: 'This strong sense of unused capacities constitutes to my mind one of the strongest intimations of our immortality. If this life be the be-all and the end-all, our aspirations seem out of all proportion with the realities of our existence.'[26] Maurice, however, had argued that eternal life was a quality that could be experienced on earth in close rapport with God, while eternal punishment was simply the absence of God. For Julia this was not enough: 'We cannot call to mind another religious teacher who so consistently refused to contemplate the world beyond the grave.'

He had also failed to respond to the challenge of Darwinism. He was, she suggested, as little interested in 'the aggressive, dogmatic science of our day' as Darwin was in its 'aggressive, dogmatic theology'. This, Julia suggested, helped to explain the remarkable phenomenon that confronted all his defenders: the prevalence of agnosticism and freethinking amongst his associates at the Working Men's College. 'Hence it has come to pass,' she wrote,

> that some men who have been learners from one whose life was an exhibition of the power and meaning of Christianity intelligible to a peasant, and impressive to the most profound scholar, are to be found in the ranks of those who have most decidedly turned their backs on the truth he shared, not only with his lips, but with his life.[27]

The confidence of his convictions had alienated men like Litchfield, Furnival, Vernon Lushington, Clough and Fitzjames Stephen and reduced his influence.[28]

Another who was unconvinced by Maurice was George Eliot, who found his theology 'dim and foggy'.[29] For Julia, reflecting on her fallible idols of the 1870s, Eliot was even more confounding than Maurice. Here was a woman of unequalled moral influence who preferred Comtism to Christianity and lived openly with a married man. Like Darwin, Eliot became one of Victorian Britain's secular saints, but unlike Darwin, she was refused burial in Westminster Abbey.[30] Julia never doubted her stature. Eliot was 'the greatest woman I have ever known'.[31] For almost three years at the time Eliot was planning and writing *Middlemarch*, they met regularly when she was in town. Initially overwhelmed by the force of her intellect and the appeal of her sympathetic presence, Julia held to her own very different moorings as the friendship ran its course.

Julia and Mary Ann Evans (George Eliot) had briefly coincided at Bedford College in 1852 where both attended Frank Newman's lectures. Though they may scarcely have known each other then, Julia would certainly have been aware of her work at the *Westminster Review* in the 1850s and heard the gossip when Evans set up with the married George Henry Lewes, whose wife had become involved with Leigh Hunt's eldest son, Thornton. Evans's first novel *Adam Bede*, published pseudonymously in 1859, was a huge success. Inevitably, there was speculation about the identity of 'George Eliot'. Like Mrs Gaskell, Julia was incredulous at the suggestion that this sympathetic and essentially moral novel could have been written by 'the strong-minded woman who <u>went abroad</u> with Geo. Lewes after the family fracas' (as Julia Sterling described her). 'Who will people invent for it next?' an amused Julia asked Effie.[32] Though the truth of the rumour was soon confirmed, her enthusiasm for *Adam Bede* remained. She read it aloud to Erskine until he stopped her, sensing that the plausible Arthur Donnithorne, who could not bear 'not to be smiled on', was too like himself. She kept up with Eliot's novels as they came out, particularly admiring *Romola*, and when the old circle gathered around Erskine's empty chair at Linlathen after his death, she chose to read them the opening section of *Middlemarch*.[33] This took her back to the time when she had been closest to the author.

Their friendship began when Eliot was first struggling to make a start on what would become her greatest novel. Though Lewes protected her from all but a very small circle, he understood the way that the admiration of younger women boosted Eliot's flagging confidence and encouraged several of these friendships. Eliot could be sharply dismissive with those seeking her advice on their literary ambitions[34] but took Julia seriously, mentoring her and passing on thoughts about the critic's art that had a lasting impact on the younger writer.

Eliot's great friend Barbara Bodichon engineered their first meeting by passing on Julia's enthusiastic letter about *The Spanish Gypsy*. When Bodichon enquired whether Julia might call, Eliot, who was feeling bruised by the critical reception of her long poem, immediately confirmed that she 'was very happy to see her'. Two weeks later on 5 January 1870, Julia presented herself at the Priory, the smart new home close to Regent's Park that Eliot shared with George Henry Lewes.[35] Finely furnished and decorated by the leading interior designer Owen Jones, it would become an attractive setting for the Sunday afternoon 'At Homes' that flourished after the immense critical and popular success of *Middlemarch*.

At the time Julia got to know Eliot, however, the question of whether or not to visit was more vexed. Some, like Browning, never held back, while even Maurice, another admirer of *Romola*, asked for an introduction in 1864.[36] Married men, however, generally left their wives behind though Lady Amberley and Mrs Mark Pattison had few qualms about coming. The rules for single women were more complicated. Charles Eliot Norton thought he understood the system: 'the women who visit her are either so emancipée as not to mind what the world says about them or have no social position to maintain'.[37] This hardly applies to Julia or to Emily Davies and Octavia Hill, who called on Eliot in the late 1860s. All three would have been appalled at being seen as lacking social caste or being indifferent to social conventions. Davies, who wanted Eliot's support for her new college, anxiously discussed the propriety of a call. Emily Gurney, knowing that George Eliot would always be out of bounds for her, was encouraging. 'She says it would be like a gin palace to her to have the temptation so close at hand & prophesies that now I have once crossed the threshold I shall be constantly going,' Davies told Charlotte Manning.

'She takes the [...] view that it is justifiable to go & see Mrs Lewes herself but not to meet people at her home.'[38] That was also Julia's conclusion.

She got to know Eliot at what was for both of them a difficult time. Julia was struggling with the final rupture with Browning and Erskine's last unhappy months, while Eliot's fitful progress on her new novel was halted in the middle of the year by the need to nurse Lewes's eldest son, Thornton, who died in October at the age of only 25. At the time they began meeting, however, these troubles lay ahead. Julia was dazzled by her initial encounter with Eliot in January 1870. 'The first contact with such a mind as hers', she later wrote to Emily Gurney, 'has an overwhelming impact.'[39]

They had a good deal in common temperamentally and intellectually. Though Eliot now had more poise, both remained needy and conscious of their unattractiveness. They suffered from poor teeth, migraines and a tendency to depression, intensified by their sensitivity to criticism. They shared too a passionate interest in religion and a high seriousness, and both had read widely in German philosophy and learnt several languages. A woman who found that Darwin's 'Development Theory' produced only 'a feeble impression compared with the mystery that lies under the processes' was always going to appeal to Julia, as was someone who when young avoided balls, preferring 'the intimacy of dinner parties where people think only of conversation' and 'one doesn't mind being a dowdy'.[40] Though Julia would never have compared her intellect with Eliot's, she could keep up with her just as she had with Browning and relished her mix of charm, sympathy and cleverness and her attentiveness as a listener. For her part, Eliot offered Julia the respect of a fellow-author sympathizing with the demands that a writing career placed on a woman and leaving her with inspiring maxims that Julia often quoted such as her favourite that 'good criticism was as rare as original creation'. And Eliot thought well enough of Julia's opinions to pass them on to others.[41]

Julia reported their têtes-à-têtes to Emily Gurney, who enjoyed this vicarious nip of gin. The first was dated 5 January 1870. Julia had been feeling earthbound and unable to write amid 'a clamour of mere <u>thoughts</u> which lead to nothing'. Eliot sympathized: '"how poor one feels on those days when the whole experience has been of expansion of the self, and one has received nothing" – she was saying that she felt it such a difficulty to silence herself and <u>receive</u> and how she envied Mr L for doing so'.[42] At the end of her tutoring stint at Hitchin, Julia called again in June 1870, soon after the Leweses had returned from a trip to Berlin and Vienna, where he had been particularly keen to visit some 'lunatic asylums': 'I felt in her the great sympathy with every form of mental illness; they had been seeing a sort of German <u>Cowper</u> in the asylum'.

Eliot was keen to hear about the new women's college. Though she had given £50 towards it in 1868, she shared some of Julia's ambivalence about university education for women, worrying that it might weaken 'the bonds of family affection and family duties', but she was very ready to listen and learn.[43] They talked about Emily Davies. Julia, who was usually reluctant to criticize her, was more open with Eliot. 'I found she had something of the same feeling about Miss Davies. A great admiration but a sense of divergent sympathy.' Eliot detected 'a want of a due sense of submission'. Julia agreed but suggested that had Davies had it, she would have achieved less. Eliot picked up the thought, comparing Davies to an airgun: the greater the compression, the further it fired. She, by comparison, felt 'nothing but counteracting truths'. 'Then she got into her old vein,' Julia wrote, 'the duty of resignation.'

Julia was entranced: 'Oh how I felt when I sat by that wonderful creature, George Eliot, and heard her shrinking modesty of voice as she limited all her assertions to a confession of ignorance and felt in my soul at the same time a flood of conviction that an invisible person was with us.' The wish fulfilment was fleeting. Julia was soon 'silenced by the sense that the words which rose in my heart as <u>knowledge</u> turned to opinion as they met her ears'. Eliot had shared Julia's faith as a girl and young woman but turned irrevocably away from it under the influence of her reading of Feuerbach, whose *The Essence of Christianity* she translated, Comte and Spinoza. Tantalizingly for Julia, Eliot had rejected the metaphysics of Christianity but retained its ethics alongside a keen understanding of religious feeling. What Eliot called 'resignation' was, Julia ventured, 'submission to God'. 'I wish I could reproduce the effect of her answer upon me,' Julia wrote,

> It was something I c[oul]d hardly have imagined. She s[ai]d that the one form of faith with which she had sympathy was Dogmatic Christianity and that of all theological positions, Philosophical Theism was that which appeared to her least tenable. 'The whole conception is anthropomorphic, and pure Theism is a mere extract of that, omitting all that makes it coherent [...]' But Christianity, she went on to say with a wonderful mournfulness and humility, she could not continue to hold, – and giving up that, she could only feel that her faith must be founded on human relations. With regard to what lay beyond, her only sense of duty was in resignation to inevitable ignorance, but there was an instinct which demanded Religion, and which shared in the 'illimitable of all human instincts, far overflowing all that we call its <u>reasons</u>, – as indeed is the case with every individual love'.

Like Darwin's late confession to Julia that 'we are all naturally inclined towards belief in a first cause', this sounded close to Julia's own convictions, obliged though she was to recognize how far apart they really were. 'I feel as if with her I were traveling a long familiar road that led homewards, and then she suddenly turned off on a wild heath just as the home came into view, and the daylight faded.'[44] Frederic Myers experienced the same disillusionment in a conversation in Trinity College gardens three years later as Eliot earnestly pronounced God 'inconceivable', immortality 'unbelievable' but Dduty 'peremptory and absolute'. 'I seemed to be gazing,' he famously wrote, 'like Titus at Jerusalem, on vacant seats and empty halls.'[45] They were on firmer ground when Eliot talked to Julia about the oppressive effect of other people's opinions. 'I never met anyone but her who matched my sense of helplessness under the influence of certain personalities.' (Was she thinking of Aunt Rich?)[46]

The next time Julia called for 'a delightful hour', she was both intrigued and discomfited by the presence of Lewes, a man who troubled many of the callers at the Priory with his mix of devotion to England's leading Sybil, high spirits and what some saw as vulgar showmanship. Julia did her best to be fair-minded. 'I had heard such odious descriptions of him that the reality was something of a relief to me,' she reported to Emily. 'I think I saw the best of him – yet there was – Oh such a chasm to traverse when I turned from one to the other and then her deferential attention to every word that fell from his lips.' She put a sentimental gloss on the relationship but could not altogether conquer her distaste.

They sat close together and her voice softened so tenderly when she said 'dear' – and I felt there was something there that was an element in the holiest conjugal union, though one could not but feel as if there was also an element of something very different. I am sure they are united by true love, though perhaps it was a flaw in her that bound them in one.

In Lewes's company, they drifted inevitably into Comteian analysis, while Eliot drew on Feuerbach to insist that the instinctive need for religion and its 'vehement reiteration' until religion became a fact were one and the same thing. For Julia the need was fundamental: how it was framed an irrelevant test of its validity.[47]

When she called again the following March, she was becoming a little disillusioned and blamed her disappointment on Lewes's hold over Eliot. She

> was very interesting and animated, but there was less in our conversation than before that I felt was coming from a first rate mind. It seemed to me as if the second rate mind to which she had surrendered herself was telling upon her, – and indeed much of her conversation was only a more graphic and poetic rendering of his ideas. [...] I felt as if I were watching a soul turned back from Paradise. [...] She has entered and explored it – and turned away to look for something better.[48]

By then in the spring of 1871, Eliot was beginning to make progress on *Middlemarch*, and the Leweses were actively seeking a country retreat where she could devote herself to the novel. Although it was far from finished, Blackwood's began its publication in what would become eight instalments on 1 December that year. Julia did not wait for the final instalment published a year later before writing a letter of appreciation. 'I wonder whether you are stifled by letters about Middlemarch, dear friend. If so throw mine in the fire, for I doubt not that many have said something very like what I feel about it.' For Julia, Eliot had achieved what Browning had failed to do in *The Ring and the Book*. She had painted 'so clearly the borderland of Evil where most of us, in this undramatic world, spend the chief part of our lives, [...] on that slope which seems so gentle, & which you show us to be so marvelously & fatally steep just where it ceases to be imperceptible'. As a result, *Middlemarch* was truly redemptive. 'What do we need to lift us above the latent grudge or the subtle self-flattery, but the perception that they end in hate and lying.' Something else in Eliot's portrayal that bore on Julia's insecurities had also struck her: 'the horror of unlovingness which makes one realize the comparative of what otherwise wd seem the supreme dread of being unloved'. The first part of these comments echoed what Eliot herself had told her publisher about 'my design which is to show the gradual action of ordinary causes rather than exceptional'.[49]

Eliot immediately invited her to tea.[50] But Julia was disappointed by her customary reluctance to talk about her work. She had been particularly keen to discuss the deteriorating marriage of Lydgate and Rosamund Vincey and the downfall of Bulstrode. Why were failing relationships so much more dramatic a subject for the novelist than aspirational ones? Eliot deflected the question with a generalization that 'tragedy was the most interesting form of human art'. She did, however, confide that she planned to write about the 'one great exception in history' to the rule that 'what one <u>saw</u> in the development of a great career was deterioration'. 'It must be someone I should never have pitched on,' a mystified Julia commented many years later.[51]

This was almost the last time Julia had an intimate conversation with Eliot. When Emily suggested that she was distancing herself from her famous friend, she denied it with a mock Comteian analysis: the initial impression had been so overwhelming that a negative reaction was inevitable. Now she had reached the 'positive stage and this abides'. In March 1873, Julia got 'a sweet little note' from the author explaining that she was 'too busy and unwell' to see her but, characteristically, asking for a reply, confirming 'that our spiritual relation is unbroken'.[52] That same week, 20 people called on Sunday afternoon, including Darwin, the great violin virtuoso Joachim, Blanche and Annie Clough, Browning's friend Mrs Sutherland Orr, the actor-manager George du Maurier and Madame Novikoff. Two Sundays later the Litchfields were amongst the many callers.[53]

Julia was, as she recognized, being gently edged out. She complied with the request for a valedictory letter (which does not seem to have survived) but volunteered to Emily that she had decided not to take 'the initiative in seeing her, now that I know how besieged she is with grandees'.[54] Other regulars also stopped coming as Belgravia 'forced an entrance into the Priory'.[55] The crowded Sunday salons (where Julia ran the risk of bumping into Browning) were not to her taste in her middle years when deafness kept her away from large gatherings.

The triumph of *Middlemarch* had marked a turning point in Eliot's life. The great and the good could no longer stay away, and wives were now as anxious to meet the famous authoress as their husbands. On 16 March 1873, when Eliot told Julia she was too busy to see her, the Hon. Mrs Frederick Ponsonby, wife of Queen Victoria's private secretary, came to call, dropping a deep curtsey before Eliot (who noted the call, if not the homage, in her generally sparsely kept diary). Shortly afterwards, Edith Simcox, a pioneering trade unionist and gifted writer, paid her first call at the Priory and fell hopelessly in love with Eliot. Emily Faithfull was another in the new circle of younger more malleable acolytes of the inappropriately named Madonna. Julia would not have felt comfortable with them.

Their friendship had run its course. In the troubled mid-1870s, Julia was conscious of the need to protect herself from a seductive idol. Though she had sometimes felt in the presence of God when talking to George Eliot (as she had with Browning), it was His absence from her thinking that she found 'so chilling'. 'Now time is so short,' she wrote philosophically to Emily, 'I cannot desire much communion with one who does not directly help the aspiration after God.'[56] But they ended their active friendship without reproach. As Julia had said when writing about *Middlemarch*, 'I sometimes feel almost ashamed of having been so presumptuous as to know you, but now there is no help for it that I must be always affly yrs FJW.'[57]

Not all contemporary female writers felt the same warmth towards George Eliot. Her pre-eminence could feel oppressive to those whose literary careers and private lives had been tougher and more troubled. Eliza Lynn Linton, who had been more forcefully pushed out of the Eliot circle, was characteristically acerbic. The hard-working widowed Margaret Oliphant mixed admiration with resentment. She recognized that she was not in the same league as Eliot but could not help wondering: 'Should I have done better if I had been kept like her, in a mental greenhouse and taken care of?' 'She took herself

Figure 24 George Eliot listening to music, sketched at a concert in 1872 by Lowes Cato Dickinson, Julia Wedgwood's great friend. Courtesy of the National Portrait Gallery.

with tremendous seriousness […] and was always on duty, her letters ponderous beyond description.'[58] Julia could be more generous. She was never under the same financial pressures as Margaret Oliphant or in competition as a novelist. For her, Eliot's 'tremendous seriousness' was one of her greatest attractions.

She later described their friendship modestly enough as something that might have happened to anyone 'had chance thrown it in their way'.[59] But she was proud of the connection and liked to include snippets from their conversations in her articles. She recalled Eliot's envious admiration of Mendelssohn's ability to communicate directly with a vast audience through his playing; her doubts about whether Mill had given enough weight to the effect of female physiognomy in the *Subjection of Women*; her disclosure that she always mapped out the physical background of her characters before starting to write; her sense that Turgenev's art had benefitted from the constraints under which he had to write because 'it was a literary gain to have to understate one's case'; and her reference to Browning, 'I always think of him as the husband of the dead wife'. (Remembering this gave Julia the opportunity not only to pay tribute to Browning's undying love but also to place him even above Eliot as a writer.)[60] Above all, she regularly reminded herself of Eliot's dictum that the best criticism required the careful gradation of praise and blame.[61]

The apparent contradiction between Eliot's work and her beliefs, however, continued to trouble Julia. She tried to address the conundrum in a long article in the *Contemporary Review* shortly after Eliot's death. Unusually, she signed it only as 'By One Who Knew Her' though later she republished it under her own name in *Nineteenth Century Teachers*. Her choice of anonymity may have reflected her concern not to upend the expectations of her regular readers. Most of the religious press struggled with its assessments of the phenomenon of George Eliot. Some put much weight on the fact that a copy of Thomas à Kempis's *The Imitation of Christ* had been found at her bedside after her death. Did this suggest a last-minute conversion or, at least, a yearning for union with God?[62] Julia avoided this wishful thinking, regretting the way that Eliot's admirers 'conceal[ed] from themselves or others, the vacuum at the centre of her faith'. At the same time, however, she was certain that 'no preacher of our day has done so much to mould the moral aspirations of her contemporaries as she has. [...] Her influence was as wise as it was profound.'

Confronting Eliot's irregular private life was easier. Eliot, Julia loyally maintained, had not set up with a married man out of arrogance or from the belief that genius gave her the right to ignore social conventions. Her best defence lay in her work:

> She was no doubt responsible for the fact that English public opinion in its idolatry of her, left in abeyance some of its most cherished principles; but her reverence for human bonds and her abhorrence of a self-pleasing choice as against a dutiful loyalty have been set forth with such eloquent conviction in her books that their testimony has outweighed even her own adverse example.

She then recalled Eliot's humility: 'the slow, careful articulation and low voice suggested something [...] almost like diffidence'. But her power was undeniable: 'one sometimes felt as if in the presence of royalty'. She had, however, a ready sympathy, especially for 'the failures of life'. Above all, she saw 'the duty of resignation' as 'the remedy for all the ills of life'. For Julia's readers, 'resignation' was a Christian obligation: for Eliot, it was a moral imperative.

Her sympathetic understanding of religion could mislead, however. She understood even 'the least cultivated Evangelical [...] there was nothing wanting to her appreciation of the faith of the humble and the poor but a sense of its reasonableness'. As she had told Julia, her only objection to Christianity was 'its want of evidence'. Julia strained for an explanation of this lack of faith. Perhaps, she argued rather unconvincingly, it lay in Eliot's limited ability to portray aspirational love (the point she had wanted to broach with Eliot when they discussed *Middlemarch*): 'where love looks <u>downwards</u>, whether for good or evil, her power is at its highest. Where it looks upwards, with few exceptions, her power seems to ebb'. Love, as Eliot showed it, had the energy of the plant cut from its stem and brought into a warm room to bloom: the flower left on the rooted stem came out more slowly but lasted longer.[63] 'Fame promises in gold but pays in silver,' she had cautioned Julia: 'if we must accept some parts of her creed,' Julia warned her readers, what was promised in gold will be 'paid in lead'.[64]

Edith Simcox was contemptuous of Julia's mix of admiration and caution. 'All that Miss Wedgwood [...] half complains of reminded me of all that I rejoice in – when others demur or doubt, I am stirred to take my Darling's part – to prove by word and deed how truly, wholly right she was,' she wrote to Eliot's widower.[65] But Simcox, unlike Julia, never had to face the challenge of recognizing that the most powerful moral teacher of the age had disavowed the faith that remained of central importance to her.

As Julia's idols fell away, one survived. 'Not all your kindred spirits have gone so long as Mr Hutton remains,' Emily Gurney reminded her when she felt overwhelmed by religious doubt in 1876.[66] Unlike more fallible idols, he did not evade the big questions. Hutton was, Julia came to believe, 'the religious teacher of our generation'.[67]

Their intellectual formation was remarkably similar. Both came from Unitarian families, both were influenced at an early stage by James Martineau and both then came under Maurice's spell. Both also moved steadily towards the High Church with Hutton, in particular, feeling drawn to Newman. Only his 'intellectual severity' held him back from going over to Rome despite 'his emotional yearning for the sort of certainty offered by Roman Catholicism'.[68] Julia would turn instead to the English mystical tradition and, later, the seductions of Spiritualism.

She was particularly drawn to Hutton's understanding of suffering. Unlike Maurice's resigned acceptance or the facile optimism she would later encounter in James Hinton's work, Hutton's sense of pain as providential consoled Julia because it derived from his own experience of tragedy. In 1851 when his health broke down, he had gone to convalesce in the West Indies, where his wife, Ann Mary Roscoe, contracted yellow fever and died. Seven years later, he married her cousin, Eliza Roscoe. She was injured in a carriage accident in 1888 and spent the last nine years of her life depressed and uncommunicative though they still played the occasional game of chess. They died within months of each other. 'A great sorrow,' Julia wrote in her posthumous tribute to him, 'either destroys trust in God, or allies it with a sense of mystery. [...] Those who can trust God through anguish enter on new views of His relation to the world.' Hutton had survived, as would she: 'when [a man] resigns himself to a higher Will and accepts the allotment of a hard fate, [he] draws on a spring of strength that is in very truth divine'.[69]

Faith, tested by personal suffering, but combined with an acute intellect, made Hutton Julia's ideal guide. He had not shirked the challenge of confronting Darwinism, and unlike some of the scientists she complained about, he engaged in the argument. As a result, Julia suggested, faith had emerged stronger, no longer relying on authority, conventional standards of behaviour, the veracity of miracles or the literal word of the Bible, but on the assertion of the validity of inner experience and personal apprehension of the divine. In the sterile theological arguments of her day, Hutton's writings were an unmatched 'refreshment' as she listened 'week by week for his voice in the Spectator'. It was his praise for *The Ring and the Book*, qualified though it was, that first made her wonder if she had missed the point in her comments to Browning. Similarly, an article by Hutton on the character of the Old Testament writers that she read in 1869 sowed the seed for the book she would write over twenty years later, *The Message of Israel*.[70]

The respect was mutual. From the time when he first responded to her letter on female suffrage in May 1870, Hutton engaged in public debates with her in the columns of the *Spectator*. While he was in charge, her letters were always prominently placed (which was not always the case under his successors). In 1888 he would go to considerable trouble to draw attention to her magnum opus *The Moral Ideal*, which had baffled some of the critics, unused to encountering a woman who chose to write comparative history, moral philosophy and theological commentary. Hutton wrote not one but two very favourable reviews of it, praising her 'largeness of grasp' and 'the masculine breadth and truth' of many of her observations.[71] A decade later he emerged from retirement to comment on a 'profoundly interesting' article she had contributed to the *Contemporary Review*, 'The Old Order Changeth'.

Perhaps, Hutton was consciously making up to Julia for her exclusion, on the grounds of her sex, from the most distinguished debating club of the 1870s, the Metaphysical Society. With the notable exceptions of John Stuart Mill, Herbert Spencer, Mathew Arnold, George Henry Lewes, John Henry Newman and, inevitably, Darwin, this attracted all the leading Victorian intellectuals. They considered many of the subjects that absorbed Julia: the relationship between morality and religious belief; the soul and the afterlife; the competing claims of intuition and empiricism; and the place of popular judgement in politics. Though its debates were rarely conclusive and it failed to make the headway its founders had hoped for in narrowing the gap between science and religion, James Knowles, its initiator, allowed the public occasional access to its debates by publishing what he called 'Modern Symposia' in his new and very successful *Nineteenth Century*. Others published versions of their papers for the Society in the *Contemporary*, the *Fortnightly*, *Macmillan's Magazine* and *Mind*. Their authors were men Julia knew like Martineau, Arthur Stanley, Maurice, Leslie Stephen, Ruskin, the Duke of Argyll and Huxley as well as Tennyson, Gladstone and Cardinal Manning.[72] Excluded though she was from this appealing intellectual company, androgynous anonymity admitted her to the columns of the *Spectator* on equal terms to discuss the same central but intractable problems.

One of Hutton's last published pieces was a commentary he wrote in the *Spectator* in September 1896 on Julia's attempt to identify the most significant developments of her century and analyse the fin de siècle *zeitgeist*. Her conclusions in 'The Old Order Changeth', published in the *Contemporary Review*, were visionary and remarkably positive. Hutton was far less confident. He regretted the passing of the age of great men, like Tennyson, Carlyle, Ruskin, Chalmers, Maurice, Kingsley, Newman and Manning, and the decline of authority. Nor did he have Julia's confidence in the progress of what Carlyle had called 'dim, common populations'. 'She is', he concluded, 'quite too optimistic when she is disposed to regard the dying out of men of genius as in any way favourable to the elevation of the masses of our people.'[73]

Hutton's verdict, written very shortly before his death, made Julia pause. She did not reprint her article in the collection of her key essays *Nineteenth Century Teachers* that does include her eloquent tribute to Hutton. She knew that she owed him much. He had steadied her in the great debate over Darwinism; reassured her about the value of thoughtful doubt; drawn attention to her major work; and invited her in to the debate over the great questions of the day, confident that what she had to say was worth hearing. He had also helped her find some positive meaning in the pain she had to bear.

Hutton's absolute reliability through the 1870s contrasted with her growing disillusionment with the greatest of the idols to whom she had been close, Charles Darwin. In her article on 'The Natural and the Supernatural' in the *Spectator* in November 1871, she drew a disguised portrait of him: 'The study of Nature seems to absorb and to a great degree almost satisfy the whole being; he who is sustained by that continued contact with large ideas and observations of unvarying sequence is secured, to some extent, from keen desires and permanent suffering. The intellectual life shelters the soul from strong emotion.'[74] By the end of the decade, when she had surmounted some of her own doubts, she wrote more confidently in disposing of the claims of the intellect to explain the world and the existence of evil. The naturalist could trace the factors that influenced the development of moral character (as Darwin had in *The Descent of Man*) but could not account for the origin of sin and man's consciousness of it. Even Plato had fallen short.

> To distinguish the permanent from the transitory, reality from appearance, significance from insignificance, – this is what is promised to the student of Plato, and in many states of mind it seems all we need. Where we are longing for deliverance from evils that seem the most real and permanent things in the world of human experience, promises like these are the bitterest mockery of the spirit's deepest needs.[75]

If she had intended this as a private message to the Darwins, she failed to hit the mark. They settled down to read her article after dinner but gave it up three quarters of the way through as too 'fatiguing'.[76] Episodes like this have encouraged Darwin's biographers, Adrian Desmond and James Moore, to suggest that Darwin saw his niece as nothing more than 'an opinionated bore'.[77] That is not the whole story.

Chapter Twelve

DOMESTIC CONTENTMENT

Just as the 1870s were Julia's time of greatest religious doubt, so, too, her relations with her family reached breaking point. Both of her sisters contracted marriages that, in their different ways, disappointed her and also left her feeling yet more isolated and unfulfilled. She responded at the end of the decade by moving out of the family home to create her own household, an unusual step for an unmarried eldest daughter with aging parents in poor health. Even more singular was her choice of a younger, uneducated Welsh woman she had first spotted as a housemaid to act as her companion and take domestic charge. Once the new arrangement settled down, it was the making not just of Marian Hughes but of Julia too.

In November 1869 Julia went on holiday with Effie and Hope to Caerleon in South Wales, delighting in the company of her two sisters, 'the two people whose society is the most welcome to me'. 'It is so rare that we have nothing to think of but each other, as we have here,' she enthused to Aunt Rich.[1] More than thirty years would elapse before she rediscovered that pleasure. By then both Effie and Hope were widows.

Lively, self-confident and her mother's favourite, Effie had never been short of suitors. There was an unnamed Frenchman when she was studying in Paris, J. R. Seeley, who was always pressing her to come to Oxford and, unbeknownst to Julia, cousin Godfrey in Barlaston. But, like her mother, Effie took time to get round to marrying. Godfrey had come close to proposing early in 1862 but fearing that she would reject him stayed silent. In June he married Mary Hawkshaw, a distant relative of whose love he felt more certain. The marriage was a happy one until Godfrey blurted out to his wife his continuing feelings for Effie. Mary died in 1863 soon after giving birth to their only child, Cecil. Godfrey's grief and guilt kept him away from the Hensleigh Wedgwoods after that.

Hensleigh knew nothing of this when he despatched Julia and Effie to Barlaston in October 1871 in the hope of improving relations with his brother Frank and his children. The two sisters' very different experiences there show poignantly how easily Julia, handicapped by her deafness, could misread what was happening around her. Though she sensed a new reserve in Godfrey's manner, she misattributed its reason: 'I think he is afraid of any deep intercourse – that part of his nature has shut up & will never open to anyone, I believe. I think he cares more <u>now</u> for you than he does for me,' she suggested to Effie. She regretted his resistance to her attempts to rekindle the faith he had lost after his wife's death. Godfrey, whose cast of mind was far more literal and phlegmatic than Julia's, had told her that 'seeking God was too arduous a search for one who has the business of everyday work of life to do'.[2] The real drama at Barlaston, however, was not about Godfrey's lost faith but his continuing feelings for Effie.

Emily Wedgwood, Godfrey's sister-in-law, had taken Effie aside at the outset to tell her that Godfrey was still in love and wanted to marry her. Effie agreed to go for a ride with him. He stumbled through his explanations of why he had kept away from her. 'Then,' as Effie wrote in her fervent account of the visit, he looked 'very hard down on the horse's neck [and said] "I've been a brute. I've felt it for years and been miserable". He asked if he might call on her in London. 'I raised my eyes to his and we took one unutterable look and then Sno came in.' After dinner, Godfrey showed Julia some prints, holding them at the angle that enabled him to gaze on Effie as she sang song after song to avoid having to talk. An unsuspecting Julia was captivated. 'What a sweet two days we have had together,' she wrote to her sister on the train back to London. She would never forget her singing of 'Cherry Ripe'.[3]

Julia had always had a soft spot for Godfrey. 'Whenever he comes into the room it is like a burst of sunshine,' she wrote to Effie in 1854, and again in 1858, 'I am glad you do appreciate him. Strange to say I think he is very little appreciated as everybody thinks he is commonplace which, when you get below the surface, he is not. If he had a backbone I shd think him perfect.'[4] She particularly admired his calm and his popularity amongst his workforce. Unlike many in her family, she liked to see him in action in the factory. For his part, Godfrey was conscious in Julia's company of his lack of a university education and rather in awe of her intellect and career as a writer. Some in the family may have expected the two to make a match. Whatever proprietary feelings Julia had towards him would be severely tested over the next five years as Effie, not she, determined Godfrey's future.

After Barlaston, Effie went to stay with the Gaskells. Meta relished the drama of Godfrey's declaration but did not think him good enough: 'I cannot bear to think of you, risking your happiness, and worse than that, risking yourself – your highest self – by a marriage which did not fully satisfy your noblest demands'. She thought up further objections: Godfrey's loss of faith and the risk of inherited defects in the children of cousin marriages. Effie consulted Dr Radcliffe, who advised against the marriage. And so when Godfrey finally proposed just before Christmas, Effie refused him. 'My darling Effie – I don't wonder at the remembrance of his "almost contorted face" haunting you,' wrote Meta.[5]

Godfrey sank back into depression, withdrawing from local affairs in the Potteries and keeping only half a mind on the Wedgwood business.[6] Effie soon had another suitor. Thomas Henry Farrer, generally known as 'Theta' or 'TH' in the Wedgwood family, was another widower but one with much more self-confidence and persistence. Born in 1819, he was closer in age to Hensleigh than to Effie and had been a fixture at the Wedgwood dinner table for as long as the girls could remember. Julia described him to Effie at a dinner party in November 1869.

> We had a large assortment of old beaux – viz. H Parker, H Allen, T.H., Mr Lawrence, Wm [?Darwin] & Eras. I glanced round the table while they were all busy with their food & thought what a minute it seemed since I remembered 'em all young sparks, & now there was only one that wasn't grey or bald & that was Mr Lawrence – & he was never a young Spark. TH was partickler nice and respectful to me.

Julia had always appreciated Farrer's 'pleasantness' and sense of purpose and was pleased when Effie started to like him in 1865. 'Of course he's selfish,' she wrote to her sister, 'but lor bless us he is a man & what can you expect?'[7]

After failing to make his name at the Bar, Farrer had found his métier in the civil service. On the recommendation of his brother-in-law, Stafford Northcote, he was given the task of amending the legislation on merchant shipping in 1849. This was the start of his steady climb up the expanding hierarchy of the Board of Trade until he became its Permanent Secretary in 1867, a post he retained until 1886. Farrer was a convinced Gladstonian, attracted by his free trade reforms in the early 1840s but later following him even on Irish Home Rule in a display of loyalty that helped earn him a peerage in June 1893. The Hensleigh Wedgwoods first got to know him well in 1849 when he agreed to serve alongside Hensleigh and Ras Darwin as a trustee at what became Bedford College. In 1854 he married Mary Rich's niece, Fanny Erskine, Julia's great teenage friend. She died in 1870, leaving four children. The eldest, Ida, enchanted all who knew her.

The Wedgwoods took pity on the widowed Farrer and invited him to dinner. Effie, as usual, entertained the company by singing after the meal. Farrer, whose wife had also been an accomplished singer, listened intently, barely concealing his tears. Julia probably sensed what was coming and warned her sister that, as Fanny Erskine had told her, TH was a peremptory wooer. Less than a year after his wife's death, he proposed to Effie. She rebuffed him. Julia did her best to console him. 'I saw in his face', she wrote to Emily Gurney, 'that grim look one knows so well in a man's face, when he wants oblivion, and one has offered sympathy'. Fundamentally, Julia did not think Farrer good enough for her sister. She was repelled too by his hasty courting which Mary Rich saw as an affront to the memory of her niece. Unwisely, Julia let Effie know what she thought: 'I am deeply grieved about the great waste to spend any feeling on a man who will find a substitute within the year, but I can't help it.' But since Farrer was clearly intent on remarrying and providing a mother for his children, Julia had a suggestion to make. 'I suppose you couldn't promise to choose for him? One could fill the place so beautifully.'[8]

The time had not yet arrived for Effie to choose other people's mates. Under steady pressure from Farrer and the pleas of his children led by Ida, the 33-year-old Effie gave way in late October 1872. Julia was agog with excitement as the wedding approached, worrying about the cake and whether Benjamin Jowett would be invited and answering enquiries from her friends about appropriate wedding presents. 'When I am married,' she wrote to Effie, 'I mean to have a neat Schedule printed, divided into Jewelry, Upholstery & nicknackery, & everybody then to fill one in with what they choose to give and return.'[9] (As with her idea of setting up an agency to advise on social introductions, she was ahead of her time.) Ras Darwin lent Effie a kitten to calm her nerves in the fortnight before the wedding. Though she nearly fainted during the ceremony, she got through it and TH was able to take his bride to his home at Abinger Hall in Surrey. It was, E. M. Forster recalled, 'a hideous mansion', which had been remodelled for Farrer by Alfred Waterhouse.[10]

The romantic in Julia rebelled against this passionless marriage and what she saw as Effie's sacrifice. 'I now feel as if she had turned away from her vocation,' she wrote to Emily Gurney.

Figure 25 Effie Wedgwood, the favourite Wedgwood daughter.

I never thought before that any woman could have too little inclination for marriage but I feel as if it were so with her. Her strong affection for him, her appreciation for his intellectual superiority, and her taste for his society seem to me only to need the spark of a readiness for the kind of union to have blazed up into a good steady fire – not brilliant, but glowing, and not to be put out. Now I see the fire laid and no match-box at hand and it makes me feel chill.[11]

However unromantic the match, Effie took to her new responsibilities. The children adored her and she proved a confident hostess at Abinger Hall. She adopted her husband's politics and would become increasingly radical just as Hope and Julia moved in the opposite direction. Emma Darwin, ever the shrewd observer, found her 'happy but not absorbed in THF'. Hope was impressed with her sister's 'farrification' when Effie came to London in the carriage to take her to a concert. 'She brought out a huge basket stocked with lordly viands & drink. In her single days she would not only have scorned to do so, but wd. have scorned those who did.'[12]

Effie had moved up in the world as a description of the Farrers in their pomp by E. M. Forster suggests. He was not an objective witness. His mother had worked as a governess to the Farrer children. He and she led an insecure existence in the house his father had built for his sister, Laura, just outside the Abinger Hall gates. The Farrers owned the land on which it stood and proved reluctant to extend the original 60-year lease. When Forster's mother died in 1945, he was turned out. His jaundiced description of Effie and TH mixed shrewd novelistic observation with long-standing resentment.

Lord Farrer he remembered as 'a civil hesitating old man with a beard who always tried to get away from the person he was speaking to in order to speak to someone better, & who relied much on his wife'. She was 'amusing, incisive, generous in large matters, mean in small'. As a child, Forster had adored her hair 'bright and beautiful, like a bird of paradise'. By the time she married, it had become 'carroty and crimped'.

> She was ugly like most of the Wedgwood women, but she was vivid and graceful and an assured hostess. [...] She was capricious; she would invite people to see her, and when they arrived it wasn't their day, and she would make small talk in exasperating lilting tones her chin raised and her mind elsewhere the whole time. [...] Though outstandingly intelligent and amusing she was not brainy or even clear-headed; she would get muddled, and at the end of her life she constantly forgot names, and apologized charmingly.

His Aunt Laura was, Forster thought, inspired by the example of the Wedgwood sisters to make a more independent life for herself than some of her friends. She remained close to all three but came to rate Effie below her 'more vindictive sister, Hope' and 'the formidable Snowie', Forster's own favourite.[13]

Marriage weakened the bond between Julia and Effie. Very few letters between them survive from the period after it, and Julia no longer treated Effie as her confidante. She put the best construction she could on her sister's new estate. Farrer was 'most devotedly in love with her. I have never seen livelier affection in a young man, which is a stupid thing to say however for affection is altogether livelier in the old.' Nor had she ever known a marriage with 'so much friendship' (if, by implication, so little passion). Effie's feeling for her husband, such as it was, would always come second to her attachment to Hope.[14]

Hope spent as much time as she could with her sister and resented the aimlessness of her life when they were apart. She and Julia both set about getting on good terms with their new step-niece, Ida. They did it in very different ways: Hope was more successful. While she wrote frequently to her 'very dear pseudo child' singing Effie's praises, Julia took the contrary step of writing about Ida's birth mother and sending her all the letters Fanny

Figure 26 Julia Wedgwood's water colour of the sitting room at 1 Cumberland Place in which she received Robert Browning. Courtesy of the V&A Wedgwood/Mosley Collection.

Farrer had written to her before she was married. 'Dearest child,' she wrote shortly before Effie's wedding, 'how I long to know that all may be under the new regime what your Mother can look upon from her distant home without pain or regret!'[15] Julia's insistence on reminding Ida of her dead mother just when Hope was talking up the attractions of a new one was not good psychology.

With Effie off their hands, the Hensleigh Wedgwoods began to think about their own accommodation and looked for a place in the country. Julia had always associated Cumberland Place with the Sunday mornings when she had sat at the window waiting to see Browning stepping through the park. 'The keenest joy and the keenest pain of my life have looked through those windows with me and neither can return,' she reflected in a letter to Emily Gurney.[16] She made a nice water colour of the sitting room where they had talked. Leaving Cumberland Place was a particular wrench for Julia.

Finding the right house in the country did not prove easy. Their first choice was the picturesque, moted Tudor castle Ightham Mote in Kent, which they rented for a year. Julia adored it, and both she and her father relished its historic and literary associations. But for all its charm, it proved damp and inaccessible. They soon moved to another rented house at Ravensbourne close to the Darwins. Hensleigh, however, wanted to build his own and found a site near Dorking half-way between the Wedgwood family home at Leith Hill Place and the Farrers at Abinger. It would cost far more than he expected. As its name 'Hopedene' suggested, it was intended not only as a permanent home for Hensleigh and Fanny but one that could engage Hope's unfocused energies. She set about making a garden there with her usual flair.

If Julia had hoped that Effie's marriage would bring Hope closer to her, she was soon disillusioned. Her relations with her sisters remained 'a half-healed wound', as she told Henrietta Litchfield in the summer of 1875.[17] That wound was about to deepen.

Effie, as E. M. Forster remembered, 'was managing; she loved planning'.[18] Now she decided to organize her younger sister's future, thinking up a plan that resolved some of her own anxieties too: Hope and Godfrey should marry. Effie may well have felt guilty about Godfrey's hurt feelings when she not only rejected him but also went on to marry another so soon after. Hope had always been the most positive of those she had consulted about marrying Godfrey. For Godfrey, marriage to Hope was a way of staying in touch with Effie. Hope, who was aware of the 'the dangers of Old Maidism',[19] was more than happy to copy her sister's lifestyle with her own house and garden to run. The Farrers invited Godfrey and Hope for a weekend at Abinger in the summer of 1876. By the end of it, they were engaged.

Not everyone approved. Godfrey's sisters, who were never on good terms with Hope, opposed the marriage, while Fanny worried that it would create jealousies among her daughters. While she was probably most concerned about tension between Hope and Effie given Godfrey's continuing attachment to the sister he had not married, she may also, for once, have sensed that the marriages of her two younger daughters could only increase Julia's feeling of exclusion. Emma Darwin certainly sensed that and went out of her way to sit for half an hour with the solitary Julia at Hopedene. As she told her daughter she felt sorry for her. Hope, too, she found 'anxious and depressed', feeling that Godfrey 'dreads the marriage instead of wishing for it'.[20] Apart from her taste for extravagant living, the marriage, however, turned out a happy one upheld by Hope's devotion to Godfrey and the unexpected birth of a child, Mary Euphrasia, in 1880, 'our child' as the childless Effie often called her. Julia spoiled her niece as much as anyone and would in time find the house that Godfrey and Hope built for themselves at Idlerocks near Modershall, the place where she was happiest. But in the summer of 1876, she felt hurt and unloved.

Figure 27 Hope, Julia Wedgwood's youngest sister.

For all Hensleigh's characteristically Wedgwood hankering after the life of a country squire, neither he nor Fanny could do without a London base. In 1874 they began renting 31 Queen Anne Street, a few doors up from Ras Darwin. Here Julia had her own upstairs sitting room where she could invite guests to join her after dinner with her parents. One of her most regular callers was Arthur Munby, and his diaries, now best known for quite other reasons, give a good idea of what it was like to visit her. Munby was 5 years older and had, like her father, studied at Trinity College, Cambridge, where his close friends included Richard Litchfield and Vernon Lushington. He joined Litchfield at the Ecclesiastical Commission, which managed the Church's estates, and also taught evening classes alongside him at the Working Men's College. He became a devotee of Maurice while still at Cambridge but unlike other early Christian Socialists never lost his faith. 'There is nothing left but to let the heart stand up & answer, "I have felt,"' he wrote in his diary in 1859, a sentiment that would also help Julia through her religious doubts in the 1870s.[21] She and Munby had many friends in common, including Cato Lowes Dickinson, who taught art at the Working Men's College alongside Ruskin and Dante Gabriel Rossetti, the Cloughs, Octavia Hill, Emily Davies and Anne Thackeray, at whose house Munby met Browning in 1875, 'airy and sprightly and affecting commonplace fashion'.[22] Munby had also attended the Meeting of the British Association at Oxford in 1860 and heard the debate between Huxley and the Bishop of Oxford about *On the Origin of Species*. He and Julia shared artistic tastes too. He was a minor poet whose work was much admired by Browning, an amateur artist and member of the Pen and Pencil Club and a music lover. They regularly attended the gatherings of the Home Quartett, a private club of music lovers who met in each other's homes, including the Hensleigh Wedgwood's. And both were passionately interested in the Classics and in theology.

She first appears in his diary at a dinner party at the Litchfields in January 1875 where Fenton Hort was also a guest. 'Much able talk on general subjects, and on poor Kingsley' (who had just died), he recorded. After that, he called regularly at Queen Anne's Street sometimes seeing Julia alone and sometimes dining with her parents. He became a firm favourite with them all and was occasionally invited to Hopedene or Abinger for the weekend as Julia's escort. A diary entry for 17 January 1879 contrasts the talk downstairs with that in Julia's 'quiet little bower upstairs':

> To Queen Anne Street at 5, and called on the Hensleigh Wedgwoods. Found Mr and Mrs W alone in the large lofty drawing room – the clever vivacious old lady lying on a sofa by the fire, wrapt in shawls & with books around her: and had a pleasant talk with her & him of books & manners & ghosts. Then upstairs to Miss Julia Wedgwood's room, and a tête à tête with her of more serious kind: of Maurice & Ecce Homo, & Philoctetes & that which these suggest.

Another day he called at teatime and found her 'in a twilight tête à tête with stout and cheery Miss F P Cobbe'. Most often, however, he discovered their mutual friend, Cato Lowes Dickinson, already in his usual chair and 'as charming as ever'.[23]

From the Wedgwoods, Munby might go on to the Athenaeum, and find himself sitting next to the future prime minister, Lord Salisbury, or walk home, stopping for a chat with a milk maid on the way.[24] Working women fascinated Munby. In his own day he was seen as a cultured, courtly and respectable man-about-town. Apparently unattached, he was popular with hostesses. Now he is was primarily remembered for his remarkable double life. Only three of his closest friends knew that the woman they regularly saw at his chambers at the Inner Temple swilling down the stairs or vigorously blacking the grate was his wife. Munby first met Hannah on the streets in 1854. He married her in 1873 but, for all his efforts, failed to persuade her to try and move to his social level or see herself acknowledged as 'Master's' wife. It is very unlikely that Julia, who had her own secrets to keep about Browning, knew anything of Munby's unconventional domestic life until the inevitable scandal emerged after his death in 1910. She left no comment but was probably more intrigued than shocked. She too had come to rely on a relationship that broke the normal rules and outraged several members of her family.

In May 1877 Fanny became seriously ill with an ulcerated leg and heart problems and took to her bed. She was not expected to recover. Julia took over the running of 31 Queen Anne Street and quickly worked a domestic revolution. 'Marian is housekeeper now,' Emma Darwin reported, 'cook is gone and the kitchen maid cooks.'[25] 'Marian' was Mary Ann Hughes, born in Radnorshire in the Welsh Marches in 1848 of a modest family. She went into service early: the 1861 census shows her working as a housemaid in nearby Brecon. Quite how she first came to work for the Wedgwoods is unclear. It is possible that Julia first met her at Caerleon in 1869 or that she was initially employed by Mary Rich, perhaps on the recommendation of one of the Allen sisters. She first appears in Wedgwood family correspondence in 1876 when she nursed the dying Rich. Though without any professional nursing qualifications, she had a gift for it and was regularly loaned out to care for friends and family members or accompany them on their convalescence. When Fanny fell ill, Marian was the one who sat up with her at night. Julia always admired her practical, unemotional way of nursing, as did her mother. It 'begins where sympathy ends', she wrote, defending Marian to Emily Gurney. She was particularly grateful to her for the account she was able to give of Mary Rich's reassuringly peaceful last days. (Once again Julia's deafness had disqualified her from spending time at a deathbed.)[26] Her promotion of Marian to housekeeper was a success. She quickly became indispensable.

By late October 1877, Fanny was well enough to go to Abinger to convalesce, and Julia went on her first visit to Hope and Godfrey since their marriage. Marian travelled with her. Hope was anxious to impress and prove to her oldest sister that she was on top of her new responsibilities. 'Snow's visit was really magnificent & I believe she quite liked me!' she told Ida Farrer with relief. But if Hope felt that she had passed a stiff test, she was more caustic about Marian's chances of success in her new role as Snow's companion: 'I see a cloud not so big as a man's hand in the offing in Marian's want of piety. She called Saint Gourlay the worst old woman she ever knew. [...] She also says it's abominable that clergymen talk such rubbish in the pulpit.'[27]

Hope's awe at her sister's exacting standards misled her. One of the qualities in Marian Hughes that most appealed to Julia was her freshness and lack of undue respect for the elevated intellectual world in which she moved. 'Marian said to me on Good Friday,' she told Jane Gourlay in 1877, 'I never can believe that the text about the camel & the needle has anything to do with money. [...] I think it must be <u>knowledge</u> that is the great difficulty. <u>How</u> hard for clever people to believe there is anything they don't know!'. This scepticism about the claims of the intellectual life mirrored Julia's own anxieties about its limitations. 'I wish I could avoid the sins of intellectualism,' she had written to Effie in 1872. 'I feel the opposite so much that I am sure I must be in danger, and the worst of it is that I do not feel the <u>gains</u> of intellectuality at all securely mine.'[28] With Marian, Julia could relax. Both of them adored animals, and Marian not only was good at nursing the sick and elderly but had a way with children too as Emma Darwin noticed. 'Gwennie' (Raverat as she would become) could hardly be separated from her, she told her daughter. At the same time, she had been surprised to discover how poorly Marian performed at the regular evening sessions of reading aloud, particularly 'as she is Welch [*sic*]'. 'I suppose Snow does not hear,' she speculated.²⁹

Life at 31 Queen Anne Street became increasingly troubled. The still unmarried Erny hung around, while Alfred, who had married precipitately the daughter of a civil engineer in Chile, Rosina Ingall, was attempting the life of a country gentleman in Surrey. The marriage quickly deteriorated. Both liked to come to London to complain about the other. Rosina was also jealous of the liking her son, Berry, had taken to Aunt Snow. By March 1880 Julia had had enough of the strained atmosphere. She moved out, taking Marian with her and set up her own modest household in rooms at 56 George Street, Portman Square, a few minutes' walk away from Queen Anne Street. This was a bold and unconventional move for a spinster with elderly parents. Emma Darwin's eldest sister, Elizabeth, who had stayed with her parents till they died, was outraged. To Emma's annoyance, she wrote to Effie begging her to intervene and put a stop to it.³⁰

Writing about Julia many years later, E. M. Forster picked out her decision as an unusual achievement. 'She had fine qualities of the heart as well as of the head [...] she could, for instance, make a close friendship outside her own class, and though it is easy enough to do this today, owing to the social break-up, it was not easy to do in the nineteenth century.'³¹ The snobbish references to Marian in some Wedgwood family letters show just how difficult it was.

Julia had always longed to be in charge of her own household. Now she had the satisfactions of domestic independence but with Marian taking on the practical cares and leaving her free for her writing. It was not uncommon for widowed and single women to take a companion, though the nature of the relationship varied. Maurice's widow, who became a trouble to everyone after the death of her husband, was obliged to advertise and take whoever she could find. Octavia Hill had a very different relationship with her 'companion' Harriet Yorke, who had her own means and played a much more equal though still supportive role. Marian Hughes like Yorke sat at the dinner table talking to Julia's guests but also ensured each course arrived on time.

Initially, the relationship did not run smoothly. In August 1881 there was a crisis, and Marian, who was often restless, moved out to try something new. Julia was heartbroken. 'I feel so stupid, I am ashamed to write to you,' she told her old confidante Ellen Tollet.

> I did think that here was a life I might make less dreary – but I think there must have been presumption somewhere or I shd. not have been allowed so to miscalculate. Of course there is no disturbing element now Marian is gone – but then I'm afraid that neither is there any love! & so the poor soul finds <u>nothing</u> that she wants in me, for service of course there never was.³²

The recognition of the patrician assumptions she had made in starting the relationship and her vulnerability and emotional isolation are touching aspects of Julia's modesty about herself in middle age. Happily, Marian soon returned. In her later years Julia would refer to her as 'the dear one who shares my life so fully & fills out all my needs'.³³ Marian Hughes was only a little less effusive: 'Dearest Miss Wedgwood. [...] Much Love Yr own

Figure 28 (a) The Wedgwood Home at 31 Queen Anne Street that Julia Wedgwood moved out of. (b) The building at 56 George Street where Julia Wedgwood set up her first independent household.

Figure 28 (continued)

Marian,' she wrote to her in 1897 in a rare surviving letter neatly combining her affection with a dutiful respect.

This unconventional relationship kept Julia anchored to the real world. Marian's letters are full of gossip and sometimes sharp comments on the Wedgwoods, as when she stayed with Hope and Godfrey at Idlerocks with 'a protest going on inwardly to the old-fashioned ways of the family'.³⁴ She enjoyed passing on servants' talk about Julia's grand friends just as Julia, increasingly isolated by her deafness, liked hearing it. Henrietta Litchfield was a particular bugbear, as seen in this quote:

> Mrs Cecil [the family governess Cecil Wedgwood had married] told us a good thing against Mrs L today. I was saying Mrs L had told me her place was a better & easier one than yours for a maid. Georgina (whose sister has lately left Mrs L) Mrs Cecil said, asked Lily one day whether she thought Servants would become mistresses in another life & the Mistress of this life their servants for if so her sister had said she would <u>chivey</u> [sic] Mrs L all over the place if she was her servant. I answered Mrs Cecil that no maid who had ever lived with you would feel like that to you.³⁵

Marian was positive and practical and unlike Arthur Munby's wife had no qualms about assuming her place in company. She also proved particularly good with Julia's nephews, Jem and Berry. Their parents split up in 1885. Alfred, feckless as always, took himself abroad, entrusting the care of his two sons to Julia. Difficult though she found the charge, she took her responsibilities seriously, worrying about finding the right schools for the boys and anxious to keep them away from their mother, who she thought of as 'an evil power'.³⁶ Berry, the older boy, proved more tractable and eventually settled to a respectable career in the army advised by Godfrey on how to keep his mess bills under control. Jem proved much more of a challenge. He was handsome, suave and gifted and would pursue an extraordinary career in the Theosophical Society and as Presiding Bishop of the Old Catholic Church.³⁷

While Julia was able to teach Berry Latin and read Caesar's *Gallic Wars* with him, she was never as comfortable with Jem. 'The care of children not one's own is fraught with too great anxiety,' she confided to Henrietta Litchfield. 'The least successful mother has a certain understanding of her child that I feel so utterly lacking with Jem [...] somehow the very naughtiest child I ever had to do with among us had a sense of kindred with me utterly lacking here.' She blamed the lack of sympathy on his 'half-caste blood' and was upset by his regular returns to his mother.³⁸ Marian had an easier relationship with him and was always on hand to take the boys to the seaside, while the family rallied round inviting them for holidays at Abinger or Idlerocks and contributing to the cost of their education. Whatever the challenges, Julia felt a sense of pride in her ability to offer her own home as a base for her two abandoned nephews.

When Hensleigh came to live with her after Fanny's death in 1889, he was apprehensive about her unusual household. 'I regarded Marian as a necessary drawback,' he wrote to his sister, Emma, 'but I have quite changed my views. I now regard her as a great advantage, adding much to the cheerfulness of the house and making everything so smooth. She is extremely handy in making all arrangements so that neither Snow nor I have the least trouble in housekeeping and she is a very pleasant companion.' While Hensleigh learned to abandon his prejudices and Emma Darwin never had any, others retained their snobbery. Her much younger second cousin, Eliza Wedgwood, thought the whole relationship sprang from Julia's 'Sentimentality' which 'showed itself to her own discomfort'. Hope recognized that Marian's 'rise in life' had cut her off from her own kin but thought she had 'never really assimilated the "culture" (horrid word) that divides one section of persons from another'.[39]

Marian did indeed pay a heavy price for her social dislocation after Julia's death. In the years they were together, however, she gave Julia stability, affection and the all-important sense that another human being depended on her. And Julia trusted her management skills. When she moved early in 1897 from unloved Gower Street to a large house in Holland Park with a welcome view of trees, she left the practical arrangements to Marian, staying at Idlerocks for a couple of months till all was in place at her new home. Domestic contentment freed her to concentrate on her work and cultivate her own social circle. In the 1880s and 1890s, she was at her most settled and productive.

Chapter Thirteen

COMING TO TERMS WITH DARWIN AND HIS LEGACY

Julia struggled to reach an accommodation with Darwinism for well over thirty years. As long as her uncle was alive, she avoided an open attack on him, clinging to the hope that he was more open to religious feeling than he was willing to admit. She, unlike her sisters, walked with pride in the family procession at his funeral in Westminster Abbey but grew increasingly restive over the Anglican establishment's readiness to promote Darwin to secular sainthood. Her frustration at this downplaying of the impact of his ideas erupted when Frank Darwin published a biography of his father. Darwin, she wrote in a review of it in the *Spectator*, had been 'a destroyer'. Only as thoughtful Churchmen like Aubrey Moore found a new basis for reconciling Darwinism with religion did Julia rediscover her original excitement about the promise of her uncle's discoveries.

By contrast, her relationship with Emma Darwin remained remarkably stable. They understood each other well. Emma was readier to make allowances for her niece's singularity than most in the family. She respected Julia's determination to make a career for herself as a writer and set up her own household. As Julia wrote just after her death, she had a 'wonderful power of [...] always remembering that I was I' and giving 'what I wanted'.[1]

Darwin could be less tolerant. Once out of his study, he wanted only to relax, strolling up and down his Sand Walk, playing backgammon with his wife or sitting absorbed as she read aloud some trashy novel with a pretty heroine. Talking about metaphysics into Julia's ear trumpet was wearisome by comparison. Even old Aunt Elizabeth, who had moved to live close to the Darwins in 1868, chafed under the need 'to keep down trivialities & gossip' when her niece was a guest.[2] Emma's first duty was to protect her husband. She told Etty about his gloom one Sunday afternoon in 1870 when the doorbell rang and he feared it was Snow. He brightened up immediately when the statistician William Farrer was announced, who had come to discuss the grim subject of how far the Census might throw light on whether cousin marriages were as harmful to their descendants as Darwin feared. This was much more agreeable than talking about whether Origen was an Epicurean or a Platonist and why it mattered.[3] Darwin had little experience of discussing 'hard' subjects with women. When Emma had thought to read Lyell's *Principles of Geology* as a way of understanding the subjects that absorbed her future husband, he discouraged her.[4] He was delighted with his daughter Etty's work on editing the text of *The Descent of Man* but confined discussion of its substance to Hensleigh, leaving Etty and Julia to conduct a parallel debate. Similarly, when his son, George, helped with revisions to the second edition, Darwin advised him that 'rather rugged sentences do not signify, if they are perfectly clear (i.e. as unlike Snow's as possible)'.[5]

Even so, Julia proved a special case in Darwin's dealings with intellectual women. Just as he had admired her review of *Origin*, so he was greatly struck by her review of *Descent*. He consulted her about the nature of religious feeling, enlisted her help in the research for *The Expression of the Emotions in Man and Animals* (though without fully acknowledging her contribution in his book) and unburdened himself to her late in life on his loss of aesthetic and religious sensibility. Janet Browne, Darwin's biographer, has suggested that 'he felt protective about Julia's literary career, successfully combining the indulgence of a close relative with the intellectual attention he usually reserved for male colleagues'.[6] As Darwin knew, Julia was an influential apologist for his work with an audience he could not address directly.

She had other uses too. He drew on her Classical expertise to commission a translation of Linnaeus and looked to her for examples in the Classics of the expression of emotion; he enjoyed her refutation of Max Müller and thought of including some of her ideas in his own work until she told him Müller was too 'rubbishy' to bother with; and he quizzed her in 1870 about the nature of religious feeling, pressing her hard to admit that this included fear. Julia conceded very reluctantly while Darwin took to his bed after their tortuous discussion.[7] But he had got what he wanted. In *The Descent of Man* he would write about Etty's pet terrier, Polly, being frightened by the sight of a parasol waving in the wind into believing it was being manipulated by some invisible spirit. Savages, he suggested, would have reacted to natural phenomena in the same way though fear then gave way to reverence for unseen powers, which, in turn, grew into love, rather like the feelings a dog had for its master.

Now Emma was unhappy. 'F[ather] is putting Polly in his Man book,' she complained to Etty, 'but I doubt whether I shall let it stand.'[8] The suggestion that devotion to God differed from a dog's feelings towards its master only in degree, not kind, always upset Emma. As she wrote about *Descent* to her daughter, 'I think it will be v. interesting but that I shall dislike it v.m. as again putting God further off.'[9] Julia approached her uncle's book in a more positive spirit. 'Oh Emily,' she wrote to Emily Gurney, 'I cannot tell you how thankful I feel for such books as my Uncle's that drive us from the miserable little corner where we seek to shut up all divine energy and force us to listen to the voice at our ear.'[10]

Darwin had promised at the end of *Origin* that 'light will be thrown on the origin of man and his history'. He collected material for his 'Man book' throughout the 1860s. Some of it on the operation of sexual selection he initially included in *The Variation of Animals and Plants under Domestication* published in 1868. He treated the subject more extensively in *The Descent of Man and Selection in Relation to Sex* published two years later. This dealt not only with man's descent from animal forebears but also the many links and resemblances between the human, animal, avian and insect kingdoms. In the more densely worked second volume, which attracted less attention than the first, he presented sexual selection as of possibly even greater importance than natural selection in determining the evolution of species.[11]

No one could accuse him of sticking narrowly to biology in *Descent*. He courted critical reaction in his theorizing about the distinctions between the sexes and the innate intellectual inferiority of women, the rise and fall of civilizations and the persistence of savagery, the advantages of primogeniture and inequality, the nature of religious feeling, the origins of morality and the moral superiority of some animal species to savage human tribes. *Descent* was in many ways Darwin's most controversial book (as well, perhaps, as his least convincing). He predicted that it would 'be denounced by some as highly irreligious'[12] as, indeed, it was with the *Times*, reasserting its own 'profound conviction of the essential difference between man and the rest of creation'.[13] Cobbe, too, who accepted the theory of man's descent from the animals objected to Darwin's 'simious theory of morals'. (Her reward was a letter from Emma Darwin privately agreeing and describing herself as 'a traitor in the camp'.)[14] Most of the reviewers attacked his ideas about the fundamental lack of distinction between man and the rest of creation and about how morality had developed. But their tone was generally respectful.

Soon after publication, Darwin singled out two that had caught his eye. One was Alfred Wallace's in the *Academy*. The other was in the *Spectator* (whose first review had been highly critical of Darwin's naturalistic explanation of the development of morality).[15] 'I have been greatly interested by the second article in the Spectator,' he wrote to Etty.[16] Though it contained a number of Julia's authorial fingerprints, Darwin initially failed to recognize it as hers. Perhaps he was surprised by her ability to explore aspects of his argument that other reviewers missed.

Had she chosen, she could have challenged her uncle's views on the female sex. In *Descent* he wrote of women's mental inferiority to men. Though he admitted their greater powers of 'intuition [...] rapid perception, and perhaps of imitation', he dismissed these as 'faculties [...] characteristic of the lower races, and therefore of a past and lower state of civilisation'. Sexual inequality would, Darwin predicted, intensify because sexual characteristics were transmitted at an early stage from parents of the same sex. For the time being, Julia avoided this contentious area, reserving it for one of her most original articles 'Male and Female Created He Them' written nearly twenty years later where she played with Darwin's ideas about the parental dissemination of sexual characteristics to develop a feminist theology that would have surprised him.[17]

She also avoided Darwin's naturalistic explanation of religious feeling and the development of morality. This was not out of lack of interest. When Darwin corresponded about it with her father when he was preparing a second edition of *Descent*, Julia and Etty followed their dialogue closely.[18] But this was a debate for private family consumption. In her review she avoided both the issue of morality (which attracted a great deal of attention) and the question of innate sexual inequality (which attracted very little). Instead, she focused on the disagreement between Darwin and the Duke of Argyll over what Argyll called 'creative evolutionism'. This enabled her to argue that her uncle was still, at heart, a Theist.

Argyll, a leading politician and exceptionally large landowner, was also a writer on evolution whose books and articles in *Good Words* were widely read. He argued that man's evolution could only have been the outcome of divine intervention. How, he asked, could primitive man, still developing his superior mental faculties, have prevailed against the greater physical strength of the apes without divine help? Nor could he accept Darwin's views on the way sexual selection worked to support natural selection. The colour, beauty and diversity of avian plumage were not there to serve the utilitarian function of attracting a mate but proof of the aesthetic sense of the Creator which was shared by his Creation.

Huxley refused to read Argyll and Hooker was dismissive: Darwin was more cautious. It did not do to offend a leading aristocrat and influential writer who broadly accepted the mechanism of natural selection even though he saw it as operating by design rather than accident.

Julia, like Charles Kingsley and Asa Gray, was fond of Argyll's writings, though she knew he could not compare with her uncle as a scientist.[19] She introduced Darwin with a flourish at the start of her article as 'our great philosophical naturalist' before turning to his disagreement with the Duke. Both pointed to the extraordinary diversity and beauty of the natural world. The question this raised was whether it was 'accidental'. Darwin had given many examples from the avian and human kingdom of the multiplicity of small variations. 'The tendency to vary within the limits of a certain uniformity is implanted in the Creative force itself.' Why were 'mischievous variations' 'quickly extinguished' while beneficial ones were 'perpetuated and accumulated' under natural selection? Though most of the reviewers ignored Darwin's views on sexual selection, Julia correctly picked them out as 'a very strong subsidiary selecting cause' in natural selection. Some of the examples he had given of animal preference for strength and beauty as well as variety delighted her. 'The most inconveniently long tail of the peacock, which must be as bad as Court dress that cannot be taken off, is the commonest instance of such a variety.' She quoted too Darwin's description of the female Argus pheasant's appreciation of the ball-and-socket ornaments of the male. Argyll claimed that these were aesthetically so subtle they could only be God-given: Darwin had a naturalistic explanation: 'the female having preferred through many generations the more highly ornamented males; the aesthetic capacity of the females having been advanced through exercise of habit, in the same manner as our own taste is gradually improved'. Here, Julia argued, was another part of 'the great central law of creation'.

While agreeing with Argyll that the operation of natural selection was not accidental, Julia sided with her uncle on the fundamental point of whether man should be distinguished from the rest of creation. The anthropomorphism of *Descent* with its affectionate references to dogs and case studies of simian bravery delighted rather than appalled her. Like her uncle, she was drawn to examples of social values and community cohesion in the animal world. She quoted at length his appealing description of a colony of ants[20] which made her think of the similar degree of 'most extraordinary industry and the most wonderful co-operation' in ancient Egypt. Similarly, the bowerbird's habit of decorating her nest with an ever-varying collection of shells to attract a mate was an 'anticipation in the lower animal world of the sort of sudden flush of artistic civilization among the Greeks'. But neither social instinct nor aesthetic sense was uniformly distributed in the natural world: apes had less appreciation of beauty than birds, while dogs lacked the organizing ability of ants but were more likely to be affectionate. Similarly, not all humans had advanced at the same rate.

In drawing conclusions from this multiplicity and looking for underlining laws or principles, Julia relied on both Natural and Christian Theology.[21] Darwin's suggestion that it was man's physical weakness that had accounted for his compensating development of superior mental power and recognition of the need to cooperate for the common good reminded her of St Paul's 'paradox of weakness being stronger than strength'. Similarly, she found in Darwin's awkward explanation of why savagery remained in some primitive tribes a faint suggestion of Argyll's supposition of a primal state of perfection from which man had fallen. She went even further, finding in Darwin a possible explanation of the origin of sin.

Darwin's universe, she concluded, was one in which 'a Creative force' had tentatively brought into being a vast number of variations to see which would predominate,

> creating very high forms of intellectual instinct at the very threshold of the world of life, – gradually mingling the love of beauty with the instinct of self-preservation [...] rooting, however, all its greatest achievements, both intellectual and moral, in the sense of weakness, and overcoming this sense of weakness only by the most wonderful and noble of all the forces of the universe, disinterested affection, – finally, when this moral affection is once fairly generated, gradually depriving the higher beings of the instincts by which the lower had been preserved, and giving them in the place thereof the power to create and mould their own instincts, and even to spoil and grievously sin against such instincts as were left them, if they would, – in other words, giving them love, reason, freedom, conscience, the power to sin.

'Is this', she triumphantly asked, 'in any sense whatever – even conceivably an atheistic philosophy?' The only question that remained was why the creative force was so 'tentative'. The answer, she suggested, lay in 'a future still far beyond our comprehension'.

She ended with a teasing but considered signal to her uncle that Darwinism was part of the best tradition of British science in its demonstration of God's purposes for His creation through the enlightened study of the natural world: 'For our own parts,' she wrote, 'we find Mr Darwin's investigation of the origin of man a far more wonderful vindication of Theism than Paley's Natural Theology, though we do not know, so reticent is his style, whether or not he so conceives it himself.'[22]

Accurate or not, Darwin was not likely to object to an article in the *Spectator*, reclaiming him as a Theist. 'He thinks it most remarkable, "It is very clever" he said twice over,' Fanny reported. Emma was deputed to write and congratulate Snow:

> 'Charles tells me to say that he has been much pleased with your notice of his views & he thinks you have given it very correctly as far as a few words could do so.' Snow was also 'the sole person, except pure naturalists, who have noticed this part [on the importance of sexual selection] with approbation'.[23]

Despite his admiration for her review, Darwin chose to discuss the question of how man's moral sense developed with Hensleigh rather than his daughter when he wanted to clarify his argument for the second edition of *Descent*. Their discussion was not productive. Though Hensleigh advocated an exclusively naturalistic view of the development of human speech, he was not to be persuaded that man's moral sense originated in the conflict between what Darwin described as permanent and transient instincts. In a lengthy correspondence, neither convinced the other. Hensleigh's conclusion was terse, 'I do [not] see how the notion of a moral God would arise out of your premises.'[24]

Julia and Etty followed these exchanges from the sidelines. Though Julia longed to join in, she did not want to trouble her uncle directly. Instead, she 'tumble[d] out' her concerns to her cousin. She was particularly anxious to dismiss Darwin's concept of 'self-regarding virtues' which he described as the sort of behaviour, like temperance, that society rewarded. For Julia, virtue was an absolute. 'I do so thoroughly feel <u>nothing</u> is self-regarding in that sense. We radiate whatever we are,' she wrote, recalling what her grandfather, James Mackintosh, had written about 'innate disposition' rather than utility as the motive of right conduct. Etty was troubled by her certainties and even more confused after a long conversation. 'The difficulty', Etty wrote when attempting to summarize their discussion, 'is to trace [God's] influence in the world around – this to her is lessened by Development theory. The making of it one whole far from making God recede brings him into an ever present attitude to the world.' But Etty was left wondering whether Huxley was not right to say that questions about the afterlife, the coexistence of good and evil and free will were 'hopeless', even though 'the preachers of science try to conceal that they are taking away what they have no equivalent for'.[25]

How we express 'whatever we are' was something that had long fascinated Darwin. In *Descent* he had commented on the similarity between human and simian faces and the way they expressed emotion. He explored this further in *The Expression of the Emotions in Man and Animals* (1872), his least theoretical but most accessible and popular book. He enlisted lots of collaborators, not just scientists and anthropologists but also family and friends, including an unusually large number of young women who delighted in describing the facial expressions of their children or the mannerisms of foreigners encountered on their travels.[26] Julia was as enthusiastic as any.

She became directly involved in Darwin's consideration of whether humans covered their faces when ashamed and his wish to trace this as far back as possible. Etty was sure there were examples in the Old Testament but could not pin them down. Julia with her greater knowledge of Biblical and Classical sources disagreed. Shame, she curiously suggested (quietly undermining one of her uncle's explanations for the development of a moral sense in man), was a 'nineteenth century bit of picturesqueness' and not an emotion known to the Greeks.[27] Reflecting further, she did come up with an obscure though ambiguous reference in Macrobius's *Saturnalia*. Darwin used it without acknowledgement, though he did refer in a footnote to a translation she made for him from Antoine Charma's *Essai sur Langage*. (Hensleigh, by contrast, got several citations in the main text.) For obvious reasons, however, he could not attribute to Julia some information that interested him much more. She had told Etty about a meeting that her friend Jane Gourlay had had in a hospital for venereal diseases when she visited a young 'fallen woman'. The girl had pulled up the sheet on her bed and refused to show her face. Darwin included this incident (in sanitized form) in his text, acknowledging only 'a lady' as his source.[28]

The Expression of Emotions was Darwin's least doctrinaire book. Its suggestion of a continuum between animal and human expressions of pain, fear and satisfaction appealed particularly to Julia as her concern with animal causes continued to grow. In 1871 she had written to Emily Gurney that though scientists did not yet recognize what they were doing, 'I think in the conviction that they are deepening in all our minds – of the unity of Nature, they are preparing the way for our reception of it as a Parable, though meanwhile their refusal to see it as this tells hurtfully on them'.[29]

After the publication of *The Expression of Emotions*, Darwin abdicated any claim to be a 'philosopher', turning to the study of insectivorous plants, orchids and, later, earthworms. He was far more comfortable with facts than metaphysics. For Julia, constantly looking for some new development of thought that would revive a complacent Church, her early hope that Darwin's revelation of a purposive improving creation would provide this was increasingly frustrated. In 1872 when she was staying at Down, she wrote to Emily Gurney: 'You know how I cling to these "sermons in stones" here feeling so much the painful atmosphere of a mind that has explored Nature only to find no trace of mind there – nothing but the working of chance.'[30]

Darwinian biology was not the only new area of science where Julia looked for theological meaning. Many saw the developing theory of conservation of energy, later formalized as the first law of thermodynamics, as of equal importance to Darwin's theory of evolution and far more easily accorded religious significance. The 'correlation of forces', as Julia usually called it, posited that though energy could be neither created nor destroyed, it could be converted from one medium to another, as with heat from light or steam from the interaction of heat and water. In his controversial presidential address to the British Association for the Advancement of Science in Belfast in 1874, John Tyndall described the discovery of the 'latent powers' in matter as 'the manifestation of a Power absolutely inscrutable to the intellect of man'.[31] But while Tyndall saw this as 'a higher materialism' with the operation of a self-contained system of energy exchange confirming that the scientist could exclude the supernatural, others saw it very differently. The most widely read exponents of a spiritual interpretation of the conservation of energy came from the northern universities: Peter Tait, the Professor of Natural Philosophy at Edinburgh, and Balfour Stewart, the Scottish Professor of Physics at Owens College, Manchester. In their *The Unseen Universe or Physical Speculations on a Future State*, first published in 1875 anonymously, like several of the most influential nineteenth-century best sellers, they attacked Tyndall's deterministic naturalism. For them the energy operating throughout the visible world of matter originally came from the invisible ether to which it would return.[32]

Grounded in German *Naturphilosophie* with its sense of an essential unity of structure and purpose in the universe, *The Unseen Universe* had an immediate appeal for Julia. Here was the reconciliation between science and religion she had hoped to find in Darwin's work, a demonstration of the connection between the visible and the invisible, the natural and the supernatural. In 1877 in an article on one of her favourite writers, the eighteenth-century mystic William Law, she would suggest that he had prefigured the discovery of 'the correlation of forces', while even as late as 1907 when physics had moved on, she could still describe the theory as a source of 'a new imaginative delight'.[33]

According to Julia, Darwin recognized that the conservation of energy theory might even prove a more important discovery than his own or the law of gravitation. The contentious professional discourse on the implications of the new theory, however, could only have confirmed his reluctance to weigh down his own science with theology.[34] In his last years, Julia became increasingly frustrated by her uncle's refusal to look beyond the natural world. Surprisingly, however, he initiated a long conversation with her shortly before he died about why he was no longer the Theist he had believed himself to be at the time he was writing *Origin*. She described the conversation at the time to Ellen Tollett and again, after his death, in a letter to his son, Frank:

> One day when I was standing in the dining room [...] he came up quite abruptly & began without any preface in a way as if the subject had been much in his mind –'The reason that I can never give in to the belief that <u>we are all naturally inclined to</u>, of a first cause' he did not say a personal first cause, but he gave the impression of meaning that 'is that I look upon all human feeling as traceable to some germ in the animals' & then he went on to tell me why this seemed to him to conflict with the other.

For Julia, who had delighted in his descriptions in *The Descent of Man* of the similarities between human, animal, avian and insect species, this had never been the problem that it became for Darwin. 'I never understood', she wrote to Frank, 'what he did mean in that, why it should be any difficulty in the way of belief in God that we were descendants of the animals & the inheritors of their impulses.'

She connected this conversation with an earlier one when Darwin had described to her his steady loss of aesthetic feeling.

> He twice referred to his turning back to books he had read with great interest in youth and finding the interest was gone. One was Wordsworth's Poems, wh. as you know are full of his marks / as a young man / & yet he sd. that at the time he spoke (about 1874 or 5) he could not possibly read them, & that he was always finding obscurity where he never remembered any difficulty in the past.

Julia had suggested to him that this was because the meaning of a line of poetry could not be put into other words. 'Ah yes,' her uncle had replied, 'I suppose it is just that, & nobody understands Science unless they can. The habit of looking for one kind of meaning I suppose deadens the perception of another.' 'I felt', Julia concluded, 'this conversation threw a strong light on his Religion.'[35]

Whatever her disillusionment, Julia tried to take comfort from the manner of Darwin's dying less than nine months after the death of his older brother Ras on 26 August 1881. By then two of their sisters were dead as were Emma's oldest brother, Joe, who had married Darwin's sister, Caroline, and Emma's oldest sister, Elizabeth. Ras had been in poor health and low spirits for some time. 'I wish', he wrote to Fanny, 'we had a telephone between our respective beds & then at 2 AM we might ask Is life worth living & ascertain the decreasing value as the hours went on.' She was with him at the end. Everyone respected her right of first choice of a keepsake: she wanted only 'a little low what-not' and his pocket edition of her father's favourite poet, Milton.[36] She did not attend his funeral.

At Down the following summer, she asked Emma to show her the grave. Emma complied a little uncomfortably wondering whether Fanny might rather have been alone with her memories of the friend who had done so much over the years to make up for the shortcomings in her marriage.[37] The family chose Julia to memorialize Ras. She wrote a letter of appreciation to the *Spectator* and later expanded it into an article for the *Bedford College Magazine*. She took her cue from a comparison Charles Darwin liked to make between his older brother and another gifted but idiosyncratic bachelor, Charles Lamb, one of Julia's personal heroes. 'The society of Erasmus Darwin had, to my mind, much the same charm. [...] There was the same kind of playfulness, the same lightness of touch, the same tenderness, perhaps the same limitations.' 'His memory', she wrote, thinking back to her closeness to him as a girl, 'retains something of a youthful fragrance, his influence gave much happiness, of a kind usually associated with youth.' Frank Darwin would later reproduce this gentle tribute in his biography of his father.[38]

Standing heavily wrapped up as the snow fell at Ras's funeral, Charles Darwin knew his own end was close. He died at home in the afternoon of 19 April 1882 with Emma and three of his children at his side. The family prepared to bury him next to Ras in the Downe churchyard. Huxley, John Lubbock and Francis Galton were never going to allow that. They wanted to see Darwin interred in the English Pantheon, Westminster Abbey.[39]

Emma did not attend her husband's funeral there. Effie and Hope also stayed away, but though she was too immobile to take part in the procession, Fanny headed the list of lady mourners who were given seats close to the grave.[40] Julia walked ahead of her father and brothers, alongside Margaret Vaughan Williams, the widowed mother of a 10-year-old boy who would turn out to be the next great Wedgwood genius. (Only Emma Darwin seems to have noticed anything special about young Ralph at this stage.)[41]

The Abbey was thronged with Britain's intellectual aristocracy, and tributes in the newspapers were uniformly respectful. Indeed, the *Times* went so far as to suggest that 'the Abbey needed [the body of the great naturalist] more than it needed the Abbey'.[42] In his Sunday sermon, just three days before the funeral, Canon Alfred Berry had reassured his congregation that 'the principle of selection was by no means alien to the Christian religion, but it was selection exercised under the Divine intelligence and determined by the spiritual fitness of each man for life hereafter'.[43]

Julia was uncomfortable with Darwin's sanctification. Berry's sermon in the Abbey was just the sort of theological claptrap she distrusted. A week after the funeral, she explained her confusion to Asa Gray. But first she described her uncle's death, making as much as she could of his last words to Emma, 'I am not the least afraid to die. Remember what a good wife you have been.' 'I love to dwell on [them],' she told Gray, 'for they conveyed to me, but perhaps wrongly, the impression that the grave did not close all anticipation to him so absolutely as I feared.' The words were indeed deeply loving and comforting – but less than Julia, with her intense investment in the reality of an afterlife, implied.[44]

Asa Gray would write to her that Darwin's death was 'like the annihilation of a good bit of what is left of my own life'. Julia shared his sense that the death marked the end of an epoch:

> What a blank it is! One looks up & the whole horizon seems changed by the absence. His figure was like a lofty tree, a principal object of interest to those who had not much else of common contemplation / & who looked in totally different directions/. It was a very interesting nature, very far from faultless in my opinion, but richly endowed in some directions, & singularly free from some of the most ordinary failings attendant on great fame. My intercourse with him was very slender [she wrote with her usual fairness] but it tinged, I now feel, a large part of my life.

Though she would not particularize his faults so soon after his death, she reacted strongly against the uncritical praise of Darwin:

> I wish obituary notices were less indiscriminately eulogistic. One wants, at such a time, no approach to censure, but the very fact that all censure is excluded should make praise temperate, for where so much is said one wants the whole said.[45]

Saying 'the whole' was a challenge Julia would mull over for five years. In the immediate aftermath of her uncle's death, she paid a more personal tribute. She asked her aunt to let her paint his study. Emma steeled herself to go in for the first time since her husband's death and ensure that everything was in its usual place as Julia prepared her record of Darwin's dedication to his scientific calling.

In the customary Victorian way, a biography prepared by a close associate or family member was set in train. Frank Darwin, the Darwins' third son, who had acted as his father's secretary and scientific assistant, was the obvious choice to write it. He knew from the start that presenting his father's views on religion would be the most difficult part of his assignment.

He asked Julia to share her understanding of his father's views. She responded with alacrity. 'It is a deeply interesting subject to me and my ideas about it are rather definite […] the attempt to gather up the fragments of memories & thoughts extending over about 40 years is a valuable one to myself,' she replied while courteously admitting it ' is very likely what I say shd prove worthless to you'.[46] She pointed him to a letter from Darwin to William Graham, the author of *The Creed of Science*. As Julia read it, this hinted at an ambivalence between Theism and agnosticism in Darwin's thinking. Frank later included it in his biography. He made less use of Julia's account of his views on religion.

Her letter mixed shrewd suggestions with wishful thinking. She began by identifying his refusal to take up the sort of confrontational stance Huxley enjoyed as the key to his standing and influence:

> What strikes everyone in your father's writings is his complete neutrality on [religion]. […] I do not know any other great man of science of whom we could say this, & in my opinion it has been a great source of his influence. […] His books […] are a manifestation of Science in its absolute purity. This gives them a coolness & repose, unlike any other written in the last 30 years.

But in private she had sensed a growing hostility towards religion. What surprised her was the inverse relationship between organized religion's attitudes to Darwin and his to it. 'He was far more sympathetic with religion when his books were considered wicked by the religious world, than when (as was the case for some years before he died) the dignitaries of the Church were eager to pay him the highest honour.' To explain the contradiction, she went back to a conversation in the 1850s when Darwin had first explained to her his ideas on natural selection and she had reacted with horror. 'I […] remember […] his last words "I cannot conceive any <u>wish</u> about the matter one way or the other."' Religion, Julia suggested, was for Darwin a disturbance from the scientific task, an influence '*that adulterated the evidence of fact.* And I think he felt this all the more because he was not so entirely without it himself as he thought he was'.

She sensed a struggle in Darwin's mind, laying great stress on his words to her in their late conversation that 'we are all naturally inclined' to belief in 'a first cause'. She had, she said, 'heard them with extreme surprise'. They reinforced her view that her Uncle 'recognized with a certain sympathy' the 'tendency to look back to some initial Will beyond the forces of Nature'. But though he may have remained a reluctant Theist, Julia acknowledged his growing aversion to the idea of God's continuing intervention.[47]

She also linked her uncle's changing attitude towards religion to his declining aesthetic sensibility, a point that Darwin also made in his 'Recollections of the Development of My Mind and Character'. Frank wanted to include this in his biography, sensibly concluding that the fairest way of explaining Darwin's views on religion was to present them in his own words. In his 'Recollections', Darwin ran through his growing doubts starting with the Old Testament's portrayal of a vengeful God. He had then questioned the uniqueness of the Christian revelation; the evidence for miracles; and the reliability of the New Testament. The doctrine of eternal punishment for non-believers was particularly 'damnable'. Nor could he believe in 'a personal God'. But though he inclined towards thinking that natural selection occurred by accident rather than design, he avoided taking a firm position on whether the extent of suffering he had observed in the animal world proved or disproved the existence of an 'intelligent first cause'. The 'most usual argument' for God, he wrote, was 'the deep inward conviction and feelings which are experienced by most persons'. But these were not confined to Christians. Similarly, although as a young man, he had seen the sublimity of nature as confirmation of his belief in God and the immortality of the soul, his appreciation of natural beauty had dimmed. At the time that he wrote *Origin* he had seen himself as a Theist. Now he was less certain. Was it possible, he wondered, for man to reach valid conclusions on belief in God given man's origins in the lowest animals? Perhaps, this was simply an inherited feeling arising from the ideas with which children were inculcated from an early age. 'The mystery of all things', he concluded 'is insoluble by us; & I for one must be content to remain an Agnostic.' But, with or without religious convictions, man should always act for the good of others and follow 'his inmost guide or conscience'.[48]

Julia read Darwin's account intently, welcoming its 'absolute sincerity & directness'. Like the great scientist he was, Darwin had written 'with a singular attention to truth', offering 'an impartial record of the attitude of an important mind to an important subject'. Much of what he wrote was familiar territory. She particularly liked the fact that his objections to Christianity centred on the moral unacceptability of some of its dogmas and his recognition that the origin of Creation remained a mystery. 'I have been very glad myself to read the sketch in its integrity,' she wrote to Etty, '& feel that it has done as much to fortify my beliefs in the ultimate truths which seem to me more valuable than Science as to raise my appreciation of the fine qualities of his nature some of which I had never seen so clearly exhibited before.'[49] Like Frank, she thought it should be published as it stood.

So did Darwin's sons subject only to any omissions their mother wanted. Etty disagreed provoking a furious family row. In essence she was trying to reassert the role of editor she had successfully played for her father. But her concern to turn his attractively informal script into the sort of finished piece of writing she had previously helped him create irritated her brothers, though Frank did his best to answer her criticisms.[50] While he brought in Leslie Stephen as a respected outside authority, Etty invited Julia to mediate.

The outcome was not what she expected. Julia favoured publishing a largely unamended text but, in an effort to be helpful, prepared an edited version. This omitted a few 'slap-dash sentences' and uncharacteristic statements, added a few glosses such as comparing Darwin's declining aesthetic sensibility with colour blindness, but kept most of the original. 'I wish as much as possible of what he said here to be given to the world,' she wrote to Etty. 'What he has here written would be of service to Christianity.'

The largely anodyne statement she produced of Charles Darwin's growing reservations about religion could almost have been written by a thoughtful Liberal Anglican of the day. 'All I have here copied is what I am sure he <u>deliberately</u> thought & the greater part is what all must feel an objection to Christianity, as far as it goes,' she assured Etty. So she retained Darwin's abhorrence of eternal damnation; included his objection to reconciling the idea of a beneficent God with the extent of suffering in the world, especially amongst animals; and his admission that the eventual end of the world predicted by scientists would not be so terrible if one believed in the immortality of the soul. And she kept Darwin's statement that even those who did not believe in a personal God or in the afterlife should observe moral imperatives. In essence, this presented Darwin as the man of science patiently testing the evidence as he confronted the greatest questions of all but confessing his failure to find definitive answers while nonetheless asserting the pre-eminent importance of morality.[51]

Etty liked Julia's version: 'it is far less crude, misrepresenting arrogant and unworthy of the best part of his mind – so that if he had written what she has put down, I shd. have felt differently about it'. But that was the problem: Julia's text was not what Darwin had written. Richard Litchfield, a bolder free-thinker than either his wife or his father-in-law, immediately objected. 'She is more biased than she thinks,' he excitedly complained, 'by her <u>triumphant delight in feeling the case against Christianity to be so poorly set out</u>'. Her proposed redraft was 'absolutely & <u>utterly impossible</u>'.[52] Etty sent it on to Frank, nonetheless. Given Litchfield's reservations, he did not use it.

The family battle continued without Julia as Etty threatened to go to court.[53] Emma insisted on just two omissions: Darwin's condemnation of the 'damnable doctrine' of everlasting punishment for unbelievers and his suggestion that children were so inculcated with religious belief that it was as hard for them to throw it off as for a monkey to give up its fear of a snake.[54] But Etty wanted more. Under pressure Frank conceded, including the deletion of Darwin's concluding paragraph about his devotion to the scientific life, which Julia particularly hoped to retain but Etty thought too private.

Though the intensity of the family disagreement had marginalized Julia's attempt to resolve it, Frank was glad to accept her professional opinion that they could publish an edited text without indicating where omissions had been made. The text of his father's autobiography, apart from the section on religion, was included near the beginning of the *Life and Letters*. A separate short chapter on religion contained the censored section from the 'Recollections', Darwin's letter to Julia in 1861 on accidental versus providential design, another to Asa Gray on the same subject, an 1879 letter to John Fordyce, denying that he had ever been an atheist but describing himself 'generally (& more & more as I grow older), but not always [...] an Agnostic' and the letter to W. S. Graham.[55]

Frank Darwin's hesitancy in making pronouncements about his father's views on religion[56] fit nicely with the appealing image of Darwin he evoked elsewhere. His chapter on domestic life at Down House presented an unthreatening figure readers could warm to: a man who was indulgent to his dogs; a wise, understanding and generous father; someone who preferred 'Miss Austen' to George Eliot and got fussed before he had to travel; a country gentleman who treated servants with consideration and did his duty to the villagers of Downe. Frank also described his father's careful scientific methods, his economical use of time and his discipline in keeping up a massive correspondence. Darwin emerged as the epitome of unshowy English virtue.

Though Etty had warned Frank of a hostile reaction to publication of the 'Recollections', Julia's prediction proved more accurate. Darwin's account of himself has become one of the classics of autobiography. Its approachable style and modest record of the author's hard-working life and love for his family softened the harsh implications of his scientific discoveries. His air of genuine puzzlement was far removed from the combative world of Huxley's Agnosticism let alone the atheism of Edward Aveling, who tried to claim him for his own persuasion, a claim politely but firmly dismissed in the biography.[57]

There was, however, one jarring note in the *Life*. Frank had invited Huxley to contribute a chapter on the reception of *On the Origin of Species*. This gave an interesting account of the changing climate of scientific opinion before and after the publication of *Origin*, alongside Huxley's usual triumphalism about the victory of science over dogmatic religion. Evolution, he argued, was 'a more adequate expression of the universal order of things than any of the schemes which have been accepted by the credulity and welcomed by the superstition of seventy later generations of men'.[58]

The biography was published in November 1887. Emma liked the look of it and ordered up 150 copies to give to friends and family. They would have been stacked up at the Grove awaiting despatch when Julia came to stay for two days late in the month. 'I have enjoyed nice talks with Snow,' Emma reported to Etty, though she was puzzled when she suddenly got up and left the room when Frank looked in on one of his regular evening calls.[59] The reason became clear when the *Spectator* published a third review of the *Life and Letters* on 10 December.

It was one of only two hostile reviews. The other by the Catholic naturalist, St George Mivart, in the *Edinburgh Review* was expected. Julia's in the *Spectator* was not. The Darwin sons saw it as an act of treachery, particularly as she went out of her way to leave clues about her authorship that could have been picked up outside the family circle. She referred to her late conversation with Darwin; she drew attention to his letter to Graham; and she trotted out her theory that Lucretius had got to the theory of evolution before Darwin (something she had already written about in the *Spectator*).[60]

Though her article was dense, its argument was forthright: Darwinian evolution could be reconciled with Christianity, but Darwin had chosen not to try. However admirable his personal qualities, she wrote, Darwin was 'a destroyer'. And yet, to believe in a Heavenly Father and in miracles like the parting of the Red Sea was, she defiantly asserted at the outset, to 'think more truly of this universe in which we live than Charles Darwin thought of it'.

She began by describing the sort of comfortable, unquestioning religion familiar to many of her readers that Darwinism had destroyed. 'The average Christian in the pre-Darwinian age felt that he knew very little about religion, and that if he tried to think much on the subject, he found it dull,' she wrote, describing the faith that had nurtured Emma Darwin. 'He might not have much religious conviction at first-hand, but he felt dimly that greater and better men had it, and that he wished to be one with them. [...] This is the kind of Christianity that modern science has made impossible [...] the works of Darwin and his contemporaries have been a torpedo-touch to the life of faith.' Yet though Darwin's theories contradicted the Bible account of creation, belief in the literal truth of the opening chapters of Genesis was not essential to Christian faith. Had he wished, his discoveries might have become part of 'our religious education'. His move away from Theism, and the potency of his example, however, had forestalled that. 'Charles Darwin's Theism', she wrote, reflecting a passage in the 'Recollections', 'faded from his mind without disturbance, without perplexity, without pain. [...] He denied nothing, he consciously opposed nothing; but so far as he swayed men's thoughts, they turned from the Invisible.'

She allowed that though some of his followers welcomed their liberation from religion, Darwin did not. But any distinction between true and false Darwinism became insignificant in the context of the new antagonism that had developed between science and faith. The old understanding of science and religion as different aspects of a universal truth had been broken when scientists like Darwin concentrated only on the visible and denied the existence of the invisible. Julia made her point with a quotation from St Paul: ' "The Invisible things of God are clearly seen, being understood by the things that are made" said St Paul. "The invisible things of God are possibly nothing at all", say, and say quite sincerely, those who know much more of the things that are made than St Paul did.' This new materialism, rather than concerns over theodicy, lay at the heart of 'that great antagonism of our day which he did so much to further'.

Evolution was essentially progressive. This, Julia argued, expanding on what she had written in her early review of *Origin*, focused attention on the afterlife. The very fact that man, though improving, was still imperfect demonstrated the need for another world of completion: 'death is an end of nothing but our relation to the things we see. [...] A God exhausted in his creation is no inevitable part of evolution, however much for the moment it be the creed of evolutionists.' Of course, the 'struggle for existence', a description she preferred to 'survival of the fittest', raised 'lacerating' questions about the meaning of suffering. But for Julia and her readers, this was not a new concern. The existence of evil and pain would always be a 'vast' 'obstacle to faith'. But for 'the spirit which feels itself in contact with the Infinite' some explanation was always possible. Only for those, like Charles Darwin, who had turned away from the invisible, did faith fail to provide an adequate answer.[61]

Why did Julia go out of her way to attack her uncle's influence and ideas? Why was the tone of her review harsher than the comments she had given Etty about her father's memoir when she first read it? She may well have felt piqued about the way her suggestions on how to present Darwin's views on religion had mostly been ignored at the same time as Huxley had been allowed his combative say. The reverential consensus emerging around Darwin's posthumous standing also provoked Julia's passion for contrary truth-telling. Perhaps, too, she was influenced by Etty's overheated concerns that publication of her father's 'Recollections' would turn him into 'an assailant of the ordinary faith of England'.[62] Above all, however, in insisting on inserting a third much more critical review of the Darwin biography in the *Spectator*, Julia was assuming her duty to her readers. Her obligation to acknowledge the damage done to the faithful by Darwinism and to try now to guide and console them was one she would not shirk even at the price of upsetting her cousinage.

Emma Darwin never commented on the substance of Julia's review, though she did criticize its tone: 'There is a great assumption of superiority in it which sets Frank's back up tremendously,' she wrote to Etty, also enclosing an outraged letter from Leonard Darwin.[63] But though she disliked her niece's authorial voice, she could not discount the sincerity of her attempt to reinstate a faith that both believed had been undermined by his work. She also shared much of Julia's theodicy. When the Darwin family was in one of its many crises in June 1861, she took the unusual step of writing to her husband: 'the only relief to my mind is to take it from God's hand, and to try to believe that all suffering and illness is meant to help us to exalt our own minds and to look forward with hopes to a future state'.[64] Unlike her more sceptical children, Emma was not disposed to condemn. In writing later about this difficult period in her mother's life, Etty chose her words carefully: 'It was a time of intense feeling for her, but I think there were no reviews that vexed her.'[65] Clearly, this was intended to cover the most controversial of them all, her niece's attack on her husband's legacy.

Emma's overriding feeling was regret at the upset that publication of Darwin's thoughts on religion had caused to family members like her sister-in-law, Caroline, who died that year. Though she saw little of the Darwin sons, Julia soon resumed her visits to her aunt and would spend Christmas 1894 with her and the Litchfields in Cambridge.[66] In January 1895 she scribbled a note to Emily Gurney while on the train to Cambridge for her fourth visit in as many months: 'I am glad of every one in its way [...] it always seems to me very strange that she can so much care for me.'[67] Though Emma liked to have Julia in measured doses, she was always pleased to see her and curious about her life. She respected what her niece had made of herself, despite her disability, and was intrigued by the way she had established an independent identity in her brother's fractious family.[68]

They swapped reading recommendations, enjoyed family news and, happiest of all, compared notes on the ways of older Wedgwoods and Darwins or the Allen sisters. Julia discovered a description of life at Maer written by Anne Caldwell. She passed it on to Aunt Emma. 'I cannot tell you what vivid pleasure this has given me,' she wrote to her niece. Caldwell's description of Emma and her much-missed sister Fanny as girls was particularly precious: 'happy gay – amiable & sensible & though not particularly energetic in learning yet still [they] acquire all that is necessary by their steady perseverance'.[69]

Hensleigh was Emma's last surviving sibling. She knew that he could be difficult, 'a most provoking man' as she once described him to Etty,[70] and was grateful to Julia for offering him a congenial home when Fanny died and for sending her regular reports when

Figure 29 Emma Darwin in old age. Courtesy of the National Portrait Gallery.

he was dying. 'I trust you will see him fall asleep like a child,' she reassuringly wrote. 'He always was childlike in his transparency.' After his death, she sent her niece a pair of kittens as a distraction. 'They come up every evening & afford a topic for us all it really seemed as if they were exerting themselves especially to amuse us yesterday,' Julia gratefully told her aunt.[71]

Emma herself had a gentle death in September 1896 at the age of 88. Julia sent her letter of condolence to Etty. She knew that the spiritual consolation she normally offered would be out of place. Instead she offered sympathy for what she diagnosed as the double loss involved in a mother's death: the loss of the person and the loss of one's own status as a child. Emma, she wrote, '<u>was</u> exceptional. [...] I think her quite as remarkable as yr father'. As a girl she had been shocked to learn that she had not been married till 'she was 30 (which I thought so indecently old)'. But the breadth of Emma's interests and sympathies were, in part, the outcome of the independent life she led before marriage. 'How touchingly little words come back to me!' she continued, lighting on two very different memories. ' "I dare say you think it is easy to bring up children" she said once when you were a baby – & I was 11.' The other, much more recent, was of her aunt arranging Darwin's study after his death so Julia could sketch it. 'What it must have been to her to cross that threshold,' she mused. In fixing her special qualities, she picked out 'her entire freedom from vanity' as 'something I have hardly known in another human being', as well as her 'forbearance, liberality' and, tellingly, her 'motherly kindness' towards her, a 'magnanimous approximation'.[72] Julia's tribute to her aunt was the most tender she ever wrote.

As the family recognized, Emma's faith had dimmed over time. While Etty suggested that living alongside constant speculation about the workings of an amoral natural world had taken its toll, Julia had a more original explanation: her aunt's own goodness. 'Her excellences blind her [to Christianity] as well as her limits. I can hardly conceive how it would present itself to one who had not the sense of sin.' Unlike Julia's other idols, Emma was so close to perfection that she had little need of the refinement that would come in the afterlife. Communication with her was so natural and complete that it approached the ideal Julia could anticipate with others only in eternity.[73]

Julia was also inclined to attribute the success of the Darwin marriage to her aunt. As she told Emily Gurney in 1874,

> Her feeling for him is almost the most remarkable I know in a wife, the union of absorbing devotion and perfect impartiality is so striking. I don't know any wife quite so absorbed in her husband – of course there is not often so much to be absorbed in – and her time is quite taken up by ministration to him, and yet there is something peculiar in her clear sightedness to his narrowness of view.

Two years later she returned to her theme, describing Emma Darwin as 'almost the purest spirit I know, and the most unselfish, and in many respects showing forth that rare and priceless excellence – love without partiality'.[74] Julia too had benefitted from her favourite aunt's 'love without partiality'.

For all her concerns about his legacy, she also retained a personal respect for her uncle. Two months after Darwin's death, she tried to sum up in a letter to Asa Gray her frustration at what seemed to her the missed opportunity in his work:

> I feel all the Evolution philosophy (as it calls itself) wants nothing to become the foundation of a true philosophy but a sense of incompleteness. [...] If ever the time should come when

Figure 30 Julia Wedgwood's water colour of the view from the Grange, George and Maud Darwin's home in Cambridge. Courtesy of the V&A Wedgwood/Mosley Collection.

men joined to my Uncle's patient industry of observation & minute accuracy respecting <u>facts</u>, a spirit of aspiration after truth rather than facts & a thirst for those truths which are by their nature ultimate, then I think all that he has ever written might take its place as a marvelous illustration of & addition to the text 'in the beginning God created the heavens and the earth. [...] [Then] we should feel that He not only created, but <u>creates</u>, that the work of creation is continuous'.[75]

Julia clung to Gray as the only scientist she knew who might provide the 'religious education' Darwin had avoided. She corresponded with him, asked for his photograph (that 'most Victorian courtesy' as James Moore has well said)[76] and drew attention in the *Spectator* to two lectures he had delivered to Yale University divinity students on natural science and religion, welcoming both his insistence on the unity of creation and his conviction that Theism and Darwinism were not incompatible. As Janet Browne has suggested, Gray's confidence that the two could be reconciled smoothed the way for the readier acceptance of Darwinian ideas in America than in the UK, where the debate was initially overtaken by the row over the competing claims of science and religion.[77] Julia was more attuned to the divisive British debate than the constructive American one. Though praising Gray's contribution, she still regretted that his influence had not forestalled the stimulus given by the new science to 'the dominant materialism'. But perhaps there would be a reaction: 'To know the seen order, and discern the unseen [as Gray did] is a distinction in our time wonderfully rare. It has not always been so and the time will come when it will cease to be so.'[78]

Her prediction was realized sooner than she expected as idealism took both a cultural and a practical hold in the 1890s.

For Julia the publication of *Origin* was one of the seminal events of her life. The eruption of Darwinian theory had, she suggested, led to a more dramatic change than the Reformation: 'men having been taught to think differently of the method of their origin, have come to think differently of their ideal aims'. Her description in 1897 of Darwinism's reception, however, more accurately portrayed her own reaction than the general response: 'A change welcomed with rapture, followed with great disappointment, and now recalled with feelings combining both.'[79] Her intellectual excitement in the 1860s was less common among the faithful than this implied. Equally, the disillusionment over a missed opportunity that underlay her review in 1887 of Frank Darwin's biography of his father stood out at a time of growing accommodation with Darwin's legacy.

Shortly after this appeared, the *Guardian* published a much more sympathetic review of *The Life and Letters of Charles Darwin* by the Oxford academic, botanist and High Church clergyman Aubrey Moore. Moore had taken a double first in Classics but then devoted much of his career to lecturing on church history. He also developed sufficient expertise in botany to be appointed warden of the Oxford Botanical Gardens. As a result, he moved with ease amongst Oxford classicists, theologians and scientists. His intellectual influences were similar to Julia's: the Cambridge Platonists, William Law, Wordsworth, Coleridge, Maurice, Frank Newman and B. F. Westcott.[80] Even the starting point of his review might have seemed the same: his conclusion, however, was very different. While Julia wrote feelingly about Darwin as a 'destroyer', Moore suggested that 'the inrush of new truth means unsettlement, and perhaps, in the reconstruction, a renouncing of something which has been associated with spiritual truth, though not of the essence of the truth itself'. But evolution, he argued, was not an alternative to the idea of divine creation but only to the concept of special creation, an idea which had largely been invented by scientists in the seventeenth century and bolstered by Miltonian rhetoric. Darwinian theory was, in fact, 'infinitely more Christian' because 'it implies the immanence of God in nature, and the omnipresence of His creative power'. Its focus on 'the universality of law and order' in the evolutionary process was 'the scientific analogue of the Christian's belief in Providence'.[81] He took this argument further in his contribution to *Lux Mundi*, an influential collection of essays reflecting the best of Anglican thought published in 1889. Darwinism, he there suggested, had moved the understanding of God on from the mechanistic theism of Paley: 'Science had pushed the deist's God further and further away, and at the moment when it had seemed as if He would be thrown out altogether, Darwinism appeared and under the disguise of a foe, did the work of a friend. [...] Either God is everywhere present in nature, or He is nowhere.'[82] He developed this thinking in a paper delivered to the Church Congress in 1883. The choice between evolution and creation was a false antithesis: 'God cannot interfere with Himself. [...] *For the Christian theologian the facts of nature are the acts of God*'. Evolution demonstrated the marvellous unity of nature and so 'restore[d] the belief that real knowledge, the knowledge of God and his working, is possible'.[83]

Moore, the most 'penetrating' of what James Moore has identified as the Christian Darwinians,[84] had the imaginative appeal for Julia that Asa Gray with his more orthodox theological stance and narrower horizons never quite managed. He was also in close touch with the idealist world of thinking at Oxford that increasingly attracted her.[85] He, like T. H. Green, one of its leading exponents, died sadly young in 1890, with most of his writings published after his death. His skilful reconciliation of Darwinism and Christianity had, nonetheless, a profound effect on troubled believers like Julia. Edward Poulton described him in his survey of 'Fifty Years of Darwinism' in 1909 as 'the clergyman who more than any other man was responsible for breaking down the antagonisms towards evolution then widely felt in the English Church'.[86]

Though Julia took time to relearn her initial sense of evolution as a purposeful process with an immanent God continuing the work of creation as man steadily improved, two articles, 'Ethics and Science' and 'The Old Order Changeth', published in 1897 reflected the new understanding she had reached between Darwin's work and her own faith.

By then she could even welcome the way that Darwinism had disrupted the comforting but intellectually undemanding ways of a Broad Church that was strong on organization and works but 'went for almost nothing' 'as a force in thought'.[87] The sudden publication of a new truth, she wrote echoing the thought in Moore's 1888 review of the Darwin biography, 'is like the shock of some vast earthquake. […] It reveals to men doubts and convictions which it could never create – doubts and convictions which have slumbered in their own hearts, and which the shock awakens to vivid life.' But faith had triumphed over science because science had no answers to questions about free will and teleological purpose, the existence of a Creator and the possibility of an afterlife. The challenge to conventional theology had obliged men to seek a surer base for their faith.

> The difficulty in the way of any Christian acceptance of the idea of evolution – the fact that two millenniums after the Divine took human shape, we live in such a world as we see around us – this difficulty was just as forcible when we thought the creation began on a Sunday, about the time we now assign to the building of the Pyramids, as it is now.

In reassessing the meaning of Christianity, men had come to see that 'both Christianity, truly understood, and evolution have an air of promise'.[88]

In 'The Old Order Changeth', she went further. Darwinism, she suggested, had fundamentally transformed man's view of himself. No longer was he travelling away from an initial act of divine creation: he was now moving steadily towards its completion.[89] Disregarding her uncle's concern with the possible randomness of natural selection, she suggested that Eden, far from lying behind man, had become the goal to which he could aspire. It might even be achieved on earth rather than in the afterlife she proposed in a surprising reflection of Herbert Spencer's optimism about ultimate human perfectibility. She would never, however, have accepted his belief that man could reach this alone as her next sentence showed.[90] 'With confidence thus fortified by the teaching of science, as well as by a message speaking to a part of our being which science cannot reach we venture to look not only for a new heaven, but also for a new earth, wherein dwelleth *righteousness*' (her favourite word).[91]

Julia's two articles were informed not only by the Victorian confidence in progress but also with the values of idealism, which by then extended into many areas of both intellectual and practical life, countering the aggressive materialism of Huxley's Darwinism. As the appeal of Darwinism declined, many were happy to settle for a compartmentalization of science and religion.[92] Others, like the gifted scientific popularizer, Arabella Buckley, whose work Darwin much admired, were able to import an optimistic moral perspective into explanations of his theories, pointing up the way that natural selection had produced 'the overwhelming preponderance of healthy, happy, and varied existence'.[93]

By comparison with this colouring of the Darwinian universe with comforting values of community, altruism and, above all, sympathy, Julia concentrated on the broader philosophical picture, grappling with theodicy, absorbing the theological implications of continuous creation and rediscovering her sense of a Darwinian teleology. In this she could rely not only on a more sympathetic intellectual context than in the 1870s but also on the strength of her rediscovered faith. 'Belief', she had written to Emily Gurney in 1883, 'is personal. Science is one of those things of which we must say they are certain. Faith is one of those things of which we must say I am certain.'[94]

Part IV

The 'Thoughtful Woman Par Excellence'

Chapter Fourteen

THE MESSAGE OF JULIA WEDGWOOD

In her later years Julia was usually identified in print as 'Miss Julia Wedgwood, the author of The Moral Ideal'. Published in 1888 after 20 years of work and reflection, *The Moral Ideal: A Historic Study* was the most characteristic of her books and the one she herself saw as her magnum opus. She thought it important enough to rework it for a younger generation with the help of E. M. Forster, publishing a revised and extended version in 1907. It contained the essence of her thinking about what she saw as man's instinctive search for spiritual meaning and closer union, one with another and with the divine.

The Moral Ideal was a remarkably ambitious book. The extent of learning it displayed, particularly in its footnotes, gave her a claim to be the best-read woman in England after the death of George Eliot. She considered not just Homer, Sophocles, Plato, Virgil, Lucretius and Marcus Aurelius but also the Rig Veda and the Upanishads, Zoroaster, the Gnostics, Epictetus and Philo, St Augustine and Julian the Pelagian. Except when she referred to foreign commentaries, she rarely dealt with secondary works, going instead to the primary sources and quoting from Greek, Latin, German, French and Italian. Sometimes, as with the Rig Veda or the Alexandrian philosopher Philo, she preferred older translations in German to the more accessible English texts. Nor did she hold back from disagreeing about Plato with the pre-eminent authority Benjamin Jowett. At a time when 'the amateur scholarship that had been the byword of the mid-century' had been replaced by increased academic specialization in the study of the classics, Julia boldly entered this newly reserved territory.[1] For a woman, her book was an extraordinary achievement. Some of the reviewers hardly knew what to make of it: others were lavish in their praise, none more so than Hutton. An eclectic mix of intellectual influences was detectible in it: Kant and Hegel, Carlyle, Erskine, Maurice and Cobbe, Matthew Arnold, Jowett and Walter Pater as well as more esoteric writers like Mary Everest Boole and Balfour Stewart. One influence was never overtly mentioned but frequently discernible: Browning.

She dedicated the book to him in the guise of 'An Old Friend' and addressed him uninhibitedly. Perhaps, she suggested, he would be more sympathetic to 'the worker than the work', but if he cared for it, others too would 'find its meaning, and enter into the vast consolation and hope bound up in the thoughts I have striven to follow'.[2] If he did dip into it, Browning would have found a continuation of some of his lively exchanges with Julia in 1864–65, and in writing that a more appropriate title might have been 'A History of Human Aspiration', she was acknowledging her continuing debt to the man often seen as the poet of aspiration.[3] 'You believe, even more firmly than I do, that a partial and incomplete revelation of what men have sought to be, tells us more of their true nature, than does the most exhaustive record possible of what they have accomplished!'[4] Modestly, but incautiously, she also drew his attention to the structural weaknesses of her book, claiming

Figure 31 Julia Wedgwood at work in her later years.

that he would understand why she had adopted what others might see as 'apparent desultoriness' in 'the debris of a gigantic scheme, without a centre and, without a scale, begun at intervals here and there, and abandoned as often'.[5] This gave the *Saturday Review* critic a ready pretext for dismissing *The Moral Ideal* as 'a book in ruins'.[6]

Others compared it to Maurice's five-volume *Moral and Metaphysical Philosophy*, which traced the history of God's cumulative revelation of Himself to man, starting with the ancient Greeks.[7] Unlike Maurice, however, Julia did not suggest a linear progress in the search for the truth, and while he wrote about God revealing Himself, Julia started from the opposite perspective of how man apprehended the divine. Her methodology too was different. As she explained in her dedication, at some points she chose to follow the history of a race, at others the thoughts of individuals and in others the spirit of an age. 'A moral history', she wrote, 'follows no obvious scale' but rather encapsulates 'those throbs and pulsations that make up the true life of Man'.[8] And so her history was, by turns, a study in comparative religion, an analysis of the rise and fall of civilizations, a literary and philosophical critique, a spiritual treatise and a contribution to moral philosophy. It was also an early work of feminist theology as well as a rebuttal of Comtism and her answer to Darwinism.

Julia did not explain what she thought the moral ideal was. By implication it was man's instinct towards unity and his awareness of a divine aspect to existence. It also touched on his appreciation of good and recognition that this was in conflict with evil. By tracing the persistence of these concerns back to the earliest recorded civilizations and showing man's upward path towards an ideal, Julia presented a parallel to Darwinian evolution, challenging Darwin's contention that morality was a learned behaviour derived from human and animal biology.

Her view of history relied on a Hegelian dialectic. Truth for her lay in the unity of knowledge and experience as discovered through definition, reaction and progressive redefinition. She compared the process to a zig-zag climb up a mountainside but, unlike Hegel or Comte, did not speculate on how close humanity was to the summit. For all its individual insights and occasional idiosyncrasies, *The Moral Ideal* was also a recognizable product of the late-Victorian school of idealism. British idealism developed in opposition to utilitarianism, drawing on the philosophy of Kant and Hegel as mediated by Coleridge, James Martineau and others. Its concern was with the apprehension of reality not through the investigation of the material world but through a mental recognition of spiritual values that transcended sensory awareness. As taught by T. H. Green, Benjamin Jowett's most brilliant pupil, the immanence of the divine in everything pointed to an underlying unity in creation and called for a metaphysics based on the existence of a common good and the recognition that the individual could only fully realize himself through connection with others. Family, community and the nation were moral entities rather than social or economic units and capable of constant improvement. While some criticized idealism as too mystical, that was part of its appeal to Julia, as was its optimism. As she would write in 'The Old Order Changeth', 'the world of the ideal is […] most truly the world of the real'.[9] Frank Turner has described its influence on a wide spectrum of disciplines towards the end of the century. Idealism, he writes, was

> an outlook that emphasized metaphysical questions in philosophy, historicist analysis of the past, the spiritual character of the world, the active powers of the human mind, intuitionism, subjective religiosity, the responsibility of individuals for undertaking moral choice and action, the relative or even absolute importance of communities and communal institutions over individual action or rights, and the shallowness of any mode of reductionist thought.[10]

'The Moral Ideal' was not, however, exclusively a work of the idealist school. Julia's concern to detect the spirit of an age owed much to her old friend, Carlyle, as well as to her new one, Hutton, while her reference to 'throbs and pulsations' reflected the theories of Mary Everest Boole, whom she later acknowledged as her 'greatest helper'.[11] Partly mystical, like much else in Mrs Boole's thinking and partly based on acute observation of the psychology of learning, the 'law of pulsation', which she credited to her late husband, the brilliant mathematician George Boole, was designed to explain the cognitive processes that made it possible to reconcile conflicting impressions. 'The mind of man', she wrote,

> is encased in a mechanism which, besides receiving information through […] the senses, receives information also from some source, invisible and undefinable, the access to which opens whenever the mind, after a period of tension on the difference, contrast, or conflict between any elements of thought, turns to contemplate the same elements as united, or as forming parts of a unity.[12]

The notion of a fusion of divergent concepts at critical points in man's search for the truth plays an important part in *The Moral Ideal* as does the role of the mediator. Alongside Julia's accounts of conflicting nations and ideologies or representative figures like Plato, Virgil or Marcus Aurelius, she also considered less familiar mediators between opposed philosophies like Epictetus or Philo. Nothing was ever lost, she maintained. Historical development was a cumulative but far-from-regular process with great leaps forward, as at the time of the French Revolution, and long periods of stasis as in the Middle Ages. She quoted in her dedication from James Martineau: 'It has been finely said, "God has so arranged the chronometry of our spirits that there shall be thousands of silent moments between the striking hours."'[13] Julia set herself to identify 'the striking hours' in man's search for moral truth.

The most obvious influence on her work was Maurice. Her book is permeated with his insistence on unity and the mediation required to achieve it, with both the family and the nation seen as expressions of the universality of the divine. Julia devoted some of her most elevated prose to this theme, hymning the unity of mother and child, of men and women in marriage, of the family, the community and the nation and, encompassing all, the union of the human with and the divine. She also reserved her severest criticisms for what undercut it: the caste system in India, slavery and the subordination of women in Greece, the unnatural role assigned to women in Augustinian theology and the divisive doctrine of pre-destination.

Richard Hutton described *The Moral Ideal* with some justice as a collection of essays on a related theme rather than a straightforward history.[14] It did, however, proceed chronologically, beginning with an account of Indian philosophy, which she saw as a pale reflection of the ultimate unity to which man aspires. Interest in Indian religions had been stimulated by Max Müller's translations of the Rig Veda and a series he edited of *The Sacred Books of the East*. Through them the reading public accustomed itself to the idea that religious truth was not confined to the pages of the Bible, a message that Maurice had also popularized in his *The Religions of the World*.

Julia welcomed the focus in Indian philosophy on calm and the distinction between reality and unreality rather than the conflict between good and evil. 'The primeval Aryan faith held in solution the religion of the conscience, and that of nature, combined in a seemingly homogeneous unity. The religion of nature recognized imperfection, the religion of conscience did not emphasize sin.' And in the Upanishads she found that 'all that seems to separate man from God belongs to the realm of illusion; in proportion as man approaches the true he recognizes his own being as embraced and interpenetrated by the Divine'. Ultimately, however, the Indian sense of primal unity was possible only in simple agrarian societies where life was 'much less full of struggle'. Nor did it confront the problems of the existence of evil and the nature of free will, which Julia dubbed in a footnote 'rather an infirmity than a power'.[15]

Persian philosophy she saw as a reaction against Vedic thought. It set good and evil in opposition and portrayed life as conflict and confrontation. But she did not dismiss the dualism of Zoroastrianism out of hand. The contemporary lack of awareness of life as a struggle between light and darkness had, she asserted, left 'a great vacuum'. Religion now missed 'much of what is most essential to it.'.[16]

From Zoroaster she turned to the more familiar world of Classical Greece and the part of her study that attracted the most plaudits from the reviewers. Though it was still rare for women, excluded from public schools and the ancient universities, to read ancient Greek, several had made a mark with their translations of the Greek dramatists. The best known was Julia's friend 'dear Miss Swanwick'. But while she looked primarily for pre-echoes of Christianity in the Greek dramatists searching out accessible prototypes of female devotion, self-sacrifice or elevated moral behaviour,[17] Julia set out to appreciate the Greeks for themselves. Greek thought was not a foreshadowing but a respite from the Christian preoccupation with good and evil, conscience and the exercise of free will. Its 'spirit of balance, of harmony, of rhythm' was 'the ideal of genius' and the 'perennial aspect that life bears to the Poet'.[18]

Here was a statement designed to catch Browning's eye as she developed the discussion they had had in the summer of 1864 about the 'charm' and 'curious satisfaction' of Homer's natural 'unfeelingness'. 'Genius', she now wrote, 'is [...] utterly immoral.' Greek genius portrayed 'all antagonism as the harmonious play of opposite emotions'. It was also non-theistic. As she pointed out, Homer's deities were often shown as being 'from a moral point of view, inferior to the objects of their capricious protection and dislike'.[19]

Greek ambivalence towards the Gods reflected distrust of individual authority, just as the Greek idea of freedom was not so much about personal liberty as collective civil action and respect for the law. Here Greece offered 'a lesson for the world'. Though Julia sidestepped the tendency of many of her contemporaries to see Greek history as a proxy for ideological battles over radical and liberal values, she still looked for instructive parallels.[20] Just as she had contrasted the torpidity of the Hindu caste system with the vitality of a British aristocracy open to new wealth and talent, so she compared the Greek sense of national identity with the British. In this case the older civilization had the advantage. Both claimed a 'national vocation', but while the British could only associate theirs with moral purpose by falsifying the facts, Greece stood for 'the triumph of the resolute few, the downfall of the barbaric armament, the Nemesis of arrogance, [and] the vindication of the spirit of liberty'.[21]

Its weakness lay in the way that the Greek citizen's liberty depended on the existence of slavery and an artisanal class kept outside the polity, while the state concerned itself with public, not private, virtue and excluded women. 'An Englishman is asked first whether he is a good son, a good father, a good husband; if he be all of them, the fact that he is not a good citizen is viewed indulgently. A Greek was asked first whether he was a good citizen.' This elitism condemned the Greeks to eventual decline. 'The love of country', wrote Julia, setting out her own ideal of a liberal, inclusive society,

> is the love of the neighbor. It sets us in kindly relationship with those of whom we know most, for whom we can do most; it includes every variety of opinion, of circumstance, of character; it contains within itself lessons of tolerance and forbearance, and it becomes in a healthy mind an expansive feeling, passing beyond its own large boundaries, and ready to embrace the world.[22]

(When E. M. Forster helped Julia tone down the language in the revised version of *The Moral Ideal* this passage remained untouched.)

Few Victorians rated Roman civilization as highly as Greek culture. For some, the best that could be said for the Roman Empire was that its size and efficient transport links had facilitated the rapid spread of early Christianity.[23] Julia saw it as a preparation for Christianity in a more original way. 'Rome', she wrote, 'was a sort of anti-type of the God made known in Christ.' It was 'monotonous, prosaic, intellectually commonplace, wanting in vividness and individuality'. Its only original feature was its system of law and obedience to it. That, and the onward march of Empire, produced 'a profound feeling of resignation' which proved the perfect preparation for Christianity. The first Christian martyrs drew on 'the stored up force of generations of patient, resolute endurance'.[24]

She detected the spirit of the age in four writers: Lucretius, Virgil, Marcus Aurelius and Epictetus. Lucretius was a controversial figure for the Victorians. George Eliot found him beguiling; Tennyson wrote a long poem about him; Matthew Arnold appreciated his sense of ennui; W. Y. Sellar thought he foreshadowed the Romantic poets.[25] Julia avoided some, but not all, of these debates. She recognized his apparent modernity but placed him in her own scheme of the way scientific knowledge had developed, oscillating between a mechanistic and organic view of nature. Lucretius, like Darwin, she said, favoured the mechanistic. His impersonality, however, marked a distinction between his science and ours. 'We see the anthropomorphism of our scientific ideas', she suggested, 'when we contrast them with his; we are forced to realize that it is not less in the world without than the world within that we have grown more personal.'[26]

She moved on to her favourite contention that Lucretius had anticipated Darwin. Not many writers could make their point by referring to a conversation on the subject with Darwin himself and then go on to disagree with him. 'I once showed the passage [in *De Rerum Naturae* V 837–877] to Mr Darwin, but the dialect was too unscientific for him, and I do not think he recognized it for the anticipation of his own views, which unquestionably it is.'[27] Julia also praised Lucretius's power as a nature poet: 'a few passages of exquisite pathos' anticipated 'the pure, delicate, natural sympathies of Wordsworth' even if they were only 'rare gleams when a finer self seems to break through the habitual self'. In Virgil, by comparison, a poet with whom Julia had much more sympathy, pathos expanded 'to colour the whole'.[28]

Hutton was lavish in his praise for this part of *The Moral Ideal*. 'We have seldom read anything more impressive than [her] criticism of the leading idea of Lucretius', while 'the criticism on Virgil [...] is even finer and more impressive'.[29] For Julia, Virgil was a more pivotal figure than Lucretius. She noted his 'resolute avoidance of originality' but attributed this to his recognition that 'to adapt, to embody, to imitate' the inheritance of Greek literature was 'the only possible intellectual aim' for a Roman writer. Virgil not only admired the past but also looked forward in his appreciation of the world as unity and history as embodying 'the idea of purpose'. This together with his submission to power and the law was an indication of 'the sort of reverence that passed into religion'.[30]

The Victorians tended to think of Virgil as only 'a pale shadow of Homer'. Gladstone dismissed him as 'a courtier', pointing to 'the intellectual mediocrity' of Aeneas and his 'vile' treatment of Dido.[31] Julia disagreed. Virgil's unquestioning loyalty to empire went hand in hand with 'a deep sympathy for its subjects and victims'. Above all, his attitude to women marked a critical change from the Greeks. 'The Iliad', she wrote, 'is a story of *men*.'

The women in it were 'mere accessories to the male actors'.³² But 'the most impressive figure' in the *Aeneid* was Dido, a tragic figure presented with 'pathos'. She also saw Virgil's depiction of Venus, Aeneas's mother, as prefiguring the cult of the Virgin Mary.

Portraying Virgil as, in this respect, a precursor of Christianity required an imaginative stretch but inspired Julia to one of her most rhapsodic depictions of the sanctity of maternal love:

> The worship of the Divine mother links in wondrous harmony the worlds that lie beneath and above humanity. In the mother's love some ocean seems to break through the shallow vessel which holds ordinary love, as though the Infinite came welling through the limitations of individual human nature; what exalted virtue hardly produces in any other relation, the mere conditions of physiology seem to ensure between mother and child. Here we seem to have reached a law wider than humanity; here we come down to the primal rock of sentient nature, and discern the elements of morality that are older than man.³³

From Virgil, Julia turned to what she described as the Age of Death, a time when men were driven in on themselves because they could no longer associate with the interests of Empire. The Empire, she wrote in a salutary warning to her British contemporaries, survived only as 'negation [...] it lives on the crushed lives of the races that were submitted to it; and the moment they awaken to energetic self-assertion it must perish'. As a result, men became preoccupied with Death and what lay beyond it. Marcus Aurelius best represented this new concern with 'a refuge for [the] need for permanence'.³⁴

Marcus Aurelius was a favourite of the Victorians. But while Arnold thought he had come close to 'the effusion of Christianity [...] for which his soul longed',³⁵ Julia found his resignation 'dreary and joyless'. Though a sense of order in Nature and of common humanity sustained him, his loneliness was that of a man set above all others. Even God, she pointed out, needed the companionship of the Trinity. 'We know the meaning of Self for the first time', she suggested in a characteristic pronouncement, 'when we know the meaning of another than Self.'³⁶

Much of the later part of *The Moral Ideal* is concerned with what Julia saw as the underlying concerns of theology: the nature of God, the existence of evil, the conflict between free will and determinism, the prospect of eternity and the human instinct towards unity with the divine. A number of the reviewers found it strange that in a history of man's growing moral awareness, she chose to say nothing about the birth of Christ and little about St Paul. As she herself wrote in her dedication to Browning, her study was 'without a centre'. By omitting any reference to Christ's life, however, she underlined its character as a unique, ahistoric moment of divine intervention outside the cyclical progress she elsewhere described. She also avoided the busy but largely masculine area of contention about Christ's significance as the human personification of God (as in J. R. Seeley's *Ecce Homo*) or as His vehicle for man's atonement after the fall (as with standard mid-century theology). For her the critical period was not the time of the birth of Christ but rather the point at which Greek, Judaic and early Christian thought came together. Their fusion was 'in some sense the key to the history of the human race'.³⁷ Judaism and Hellenism had been 'the great antithesis of all human thought': Christianity, in the form of St Paul, was the intermediary between them.³⁸

Rather than focus on St Paul, however, she found her representative figure of the age in Philo, the Jewish philosopher living in Alexandria at the time of Christ, whom she nicely described as 'an attentive traveller along the highway, studious of all that was revealed to the eye of average power'. Philo, she suggested, discovered in the Old Testament not simply the history of a people but the presence of divine law, will and creation, and 'Human Will takes on new meaning when men believe in Divine Will.' She now got to the heart of her message: the complementarity of human and divine will as paralleled in the complementarity of the sexes:

> The distinction of the passive and active, suggested by the two halves of humanity, is ideally complete in the relation of humanity to that which lies above it. Israel was the spouse of the Lord; the ideal Humanity needed the Divine for its counterpart, as a bride her groom. And thus the religion of the Jew held in germ all that elevation of women which is most characteristic of modern, and most unlike classic thought [...] the feeling which prostrates man before God has a deep and hidden connection with that in which man and woman find, each in each, the complete explanation of their being.[39]

At the root of morality lay the need for humans to be at one not only with God but also with each other. 'We *are* members of one another,' Julia affirmed. '*We* is a reality as much as the *I*,' 'when the We swallows up the I we touch on the solution of all morality.'[40]

From this central assertion, Julia moved to a central preoccupation: the problem of evil. Darwinian science, she suggested, dismissed it as an incidental aspect of an improving world. For the Greeks, too, the problem barely existed, while for the Jews, man's inherently evil nature was redeemed by God's goodness. The contemporary view that evil was necessary if man was to use free will to choose between it and good was 'an inadequate answer', but like Maurice, Julia had little to offer in its place as an explanation of that 'unintelligible thing'.[41]

Pain, however, proved that evil existed, separating the sufferer from others and overwhelming every sensation. She looked for relief to ancient Greece. For Plato life was only a shadow and yet the Greeks had left behind great art: in their statues, man appeared beautiful and 'at home in the bright world around him'. Judaism, by contrast, had taught man to wonder why the world was not all good. 'The myth of Eden', she wrote, 'holds a perennial truth [...] from the knowledge of Evil springs the knowledge of a higher good. We seem to know God and sin together.'[42]

Belief in the fall of man brought with it 'a whole system of theology' centred on immortality and redemption. While early Christianity had made eternity available to all, however, under the influence of St Augustine, salvation became confined to the few. His remodelling of Christianity, she wrote, had 'lasted for centuries and still remains as a picturesque ruin'. She objected to his spiritual elitism but even more to his attitude to women. 'Perhaps all that is most hurtful in the spiritual history of mankind comes from the endeavor of great men to exhibit the truth that has been felt in experience as part of a logical scheme.'[43]

Augustine's stress on the need for redemption sprang from his sudden awareness of his sinfulness and need for deliverance from sexual temptation. In response he repudiated the mother of his son and elevated his own mother to a position above that she merited.

'Man's fall was commemorated in sexual desire, and his regeneration was to be manifest in sexual separateness.' As she sharply noted, Augustine 'made the order of things in which we live take its rise in a crime, the shadow of which fell on all subsequent exercise of human activity, and was commemorated in every new life'.[44]

She passed over the next thousand years of history quickly, picking out as salient features the rediscovery of the Classical world at the time of the Renaissance, the unnecessary splintering of the Catholic and Protestant Churches, the first scientific revolution, the rediscovery of man in the French Revolution and the challenge of the new science. Her final chapter, 'The Heritage of Today', was a riposte to Darwinism and a statement of her personal credo.

She began with a statement about aspiration which reads like a paraphrase of Browning: 'That which gives life its keynote is, not what men think good, but what they think best,' 'the dominant influence of life lies ever in the unrealized.' She discerned a steady improvement both in man's civic relations and in the marital bond. Man joined with others in society 'by the principle of resemblance' and in marriage 'by the principle of difference' on which 'the charm of conjugal happiness' rested. Though marriage was sometimes no more than 'a mere magnified selfishness', at its best it combined private and civic virtue: 'the man who is faithful to one woman, who has brought no children into the world without endeavouring to ensure their welfare, who has paid back to his parents that tribute of protection and care he has received from them – such a man may be counted by the State among her true sons'.[45] Judaism had recognized the importance of the family: for centuries Christianity had not. The cult of the Virgin Mary was the outcome of the failure to give woman her proper place.

Both the rediscovery of Classical literature and the discoveries of Galileo and Newton had freed humanity from the distortions of Augustinian theology. 'Man entered upon the rehabilitation of nature. His home was no longer overshadowed by the recollection of a pristine crime [the Fall of Man]. It was a glorious palace, and its inhabitants must be a royal race.' 'Human nature became interesting for its own sake.' Attitudes towards women were transformed. 'The love of woman changes from the centre of human temptation to the centre of human aspiration.'[46]

But progress had not been uninterrupted. Protestantism, with its emphasis on sin and conversion, had revived Augustinianism. Against the individualism of the Protestant revival, she, remembering her debt to James Mackintosh, praised the spirit of universal humanity in the French Revolution and Rousseau's reverence for natural man. Darwinian science, however, had taken reverence for nature too far. While 'nature had been the invading, disturbing influence in Creation; she is now enthroned as the Creator'. A recoil from Christianity had been its result. 'The men of our day turn away from Christianity […] because […] the idea of Evolution, as they hold it, implies a sanction on all desire and choice.'[47] But Darwinism was an overreaction that would, in time, be corrected.

Science, Julia suggested, now stood in the same relationship to time as it had to space in the sixteenth century. But while cosmologists and explorers had seen their discoveries as 'an enormous expansion of the Divine', the discovery of 'the seemingly undivine' processes of evolution had tended to 'eliminate' God. To see God acting in time, rather than space, required more faith since it called for belief not only in divine will, as in the act of creation, but also in divine character, as in God's continuing operation in a world where evil existed. This could only come from 'a consciousness in man [...] of something that seems eternal'. Comtism was not the answer: 'Men think in our day that this centre can be found in the ideal of Humanity. They have yet to learn that no ideal is possible if that which is idealized knows no Beyond.'[48]

Julia's conclusion was confident. There was, she wrote, a new recognition that 'the fragmentary I had become part of a larger whole' in an 'organic, rational Unity' resting on 'the greater Unity beyond that'. Her closing sentences, with their echoes of Maurice, Carlyle and Goethe, were resonant and affirmative:

> They who [...] feel that Nature exhausts God, that the summits of human virtue are the summits of moral excellence, that reverence is the provision for inferiority, and fades away before Man reaches those heights towards which he is always striving – they can find in the moral thought of the Past little but a collection of errors. Man, if we judge him by history, knows himself only so far as he turns towards the eternal Other of the human spirit: he finds his true Unity only as he finds a larger Unity which makes him one with himself and with his brother man.[49]

The Moral Ideal, which headed Trubner's list in autumn 1888, was reprinted the following spring. It was both extravagantly praised and dismissed out of hand. Hutton devoted two reviews to it in the *Spectator*: the Methodist *London Quarterly* reviewer also took it seriously. 'After so much from female pens', he wrote, 'which gallantry itself cannot help stigmatizing as mere rubbish it is a treat to come to such a very full and suggestive volume.' Those prepared to engage with the work all agreed it was not an easy read. The *Monthly Packet*, staple fare in country rectories, warned that it could not be skimmed. There was 'scarcely a page [...] without an epigram which in itself would be a subject for an essay on its own'. Most critics, however, regretted the thinness of her chapters on Christian thinking by comparison with her analysis of non-Christian thought. Even so, as the *London Quarterly* commented: 'there is much more in this volume than wide and deep reading; there is a rare breadth of thought and a still rarer appreciation of the purpose which, we as Christians are bound to believe, runs through the ages'.[50] Many recognized her debt to Maurice but also her own authorial voice. When Octavia Hill and her mother read it aloud, she wrote to her sister, 'It reminded me a little of things that Mr Maurice had said, but was very different too.'[51] Similarly, the *London Quarterly* wrote, 'If Miss Wedgwood has got saturated with Maurice, she has not in the least lost her individuality [...] in matter and treatment, though not in style, Miss Wedgwood is wholly original.'

Hutton went further in his first review headed 'Miss Wedgwood's Apophthegms'. With his experienced editorial eye he noted that her chapter openings could be 'cumbrous'. Once she got into her subjects, however, the reader became aware that 'he is studying the writings not only of a profoundly reflective mind, but of one of great imaginative grasp. [...] Scattered through her pages are apophthegms that deserve to be separated from them [...] for their masculine breadth and truth.' He went on to pick out two full columns of them.[52] A week later he was back with an even longer review addressing some of Julia's wider themes, including Virgil's and St Augustine's attitudes to women, where Hutton found her analyses 'shot through with fine criticisms' that were 'both true and original'.

His only reservations about 'a very remarkable and powerful book' were over Julia's treatment of the problem of evil and its relationship to free will. But even Hutton's answers to her 'perennial problem' were no more than tentative.

The Moral Ideal was a book for its times. While some of its insights may have crept into sermons, provoked discussion at church study groups or stimulated private reflection, its analysis had no lasting influence. It was nonetheless a remarkably ambitious book for a woman to have written in the 1880s. High-minded and idealistic, sometimes repetitive and obscure, but always resonant and drawing on a telling use of natural metaphor, *The Moral Ideal* was also enlivened by unique personal touches. Who else would have likened Julian the Pelagian to Charles Kingsley, or drawn attention to some 'enriching' manuscript markings by Bentley in the copy of Epictetus she had read in the British Museum or referred to conversations with Charles Darwin? Few women would have taken on Jowett and Nettleship in print or pointed out the rather obvious structural weakness of her study in its disproportion between the treatment of pre- and post-Christian philosophy. Even fewer would have brought a historian's eye to her contrasting descriptions of Herodotus and Thucycides, the one gossipy, humorous and confident, the other reflecting the scepticism of his times in a surprisingly modern way. For all her seriousness there was charm too in her study.

The feminist thinking that permeates *The Moral Ideal* particularly appealed to Octavia Hill,[53] but few others commented on it. Male reviewers may have accepted it as the price they had to pay for a work whose 'masculine' ability to confront difficult issues about the Greek or Judaic traditions or Augustinian theology deserved their attention. Female reviewers were rare: they veered from the brief but respectful like Charlotte Yonge to the eccentric like Mrs Boole.[54]

In an essay called 'Plutarch and the Unconscious Christianity of the First Two Centuries', which was probably an off-cut from her work on *The Moral Ideal*, Julia had written appreciatively about Plutarch's philosophical works, finding in them a sympathy towards women and the family, a sense of man's corruption but also his immortality and a belief in a mediator, all of which she saw as characteristics of a period preparing itself to receive Christianity. But she was stern about his prose style: 'his words always overflow [...] his thoughts therefore appear to more advantage in detached extracts than in their original context – a sure condemnation as far as literary value is concerned'.[55] The same criticism would be made of her own work. Most reviewers found it easier to select individual insights than to engage with the overall argument of *The Moral Ideal*.

The family, however, took its responsibility to get to grips with it seriously. Effie read it aloud for an hour every evening to her mother, who was convalescing at Abinger. Emma Darwin made several attempts to get into it, initially finding it 'almost too fatiguing – She refines & refines till I lose all comprehension.' But once she got to the chapters on Greece, she was entranced. 'Now I must go to my Moral Ideal,' she wrote to her daughter. 'I always feel inclined to call it Typical Developments' (a reference to a popular weekly column in *Punch* magazine). She was cross, too, about a negative review ('Is it too Christian or because it is written by a woman') and concerned about the *Spectator*'s slowness in reviewing it.[56] Her brother, by contrast, was intent on lowering the family's expectations: 'her book [...] I am afraid will be a gt. Disappointment to her', Hensleigh wrote to Emma, 'tho' I look at everything in so radically differing a point of view that I am perhaps not a fair judge'. He later claimed credit for helping Julia correct her proofs and persuading her 'to omit a good deal'.[57] The deadening hand of dismissive paternal control still lay on Julia's shoulder but now had less power to demoralize than in the 1850s.

Though *The Moral Ideal* attracted few female reviewers, an article Julia published in the *Contemporary Review* in July 1889, 'Male and Female Created He Them', was immediately seized on by the leading feminist periodical *The Englishwoman's Review*. Their reviewer (perhaps Jessie Boucherett) wrote: 'for those who wish to go down into the deepest meanings of society, those who would the better understand the inner workings of the present by tracing back its links into a far remote past, this paper of Miss Wedgwood's is the most valuable contribution that the literature of the woman question has yet received'.[58]

'Male and Female Created He Them' developed some of the implicit themes in *The Moral Ideal*. In it she took on not only J. S. Mill and, even, briefly, George Eliot, but also Darwin, whose ideas she turned on their head, finding a partial sanction for her theories in some manuscript notes he had made on an obscure French book in his library. She also drew on her Classical learning to supplement an argument about the persistence of women's superior moral sense that grew out of her reading of Darwin. Her starting point was the suggestion that women were more various than was generally assumed. The stereotyping that presented men as representative of humanity and women as a class apart was misleading. For the purposes of her argument, however, she was prepared to work from the general perception that women were less selfish than men.[59] But while Cobbe saw female moral superiority as an innate attribute, Julia looked for a biological explanation of women's 'moral seniority'.

Cobbe records in her autobiography that she once encouraged Darwin to read Mill's *On the Subjection of Women*. But Darwin, who read more of Mill than he sometimes admitted,[60] told Cobbe that Mill had much to learn about women from science. Julia, like George Eliot, was of the same view. In her article she objected to Mill's depiction of women as 'subject' as over-reliant on the position of married women. He was, in any case, outdated, she wrote, since he had failed to take account of Darwinian science. In *The Descent of Man*, Darwin had produced evidence that while sexual selection was the prerogative of the female in the animal kingdom, when it came to humans, it was the man who chose. This was, he suggested, a mark of advance. 'The superior male intelligence' had been sharpened by hunting and the struggle to possess the female and defend them and their young.

Eliza Lynn Linton found Darwin's statement of the natural limits on female aspiration reassuring.[61] Julia did not. She put a different slant on his ideas by going back to the suggestion he had made in 1868 in *The Variation of Animals and Plants under Domestication* that some sexual characteristics were inherited only from parents of the same sex. For Julia the most significant inherited female characteristic was the maternal sense. With it came not what George Eliot had declared to be the foundation of moral sense, feeling the need of another, but rather feeling needed by another.[62]

The maternal instinct, Julia suggested, was much older than the paternal. In primeval times, 'the care of a helpless being' fell exclusively on the mother, with fathers not necessarily recognizing any connection with their offspring. Paternity was a learned responsibility: maternity both a physical and an instinctive one. It then passed down a Darwinian 'line of accumulative idiosyncrasy', applying to all women whether mothers or not.[63]

Before attempting to define 'The Spirit of the Mother', however, and its significance for contemporary society, Julia moved on from considering the maternal role in primitive societies to examining the broader position of women in early civilizations and the relationship between religious feeling and reverence for women. Here she drew on Giraud-Teulon's *La Mère chez certains Peuples de l'Antiquité* published in 1867 and Bachofen's *Das Mutterrecht*, but also on Darwin's pencilled notes on the French text. Giraud-Teulon had argued that in pre-history, a woman was predominant not only in the family but also in religion, civil life and even the activities of the state. Darwin summed this up as 'a gynocratic period'. Bachofen offered a raft of examples of female dominance including Herodotus's suggestion that in Egypt women conducted business while the men stayed at home to work the loom. Theseus, Julia pointed out, only acquired his position as founder of his nation after defeating the Amazonians in battle. Similarly, the oldest Greek deities were female: Demeter, the Earth goddess, who, unlike Zeus, had no parentage, and the Eumenides. 'The moral life', she concluded, 'is older in women than in men.' To Darwin's pencilled question about whether there was a period when 'the gentler virtues rose into eminence?' Julia answered that they had always been paramount: 'the protective impulse to which humanity turns was inevitably female'. From Demeter onwards, worship had often centred on the female, as with the cult of the Virgin Mary. Protestantism had reacted against this, but Evangelicanism had reinstated a meek and mild unmanly Jesus.[64] Now in an 'effeminate age', 'the Divine Feminine' (as described by Goethe from whom she quoted at the head of her article) was reverenced again.

In the concluding section of her article, however, Julia drew a different conclusion from Darwin's patriarchal assumptions by redefining the nature of women's inherited moral sense. While the influential American feminist Eliza Burt Gamble equated maternal sense with altruism, Julia linked it to justice, that 'rare virtue' which lay at the heart of a progressive society.[65] This, she argued, had grown out of the 'Spirit of the Mother'. She defined this as 'love measured by need, unchilled by neglect, careless of external attraction, and at leisure to pursue the good of the object, apart from distractions of vanity, jealousy, or selfish interest'. But despite the origin of justice in the maternal feeling that all women inherited, its exercise was confined within the family. A woman's 'relations with those *not her own*, show the sterile waste coming up to the very edge of the cultivated garden'. Men, by contrast, dealt with 'those beyond the pale of kindred, preference, or compassion'. Which model would prevail in the search for justice, the civil or the domestic? Julia's answer was clear. Justice was 'not civil relation drawn closer, but family relation spread wider'. Would it not be 'disastrous' to 'ignore' 'this inexhaustible spring of knowledge and of power [that] belongs to half the human race?'[66]

Unlike Cobbe, Julia was not advancing an argument for specific recognition of women's rights. Even less was she following Mary Carpenter's belief that engaging in charitable work enabled women 'to be mothers in heart though not by God's gift on earth'.[67] As with her article on female suffrage in *Woman's Work and Woman's Culture* in 1869, where she argued for the normalization of relations between the sexes, so here she relied on the general consideration that the failure to provide a wider outlet for women's superior moral sense was not only ahistorical but also disadvantageous to society.

Her article written in the immediate aftermath of her mother's death had a deeply felt personal significance. Like her daughter, Fanny Wedgwood shared a passion for justice. In arguing that there was a close association between inherited maternal feeling and awareness of social justice, Julia was making an emotional as well as an intellectual connection between them and drawing on her mother's example. Though Fanny was less confined to her 'cultivated garden' than most women of her generation, did Julia sense that ultimately she had failed to realize her potential? In 'Male and Female Created He Them', she made peace with her mother, celebrating her inheritance from her and highlighting the dangers of not allowing women to use their talents to the full.

In *The Moral Ideal* Julia had made clear her admiration for the Judaic tradition on monogamy, the family and the place of women. Though she discussed Judaism only in passing there, her interest in the history of Israel was of long standing. She and Erskine had read Heinrich Ewald's *History of Israel* together in 1869. For Erskine this was 'the history of Israel divested of miracle [...] it is a very ingenious and gravely written book'.[68] Both wondered at the fact that God had chosen to give his exclusive trust to a 'wandering Arab tribe' settled in an area not much bigger than Wales.[69] But the history of Israel was an exception to the dialectical scheme of *The Moral Ideal*. While other civilizations had developed their system of moral values by reacting against the assumptions of their predecessors, the obscure Hebrew race had been entrusted with the truth from the first but not always perceived it.

The Message of Israel, published in 1894, went beyond filling an apparent gap in her earlier book, however. Julia's principal concern was to make the results of recent Bible criticism accessible to the general reader and so contribute to a renewal of faith. The new criticism was often seen as even more of a threat to established beliefs than Darwinism. It also acquired its martyrs, of whom William Colenso, the Bishop of Natal, was the most prominent. In his seven-volume study of the Pentateuch, published between 1862 and 1879, Colenso put his mathematical training to use to prove that the accounts of Noah's Ark and the flood in *Genesis* and the Israelite wanderings in the desert in *Exodus* could not be true. Though the South African church hierarchy failed in its attempts to strip him of his Bishopric, he was left impoverished and ostracized. One of those who disowned him was Maurice, a disavowal Julia found hard to forgive. 'A brave missionary', she later wrote, 'had admitted the atmosphere of rational judgment to that closed chamber where the notion of total inspiration, like the corpse in a hermetically sealed tomb, crumbled to dust at that admission.' 'And what was his reward? – but I will not dwell on thoughts raising indignation against some I loved much,' she wrote in 1909.[70]

Maurice, who was anxious not to undermine the continuing relevance of the Bible to the Christian life,[71] had dipped his toes in the new waters of Bible criticism far more cautiously than Frank Newman, who first drew attention to the new German scholarship in his *A History of the Hebrew Monarchy* published anonymously in 1847, or W. R. Greg, whose *Creed of Christendom* argued against the literal inspiration of the Bible.[72] Maurice admitted the self-evident point that Genesis contained two divergent accounts of the creation. His suggestion that one was the creation as seen by God and the other as understood by man was far from the rigour of the new German textual criticism. In Scotland its most effective promoter was William Robertson Smith, the Professor of Hebrew and Old Testament Exegesis in Aberdeen, and a leading exponent of the work of Julius Wellhausen. He was forced out of his chair in 1881, finding a more congenial berth in Cambridge.

In Oxford, Samuel Rolles Driver, the Regius Professor of Hebrew, and Thomas Cheyne, the Oriel Professor of the Interpretation of Holy Scripture, were influential exponents of the Wellhausen thesis on how and when the Old Testament had been put together. By the time Julia immersed herself in Old Testament criticism, German thinking was even being taught in Anglican training colleges but was kept out of the pulpit for fear of bewildering already unsettled congregations. Julia determined to fill the void confident that a wider understanding of the new scholarship would revive faith. She was, as she knew, entering an area where the discourse had until then been exclusively male.[73]

As she wrote near the outset of her study, the Old Testament was 'the most important book that was ever written'. Reading it, however, could be both confusing and disappointing. 'The Bible recalls to many persons dreary hours of childhood, when the attempt to carry on into Leviticus the reverence with which the story of Joseph had at first been heard, ended by associating that also with tedium and disgust.'[74] Some parts were so repellent or obscure they could only be read with 'devout inattention'.[75] Accepting that the Old Testament was not the literal word of God required the reader to distinguish 'the precious from the vile'.[76] Understanding how it had been put together was essential to recognizing it as an account of a historical interaction with the divine but not itself divinely inspired. Understanding the new criticism would, she assured her readers, have the same energizing impact on faith as the wider availability of the Bible had had at the time of the Reformation.

Her approach also reflected the new historicism with its interest in the study of ancient Middle Eastern civilizations. Like Jowett and others, she read the Old Testament in the context of contemporaneous literature like the *Iliad*, appreciating it not just as a historical text but also as a collection of 'a nation's legendary and mythical lore'. She pointed up similarities with Plato or the Egyptian Book of the Dead, whose treatment of the afterlife she found more suggestive than that of the Hebrew text, just as Socrates's dying thoughts were more interesting than those recorded of Moses. Her range of sources was wide and mostly up-to-date. It included not just Ewald, Driver, Robertson Smith and Cheyne but also Alexandre Westphal, Frantz Buhl, Friedlander, Renan, Schenkel and what she described as Ruess's 'noble edition' of the Old Testament in French. As usual, her footnotes included an impressive number of quotations from German, French and Greek.

Wellhausen's synthesis of earlier critical work concluded that the text of the Pentateuch (the first five books of the Old Testament) had not been finalized until the middle of the fifth century BCE after the Jews' return from exile in Babylon. He also identified at least three contributors to it, the Jehovist and the Eloist in the ninth century BCE and the Priestly Code drawn up after the building of the Temple in Jerusalem in the fifth century BCE. Deuteronomy he dated to the time of the Hebrew exile in the sixth century BCE, while the Psalms, far from being the work of David, were ascribed to the time of the Maccabees in the second century BCE.

These datings offered a way of accounting for the discrepancies in the Genesis account of the creation, the fall of man and the flood. They also suggested that the presentation of Moses and subsequent Jewish history had been determined by the emotions of exile and the creation of an ideal past, 'an artificial memory distilled from hope' as Julia described it. Alongside this was another kind of memory, the potent force of myth, that 'common stock of traditions busy with dim memories of some dawning civilization'. For Julia its influence on the Jewish people was profound. 'The truth of parable to the Eastern mind is perhaps more real than the truth of history. […] An accurate narration of facts embodies, in most cases, much that is incidentally misleading. A true parable has nothing that is not true.'[77]

Much of her study dealt with the account of creation in Genesis, 'a jumble of parable and science which became inevitably a stumbling block in the way of science', with its incompatible accounts in chapter 1 and chapters 2–5 of 'an event which cannot have happened twice'. Though she was generally critical of the Priestly Code, she preferred its more systematic account of creation in chapter 1 to the Eloist's account that follows. The Code's description of the six days of creation might, she suggested, be seen 'as an interesting first sketch of the theory of evolution'.[78] She also much preferred its account of the creation of woman.

As Marion Ann Taylor and Heather Weir have rediscovered, female writing about the Old Testament in the nineteenth century was extensive but largely concerned with its portrayal of women.[79] Eve was inevitably a problem as not just the first woman and mother but also the one who succumbed to the serpent and then tempted her husband, leading to her and Adam's expulsion from Paradise. Few women commentators could forget Milton's vivid characterization of her failings in *Paradise Lost*. Some saw her as a victim, some pointed out that by accusing his wife before God, Adam had committed the greater sin, others emphasized her pivotal role in securing the eventual redemption of all mankind, while clever American feminists like Lillie Devereux Blake and Clare Bewick Colby avoided all that they found objectionable in the presentation of Eve and, later, Abraham's wife, Sarah, by omitting it from their Women's Bible.[80]

Julia was more ambitious. By focusing on the disparate origins of the Genesis text, she could present the traditional figure of Eve not as God's creation but as the invention of the Eloist and compare his version with the more positive story told in the Priestly Code. Far from the Eloist's 'grotesque account' of Eve emerging from Adam's rib, the Priestly Code took a 'coeval' view of man and woman as both created by God. 'Woman is no afterthought […] and derives her being directly from Him.' The instruction 'to go forth and multiply' was similarly more acceptable than the prediction that 'in sorrow shalt though bring forth children'. The Eloist's account of Eve's origin and conduct, which was, as she said, faithfully reflected in *Paradise Lost*, had long troubled Julia: 'to judge from the result it would have been far better for man to have been alone than to have had Eve for a companion'.[81] Nor did the stories that followed improve matters. Except for Cain's murder of Abel, women were implicated in all the subsequent disasters that befell the Hebrew race as recorded in Genesis. By presenting these uncomfortable models of feminine behaviour in a critical, historicist context, Julia cut through the exculpatory discourse of most female commentators.

She presents the Jewish people as a race that was often fallible but inspired by a desire for unity through completion with God. Their destiny was not to be a powerful nation but to preserve the remnant from which the longed-for Messiah would come. But the priestly era after the return from exile had saved the 'outward unity' of Judaism only by confining worship to the Temple in Jerusalem and establishing a priestly caste separate from the rest of the nation. Judaism's 'inner unity' had survived, however, in the remnant. Jesus was 'the ideal Jew', rejected though he was by a 'renegade Judaism' reliant on its clerical exclusivity and readiness to compromise with imperial Rome.[82] Julia deployed a suggestive metaphor, writing of the sheath that conceals the setting seed. The husk withers as the Jews are dispersed after the destruction of the Temple: the seed germinates as the exclusivity of God's promise to the Jewish people is extended to all nations through Christ.

Once again, she focused on the need for unity, concentrating this time on the unity of the nation. By comparison, the unity of the church was no more than an 'external unity'. Insofar as the Psalms 'express a passionate race-unity we need not turn from them'. 'The man who loves his country cares 'for all sorts and conditions of men' rather than the narrow interests of his order', unlike the established Church.[83]

Julia wrote well about the way that history is as much a reflection of the present as a record of the past and about the role of myth in its formation. She also enjoyed drawing idiosyncratic parallels between Old Testament and Classical literature. Jacob reminded her of Ulysses, the discussion of sexuality in the *Symposium* was more sophisticated and interesting than that in *Genesis*, Tubalcain was reminiscent of Vulcan and the Eloist's God was a kind of Prometheus.

Her conclusion blended critical force with optimistic mysticism. Like Maurice, she wanted to demonstrate the continuing relevance of the Old Testament. She found a warning in the 'renegade Judaism' of the priestly cast, its accommodation with Rome and rejection of the Messiah, but a promise in the survival of 'the Remnant' from which Christ had come. Something similar, she suggested, had happened in England. Faith had been assailed and the established Church challenged. Those who had survived were the stronger for it. 'The Church has lost something and gained something. There has been an outward surrender – an inward accession of strength.'[84] But Christ, Julia reminded her many clerical readers, had not turned away from the Temple. 'We may feel our loyalty not less claimed by the Church of our race than was His by the Temple of His race.' Faith, however, had already reached the zenith of its 'external impressiveness'. An invisible transformation was occurring. 'The change from the religion of a Remnant is always externally despicable, but it is a change from second hand to first hand – from trust in an Order, a Temple, a Book, to trust in God.'[85] The quiet confidence of this conclusion reflected the reliance on inner religious experience that Julia had learnt in her spiritual crisis of the 1870s.

The Message of Israel was published in 1894 by Isbister and Company, who had recently published a book of Old Testament studies by Gladstone. The topicality of the new Bible criticism ensured that it was widely reviewed. A few of the reviews were respectful and admiring, others condescending and the rest hostile. Though her good intentions were generally recognized, her competence was often questioned. For the *National Observer*, published in Edinburgh, the Old Testament was 'a sacred text'. It was 'thoroughly misleading from end to end' for 'the authoress' (as her more critical reviewers tended to describe her) to suggest that acceptance of the new Bible criticism could be an aid to faith. The *London Quarterly Review* shared its contempt.[86]

This condescension would not have surprised Julia. The *Athenaeum* criticized her Hebrew, recommending its readers to stick with 'the learned conclusions of Dr Driver'. Since she had acknowledged her debt to Driver, this was no more than a way of putting her in her place as a writer outside the world of professional scholarship and a woman to boot. Predictably, the *Saturday Review* objected to her temerity: 'She throws herself into the area of the higher critic with perhaps too little reserve, and certainly too many words.'[87]

More knowledgeable reviewers treated her with greater respect. Two leading scholars in the Free Church of Scotland and supporters of William Robertson Smith, Marcus Dodds in *The Bookman* and Alexander Balmain Bruce in a 14-page essay in the *Contemporary Review*, applauded the skill with which she had made the findings of the new criticism more widely available and the spirit in which she had approached a necessary but difficult task.[88] Bruce acknowledged her 'freshness and originality' and a 'wide range of knowledge which enables her to illuminate her arguments by many a comparison drawn from other peoples, and last, but not least, the curious felicities of style which one has occasion to admire on every page'. Dodds noted that 'the Old Testament has been studied from end to end with care, intelligence, and fruit. The style, though sometimes slightly involved, is frequently illuminated with brilliant and memorable sayings.'[89] Bruce, who explained Julia's argument at length in the *Contemporary Review*, found her suggestion that the importance of faith, rather than the search for righteousness, was the dominant element in the message of Israel, more convincing than Mathew Arnold's contrary assertion. Though *The Message of Israel* was not 'easy holiday reading', he recommended it to clergymen as a book that would 'help them help their people'.[90]

The reviewer in the *Academy* was more critical, picking up errors in Julia's Classical references. Nor did he accept what he misleadingly described as the argument of the book that 'what Israel proclaimed was the intimate interdependence of monotheism and monogamy'. But he found 'her observations on human life' 'just and penetrating'. 'Her style,' he wrote, 'though too labored and sometimes wanting in clearness, always has dignity and distinction, and occasionally a certain eloquence, at once feminine and austere.'[91] The author of this nice description of Julia's mature prose was Alfred Benn. As Julia may have known, he was a Comtean like his friend Vernon Lushington and the author of a two-volume study of *The Greek Philosophers* published in 1882.

True to form, she appreciated his review the most. 'I was particularly grateful for a list of mistakes,' she wrote to him. Could he let her have the names of the more recent historians of Greece to whom he had referred? Benn quickly supplied them and invited Julia to visit him in Florence. The invitation, she charmingly replied, added 'one more to the many attractions of that (to me) unvisited city. Will you remember my address [94 Gower Street] as at any rate a striking contrast to all that meets your eye. (Ruskin rightly chooses Gower St. as the focus of London ugliness.)'[92]

Fifteen years later, Benn got in touch to suggest meeting in London. So began one of Julia's most rewarding friendships in her last years. The fact that it had begun with genuine gratitude for the care he had taken in pointing out her errors was an indication not just of her essential modesty but also of the extent to which she felt isolated from academic contacts. 'My scholarship is so shallow & partial', she wrote to him in September 1906, 'that in face of the real thing [a planned meeting to discuss Hellenism] I am always more anxious to learn than to argue.'[93]

The precariousness of her learning, excluded as she was from the academic community, makes the daring of *The Message of Israel* more striking. But had she, as Dodds implied, fallen between stools? Was *The Message of Israel* too expert and exegetic for the general reader but too personal and un-academic for the specialist? The errors that Benn and others identified could have been corrected in a second edition. But there was none. The copies of her book that she gave to members of the family still sat on their shelves, the pages uncut, 90 years later. Emma Darwin, however, read hers though with less than her usual attention. What caught her eye was not the general argumentation but Julia's abuse of Esther ('hard, cruel, immodest') and her love of the Psalms.[94]

The literary world was moving on as Julia continued to mull over the preoccupations of her own aging generation. Perhaps, she feared, she was losing her audience. Her friend Harold Herford, the Professor of English at Manchester, tried to reassure her:

> You were speaking the other day of the apparent lack of those who understood & listened to you. I am confident that you exaggerate this 'solitude' and that there are many chosen souls throughout the country to whom your voice appeals as few other contemporary voices do; they are not of the kind which makes a noise in the press.[95]

Herford was less prescient than Julia. The space for the still small voice in the more unbuttoned and fragmented world of the 1890s was shrinking.

Chapter Fifteen
'THE OLD ORDER CHANGETH'

The end of the nineteenth century was, inevitably, a time for both taking stock and trying to look forward. For some, particularly in the younger generation, it brought the exhilaration of freedom from old orthodoxies. While older generations had more regrets over the loss of settled authority, they too sensed the possibility of re-definition in the aftermath of a heroic age of dominant personalities in politics, religion and literature. In this freer climate the antagonism between science and religion became less acute, while agnosticism was more pervasive and less guilt-ridden. In politics, Gladstone's adoption of Home Rule broke up old party loyalties, while concern about social disintegration was met with a new emphasis on the importance of family and community and more diverse approaches towards tackling the problems of the poor. In literature, new and distinctive voices emerged, ranging from Oscar Wilde to H. G. Wells, Robert Louis Stevenson to Walter Pater, Algernon Swinburne to Thomas Hardy. The fluidity was equally evident in religion, where, as José Harris has suggested, a 'disorderly pluralism' prevailed. Julia observed the same phenomenon: 'ideas and aspirations which we have hitherto recognized under the name of Christianity are taking up new aspects and appearing in unexpected quarters'.[1] Alongside the traditional forms of faith, Theosophy, Transcendentalism, Eastern mysticism and other 'varieties of religious experience' attracted new adherents, while interest in Spiritualism revived. With old doctrinal certainties weakening and Darwinism losing some of its assurance, the 1890s were, Julia believed, a time when people had to think for themselves.

Politically, she moved to the right after the Home Rule split. Dicey's critique of the destabilizing effects of the establishment of a separate Parliament in Dublin impressed her. In 1890 she published what can only be described as a reactionary article in *Murray's Magazine*, warning of the dangers of majoritarian democracy. Home Rule, she claimed, would legitimize the Irish Land League that had 'martyred' the law-abiding Irish minority.[2]

For all her nostalgia over what had been lost, however, she welcomed the new challenges in her own stock-take of the nineteenth century, 'The Old Order Changeth' published in 1897 in the *Contemporary Review*. Though she highlighted the dangers of 'eccentricity', she looked forward to the new age of individuality with excitement. She had no doubt that fundamental change was in store. 'New centres, new groupings, new forms of divine teaching are upon us now. The powers, the perceptions of an individual life are widened. [...] The very lack of exceptional eminence among us is an aid in guiding our attention to the powers and opportunities that are common to every child of man.'[3]

'Eccentricity' was not something Julia entirely avoided in her last two decades. For a time she was drawn into Hintonism until it was undermined by scandal; she followed her father in his devotion to Spiritualism, seduced by a well-meant trick; she spent much time with her 'strange friend' Mary Everest Boole; and was drawn to the eclecticism of another friend, Victoria, Lady Welby. In the last two decades of her life, she could be found in surprising places: lecturing at the Christo Theosophical Society alongside the young G. K. Chesterton or in Edinburgh at the annual meeting of the International Society of Ethics with Patrick Geddes, cooperating with Arthur Munby against legislation that would have prohibited women from working at pitheads or supporting a campaign in the *Spectator* to raise money for the training of reservists at a time of concern about the lack of military spirit in the nation's young men.[4] But there are more orthodox sightings too. She became an active supporter of the work of the Charity Organisation Society and was, like Frances Power Cobbe, a passionate anti-vivisectionist. Her critical acumen generally prevailed, tinged though it was by an optimism that sometimes shaded into sentimentality. She was never as credulous about Spiritualism as her father, always more restrained than Cobbe in her campaigning against vivisection, wary of Boole's devotion to James Hinton and cautious about Welby's modernist attempts to reconcile science and religion. Despite her sisters' curiosity about Theosophy, she steered clear of Madame Blavatsky as well as Mary Baker Eddy. Though eugenics attracted several in her wider family, Julia's instinctive sympathy for the weak made her more cautious.

In 1889 she moved to a tall dark house on Gower Street where she could offer a home for her widowed father. She was close to the British Museum, where she still put in regular hours. Harold Herford remembered seeing her there: 'the small, slight figure with the grave, absorbed eyes under the massive brow [...] noiselessly moving along the catalogue shelves in the reading-room'.[5] On Saturday and Sunday afternoons, she was 'at home', ready for whatever company came to call. David Erskine recalled the scene: 'You in the little wicker chair. [...] The photos along the edge to the right of the fireplace "the Herakleion" the watercolours of home. The clock, the green glasses with daffodils.'[6] A watercolour portrait she did of her father shows an airy, unfussy sitting room, free of the heavy Victorian mahogany furniture she disliked. Staying with the Salis Schwabes at their holiday home overlooking the Menai Strait, she had been appalled at

> how vast expense has been incurred to shut out all the outer beauty [...] everywhere lace hangings, deep mullions, & painted glass shut in one's gaze to the expensive & tasteless interior of a big villa, & make one wonder how such a spot was selected when all its beauty was treated exactly as if it had been Gower St.[7]

Whatever its drawbacks, Gower Street was a magnet for independent able women. Mary Robinson and her family hosted a famous literary salon at No. 84 in the early 1880s, while Agnes Garrett and her cousin, Rhoda, set up an interior-decorating company on the Street. After Rhoda's early death, Millicent Garrett Fawcett and her daughter, Philippa, came to live with Agnes. The Ladies Residential Chambers built on nearby Chenies Street just before Julia moved away, included among its residents Jane Harrison, Olive Schreiner and Emily Penrose, the head of Bedford College.[8]

Offering her father a well-run home pleased Julia. She followed Hope's sensible advice not to subordinate her own work to looking after him: 'the diffused cheerfulness of your

Figure 32 Julia Wedgwood's watercolour of her father, Hensleigh, in the sitting room of her house on Gower Street. In the possession of the author.

having something in hand that is being done advantageously will be more valuable to Father than personal attendance'.[9] He continued to write for the *Journal of the Society for Psychical Research* and articles on philology. He also brought with him his massive collection of rare dictionaries and books on language that Julia would later donate to what became the Birmingham University Library, after carefully cataloguing each volume.[10] Hensleigh survived his wife by just two years. In his last year his sight was so poor he needed a secretary to read to him and take dictation though his mind remained alert. 'I incline to place this year of semi-blindness and weakness among the happiest of his life,' Julia remembered. 'The heart and mind kept their activity, and the failing bodily powers seemed but closing doors that shut him in with peaceful thoughts and loving care.'[11] He died quietly at home on 1 June 1891.

Thanks to his family inheritance, directorships and careful investments (on which Ras Darwin had offered shrewd advice), Hensleigh died a rich man, leaving £123,694. Unlike his father and grandfather, he chose to divide his estate equally between his five surviving children, though the unreliable Alfred's share was to be held in trust. Ernest was made his father's principal executor and got his gold watch and chain and fur coat, while Alfred received only some silver desert spoons and forks. The bulk of Hensleigh's personal possessions went to Julia. After a few individual bequests, including £100 to John Scott, the 'son of my old friend A. J. Scott', the money was split between his three daughters and two sons after loans that had already been advanced were deducted. Hope had borrowed the most, £4,550, a substantial sum, with Ernest taking £2,000, Effie £1,300 and Alfred £600. Only £250 had been advanced to Julia, reflecting not just her reduced needs as a single woman but also her ability to earn useful amounts from her articles and royalties on her books. She was always discreet about her earnings. There is just one reference to them in her surviving correspondence. In 1880 she told Ellen Tollett how pleased she was at having earned £20 from the *Spectator* the previous year.[12] The *Contemporary Review*, to which she regularly contributed, was known to pay well, and *The Moral Ideal* had been quickly reprinted. With these and other earnings and an allowance from her father, Julia had lived comfortably even before Hensleigh died.

His death freed Julia to go on a holiday she may have had in mind since Browning's death in Venice on 12 December 1889. She had not attended his funeral, a largely masculine affair in a dank Westminster Abbey on 31 December. Arthur Munby, however, was among the mourners and braved the persistent thick fog to call on her three days later to tell her about it. As the *Pall Mall Gazette* reported, streams of female admirers came to pay homage at Browning's grave in the days after his interment.[13] Julia and Marian Hughes may well have been among them.

After the disastrous family holidays of the 1840s and 1850s, Julia rarely travelled abroad. She accompanied her invalid mother to Grasse in 1888 and would go for a cure at Aix-les-Bains in 1895.[14] Her 1893 trip was more leisurely than either of these, travelling with Marian under cousin Godfrey's protection to Greece and Italy. In Venice she made several fine sketches of the Grand Canal, visited San Rocco to see the Tintorettos (with Ruskin in hand) and was entranced by St Marks. It felt like a tent, 'gorgeous hangings as it were & the windows mere chinks in them'.[15] But, though she said nothing of it, the sight of Ca' Rezzonico, where Browning died, probably had an even greater impact on her than the fabled city and its rich artworks.

Back in England, she spent more time with Hope and Godfrey at the large mock Tudor house they built at Idlerocks near Stone. It was sited on a hilltop, from which they could see 'six counties or at all events a good round number' with lots of space for the fine garden Hope created.[16] A visit from Julia was not, as E. M. Forster remembered, something to be taken lightly: 'Snowie was too serious, too authoritative, too exacting, too learned, too cross, and too deaf, and eyebrows would be (humorously) raised in later years when she was due for a visit.'[17] While Julia liked nothing better in the late afternoon than 'getting into my armchair with a book of philosophy till dressing time', Hope fretted over her reluctance to go for walks.[18] Snow's presence quickly revived the old mix of resentment, rebelliousness and respect in her youngest sister. 'I stretch my arms & legs & shriek – in reaction to the previous experience of physical mental & moral cramp,' she told Charlotte Massingberd after one visit.[19] But they agreed on politics, both becoming enthusiastic Liberal Unionists. Julia was outspoken in her criticism of Thomas Farrer: 'men like my brother-in-law terrify me', she told Albert Dicey in 1893.[20] The breach over Home Rule was intensified by disagreements over the Boer War. Effie opposed it, despite the fact that her nephew, Cecil, Godfrey's eldest child, was fighting in it. Julia was horrified when a young friend, May Crum, also showed sympathy for the Boers. 'I am obliged to keep a chamber in my heart for them because of my sister,' she wrote, 'but I shd. be sorry to have to put another bed in it.'[21] Despite the tensions, Idlerocks became the sort of haven that Maer and Down House had been. She had no compunction about inviting Alfred Benn and his wife to join her there, 'if you would like to escape

Figure 33 Julia Wedgwood's unfinished water colour of Idlerocks, the house that Godfrey and Hope Wedgwood built near Modershall, Staffordshire. Source: V A Wedgwood/Mosley collection.

from London heat to a green Hilltop looking towards Welsh hills & the society of a good many elderly ladies, all worthy persons, & one yr affte friend F Julia Wedgwood'.[22]

Godfrey died in 1905 after several years of ill-health, including the amputation of his right leg (like his great grandfather, Josiah Wedgwood, he wore a wooden leg). Hope found particular comfort in Julia's letters and their conversations. 'No one speaks of him <u>but you almost</u>,' she wrote two years later. The Victorians took trouble over their letters of condolence. Julia's were particularly prized. In some she shared her growing confidence in the prospect of reunion with loved ones, but with others she recognized this promise would be meaningless. Cato Lowes Dickinson frequently turned to her letters for spiritual reassurance after his wife's early death.[23] Henrietta Litchfield, by contrast, received a touching letter that avoided religious consolation when her mother died.

Julia had a theory that grieving was often at its most desolate and intense after the initial shock of separation had faded. Effie copied round a letter she had written to a bereaved mother. A sense of communion with the dead, Julia wrote, took time to emerge after a death just as stars were visible at twilight, not in the sunset's glow.[24] Similarly, her letters of condolence to Victoria Welby on her husband's death were the only ones her daughter chose to publish. 'We dwell in houses not made with hands long before we quit those of material building, and as our dearest pass away from us those unseen habitations grow more definite to us.'[25]

Though she was happy to act as a spiritual counsellor to those who sought her advice, Julia's circle in her later years was eclectic. It included Positivists, like Alfred Benn, the Lushington brothers, Vernon and Godfrey, and Harold Herford; the free-thinking Litchfields, and, later, the young atheist Morgan Forster, alongside devoted Churchmen like Arthur Munby and Cato Lowes Dickinson. What mattered to her was that they had lively minds and were good talkers. Roger Fry sent her copies of his books, and from time to time, she encouraged him and his wife to visit her though always gracefully acknowledging that they might have better things to do. 'How pleasant is the unexpected remembrance of the young to the old,' she wrote to them in 1901.[26] She was also in touch with Alice Meynell, whose interests in art, religion and literature she shared.[27] Coming a generation after Julia, Meynell had become by the 1890s the first wholly successful 'woman of letters'. Her literary persona, playful but expert and always persuasive, was, like Julia's, consciously constructed but would win her greater rewards and wider critical esteem.[28]

New friendships compensated for the loss of older friends. After several months of ill-health, Emily Gurney died in 1896 at the convalescent home for the needy that she and her husband had founded 20 years earlier in Bayswater. By then Julia saw much less of her though they wrote regularly. The authoritative tone of her later letters and their wide range of subjects show how far she had moved on from the needy confessions of the 1870s. But Emily's influence was still important. She introduced her to a young woman who became one of her closest friends and set her an example through her support for the Charity Organisation Society.

The idealist emphasis on the importance of community, self-realization through cooperation, and the development of personal responsibility were a major input in the Society's work.[29] Like her friend Octavia Hill, who had also grown up in Christian Socialism, Julia believed in helping the poor to help themselves. With funding from Ruskin, Hill had acquired some run-down properties in Marylebone, done them up and rented them out to tenants willing to pay rent regularly and keep their properties in order. Further purchases followed in Notting Hill and south of the river, with supporters like Caroline Stephen and Emily Gurney also buying properties and handing them over to the Society for it to manage once they had been refurbished and tenants installed. Julia gave a house in Marylebone in 1908.[30]

'Sympathy widens downwards,' she wrote in 'The Old Order Changeth'. 'We cannot ignore the sufferings of the weak and the poor as the best men of former ages ignored them.' The ethos of the Charity Organisation Society with its emphasis on the development of character, acceptance of family responsibilities and friendly contact between upper and middle class visitors was far more to her taste than the workhouse visiting Maurice had promoted. Sunday afternoons with 'torpid old creatures' at the St Pancras Workhouse always depressed her. 'A Skye terrier was more sympathetic,' she complained to Emily about one. But she spoke up for the Workhouse when it was threatened with removal to the country, arguing in her letter to the *London Daily News* that the move would make it harder for visitors to 'relieve the dismal monotony of workhouse life' by keeping in touch with the inmates.[31]

Julia was defensive about the charge that she and Emily had grown apart, though the desperate tone of some of Emily's last letters to 'Beloved Snow' tends to confirm it.

Watching the tensions between 'MiLady' Inglis and Mary Rich in 1872, she had wondered whether she and Emily might want 'some now young Stephens' to reconcile them if they survived into their 80s.[32] When the Gurneys narrowly escaped drowning on the Nile in 1876, she had felt that she would 'have lost something that is almost like water or air to my soul' if Emily had died. Rereading this in 1896, she commented: 'It was not so when she did go, tho' I loved her even more.' The explanation lay in something she had written many years before: 'We love most when we need least.'[33] By the 1890s Julia was no longer the demanding, self-absorbed friend she had been in the 1870s. She enjoyed a network of friendships, she was the head of her own household and she had an established place in the literary world. Now she could respond to the needs of others, offering herself as sage and spiritual counsellor and attracting a circle of young women she could mentor.

The most important was Kathleen Jervois, who had been introduced to her by Emily, a fact that gave a special aura to the friendship almost as if Emily had given her a daughter. Their mutual liking had been 'sudden' as with all Julia's most important friendships.[34] Though only a few extracts from her letters to Jervois remain, what was probably a similar, though less intense correspondence with another young woman, May Crum, has survived.[35] Crum, who lived in Cambridge, was the maternal granddaughter of Rev. John McLeod Campbell, the great Scottish religious leader whom Julia had met at Linlathen. She was young, in rather poor health, keenly interested in the arts and hoping to become a writer.

Julia's letters to her are affectionate, encouraging and wise. She advises her on how to find a publisher for an article on bull-fighting and whether to refer to the supposed views of the Queen on animal welfare. She helped her through a crisis of religious doubt and passed on her passion for art. At the outset of their friendship, she suggested they make a special study of the paintings in the National Gallery. Perhaps it was Crum that Herford spotted there with Julia. 'Pictures', he wrote, 'were a peculiar delight to her; and at the London galleries a little crowd might often be seen attending her while she, wholly unconscious, expounded and interpreted, in the unsubdued voice of the deaf, to some privileged but slightly embarrassed young friend.'[36]

Someone else with an interest in the arts that Julia grew close to was her younger cousin, Eliza, the granddaughter of John Wedgwood. She was a friend of John Singer Sargent and his sister, Emily, and an expert folksong collector. Though she briskly dismissed Julia's fondness for reminiscing about her famous friends of earlier days and could not get on with her published work, as she told her friend, Ruth Draper, many years after Julia's death, 'I very much appreciated her letter writing powers.'[37]

Another young Wedgwood with mixed feelings about Julia was Mary Euphrasia, Hope and Godfrey's only child. Spoilt and rather aimless, 'Bim', as she was known in the family, received lots of attention from the childless Julia and Effie. Julia was keen to give her a sense of the Wedgwood family inheritance, compiling for her the Family Album of letters written by their distinguished literary and political connections.[38] She invited her to stay for long periods, encouraging her to visit the galleries and giving her and her friends theatre tickets so she could have the 'vicarious' pleasure of attending performances she could no longer hear. The results sometimes disappointed. After receiving one rather laboured thank you letter, Julia wrote in the margin, 'I wish she would learn to write letters. She wd find it a great escape from loneliness.'[39]

Hope and Godfrey were keen for their daughter to apply to Newnham College. Julia did her best to prepare her for the interview. 'I am acting as Lady Assessor to an Examining Board,' Hope reported to Effie, 'consisting of Aunty Sno with one small examinee – who began by being cross, but I am glad to say the crossness melted away under the interest of Sno's questions & now she is in high glee over it which is better luck than I had ventured to hope for.' 'Bim', not a natural intellectual, eventually applied to Newnham in 1902 but was not accepted. Julia was relieved. Both Hope and Godfrey were in poor health at the time. Julia, still ambivalent about the value of university education for women, wanted their daughter to stay at home and look after them.[40]

In her 60s and 70s, she lectured occasionally, mostly to female audiences. In 1896 she gave a talk on maternal self-sacrifice at Broughty Ferry. In 1893 she addressed the St Andrews Club, a female Shakespeare appreciation society. Rather more surprisingly, she also lectured in Edinburgh in 1896 alongside Patrick Geddes, whose sensational views on the biologically determined limits on women's intellectual capabilities had attracted much attention.[41]

In autumn 1902, May Crum engineered an invitation for her to give a lecture at Newnham. Julia was in two minds about accepting. Though she had a talk ready about Greek drama, 'I feel myself that so much of the life of this sort of address depends on the subsequent discussion my deafness makes impossible,' she wrote, but if May and her sister, Jessie, were there to support her, she would brave Newnham and looked forward to spending a couple of quiet hours in its library. Jessie, who had won a first in the second part of the Classical Tripos in 1901 before going on to marry Rev. Hugh Stuart, the chaplain at Trinity College, was, at the time, the favourite protégée of Jane Harrison, the Classics tutor at Newnham. Though Harrison had not yet published the books on Greek religious ceremonial that made her famous (or been canonized by Virginia Woolf in *A Room of One's Own*), she was already well-known as a daring and flamboyant lecturer. As Mary Beard has suggested, the most influential part of her teaching was 'that somewhere underneath the calm, shiny, rational exterior of the classical world is a mass of weird, seething irrationality'. Julia's view of the Greeks was more traditional. Judging from Jane Harrison's letter of thanks, she chose to lecture on her familiar theme of the sense of proportion in Greek thought. 'Your idea', Harrison wrote, 'about the fresh mind being concerned with a sympathetic balance of realities instead of right and wrong is most suggestive & goes very deep down – it is I am <u>sure</u> right & I am most grateful to you for your emphasis on it'. Julia liked the letter rather more than Harrison's suggestion that she read the *Bacchae*, a play she had always avoided.[42]

Both Julia and Jane Harrison had contributed to *The Woman's World*, a monthly periodical whose editorship Oscar Wilde took on in 1887.[43] His remit was to revive a publication focused on fashion and society by appealing to the much talked-about 'Girton girl' and her kind. He invited a wide range of women writers to contribute, including Anne Thackeray Ritchie, Ouida, Amy Levy, Olive Schreiner, Edith Simcox and Emily Faithful as well as titled ladies like the Countess of Portsmouth and Lady Archibald Campbell, and extended the magazine's range with reviews of Greek drama at Oxford and Cambridge and articles on women in Classical times. Julia was given a lead article in 1888 and chose as her subject 'Women and Democracy'. She enjoyed addressing a readership of young, educated, independent, middle-class women who might, or might not, become wives and mothers and happily launched her article with a rather obscure reference to 'the ages of the Pisistratides and the Tarquins', confident that her audience would pick it up.

The more restricted space Wilde was able to offer her by comparison with her usual pieces in the *Contemporary Review* scarcely allowed room to develop all the themes she launched in her article. Some she would work up more fully in 'Male and Female Created He Them'; others, like her attack on the over-influential but unrepresentative views of upper-class women, she had already tackled and now sharpened up with a critique of the 'vulgarity' of class feeling. The most striking aspect of her article, however, is its silence about female suffrage. Despite her title 'Women and Democracy', she sidestepped the issue, suggesting that women were already having an increasing impact in the polity. Democracy was, she claimed, advancing everywhere not just as a political or social force but also in the intellectual world: 'even by the domestic hearth, and in the solitude of the study, it is still impossible for us to forget that the idea of authority has grown dim'. As a result, 'obedience' was 'no longer the ideal of marriage', and the world of knowledge had become 'one vast Republic' where 'one fact is as good as another'. In this less-structured environment, 'the new development of female influence' was 'characteristic of our day'. Woman, she wrote in a long-delayed but implicit acceptance of J. S. Mill, 'has been the slave of man; and now in her newly won freedom she gives thanks for standing as the spokesman of all the enslaved'. Above all, she had retained 'the virtue of the slave, the passionate devotion to self-obliterating interest'. Women had not only a superior moral sense to men but also the ability to reconcile. 'In her sense of incompleteness, in her craving for the presence of an opposite nature, in her continual yearning to exchange the *I* for the *We*, lies the true medicine of the ills of Democracy,' she concluded in familiar Maurician terms.[44]

Though Julia portrayed the development of democracy as liberating, she had increasing reservations about female suffrage. The likelihood 20 years later that women would only get the vote as part of a move towards universal suffrage dampened her enthusiasm. When Emily Davies sought her signature in 1910 on a circular letter supporting the first Conciliation Bill, which proposed a limited, property-based franchise for women, Julia reluctantly declined. She admired the tone of the draft with its 'power of temperance & understatement, the freedom from all incitement to emotion [...] which is supposed to be an inaccessible eminence to women'. But it could not hide the reality 'that the momentum of this movement is not with you [...] & that it's vain for the wise tens to point out the way beside the precipice if the foolish thousands are rushing towards it'.[45] Majoritarian democracy with its incentive for 'uneducated or half-educated men' to rely on opinions picked up from a hasty reading of the *Star* or the *Echo* was something Julia had learnt to distrust in the debates on Irish Home Rule.[46]

Women aged 30 and above who satisfied a modest property requirement finally got the vote in 1918. Davies, like Millicent Garrett Fawcett, survived to go to the polls in 1921: Julia did not. Had she lived long enough, she would doubtless have exercised her new right but might well have felt uncomfortable with the company she was obliged to keep at the polling station (and even more so in 1929 when the franchise for women was further extended). Despite her resistance to majoritarian political democracy, however, Julia's heart could overcome her head. Late in life she was asked to donate to a Suffragette Bazaar. She explained to the organizers that she no longer sympathized with their cause but contributed all the same, 'just as a personal luxury'.[47]

Like Cobbe, Julia had moved from 'The Claims of Women' to 'The Claims of Brutes', a group less able to defend themselves. As Cobbe noted in her *Autobiography*, the Wedgwood family's concern with animal welfare was long and honourable. Both James and Kitty Mackintosh had been early supporters of the Royal Society for the Prevention of Cruelty to Animals. Cobbe was delighted to have their daughter, Fanny, serving on the executive committee of the Society for the Protection of Animals Liable to Vivisection (generally known as the Victoria Street Society) that she set up in 1875. Though Julia did not take her mother's place when ill-health obliged her to stand down, she became more passionately attached to the causes of animal welfare and anti-vivisection than any other. 'The indifference of almost everyone to the sufferings of those of our fellow creatures who seem to have nothing but suffering here has been the greatest sorrow of my life,' she wrote in 1897. She joined the Victoria Street Society; contacted distinguished clergymen she knew, seeking their support for moves to stop the development of physiology laboratories conducting experiments on live animals; and wrote regularly to the *Spectator*, objecting to vivisection as a perversion of science and the cause of unnecessary suffering.[48] In 1910 she broke off from work on her biography of Josiah Wedgwood to write a pamphlet for the National Anti-Vivisection Society.

Vivisection was a divisive subject. Though the Wedgwoods were largely united in their opposition to it, the Darwins were not. So fraught did the subject become at Down House that Darwin warned visitors 'when in the presence of my ladies do not talk about experiments on animals'. Adopting even more of a sexual stereotype than usual, he suggested that female concern with vivisection was due to the 'tenderness of their hearts' and 'profound ignorance'.[49] But anti-vivisection feeling was not confined to women. Several of the men Julia admired, including Browning, Tennyson, Ruskin, Carlyle, Jowett, Frank Newman and James Martineau, were prominent opponents of vivisection. The most influential was Hutton, who served on the Royal Commission alongside Huxley and others and was responsible for its recommendation that live experiments on dogs and cats be prohibited.

Though provision for this was made in the Cruelty to Animals Bill introduced in May 1876, the exclusion was steadily whittled away as the legislation went through Parliament. Far from stopping vivisection, the Act, as finally adopted, introduced a loosely administered system for facilitating it. Cobbe and the Victoria Street Society monitored its implementation, exposing the growing incidence of live experimentation and the abuses that arose. In 1878 it called for the total prohibition of vivisection, a policy the Society maintained until 1894 when it backed away from its demand for an immediate end to the practice. Cobbe withdrew to set up the British Union for the Abolition of Vivisection but attracted only 5 per cent of the Society's membership. Julia, like Anna Swanwick, remained with the majority.

Cobbe's campaigning against vivisection was always highly emotive. Her torrent of articles and pamphlets contained horrifying descriptions and images of live animals, especially dogs, pinned to the operating table. As with her campaign for the removal of female disabilities or sanctions against abusive husbands, she saw herself as speaking for the powerless against the powerful, amongst whom she now included over-mighty doctors, all too ready to determine what happened to women's bodies without consulting them and abuse animals in experiments designed to further their careers.

Like Cobbe, Julia defended the right to hunt animals but not what they both described as the right to 'torture' them. In a letter to the *Spectator* in 1879 she pointed out that no one argued for medical experimentation on condemned criminals even though this might produce more effective results than experiments on live animals. Presumably, the assumption was that 'an immoral being cannot forfeit the rights which an unmoral being cannot possess'. In 1906 she argued more passionately that failure to put oneself in the place of a sufferer as with 'the majority of sentient inhabitants of this planet' was 'to seal the springs of pity against those who have the least power to open them, and to harden the average heart where it is already most callous'.[50] In her 1910 pamphlet 'Why Am I an Anti-Vivisectionist?' she deliberately adopted a moderate tone criticizing the medical profession in far less emotive terms than Cobbe but sharing her ethical concern about the brutalizing effect on practitioners of conducting experiments on live animals. 'I have come to feel', she wrote at the outset, 'that those who oppose [vivisection] are endeavouring to protect, not only the bodies of animals, but the souls of men.'

Julia's attitude towards doctors was one of guarded respect. Like her father, she left a generous bequest to her personal physician but she could also entreat her friend Annie Erskine 'to try the novelty of a rest-from-doctors-cure'.[51] In her pamphlet she pointed to the risk that the medical profession was being compromised in its search for new cures by the seductions of fame and money. The search for cures, together with light regulation, had led to a dramatic increase in vivisection. Of the 89,581 experiments conducted on live animals between 1903 and 1905, only 93 had been inspected. Delving into the Registrar General's records of rates of mortality for those diseases where it was claimed that vivisection was most likely to help find a cure, she found no correlation. Rates for cancer, anthrax, diabetes and diphtheria had all increased, while the fall in deaths from tuberculosis was, she claimed, the result of the adoption of open-air treatment, not Professor Koch's 'tuberculin'. 'No tortured animal laid down its life to secure that result, but it might have been approached more than a century earlier if physicians had [...] simply yielded to the longing of patients whose lives they had no hope of saving, and opened the window.' Similarly, if doctors had tried 'a little imagination and experiment on invalids', they might have found dietary cures for diabetes without the need to experiment on animals.

Julia's argument, however, went beyond the need for more responsive medical attitudes. Her concern was with the equivalence of God's creation. Suffering caused to an animal did not differ in kind from human suffering. Even if vivisection could find a cure for cancer, she would still oppose it. 'Truth is one of the few things that are better than health. We must all die, few painlessly.'[52] At the time she made this brave assertion, she faced an operation for cancer. In preparation for that, she rewrote her will, leaving substantial sums for the reform of slaughterhouse practices, the provision of drinking troughs for horses and the continuing campaign against vivisection.

The contrast between Julia's high-minded advocacy and Cobbe's campaigning designed to shock reflected their very different temperaments. They remained good friends, however, and appreciated each other's work. Cobbe's praise for *The Moral Ideal* meant a lot to Julia, who had been an early admirer of Cobbe's Kantian-inflected *Theory of Intuitive Morals*.[53] In her *Autobiography*, Cobbe drew up a list of her 'beloved and honoured friends' designed to impress. Julia was there alongside Lady Mount-Temple, who convened the Broadlands revivalist meetings that Emily Gurney and, occasionally, Julia attended, Emily Shirreff, Millicent Garrett Fawcett, Caroline Stephen and Octavia Hill. Similarly, when a congratulatory message was prepared for Cobbe's 80th birthday in 1902, Julia's name headed the list of distinguished female signatories, who included Florence Nightingale, Josephine Butler and Anne Thackeray Ritchie.[54]

Just as Darwin took a different view on vivisection from his Wedgwood cousins, so he, unlike Hensleigh and his daughters, remained deeply suspicious of Spiritualism, which reached an initial peak of interest in the 1860s and 1870s as séances became as popular in middle-class drawing rooms as working-class parlours. Though the exposure of several frauds discredited some of the more theatrical happenings, interest in Spiritualism remained. Towards the end of the century, it acquired a new emphasis on telepathy, automatic writing at the planchette board and communication with the dead via mediums.

The interests of those attracted to Spiritualism were diverse. Some, like Frederic Myers, Oliver Lodge, Henry Sidgwick, the distinguished Cambridge academic, and Edmund Gurney, Emily's nephew, looked to find a substitute for the faith they had lost. Others, like Julia and Hutton, saw it as reaffirming their faith. For him Spiritualism suggested an unexplained dimension beyond the visible and material world as well as the existence of unrealized mental capacities. Perhaps it could answer 'the age-old difficult questions about the identity of mind and spirit, the distinction between body and soul, and the ability of intellect truly to fathom the working of natural laws by empirical evidence alone'.[55] Julia's commitment, by contrast, was more emotional than intellectual.

Hensleigh was increasingly obsessed by Spiritualism. He made friends with professional mediums and probably arranged for Charles Williams to act at a séance Ras and George Darwin organized in January 1874. It attracted a remarkable attendance: the Darwins, the Litchfields, George Eliot and George Henry Lewes, Francis Galton and Frederic Myers, and *in cognito* T. H. Huxley. Julia too was there with her parents. Darwin and the Leweses left early, suspecting trickery, but Hensleigh was entranced, vigorously defending Williams when Huxley complained about sharp practice. Talking to Aunt Emma after the séance Julia, though still not fully convinced, was more open-minded than her 'bigoted' Uncle Charles.[56]

In 1882 Hensleigh became a founding vice president of the Psychical Research Society, which would list among its honorary members Gladstone, Tennyson, Ruskin and Alfred Wallace, with A. J. Balfour and William James as two of its vice presidents. The Society's most active adherents were Henry Sidgwick and his wife Eleanor, Frederic Myers, Frank Podmore and Edmund Gurney. Hensleigh regularly contributed accounts of spiritualist happenings to the *Journal* and *The Proceedings of the Psychical Research Society* but fell out with Elinor Sidgwick over his admiration for William Eglinton, who specialized in producing writings on the inside of sealed pairs of slates.[57] When Eglinton was exposed as a trickster in 1885, some members of the Society resigned: Hensleigh stayed.

His credulous obsession with Spiritualism became a family joke. Emma Darwin wrote wryly to her daughter about him going up to town 'to meet some ghosts at dinner at 31 Queen Anne Street'.[58] Lily Whichelo, the future mother of E. M. Forster, who worked briefly as governess to the Farrer children in 1876, was more outspoken:

> Mr and Mrs Wedgwood are staying here at Abinger Hall, he really hardly looks human, he is so screwed up and wizen looking, more like one of his own spirits than anything else. He is as spirit mad as ever and has now another spiritual grandchild who is also black named 'Cissy'. If you remember he had one named Pokey without a head – Oh! The nonsense of it is too dreadful!! The spirits sometimes take his spectacles off and put them on someone else which makes Mr W. rather nervous and he calls out to the spirits to 'take great care of them'.[59]

But, for all the scoffing, Effie who, like Hope, would later become a convinced Spiritualist, helped her father when he had a photo taken of himself with a 'spirit'. Hensleigh unwisely sent it to Huxley as proof of the existence of worlds beyond the scientist's ken. The rather obvious double exposure did not survive Huxley's scrutiny.[60]

Julia's deafness probably kept her away from her father's sessions with two well-known mediums, Mrs Everett and her sister, Mrs Turner, but Marian Hughes sat with them at the planchette table. Julia did, however, verify the information they picked up there, checking out the cases of Alice Grimbold, who had been hanged for murder in 1605 but now protested her innocence, and John Gurwood, a veteran of the Peninsular Wars, who explained how his unhappy military conduct had led to his suicide.[61]

Though she recognized her father's 'credulity', emotionally Julia was more than ready to commit to Spiritualism. Both she and Emily Gurney knew that it bore a transgressive taint, with Emily confessing her 'proclivities' whenever she indulged in a round of automatic writing with her nieces, the orphaned sisters of Edmund Gurney. But Julia sympathized with Emily's longing to see her mother again after her death. 'A faint voice from that unseen world would make all the difference if once, only once, the Dead could send some unmistakable communication the horror of the grave would be gone,' she wrote to her in 1867. Rereading her letter in 1898, Julia wrote in the margin, 'That I have had now'.[62]

The trigger was the death of her mother in May 1889. Fanny had been ailing for several years, spending much of her time on the sofa at Abinger Hall or Queen Anne Street or getting around in a wheelchair. The three sisters were together at her deathbed and each contributed affecting accounts of their mother's last hours to a joint diary. Effie was struck by her consideration for her servants, telling 'Farqhar and Jane' shortly before she lapsed into her final coma, 'I'm not dying yet, but it won't be long & I mayn't be able to speak again & I want to thank you both for all yr goodness to me.' Hope recorded, 'She was v full of a journey – & asked about the preparations for one & was anxious to be ready in time.' Julia's diary entry was the most subjective:

> I sd. a few words as to what I felt about the parting. That it wd. be for a short time, & I so longed for some word from her that I added, rather unwisely, 'And you believe that too don't you?' I wish I cd. write down the tone & manner of her answer, for it expressed something different from what the words say 'I feel a vicarious confidence in your hope, & it is enough for me.'[63]

In her last weeks, Fanny gave Julia her watch and chain. A few months later, Mrs Turner picked up a message from her at a séance where Julia was not present: 'I am glad Snow is wearing my chain.' It is easy to imagine the medium and Marian Hughes concocting together this way of offering comfort to the grieving daughter. It worked. The message, Julia wrote to Frederic Myers, was 'a source of consolation so deep & sacred that I scarcely dare to speak of it [...] [it] moves me to remember more than any event of my life.'

Her letter describing it was unusually defensive. She knew enough of the conscientious examinations and cautious analyses of psychic events in the publications of the Society for Psychical Research to see how easily even a sensitive researcher like Myers might expose the flimsy credibility of the message. As she admitted, Mrs Turner might be 'a clever cheat' acting on inside knowledge. 'A scientific person, who was nothing more would say that we must try if this hypothesis wd. explain the facts before trying that which finds an element of the supernatural.' But Julia was not prepared to concede the validity of Myers' method in her own case. Experiments to test the existence of paranormal powers would never succeed: 'those who are gone into the Invisible can use these abnormal means of communication only in accordance with peculiar conditions. [...] They can reinforce the hope of re-union, to those who already possess it,' but would 'never pierce the wall of a strong negative belief' except with some broken message. In short, for Spiritualism to work, you had to believe in it.[64]

Julia's sense of the dead as essentially unchanged – 'those who were frivolous before it seem to remain frivolous after' – was in tune with the usual Spiritualist imaginings of the 'Sunny Land' beyond death.[65] She now had many sessions at the planchette, sometimes with Kathleen Jervois, probably with Mary Boole and almost certainly with Marian Hughes. Her father proved harder to contact than her mother. As she explained to Myers, a malign spirit called 'Julie' tried to get in the way, but 'vague & obscure as they are', she passed on to him some 'fragmentary' messages. The fact that they contained so many apparently foreign words was, she suggested, proof of their authenticity.[66]

Julia's uncritical attachment to Spiritualism was uncharacteristic. In general, as she navigated the uncharted waters of late nineteenth-century religious and pseudo-religious thought, she kept her ability to discriminate. Briefly, however, both she and Emily Gurney were attracted to Hintonism through her friendship with Howard Hinton's mother-in-law, Mary Boole.

Boole is now popularly remembered as the woman who contributed to the early death of her husband, the brilliantly inventive mathematician, George Boole, by following her homeopathic principles and wrapping him in damp sheets after he caught a chill.[67] Despite her crankiness, however, her innovative work on educational psychology was much admired by William James.[68] Julia was protective: 'She is as noble a being as I have ever known, though streaked with what is not noble,' her 'extraordinary arrogance'.[69] When she introduced her to the family, Hope was charmed and even engaged her to serve as her stepson Cecil's tutor in the summer holidays, but Bessie Darwin thought her 'the most unpleasant woman she ever saw'.[70]

The Booles had married in 1855 when he was 40 and she 23. His death nine years later left her with five unusually gifted daughters to bring up on her own. She threw herself on the mercy of Maurice, a man she revered but had never met. He created a post for her as Librarian at Queen's College and gave her the tenancy of 68 Harley Street to run as a boarding house for students at the College. Here she organized an adventurous series of Sunday evening discussions, approaching leading figures for their views on problems in mathematics, the links between natural history and psychology and the work of Renan and Darwin. Though she succeeded in tempting Darwin into a rare excursion into theodicy, Maurice became increasingly troubled by her eccentricity.[71] In 1873 she went to work for a more sympathetic employer, James Hinton.

Though a brilliant ear specialist, Hinton preferred to devote himself to high-flown, pseudo-religious writings. Seth Koven has presented him as a key figure for his times and a martyr in the cause of sexual liberation.[72] Hutton, a fellow member of the Metaphysical Society remembered rather his 'wistful, sanguine, I had almost said, hectic idealism'.[73] From time to time he abandoned his medical career to live in the East End of London and concentrate on philosophical writing. He shared the Booleian passion for finding the middle way between conflicting positions. The idea of God he argued had been overtaken by the concept of a universal spirit whose 'actuality' resolved the conflict between idealism and materialism. In his most popular book *The Mystery of Pain* (1866) he proposed that pain be seen as a good not an evil. When it involved sacrifice for others, as with a mother's self-obliterating care for her children, it could be welcomed as the highest joy. Hinton's commitment to altruism was practical as well as theoretical. He helped various women in his circle achieve self-realization through sexual satisfaction. He died in the Azores in 1870, possibly of syphilis.

Despite their vagueness, Hinton's ambitious ideas were strikingly influential. The 20-year-old Havelock Ellis was teaching in the Australian outback when he first read one of his books. He immediately dropped everything to return to England and follow Hinton in training for a medical career. He also collaborated with Hinton's widow, sister-in-law Caroline Haddon, and son, Howard, to get his work published.[74]

Howard Hinton, who married Mrs Boole's eldest daughter, Mary Ellen, and had four children by her, had been one of Jowett's brightest students at Balliol and became a science master at Uppingham. His main interest was publicizing his father's work and developing new theories of what he called higher dimensional space. He also followed his father's ways, siring twins with the woman who had nursed his wife in her last pregnancy, bigamously marrying her and then deciding to make his views on the desirability of altruistic polygamy public. Astonishingly, his mother-in-law encouraged him.[75] He got himself arrested at St Pancras Hotel in the company of his second 'wife', admitted his bigamy and was jailed for three days. On release he left the country with Mary Ellen to pursue a successful academic career in Japan and North America. Mrs Boole was put under the care of Henry Maudsley, taking with her only a Hebrew grammar, her embroidery and a notebook for the reams of poetry she was composing. Julia was left to pick up some of the pieces.

Everyone had a view about the Hinton scandal. Alice Bonham Carter and her brother-in-law, Albert Dicey, thought Hinton's polygamy a reversion to the old Adam: 'I suppose the Mormons call it moral & the Spiritualists of America also call it a "higher law" but [...] they are all seductive blackguards.'[76] Emily Gurney had heard rumours about James

Hinton's sexual permissiveness, but fallen for his son's 'suffusedness' and was readier to excuse his crime than Julia. Seeing the headline 'Extraordinary Bigamy Case' as she sat on a train opposite another traveller absorbed in the report in his *Morning Post*, she felt both 'regret and indignation', but above all, 'immense curiosity as to his motives [...] & [...] courage in letting all his reputation & living go for the sake of not keeping up appearances before the world'.[77]

Julia was less forgiving. Though she had thought him 'an attractive and interesting personality', his 'loathsome' behavior and 'morbid love of notoriety' now reminded her of 'some nauseous German novel'.[78] But she secured Boole's release from Maudsley's care and arranged for Marian Hughes to take her to the seaside to convalesce. People, Julia wrote, would just have to get used to her 'odd ways'.[79] The whole episode, 'a tragedy too interesting to destroy', as Julia labelled the papers she collected about it, was a warning about the dangers of unorthodox thinking.

The friendship between Julia and Boole survived the scandal. As Eleanor Cobham, who knew them both, wrote: 'they saw each other often [...] they read each other's manuscripts and criticized each other's work with relentless faithfulness [...] they often differed in opinion and sometimes quarrelled, but they had a deep sympathy in ultimate aims and a great appreciation of the value of each other's work'.[80] Wayward though many of Boole's ideas were, she was a gifted educationalist using practical activities to stimulate a child's unconscious imagination: gardening or caring for animals if they were studying natural science, curve stitching on cards when learning geometry. The careers of her daughters were evidence of the success of her methods. Apart from Mary Ellen, who committed suicide after Howard Hinton's sudden death in 1908, one trained as a concert pianist, one became a best-selling writer, another an expert in four-dimensional geometry, while the fourth, Lucy, was the first woman fellow of the Institute of Chemistry.

Boole's intellectual sympathies mirrored Julia's. She was interested in Judaism and Indian religion; she was also a committed Spiritualist, with a particular interest in telepathy; and opposed vivisection as a one-dimensional science.[81] Her support for the Mortisection Society, which promoted the use of long-term clinical observation supplemented by post-mortem inspection for both humans and animals, almost certainly influenced Julia's decision to call for a post-mortem examination in her will.

Through Boole, Julia also made an important new intellectual friendship with Victoria, Lady Welby. Boole had been attracted by Welby's first book, *Links and Clues* (1881), a collection of unorthodox thoughts on religion. She wrote to her, and the three of them met soon after. Boole's hopes that they might use their 'women's fingers to unpick' 'the antagonism between science and religion' were soon frustrated by her indiscipline. Welby, however, remained friends with Julia until her death in 1912 even though they did not always agree. 'I care so much for all you give us by being as well by working, that I feel unable to bear the idea that we must differ in a matter so vital as the ultimate significance of physical science,' Welby wrote to Julia shortly before she died.[82]

She had had little formal education but travelled extensively before her marriage in 1863 to William Earle Welby, a military man and MP who encouraged her writing. A voracious reader with the auto-didact's exuberant ambition and openness to new ideas, Welby was particularly good at spotting ability in others and maintained an extensive correspondence with a remarkable collection of the best minds of her day. In her earlier years, they ranged from Huxley to Dean Church, Frederic Harrison to James Martineau, Leslie Stephen to Bishop Westcott and Max Müller to John Tyndall. Later she cultivated Bertrand Russell, whose importance she was quick to spot, Henri Bergson, William and Henry James, and H. G. Wells. In her letters to them, she coaxed, explained, challenged and, above all, questioned. Mary Warnock, who included her in a collection of the writings of leading women philosophers, praised her 'genuine originality' despite her 'markedly non-professional style'.[83] As well as six books, she wrote for a wide range of periodicals including the *Spectator* and *Fortnightly Review*, *Nature* and *Mind* on science, mathematics, anthropology, philosophy, education and social issues, as well as contributing an important article on 'significs' to the *Encyclopedia Britannica*.[84]

Julia shared many of her concerns: the significance of pain and evil; the condition of the Church; the nature of immortality; the relationship between language and meaning and the role of symbols; and, above all, whether conflict between science and religion was inevitable. Welby tended to blame the latter on the Church's empty language and ossified thinking. Julia was more cautious. Like Hutton, she was deeply attached to the Anglican liturgy. For her its age was not, as Welby claimed, a sign of its outmodedness but rather of the potency of long usage and accumulated reverence.[85] Similarly, though both suffered acute bouts of ill-health, Julia never went along with Welby's enthusiasm for Hinton's belief in suffering as a form of purification. She conceded only that there was sometimes 'a moment' when the pain ebbed that could give way to 'a new transparency' of understanding like the clear skies that followed a storm.[86]

While Welby wrote about gravitation or the movement of light as analogous to religious experiences if only the right language could be found to identify the spiritual element in these material phenomena, Julia countered with familiar metaphors about the effects of light. Biblical criticism, she suggested, meant that the 'records of Christianity' had lost their 'old halo' but now stood out more clearly. At the same time, 'the dazzling blaze which in our time has been thrown on the laws of the Outward has made the Inward so difficult to contemplate that we cannot see the stars for the gas'.[87] As Welby tried to cajole Julia into sharing her enthusiasm for the potential of the new science, whether in mathematics, psychology or eugenics, she resisted. 'You are in sympathy with the scientific spirit of our time in a way I never could be,' Julia wrote to her in the late 1880s.[88] In 1904 Welby was still encouraging her to be more open-minded. She blamed Julia's resistance on 'experiences in earlier life', perhaps a reference to Julia's tortuous reaction to Darwinism, and proposed a Booleian way of resolving their difference. 'Let us help one another in this, and make our unlikeness serve: not clinging in bondage to pasts, nor rushing in licence to futures.'[89]

The comparison was apt: as an excited Victoria Welby looked to the future, Julia fondly looked back. By the end of the century she had come to think her writing career all but over. She contributed fewer periodical articles once the editors who had nourished her career withdrew, and though she regularly submitted letters to the correspondence columns of the *Spectator*, her increasingly right-wing views were not always welcomed by Hutton's successors.

Many of her letters were about keeping the record straight as with her defence of Coleridge or authoritative restatement of Maurice's views on the importance of national unity or the toleration of stupidity. Others were delicate reminiscences about people she had known. There was Robert Darwin's recognition as early as the 1820s that TB might be infectious; Jessie Sismondi's story about the respect shown to Nelson's widow by French customs officers hearing her surname; and some wise words by Rusell Gurney on the need to temper compassion with justice in homicide cases.[90] She was always ready to join the debate on vivisection but got into yet more perilous territory when she intervened in an intense correspondence about whether a mother could ever be forgiven for infanticide. Julia's sympathies lay with desperate mothers saving their illegitimate children from miserable lives. 'There is muddle-headed sentimentality, not justice, in such an attitude of mind,' the editor declared. 'This correspondence must now cease.'[91] After that she wrote less often. Her last two letters to the *Spectator* in September 1911 and April 1912 defended the rights of non-unionized workmen and criticized the *Spectator's* praise for the forbearance of striking miners. Under the heading 'What Is Liberty?' she complained, 'It is such language as this on the part of the thinkers which induces, on the part of the thoughtless, acquiescence in the supra-legal position of a class and the surrender of honest labour to tyranny.'[92] The editor, maintaining the *Spectator's* credentials, politely, but firmly disagreed with both her letters. Like her grandfather, James Mackintosh, she had responded to troubling times by moving to the right. The prospect of majoritarian democracy and the statutory recognition of trade union rights completed her transformation into 'the most tremendous old Tory' as she now liked to describe herself to friends.

The literary climate had changed. As Alexis Easley has written, women were being marginalized in the high culture literary establishment.[93] Both George Eliot and Elizabeth Gaskell were now out of fashion and Harriet Martineau largely forgotten. A new generation of female writers was attempting to make its name in a more professionalized marketplace, writing for the newspapers or women's magazines or delivering sensation fiction. As early as April 1890, Eliza Lynn Linton complained in her usual aggrieved fashion that 'literature which was once a grave and honourable profession has now degenerated into a noisy, pushing, self-advertising trade'.[94] In 1889 she had become one of the first five female members of the Society of Authors, alongside Charlotte Yonge and Mary Ward. Though Julia would not have been unhappy in Yonge's company, she did not join. Her distinctive place in the upmarket periodical world was already secure, and with her active career winding down, as she thought, she had no need to promote herself by association with its professionalization.

She had even less in common with a group of women writers led by Mathilde Blind who set up the Women Writers' Dinner Club and spoke at its first dinner at the Criterion on 31 May 1889. Guests included Mona Caird, Rosamund Watson, Amy Levy, Katherine Tynan, Clementia Black and Alice Meynell.[95] Even if deafness had not excluded her, Julia would not have found their company sympathetic with the exception of Meynell. Though Blind was only 8 years younger than Julia, she was, in many ways, her polar opposite. They confronted many of the same issues but reached very different conclusions on Italian unification, Darwinism, the influence of John Stuart Mill, Irish Home Rule, universal suffrage, Comtism, marriage and the divergence between science and religion. Blind was radical and passionately devoted to subversive causes. Julia was increasingly conservative.

Even on the one subject on which they did agree, their admiration for George Eliot, whose biographer Blind became, they assessed her achievement very differently.

Blind's radical, forward-looking world was not Julia's as the century drew to a close. The mental and physical effort her writing career involved had become more taxing. By 1896, just two hours work a day left her feeling like the Queen of Sheba with 'no more spirit in me [...] an odd result of conversation with Solomon', as she remarked to May Crum.[96] But the habit of writing proved harder to abandon than she had expected. She would spend her last decade reworking *The Moral Ideal*, republishing some of her best essays about the remarkable Victorians she had known and delving into her Wedgwood family inheritance. Her 'bondage to the past', far from holding her back, became a source of personal renewal.

Chapter Sixteen

'A SATISFIED GUEST'

Julia first wrote about the satisfactions of old age when she was not yet 50. In an article about Cicero's *De Senectute* in the *Spectator*, she described it as a time of narrowed perspectives: 'long before we receive such telling notice [from 'dim sight, dull hearing, weakened powers of locomotion and failing memory'] that our mansion here is getting out of repair, and must be shortly abandoned, we have parted with some of the attractiveness and interest of life. We have lost its store of infinite possibility'. There were, however, compensations. Old age was a time for reflection, for looking back at the defeats of middle age with less emotion and more understanding. 'Some pain', she wrote, 'never loses its painfulness', but time had more power to transmute the impact of past errors than we expect. Age could also be 'vivid, intense, crowded with interest and hope'. Like childhood, it was a time of self-definition. The serenity of Julia's reflections on old age rested on her confidence in the 'almost audible promise' of a future life. 'As the windows are darkened, and the grasshopper become a burden, and as desire failed, have we not all witnessed a revelation of new possibilities within a character long familiar, rendering the notion that it shall cease to be [...] impossible?'[1]

As she anticipated, Julia enjoyed her final years. 'Age', as she wrote to Henrietta Litchfield, 'has all the advantage in point of happiness.'[2] Her hearing steadily deteriorated, she underwent an operation for cancer, she worried that her eyesight was failing and could no longer work long hours, but she was content in her domestic life, her friendships with younger women and her correspondence with a varied circle. Above all, she enjoyed thinking back to the great writers and teachers she had known as well as looking forward to reunion with those she had loved. As she told Alfred Benn the year before she died, she was ready to 'rise from the banquet a satisfied guest', if only she could first finish the book she was writing.[3] She had not expected to be quite so busy in her last decade.

The revised edition of *The Moral Ideal*, published in 1907, was designed to take account of new scholarship since the first edition of 1888 as well as intervening social and political developments and changes in her own thinking. She had high hopes for it. 'It has been my life's work,' she wrote to May Crum, '& the last years have been, I believe, more fruitful than the first but you shall judge.'[4] She was particularly keen to convey her message to a new generation. 'There comes a time', she wrote, 'in the lives of most persons who live to an old age when strong desire is recalled with a smile, and successful effort with a sigh; when we turn from the spectacle of change and decay to seek some enduring reality.'[5] The new edition of *The Moral Ideal* aimed to capture that 'enduring reality'. Its layout and language were more accessible than the original, and she recruited two younger men to help her, Harold Herford and E. M. Forster.

Figure 34 Julia Wedgwood's water colour contrasting the passions and serenity of 'Youth and Age'. By courtesy of the V&A Wedgwood/Mosley Collection.

Julia had known Morgan Forster all his life. His mother, Lily Wichelow, a protégée of Marianne Thornton, had been governess to the Farrer children before catching the eye of Eddie Forster, one of Thornton's nephews. They married in 1877. Their only surviving child was born in January 1879, less than two years before Eddie died. An array of middle-aged women stepped in to support the widow and child, including his aunt, Laura Forster, Maimie Aylward, the widow of one of Marianne Thornton's nephews and his mother's best friend, and Thornton herself, who lavished money, affection and perhaps too much attention on the child. Julia watched it all rather critically. When Thornton died in November 1887, she wrote to Emily Gurney: 'Her fondness for children was rather disastrous of late years for I think it became oppressive to little Morgan Forster.'[6] But though Forster tried to create his own space amongst the doting women who surrounded him, he also became a shrewd observer of the frustrations of their lives and limited expectations. His last book, a biography of Marianne Thornton, resurrected a gallery of women who might otherwise have remained forgotten. They were drawn from her generation and the more troubled one that succeeded it. As Forster saw it, the younger women like Henrietta Synot, Henrietta Darwin and the Wedgwood girls were spikier and less generous than their predecessors. All, however, had become gentler and more confident as they grew older.[7]

Forster might not have warmed to Julia had he known her in her troubled earlier years. He read some of her correspondence with Emily Gurney and was put off by its emotional intensity. 'So feminine a woman repels me, and even Miss Wedgwood's in reply have caught this exotic taint.'[8] He knew her best, however, when she had attained the poise of her late years and had nothing but praise for her.

They moved in overlapping circles. When Forster went up to King's College in 1899, Laura Forster gave him introductions to Horace and Frank Darwin and to Caroline Stephen, Leslie Stephen's formidable Quaker sister and a good friend of Julia's. He found himself drawn to the circle around Goldsworthy Lowes Dickinson, the son of Julia's great friend in London, Lowes Cato Dickinson, and was invited to join the Apostles. Nervously, but successfully, Forster moved amongst the Cambridge intellectual élite. His degree was not good enough, however, to win him a fellowship and he spent some unsettled years after university. His work at the London Working Men's College teaching Latin brought him again into Julia's orbit. In 1903 when he went back to Cambridge to stay with his friend Edward Dent, he took her to a production of Aristophanes's *The Birds*. The following year she returned the hospitality, inviting him to stay at Idlerocks for the opening of Modershall Church whose construction she had largely funded. Hope fussed over the fact that her daughter was away and that she had been unable to rustle up any other young woman to entertain Morgan.[9] She need not have worried. He was more than content to come to Staffordshire as Julia's escort.

By then he had begun working with her on the revised edition of *The Moral Ideal*. Julia was always sensitive to the criticism that her scholarship was out-of-date. Forster, who had graduated in Classics and History and was working on an edition of the *Aeneid*, was her talisman against that criticism and a means of reaching out to a younger generation.

He gave various accounts of his work on *The Moral Ideal*. He described himself as 'devilling' for her which might imply that his main contribution was research for the new and extended chapters; at another time he wrote that he 'redrafted certain passages with the author's approval'; and on another recalled that 'Snow' always agreed with what he did but sometimes forgot what it had been.[10] He began his work for her in 1904 and then put in several intensive sessions starting in spring 1907, by which time he had published two novels. 'Much labour over The Moral Ideal, to which I look back with pleasure,' he wrote in an end-of-year roundup in his diary.[11]

Harold Herford, the professor of English at Manchester University, whom Julia also co-opted, had been part of her circle since the early 1880s. Like a surprising number of her friends, he was a Comtian. Beginning as a regular at her Sunday afternoon at-homes when he happened to be in town, he graduated to calling her home his 'Hotel' when he served as an external examiner at London University in the 1890s. Just after her 70th birthday, Julia invited him to consider himself as her 'honorary nephew'. In 1900 he was commissioned to write a study of Browning for the Modern Writers series. It was probably not until after he had finished it that Julia told him of her earlier closeness to the poet and disclosed the identity of the dedicatee of *The Moral Ideal*. Initially, he was hesitant about helping Julia on her revision but by June 1903 was sending detailed comments on her chapter on the Greeks. By February 1905 her re-written final chapter was ready in proof for him to consider once Forster had read it. Herford, a genuine admirer of Julia's work but also a natural courtier, described the acknowledgement of his and Forster's help in the notice at the front of the new edition as 'the greatest honour I have ever had'.[12]

In her pursuit of a new audience, Julia adopted a more discursive style, softening both the density of thought and the heightened language of the original. Side-headings, probably prepared by Forster, were introduced to summarize the argument of each paragraph,

Figure 35 The young E. M. Forster. By courtesy of the Provost and Fellows of King's College, Cambridge.

an expertly compiled index (Forster's work again?) replaced its sketchy predecessor and the footnotes were simplified. Though that meant fewer of the idiosyncratic touches that had enlivened the first edition, the decision to relegate the showy quotations from Greek, Latin and German to footnotes with translations provided in the main text was a gain. There was more storytelling too as she narrated the stories of Isis and Osiris, Oedipus or the Eumenides, and Rama and his wife Sita, and more physical description as well as a better-ordered treatment of the Greek dramatists and philosophers (probably at Herford's suggestion). Julia also reflected the growing interest in Egyptology and Sanskrit literature with a new chapter on Egypt and a more extended treatment of Vedic texts, where she took the advice of Romesh Chunder Dutt, the Indian writer and civil servant who had produced a version of the Mahabharata in 1899.[13] The most important change was a completely re-written final chapter 'Male and Female Created He Them', which presented a less overtly feminist view than her article with the same title in *The Contemporary Review* in 1889.

Just as she toned down her feminism, so, too, Julia diluted her Hegelian dialectic. In part this reflected the difficulty of trying to fit early Egyptian culture into the pattern of action and reaction she had earlier adopted. For Julia, Egypt stood alone, a precocious phenomenon, focused on death and an attenuated sense of the afterlife but upholding values that had always been important to her, such as the importance of work and close family life. Egyptian epitaphs showed a sense of neighbourliness and consideration for those in distress: 'goodness of character meant to the Egyptian what it does to us, and we could say the same of no other ancient people, except the Hebrews'. But Egyptian civilization was not reacting to any other nor did it provoke a countervailing reaction: it was rather a pale foreshadowing of aspects of contemporary culture.[14]

Once again she hymned the importance of the family but reserved her most rhapsodic language for the union of man and woman in marriage. Against the rise of collectivism, and what she saw as the tendency of modern democracy to discount the lessons of the past, she set 'the impulse that seeks unity', the human instinct to feel 'members of one another'. This found its highest expression in marriage. 'The lesson of our incompleteness, the fragmentary nature of each one of us alone, is enforced by the law which gives creative power to the union of male and female."'. Indeed, she now extolled the power of sex beyond its procreative function, quoting approvingly its Biblical description as 'to know' someone.[15]

The most marked change between the two editions of *The Moral Ideal* was her reluctance to criticize Darwinism. She was, however, forthright in her condemnation of the new antagonism between scientific and spiritual truth. They were, she suggested, at odds with each other not only in substance but also in their manner of discovery. Scientific truth proceeded in a straight line as a result of a cumulative, collective effort: spiritual truth followed a zigzag individual upward path. While the first 'can be transferred from one mind to any other as water is poured into a cup, the other truth must be approached and entered as a man enters a house'.[16]

In her first edition she had avoided defining the 'Moral Ideal'. Now she referred to it not as a hankering after eternity or apprehension of the divine, but as 'The Other of Science'. 'Science', she concluded, 'can say of every ascertained decision, "It is certain." [...] The Other of Science never affords that external and transferable certainty which can adhere to words; the truth it opens is one of which a man must say, "I am certain."' As a result, spiritual truth was never absolute and man's apprehension of it varied: 'It is one thing', she wrote, thinking back to her doubts and depressions in the 1870s, 'in moments of vigorous health when the body makes claim on the spirit, another in dark dim hours when nothing seems real but miserable sensation.'[17] Explaining the existence of evil and its physical manifestation in pain was no easier in 1907 than it had been in 1888.

Once again she defended the importance of doubt, describing it as 'a rare and arduous state of mind'.[18] The path from doubt to a denial that had become 'loud and emotional' was all too easy. Her appreciation of the continuing value of doubt tempered her conclusions. She described her own age in 1907 as transitional. 'Men never rush to build as they rush to demolish' but 'construction always substitutes Unity for Plurality'. The process of moral evolution was 'a sense of successively overcome incompleteness'. Instead of the resonant assertions with which she had concluded the first version of *The Moral Ideal*, she now posed three questions. Would man's sense of completion in the family, the nation and the church grow or diminish as he 'rises towards the summit of humanity'? Would he become more or less aware of aspirations beyond his power to realize? And as collective sympathy grew, would he be 'more or less conscious of the need for that sympathy which is Divine'?[19]

Though Herford was quick to reassure her that friends at his university had eagerly seized on the revised version of *The Moral Ideal*, his letter of congratulation implied that he knew it would have less impact than the original. 'I cannot help being reminded, when

I consider how rare – how lonely – massive thought & weighty expression like yours are in this age of flippant epigrams & the "Daily Mail" – of Milton amid the dissonant revelry of the Restoration.' Forster was much more succinct in his end-year review: 'It has been scantily reviewed.'[20] By 1907 no cheerleaders with the influence of Hutton remained though the *International Journal of Ethics* gave it a glowing review, praising its 'many fresh and stimulating *aperçus*' and 'the writer's strong personality'.[21]

In attempting to make her book more accessible and tone down its Carlylean rhetoric, Julia had produced a work of more muted impact. There were fewer apopthegms, and the thought and its expression were not as well-matched as in the denser, more rhetorical original version. Above all, its preoccupations with the challenge of the new science or the role of religious doubt were those of her own generation rather than the early twentieth century, where many were excited by the new vistas opened up by men like H. G. Wells, a writer Julia 'read' but predictably 'hated'.[22]

The Edwardian period was a time of more diverse attitudes towards religion as accommodations were reached between it and science. For many scientists and professional men, religion had become 'a Sunday hobby [...] divorced from the practice of weekday affairs'.[23] Nor could Julia's book be easily pigeonholed. It retained a strong element of idealism but also reflected the concern of modernist theology with subjective religious experience. Its underlying ethos, however, remained Maurician, and as such, it appeared old-fashioned. Julia was also competing in an increasingly specialized academic environment where few now attempted to survey the entire course of moral history. But despite the muted interest in her revision of *The Moral Ideal*, her earlier reputation as a writer on the classics remained. The *School Review* in January 1908 ranked her with (male) authorities like Sellar, Nettleship, Saint-Beuve, Rohde and J. R. Green as a commentator on Virgil, while *The Classical Weekly* repeated the accolade in 1920.[24]

Perhaps the most easily detectable impact of *The Moral Ideal* is to be found in the early work of E. M. Forster. His thinking was in many ways different from Julia's. He was critical of the restricted horizons of her social milieu and aware that his sexuality did not conform to its expectations. He had also lost his religious faith at Cambridge without undergoing the agonies of some of Julia's contemporaries. But he respected 'the formidable Snowie' and was particularly impressed by her unconventional relationship with Marian Hughes, a relationship that may have influenced his own later one with a policeman, Bob Buckingham. The connection, however, goes deeper. On 18 July 1904 he wrote in his diary: 'Today have been working again at Miss Wedgwood's.' Back home that same evening he jotted down an outline of what became his most original and deeply felt novel, *The Longest Journey*.[25] The plot changed significantly from his original outline, but its central element of the Manicheaen struggle between two half-brothers (who do not know of their relationship) remained, as does the idea of the weaker brother passing on his physical defect of lameness to his short-lived daughter.

Elizabeth Heine, the editor of the Abinger edition of *The Longest Journey*, has detected a strong Hegelian influence on the novel that Forster could not have absorbed through his Cambridge circle and suggested too that the main character, Ricky's Cambridge friend, Ansell (who was modelled on George Moore), probably acquired his knowledge of Schopenhauer from *The Moral Ideal*. She also points to Julia's poetic descriptions of the constellations, including Orion, which she finds reflected in both *The Longest Journey* and *A Passage to India* and suggests that her extended chapter on Indian philosophy and literature might have contributed to Forster's growing interest in India. But perhaps the most potent influence was on his understanding of human relations. Julia is far from the only influence on this, but it is not fanciful to see a connection between Forster's most famous aphorism 'Only connect' and Julia's 'sense of an indefeasible claim on human sympathy in every human being'. *Howard's End*, a book Julia very much admired, shares some of the same ethos as *The Moral Ideal*.[26]

She gave him £50 to thank him for his work. Some in the family thought it rather little, but Forster was delighted and went on holiday to Italy. Julia took her disappointment over the reception of *The Moral Ideal* philosophically. 'I am well, but solitary. [...] I am feeling very old,' she wrote to May Crum.[27] Though she put together a collection of her articles and related pieces about some of the great Victorians she had known, she was preparing to settle to that 'candle light & drawn curtain time of life' she thought characteristic of everyone's eighth decade.[28] Her sisters had other ideas. They were determined she should rescue their family's honour by writing a biography of their great grandfather, Josiah Wedgwood.

To the family's embarrassment, Gladstone had drawn attention to the absence of a biography of Josiah Wedgwood when he laid the foundation stone for the Wedgwood Institute at Burslem in 1863. Eliza Meteyard quickly stepped forward to fill the gap, publishing a massive two-volume life in 1865 and 1866 and dedicating it to Gladstone. She followed this up with a study of Wedgwood's sons and their friends, *A Group of Englishmen (1795–1815)*. Whilst her first volume contained a glowing acknowledgement of help from the Wedgwood and Darwin families, her last outspokenly criticized their failure to write their own history. As she knew from her researches, the Wedgwoods had been careless about preserving their archive. Happily, Joseph Mayor in Liverpool had acquired the mass of the firm's business papers Uncle Frank had thrown out. He made them available to Meteyard, who also tracked down the most revealing of all the sources on Wedgwood's life, his letters to his friend and business partner, Thomas Bentley. Her biographical studies of Wedgwood and his sons are, as Robin Reilly has written, an 'astonishing' 'achievement by any standards (let alone those of Victorian ladies past middle age)'.[29]

The family saw it differently. Emma Darwin objected to her revelations about James Mackintosh's attempt to cadge yet another loan from her father. Richard Litchfield, who wrote a rather feeble biography of Tom Wedgwood, dismissed *A Group of Englishmen* as 'full of inaccuracy, the authoress habitually mixing up guesswork with fact'.[30] Effie countered with her own 'erratic' edition of the Bentley–Wedgwood correspondence, misdating letters, splicing others together and giving credence to a myth about Wedgwood's altruistic suicide.[31] Even Boole joined in with a slim edition of Tom Wedgwood's philosophical writings *A Maimed Life* in 1912. Only Josiah C. Wedgwood, Frank's grandson and a campaigning Radical MP, succeeded in producing a worthwhile addition in his *A History of the Wedgwood Family* in 1909.

Julia shared the family's distaste for Meteyard's work, complaining to Effie in 1871: 'One feels vexed at having one's unpretentious ancestors being brought forward in that way.' Forty years later she was just as critical, describing the biography as 'tasteless and gushing' and not 'even the most modest contribution to literature'.[32] This was uncharitable. As she knew, Meteyard was, like her, profoundly deaf and had had a much harder time pursuing a literary career. To create time for her work on the Wedgwoods, she turned out mediocre fiction in a vain attempt to pay the rent, worked hard on articles for poorly paying periodicals and regularly appealed to the Royal Society for Literature for financial support.[33]

The testy defensiveness of the family's reaction to Meteyard's rediscovery of Josiah Wedgwood reflected not only guilty conscience about their own failure to honour their famous ancestor but also an underlying ambivalence about the commercial origin of their fortunes. When Samuel Smiles set Wedgwood up as a model of his gospel of self-help in 1895, Hope was horrified that anyone would pay 'six shillings for that wretched twaddle'.[34]

Josiah Wedgwood was not a natural subject for Julia. In compiling her album of family history, she had concentrated on her family's distinguished literary and political connections and included only one letter from Wedgwood himself. In her own work she was drawn to mystics like William Law and Thomas Erskine. Wedgwood, by contrast, was a practical man whose religion 'exceed[ed] as little as possible the simplicity of pure Deism' and to whom 'mystery was distasteful and suspect'.[35] Nonetheless, she soon fell under his spell. 'I love him as much as is possible to do to a man who has been unseen of men for 116 years,' she wrote to Alfred Benn in June 1911.[36] His personality and relations with his family and friends intrigued her just as much as his achievements as a craftsman and entrepreneur. Though she sketched in his political ideas and intellectual contacts with fellow members of the Lunar Society, she spent more time on his character. She presents him as shrewd and level-headed, a man making up for his own limited education with a steadily acquired culture that left him un-phased by the claims of aristocratic society and very much his own man, hard-working, conscientious, innovative and highly skilled.

In taking on a new biography, she knew she was in a race against time. In February 1912 she underwent an operation for cancer. She was not afraid of dying but troubled that she might not finish her book.[37] When she remade her will in 1913, its first substantive provision reflected her sense of obligation to tell her great grandfather's story. She left £500 to Harold Herford to complete her biography, if it remained unfinished at her death, and also provided that the costs of publication could be drawn from her estate.

After her death, Herford willingly stepped in to finish the book, which was published by Macmillan as *The Personal Life of Josiah Wedgwood* in a nice, well-illustrated edition in 1915. It did not replace Eliza Meteyard's work. As with Julia's Wesley biography, its proportions are uneven and some of the later chapters rather disjointed.[38] But the book has charm and readability. The most personal pages are those that reflect on the origin of the long-running tension in the Wedgwood family between the desire for social advancement and the responsibility to maintain the business that had made the family name synonymous with the finest in English ceramics.

Josiah Wedgwood was a self-made man. His reputation depended not just on his own technical innovations and skill in managing new industrial processes but also on his ability to attract rich patrons and cater to their tastes. The most prestigious of his commissions came from Catherine the Great in 1773 for a dinner and dessert service of nearly a thousand pieces. Meteyard gives a dutiful description of the work. Julia, who had the advantage of having seen much of the 'Frog Service' when it was brought back to England and put on display in 1909, is more alert to both the social and aesthetic niceties that troubled her great grandfather and his partner, Thomas Bentley. What perplexed them amuses her.

Though Wedgwood's international reputation relied, in part, on his reproductions of antique vases, Catherine, Julia wrote, did not want 'an English imitation [...] of the long-buried treasure of Italy' but 'an English work that should instruct her about England'. Over a thousand views of its scenery and 'statelier [...] homes' were assembled to decorate the service. Julia comments on some of them. They included, amongst other London houses, Northumberland House '(whose ugliness, here faithfully reproduced, may reconcile us to its loss)' but also 'the first Westminster Bridge [...] that crossed by Wordsworth – with its multitude of little arches, the shortest lived of all memorable bridges'. She suspected that her great grandfather's heart was less in country estates than 'in the busy, industrial, inventive England just coming to the birth, and he gratified his taste even at some risk to his interest'. He decorated one of the largest dishes with a view of his own Etruria Hall and even managed to slip in 'an excellent little study of a canal-lock' which Bentley judiciously labelled in the catalogue he prepared for the Empress as 'The Dunnington Hills, Derbyshire'. Julia was nicely alert to Wedgwood's and Bentley's anxieties over which views to place on which pieces and the risk of offending the owners of the largest properties included in the collection if they failed to get due prominence. 'Unluckily,' she wrote, 'the small plates far outnumbered the great dishes, and there were more noble lords than soup tureens.' 'Kew Gardens should not have afforded a delicate illustration for a sauce-ladle, nor Holland House appear on a dish cover.'[39]

The inclusion of Etruria Hall in the 'Frog Service' reminded Julia of the damage that expansion of the Potteries had done to the surrounding countryside. Not many in 1912 could remember the Hall as she had known it as a child with its 'green sweeps of lawn and tall trees' by the new canal 'where all is now cinders and oven-refuse' and the Hall left 'conspicuous [...] in a treeless and verdureless waste'. Burslem, too, had changed out of recognition from the days when Wedgwood's successful father-in-law, Richard Wedgwood, had lived at 'The Big House': 'The name attests both their own importance and the insignificance, at that time, of the town in which one house could be so singled out.'[40] But though she lamented the deterioration of the local landscape, Julia applauded her great grandfather's entrepreneurial spirit, constant pursuit of innovation and willingness to take risks. She also portrayed him as a firm but sympathetic employer, requiring discipline from his workforce but rewarding them with good housing and some opportunities for self-improvement.

'My Ancestor [...] more and more attracts me,' she wrote to Benn in August 1911. 'He is modest, fervent, exuberant in sympathy and compassion for all men. Only I'm afraid a little classish but how few businessmen are not.'[41] By '*classish*' she did not mean snobbish but concerned with the economic self-interest of entrepreneurs like himself. This made his support for the abolition of slavery the more remarkable. Something else she particularly admired was his attitude towards pain and ill-health. A childhood attack of smallpox had left him with a weakened right leg. His lameness was exacerbated by a fall from his horse in 1762. In 1768 he decided to have the leg amputated at the knee. Julia followed Meteyard's convincing if unauthenticated account of the operation conducted without anaesthetic. He underwent it, she wrote, 'without a groan'. 'The buoyant tone' of his letters at this time was impressive. 'To our mind,' she wrote, they 'are a model of the way to speak in correspondence of one's physical ailments, and above all of the way to leave them unspoken.'[42]

'As with many other men,' she wrote to Benn in May 1912, 'what interests me most in him is his failures.'[43] Chief of them was his relations with his sons. Her final chapter, 'Wedgwood and His Children', is the most personal in her book. She was writing about a generation, some of whom she had known as a child: Jos Wedgwood, who had reluctantly taken on responsibility for the business, his youngest sister, Sarah, 'a woman of noble though somewhat forbidding character', and Robert Darwin, who married Wedgwood's eldest daughter, Sukie. Like Emma Darwin, Julia remembered him as 'irascible, sometimes unreasonable and exacting, often formidable to his juniors, and, capable of making himself so to his patients – a power which he often exercised to their great advantage'.[44]

One much talked-about member of this generation that Julia had not known was Tom Wedgwood. Reputedly the most brilliant of the Wedgwood sons, he had been a friend of Coleridge, Wordsworth, Southey, Mackintosh, John Leslie and others. Though he scorned an active part in the Wedgwood business, he was, like his father, an innovative scientist and had a claim to have invented photography though he was never able to fix the images he obtained on paper sensitized with a solution of nitrate silver. At his death aged 34 after years of ill-health, Mackintosh had promised to edit the philosophical jottings he had left behind. He soon found that they did not amount to much (though Boole would do her imaginative best to identify a coherent Hartleyan philosophy in them). Nor, reading his letters, full of complaints about his ailments and depressions, is it easy to discover the charisma that captivated his contemporaries. Like Eliza Meteyard and Richard Litchfield, Julia was obliged to fall back on romantic assertions about his 'spiritual beauty of character' and present him as 'tormented by chronic ill-health',[45] rather than the drug addiction that killed him.[46]

One aspect of Tom's life that remained an issue of lively discussion in the family was the annual pension of £150 that he and Jos had awarded Coleridge from 1795. Seven years after Tom's death, Jos stopped it without explanation. When Hensleigh asked his father why, he refused to discuss the matter, saying 'only that he had good reasons'. Meteyard excused Jos on the grounds of Coleridge's neglect of his wife and children, while Litchfield speculated that he had hoped that the peremptory withdrawal of the pension would shock Coleridge into ending his opium addiction. But, as Julia pointed out, the pension was stopped after, rather than before, Coleridge's return to literary form. She saw the explanation in Jos's stolid temperament. Having first taken his decision in 1810, he did not act on it till 1812. 'Josiah was a just man [...] his absolute rectitude of intention was fortified by a massive inertia, which held him obstinately in a course he had once accepted as right.'[47]

Of all the second generation of Wedgwoods, Jos was the one Julia knew best. She describes him as she had known him as a girl: silent and unemotional but devoted to his wife, a man that some children, though not she, found intimidating. Her analysis of the 'coolness' of his relations with his father, however, went to the heart of the Wedgwood dissonance between social status and commercial success. Josiah Wedgwood came from a modest background, making up for a very limited education through his own careful reading, willingness to learn from others like his friends in the Lunar Society and openness to his partner Thomas Bentley's ideas on how to cultivate royal or aristocratic patrons. Etruria Hall, though situated in the middle of the Potteries, was designed and furnished like the home of the rich gentleman Wedgwood had become in the course of his innovative but determined career. From the time that he first thought about the education of his sons, he accepted that their lives would be different from his own. His eldest, John, might become a 'gentleman farmer [...] with as many acres for himself and his tenants to improve as I can spare him', while Jos and Tom were to follow in the family business, one as a manufacturer, the other as a salesman.[48] How to educate them for these different careers was a subject of anxious discussion with Thomas Bentley and Erasmus Darwin. Julia criticized Wedgwood's decision to educate them at home, suggesting that his own ability to make up for his inadequate schooling blinded him to the need to give his sons the polish of a university education commensurate with their personal wealth and social ambition.

She dated the strains between Jos and his father to the time when Josiah sent him and Tom Byerly on a mission to the Hague and Berlin to promote sales of the Portland Vase in royal and aristocratic circles. After this, Jos proved reluctant to deal with all but the most select patrons in the Wedgwood London showrooms. 'Like most sons of self-made men,' Julia wrote, 'he showed himself sensitive to social distinctions to which his father was robustly indifferent.' 'My sympathies all go with the plain straightforward father who never I think perceived the cause of a certain coldness that he must have felt,' she wrote in a letter to Benn.[49]

Robin Reilly has written harshly about the Wedgwoods in the nineteenth century. With a few exceptions, he wrote, they 'were a dullish lot, whose lethargy, solemnity, snobbishness and hypochondria, endlessly displayed in their letters, tend to eclipse upright and honourable behavior and earnest endeavor'.[50] This hardly does justice to women in the family like Emma Darwin or the three Hensleigh Wedgwood daughters. Julia's own analysis is more sympathetic. Josiah Wedgwood, she wrote, 'shrank back' from 'all that was showy, or dramatic or even eminent'.[51] His lack of vanity made him averse to flattery, a quality inherited by his Darwin grandsons, Ras and Charles, and his son Jos. But what was admirable in 'the Ancestor' had its drawbacks in succeeding generations. Josiah, she wrote to Benn, 'was entirely free from vanity. It is part of his great charm to me & so far as the generation above me goes I may say that he transmitted his modesty to his descendants, but in their case I have sometimes doubted whether it is <u>unmixed gain</u>. A little exaggeration of one's own powers is sometimes a help to exertion'. Further reflection on her family's history re-opened an old wound about which she was usually silent.

> Perhaps I feel more lenient towards the temptation [to flatter] because the very opposite is characteristic of all my blood. (I mean on my father's side.) I think the resolution never to go one inch beyond the truth in any gratifying direction ends in eliciting all that is discouraging & leaving perfectly sincere & encouraging opinion unspoken. [...] Perhaps I exaggerate it from our all having suffered it in early days from our dear Father, who could not believe that anything remarkable ever belonged to anyone belonging to him.

There was a wistfulness, too, in her reference to Josiah Wedgwood as 'always [...] a playfellow' to his children.[52] That was never Hensleigh's way.

Mulling over the past was a favourite occupation in Julia's last years. 'At 80,' she wrote to Benn in March 1913, 'one has many unseen companions – not all welcome, but all instructive.'[53] Her father's dismissal of her work was still painful. Most of her memories were warmer. As Eliza Wedgwood, John Wedgwood's grand-daughter, described: 'she used to sit over the fire, & talk of her many friendships'. E. S. Roscoe, who got to know her in the last months of her life, was charmed by the immediacy of her talk. 'Her memory of the past was so clear, and her mental alertness so considerable, that she talked of things and people of nearly a century ago as if she had met them yesterday.'[54]

She took particular pleasure in recalling for Alfred Benn, who had written a history of British rationalism in the nineteenth century, her memories of Frank Newman, Harriet Martineau, about whom she was still acerbic, Macaulay, Carlyle, Maurice, George Eliot, Mrs Gaskell, James Fitzjames Stephen, Tennyson and Uncle Charles. Occasionally, she referred to another 'old friend' but always without naming Robert Browning. Writing to Benn about Johnson's letters to Mrs Thrale in June 1911, she reflected: 'How little fiction mirrors life in the space it leaves for this sort of feeling. I mean the sense of a supreme relation between men & women which has no thought of marriage. I have known a beautiful instance of it in my own experience.' She probably also had Browning in mind when she wrote two years later: 'We find the true self when we find <u>the other</u>. [...] It is a wonderful feeling when some reflection from another soul flashes a ray upon our own that shows us something new there.'[55] The careful datings in the copy of his poems that Browning had given her show how regularly she still turned to him.[56] She was about to rediscover the younger self that Browning had known in an unexpected way.

With the one great exception of his courtship correspondence with Elizabeth, Browning kept very few letters. Though he may have forgotten that he still had them, however, he did not destroy Julia's. They came to light after his son Pen's death in 1912 when all Browning's remaining effects were put up for sale in May 1913. Julia's letters were included with some from Rev. J. D. Williams, and though her name was not mentioned in the auction catalogue, the description of the letters as referring to 'Landor, Lord Houghton etc' caught the eye of Gabriel Wells, a New York book dealer, who bought them for 14 shillings. He must have recognized at once the intimate nature of her letters and known that she was still alive. He returned them in the summer of 1913.

Her letter of thanks to him was characteristically modest but warm in its gratitude. Her overriding concern was that Wells should not think less of Browning now he had seen her letters. As always, however, she avoided naming him.

> Dear Sir,
>
> Accept my earnest thanks, & since you have quite innocently read these letters let me assure you that nothing in them need modify in the slightest degree your opinion of the person to whom they are addressed. I have done myself the pleasure of sending you one of my books in which some pages may perhaps interest you, but it is not to trouble you for any comment or thanks.
>
> I am dear Sir sincerely & gratefully yours,

Frances Julia Wedgwood[57]

Julia carefully put her letters together with those from Browning, adding tentative datings to some of them. Either she or Browning, or perhaps both of them, re-read her letter of 1 March 1864, asking him to stop calling, many times judging from its worn appearance. Re-uniting this precious correspondence must have brought a satisfying sense of completion as Julia's health steadily declined in the summer of 1913.

In July she had her last meeting with Alfred Benn at Lansdowne Road. By then her hearing was a serious problem. She had even had a painful falling-out with Herford when his efforts to put another guest at ease left her isolated at her own dinner table. She was anxious that even with her trumpet conversation with Benn might be impossible. 'Please don't make a great effort to make me hear,' she begged him. 'I have a horror of becoming a nuisance.' In the event, all was well. 'Our conversation somehow roused many scraps of memory pleasant to recall,' she assured him afterwards before coming up with an anecdote about Uncle Charles.[58] Her last letter to him was sadder as she reflected on the potency of evil and its familiar manifestation in pain and suffering: 'I mean that element of misfit, of defeat in life <u>which we find & do not bring</u>. [...] I mean that which makes wrong inevitable, which I feel myself in the uncontrollable impatience of illness, reminding me that the right relation of soul & body is inverted, & that it is the flesh which rules'. Sadly, overcome with nausea, she was unable to finish her letter. 'I wish I could write on. I have so much to say,' were her last affecting words to Benn. A few months earlier, she had written to him: 'the thought of death is like some brightly lighted mirror in a room otherwise dark, which vividly lights up the past'.[59] She was very ready to die and be reunited, as she confidently expected, with so many she had known and loved.

From the late summer when Julia fell ill with a failing heart, breathlessness and inability to sleep, Hope and Effie took turns to be with her. 'She cannot lie down & sits leaning forward in the same chair, day & night,' Hope reported to Eliza Wedgwood. The doctor had prescribed 'morfia wh. disturbs the brain sadly. [...] Every now & then we can understand what she says, but it is almost always astray. I am thankful to say she is blessed with a much larger share of patience than was her normal endowment.'[60] Julia died peacefully early in the morning of Wednesday, 26 November 1913.

Her last weeks had not been quite as tranquil as Hope suggested. Though she wrote, 'for the last 3 weeks – she has hardly been with us',[61] in that time Julia twice made important changes to her will. Word had already got round the family that she was leaving the bulk of her estate to animal causes. They did not approve. In fact, she had made generous provision for Hope's daughter, Mary Euphrasia, and set up trusts for Alfred's three children, Jem, Berry and Olive (born in 1893 after her father's death) as well as providing for Marian Hughes and her maid, Emma Morris, 'who has done so much to lighten many hours of my illness' and the rest of her household. But the National Anti-Vivisection Society (£5,000), the National Anti-Vivisection Hospital (£1,000) and the Metropolitan Drinking Fountain and Cattle Trough Association (£500) as well as the Charities Organisation Society (£500) were also beneficiaries. And the residue of her estate, which would be proved at the then-substantial sum of £63,887, was to be administered by Godfrey's eldest child, Cecil, in favour of animal causes of his choosing.

Nine days before she died, Julia altered her will to give Mary the freehold of the large Lansdowne Road house rather than a lifetime's interest in it. Six days before her death, she changed her will again to halve the bequest to the National Anti-Vivisection Society and leave the balance to her sister Effie. She also came under pressure to seek written assurances from Cecil about how he would administer the residue of her estate. Her letter of 13 November is sad reading: 'I am now very unequal to anything of the kind [...] needing sharpness of judgment and clearness of memory and no longer grasping either,' she wrote as she apologized for taking up Cecil's time. This letter was introduced as evidence when Wilfred Baugh Allen, the second of her two executors, went to court to challenge unsuccessfully the wide discretion Julia had given to Cecil as her residuary legatee.[62]

'Lady of the Wedgwood Family Leaves a Remarkable Will' was the headline in the *Dundee Evening Telegraph* on 1 January 1914. What had caught the attention of the provincial press in an age of curiosity over the wills of the wealthy were Julia's instructions that a post-mortem examination should be carried out but that no one should wear mourning or cancel engagements. The provision for a post-mortem was Julia's answer to the vivisectionists: if more human bodies were examined after death, the pressure to experiment on live animals might be reduced. The second provision, at a time when the solemn mourning observances of the high Victorians were relaxing, was characteristic of her desire to avoid fuss. Nor did she want her death to become an occasion for grief. 'I believe that "the communion of saints" and of many beside them to whom that name is due is a vast, real, vital fact, always true,' she wrote three years before her death.[63] Now she could be part of that company free, at last, from the constraints of deafness and ill-health.

Apart from the unusual provisions in her will, her death attracted little notice. The *Times* had a short obituary, possibly prompted by Henrietta Litchfield. It named the titles of her major works and quoted Darwin's approving comments on her early review of *On the Origin of Species*. It is doubtful, however, whether Julia would have chosen to be remembered primarily as an apologist for Darwinism. Harold Herford contributed a longer and more personal piece in the *Manchester Guardian* that he later expanded in a letter to the *Spectator*, regretting that more notice had not been 'taken of the departure last month, at eighty, of one of the most gifted Englishwomen of her time'. But, as he conceded, Julia had outlived her period of greatest influence and popularity as a writer. 'Yesterday is often hard put to it, in the twentieth century, to hold its own against today.' 'Girls had to struggle', he wrote, 'for the higher learning in her early days, but "Snow" Wedgwood [...] overcame most of the disabilities of her sex, and won the command of a very ample and varied learning.' Like E. M. Forster writing 20 years later, Herford also paid tribute to the brilliance of Julia's conversation, despite her deafness, and to the range of her friendships including some with whom 'she had scarcely an article of faith in common'. 'Masculine force of intellect and of will were allied in her [...] with spiritual wisdom and intuitive insight,' he continued. 'The sufferings of animals were an enduring sorrow to her. [...] Deepest of all in her was the passion for righteousness, the divine form which glowed in Greek as in Hebrew.'[64]

As she had wished, Julia's body was cremated and her ashes taken to be buried next to Godfrey in the tranquil, tree-shaded cemetery in Modershall churchyard close to Idlerocks. (Twenty years later, her sisters would be buried beside her beneath matching tombstones.) Effie and Hope chose a melancholy epitaph: 'Thou hast chastened me sore but has not given me over to death,' adding in respectful tribute, 'her words spoken or written enlightened and consoled many hearts.' This dignified description of Julia as sage and spiritual counsellor gave little sense of her originality. Effie and Hope were still rather in awe of their oldest sister.

Amongst the mourners at Modershall was Marian Hughes, whom Hope had invited to Idlerocks to recover from the strain of nursing Snow in her last illness. As Hope wrote to Eliza Wedgwood, 'Poor Miss Hughes is the real mourner – Snow was everything to her.'[65] Julia had made generous provision for the woman she described in her will, not as her 'companion' (the usual designation in Census returns) but as 'my dear friend Mary Ann Hughes'. She set up a trust fund designed to pay her an annuity of £600 for life. This was more than enough to enable her to establish her own household and live in comfort in London or Wales. But while Julia could offer the wherewithal for a solid middle-class life, she could not bequeath the necessary social standing. As Hope pointed out, Marian was in limbo, 'the circumstances having cut her off her natural allies'.[66] She emigrated to America to be with her brother, David, in Dallas, Texas, where he, like his father, worked as a stonemason. She died age 67 in 1918. Poignantly, her doctor attributed her death to dementia, which, he wrote, had lasted for five years, exactly the period since Julia's death.[67]

Cecil, too, did not long survive his aunt. Having already served in the Boer War at the head of his North Staffordshire Volunteer force, he volunteered again at the age of 52 for service in France and was killed at the Battle of the Somme in July 1916. His cousin, Berry, Alfred's son and Julia's ward, also served in the war but survived. His older brother, Jem, who Julia had always found rather troublesome, had an altogether more colourful career, becoming a prominent member of the Theosophical Society as well as being ordained in the Old Catholic Church of England. When that was dissolved, he became presiding Bishop of the Liberal Catholic Church. A drug addict and energetic homosexual, he died of tertiary syphilis in 1951 after many years of dementia.[68]

Effie and Hope lived long and happily together at Idlerocks, holding regular séances. Sometimes they intimidated tongue-tied young Wedgwoods with their instruction 'Say something' as they held out their ear trumpets. On special occasions, they handed round Julia's Album of Family History.[69] Mary Euphrasia, who was awarded an MBE for her war work in Italy, married late and unhappily. After her mother's and aunt's deaths, she put up for sale some of the books and letters she had inherited from Julia. The Darwin letters and first editions sold well: the Browning collection (some of it disfigured by her careless manuscript additions) was much less successful. Nor did the correspondence with Browning in a cursory edition prepared by Richard Curle restore Julia's reputation. In the 1930s the painful struggles of Victorian women to establish themselves in a man's world attracted little interest, with the conspicuous exception of Julia's bête noire, Florence Nightingale.

Julia's relative obscurity at the time of her death reflected the fact that she had lived on into an age that was 'impatient with Victorian earnestness'.[70] Her current neglect, however, is more surprising. While Cobbe, Alice Meynell and, above all, Harriet Martineau and the younger generation of writers like Vernon Lee, Rosamund Watson and Mathilde Blind are attracting fresh attention, interest in Julia has largely centred on her relationships

Figure 36 Hope and Effie Wedgwood together in old age at Idlerocks. Courtesy of James Wendt.

with Browning and Darwin. This fails to reflect the fact that in her literary prime she was seen as one of the great female intellects of her age.

Her mother and two sisters are good examples of the way bright, comfortably off women fared in a world of expanding opportunity. All three were clever, articulate, active and not to be ignored. But Julia wanted more than that. Beatrice Potter wrote in 1878, 'So few women have enough character to live an unmarried life, and not sink into a nobody, or still worse into a general nuisance.'[71] Julia was never a nobody and, though some in her family found her high-mindedness daunting, nor was she a nuisance. She survived the discouragement of paternal dismissal to make her own more realistic assessment of her and her father's relative abilities without losing respect for him. Her relationship with her mother was more fraught. Her recognition of her own excessive neediness, however, became a way into her understanding of the parallels between a child's demands on its mother and man's craving for God.

She would have dismissed E. M. Forster's description of her as 'formidable' with a graceful smile, however. 'Formidable' was an adjective rarely applied to women in the Victorian age. Julia was more aware of the inadequacies in her learning than the rarity of her accumulation of knowledge and wide reading. Asked to describe the influences on her early development in an article for the *Women's Herald* in 1891, she singled out Uncle Charles, James Martineau, F. D. Maurice and Francis Newman. Reflecting on their brilliance, she concluded, 'I ought to have been something larger than I am.'[72] This characteristic modesty can mislead us over the scale of her achievement in both her private and public life. For all her sensitivity to social conventions, Julia was a quiet rebel. She refused to conform with expectations about how Victorian spinsters should organize their lives, moving out of the family home when her parents were old and ailing to set up her own household and elevating a Welsh housemaid to a prominent place at her dinner table. This gave her the freedom to pursue her career as a writer, focusing on the big subjects that engrossed her: the ancient Greeks, world history, theology, mysticism, scientific and political developments, philosophy and German Bible criticism, as well as the more familiar subjects for women of literature and biography. Her response to them was not systematic. Standing to one side of an increasingly specialized discourse, she is not always easy to categorize. Her reactions to Darwinism were atypical; her dedication to female suffrage declined the closer its advocates came to achieving it; her writing about science and early ability to get to the heart of Darwinian teleology sat alongside a mystical approach to the new science of energy; her keen critique of impoverished Broad Church theology coexisted with a late and largely emotional attachment to Spiritualism. Her intellectual range, however, was remarkable. Julia wrote about what she thought important. The fact that she was venturing on to male territory to do this never deterred her. This boldness has, however, tended to conceal the place she held in the demanding world of upmarket periodical writing in the late Victorian age. Because we do not expect to find a woman writing about the variety of subjects Julia chose, we have not always seen her there.

Though she lived on even into the post-Edwardian age, Julia was essentially a Victorian. She knew that she had lived in an age of great thinkers and writers, addressing fundamental issues about religion, the nature of society, the expansion of democracy, the role of science and the relationship between the material and immaterial worlds. Whatever the limited expectations of her family, the restrictions of her deafness and her awareness of the deficiencies in her education, she too wanted to tackle them. She brought to her work a rare combination of charm and authority, high intelligence and mysticism, wide but uneven reading and a seriousness she never tried to hide as well as a constant willingness to learn and explore. From the start her mission was to lead, console and invigorate her readers. The combination was as unexpected in her own time as it is for us as we look back on a time that Julia saw as a heroic age.

ACKNOWLEDGEMENTS

My greatest debt is to Gill Sutherland at Cambridge, who first encouraged my nascent interest in Julia Wedgwood. She has since read a number of chapters offering sage comments and suggestions for further reading as well as welcome hospitality on my visits to Cambridge. Similarly, Valerie Sanders at Hull has taken an encouraging interest in my book from its early days and commented on a number of chapters. My debt to her own work will be clear to the reader. Jane Stabler at St Andrews kindly made time in a very busy schedule to comment on my Browning chapters. I also owe a particular debt to Bernie Lightman in Toronto, who generously read a number of chapters and steered me in some new directions. Samantha Evans at the Darwin Correspondence Project in Cambridge and the author of 'Darwin and Women' also read my chapters on Darwin and Julia Wedgwood, leading to some illuminating chats over coffee and cake in the canteen at the Cambridge University Library. The speed and authority with which Patricia Fara assembled an online team of international experts to enlighten me on nineteenth-century deafness was impressive. I am also grateful for the keen eyes and informed suggestions of the three anonymous assessors recruited by my publisher to appraise the full script. Needless to say, whatever errors or mis-readings remain are all my own.

Stephen Evans, Michael Meredith, Simon Avery and the much-missed Pamela Neville-Sington at the Browning Society and Sharon Connor at the Martineau Society have also been particularly helpful, and I was grateful for the early interest of Daniel Karlin, Joe Phelan, David Amigoni and John Woolford in my project. Jennifer Holmes, the expert biographer of Ray Strachey, kindly read through the whole of my penultimate draft offering very pertinent suggestions that helped shape the final script.

Janet and Alan Wedgwood and Anthony Wedgwood generously gave me access to some of their family treasures, including an album that Ras Darwin gave to Fanny Wedgwood containing three charming portraits of the infant Julia Wedgwood.

Bringing this book to completion has been a long haul. It would not have happened without the sustaining encouragement of friends. Singling out a few is an invidious process, but I must mention Ralph and Margaret Houlbrooke, Alice and Frank Prochaska, Hazel Morgan and her husband, Andy, whose genealogical expertise helped me trace Marian Hughes from her early days in Wales to her sad last years in Texas, Mary and Mike Clapinson, Jo and Liz Carey, Kate Allan, Gill Hancock, Susan Robinson, Ann Beaton, Pat Gibson, Yvonne Baker, Jill Webster, David Milne, Edward Warrington, Robert Baldock and Neil Bennett, who gave me invaluable help with formatting and illustrations.

Any biographer working from original manuscripts owes a great debt to their curators. I worked at the Wedgwood Archive at Barlaston (as it then was) at a very difficult time when its future seemed in doubt. I was particularly grateful for the keen interest in my work taken by the late Sharon Gater, the head of education, who determinedly tracked down the album of Wedgwood family history Julia Wedgwood compiled, and the helpfulness of a number of volunteers who included Lucy Lead, then about to start her postgraduate studies and now the expert archivist at the V&A Wedgwood Collection. Its value as a rich source of nineteenth-century family and cultural history alongside its outstanding importance as a source for industrial, artistic and commercial history is being increasingly explored. I was glad to be in email contact at a late stage in my work with Madison Miller, who is researching the contribution to philology of Julia Wedgwood and her father, Hensleigh. There is still much to discover about Julia Wedgwood.

I also had a rewarding visit to the excellent new Girton College Archive in Cambridge, where the Archivist and Curator Hannah Westall went to some trouble to prepare my visit and ensure I was able to make best use of my time in the Archive. Reading Arthur Munby's diaries in the magnificent Trinity College Library during a bitterly cold spell was a very different but equally rewarding experience, and I am grateful to Jonathan Smith for facilitating my visit. The curators of the Bedford College Archive now at Royal Holloway College were also very helpful. I was lucky enough to see the complete Robert Browning–Julia Wedgwood correspondence (including unsent drafts) at the Browning-Armstrong Library at Baylor University in Texas when I was an invited scholar during the Robert Browning bicentenary celebrations. Jennifer Borderud, who has now succeeded Rita Patteson as librarian, continues her tradition of expert helpfulness supported by Christi Klempnauer.

Julia Wedgwood and her mother were early members of the London Library. It remains a splendid resource that responded brilliantly to the challenges of Covid-related restrictions, always putting the interests of readers first. Others who have been particularly helpful include the staff of the Women's Library at LSE, the British Library, the Bodleian Library, Oxford and the knowledgeable staff in the Manuscripts Room at Cambridge University Library, where the Darwin Papers are housed.

I have been grateful for the early and sustained interest of Anthem Press in this book and for the care, sensitivity and professionalism with which they have brought it to completion.

Permissions for the reproduction of illustrations in various collections are noted alongside them in the text. I have also reproduced a number of family portraits included in Barbara and Hensleigh Wedgwood's *The Wedgwood Circle 1730–1897*. My various efforts to track down the current owners of these images have not all succeeded. I apologize for any resulting breaches of permission, which I shall be happy to rectify.

Permission to reproduce extracts from manuscript collections has been granted by the following: the V&A Wedgwood Collection, presented by the Artfund with major support from the Heritage Lottery Fund, private donations and a public appeal; the Syndics of Cambridge University Library; the Mistress and Fellows of Girton College, Cambridge; the Armstrong-Browning Library at Baylor University, Waco, Texas; the Master and

Fellows of Trinity College Cambridge; the Provost and Fellows of King's College, Cambridge; and the archives of the Gray Herbarium, Harvard University.

This book is dedicated to my late sister, Ruth, who shared Julia Wedgwood's sense of the vital importance of religious feeling and also had to confront the problem that always troubled her, the existence of pain.

NOTES

All underlinings in the text or italics are in the original sources, whether manuscript or printed.

Introduction: 'The Formidable Snowie'

1. *Robert Browning: The Major Works*, ed. Adam Roberts, with an introduction by Daniel Karlin (Oxford World's Classics, Oxford University Press, 2009). See especially pp. 697–702 and 704–26.
2. Browning to J W, 21 January 1869 and 8 March 1869, in Roberts, *Robert Browning*, pp. 711 and 725.
3. E. M. Forster, 'Snow Wedgwood', *The Listener*, 13 October 1937, reprinted in *Two Cheers for Democracy* (Abinger edition), pp. 195–96.
4. J W to Fanny Wedgwood, August 1880, Wedgwood/Mosley Collection at the V&A Wedgwood Collection hereinafter described as W/M 252; and J W to Emily Gurney, 18 December 1887, W/M 584.
5. J W to Laura Forster, 27 April 1906, E. M. Forster Papers Letter Book 2, EMF FF/25 vol. 8/25.
6. E. M. Forster, *Marianne Thornton*, pp. 223 and 280.
7. Adrian Desmond and James Moore, introduction to Charles Darwin's *The Descent of Man*, p. xlix; and Janet Browne, *Charles Darwin: Voyaging*, p. 375.
8. Jenny Uglow, *Elizabeth Gaskell: A Habit of Stories*, pp. 445 and 447; and 'Manuscript Moments', *Lives for Sale*, ed. Mark Bostridge, pp. 184–85, and José Harris, 'Julia Wedgwood', *Oxford Dictionary of National Biography*.
9. P. N. Furbank, *E. M. Forster: A Life*, 1, p. 115.
10. *Glasgow Herald*, 3 February 1891.
11. C. H. Herford, 'Frances Julia Wedgwood: A Memoir', prefaced to J W, *Josiah Wedgwood the Potter*, p. xxiii.
12. Julia Wedgwood, 'The Duties of the Biographer', *Spectator*, 20 December 1879, pp. 1606–7.
13. Barbara Caine, 'Feminist Biography and Feminist History', *Women's History Review*, 3 (1994), p. 251.
14. E. M. Forster, 'West Hackhurst: A Surrey Ramble', in ed. Philip Gardner, *The Journals and Diaries of E. M. Forster*, 3, p. 171.

Chapter One A Brilliant Child

1. Wedgwood Family Album XXII W/M uncatalogued.
2. Charles Darwin, 'Recollections of the Development of My Mind and Character', in *Charles Darwin Evolutionary Writings*, ed. James Secord, p. 375.
3. He later told J W that the only brief he secured was in advising a Mr Williams from Boddelwyddam about whether his brother could 'get rid of his orders' (J W's account of her father's early life in Fanny Wedgwood's album in the possession of Janet and Alan Wedgwood).
4. Quoted in Patrick O'Leary, *Sir James Mackintosh: The Whig Cicero*, pp. 148–49.
5. Ibid., 163.
6. Fanny Wedgwood to Sarah Elizabeth Wedgwood, [1832], W/M 167.
7. Barbara and Hensleigh Wedgwood, *The Wedgwood Circle*, p. 219, but see J W to May Crum, 21 February 1892, EAD/GBR/vol. 2/MS Add.7671/V/D; and Catherine Darwin to Charles

8 Fanny Wedgwood to Bessy Wedgwood, [February 1833], W/M 210.
9 Harriet Martineau to Rev W J Fox, [18 June 1833], *Selected Letters of Harriet Martineau*, ed. Valerie Sanders, p. 41.
10 Fanny Wedgwood to Elizabeth Wedgwood, [1834], W/M 167.
11 Elizabeth Wedgwood to Bessy Wedgwood, 3 March 1835, in H. Litchfield, *Emma Darwin: A Century of Family Letters*, 1, p. 355.
12 Fanny Wedgwood to Emma Wedgwood, W/M 199. The date of '1834' was later added by J W. The year 1835 seems more likely.
13 Fanny and J W to Emma Wedgwood, 28 January 1837, W/M 199.
14 Elizabeth Wedgwood to Jessie Sismondi, 5 June 1839, *Emma Darwin*, 1, p. 465. Annie Darwin, by comparison, did not start to write till she was 6 (Randall Keynes, *Annie's Box*, p. 107).
15 Charles Darwin to Emma Darwin, 24 October 1843, CUL DAR 210.8:21.
16 Fanny Allen to Emma Wedgwood, 11 May 1835, *Emma Darwin*, 1, p. 374.
17 Charles Darwin to Caroline Darwin, [7 December 1836], *Correspondence of Charles Darwin*, 1, p. 524.
18 Fanny Wedgwood to Anne Marsh, 13 February 1839, *Emma Darwin*, 1, p. 451.
19 Quoted in Barbara Wedgwood, 'Julia Wedgwood', unpublished PhD thesis, University of London), p. 57.
20 Emma Wedgwood to Fanny Wedgwood, 1830, quoted in ibid., p. 56.
21 Fanny Wedgwood to Emma Wedgwood, 6 July [1838], W/M 199; and Emma Darwin to Elizabeth Wedgwood, 29 March 1839, *Emma Darwin*, 1, p. 460.
22 Harriet Martineau, *Autobiography*, ed. Gaby Weiner, 1, p. 99; and Harriet Martineau to Fanny Wedgwood, May 1834, *Harriet Martineau's Letters to Fanny Wedgwood*, ed. Elisabeth Sanders Arbuckle, p. 1.
23 Erasmus Darwin to Fanny Wedgwood, 'Thursday', [? early 1840s], W/M 227.
24 Fanny Wedgwood to Elizabeth Wedgwood, October 1835 and 14 November 1835, W/M 167.
25 J W to Alfred Benn, 22 January 1910, W/M 627.
26 Wedgwood Family Album W/M uncatalogued.
27 Charles Darwin to William Darwin, 1 March [1853], *Correspondence of Charles Darwin*, 5, p. 121.
28 Fanny Allen to Elizabeth Wedgwood, 18 April 1851; and Charles Darwin to Emma Darwin, 19 and 21 April 1851, *Emma Darwin*, 2, pp. 133, 132 and 135. See also Randall Keynes, *Annie's Box*, pp. 170–78.
29 J W to Fanny Wedgwood, 6 December 1841, W/M 252.
30 J W to Effie Wedgwood, 3 April 1860, W/M 324.
31 Wedgwood Family Album W/M uncatalogued, Fanny Wedgwood to Elizabeth Wedgwood, 14 November 1835, W/M 167; and Barbara Wedgwood, 'Julia Wedgwood', p. 57.
32 J W to Effie Wedgwood, 15 August 1871, W/M 324.
33 Wedgwood Family Album W/M uncatalogued.
34 Ann Marsh to Elizabeth Wedgwood, 8 May 1844; Wedgwood Family Album W/M uncatalogued.
35 Harriet Martineau to J W, 30 May [1840], *Harriet Martineau's Letters to Fanny Wedgwood*, p. 34.
36 Harriet Martineau to J W, 17 February [1841], in ibid., p. 37.
37 J W, *Josiah Wedgwood the Potter*, p. 332.
38 J W to Alfred Benn, 3 September 1910, W/M 627.
39 Barbara Wedgwood, 'Julia Wedgwood', p. 68.
40 J W to Effie Wedgwood, 1 January 1863, W/M 324.
41 Christina de Bellaigue, *Educating Women: Schooling and Identity in England and France 1800–1867*, pp. 80–81.
42 Fanny Wedgwood to Elizabeth Wedgwood, 14 November 1835, W/M 167.
43 As a magistrate, Hensleigh Wedgwood had the unhappy distinction of being the last magistrate in England to condemn two young men for homosexuality though he recommended, unavailingly, that they be spared capital punishment. See the entry on him in *Wikipedia*.

(Note: entry 7 continues at top) Darwin, 27 September 1833, in CUL DAR 204, p. 88. Weather reports for 3 February 1833 record a mild day.

44 J W, 'Hensleigh Wedgwood', in *Bedford College Magazine*, 1902, p. 27.
45 *Emma Darwin*, 1, p. 405.
46 Charles Darwin to W. D. Fox, 12 December 1937, *The Wedgwood Circle*, p. 229.
47 Hensleigh Wedgwood to Jos Wedgwood, n.d., Wedgwood Family Album W/M uncatalogued.
48 Emma Wedgwood to Jessie Sismondi, 5 August 1833, *Emma Darwin*, 1, p. 355.
49 Emma Wedgwood to Charles Darwin, 21–22 November 1838, CUL DAR 254:150.
50 Emma Wedgwood to Fanny Wedgwood, 21 October 1836, *Emma Darwin*, 1, p. 384.
51 Charles Darwin's two notes on the pros and cons of marriage are reprinted in Samantha Evans, *Darwin and Women: A Selection of Letters*, pp. 30–31. They are undated. Desmond and Moore read these in the context of Darwin's interest in marrying Emma, but Janet Browne suggests early summer, 1837, and Edna Healey 'summer, 1837'.
52 See ibid., p. 36.
53 Emma Wedgwood to Jessie Sismondi, 15 November 1838, *Emma Darwin*, 2, p. 6.
54 Emma Darwin to Charlotte Langton, [15 March 1839]; and Emma Darwin to Bessie Wedgwood, 8 February 1839, in ibid., 2, pp. 32, 38–39.
55 J W to Effie Wedgwood, 9 August [1855], W/M 324; Kathryn Hughes, *George Eliot*, p. 19; and J W to Alfred Benn, 21 December 1912, W/M 627.
56 *Emma Darwin*, 2, p. 48.
57 Emma Wedgwood to Elizabeth Wedgwood, [1 February 1842], in ibid., 2, p. 65.
58 Elizabeth Wedgwood to Emma Darwin, n.d., in ibid., 2, p. 81.
59 See Janet Browne, *Charles Darwin: Voyaging*, p. 11.
60 See Loy and Loy, *Emma Darwin*.
61 *The Wedgwood Circle*, pp. 261–62. Some subsequent biographers have followed this but not Edna Healey: 'Hensleigh would not have tolerated it, nor would the fastidious Erasmus have so insulted him' (Edna Healey, *Emma Darwin*, pp. 315–16).
62 Wedgwood Family Album W/M uncatalogued; and V. Surtees, *Jane Welsh Carlyle*, p. 167; and Ras Darwin to Fanny Wedgwood, August 1842, W/M 227.
63 Ras Darwin's extensive correspondence with Fanny Wedgwood is at W/M 227.
64 Erasmus Darwin to Fanny Wedgwood 1841 and 'Thursday', W/M 227; and Fanny Wedgwood to Emma Wedgwood, 6 July [1838], W/M 199.
65 J W to Emily Gurney, 16 September 1883, and to Jane Gourlay, 26 January 1878, W/M 438 and W/M 447.
66 Leonore Davidoff, *Thicker than Water: Siblings and Their Relatives 1780–1920*, p. 167.
67 Mary Rich to Fanny Wedgwood in W/M 173.
68 Wedgwood Family History Album W/M uncatalogued. Mary and Claudius Rich's adventures are recounted in Constance M Alexander, *Baghdad in Bygone Days*.
69 *Records of Girlhood: An Anthology of Nineteenth-Century Women's Childhoods*, ed. Valerie Sanders, p. 13.
70 Mary Rich to Fanny Wedgwood, [1838], W/M 173; and J W, *Nineteenth Century Teachers*, p. 388.
71 Harriet Martineau, *Autobiography*, 1, p. 42.
72 J W to May Crum, 30 December 1896, CUL EAD/GBR/0012/MS. Add.7671 V/D 245.
73 J W to Alfred Benn, 4 December 1911 and 14 April 1912, W/M 627.
74 Christobel Coleridge, *Charlotte Mary Yonge*, pp. 60 and 96.
75 J W to Robert Browning, 9 September 1864, *Robert Browning and Julia Wedgwood: A Broken Friendship*, ed. Richard Curle, p. 84.
76 Emma Wedgwood to Elizabeth Wedgwood, 27 January 1832, *Emma Darwin*, 1, p. 244.
77 J W to Alfred Benn, 4 December 1911, W/M 627; Barbara Wedgwood, 'Julia Wedgwood', p. 66; and Wedgwood Family Album W/M uncatalogued.
78 J W to Henrietta Litchfield, December 1887, W/M 448.
79 J W to Alfred Benn, 17 March 1913, W/M627. See also George Eliot to Sarah Hennell, 1844, in *The George Eliot Letters*, ed. Gordon S. Haight, 1, p. 173.
80 J W to Fanny Wedgwood, 4 April [1846], W/M 252.

Chapter Two Mentors, Friends and Pioneers

1 See Kathryn Hughes, *George Eliot: The Last Victorian*, pp. 17–78.
2 Harriet Martineau, *Autobiography*, 1, p. 118.
3 Harriet Martineau to Fanny Wedgwood, 11 February [1843], printed in *Harriet Martineau's Letters to Fanny Wedgwood*, ed. Elizabeth Arbuckle, p. 47.
4 J W to Effie Wedgwood, 8 November [1857], W/M 324.
5 Christobel Coleridge, *Charlotte Mary Yonge: Her Life and Letters*, p. 60; and Charlotte Yonge, *The Daisy Chain*, pp. 163–64.
6 Harriet Martineau to Hensleigh Wedgwood, 'Christmas Eve', [1843]; Hensleigh Wedgwood to Harriet Martineau, December 1843; and Harriet Martineau to Fanny Wedgwood, 11 January 1844, *Harriet Martineau's Letters to Fanny Wedgwood*, pp. 69 and 77.
7 Ras Darwin to Fanny Wedgwood, 'Monday' [1846], W/M 227.
8 Ibid.
9 Rosemary Ashton, *Victorian Bloomsbury*, p. 235.
10 See Christina de Bellaigue, *Educating Women: Schooling and Identity in England and France 1800–1867*, pp. 12–21.
11 Harriet Martineau to Fanny Wedgwood, [February or March 1844], *Harriet Martineau's Letters to Fanny Wedgwood*, p. 75.
12 R. Watts, *Gender, Power and the Unitarians in England 1760–1860*, p. 68.
13 Elizabeth Cain, 'Rachel Martineau and Her School', unpublished BA thesis, Cambridge University, 2010.
14 J. Estlin Carpenter, *James Martineau*, p. 271.
15 Ibid., p. 43.
16 J W to Mary Rich, '1875 or 6', W/M 325.
17 Harriet Martineau to Fanny Wedgwood, 8 September 1846, *Harriet Martineau's Letters to Fanny Wedgwood*, p. 93.
18 J W to Effie Wedgwood, August 1862, W/M 324.
19 Mrs Gaskell to Marianne Gaskell, c. 27 November 1852, *The Letters of Mrs Gaskell*, eds J. A. V. Chapple and A. Pollard, pp. 140 and 214.
20 Jenny Uglow, *Elizabeth Gaskell*, p. 132.
21 C. H. Herford, 'Frances Julia Wedgwood A Memoir', pp. xiii–xiv, in J W, *Josiah Wedgwood: The Potter*.
22 Ralph Waller, 'James Martineau', *Oxford Dictionary of National Biography*.
23 Carpenter, *James Martineau*, p. 271; and J W, *Woman's Herald*, 23 May 1891, p. 481.
24 Eleanor Bonham Carter to Alice Bonham Carter, n.d., Bonham Carter Papers Hampshire Record Office F 571.
25 Carpenter, *James Martineau*, p. 272.
26 *Anna Swanwick: A Memoir and Reflections*, ed. Mary L. Bruce, p. 22; and *Memorials of Two Sisters Susanna and Catherine Winkworth*, ed. Margaret J. Shaen, p. 20.
27 J W, 'James Martineau and the Heterodoxy of the Past', *The Expositor*, 6th Series, 7, 1903, pp. 27–28.
28 Carpenter, *James Martineau*, p. 272; and J W, *The Woman's Journal*, 23 May 1891, p. 481.
29 Carpenter, *James Martineau*, 250; and *Contemporary Review*, 1900, p. 175.
30 Carpenter, *James Martineau*, 226; and J W, 'James Martineau', *The Expositor*, 7, 1903, p. 27.
31 Quoted in R. K. Webb, 'The Unitarian Background', *Truth, Liberty, Religion: Essays Celebrating Two Hundred Years of Manchester College*, ed. Barbara Smith, p. 11; and Carpenter, *James Martineau*, p. 106.
32 J W, 'James Martineau', *The Expositor*, 7, 1903, p. 29.
33 Jane Carlyle to Helen Welsh, c. 16 June 1846, Carlyle Letters online, JWC-HW-01; Ras Darwin to Fanny Wedgwood, 1846, W/M 227; and Wedgwood Family History Album XXXVIII W/M uncatalogued.
34 Wedgwood Family History Album XLI W/M uncatalogued.

35 Quoted in Alec R. Vidler, *F.D. Maurice and Co*, p. 205. See Brenda Collems, *Victorian Visionaries*, pp. 15–16; and J. P. Newell, 'The Other Christian Socialist Alexander John Scott', *Heythrop Journal*, 24, 1983, pp. 278–89.
36 Quoted in Alec R. Vidler, *F. D. Maurice and Co*, p. 249.
37 F. Maurice, *Life of Frederick Denison Maurice*, 1, p. 121.
38 See B. G. Reardon, *From Coleridge to Gore: A Century of Religious Thought in Britain*, pp. 398–400.
39 F. Maurice, *The Life of Frederick Denison Maurice*, 1, p. 533.
40 Quoted in E. M. Forster, *Marianne Thornton*, p. 227.
41 *The First College Open to Women: Queen's College London*, ed. Mrs Alec Tweedie, p. 113.
42 Ibid., p. 37.
43 Camilla Crundace, in ibid.
44 Quoted in Elaine Kaye, *A History of Queen's College, London 1848–1972*, pp. 22, 51–52; and *The First College Open to Women: Queen's College London*, ed. Mrs Alec Tweedie, p. 69.
45 *The First College Open to Women: Queen's College, London*, p. 37.
46 Ibid., p. 38.
47 J W to Ellen Tollet, 12 December 1869, W/M 401; and F. Maurice, *The Life of Frederick Denison Maurice*, 2, p. 536.
48 J W to A. W. Benn, 3 March 1912 and 4 March 1911, W/M 627; and J W to May Crum, 5 September 1907 CUL Add 7671 V.
49 Rosemary Ashton, *Victorian Bloomsbury*, p. 220.
50 Margaret Tuke, *Educating Women*, p. 7.
51 Ras Darwin to Fanny Wedgwood, 'Wednesday', [1849], W/M 227.
52 Ras Darwin to Fanny Wedgwood, 'About 1850', W/M 227.
53 The Bedford College Student Register in the Royal Holloway College Archive does not always distinguish between 'Miss' and 'Mrs' Wedgwood.
54 J W to Benn, 6 October 1909 and 6 January 1910, W/M 627.
55 J. W. Cross, *George Eliot's Life*, 1, pp. 93–94.
56 J W to Benn, 6 and 12 October 1909, W/M 627.
57 Godfrey Wedgwood to J W, 7 March 1852, W/M 315.
58 J W, *Women's Herald*, 23 May 1891, p. 482.
59 Frank Wedgwood to Clement Wedgwood, n.d., W/M uncatalogued; Ernest Wedgwood to J W, [1854], W/M 333; and Godfrey Wedgwood to J W, 7 March 1852, W/M 315.
60 *The First College Open to Women: Queen's College London*, p. 113.
61 Maurice is quoted in Elaine Kaye, *A History of Queen's College, London 1848–1972*, p. 24; and Mrs Reid in Margaret Tuke, *A History of Bedford College*, p. xiv.

Chapter Three Waiting

1 J W, 'A Reminiscence', *The First College Open to Women: Queen's College London*, ed. Mrs Alec Tweedie, p. 111.
2 See Sharon Connor, 'The Age of the Female Novelist: Single Women as Authors', in *British Women's Writing from Bronte to Bloomsbury*, ed. Gavin and Oulton, pp. 1, 140–43, on the extent to which the 1851 Census figures were misleading about the relative numbers of single men and women of marriageable age.
3 *Woman's Work and Woman's Culture*, ed. Josephine Butler, p. 263.
4 Ibid., p. 250.
5 J W to Ida Farrer, 10 July 1877, CUL Darwin Archive 93861: 16224. Another gifted young woman whose life was transformed by her attendance at Scott's lectures and the contact she made there with F. D. Maurice was Sara Coleridge. See Katie Waldegrave, *The Poets' Daughters Dora Wordsworth and Sara Coleridge*, p. 238.

NOTES

6. Fanny Erskine to J W, 14 November [1849], 11 March [1851] and 1 January 1849, CUL Darwin Archive 258.1522, 1512 and 1502.
7. Fanny Erskine to J W, [1 January] 1849, CUL Darwin Archive 258:1502.
8. Fanny Erskine to J W, 15 July [1853]; and J W to Ida Farrer, 10 July 1877, CUL Darwin 8904.1 3222 and 9368.1: 16224.
9. J W to Fanny Wedgwood, 29 September 1850, W/M 252. *Alton Locke* was originally published anonymously.
10. E. M. Forster, 'West Hackhurst: A Surrey Ramble', *The Journals and Diaries of E.M. Forster*, ed. Philip Gardner, 3, p. 161.
11. J W to Alfred Benn, 6 January 1910, W/M 627.
12. See Randal Keynes, *Annie's Box*, pp. 120–21 and 159.
13. J W, *Nineteenth Century Teachers*, pp. 221–22.
14. Richard Litchfield to J W, [June 1861], W/M 384.
15. J W, *Women's Herald*, Saturday, 23 May 1891 (384), p. 482.
16. Quoted in Mark Bostridge, *Florence Nightingale*, pp. 92 and 140.
17. See Leonora Davidoff, *Thicker than Water: Siblings and Their Relatives 1780–1920*, pp. 107 and 110.
18. J W to Hope Wedgwood, '1852', W/M 326, and to Effie Wedgwood, n.d. [?1854], W/M 324.
19. Ras Darwin to Fanny Wedgwood, Friday '58', W/M 227.
20. J W to Robert Browning, 21 October 1864, in *Robert Browning and Julia Wedgwood: A Broken Friendship*, ed. R. Curle, p. 104.
21. J W to Effie Wedgwood, 9 March 1865, W/M 326; and Hope to Effie Wedgwood, n.d. [1867], W/M 327.
22. E. M. Forster, *Marianne Thornton*, p. 241.
23. J W, 'James Fitzjames Stephen', *Nineteenth Century Teachers*, p. 209.
24. J W to Mary Rich, December 1854, in B. and H. Wedgwood, *The Wedgwood Circle*, ed. p. 96.
25. Fanny Wedgwood and J W to Effie Wedgwood, 5 August 1845, W/M 268.
26. Fanny Erskine to J W, 8 November 1853, CUL DAR 8904.1 3223.
27. Thomas Carlyle to Jane Carlyle, 16 July 1857, Carlyle correspondence online.
28. Ras Darwin to Fanny Wedgwood, 26 August 1857, W/M 227.
29. Fanny Wedgwood to Effie Wedgwood, 5 August 1845, W/M 268.
30. Ras Darwin to Fanny Wedgwood, 10 May 1855, W/M 227.
31. Quoted in R. K. Webb, *Harriet Martineau*, p. 48.
32. J W to Effie Wedgwood, 29 May 1855, W/M 324.
33. J W to Effie Wedgwood, 10 and 29 May 1855, W/M 324.
34. J W to Effie Wedgwood, 10 May 1855, W/M 324.
35. See Valerie Sanders, *The Brother-Sister Culture in Nineteenth Century Literature*, p. 2.
36. Fanny Wedgwood to Effie Wedgwood, 20 August 1858, W/M 268.
37. J W to Effie Wedgwood, n.d. [1855], W/M 324.
38. J W to Emily Gurney, 16 November 1890, W/M 584.
39. J W to Effie Wedgwood, 18 June 1855, W/M 324.
40. L. Davidoff, *Thicker than Water*, pp. 110–16.
41. J W to Effie Wedgwood, 9 August 1855, W/M 324.
42. Quoted in Mark Bostridge, *Florence Nightingale*, p. 349.
43. J W to Effie Wedgwood, 29 September 1854, W/M 324.
44. Mrs Gaskell to Marianne Gaskell, 15 and 22 November 1852, *The Letters of Mrs Gaskell*, ed. J. A. V. Chapple and A. Pollard, pp. 209 and 213.
45. Wedgwood Family Album W/M uncatalogued.
46. Fanny Erskine to J W, 23 November 1852, CUL DAR 258 1519.
47. Fanny Wedgwood to Effie Wedgwood, [?1854], W/M 268.
48. See Elisabeth Bennion, *Antique Hearing Devices*, p. 28.
49. Harriet Martineau, 'Letter to the Deaf', *Tait's Edinburgh Magazine*, April 1834.

50 J W to Fanny Wedgwood, [1855], W/M 252.
51 Fanny Wedgwood to Effie Wedgwood, c. 11 May 1859, W/M 268.
52 Marianne Thornton to ?Laura Forster, quoted in E. M. Forster, *Marianne Thorton*, p. 223.
53 J W to Effie Wedgwood, 10 July 1869, W/M 324.
54 J W, *Woman's Work and Woman's Culture*, pp. 251–52.
55 Mrs Gaskell to Mary Rich, 10 March [1853], *Further Letters of Mrs Gaskell*, p. 84.
56 J W to Effie Wedgwood, 17 October 1855, W/M 324.
57 Ibid.
58 J W, *Woman's Work and Woman's Culture*, p. 263.
59 J W to Effie Wedgwood, 3 November [1855], W/M 324.

Chapter Four The Young Novelist

1 Her mother was the sister of Peter Holland, whose first wife, Mary Willetts, was a niece of Josiah Wedgwood.
2 Elizabeth Stevenson to Harriet Carr, 3 May 1832, in *Further Letters of Mrs Gaskell*, eds John Chapple and Alan Shelston, p. 17.
3 Though *Mary Barton* was published anonymously, Henry Holland guessed its authorship. Mrs Gaskell blamed Hensleigh Wedgwood and Anne Marsh for spreading the rumour (Mrs Gaskell to Edward Chapman, 7 December 1848, in *The Letters of Mrs Gaskell*, eds Chapple and Pollard, p. 65).
4 Mrs Gaskell to ?Marianne Gaskell, 13 July 1851, printed in ibid., p. 158. This is the date suggested but may be too late in the year as Snow's birthday was in February.
5 Mrs Gaskell to Marianne Gaskell, 15 November 1852, in ibid., p. 211.
6 J W to Effie Wedgwood, 27 June (?) and 6 September 1856, W/M 324.
7 J W to Effie Wedgwood, 6 September 1856, W/M 324.
8 J W to Effie Wedgwood, 3 November 1855, W/M 324.
9 J W to Fanny Wedgwood, 17 November 1855, W/M 252.
10 J W to Effie Wedgwood, 3 November 1855, W/M 324.
11 *Memorials of Two Sisters Susanna and Catherine Winkworth*, ed. Margaret J Shaen, p. 24.
12 Edward Fiddes, *Chapters in the History of Owen's College*, pp. 32 and 36; Joseph Thomson, *The Owen's College: Its Foundation and Growth*, pp. 191 and 189; and Wedgwood Family Album XXIX b W/M uncatalogued.
13 J W to Ellen Tollet, 22 August 1862, W/M 401; and J W to Fanny Wedgwood, 17 November 1855, W/M 252.
14 J W to Fanny Wedgwood, 17 November 1855, W/M 252.
15 One employee reckoned in 1853 that 'about seven novels a day came in and most went back'. See B. Q. Schmidt, 'Hurst and Blackett 1853–1954', in *Dictionary of Literary Biography, 106, British Literary Publishing Houses 1820–1900*, eds Patricia J. Anderson and Jonathan Rose, pp. 155–58. J W to Effie Wedgwood, November 1856, W/M 324.
16 J W to Effie Wedgwood, 19 October 1856, W/M 324.
17 J W to Effie Wedgwood, 24 October 1856, W/M 324.
18 J W to Effie Wedgwood, 25 August 1858, W/M 324.
19 C. E. Maurice to J W, 7 January 1877, W/M 425. The suggestion by the critic in *The Observer* that Scott's *Fair Maid of Perth* was a precedent for a novel about a coward missed the point that Maurice, unlike the head of the Clan Chattan, only appears to be so.
20 *Framleigh Hall*, 3, pp. 59 and 307.
21 J W to Effie Wedgwood, 8 November 1857, W/M 324.
22 J W to Effie Wedgwood, 21 November and 24 October 1856, W/M 324.
23 *Framleigh Hall*, 1, p. 17.
24 *Framleigh Hall*, 3, p. 237.

25 *Framleigh Hall*, 3, p. 225.
26 *Framleigh Hall*, 3, p. 282; and Ernest Wedgwood to J W, 26 August 1858, W/M 333.
27 J W to Effie Wedgwood, 'November 1856', 19 October 1856; and 'November 1856', W/M 324.
28 J W to Effie Wedgwood, 'November 1856 and 12 November 1856 and 21 January 1857', W/M 324.
29 J W to Effie Wedgwood, 30 December 1856.
30 Fanny Wedgwood to Effie Wedgwood, 24 August 1857, W/M 268.
31 Ernest Wedgwood to J W, 26 August 1858, W/M 333; and J W to Effie Wedgwood, 1 and 24 August 1858, W/M 324.
32 Fanny Wedgwood to Effie Wedgwood, 24 and 29 August and 16 May and 24 August 1858, W/M 268.
33 Ras Darwin to Fanny Wedgwood, 'Tuesday', 1858.
34 J W to Robert Browning, 8 July 1864, printed in Sue Brown, 'Robert Browning and Julia Wedgwood: The Unpublished Correspondence', *Journal of Browning Studies*, 3, December 2012, p. 41.
35 *An Old Debt*, 1, pp. 6, 204 and 244, and 2, p. 25.
36 Ibid., 2, p. 227.
37 Valerie Sanders, *The Private Lives of Victorian Women Autobiography in Nineteenth-Century England*, p. 62.
38 J W, 'Contemporary Fiction', *Contemporary Review*, 1886. For a discussion of trans-gendered novel writing, see Valerie Sanders, *The Brother-Sister Culture in Nineteenth Century Literature: From Austen to Woolf*, p. 136.
39 J W to Robert Browning, 23 July 1864; and Browning to J W, 28 July 1864, in ed. Curle, pp. 39 and 52.
40 See J W to Effie Wedgwood, 18 July 1857, W/M 324.
41 Mackintosh Wedgwood to Fanny Wedgwood, 6 August 1860, W/M 268.
42 *An Old Debt*, 2, p. 314.
43 J W to Effie Wedgwood, 24 August 1858, W/M 324.
44 *Saturday Review*, 5 March 1859, 7 (175), p. 279.
45 J W to Effie Wedgwood, 14 March 1859, W/M 324.
46 J W to Effie Wedgwood, 28 August 1858, W/M 324.
47 *Athenaeum*, 5 February 1859, (1632), p. 185.
48 J W to Effie Wedgwood, 21 December 1858, W/M 324.
49 Sophia Sennett to Effie Wedgwood, 13 June 1859, W/M 324.
50 Julia Sterling to J W, 23 December 1858; Meta Gaskell to J W, 23 January 1859; and Godfrey Wedgwood to J W, 30 December 1858, in W/M 324.
51 Julia Sterling to J W, 28 January 1859, W/M 324.
52 Quoted in Loy and Loy, *Emma Darwin*, p. 144.
53 Hensleigh Wedgwood to J W, n.d., W/M 377.
54 See J W to Effie Wedgwood, 1 August 1857, W/M 324. Sadly, J W's letter to her father has not survived.
55 J W to Effie Wedgwood, 3 April 1860, W/M 324.
56 J W to Laura Forster, 27 April 1906, in E. M. Forster Papers EMF FF/25 vol. 8/25.
57 See, e.g., J W to Effie Wedgwood, September 1854, W/M 324, and note by J W dated 1897 attached to a letter to her mother of 20 September 1859 in W/M 252. Barbara Wedgwood has traced two possible suitors in Tenby in the winter of 1858, George Lort Phillips, whom Great Aunt Fanny had put in her way, and Dr Edward Wilson, who invited her for a walk. Barbara Wedgwood, 'A Critical Study of the Life and Works of Julia Wedgwood', pp. 110–12.
58 Ernest Wedgwood to J W, 'Friday', October 1856; J W to Effie Wedgwood, 24 October 1856; and J W to Effie Wedgwood, 22 May 1863, W/M 324.
59 J W to Effie Wedgwood, 24 October 1856, W/M 324.
60 J W to Effie Wedgwood, 17 June 1856, 23 May 1863, 10 January 1859 and 7 August 1872, W/M 324.
61 *Framleigh Hall*, 3, pp. 83–84.
62 J W to Emily Gurney, 19 May 1884 and 8 May 1886, W/M 584.
63 J W to Effie, 24 August 1858, W/M 324; and Fanny Wedgwood to Effie Wedgwood, 20 August 1858, W/M 268.

64 Jenny Uglow, *Mrs Gaskell*, p. 445.
65 Meta Gaskell to J W, 23 January 1858, W/M 324.
66 Harriet Martineau to J W, 4 May 1857, *Harriet Martineau's Letters to Fanny Wedgwood*, ed. E. S. Arbuckle, p. 153.
67 J W to Ellen Tollet, 22 August 1862, W/M 401; J W to Effie Wedgwood, August 1862 and 29 April 1862, W/M 324.
68 J W to Effie Wedgwood, 25 September 1865, W/M 324.
69 Reprinted in J W, *Nineteenth Century Teachers*, p. 15.
70 J W to Effie Wedgwood, 12 March 1859, W/M 324.
71 Fanny Wedgwood to J W, 'Sunday', 1860, W/M 268.
72 J W to Effie Wedgwood, 9 October 1860, W/M 324.
73 Julia Sterling to Effie Wedgwood, Friday, 1860, W/M 324.
74 Fanny Wedgwood to Effie Wedgwood, 13 September 1860, W/M 268.
75 J W to Effie Wedgwood, 3 April 1860, W/M 324.
76 F. D. Maurice to Fanny Wedgwood, 9 December 1857, W/M 425.
77 J W to Robert Browning, 21 May 1864, printed in Sue Brown, 'Robert Browning and Julia Wedgwood', *Journal of Browning Studies* 3, 2012, p. 39.

Chapter Five The Promise of Darwinism

1 See Bernard Lightman, 'Creating a New Space for Debate: The Monthlies, Science and Religion', in *Rethinking History, Science, and Religion*, ed. B Lightman, pp. 85–109.
2 Quoted in George Worth, *Macmillan's Magazine 1859–1907*, p. 33.
3 Rosemary T. Vanarsdel, 'Macmillan's Magazine and the Fair Sex', *Victorian Periodicals Review*, 33, no. 4, Winter 2000, p. 379.
4 Fanny Wedgwood to Effie Wedgwood, 13 September 1860, W/M 268. See also Edward Manier, *The Young Darwin and His Cultural Circle*, pp. 124–31 and 178–80.
5 Janet Browne, *Charles Darwin: Voyaging*, pp. 446–47.
6 See James A. Secord, *Victorian Sensation: The Extraordinary Publication, Reception, and Secret Authorship of Vestiges of the Natural History of Creation*, and Adrian Desmond, *The Politics of Evolution: Morphology, Medicine and Reform in Radical London*, especially p. 379, on Chambers' success in disassociating evolution from its previous radical context.
7 From *On the Origin of Species* in *Charles Darwin Evolutionary Writings*, ed. James Secord, pp. 210 and 211.
8 'Recollections of the Development of My Mind and Character', in *Charles Darwin Evolutionary Writings*, p. 396.
9 Harriet Martineau to George Holyoake, quoted in Adrian Desmond and James Moore, *Darwin*, p. 486.
10 Edmund Gosse, *Father and Son*, p. 122.
11 Gray, who was brought up a Presbyterian, switched to Congregationalism at Harvard though his wife remained a Unitarian.
12 Quoted in Jenny Uglow, *Mrs Gaskell*, p. 136.
13 Charles Kingsley to Darwin in Frank Darwin, *The Life and Letters of Charles Darwin*, 2, pp. 287–88. Like Maurice, he disowned the Broad Church label often attached to him, preferring to describe himself as an 'old-fashioned High Churchman' (James Moore, *The Post-Darwinian Controversies*, p. 306).
14 For a more extended discussion of Kingsley's attempt to incorporate Darwinian theory into a revised natural theology, see B. Lightman, *Victorian Popularisers of Science*, p. 80, and 'Creating a New Space for Debate: The Monthlies, Science and Religion', p. 101.
15 See Moore, *The Post-Darwinian Controversies*, pp. 90–92.
16 Charles Darwin to J W, 11 July 1861, Darwin Correspondence Project Letter 3206.
17 See Frank A. L. James, 'An Open Clash between Science and the Church?: Wilberforce, Huxley and Hooker on Darwin at the British Association, Oxford, 1860', in *Science and Beliefs from Natural Philosophy to Natural Science, 1700–1900*, eds David M Knight and Matthew Eddy.

18 T. H. Huxley, *Macmillan's Magazine* (1), p. 147.
19 See, for example, J W to Effie Wedgwood, 13 August 1854, W/M 324.
20 J W to Frank Darwin, 3 October 1884, in CUL DAR 1399.12:17.
21 C. H. Herford, 'The Late Miss Julia Wedgwood', *Spectator*, 10 January 1914. See also Janet Browne, *Charles Darwin: The Power of Place*, p. 297.
22 Charles Darwin to J. D. Hooker, 13 July 1856, in *The Correspondence of Charles Darwin*, ed. F. Burkhardt et al., 6, p. 178.
23 This was also a form often deployed by women popularizers of science in the mid-nineteenth century. See Barbara T. Gates, *Kindred Nature Victorian and Edwardian Women Embrace the Living World*, p. 38.
24 J W, 'The Boundaries of Science: A Dialogue', *Macmillan's Magazine*, 8, June 1860, pp. 135, 136 and 138.
25 See Owen Chadwick, *The Victorian Church*, 2, pp. 75–84. On the origin of the collection and the substance of the essays, see Joseph L. Althoz, *Anatomy of a Controversy: The Debate over Essays and Reviews 1858–1864*, pp. 9–33.
26 Herbert Spencer was similarly struck by the lack of adjustment between man and his environment. He, however, took an optimistic view of the social and economic possibilities arising from man's evolutionary progress towards human perfection. See Robert Young, *Darwin's Metaphor*, pp. 16–18.
27 J W, 'The Boundaries of Science: A Second Dialogue', *Macmillan's Magazine*, 21, July 1861, pp. 237, 238, 241, 245 and 247.
28 Charles Darwin to J W, 11 July 1861, in *The Correspondence of Charles Darwin*, 9, p. 200.
29 See A. Hunter Duprée, *Asa Gray 1810–1888*, pp. 376–77.
30 See John Hedley Brooke, 'Darwin and Victorian Christianity', in *The Cambridge Companion to Darwin*, ed. Jonathan Hodge and Gregory Radick, p. 203.
31 J W to Frank Darwin, 3 October 1884, CUL DAR 139(12): 17 and See below pp. 230–31, 233–34 and 236–37.
32 J W to Emily Gurney, 31 December 1872 and 22 and 31 December 1872, W/M 438.
33 See Judith Johnston and Hilary Fraser, 'The Professionalization of Women's Writing: Extending the Canon', in *Women and Literature in Britain 1800–1900*, ed. Joanne Shattock, pp. 236–37.
34 Virginia Woolf, *Three Guineas*, p. 244.
35 J W, 'Mr Hensleigh Wedgwood', *Bedford College Magazine*, 1902, p. 28.
36 J W to Effie Wedgwood, August 1862, W/M 324.
37 Fanny Wedgwood to Effie and Hope Wedgwood ('Dear Souls'), 'St Bartholomew's Day', 1862, W/M 268.
38 J W to Effie Wedgwood, 5 November 1865, W/M 324.
39 See Hans Aarsleff, *The Study of Language in England 1780–1860*, p. 221.
40 Gregory Raddick, *The Simian Tongue: The Long Debate about Animal Language*, p. 15.
41 Quoted in ibid., p. 16.
42 Charles Darwin to Asa Gray, 23 November 1862, in *Correspondence of Charles Darwin*, 10, p. 546. Darwin describes the article as having been written by 'my brother-in-law, H. Wedgwood and his daughter'.
43 Quoted in Raddick, *The Simian Tongue*, p. 32.
44 Max Müller, *Auld Lang Syne*, 1, pp. 176–77; and Raddick, *The Simian Tongue*, p. 40.
45 J W to Henrietta Darwin, 3 August 1869, W/M 448; and *Spectator*, 5 August 1871, pp. 952–53.
46 J W, 'The Origin of Language', *Macmillan's Magazine*, 7 November 1862, pp. 54–60.
47 J W, 'The Origin of Language', *Westminster Review*, 1866, pp. 88–122. Stephen Alter picks out this article as 'an important contribution' to the debate on the origins of language in *Darwinism and the Linguistic Image*, pp. 52–3. Müller's theory of the origins of speech was quickly discredited. See Linda Dowling, 'Victorian Oxford and the Science of Language', *PMLA*, 97, no. 2, 1982, p. 160.
48 See Sandra Herbert, *Charles Darwin, Geologist*.

49 Janet Browne, *Charles Darwin: The Power of Place*, p. 219.
50 J W to Effie Wedgwood, 1866, W/M 324.
51 J W, 'Lyell on the Antiquity of Man', *Macmillan's Magazine*, 7 April 1863, p. 171.
52 Wedgwood Family Album W/M uncatalogued.
53 J W, Introduction to Alexander Scott, *Discourses*, p. i; and J. P. Newell, 'The Other Christian Socialist Alexander John Scott', *Heythrop Journal*, 24, 1983, p. 282.
54 Ibid., p. xii; J W was quoting from an article in the *North British Review*.
55 Hope Wedgwood to Emma Darwin, n.d., W/M 625.
56 J W, 'The Boundaries of Science: A Second Dialogue', in *Macmillan's Magazine*, 21 July 1861, p. 238.
57 J W to Effie Wedgwood, 15 February 1864, W/M 324.
58 Emma Darwin to Henrietta Litchfield, 16 August 1872, CUL DAR 219:9:98.
59 J W to Effie and Hope Wedgwood, 5 April 1864, W/M 324.
60 J W to F. D. Maurice, 30 April 1864, W/M 425.
61 J W to Ellen Tollet, 28 June 1864, W/M 401.
62 J W to F. D. Maurice, 4 May and 24 June 1864; and Maurice to J W, 'Friday', 1864, W/M 425.
63 J W to Robert Browning, 25 June 1864; and Robert Browning to J W, 25 June 1864, in *Robert Browning and Julia Wedgwood: A Broken Friendship*, ed. Richard Curle, pp. 27 and 30.

Chapter Six 'The Era of My Life'

1 Robert to Sarianna Browning, 30 June 1861, and Browning to Euphrasia Haworth, 20 July 1861, in *Letters of Robert Browning*, eds T. J. Wise and T. L. Hood, pp. 62 and 65.
2 Browning to William Story, 18 January 1863, in *Browning to His American Friends*, ed. G. R. Hudson, p. 114.
3 J. W. to Effie Wedgwood, 12 February 1863, W/M 324.
4 Fanny Wedgwood to Effie Wedgwood, 19 May 1863, in W/M 268.
5 J W to Effie Wedgwood, 'Sunday night' [12 July 1863], W/M 324.
6 J W to Browning, 26 July 1866, in *Robert Browning and Julia Wedgwood: A Broken Friendship*, ed. Richard Curle, p. 50.
7 Browning to Elizabeth Barrett, 20 May 1845, in *The Courtship Correspondence*, ed. D. Karlin, p. 52.
8 J W to Effie Wedgwood, 'Sunday night' [12 July 1863], W/M 324.
9 Ibid.
10 Browning to Isa Blagden, 19 September 1865, in *Dearest Isa*, ed. Edward MacAleer, p. 224.
11 J W to Effie Wedgwood, 'Sunday night' [12 July 1863], W/M 324.
12 J W to Browning, 1 November 1864, and Browning to J W, 'Friday Mg', in ed Curle, pp. 113 and 115
13 Browning to Fanny Wedgwood, 9 December 1863, in ibid., p. 10.
14 Browning to Isla Blagden, 8 February 1864, in ibid., p. 11.
15 Browning to J W, n.d., in ibid., p. 25.
16 J W to Browning, May 1864, in ibid., p. 23.
17 Quoted in Pamela Neville-Sington, *Robert Browning: A Life after Death*, p. 14.
18 St Paul's companion, whose name meant 'Son of Encouragement'.
19 J W to Robert Browning, 25 June 1864, in ibid., pp. 26–28.
20 J W to Browning, 27 June [1864], in ibid., p. 31.
21 Browning to J W, 25 June 1864, in ibid., pp. 29–30.
22 Browning to Elizabeth Barrett, 19 June 1845, in *Robert Browning and Elizabeth Barrett*, ed. D. Karlin, p. 74.
23 J W to Browning, 27 June [1864], in ed. Curle, pp. 31–32.
24 Ibid., p. 32.

25 Browning to J W, 27 June 1864, in ibid., pp. 34–35.
26 Browning to J W, 27 June 1864, in ibid., p. 33.
27 J W to Browning, 1 July 1864, in Sue Brown, 'Robert Browning and Julia Wedgwood: The Unpublished Correspondence', *Journal of Browning Studies*, 3 (December 2012), p. 39.
28 J W to Browning, 8 July [1864], in ibid., p. 40.
29 J W to Browning, 1 July 1864, in ibid., p. 40.
30 J W to Browning, 8 and 20 July 1864, in ibid., pp. 41–42.
31 D. C. Somervill, *Observer*, 27 September 1937; Betty Miller, *Robert Browning: A Portrait*, p. 227; and Eliza Wedgwood to Ruth Draper [1940], Armstrong Browning Library Baylor.
32 J W to Browning, 23 July 1864, and Browning to J W, 28 July 1864, in ibid., pp. 40 and 52.
33 Browning to J W, 25 July 1864, in ibid., p. 45.
34 J W to Browning, 23 July 1864, in ibid., pp. 39–43.
35 Browning to J W, 25 July 1864, in ibid., pp. 44–46.
36 J W to Browning, 26 July [1864], in ibid., pp. 47–51.
37 Browning to J W, 28 July, and J W to Browning, 29 July 1864, in ibid., pp. 52 and 58.
38 Browning to J W, 28 July 1864, in ibid., p. 53.
39 Browning to J W, 2 August 1864, in ibid., p. 59.
40 Bonamy Dobrée, *Now and Then*, Autumn 1937.
41 J W to Browning, 12 August 1864, in Brown, 'The Unpublished Correspondence', pp. 42–44.
42 Browning to J W, 19 August 1864, in ed. Curle, pp. 63–65.
43 J W to Browning, 24 August, Browning to J W, 2 September, and J W to Browning, 9 September 1864, in ibid., pp. 70–71, 74–75 and 82.
44 J W to Browning, 24 August and 9 September, and Browning to J W, 2 September 1864, in ibid., pp. 68, 81 and 75.
45 Browning to J W, 2 September, and J W to Browning, 9 and 22 September 1864, in ibid., 77, 81 and 88.
46 Browning to Tennyson, 13 October 1864, quoted in ibid., p. 86.
47 See p. xx. Browning to J W, 2 September 1864, in ibid., pp. 78–79.
48 J W to Browning, 9 and 22 September, in ibid., pp. 84 and 87.
49 Browning to J W, 3 October 1864, in ibid., p. 95.
50 RB to JW, 2 September 1864, in Curle p. 78.
51 Browning to J W, 2 September, and J W to Browning, 9 September 1864, in ibid., p. 83.
52 J W to Browning, 22 September 1864, in ibid., p. 90.
53 Browning to J W, 3 October, and J W to Browning, 22 September 1864, in ibid., pp. 91 and 93–96.
54 Browning to J W, 3 October 1864, in ibid., p. 94.
55 J W to Browning, 14 October and 10 October 1864, in ibid., pp. 100 and 98.
56 Browning to J W, 17 October 1864, in ibid., p. 102.
57 J W to Browning, 21 October, and Browning to J W, 31 October 1864, in ibid., pp. 106–7.
58 J W to Browning, 1 November, and Browning to J W, 'Friday Mg' [1864], in ibid., pp. 112 and 114.
59 J W to Browning, 18 November 1864, in ibid., pp. 116 and 117.
60 J W to Browning, 12 November 1864 (draft), in Brown, 'The Unpublished Correspondence', p. 45.
61 J W to Browning, 18 November 1864, in ed. Curle, p. 118.
62 J W to Browning, 25 December, and Browning to J W, 31 December 1864, in ibid., pp. 120, 121 and 123.
63 Browning to J W, 9 January 1865, in ibid., p. 125.
64 J W to Browning, 4 February 1865, in Brown, 'The Unpublished Correspondence', p. 47.
65 J W to Browning, 1 November 1864, in ed. Curle, p. 111.
66 Browning to J W, 'Saturday Eg', and J W to Browning, 24 February 1865, in ibid., pp. 128–29 and 130.

67 J W to Browning, 1 March 1865, in ibid., pp. 132–34.
68 E. M. Forster, 'Snow Wedgwood', *Listener*, 13 October 1937.
69 Browning to J W [no address or date], in ed. Curle, pp. 135–37. Julia annotated the original in pencil, 'Answer to mine begging him not to come.' The use of the word 'begging' rather than 'asking' or 'telling' suggests her deep emotional involvement.
70 J W to Browning, 20 April 1865, in ibid., p. 138.
71 Ibid., pp. 138–39.
72 Julia Sterling to J W, 5 March 1865, in ibid., p. 14.
73 This helps to explain some of the excisions in the published correspondence. See Brown, 'The Unpublished Correspondence', pp. 34–35.
74 Maisie Ward, *Browning and His World: The Two Brownings*, p. 168; Betty Miller, *Browning: A Portrait*, p. 228; Iain Finlayson, *Browning: A Private Life*, p. 536; and Pamela Neville-Sington, *Robert Browning: A Life after Death*, p. 131.
75 Fanny Wedgwood to Effie Wedgwood, [20 November 1869], W/M 268.
76 *Woman's Work and Woman's Culture*, ed. Josephine Butler, p. 261.
77 J W, 'Lawrence Oliphant', in *Nineteenth Century Teachers*, p. 266; and Emily Gurney to J W, [1869], W/M 438.
78 Ibid., p. 264.
79 J W to Browning, 24 August 1864, in ed. Curle, p. 70.
80 J W to Emily Gurney, 30 June 1870, W/M 438.
81 Browning to J W, 29 March 1869, in ed. Curle, p. 201.
82 Elizabeth Barrett to Browning, 15 December 1845, and Browning to Elizabeth Barrett, 31 December 1845, in *Robert Browning and Elizabeth Barrett*, ed. Daniel Karlin, pp. 167 and 180. 'Sonnets from the Portuguese', XXIX: 5.
83 Browning to Elizabeth Barrett, 19 January 1846, in *Robert Browning and Elizabeth Barrett*, ed. Daniel Karlin, p. 198; and Browning to J W, 27 June 1864, in ed. Curle, p. 34.
84 Emily Gurney to J W, 1 January 1872, W/M 438.
85 Browning to J W, 21 June 1864, in ed. Curle, p. 36.
86 J W to Browning, 17 May 1867, and Browning to J W, 12 February 1869, in ibid., pp. 142 and 179.

Chapter Seven A Woman's World

1 Thomas Erskine to Mrs Montagu, 22 November 1828, in *Letters of Thomas Erskine*, ed. William Hanna, 1, p. 148, and 2, p. 302.
2 Fanny Wedgwood to Marianne Thornton, 'Saturday', W/M 211.
3 Thomas Erskine to Mary Rich, n.d., W/M 224.
4 Thomas Erskine to J W, 18 May and 12 June 1865, W/M 224; and see Andrew Purves, 'New Trends: Erskine of Linlathen, Irving and Macleod Campbell', in *The History of Scottish Theology, 2, The Early Enlightenment to the Late Victorian Era*, ed. David Fergusson and Mark W. Elliot, pp. 228–41.
5 Thomas Erskine to J W, 12 June 1865, W/M 224.
6 J W to Emily Gurney, 3 June 1890, W/M 584.
7 J W, in *Letters of Emilia Russell Gurney*, ed. Ellen Mary Gurney, p. 13.
8 J W to Effie Wedgwood, 19 September 1865, W/M 326; and John Campbell Shairp, 'Recollections of Linlathen', in *Letters of Thomas Erskine*, p. 365.
9 Thomas Erskine to J W, 16 February 1866, in ibid., p. 187; see Trevor Hart, *Thomas Erskine*, and Don Horrocks, *Laws of the Spiritual Order: Innovation and Reconstruction in the Soteriology of Thomas Erskine of Linlathen*.

10 *The Spiritual Order and Other Papers Selected from the Manuscripts of the Late Thomas Erskine of Linlathen*, [ed. Jane Gourlay], pp. 2, 58; and J W, 'William Law, the English Mystic', *Contemporary Review*, 1 December 1877, pp. 98 and 101.
11 J W on Linlathen, in *Letters of Emilia Russell Gurney*, p. 14.
12 Quoted in Don Horrocks, *Laws of the Spiritual Order*, p. 203; and J W, in *Letters of Thomas Erskine*, p. 167.
13 J W to Henrietta Darwin, 30 August 1869, W/M 448.
14 J W to Emily Gurney, n.d. [1870], W/M 438; and J W to Mary Rich, 11 September 1874, W/M 325.
15 See Catherine Hall, *White, Male and Middle Class: Explorations of Feminism and History*, p. 275.
16 J W to Effie Wedgwood, 4 November 1865, W/M 324.
17 J W to Effie Wedgwood, 25 September 1865, W/M 324.
18 J W to Effie Wedgwood, [October 1865] and 4 November 1865, W/M 324.
19 Emily Gurney to J W, 19 August 1886, W/M 438; and J W to Emily Gurney, 13 December 1894, W/M 584.
20 Emily Gurney, in *New Oxford DNB*.
21 Emily Gurney to J W, Bequest, 31 October 1896, W/M 438.
22 J W to Emily Gurney, 25 January 1885, W/M 584.
23 J W, preface to vol. 1 of typescript of correspondence with Emily Gurney, W/M 438.
24 J W to Effie Wedgwood, n.d. 1856?, W/M 324.
25 J W to Effie Wedgwood, 6 November 1865, W/M 324.
26 Hope Wedgwood to Effie Wedgwood, 22 June 1865, W/M 327.
27 Hope Wedgwood to Effie Wedgwood, 18 and 25 December 1866, W/M 327.
28 Emily Gurney to J W, 8 February 1866, W/M 438.
29 J W to Emily Gurney, 8 February, 3 March and 8 December 1866, W/M 438.
30 J W to Emily Gurney, 3 March 1866, W/M 438.
31 Emily Gurney to J W, n.d. 1867 and 31 October 1896, in loose papers in W/M 438.
32 J W to Emily Gurney, 7 February 1867 and [15 February 1867], W/M 438.
33 J W to Emily Gurney, 16 January 1868, W/M 438.
34 J W to Emily Gurney, [28 July 1868], and Emily Gurney to J W, 27 December 1866, W/M 438.
35 Emily Gurney to J W, 5 April 1869, and J W to Emily Gurney, 20 August 1869, W/M 438.
36 Emily Gurney to J W, 'Wedy' [1875?], J W to Emily Gurney, n.d. [1870] and J W to Emily Gurney, 16 August 1870, W/M 438.
37 Martha Vicinus, *Intimate Friends*, p. 114.
38 See Sharon Marcus, *Between Women*, p. 27.
39 J W to Jane Gourlay, 2 October 1876, W/M 447.
40 J W to Fanny Wedgwood, 11 March 1875, W/M 252.
41 J W to Effie Wedgwood, 30 June 1869, W/M 326.
42 J W to Emily Gurney, 24 November 1872, W/M 438.
43 J W to Effie Wedgwood, 19 September 1871, W/M 326, and 24 June 1872, W/M 434.
44 J W to Effie Wedgwood, 20 August 1871, W/M 434.
45 Hensleigh Wedgwood to J W, January 1876, W/M 438.
46 J W to Emily Gurney, 18 January 1876, W/M 438.
47 F. P. Cobbe, *The Life of Frances Power Cobbe as Told by Herself*, 2, p. 222.
48 J W to Effie Wedgwood, 10 July 1869, W/M 324, and preface to J W–Emily Gurney correspondence, W/M 438.
49 J W to Jane Gourlay, 2 October 1876, W/M 447, and J W to Effie Wedgwood, 19 September 1871, W/M 324.
50 Emily Gurney to J W, 6 August 1867, W/M 438.
51 J W to Henrietta Darwin, 18 August 1871, W/M 448.
52 J W to Emily Gurney, 24 November 1872 and [1874], W/M 438.

53 J W to Emily Gurney, 14 August 1872, W/M 438.
54 J W to Victoria Welby, 18 December 1886 (copy), W/M 593, and J W to Emily Gurney, 23 October 1869, W/M 439.
55 J W to Emily Gurney, 14 September 1866, W/M 438.
56 J W to Victoria Welby, 18 December 1886 (copy), W/M 593.
57 J W to Effie Wedgwood, 23 January 1867, W/M 324.
58 [J W], 'Social Reform in England', *Westminster Review*, xxxi (January 1869), pp. 163, 164, 168 and 170.
59 Reprinted in *Feminist Theorists: Three Centuries of Women's Intellectual Traditions*, ed. Dale Spender, p. 102.
60 C. H. Herford to J W, 5 February 1903, W/M 578.
61 See Susan David Bernstein, *Roomscape: Women Writers in the British Museum from George Eliot to Virginia Woolf*, pp. 113–15. For a list of women readers there, see the 'Appendix of Notable Readers'. This shows J W gaining admission on 8 April 1875. As a letter to her sister Effie shows, she became a reader at least a decade earlier. (J W to Effie Wedgwood, 25 November 1865, W/M 324).
62 Ernest Wedgwood to J W, [1872], W/M 333, and J W to Effie Wedgwood, 15 February 1864, W/M 324.

Chapter Eight The Responsibilities of the Poet

1 Browning to J W, 17 May 1867, J W to Browning, 17 May 1867, in *Robert Browning and Julia Wedgwood: A Broken Friendship*, ed. Richard Curle, pp. 140–41 and 142. J W to Emily Gurney, 3 June 1867, W/M 438.
2 J W to Browning, 2 and 5 November 1868, in ed. Curle, pp. 146 and 150.
3 Browning to Isa Blagden, 18 March and 19 August 1865, in *Dearest Isa*, ed. E. C. McAleer, pp. 212 and 220.
4 Browning to Lady Colville, 26 October 1868, quoted in Pamela Neville-Sington, *Life after a Death*, p. 94.
5 Browning to J W, 1 February 1869, in ed. Curle, p. 175.
6 Browning to J W, 30 October 1868, in ibid., p. 145.
7 J W to Browning, 5 November 1868, in ibid., p. 151.
8 J W to Emily Gurney, 30 June 1870, W/M 431.
9 J W to Browning, 28 and 18 November 1864, in ed. Curle, pp. 146 and 118.
10 J W to Browning, 2 November 1868, and Browning to J W, 5 November 1868, in ibid., pp. 146 and 149.
11 J W to Browning, 15 November 1868, in ibid., pp. 152–57.
12 J W to Browning, 15 November 1868, in ibid., p. 152.
13 Browning to Isa Blagden, 19 August 1861 and 19 December 1864, in ed. McAleer, pp. 85 and 201.
14 Browning to J W, 19 August 1864, in ed. Curle, p. 63.
15 Maisie Ward, *The Two Robert Brownings*, p. 69.
16 Betty Miller, *Robert Browning: A Portrait*, p. 245.
17 Browning to J W, 21 January 1869, in ed. Curle, p. 167.
18 Browning to J W, 19 November 1868, in ed. Curle, p. 159.
19 Browning to Elizabeth Barrett, 11 February 1845, in *Robert Browning and Elizabeth Barrett: The Courtship Correspondence*, ed. Daniel Karlin, p. 15.
20 J W to Browning, 15 November 1868, Browning to J W, 19 November 1868, Browning to J W, 15 November, in ed. Curle, pp. 156 and 158–61.
21 J W to Browning, 15 November 1868, and Browning to J W, 19 November 1868, in ibid., pp. 156 and 161.

22 J W to Browning, 3 December 1868, in ibid., pp. 163–64.
23 Browning to J W, 21 January 1869, in ibid., 166–68.
24 See Britta Martens, 'Hardly shall I tell my joys and sorrows: Robert Browning's engagement with Elizabeth Barrett Browning's poetics', *Victorian Poetry*, 43, no. 1 (2005), p. 93.
25 J W to Browning, 22 January 1869 and 30 January 1869, in ed. Curle, pp. 168–70 and 171.
26 *The Ring and the Book*, 1, pp. 1379–80. By the time Book XII was published, Browning felt able to address his readers rather differently as 'British Public, who may like me yet, / (Marry and amen!)', XII, pp. 831–32.
27 *Saturday Review*, 24 December 1868, pp. xxvi, 832–34; *Fortnightly Review*, 1 January 1869, pp. xi, 175–76; *Atlantic Monthly*, February 1869, pp. xxiii, 256–59.
28 J W to Emily Gurney, 29 July 1870, W/M 438.
29 J W to Browning, 30 January 1869, in ed. Curle, p. 173.
30 Mrs Sutherland Orr, *Life and Letters of Robert Browning*, p. 281.
31 Browning to J W, 1 February 1869, in ed. Curle, p. 178.
32 Browning to J W, 12 February 1869, and J W to Browning, 14 February 1869, in ibid., 179 and 182.
33 J W to Emily Gurney, 30 June 1870, W/M 438.
34 J W to Browning, 21 February 1869, in ed. Curle, p. 185.
35 Browning to Isa Blagden, August 1871, in ed. MacAleer, p. 345. See Pamela Neville-Sington, *Robert Browning: A Life after Death*, p. 141, for an interesting analysis of Browning's reassessment of his poetic persona by comparison with his wife's in the light of J W's comments about his undue fascination with evil.
36 Browning to Elizabeth Barrett, 24 May 1845, in *Robert Browning and Elizabeth Barrett: The Courtship Correspondence 1845–1846*, ed. Daniel Karlin, p. 59.
37 Quoted in ed. McAleer, p. 38 fn 19.
38 Browning to J W, 'Monday afternoon', [22 February 1869], in ed. Curle, pp. 189–90.
39 J W to Robert Browning, 5 March 1869, in ibid., p. 191.
40 J W to Emily Gurney, March 1869, W/M 438.
41 D. Karlin, ed., *Robert Browning and Elizabeth Barrett: The Courtship Correspondence*, pp. 128–29.
42 Browning to J W, 8 March 1869, in ed. Curle, pp. 194–96.
43 J W to Browning, 'Good Friday', 1869, and Browning to J W, 29 March, in ibid., pp. 197 and 201.
44 J W to Browning, 7 April 1869, in ibid., pp. 202–3, Emily Gurney to J W, 4 April 1869, W/M 438, and J W to Browning, 7 April 1869, in ed. Curle, p. 204.
45 J W to Browning, 5 March 1869, in ibid., p. 191.
46 J W to Browning, 11 June 1870, and Browning to J W, 14 June 1870, in ibid., pp. 205 and 206.
47 J W to Browning, 12 July 1870, and Browning to J W, 14 June 1870, in ibid., pp. 208 and 206.
48 Browning to Isa Blagden, August 1870, in ed. McAleer, p. 339.
49 Quoted in Pamela Neville-Sington, *Browning: A Life after Death*, p. 96.
50 Browning to J W, 8 March 1869, in ed. Curle, pp. 194–95.
51 See Jane Stabler, *The Artistry of Exile*, p. 222.
52 J W to Emily Gurney, 8 March 1876, W/M 438.
53 J W to Emily Gurney, 6 March and 8 February 1887, W/M 584. This collection of letters to Emily Gurney was kept separate from the bulk of the typed-up correspondence.
54 J W to Emily Gurney, 30 June 1870, W/M 438.
55 J W asked Browning what he thought of *The Spanish Gypsy* in February 1869. He did not answer on that point, perhaps out of tact. J W to Robert Browning, 21 February 1869, in ed. Curle, p. 185.
56 Barbara Bodichon to J W, n.d., W/M 438.
57 J W to Barbara Bodichon, n.d., Yale GEN MSS 963 Box 14.
58 Octavia Hill to Miss Mayo, 20 September 1868, in *Octavia Hill Early Ideals*, ed. Emily Maurice, p. 246.

59 George Eliot to Browning, 30 May 1869, in *The George Eliot Letters*, ed. Gordon S. Haight, 5, p. 41. Haight speculates that the 'nonsense' referred to Sophia Eckley.
60 Browning to J W, 8 March 1869, in ed. Curle, p. 195.

Chapter Nine Finding a Voice

1 Joanne Shattock, introduction to *Women and Literature in Britain 1800–1900*; Deirdre David, *Intellectual Women and Victorian Patriarchy: Harriet Martineau, Elizabeth Barrett Browning, George Eliot*, p. 229; and Benjamin Dabby, *Women as Public Moralists in Britain from the Bluestockings to Virginia Woolf*.
2 *Glasgow Herald*, 3 February 1891.
3 J W to Robert Browning, 29 July 1864, in ed. Richard Curle, *Robert Browning and Julia Wedgwood: A Broken Friendship*, p. 58.
4 José Harris, *New Oxford DNB* entry on Julia Wedgwood.
5 Quoted in Joan Bellamy, 'Margaret Oliphant Mightier than the Mightiest of Her Sex', in *Women, Scholarship and Criticism*, eds Joan Bellamy, Anne Laurence and Gill Perry, p. 148.
6 Valerie Sanders and Gaby Weiner, eds, *Harriet Martineau and the Birth of Disciplines*, p. 199.
7 J W to Ellen Tollett, 10 July 1871, W/M 401. Iain Crawford has seen Harriet Martineau as a 'pioneering model for the young writers who would become mid-Victorian women of letters' and referred to 'the many examples' of their recognition of their debt to her. The only one he specifically mentions, however, is Anne Thackeray Ritchie, whose written style was very different from Martineau's and whose subject matter was much narrower. See Iain Crawford, 'Harriet Martineau: Women, Work and Mid-Victorian Journalism', in *Journalism and the Periodical Press in Nineteenth-Century Britain*, ed. Joanne Shattock, pp. 326–27.
8 Wedgwood Family Album W/M uncatalogued; and J W to Mary Rich, 5 March 1869, W/M 325.
9 J W to Jane Gourlay, 17 April 1878, W/M 447; and *Memorials of Two Sisters Susanna and Catherine Winkworth*, ed. Margaret J. Shaen, p. 65.
10 Harriet Martineau to Lord Brougham, 10 October 1832, in *Harriet Martineau Selected Letters*, ed. Valerie Sanders, p. 32.
11 Linda Petersen, 'Harriet Martineau Masculine Discourse, Female Sage', in *Victorian Sages and Cultural Discourse*, ed. Thais E. Morgan, p. 175; and Alexis Easley, 'Gendered Observations: Harriet Martineau and the Woman Question', in *Victorian Women Writers and the Woman Question*, ed. Nicola Diane Thompson, pp. 80–83.
12 See p. xx and Harriet Martineau to Maria Martineau, 21 November 1869, in *The Collected Letters of Harriet Martineau*, ed. Deborah Ann Logan, 5, p. 262. This appears to refer to J W's contribution to Butler, ed., *A Woman's Work and a Woman's Culture*.
13 Charles Darwin to John Murray, 25 May 1868, and J W's enclosure, *Correspondence of Charles Darwin*, 16, p. 539.
14 J W to Henrietta Darwin, 24 May 1868, W/M 448.
15 Charles Darwin to John Murray, 25 May 1868, and J W's enclosure, *Correspondence of Charles Darwin*, 16, p. 539.
16 J W to Effie Wedgwood, 19 March 1868, 30 June 1869 and 7 September 1869, W/M 324; J W to Fanny Wedgwood, 7 August 1870, W/M 252; J W to Mary Rich, 26 October 1869, W/M 325; and J W to Henrietta Darwin, 16 June 1868, W/M 448.
17 J W to Henrietta Darwin, 24 May 1868, W/M 448; J W to Effie Wedgwood, 19 March 1869, and to Hope Wedgwood, 21 July 1869, W/M 324.
18 J W to Mary Rich, 18 October 1869, W/M 325.
19 *The Life of Wesley and the Rise and Progress of Methodism with notes by the late Samuel Taylor Coleridge*, ed. Charles Cuthbert Southey, 1, p. xiv.

20 Luke Tyerman, *The Life and Times of the Rev John Wesley, M.A., Founder of the Methodists*, 1, pp. iv and 1.
21 J W to Mary Rich, 21 September 1869, W/M 325.
22 J W, *John Wesley and the Evangelical Reaction of the Eighteenth Century*, pp. 89, 144, 45, 83 and 304.
23 J W, ibid., p. 159.
24 Ibid., pp. ii and 261.
25 Ibid., p. 223.
26 Ibid., pp. 201–2 and 203.
27 Ibid., pp. 153, 71 and 94.
28 Ibid., p. 173.
29 Ibid., pp. 118, 164, 333, 284, 208 and 145.
30 J W, 'Laurence Oliphant', in *Nineteenth Century Teachers*, p. 255.
31 *Saturday Review*, 30 (3 December 1870), p. 719; *London Quarterly Review*, 72 (January 1872), pp. 303–5; *Pall Mall Gazette* (15 December 1870), p. 22; and *Westminster Review*, 39 (1 January 1871), p. 265.
32 W. H. Lecky, *History of England in the Eighteenth Century*, 2, p. 549 fn 2.
33 Harriet Martineau to J W, 2 July 1871, in *Correspondence of Harriet Martineau and Fanny Wedgwood*, ed. Elizabeth Arbuckle, p. 306.
34 See Laurel Brake, 'Periodical Formats: The Changing Review', in *Journalism and the Periodical Press in Nineteenth-Century Britain*, ed. Joanne Shattock, p. 61. J W's reviews of contemporary fiction appeared in the *Contemporary Review* in July 1883, March and July 1884, May and November 1885 and April and August 1886.
35 J W, 'Biography', 'The Majority' and 'A Study of Carlyle', *Nineteenth Century Teachers*, pp. 327, 193 and 158.
36 *Spectator*, 10 July 1909, p. 58.
37 J W, *Nineteenth Century Teachers*, pp. 250 and 251 and 98–100.
38 Ibid., pp. 124, 82 and 122.
39 Ibid., pp. 206, 209 and 213–14.
40 Ibid., pp. 21–22 and 101.
41 Ibid., p. 204.
42 J W, iIbid., pp. 117, 196, 26–7, 25 and 26.
43 J W, iIbid., pp. 175, 176, 85 and 249.
44 J W, 'Fiction', *Contemporary Review* (March 1884), p. 454.
45 J W, 'Fiction and Faith', *Contemporary Review* (1892), p. 221.
46 J W, 'Fiction and Faith', *Contemporary Review* (1892), p. 224; and 'Fiction', *Contemporary Review* (April 1886), p. 591 and (July 1884), p. 152.
47 J W, 'Fiction', *Contemporary Review* (April 1886), p. 594; (May 1885), p. 751; and (April 1886), p. 590.
48 J W, 'Fiction and Faith', *Contemporary Review* (1892). Pp. 220 and 219; 'Fiction', *Contemporary Review* (March 1884), p. 449; (May 1885), p. 751; and (August 1886), p. 294.
49 J W, 'Fiction', *Contemporary Review* (April 1886), p. 595.
50 J W, 'Fiction', *Contemporary Review* (August 1886), p. 300; and William James to Henry James, 1907, quoted in Leon Edel, *Henry James the Master 1901–1916*, p. 311.
51 See Laurel Brake, 'Periodical Formats: The Changing Review', in *Journalism and the Periodical Press in Nineteenth-Century Britain*, ed. Joanne Shattock, p. 61; and Laurel Brake, *Subjugated Knowledges: Journalism, Gender and Literature in the Nineteenth Century*, pp. 56–58.
52 J W, 'Fiction and Faith', *Contemporary Review* (1892), pp. 222, 223 and 220.
53 J W, 'Ethics and Literature', *Contemporary Review* (January 1897), pp. 69 and 73; and see p. xx.
54 J W, 'Sir Walter Scott and the Romantic Reaction', *Contemporary Review* (1 August 1878), pp. 531, 515, 530 and 521. See also Wedgwood Family Album XIV, where she includes a letter from Scott to Mackintosh W/M uncatalogued

55 Philip Waller, *Writers, Readers and Reputations*, p. 259; and J W, 'Midsummer Night's Dream', *Contemporary Review* (April 1890), p. 585.
56 *Women Reading Shakespeare 1660–1900*, ed. Ann Thompson and Sasha Roberts, pp. 2–4.
57 J W, 'Midsummer Night's Dream', *Contemporary Review* (April 1890).
58 Joanne Shattock, 'Work for Women: Margaret Oliphant's Journalism', in *Nineteenth-Century Media and the Construction of Identities*, ed. Laurel Brake et al., p. 171.
59 Owen Chadwick, *The Victorian Church*, 2, p. 123; John Hogben, *Richard Holt Hutton of the Spectator and The Academy* 56 (1899), p. 451; J W, *Nineteenth Century Teachers*, p. 139; and Alan Willard Brown, *The Metaphysical Society: Victorian Minds in Crisis, 1869–1880*, p. 204.
60 J W, *Nineteenth Century Teachers*, p. 141.
61 Wilfred Ward, 'Richard Hutton', in *Ten Personal Studies*, p. 59.
62 E. M. Forster, *Marianne Thornton*, p. 223.
63 R. H. Tener and Malcolm Woodfield, *A Victorian Spectator: Uncollected Writings of R H Hutton*, p. 74.
64 J W, 14 May, F. P. Cobbe, 21 May, and R. H. Hutton, 14 May 1870, *Spectator*, 43, pp. 613, 603 and 640.
65 See below p. 229.
66 For a more considered look at McCosh's cautious reconciliation with Darwinism see James Moore, *The Post-Darwinian Controversies*, 245–49.
67 [J W], 'Christianity and Positivism', *Spectator* (5 August 1871), p. 952. Identifying J W's contributions to the *Spectator* is not easy now that R. H. Hutton's notebooks listing contributors in the 1870s and 1880s have been lost (John O'Neill at the *Spectator* to the author, 8 October 2018). A few were published in *Nineteenth Century Teachers*, and J W occasionally refers to her contributions in private letters as with J W to Jane Gourlay, 2 September 1871, W/M 447 (on Comte), and J W to Mary Rich, August 1872 (on Newman). The piece on 'The Natural and the Supernatural' contains several of J W's stylistic fingerprints including her claim that Lucretius pre-figured Darwin's findings.
68 See below p 204.
69 [J W], *Spectator* (5 August 1871), p. 953.
70 [J W], 'The Natural and the Supernatural', *Spectator* (4 November), p. 1342.
71 [J W], 'John Henry Newman', *Spectator* (24 August 1872), p. 1077.
72 J W, *Nineteenth Century Teachers*, p. 141.

Chapter Ten A Forgotten Feminist

1 She is not included in Olive Banks, *Dictionary of Nineteenth Century Feminists*, nor is she one of the 50 pioneers Philippa Levene considers in her *Feminist Lives in Victorian England* though Emily Gurney is.
2 For an analysis of parliamentary divisions on women's suffrage in this period, see Brian Harrison, *Separate Spheres*, pp. 28–29.
3 Alexander Macmillan to Josephine Butler, 8 June 1868, BL Add MS 358363 487996 (1868 Letter Book).
4 Emily Davies to Anna Richardson, 1 August [1867], GCPP Davies 1/2 Family History.
5 GCPP Davies 1/2, p. 562; and Emily Davies to Anna Richardson, 22 February 1868, GCPP Davies 1/2, 596.
6 Josephine Butler to James Bryce, 9 February 1869, Bryce Papers.
7 Josephine Butler, ed., *Woman's Work and Woman's Culture*, pp. xiv and xxvi.
8 J W, 'Female Suffrage Considered Chiefly with Regard to Its Indirect Results', in ibid., particularly pp. 248, 254, 259 and 263.
9 Cf. Browning, 'Oh but a man's reach should exceed his grasp.'
10 J W to Effie Wedgwood, 3 August 1869, W/M 324.
11 J W, 'Female Suffrage Chiefly Considered with Regard to Its Indirect Results', pp. 277 and 273.

12 Ibid., pp. 251–52.
13 Hensleigh Wedgwood to Alexander Scott, [1838], W/M 239; and C. H. Herford, *A Memoir of Frances Julia Wedgwood*, p. xxi.
14 J W to Effie Wedgwood, 24 June 1869, W/M 324.
15 J W to Effie Wedgwood, 10 July 1869, W/M 324.
16 J. S. Mill, *On the Subjection of Women*, pp. 471, 573 and 575.
17 J W to Effie Wedgwood, 10 July 1869, W/M 324; and J W to Alfred Benn, 31 July 1910, W/M 627.
18 See above p. 137.
19 *Macmillan's Magazine*, October 1869, 120, p. 555.
20 *The Saturday Review*, 31 July 1869, pp. 159–60.
21 J W to Effie Wedgwood, 18 September 1869, W/M 324.
22 J W to Effie Wedgwood, [November 1869], W/M 324.
23 *The Times*, Saturday, 21 August 1869.
24 J W to Effie Wedgwood, 4 February 1872, W/M 324.
25 Ibid.
26 J W to Emily Gurney, 20 August 1869, W/M 438.
27 J W to Emily Gurney, 23 October 1869, W/M 438.
28 Quoted in Daphne Bennett, *Emily Davies and the Liberation of Women*, p. 127.
29 Emily Gurney to J W, November 1870, W/M 438.
30 J W to Emily Gurney, 18 November 1870, W/M 438.
31 J W to Effie Wedgwood, 2 November 1870, W/M 324.
32 J W to Effie Wedgwood, 5 October 1870, W/M 324.
33 Patricia Hollis, *Ladies Elect*, p. 77.
34 Emily Gurney to Emily Davies, 5 December 1867, GCPP Davies 15/1/5 Family History, p. 557.
35 GCPP Bodichon 1/8, Emily Davies to Barbara Bodichon, 6 April 1867, printed in *Letters of Emily Davies*, p. 238.
36 Emily Davies to Elizabeth Garrett, n.d., quoted in Daphne Bennett, *Emily Davies*, p. 87, where 'Mrs' is mis-transcribed as 'Miss'.
37 GCPP Davies 1/2 Family History, p. 547.
38 J W to Effie Wedgwood, 19 March 1868, W/M 324.
39 J W to Effie Wedgwood, [22 February 1870], W/M 324. On Maurice's views, see Emily Davies to Anna Richardson, 4 February 1868, in GCPP Davies 1/2 Family History, p. 576.
40 See James Moore, *The Post-Darwinian Controversies*, p. 91.
41 Stephan Collini, *Public Moralists*, p. 43.
42 J W to Emily Gurney, 9 April 1876, W/M 438.
43 Emily Davies's brother, Rev. Llewelyn Davies, a Christian Socialist colleague of Seeley's, divulged the secret to R. H. Hutton, who published it in the *Spectator* in November 1866. See Ian Hesketh, *Victorian Jesus: J. R. Seeley, Religion and the Cultural Significance of Anonymity*, p. 140.
44 Emily Gurney to J W, 8 February 1866, W/M 438.
45 See Val Campion, *Pioneering Women: The Origins of Girton College in Hitchin*, p. 30.
46 Though they would certainly have discussed the idea, there is no record of this in the surviving correspondence between J W and Emily Gurney.
47 J W to Effie Wedgwood, 2 July 1869, W/M 324. For Alice Bonham Carter's contribution at Newnham, see Gill Sutherland, *Faith, Duty and the Power of Mind*, p. 95.
48 Emily Davies to Anna Richardson, 30 December 1869, in B. Stephen, *Emily Davies and Girton College*, p. 228.
49 J W to Effie Wedgwood, 10 February 1870, W/M 324.
50 J W to Emily Gurney, 13 May 1870, W/M 328.
51 George Eliot to Mrs William Smith, 25 April 1873, in *The George Eliot Letters*, ed. G. S. Haight, 5, p. 406.

52 J W to Emily Gurney, 13 May 1870, W/M 328.
53 GCPP Davies 10/3.
54 Emily Davies to Barbara Bodichon, 25 February [1870], GCPP Bodichon 1/40.
55 Sarah Woodhead to Emily Davies, 4 March 1870, GCPP Davies 15/1/5/15.
56 Isabel Hurst, *Victorian Women and the Classics*, pp. 12–24.
57 Quoted in Barbara Stephen, *Emily Davies and Girton College*, p. 240.
58 Emily Gibson to Emily Davies, 6 March 1870, GCPP Davies 15/1/5/16.
59 J W to Emily Gurney, 10 February 1870, W/M 438.
60 'Hitchin', in Louisa Lumsden, *Yellow Leaves*, pp. 188–89.
61 J W to Emily Gurney, March 1871, W/M 438.
62 J W to Effie Wedgwood, 5 October 1870, W/M 324.
63 June Purvis, *Hard Lessons: The Lives and Education of Working-Class Women in Nineteenth-Century England*, p. 173.
64 J W to Jane Gourlay, 20 May 1876, W/M 447.
65 J W continued her annual subscriptions until 1906 when she donated £100 and also persuaded Effie to give £50 and Hope £25. In 1890 she gave £123.15 probably in memory of her mother (annual reports of the College for Working Women. LMA A/FMC/AR1-32).
66 J W to Emily Gurney, 13 May 1870, W/M 438.
67 J W, *The Political Claims of Women* (published by the London National Society for Women's Suffrage [1876]), p. 8.
68 J W to Emily Gurney, 16 June 1870, W/M 438.
69 The *Spectator*, 14 May 1870 (43), p. 613.
70 The *Spectator*, 21 May 1870 (44), p. 641, and 14 May 1870 (43), p. 603.
71 Barbara Caine, *Victorian Feminists*, p. 15.
72 J W, 'Female Suffrage in Its Influence on Married Life', *Contemporary Review*, 1872, pp. 360–70.
73 Ibid., p. 369.
74 J W, *The Political Claims of Women*.
75 Emma Darwin to Henrietta Litchfield, [30 May 1876], CUL DAR 219.9.135.
76 *Englishwomen's Review*, CXXXIII, 15 May 1884, 21.
77 J W to Mary Rich, n.d., W/M 325, part printed in Barbara and Hensleigh Wedgwood, *The Wedgwood Circle*, p. 307.
78 Quoted in Susan Hamilton, *Frances Power Cobbe and Victorian Feminism*, p. 153.
79 Quoted in Ann Robson, 'A Birds' Eye View of Gladstone', *The Gladstonian Turn of Mind*, ed. Bruce Kinzer, p. 83.
80 Quoted in Constance Rover, *Women's Suffrage and Party Politics in Britain 1866–1914*, p. 120.
81 *Fraser's Magazine*, 78 (1868), pp. 777–94.
82 J W to Emily Davies, 7 October 1910, GCPP Davies 17/23.
83 For an account of anti-female suffrage feeling, see Brian Harrison, *Separate Spheres*, and on the masculinity of Victorian national politics, see Ben Griffin, *The Politics of Gender in Victorian Britain*.
84 Quoted in F. P. Cobbe, *Autobiography*, 2, p. 215.
85 'Mme […] is a very good specimen of that kind of woman – quite remote from all vulgar Saturday feeling – & yet not at all belonging to that *anti*-man band which does quite as much harm' (J W to Effie Wedgwood, 19 March 1868, W/M 324).
86 Ray Strachey, *The Cause*, p. 44.
87 J W, 'Richard Holt Hutton', *Contemporary Review*, October 1897 (72), p. 468.

Chapter Eleven Doubt and the Fallibility of Idols

1 J W to Emily Gurney, 12 June 1871, W/M 438; J W to May Crum, 31 March 1900, CUL Hugh Fraser Stuart Collection EAD/GBR/0012/MS.Add.7671/V/D 263; and J W to Jane Gourlay, 12 September 1874, W/M 447.

2 J W to Jane Gourlay, 10 September 1875, W/M 447.
3 J W to Ellen Tollet, 27 August 1874, W/M 401.
4 [J W], 'The Natural and the Supernatural', *Spectator*, 4 November 1871 (2262), p. 1340.
5 [J W], 'Doubting Doubt', *Spectator*, 20 December 1879 (2686), p. 1607; J W, 'James Martineau and the Heterodoxy of the Past', *Expositor*, 6th series, 17 (1903), p. 22; and J W, 'Richard Holt Hutton', *Nineteenth Century Teachers*, p. 144.
6 J W to Jane Gourlay, 12 October 1871, W/M 447.
7 J W to Ellen Tollett, 26 August 1871, W/M 401.
8 J W to Jane Gourlay, 18 June 1876, W/M 447; and J W to Emily Gurney, 3 November 1872, W/M 438.
9 Emma Darwin to Henrietta Litchfield, 24 August 1873, CUL DAR 219. 9:104; J W to Jane Gourlay, 25 November 1872, W/M 447; J W to Emily Gurney, 16 September 1883, W/M 584; and J W to Jane Gourlay, 22 October 1876, W/M 447.
10 J W to [Ellen Mary Gurney], 24 March 1893, W/M 584; and J W to Jane Gourlay, 5 November 1872, W/M 447.
11 J W to Jane Gourlay, 12 March 1875, W/M 447; and J W to Henrietta Darwin, 16 June 1868, W/M 448.
12 Fanny Allen to Mary Rich, n.d., W/M 208.
13 Barbara and Hensleigh Wedgwood, *The Wedgwood Circle*, pp. 288–89 and 291.
14 Thomas Erskine to J W, 27 January 1870, W/M 224; and J W to Jane Gourlay, 22 March 1870, W/M447.
15 J W, 'Thomas Erskine of Linlathen', *Nineteenth Century Teachers*, pp. 63–78; and J W to Emily Gurney, 3 April 1870, W/M 438.
16 J W to Ellen Tollet, 27 August 1874, W/M 401.
17 J W to Mary Rich, 23 September 1869, W/M 325; Emily Gurney, 3 April 1870, W/M 438; and Jane Gourlay, 22 March 1870, W/M 447.
18 J W to F. D. Maurice, 30 May 1870, W/M 425.
19 J W to Jane Gourlay, 5 August 1872, W/M 447; J W to Mary Rich, quoted in *The Wedgwood Circle*, p. 293; and J W to Emily Gurney, 21 October 1870, W/M 438.
20 Frederick Maurice, *The Life of Frederick Denison Maurice*, 2, p. 598.
21 J W, 'James Martineau and the Heterodoxy of the Past', p. 26.
22 Dr Radcliffe, who attended him, had also been Thomas Erskine's deathbed doctor (*The Life of Frederick Denison Maurice*, 2, pp. 643 and 645).
23 See ibid., p. 647. This has sometimes been corrupted into the suggestion that attendance at Maurice's funeral was the largest since Wellington's. See, for example, Alan Willard Brown, *The Metaphysical Society Victorian Minds in Crisis, 1869–1880*, p. 118.
24 J. Estlin Carpenter, *James Martineau*, p. 438 fn 1; and J W to Jane Gourlay, 5 April 1872, W/M 447. Harriet Martineau described 'the loud thrush' as the last bird song that those suffering increasing deafness could still hear (Harriet Martineau, 'Letter to the Deaf', reprinted in *Prose by Victorian Women: An Anthology*, eds Andrea Broomfield and Sally Mitchell, p. 59).
25 Margaret Shaen, ed., *The Winkworth Memorials*, p. 242.
26 Anna Swanwick, *Memoir*, p. 71.
27 J W, 'Frederick Denison Maurice', *Nineteenth Century Teachers*, pp. 29–62.
28 J W, *Nineteenth Century Teachers*, p. 222.
29 Quoted in Geoffrey Rowell, *Hell and the Victorians*, p. 83.
30 Her memorial stone in Poets' Corner, Westminster Abbey was installed only 100 years after her death.
31 J W to Alfred Benn, 9 June 1910, W/M 627.
32 J W to Effie Wedgwood, 4 August 1859, W/M 324. See also J. Uglow, *Mrs Gaskell*, pp. 462–63.
33 J W to Jane Gourlay, 10 September 1875, W/M 447, and to Emily Gurney, 21 October 1872, W/M 438.

34 See Kathryn Hughes, *George Eliot*, pp. 288 and 292.
35 George Eliot to Barbara Bodichon, 17 December [1869], in *The George Eliot Letters*, ed. G. S. Haight, 5, p. 73. Eliot's reference to J W in her letter to Browning of 30 May 1869 as 'a very rare young woman' (see pp. xx–xx) might suggest that they had already met though Eliot was more probably relying on what she had heard about her from Barbara Bodichon and on what she knew of her work.
36 Hughes, *George Eliot*, p. 249.
37 Charles Eliot Norton to George W. Curtis, 29 January 1869, in *George Eliot Interviews and Recollections*, ed. K. K. Collins, p. 77.
38 Emily Davies to Charlotte Manning, 25 November 1867, in Emily Davies, 'Family History', p. 553, Girton College Archive ECPP Davies 2.
39 J W to Emily Gurney, 31 December 1872, W/M 438.
40 George Eliot to Barbara Bodichon, 5 December 1859, printed in J. Cross, *Life of George Eliot*, 2, p. 148; and Eliot quoted in Hughes, *George Eliot*, p. 116.
41 See George Eliot to Cara Bray, 22 December 1873, in *The George Eliot Letters*, 5, p. 472.
42 J W to Emily Gurney, 5 January 1870, W/M 438. The first 12 of J W's numbered letters to Emily Gurney when the Gurneys were in America from September 1871 have not survived. Judging from Emily Gurney's replies, they contained at least one lost account of a meeting with Eliot.
43 Quoted in *George Eliot Interviews and Recollections*, p. 222.
44 J W to Emily Gurney, 3 June 1870, W/M 438.
45 F. W. H. Myers, *Essays: Modern*, [1883], pp. 268–69.
46 J W to Emily Gurney, 3 June 1870, W/M 438.
47 J W to Emily Gurney, 11 September 1870, W/M 438.
48 J W to Emily Gurney, March 1871, W/M 438.
49 J W to George Eliot, 8 November 1872, Beinecke Library GEN MSS 963 Box 14; and George Eliot to John Blackwood, 24 July 1871, in Timothy Hands, *A George Eliot Chronology*, p. 121.
50 Eliot's letters to J W have not survived. Interestingly, J W did not choose to include any in her Wedgwood Family History.
51 J W to Emily Gurney, 16 November 1872. The comment is c. 1897, W/M 438. See also Benjamin Jowett to Arthur Stanley, 29 December 1880 (the day of Eliot's funeral), 'Mr Cross tells me that she had intended to write one more great work of fiction', in *George Eliot Interviews and Recollections*, p. 233 fn 1. (Did Eliot, like Wagner, contemplate a final work about the Buddha?)
52 J W to Emily Gurney, 31 December 1872 and 31 March 1873, W/M 438.
53 Gordon S. Haight, *George Eliot: A Biography*, p. 463.
54 J W to Emily Gurney, 31 March 1873, W/M 438. She did, however, see Eliot again late in 1873 and at the séance organized by Ras Darwin in January 1874. See George Eliot to Cara Bray, 22 December 1873, referring to a conversation with J W 'the other day' in *The George Eliot Letters*, 5, p. 472.
55 Matilda Betham Edwards, *Mid-Victorian Memories*, p. 45.
56 J W to Emily Gurney, 31 March 1873, W/M 438.
57 J W to George Eliot, 8 November 1872, Beinecke GEN MSS 963 Box 14.
58 See Beth Palmer, 'Assuming the Role of Editor', in *The Cambridge Companion to Victorian Women's Writing*, ed. Linda H. Peterson, pp. 168–69; and *The Autobiography of Margaret Oliphant*, ed. Elizabeth Jay, p. 16.
59 J W, 'The Moral Influence of George Eliot', *Nineteenth Century Teachers*, p. 230.
60 J W, *Nineteenth Century Teachers*, pp. 230, 312, 315 and 231; and 'James Martineau and the Heterodoxy of the Past', 24 (on Turgenev).
61 J W, *Nineteenth Century Teachers*, p. 143; and J W to May Crum, n.d., CUL Archive 7671 V f 307.
62 See K. K. Wilson, *Identifying the Remains: George Eliot's Death in the London Religious Press*, pp. 33–46.

63 The Wesleyan, *London Quarterly Review*, 57 (October 1881), pp. 154–76, picked up this metaphor in its own long assessment of Eliot.
64 J W, 'The Moral Influence of George Eliot', *Nineteenth Century Teachers*, pp. 225–41.
65 Edith Simcox, diary entry for 2 February 1881, printed in *A Monument to the Memory of George Eliot: Edith Simcox's Autobiography of a Shirtmaker*, eds Constance M. Fulmer and Margaret E. Barfield, p. 150.
66 Emily Gurney to J W, 18 December 1876, W/M 438.
67 J W, 'Richard Holt Hutton', *Nineteenth Century Teachers*, p. 147.
68 Tener and Woodfield, *Richard Holt Hutton: A Victorian Spectator*, p. 25.
69 J W, 'Richard Holt Hutton', *Nineteenth Century Teachers*, p. 153.
70 Ibid., p. 147; and J W to Mary Rich, 7 September 1869, W/M 325.
71 Hutton's advocacy of *The Moral Ideal* encouraged its publisher, Trubner, to give it greater visibility in its periodic listings in the advertising columns of the *Spectator*, 1 December 1888, p. 1696, where it was placed fifth, and 2 March 1889, p. 317, where it headed Trubner's list of new editions. They also recommenced advertising Hensleigh Wedgwood's *On the Origin of Language*.
72 See particularly Alan Willard Brown, *The Metaphysical Society Victorian Minds in Crisis 1869–1880*, pp. 38–39; *The Papers of the Metaphysical Society 1869–1880*, eds Catherine Marshall, Bernard Lightman and Richard England, 1, p. 23; and *The Metaphysical Society (1869–1880) Intellectual Life in Mid-Victorian England*.
73 *Spectator*, 5 September 1896, p. 11.
74 [J W], 'The Natural and the Supernatural', *Spectator*, 4 November 1871, p. 1341.
75 [J W], 'The First Opponent of Christianity', *Spectator*, 30 March 1878, p. 410.
76 Emma Darwin to Henrietta Litchfield, 22 April 1878, CUL DAR 219.9: 169.
77 Adrian Desmond and James Moore, introduction to Charles Darwin, *The Descent of Man*, pp. xlxix.

Chapter Twelve Domestic Contentment

1 J W to Mary Rich, 7 November 1869, W/M 325.
2 Effie Wedgwood's 'Courtship Journal', 1 November 1871, W/M 435; and J W to Emily Gurney, 16 August 1870, W/M 438.
3 J W to Effie Wedgwood, October 1871, W/M 324.
4 J W to Effie Wedgwood, 7 August 1854 and 28 April 1858, W/M 324.
5 Meta Gaskell to Effie Wedgwood, 20 and 23 November and 29 December 1871, in Irene Wiltshire, ed., *Letters of Mrs Gaskell's Daughters 1856–1914*, pp. 182–83 and 193. Marianne Gaskell, Meta's eldest sister, had married her second cousin Thurston Holland. Both their children were born deaf.
6 Barbara and Hensleigh Wedgwood, *The Wedgwood Circle*, p. 303.
7 J W to Effie Wedgwood, [November 1869] and 25 September 1865, W/M 324.
8 J W to Effie Wedgwood, 18 July 1871, W/M 324; J W to Emily Gurney, 21 October 1872, W/M 449; and J W to Effie Wedgwood, n.d., [1872], W/M 324.
9 J W to Effie Wedgwood, 17 August 1872, W/M 324.
10 E. M. Forster, 'West Hackhurst: A Surrey Ramble', in *Journals and Diaries of E M Forster*, ed. Philip Gardner, 3, p. 163.
11 J W to Emily Gurney, 21 October 1872, W/M 438.
12 Emma Darwin to Henrietta Litchfield, 15 August 1873, CUL DAR 219.9:102; Hope Wedgwood to Ida Farrer, n.d., 1875 CUL DAR 93861.1:16262.
13 Forster, 'West Hackhurst: A Surrey Ramble', 3, pp. 162–63 and 171.
14 J W to Jane Gourlay, 'Good Friday', 1873, W/M 447, and to Ellen Tollet, 15 July 1873, W/M 401.

15 Hope Wedgwood to Ida Farrer, 8 August 1873, CUL DAR 93861.1: 16254; J W to Ida Farrer, 1 April 1873, CUL DAR 9368.1: 16222.
16 J W to Emily Gurney, 6 December 1872, W/M 438.
17 J W to Henrietta Litchfield, n.d. [1875], W/M 448.
18 Forster, 'West Hackhurst: A Surrey Ramble', 3, p. 171.
19 Hope Wedgwood to Ida Farrer, ?1875, CUL DAR 16264: 9368.1.
20 Emma Darwin to Henrietta Litchfield, 25 May 1876, CUL DAR 9:134, and 6 October 1876, CUL DAR 219.1:141.
21 Derek Hudson, *Arthur Munby Man of Two Worlds*, 23 (diary entry, 27 February 1859).
22 A. H. Munby, ms diary, 11 February 1875.
23 A. H. Munby, ms diary, 26 February 1878, 17 January 1879, 12 November 1879 and 16 November 1882.
24 A. H. Munby, ms diary, 17 January 1879.
25 Emma Darwin to Henrietta Litchfield, 14 July 1877, CUL DAR 9.152.
26 J W to Emily Gurney, 16 November 1890, W/M 438, and to Jane Gourlay, 17 August 1876, W/M 447.
27 Hope Wedgwood to Ida Farrer, 24 October 1877, CUL DAR 16293.
28 J W to Jane Gourlay, 'Easter Day', 1877, W/M 447, and to Effie Wedgwood, 17 August 1872, W/M 324.
29 Emma Darwin to Henrietta Litchfield, 3 September 1888, CUL DAR 219.9:673.
30 Emma Darwin to Henrietta Litchfield, 28 January and 15 March 1880, CUL DAR 9:221 and 9:227.
31 E. M. Forster, *Two Cheers for Democracy*, p. 196.
32 J W to Ellen Tollet, 21 August 1881, W/M 401.
33 J W to May Crum, 31 July 1898, CUL EAD/GBR/0012/MS,Add.7671/V/D 256.
34 Marian Hughes to J W, [1897], W/M 632.
35 Marian Hughes to J W, n.d., W/M 632.
36 J W to Emily Gurney, 19 January 1885, W/M 438.
37 For an account of his colourful career, See below p. 305.
38 J W to Henrietta Litchfield, 18 September 1892, W/M 448.
39 Hensleigh Wedgwood to Emma Darwin, 6 January 1890, W/M 195; Eliza Wedgwood to Ruth Draper, [1940]; and Hope Wedgwood to Eliza Wedgwood, '1913', Armstrong-Browning Library, Baylor.

Chapter Thirteen Coming to Terms with Darwin and His Legacy

1 J W to Henrietta Litchfield, 4 October 1896, CUL DAR 251:1576.
2 Emma Darwin to Henrietta Litchfield, 2 April 1880, CUL DAR 219 9:228.
3 Emma Darwin to Henrietta Litchfield, 12 July 1870, CUL DAR 219.9:90.
4 Evelleen Richards, *Darwin and the Making of Sexual Selection*, p. 48.
5 Charles Darwin to George Darwin, printed in Samantha Evans, *Darwin and Women: A Selection of Letters*, p. 145.
6 Janet Browne, *Charles Darwin: The Power of Place*, pp. 70–71.
7 Emma Darwin to Henrietta Litchfield, 4 December 1873, printed in Evans, *Darwin and Women*, p. 160, and [February 1870], CUL DAR 219.9:72.
8 Emma Darwin to Henrietta Darwin, [1870] quoted in Browne, *Charles Darwin: The Power of Place*, p. 349. See also E. Richards, *Darwin and Sexual Selection*, p. 440.
9 Emma Darwin to Henrietta Litchfield, 21 February 1870, printed in Evans, *Darwin and Women*, p. 178.
10 J W to Emily Gurney, 19 February 1871, W/M 438.
11 See Evelleen Richards, *Darwin and the Making of Sexual Selection*, especially pp. xvii–xxiv.

12 *The Descent of Man*, p. 683.
13 *Times*, 7 April 1871.
14 Evans, *Darwin and Women*, pp.178–79.
15 See *Spectator*, 11 March 1871 (2228), pp. 288–89. Though this was described as the 'First Notice', the same edition also contained a review attacking Darwin's account of the origin of aesthetic feeling. See pp. 280–81.
16 Charles Darwin to Henrietta Darwin, 28 March 1871, printed in Evans, *Darwin and Women*, p. 143.
17 See below p. 262.
18 J W summarized her understanding of Darwin's ethics in a note (which has not survived) that she showed her uncle and to which he responded. See Charles Darwin to J W, [after April 1871], summarized in *Correspondence of Charles Darwin*, 19, pp. 247.
19 J W to Henrietta Litchfield, 18 March 1897, W/M 448. Argyll was one of the pall-bearers at Darwin's funeral. See James Moore on his 'Christian Darwinisticism', in *The Post-Darwinian Controversies*, pp. 222–23 and 231–32.
20 'Ants communicate information to each other. [...] They recognize their fellow-ants after months of absence. They build great edifices, keep them clean, close the doors in the evening, and post sentries. They make roads, and even tunnels under rivers. They collect food for the community, and when an object too large is brought into the nest, they enlarge the door, and afterwards build it up again. They go out to battle in regular bands, and freely sacrifice their lives for the common weal.'
21 See John Durant, 'Darwinism and Divinity: A Century of Debate', in *Darwinism and Divinity*, ed. John Durant, pp. 12–20, on the growing emphasis in nineteenth-century Natural Theology on creative laws rather than the specific creative interventions envisaged by Paley.
22 *Spectator*, 18 March 1871, pp. 15–16.
23 Fanny Wedgwood to Effie Wedgwood, 7 November [1871], W/M 268; and Emma Darwin to J W, [March 1871], *Correspondence of Charles Darwin*, 19, pp. 112–13.
24 Hensleigh Wedgwood to Charles Darwin, 3–9 March [1870], *Correspondence of Charles Darwin*, 19, p. 134.
25 J W to Henrietta Darwin, 1 April 1871, in *Correspondence of Charles Darwin*, 19, p. 246; Robert J. Richards, 'Darwin on Mind, Morals and Emotions', in *The Cambridge Companion to Darwin*, ed. Jonathan Hodge and Gregory Radick, p. 101; and Henrietta Darwin diary, 26 March 1871, in *Correspondence of Charles Darwin*, 19, pp. 803–4. Huxley, Tyndall and Herbert Spencer were more conscious of the need to develop a competing evolutionary creed, covering teleology, theodicy and eschatology than either J W or Henrietta Darwin acknowledged. See Lightman, 'The Theology of Victorian Scientific Naturalists', in *Science without God*, ed. Peter Harrison and Jon Roberts, pp. 238–50.
26 Evans, *Darwin and Women*, pp. 123–33.
27 J W to Henrietta Darwin, n.d., *Correspondence of Charles Darwin*, 20, 597–98.
28 Charles Darwin, *The Expression of Emotions in Man and Animals*, ed. J. J. Rachman, pp. 273 fn and 323.
29 J W to Emily Gurney, 19 February 1871, W/M 438.
30 J W to Emily Gurney, 27 August 1872, W/M 438.
31 Quoted in Bernard Lightman, 'Scientists as Materialists in the Periodical Press: Tyndall's Belfast Address', in *Evolutionary Naturalism in Victorian Britain: The 'Darwinians' and Their Critics*, p. 200.
32 See Crosbie Smith, *The Science of Energy: A Cultural History of Energy Physics in Victorian Britain*, pp. 253–55; and P. M. Heimann, '*The Unseen Universe*: Physics and the Philosophy of Nature in Victorian Britain', *British Journal for the History of Science*, vi (June 1972), pp. 73–79.
33 J W, 'William Law the English Mystic of the Eighteenth Century', *Contemporary Review*, December 1877, p. 99; and J W, *The Moral Ideal* (revised edition, 1907), p. 69.

34 [J W], review of Frank Darwin, *Life and Letters of Charles Darwin*, in *Spectator*, 10 December 1887, p. 1706.
35 J W to Ellen Tollett, 2 October 1880, W/M 401, and to Frank Darwin, 3 October 1884, CUL DAR 139 (12):17.
36 Ras Darwin to Fanny Wedgwood, n.d., but annotated '1880 or 1881' by J W, W/M 227; and Loy and Loy, *Emma Darwin*, p. 279.
37 Emma Darwin to Henrietta Litchfield, 8 June 1882, CUL DAR 219.9:293.
38 Frank Darwin, *Life and Letters of Charles Darwin*, 1, pp. 23–25.
39 See James Moore, 'Charles Darwin Lies in Westminster Abbey', in *Charles Darwin: A Commemoration 1882–1982*, ed. R. J. Berry.
40 CUL DAR 215 (Album about Darwin's funeral), 3b and 4. There is also a small collection about the funeral in the American Philosophical Society Library in Philadelphia. This includes some notes to the ushers at the funeral. One is an instruction to take special care of '4 Ladies' who may perhaps have included Fanny and Julia Wedgwood. Emma Darwin had advised Fanny Wedgwood to stay away as the Abbey would be cold (E D to F W, [22 April 1882], in H. E. Litchfield, *Life of Emma Darwin*, 2, p. 102).
41 Emma Darwin to Henrietta Litchfield, 12 June 1882, tells a charming story of R V W's generosity in offering to give a lark's egg he had discovered to the Darwins' grandson, Bernard. CUL DAR 219.9:296.
42 *Times*, 26 April 1882.
43 Quoted in James Moore, 'Charles Darwin Lies in Westminster Abbey'.
44 Litchfield, *Emma Darwin*, 2, pp. 328–29. See also Janet Browne, 'There were no famous last words.' (*Charles Darwin: The Power of Place*, p. 495).
45 Asa Gray is quoted in Browne, *Charles Darwin*, p. 496. J W to Asa Gray, 4 May 1882, Gray Herbarium.
46 J W to Frank Darwin, 3 October 1884, CUL DAR 139 (12):17.
47 Ibid.
48 Charles Darwin, 'Recollections of the Development of My Life and Character', printed in James A. Secord, *Charles Darwin Evolutionary Writings*, pp. 396–97.
49 J W to Henrietta Litchfield, 4 April 1885, CUL DAR 199.1:16.
50 See Frank Darwin's marginal comments on Henrietta Litchfield's commentary at CUL DAR 199.1:2; and William Darwin to Frank Darwin, 27 January [1885], CUL DAR 199.1:13.
51 J W to Henrietta Litchfield, 4 April 1885, CUL DAR 199.1:16. J W's comments on Henrietta Litchfield's comments on the draft are marked in purple ink on CUL DAR 199.1:1. J W's redraft which has not previously been attributed to her is at CUL DAR 199.1:24.
52 Henrietta and Richard Litchfield to Frank Darwin, n.d., CUL DAR 199.1:7.
53 Nora Barlow, *The Autobiography of Charles Darwin*, p. 12.
54 Emma Darwin to Frank Darwin, 1885, printed in ibid., pp. 87 and 93 fn 2.
55 Frank Darwin, *The Life and Letters of Charles Darwin*, 1, pp. 304–17.
56 Ibid., p. 304.
57 Ibid., p. 317.
58 Ibid., 2, pp. 180–81.
59 Emma Darwin to Henrietta Litchfield, November 1887, CUL DAR 219.9:633.
60 See [J W], 'The Natural and the Supernatural', *Spectator*, 4 November 1871, pp. 1340–44.
61 *Spectator*, 10 December 1887, pp. 1705-7.
62 Henrietta Litchfield to Frank Darwin, 20 January 1885, CUL DAR 199.1:10.
63 Emma Darwin to Henrietta Litchfield, [December 1887], CUL DAR 219.9:634.
64 Emma Darwin to Charles Darwin, n.d. [1861], printed in Litchfield, *Emma Darwin*, 2, p. 190.
65 Ibid., p. 379.
66 Emma Darwin to Henrietta Litchfield, 8 January 1888, CUL DAR 219.9:639; and Barbara and Hensleigh Wedgwood, *The Wedgwood Circle 1730–1897*, p. 340.

67 J W to Emily Gurney, 3 January 1895, W/M 584.
68 See, for example, Emma Darwin to Henrietta Litchfield, 3 September 1883 and 31 July 1883, CUL DAR 219.9:374 and 366. Loy and Loy, *Emma Darwin*, gives a consistently negative but misleading picture of Julia Wedgwood's relationship with Emma Darwin. See, for example, p. 352.
69 Emma Darwin to J W, [Autumn] 1891, printed in Litchfield, *Emma Darwin*, 1, pp. 59–60.
70 Emma Darwin to Henrietta Litchfield, February 1877, CUL DAR 219.9:145.
71 Emma Darwin to J W, 1 June [1890], W/M 644; J W to Emma Darwin (copy), n.d., W/M 423.
72 J W to Henrietta Litchfield, 4 October 1896, CUL DAR 251:1576.
73 J W to Emily Gurney, 27 March 1876, W/M 438.
74 J W to Emily Gurney, 9 July 1874 and 27 March 1876, W/M 438.
75 J W to Asa Gray, 11 June 1882, Gray Herbarium.
76 James Moore, *The Post-Darwinian Controversies: A Study of the Protestant Struggle to Come to Terms with Darwin in Great Britain and America 1870–1900*, p. 190.
77 Janet Browne, 'Asa Gray and Charles Darwin: Corresponding Naturalists', *Harvard Papers in Botany* 15(2), p. 3.
78 *Spectator*, 22 April 1882, pp. 536–38.
79 J W, 'The Old Order Changeth', *Contemporary Review*, 1897, p. 422.
80 See Timothy Maxwell Gouldstone, *The Rise and Decline of Anglican Idealism in the Nineteenth Century*, p. 120.
81 Quoted in Moore, *The Post-Darwinian Controversies*, pp. 263 and 265.
82 Quoted in Gouldstone, *The Rise and Decline of Anglican Idealism in the Nineteenth Century*, p. 120. For his discussion of Moore's idealism, see pp. 110–33.
83 Quoted in Moore, *The Post-Darwinian Controversies*, p. 261.
84 See Moore, *The Post-Darwinian Controversies*, p. 263. For an illuminating analysis of Moore's thinking on Darwinism, see 259–69.
85 Gouldstone refers to his 'impressive attempt to combine faith, science and idealist philosophy' (*The Rise and Decline of Anglican Idealism*, p. xvi.) For a fuller discussion of idealism, see pp. xx–xx.
86 Quoted in Moore, *The Post-Darwinian Controversies*, p. 259.
87 J W, 'Richard Holt Hutton', *Contemporary Review*, October 1897 (72), p. 463.
88 J W, 'Ethics and Science', reprinted in *Nineteenth Century Teachers*, pp. 304–23, especially pp. 318–20 and 323.
89 J W, 'The Old Order Changeth', *Contemporary Review*, 1897, p. 428.
90 A sense of man as ill-adapted to his current environment was central to both J W's and Herbert Spencer's thought, but while the one primarily thought of perfection as possible only in the afterlife, the other saw it as the end of the progressive evolutionary process on earth (see Lightman, 'The Theology of Victorian Scientific Naturalists', pp. 245–48).
91 J W, *Nineteenth Century Teachers*, p. 323.
92 Owen Chadwick, *The Victorian Church*, 2, p. 35. See also J. H. Brooke, *Science and Religion*, pp. 317–19.
93 Quoted in Barbara T. Gates, *Kindred Nature: Victorian and Edwardian Women Embrace the Living World*, p. 67. See also Thomas Dixon, *The Invention of Altruism*, pp. 155–57. On the more visionary aspects of Buckley's evolutionary thought derived from her private attachment to Spiritualism, see Bernard Lightman, *Victorian Popularizers of Science*, pp. 239–53.
94 J W to Emily Gurney, 23 September 1883, W/M 438.

Chapter Fourteen The Message of Julia Wedgwood

1 F. M. Turner, *Contesting Cultural Authority Essays in Victorian Cultural Life*, p. 360.
2 J W, *The Moral Ideal*, p. viii.
3 See, for example, what Anna Swanwick, a good friend of Browning's in his later years and a vice president of the Browning Society, wrote: for Browning, man is 'a two-fold being, allied to

NOTES

God by his spiritual nature, destined accordingly for endless progress, and haunted forever by visions of perfection transcending his experience. These, with passionate earnestness, he strives to realize, but finds to his disappointment that they elude his grasp.' Anna Swanwick, *Poets: The Interpreters of Their Age*, pp. 387–88.

4 c.f. "'Tis not what man Does which exalts him, but what man Would do!' Browning, *Saul*, p. 295.
5 *The Moral Ideal*, p. vii.
6 *Saturday Review*, 8 December 1888, p. 693.
7 *London Quarterly Review*, July 1889, p. 391.
8 *The Moral Ideal*, p. vii.
9 J W, 'The Old Order Changeth', *Contemporary Review*, 1897, p. 433.
10 Turner, *Contesting Cultural Authority*, p. 322.
11 Acknowledgements in revised edition of *The Moral Ideal*, 1907.
12 M. E. Boole, *Collected Works*, 2, p. 789. See also K. G. Valente, 'Giving Wings to Logic: Mary Everest Boole's Propagation and Fulfillment of a Legacy', *British Journal for the History of Science*, 43 (March 2010), pp. 49–74.
13 *The Moral Ideal*, p. vii, quoting from James Martineau, *Hours of Thought on Sacred Things*, 1: 10 (1880). Rather surprisingly, J W did not name Martineau as her source.
14 [R. H. Hutton], 'Miss Wedgwood's Apopthegms', *Spectator*, 17 November 1888, p. 11.
15 *The Moral Ideal*, pp. 17, 26, 27 and 47 fn 7.
16 Ibid., p. 80.
17 See Lorna Hardwick, 'Women, Translation and Empowerment', in *Women, Scholarship and Criticism Gender and Knowledge c1790–1900*, eds Joan Bellamy, Anne Laurence and Gill Perry, p. 188; Isobel Hurst, *Victorian Women Writers and the Classics*, p. 143; and Jennifer Wallace, 'Greek under the Trees: Classical Reception and Gender', in *The Oxford History of Classical Reception in English Literature vol. 4 (1790–1880)*, eds Norman Vance and Jennifer Wallace, p. 251.
18 *The Moral Ideal*, p. 82.
19 J W to Robert Browning, 24 August 1864, in R. Curle, ed., *A Broken Friendship*, p. 69; and *The Moral Ideal*, pp. 83–84 and 87.
20 *The Moral Ideal*, p. 107; and see F. M. Turner, 'The Triumph of Idealism in Victorian Classical Studies', in *Contesting Cultural Authority*, pp. 327–30 and 349–53.
21 *The Moral Ideal*, pp. 33–34, 107 and 118.
22 Ibid., pp. 138 and 118.
23 F. M. Turner, 'British Politics and the Demise of the Roman Republic: 1700–1939', in *Contesting Cultural Authority*, pp. 248–50.
24 *The Moral Ideal*, pp. 151, 148, 161, 152 and 186.
25 See Norman Vance, *The Victorians and Ancient Rome*, pp. 84–97.
26 *The Moral Ideal*, pp. 171 and 166–67.
27 Ibid., p. 168 fn 1. See also [J W], 'The Natural and the Supernatural', *Spectator*, 4 November 1871, p. 1341.
28 *The Moral Ideal*, p. 172.
29 [R. H. Hutton], *Spectator*, 26 November 1888, p. 15.
30 *The Moral Ideal*, pp. 173 and 182.
31 Norman Vance, *The Victorians and Ancient Rome*, p. 134; and Turner, *Contesting Cultural Authority*, pp. 294–95.
32 *The Moral Ideal*, pp. 183 and 184.
33 Ibid., p. 185. See also J W, 'Virgil as a Link between the Ancient and the Modern World', *Contemporary Review*, July 1877, pp. 199–218.
34 *The Moral Ideal*, pp. 189 and 207.
35 Quoted in Turner, 'Virgil in Victorian Classical Contexts', in *Contesting Cultural Authority*, p. 319.
36 *The Moral Ideal*, pp. 207 and 217.
37 E. S. Talbot, the future Bishop of Winchester, made a similar claim a year later in an influential essay 'The Preparation in History for Christ', in *Lux Mundi*.

38 *The Moral Ideal*, p. 245
39 Ibid., pp. 251, 265 and 269. On Philo's significance, see John Barton, *A History of the Bible*, pp. 152–54.
40 *The Moral Ideal*, p. 272.
41 *The Moral Ideal*, p. 289; and see Olive J. Brose, *Frederick Dennison Maurice Rebellious Conformist*, p. 282.
42 *The Moral Ideal*, pp. 293, 299 and 304.
43 Ibid., pp. 326, 348 and 351.
44 Ibid., pp. 358 and 361.
45 Ibid., pp. 370 and 373.
46 Ibid., pp. 379 and 378.
47 Ibid., pp. 382 and 383.
48 Ibid., pp. 384, 388 and 390.
49 Ibid., p. 390.
50 *The London Quarterly*, 1889, p. 391; and *The Monthly Packet*, 1 June 1889.
51 Octavia Hill to Miranda Hill, 18 February 1889, in ed. C. Edmund Maurice, *Life of Octavia Hill as Told in Her Letters*, p. 487.
52 *Spectator*, 17 November 1888, p. 12. The OED describes an apophthegm as a 'pithy maxim' or 'terse saying'.
53 Octavia Hill to Miranda Hill, 18 February 1889, in Maurice, ed., *Life of Octavia Hill*, p. 487.
54 Boole described J W as the latest representative of a distinguished Wedgwood intellectual tradition going back to Erasmus Darwin. Her book was both 'The Origin of Species of Moral Ideas' and an 'exquisite series of cameos'. *Collected Works of Mary Everest Boole*, 1, pp. 390–93.
55 *Contemporary Review*, January 1881, p. 56.
56 Emma Darwin to Henrietta Litchfield, 'Thursday', July 1888, 3 November and 6 November 1888, 23 January 1889, CUL Darwin Papers 219.9:671, 685, 686 and 690.
57 Emma Darwin to Henrietta Litchfield, 8 May and July 1888, CUL Darwin Papers 219.9:657 and 671.
58 J W, 'Male and Female Created He Them', *Contemporary Review*, 56 (July 1889), pp. 120–33; and *The Englishwoman's Review*, CXLIV, Monday, 15 July 1889, p. 308.
59 Fiona Erskine has argued in an illuminating article 'The Origin of Species and the Science of Female Inferiority' that in taking this starting point J W was going along with the new post-Darwinian patriarchal assumption that 'the existence of innate sex differences was no longer open to question.' (*Charles Darwin's The Origin of Species New Interdisciplinary Essays*, eds David Amigoni and Jeff Wallace, p. 115). Other comments by J W, however, suggest that this was not an issue on which she ever took a firm position.
60 J W in *The Women's Herald*, 23 May 1891, (324), p. 481.
61 For an incisive discussion of Darwin's attitudes and the reactions of Linton and Cobbe to them, see Evelleen Richards, 'Redrawing the Boundaries: Darwinian Science and Victorian Women Intellectuals', in *Victorian Science in Context*, ed. Bernard Lightman, pp. 119–20 and 129–30. See also Evelleen Richards, *Darwin and the Making of Sexual Selection*, pp. 442–46.
62 J W, 'Male and Female Created He Them', p. 124.
63 Ibid.
64 Ibid., fn p. 125, 130 and 132.
65 See Rosemary Jann, 'Revising the Descent of Woman: Eliza Burt Gamble', in *Natural Eloquence Women Reinscribe Science*, eds Barbara Gates and Ann B. Shteir, p. 152.
66 J W, 'Male and Female Created He Them', pp. 132 and 133.
67 Quoted in Sue Morgan, *Women, Religion and Feminism in Britain 1750–1900*, p. 14.
68 Thomas Erskine to Jane Gourlay, 14 August 1869, in William Hanna, ed., *Letters of Thomas Erskine*, p. 219.
69 J W to Mary Rich, 5 August 1869, W/M 325; and J W, *The Message of Israel*, p. 55.

70 J W, 'Richard Holt Hutton', in *Nineteenth Century Teachers*, p. 144; and J W to Alfred Benn, 29 November 1909, W/M 627.
71 See John Rogerson, 'What Difference Did Darwin Make? The Interpretation of Genesis in the Nineteenth Century', in *Reading Genesis after Darwin*, eds Stephen C. Burton and David Wilkinson, pp. 79–85; and *The Bible and Criticism in Victorian Britain: Profiles of F D Maurice and William Robertson Smith*, pp. 16–54.
72 J W to Alfred Benn, 29 November 1909, W/M 627. See B. M. G. Reardon, *From Coleridge to Gore*, p. 254.
73 See Owen Chadwick, *The Victorian Church*, 2, pp. 107–10.
74 *The Message of Israel*, pp. 20, 5 and 16.
75 Ibid., p. 19. See also her reference to 'reverent inattention' in 'The Unfaithful Steward', *Contemporary Review*, January 1890, p. 52.
76 *The Message of Israel*, p. 14. This is a quotation from *Jeremiah*, pp. xv, 19.
77 Ibid., pp. 246, 116 and 175–76.
78 Ibid., pp. 76 and 250.
79 Marion Ann Taylor and Heather E Weir, *Let Her Speak for Herself: Nineteenth Century Women Writing on Women in Genesis*, pp. 1–25.
80 Ibid., pp. 96–97 and 184.
81 *The Message of Israel*, pp. 86, 261 and 85.
82 Ibid., pp. 298 and 302.
83 Ibid., pp. 298 and 241.
84 Ibid., p. 309. J W, 'The Unfaithful Steward', expands this theme.
85 *The Message of Israel*, p. 310.
86 *The National Observer*, 20 June 1894, 12 (293), pp. 180–81; and *The London Quarterly Review*, October 1894, 23(1), pp. 154–55.
87 *Athenaeum*, 20 October 1894 (3495), pp. 526–27; and *Saturday Review*, 16 December 1894, 18(2042), p. 643.
88 Dodds was Professor of New Testament Exegesis at New College, Edinburgh, and Bruce, who had been a minister at Broughty Ferry in Thomas Erskine's last years, held the Chair of Apologetics and New Testament Exegesis at the Free Church Hall, Glasgow. Both had been called before their Church's general assembly in 1890 to account for their openness to the new criticism, but grudgingly acquitted.
89 *Contemporary Review*, July 1894 (66), pp. 77 and 78; and *The Bookman*, August 1894, 6 (35), p. 149.
90 *Contemporary Review*, pp. 83 and 90; and *The Bookman*, p. 149.
91 *The Academy*, 6 October 1894, 1170, p. 247.
92 J W to Alfred Benn, 2 November and 6 December 1894, W/M 627. Benn's letters to J W have not survived.
93 J W to Alfred Benn, 26 September 1906, W/M 627.
94 Barbara Wedgwood, 'A Critical Study of the Life and Works of Julia Wedgwood', p. 244; and Emma Darwin to Henrietta Litchfield, 9 August 1894, printed in H. Litchfield, *Emma Darwin*, 2, p. 434.
95 C. H. Herford to J W, 11 April 1894, W/M 578.

Chapter Fifteen 'The Old Order Changeth'

1 José Harris, *Private Lives and Public Spirit*, p. 175; and J W, 'The Old Order Changeth', *Contemporary Review*, 1897, p. 433.
2 J W, 'The Irish Patriots and Professor Dicey', *Murray's Magazine*, November 1890, 8 (47), p. 586.
3 J W, 'The Old Order Changeth', *Contemporary Review*, 1897, p. 433.
4 *Spectator*, 4 November 1905, p. 13.
5 C. H. Herford, 'Frances Julia Wedgwood: A Memoir', pp. xxix–xxx.

6. David Erskine to J W, 16 September 1894, W/M 623. Richard Davenport-Hines identifies Erskine as one of Maynard Keynes's early lovers in *Universal Man: The Seven Lives of John Maynard Keynes*, p. 218.
7. J W to Eliza Wedgwood, 9 December 1892, Baylor.
8. Jennifer Glynn, *The Pioneering Garretts*, pp. 58 and 170.
9. Hope Wedgwood to J W, n.d. [1889], W/M 550.
10. Many of these slips still survive there.
11. J W, 'Mr Hensleigh Wedgwood', *Bedford College Magazine*, 1902, p. 28.
12. J W to Ellen Tollett, 2 October 1880, W/M 401.
13. Arthur Munby, ms diary, 3 January 1880, Trinity College, Cambridge, and *Pall Mall Gazette*, 30 December 1889.
14. David Erskine to J W, 2 November 1895, W/M 623.
15. J W to May Crum, 24 April 1899, CUL EAD/GBR/0012/MS Add.7671/V/D 260.
16. Hope Wedgwood to Effie Farrer, n.d., W/M 562.
17. Philip Gardner, ed., *Journals and Diaries of E. M. Forster*, 1, p. 161.
18. J W to Henrietta Litchfield, 18 March 1897, W/M 448; and Hope Wedgwood to Charlotte Masingberd, 14 June 1911, W/M uncatalogued.
19. Hope Wedgwood to Charlotte Massingberd, 11 July 1911, W/M uncatalogued.
20. J W to A. V. Dicey, 7 June 1893, Nightingale Collection LMA A/NFC 109/55.
21. J W to May Crum, 29 July 1902, CUL MS Add.7671/V/D/269.
22. J W to Alfred Benn, n.d. [?1911], W/M 627.
23. Hope Wedgwood to J W, 3 September 1905 [1906] and 9 June 1907, W/M 550; Pat Jalland, *Death in the Victorian Family*, p. 307; and Arthur Munby, ms diary, 20 November 1882, Trinity College, Cambridge.
24. Copy of J W to unknown recipient annotated by J W, W/M 615.
25. J W to Lady Welby, c. 1898, printed in Nina Cust, ed., *Other Dimensions*, p. 38.
26. J W to Roger Fry, 22 December 1901, Roger Fry Papers, viii W, King's College, Cambridge.
27. Alice Meynell to J W, 20 July [no year], W/M 622.
28. See Ann Ardis, 'Organizing Women: New Woman Writers, New Woman Readers, and Suffrage Feminism', in *Victorian Women Writers and the Woman Question*, ed. Nicola Diane Thompson, pp. 195–96; and Linda Peterson, *Becoming a Woman of Letters*, pp. 171–86.
29. See Andrew Vincent and Raymond Plant, *Philosophy, Politics and Citizenship: The Life and Thought of the British Idealists*.
30. See C. Edmund Maurice, *The Life of Octavia Hill as Told in Her Letters*, p. 524; and *Octavia Hill's Letters to Co-Workers 1872–1911*, ed. Robert Whelan, pp. 555 and 582 (1906 and 1908 Letters).
31. J W, 'The Old Order Changeth', p. 432; J W to Emily Gurney, [1871], W/M 438; and J W to editor of *London Daily News*, 10 February 1890.
32. J W to Emily Gurney, 19 November 1872, W/M 438. She was probably thinking of James Fitzjames's four daughters, one of whom, Katherine, became principal of Newnham College, not Vanessa and Virginia Stephen, who were both born after this comment.
33. J W to Emily Gurney, 18 January 1876 and 19 November 1872, W/M 438.
34. J W to Emily Gurney, 13 December 1894, W/M 584.
35. Extracts from J W's letters to Kathleen Jervois are printed in C. H. Herford, 'Memoir of Julia Wedgwood', pp. xxvi–xxvii.
36. J W to Jean Crum, 31 January 1895, CUL Hugh Fraser Stuart Papers MS Add.7671/VIII/A 239; and C. H. Herford, *Manchester Guardian*, 28 November 1913.
37. Eliza Wedgwood to Ruth Draper [1940]. Armstrong Browning Library, Baylor.
38. J W to Mary Euphrasia Wedgwood, 14 February 1897, W/M uncatalogued.
39. J W in margins of Mary Wedgwood to J W, [?1907], W/M 597.
40. Hope Wedgwood to Effie Farrer, 28 December 1891, W/M 562; and J W to May Crum, 15 June 1902, CUL EAD/GBR/0012/MS Add.7671/V/D 268.

41 *The Parents' Review*, 7(1896), p. 77; see p. x; and Evelleen Richards, *Darwin and the Making of Sexual Selection*, pp. 503–4.
42 Mary Beard, *The Invention of Jane Harrison*, p. 7; Jane Harrison to J W, October 1902, W/M 674; and J W to May Crum, 27 December 1902, CUL EAD/GBR/0012/MS Add.7671/V/D 275.
43 See Isobel Hurst, 'Ancient and Modern Women in the *Woman's World*', *Victorian Studies*, 52, pp. 1, 42–51; and Laurel Brake, S*ubjugated Knowledges: Journalism, Gender and Literature in the Nineteenth Century*, pp. 128–43.
44 J W, 'Women and Democracy', *The Woman's World*, 1888, pp. 338–39.
45 J W to Emily Davies, 7 October 1910, GCPP Davies 17/23. See also Herford, 'Frances Julia Wedgwood', p. xxvii.
46 J W, 'The Irish Patriots and Professor Dicey', *Murray's Magazine*, November 1890 (47), p. 578.
47 Quoted in Herford, *Julia Wedgwood*, p. xxvii.
48 J W to May Crum, 18 and 12 July 1897, CUL 7671/V/D 253 and 252; J W to Emily Gurney, April [1883], W/M 584; and J W to *Spectator*, 8 June 1878 (2606), p. 728, 26 July 1879 (2665), pp. 947–48, 30 June 1906 (4070), p. 1037, and 15 January 1910 (4255), p. 94.
49 Janet Browne, *Charles Darwin: The Power of Place*, p. 421; and Charles Darwin, Correspondence 10546.
50 J W to the *Spectator*, 26 July 1879 (2665), p. 947 and 30 June 1906 (4070), p. 1037.
51 J W to May Crum, 3 July 1906, CUL MS Add.7671/VIII/A.
52 J W, 'Why Am I an Anti-Vivisectionist?' 1910, pp. 1–4.
53 Emma Darwin to Henrietta Litchfield, 3 October 1888, CUL DAR 219.9:684; and J W to Ellen Tollet, 22 October 1872, W/M 401.
54 F. P. Cobbe, *Autobiography* (one-volume edition), p. 578; *The Abolitionist*, 15 December 1902, 9 (3), p. 100.
55 Janet Oppenheim, *The Other World: Spiritualism and Psychical Research in England 1850–1914*, p. 129.
56 Hensleigh Wedgwood to Frederic Myers, 28 January 1874, Myers Papers. See also Browne, *Charles Darwin: The Power of Place*, pp. 404–6 and p. x.
57 *Journal of the Society for Psychical Research*, 2, 1885–86, p. 460.
58 Emma Darwin to Henrietta Litchfield, 31 July 1883, CUL DAR 219.9.366.
59 Lily Whichelo to Marion Southey, n.d., printed in P. N. Furbank, *E. M. Forster: A Life*, 1, pp. 5–6.
60 Reprinted after p. 442 in Janet Browne, *Charles Darwin: The Power of Place*. See also *The Wedgwood Circle*, p. 355, on Effie and Hope Wedgwood's later devotion to Spiritualism.
61 *Proceedings of the Society for Psychical Research*, 9, 1893, pp. 93–103.
62 Emily Gurney to J W, n.d. [1869]; and J W to Emily Gurney, 7 March 1870 and 7 February 1867, W/M 584.
63 J W's engagement diary, 1889, W/M 1260.
64 J W to Frederic Myers, 27 April 1890, Frederic Myers Papers, 4, p. 140
65 See Georgina Byrne, *Modern Spiritualism and the Church of England 1850–1939*, especially pp. 84–85 and 100–01; and Pat Jalland, *Death in the Victorian Family*, 268–73.
66 J W to Frederic Myers, n.d., Myers Papers, 4, p. 138.
67 Desmond MacHale, *George Boole: His Life and Work*, pp. 242–3.
68 E. M. Cobham, *Mary Everest Boole: A Memoir*, p. 60.
69 J W to Emily Gurney, 16 September 1883, W/M 584 (unbound letters); and J W to Lady Welby, c. 1882, in Mrs Henry Cust, ed., *Echoes of a Larger Life*, pp. 97 and 86 fn1.
70 Hope Wedgwood to Fanny Wedgwood, 1877, W/M, and to Ida Farrer, 6 September 1879, CUL DAR 9368.1:16310; and Emma Darwin to Henrietta Litchfield, October 1888, CUL DAR 219.9: 683.
71 The correspondence with Darwin is printed in Samantha Evans, ed., *Darwin and Women: A Selection of Letters*, pp. 175–77. Evans describes Boole's letter as 'one of the most searching he ever received', p. 174.

72 See Seth Koven, *Slumming*, p. 14.
73 Quoted in Alan Willard Brown, *The Metaphysical Society*, p. 60.
74 See Phyllis Grosskurth, *Havelock Ellis: A Biography*, pp. 42–43 and 52–54.
75 Marian Hughes to J W, [April 1887], W/M 595.
76 Alice Bonham Carter to J W, 26 October 1866, W/M 595.
77 Emily Gurney to J W, 11 October 1886, W/M 595.
78 J W, covering note to papers on the Hinton affair; and Emily Gurney to J W, 11 October 1886, W/M 595.
79 Marian Hughes to J W, April 1887; and J W to Mary Ellen Hinton, 7 October 1886, W/M 595.
80 E. M. Cobham, *Mary Everest Boole: A Memoir*, p. 50.
81 K. G. Valente, 'Giving Wings to Logic: Mary Everest Boole's Propagation and Fulfillment of a Legacy', *British Journal for the History of Science*, March 2010, pp. 43, 156 and 71.
82 M. E. Boole to Lady Welby, c. 1882, in Mrs Henry Cust, ed., *Echoes of a Larger Life*, pp. 89, 247 and 260.
83 Mary Warnock, *Women Philosophers*, p. xxxviii.
84 Susan Petrilli, 'Three Women in Semiotics: Welby, Boole, Langer', *Semiotica*, 2010, 1821/4, p. 328.
85 J W to Victoria Welby, c. 1885, in Mrs Henry Cust, ed., *Echoes of a Larger Life*, pp. 163–64.
86 Victoria Welby to Lady Mount Temple, c. 1881; and J W to Victoria Welby, c. 1888, in Mrs Henry Cust, ed., *Echoes of a Larger Life*, pp. 77 and 242.
87 J W to Victoria Welby, c. 1885, in Mrs Henry Cust, ed. *Echoes of a Larger Life*, p. 163.
88 J W to Lady Welby, c. 1888, in ibid., p. 240.
89 Victoria Welby to J W, c. 1904, in Mrs Henry Cust, ed., *Other Dimensions*, p. 260.
90 J W to the editor, *Spectator*, 25 May 1895 (3491), pp. 718–19, 22 November 1879 (2682), p. 1474, 10 April 1897 (3589), 14 July 1906 (4072), p. 57, 28 October 1905 (4035), p. 650, 20 April 1907 (4112), p. 619.
91 J W to the editor, *Spectator*, 24 October 1908 (4191), p. 627.
92 J W to the editor, *Spectator*, 2 September 1911 (4340), p. 340, and 6 April 1912 (4371), p. 545.
93 Alexis Easley, *First Person Anonymous Women Writers and Victorian Print Media, 1830–70*, p. 182.
94 Quoted in Philip Waller, *Writers, Readers and Reputations*, p. 322.
95 See James Diedrick, *Mathilde Blind: Late Victorian Culture and the Woman of Letters*, p. 204.
96 J W to May Crum, July 1896, CUL EAD/GBR/0012/MS. Add.7671/V/D 244.

Chapter Sixteen 'A Satisfied Guest'

1 J W, *Nineteenth Century Teachers*, pp. 404, 407, 412.
2 J W to Henrietta Litchfield, 18 March 1897, W/M 448.
3 J W to Alfred Benn, 5 May 1912, W/M 627.
4 J W to May Crum, 7 June 1903, CUL Add.7671/V.
5 J W, *The Moral Ideal*, revised edition, p. 42.
6 J W to Emily Gurney, 18 December 1887, W/M 584.
7 E. M. Forster, *Marianne Thornton*. This theme runs throughout the book, but see particularly p. 220.
8 E. M. Forster Diary, 23 June [1908], in *The Journals and Diaries of E. M. Forster*, 1, p. 161. Julia may have sought Forster's opinion on whether the correspondence should be published.
9 Hope Wedgwood to Mary Wedgwood, 22 April 1904, W/M 618.
10 Quoted in Elizabeth Heine introduction to *The Longest Journey*, Abinger edition, 1984, p. xl; and P. N. Furbank, *E. M. Forster*, 1, p. 115. Furbank does not give a reference for this comment, which probably reflects something Forster told him in conversation.
11 31 December 1907, *The Journals and Diaries of E. M. Forster*, 1, p. 157.

12 C. H. Herford to J W, 12 May 1907, W/M 578. 'The present edition,' J W wrote, 'owes more than I can say to two who have put aside their own work to help mine – Edward Morgan Forster and Charles Harold Herford.'
13 This presents it as a 'moralizing version of ancient India's origins.' *TLS* November 2016, p. 32.
14 J W, *The Moral Ideal*, p. 25.
15 Ibid., pp. 473, 476 and 479.
16 Ibid., p. 467.
17 Ibid..
18 Ibid., p. 470.
19 Ibid., p. 481.
20 C. H. Herford to J W, 11 July 1907, W/M 578; and E. M. Forster, 31 December 1907, *The Journals and Diaries of E. M. Forster*, 1, p. 157.
21 Melian Stawell, *International Journal of Ethics*, 18 (3), April 1908, pp. 394–97.
22 J W to Alfred Benn, 9 October 1910, W/M 627.
23 José Harris, *Private Lives, Public Spirit: A Social History of Britain 1870–1914*, p. 176.
24 *School Review*, 16 (1), January 1908; and *Classical Weekly*, 1920.
25 P. N. Furbank, *E. M. Forster: A Life*, 1, p. 118.
26 J W, *The Moral Ideal*, p. 459; and P. N. Furbank, *E. M. Forster: A Life*, 1, p. 190.
27 J W to May Crum, 12 August 1907, CUL Add.7671/V/300.
28 C. H. Herford to J W, 5 February 1903, W/M 578.
29 R. Reilly, *Wedgwood*, pp. 1, 7.
30 Barbara and Hensleigh Wedgwood, *The Wedgwood Circle*, p. 300; Samantha Evans, *Darwin and Women*, p. 151; and R. Litchfield, *Tom Wedgwood: The First Photographer*, p. ix.
31 This was that when Wedgwood sensed he was close to death, he locked himself away from his family to spare them. Godfrey Wedgwood, Effie claimed, had heard it from 'the old carpenter, Greaves' who had broken the door down (*Letters of Josiah Wedgwood*, 1, pp. viii). J W was moved by the story but did not include it in her biography (J W to A. Benn, 5 May 1912, W/M 627).
32 J W to Effie Wedgwood, 4 November 1871, W/M 324, and to Alfred Benn, 12 March 1911, W/M 627.
33 See Kay Boardman, 'Struggling for Fame: Eliza Meteyard's Principled Career', in *Popular Victorian Women Writers*, eds Kay Boardman and Shirley Jones, pp. 46–54. Both Charles Darwin and Hensleigh Wedgwood signed the petition that won Meteyard a much-needed Civil List pension.
34 *The Wedgwood Circle*, p. 342.
35 J W, *The Personal Life of Josiah Wedgwood the Potter*, p. 36.
36 J W to Alfred Benn, June 1911, W/M 627.
37 J W to Alfred Benn, 5 May 1912, W/M 627.
38 A small file of drafts for the biography marked by J W 'LIMBO' is at W/M 1340.
39 J W, *The Personal Life of Josiah Wedgwood the Potter*, pp. 141, 153, 154, 158 and 161.
40 Ibid., pp. 111, 110 and 60.
41 J W to A. Benn, 29 August 1911, W/M 627.
42 J W, *The Personal Life of Josiah Wedgwood the Potter*, p. 105.
43 J W to Alfred Benn, 5 May 1912, W/M 627.
44 J W, *The Personal Life of Josiah Wedgwood the Potter*, pp. 362–66 and 264–65.
45 Ibid., p. 329.
46 Eliza Meteyard, *A Group of Englishmen*, pp. 215–17, unwittingly dropped some hints about this. In 1882 J W wrote to the *Spectator* reporting that a box of Thomas Wedgwood's papers had been discovered and asking anyone with further information about him to contact her cousin, Arthur Wedgwood. This would, she suggested, help the family decide whether to produce an account of his life. J W to *Spectator*, 30 September 1882 (2831), p. 1255.

47 J W, *The Personal Life of Josiah Wedgwood the Potter*, p. 339; Richard Litchfield, *Tom Wedgwood the First Photographer*, pp. 257–59; and J W, *The Personal Life of Josiah Wedgwood The Potter*, p. 340. A different account circulated on the Darwin side of the family. Gwen Raverat wrote in a manuscript note in her copy of *The Personal Life of Josiah Wedgwood the Potter*, which came to her from her aunt Henrietta Litchfield: 'Bernard Darwin told me in 1933 that he believed that Josiah had discovered that Coleridge had induced Tom to take opium, & that this was the reason that he stopped the pension – There were various reasons for this theory, though no absolute proof. But it also accounts for the way in which Tom's very serious illness is never explained' (copy in the author's possession).
48 Brian Dolan, *Josiah Wedgwood*, p. 323.
49 J W, *The Personal Life of Josiah Wedgwood the Potter*, p. 316; and J W to Alfred Benn, 14 October 1912, W/M 627.
50 Robin Reilly, *Wedgwood*, 1, p. 7.
51 J W, *The Personal Life of Josiah Wedgwood the Potter*, p. 191.
52 J W to Alfred Benn, 14 April 1912 and 1 September 1912, W/M 627; J W, *The Personal Life of Josiah Wedgwood the Potter*, p. 64.
53 J W to Alfred Benn, 17 March 1913, W/M 627.
54 Eliza Wedgwood to Ruth Draper, Armstrong–Browning Library, Baylor; and E. S. Roscoe to *Spectator*, 17 January 1914, p. 17.
55 J W to Alfred Benn, 23 June 1911 and 17 March 1913, W/M 627.
56 Now in the Armstrong–Browning Library at Baylor University.
57 The text of this letter is taken from Barbara Wedgwood, 'A Critical Study of the Life and Works of Julia Wedgwood', unpublished PhD thesis, London University, 1983, pp. 271–72. Though this claims that the original is at the Armstrong–Browning Library at Baylor University, it has not been found there.
58 J W to Alfred Benn, 4 and 8 July 1913, W/M 627.
59 J W to Alfred Benn, 12 August 1913 and 21 December 1912, W/M 627.
60 Hope Wedgwood to Eliza Wedgwood, 'November' 1913, Baylor.
61 Hope Wedgwood to Eliza Wedgwood, 28 November [1913], Baylor.
62 Wilfred Baugh Allen vs. Cecil and Bertram Hensleigh Wedgwood and HM Attorney General in High Court Chancery Division, 1914, W No. 384 (Stoke City archive SD 4842/40/1, 1930).
63 See Pat Jalland, *Death in the Victorian Family*, p. 371; and J W to Jean Stuart, 6 December 1911, CUL Hugh Fraser Stuart Papers MS Add.7671/VIII/A242.
64 *Manchester Guardian*, 28 November 1913; and *Spectator*, January 1914.
65 Hope Wedgwood to Eliza Wedgwood, 28 [November] 1913, Baylor.
66 Ibid.
67 Texas death certificate of Mary Anne Hughes, 10 January 1919.
68 See the lively account of his life in Wikipedia.
69 *The Wedgwood Circle*, p. 355.
70 Sandra M. den Otter, *British Idealism and Social Explanation: A Study in Late Victorian Thought*, p. 211.
71 Quoted in Pat Jalland, *Women, Marriage and Politics 1860–1914*, p. 287.
72 A commissioned letter from J W printed in *Woman's Herald* Saturday, 23 May 1891, p. 482.

BIBLIOGRAPHY

Archival Sources

Armstrong-Browning Library, Baylor University, Waco, Texas: Robert Browning–Julia Wedgwood correspondence, Eliza Wedgwood correspondence, Julia Wedgwood's annotated copies of the works of Elizabeth and Robert Browning.
Bodleian Library, Oxford: James Bryce Papers.
Botany Libraries, Gray Herbarium Library, Harvard University: Asa Gray correspondence with Julia Wedgwood (seen in photostat).
Cambridge University Library: Charles Darwin papers, including correspondence of Emma and Henrietta Darwin, papers about the presentation of Darwin's views on religion, correspondence between Julia Wedgwood and Charles and Emma Darwin and Fanny Erskine's correspondence with Julia Wedgwood.
———. Hugh Fraser Stuart Collection: May Crum–Julia Wedgwood correspondence.
Girton College Cambridge: Emily Davies papers.
King's College, Cambridge: E. M. Forster and Roger Fry Papers.
Metropolitan Archive, London: London Working Women's College records.
Royal Holloway College, London: attendance registers for early years of Bedford College and related papers.
Stoke on Trent City Archive: papers relating to dispute over Julia Wedgwood's will.
Trinity College, Cambridge: Arthur Munby diaries and letters and Frederic Myers papers.
V&A Wedgwood Collection, presented by the Artfund with major support from the Heritage Lottery Fund, private donations and a public appeal, in particular the Wedgwood/Mosley Collection (referenced as 'W/M'), including family correspondence of Hensleigh and Fanny Wedgwood and their children, Julia Wedgwood's correspondence with A. W. Benn, Emma Darwin, Erasmus Darwin, Thomas Erskine, Jane Gourlay, Emily Gurney, Henrietta Litchfield, Harriet Martineau, Marian Hughes and Emma Tollet, papers concerning the publication of the Julia Wedgwood–Browning correspondence, papers on the Howard Hinton affair and the Wedgwood Family History Album.
Winchester Record Office: Bonham–Carter family correspondence.
Women's Library, London School of Economics: Josephine Butler correspondence (on microfilm).

Contemporary Memoirs, Letters, Biographies and Other Source Materials

Bennett, Arnold. *Journalism for Women: A Practical Guide*. London: John Lane, 1898.
Betham-Edwards, M. *Mid-Victorian Memories with a Personal Sketch by Mrs Sarah Grand*. London: John Murray, 1919.
Boole, Mary Everest. *Collected Works*, 4 vols, edited by E. M. Cobham. London: C. W. Daniel, 1931.
———. *The Value of a Maimed Life: Extracts from the Notes of Thomas Wedgwood*. Selected by Margaret Olivia Tremayne with an introduction by Mary Everest Boole. London: C. W. Daniel, 1912.
Bruce, Mary L., ed. *Anna Swanwick: A Memoir and Recollections 1813–1899*. London: T. Fisher Unwin, 1903.
Butler, Josephine, ed. *Woman's Work and Woman's Culture: A Series of Essays*. London: Macmillan, 1869.
Carpenter, J. Estlin. *James Martineau Theologian and Teacher: A Study of His Life and Thought*. London: Philip Green, 1905.

Chesterton, G. K. *Robert Browning.* London: Macmillan, 1903.
Cobbe, Frances Power. *Darwinism in Morals and Other Essays.* London: Williams and Norgate, 1872.
———. *Life of Frances Power Cobbe, by Herself.* London: R. Bentley, 1894.
———. *The Duties of Women: A Course of Lectures.* London: T. Fisher Unwin, 1894.
———. *An Essay on Intuitive Morals*, 2 vols. London: privately published, 1855–57.
Coleridge, Christabel. *Charlotte Mary Yonge: Her Life and Letters.* London: Macmillan, 1903.
Cross, John W. *George Eliot's Life as Related in Her Letters and Journals Arranged and Edited by Her Husband J.W. Cross.* London: William Blackwood and Sons, 1885.
Darwin, Frank. *The Life and Letters of Charles Darwin Including an Autobiographical Chapter*, 3 vols. London: John Murray, 1887.
Davies, J. Llewelyn, ed. *The Working Men's College 1854–1906: Records of Its History and Its Work for Fifty Years by Members of the College.* London: Macmillan, 1904.
Dicey, A. V. *A Leap in the Dark or Our New Constitution.* London: John Murray, 1893.
Edgeworth, Maria. *Harry and Lucy.* Illustrated edition. London: George Routledge, 1858.
———. *The Parent's Assistant: Or Stories for Children. In Six Volumes.* London: printed for J. Johnson, 1804.
Eliot, George. 'Silly Novels by Lady Novelists', *Westminster Review*, October 1856.
Gurney, Ellen Mary, ed. *Letters of Emelia Russell Gurney.* London: James Nisbet, 1902.
Erskine, Thomas. *The Spiritual Order; and Other Papers Selected from the Manuscripts of the Late Thomas Erskine of Linlathen*, edited by Jane Gourlay. Edinburgh: n.p., 1871.
———. *Letters of Thomas Erskine of Linlathen*, 2 vols, edited by William Hanna. Edinburgh: David Douglas, 1878.
Herford, Charles Henry. 'Frances Julia Wedgwood: A Memoir', preface to Julia Wedgwood, *The Personal Life of Josiah Wedgwood the Potter.* London: Macmillan, 1915.
———. 'The Late Miss Julia Wedgwood', *Spectator*, 10 January 1914.
Litchfield, Henrietta. *Emma Darwin Wife of Charles Darwin: A Century of Family Letters*, 2 vols. Cambridge: Privately printed at Cambridge University Press, 1904.
Litchfield, Richard. *Tom Wedgwood the First Photographer: An Account of His Life, His Discovery and His Friendship with Samuel Taylor Coleridge.* London: Duckworth, 1903.
Lumsden, Louisa. *Yellow Leaves: Memories of a Long Life.* Edinburgh: W. Blackwood & Sons, 1933.
Mackintosh, Robert James. *Memoirs of the Life of the Rt. Hon. Sir James Mackintosh*, 2 vols. London: Edward Moxon, 1835.
Malleson, Elizabeth. *Elizabeth Malleson 1828–1916: Autobiographical Notes and Letters with a Memoir by Hope Malleson.* Privately printed, 1926.
Martineau, Harriet. *Autobiography*, 2 vols, edited by Gaby Weiner. London: Virago Press, 1983.
———. 'Letter to the Deaf', *Tait's Edinburgh Magazine*, April 1834. Reprinted in Andra Broomfield and Sally Mitchell. *Prose by Victorian Women: An Anthology.* London: Garland, 1996.
Maurice, C. Edmund. *Life of Octavia Hill as Told in Her Letters.* London: Macmillan, 1913.
Maurice, Emily, ed. *Octavia Hill: Early Ideals from Letters.* London: G. Allen & Unwin, 1928.
Maurice, F. D. *Lectures on Social History: Twenty-One Lectures Delivered in the University of Cambridge.* London: Macmillan, 1869.
Maurice, Frederick. *The Life of Frederick Denison Maurice Chiefly Told in His Own Letters*, 2 vols, 3rd edition. London: Macmillan, 1884.
Muller, Max. *Auld Lang Syne.* London: Longmans Green, 1898.
Orr, Mrs Alexander. *Life and Letters of Robert Browning.* London: Smith & Elder, 1891.
Perris, H. S. *A Sketch of the History of Little Portland Street Chapel London.* London: McQuorquodale, 1900.
Podmore, Frank. *Modern Spiritualism: A History and a Criticism.* London: Methuen, 1902.
Ritchie, Anne Thackeray. *Records of Tennyson, Ruskin and Browning.* London: Macmillan, 1892.
Shaen, Margaret S., ed. *Memorials of Two Sisters Susannah and Catherine Winkworth Edited by Their Niece Margaret J Shaen.* London: Longmans, Green, 1908.
Sieveking, I. Giverne. *Memoir and Letters of Francis W. Newman.* London: Kegan Paul, Trench, Trübner, 1909.
Simcox, Edith. *A Monument to the Memory of George Eliot: Edith Simcox's Autobiography of a Shirtmaker*, edited by Constance M. Fulmer and Margaret E. Barfield. London: Garland, 1998.

Thompson, Joseph. *The Owens College: Its Foundation and Growth, and Its Connection with the Victoria University, Manchester.* Manchester: J. E. Cornish, 1886.
Tweedie, Mrs Alex, ed. *The First College Open to Women Queen's College London: Memories and Records of Work Done, 1848–1898.* London: Queen's College, 1898.
Ward, Wilfrid Philip. *Ten Personal Studies.* London: Longman's, 1908.
Wedgwood, Hensleigh. *On the Development of the Understanding.* London: Privately printed, 1848.
Wedgwood, Frances Julia. *John Wesley and the Evangelical Reaction of the Eighteenth Century.* London: Macmillan, 1870.
———. *The Moral Ideal: A Historic Study.* London: Trübner, 1888.
———. *The Message of Israel in the Light of Modern Criticism.* London: Isbister, 1894.
———. *The Moral Ideal.* New and revised edition. London: Kegan Paul, Trench, Trübner, 1907.
———. *Nineteenth Century Teachers, and Other Essays.* London: Hodder & Stoughton, 1909.
———. *The Personal Life of Josiah Wedgwood the Potter.* Revised and edited, with an introduction and prefatory memoir of the author by C. H. Herford. London: Macmillan, 1915.
———. *The Political Claims of Women.* London: National Society for Women's Suffrage, 1876.
———. *Why Am I an Anti-Vivisectionist?* London: Animal Defence & Anti-Vivisection Society, 1910.
——— [as W. J.]. *Framleigh Hall.* London: Hurst & Blackett, 1858.
——— [as Florence Dawson]. *An Old Debt.* London: Smith, Elder, 1858.

Secondary Sources

Aarslaff, Hans. *The Study of Language in England, 1780–1860.* Princeton, NJ: Princeton University Press, 1967.
Ablow, Rachel. *Victorian Pain.* Princeton, NJ: Princeton University Press, 2017.
Alexander, Constance. *Baghdad in Bygone Days.* London: John Murray, 1928.
Alter, Stephen G. *Darwinism and the Linguistic Image.* Baltimore: Johns Hopkins University Press, 1999.
———. 'Darwin and the Linguists: The Evolution of Mind and Language Part 1: Problematic Friends', *Studies in History and Philosophy of Biological and Biomedical Sciences*, 38 (3), September 2007.
Amigoni, David, ed. *Life Writing and Victorian Culture.* Aldershot: Ashgate, 2006.
Amigoni, David, and Jeff Wallace. *Charles Darwin's The Origin of Species: New Interdisciplinary Essays.* Manchester: Manchester University Press, 1990.
Annan, Noel. *Leslie Stephen the Godless Victorian.* New York: Random House, 1984.
———. 'The Intellectual Aristocracy'. In *Studies in Social History: A Tribute to G. M. Trevelyan*, edited by J. H. Plumb. London: Longmans, Green, 1955.
Ardis, Ann. 'Organizing Women: New Women Writers, New Women Readers and Suffrage and Feminism'. In *Victorian Women Writers and the Woman Question*, edited by Nicola Diane Thompson. Cambridge: Cambridge University Press, 1999.
Anderson, Patricia J., and Rose Jonathan, eds. *Dictionary of Literary Biography: 106 British Literary Publishing Houses, 1820–1880.* Detroit: Gale Research, 1991.
Arbuckle, Elisabeth Sanders, ed. *Harriet Martineau's Letters to Fanny Wedgwood.* Stanford, CA: Stanford University Press, 1983.
Armstrong, Isobel, ed. *The Major Victorian Poets: Reconsiderations.* London: Routledge & Kegan Paul, 1969.
Ashton, Rosemary. *Thomas and Jane Carlyle: Portrait of a Marriage.* London: Chatto & Windus, 2002.
———. *Victorian Bloomsbury.* London: Yale University Press, 2012.
Atkinson, Juliette. *Victorian Biography Reconsidered: A Study of Nineteenth-Century 'Hidden' Lives.* Oxford: Oxford University Press, 2010.
Beer, Gillian. 'Darwin and the Growth of Language Theory'. In *Nature Transfigured Science and Literature, 1700–1900*, edited by John Christie and Sally Shuttleworth. Manchester: Manchester University Press, 1989.
Beetham, Margaret. 'Periodical Writing'. In *The Cambridge Companion to Victorian Women's Writing*, edited by Linda H. Peterson. Cambridge: Cambridge University Press, 2015.

De Bellaigue, Christina. *Educating Women: Schooling and Identity in England and France, 1800–1867.* Oxford: Oxford University Press, 2007.
Bellamy Joan, Anne Laurence, and Gill Perry, eds. *Women, Scholarship and Criticism Gender, c. 1790-1900.* Manchester: Manchester University Press, 2000.
Bennett, Daphne. *Emily Davies and the Liberation of Women, 1830–1921.* London: André Deutsch, 1990.
Bennion, Elisabeth. *Antique Hearing Devices.* Brighton: Vernier Press, 1994.
Berry, R. J., and T. A. Noble, eds. *Darwin, Creation and the Fall: Theological Challenges.* Nottingham: Apollos, 2009.
Beard, Mary. *The Invention of Jane Harrison.* London: Harvard University Press, 2000.
Bernstein, Susan David. *Roomscape: Women Writers in the British Museum from George Eliot to Virginia Woolf.* Edinburgh: Edinburgh University Press, 2013.
Billings, Malcolm. *Queen's College: 150 Years and a New Century.* London: James and James, 2000.
Binfield, Clyde. *Belmont's Portias: Victorian Nonconformists and Middle-Class Education for Girls.* London: Dr William's Library, 1981.
Binckes, Faith, and Carey Snyder, eds. *Women, Periodicals, and Print Culture in Britain, 1890s–1920s: The Modernist Period.* Edinburgh: Edinburgh University Press, 2019.
Boardman, Kay. 'Struggling for Fame: Eliza Meteyard's Principled Career'. In *Popular Victorian Women Writers*, edited by Kay Boardman and Shirley Jones. Manchester: Manchester University Press, 2004.
Bostridge, Mark. *Florence Nightingale: The Woman and Her Legend.* London: Viking, 2008.
Bowler, Peter J. *Evolution: The History of an Idea.* Berkeley: University of California Press, 1983.
———. *Reconciling Science and Religion: The Debate in Early Twentieth Century Britain.* Chicago: University of Chicago Press, 2001.
Brake, Laurel. *Subjugated Knowledges: Journalism, Gender and Literature in the Nineteenth Century.* Basingstoke: Macmillan, 1994.
———. 'Periodical Formats: The Changing Review'. In *Journalism and the Periodical Press in Nineteenth-Century Britain*, edited by Joanne Shattock. Cambridge: Cambridge University Press, 2017.
Brake, Laurel, Bill Bell and David Finkelstein, eds. *Nineteenth Century Media and the Construction of Identities.* Basingstoke: Palgrave, 2000.
Brooke, John Hedley. *Science and Religion.* Cambridge: Cambridge University Press, 1991.
———. *Science and Religion: Some Historical Perspectives.* Cambridge: Cambridge University Press, 2014.
———. 'Darwin and Victorian Christianity'. In *The Cambridge Companion to Darwin*, edited by Jonathan Hodge and Gregory Radick. Cambridge: Cambridge University Press, 2003.
Brooke, John Hedley, and Geoffrey Cantor. *Reconstructing Nature: The Engagement of Science and Religion.* Edinburgh: T&T Clark, 1998.
Brose, Olive J. *Frederick Dennison Maurice: Rebellious Conformist.* Athens: Ohio University Press, 1971.
Brown, Alan Willard. *The Metaphysical Society: Victorian Minds in Crisis, 1869–1880.* New York: Columbia University Press, 1947.
Brown, Sue. 'Robert Browning and Julia Wedgwood: The Unpublished Correspondence', *Journal of Browning Studies*, 3 (December 2012), 29–52.
———. 'Julia Wedgwood on Robert Browning's "Italian Murder Thing"'. *Journal of Anglo-Italian Studies*, 13–14 (2014), 65–76.
———. 'Harriet Martineau and Julia Wedgwood: A Study in Disillusionment'. *The Martineau Society Newsletter*, 41 (February 2018), 20–29.
———. '"[Your novel] quite gives me a pain in the stomach": How Paternal Disapproval Ended Julia Wedgwood's Promising Career as a Novelist'. In *British Women's Writing from Brontë to Bloomsbury, 1840–1940*, 229–43, edited by Adrienne E. Gavin and Carolyn W. de la L. Oulton. Basingstoke: Palgrave Macmillan, 2018.
Browne, Janet. *Charles Darwin: Voyaging.* London: Pimlico, 1996.
———. *Charles Darwin: The Power of Place.* London: Pimlico, 2003.
———. 'Asa Gray and Charles Darwin: Corresponding Naturalists'. *Harvard Papers in Botany*, 15 (2).
Butler, Marilyn. *Maria Edgeworth: A Literary Biography.* Oxford: Clarendon Press, 1972.

Byrne, Georgina. *Modern Spiritualism and the Church of England, 1850–1939*. Woodbridge: Boydell, 2010.
Caine, Barbara. *Victorian Feminists*. Oxford: Oxford University Press, 1992.
———. *English Feminism, 1780–1980*. Oxford: Oxford University Press, 1997.
———. 'Feminism, Journalism and Public Debate'. In *Women and Literature in Britain, 1800–1900*, edited by Joanne Shattock. Cambridge: Cambridge University Press, 2001.
———. 'Feminist Biography and Feminist History'. *Women's History Review*, 3 (1994).
Cain, Elizabeth. 'Rachel Martineau and Her School', unpublished Cambridge BA thesis, 2010.
Campion, Val. *Pioneering Women: The Origins of Girton College in Hitchin*. Hitchin: Hitchin Historical Society, 2008.
Carpenter, Mary Wilson. *Health, Medicine, and Society in Victorian England*. Oxford: Praeger, 2010.
Chadwick, Owen. *The Victorian Church, 1860–1901*, 2 vols. London: Adam and Charles Black, 1966.
Chapple, John. *Elizabeth Gaskell: The Early Years*. Manchester: Manchester University Press, 1997.
Chapple, John, and Arthur Pollard. *The Letters of Mrs Gaskell*. Manchester: Manchester University Press, 1966.
Chapple, John, and Alan Shelston. *Further Letters of Mrs Gaskell*. Manchester: Manchester University Press, 2000.
Christ, Carol T. 'The Hero as Man of Letters: Masculinity and Victorian Nonfiction Prose'. In *Victorian Sages and Cultural Discourse*, edited by Thais E. Morgan. New Brunswick, NJ: Rutgers University Press, 1990.
Cobham, E. M. *Mary Everest Boole: A Memoir*. Ashington: C. W. Daniel, 1951.
Collini, Stefan. *Public Moralists: Political Thought and Intellectual Life in Britain, 1850–1930*. Oxford: Clarendon Press, 1991.
Collins, K. K., ed. *George Eliot: Interviews and Recollections*. Basingstoke: Palgrave Macmillan, 2010.
———. *Identifying the Remains: George Eliot's Death in the London Religious Press*. Victoria, BC: ELS Editions, 2006.
Colloms, Brenda. *Victorian Visionaries*. London: Constable, 1982.
Connor, Sharon. 'The Age of the Female Novelist: Single Women as Authors'. In *British Women's Writing from Bronte to Bloomsbury*, vol. 1, edited by Adrienne Gavin and Carolyn Oulton. Basingstoke: Palgrave Macmillan, 2018.
Culler, A. Dwight. *The Victorian Mirror of History*. London: Yale University Press, 1985.
Curle, Richard, ed. *Robert Browning and Julia Wedgwood: A Broken Friendship as Revealed in Their Letters*. London: John Murray and Jonathan Cape, 1937.
Cust, Mrs Henry. *Echoes of a Larger Life: A Selection from the Early Correspondence of Victoria Lady Welby*. London: Jonathan Cape, 1929.
———. *Other Dimensions: A Selection from the Later Correspondence of Victoria, Lady Welby*. London: Jonathan Cape, 1929.
Dabby, Benjamin. *Women as Public Moralists in Britain from the Bluestockings to Virginia Woolf*. Suffolk: Boydell Press, 2017.
Davenport-Hines, Richard. *Universal Man: The Seven Lives of John Maynard Keynes*. London: William Collins, 2015.
David, Deirdre. *Intellectual Women and Victorian Patriarchy Harriet Martineau, Elizabeth Barrett Browning, George Eliot*. London: Macmillan, 1987.
Davis, John R. *The Victorians and Germany*. Oxford: Peter Lang, 2007.
Davidoff, Leonore. *Family Fortunes: Men and Women of the English Middle Class, 1780–1850*. London: Routledge, 2002.
———. *Thicker than Water: Siblings and Their Relatives, 1780–1920*. Oxford: Oxford University Press, 2012.
Davis, Philip. *The Transferred Life of George Eliot: The Biography of a Novelist*. Oxford: Oxford University Press, 2017.
Den Otter, Sandra M. *British Idealism and Social Explanation: A Study in Late Victorian Thought*. Oxford: Clarendon Press, 1996.

Denisoff, Dennis, and Talia Schaffer, eds. *The Routledge Companion to Victorian Literature*. New York: Routledge, 2020.
Desmond, Adrian. *The Politics of Evolution: Morphology, Medicine and Reform in Radical London*. Chicago: University of Chicago Press, 1989.
Desmond, Adrian, and James R. Moore. *Darwin*. London: Michael Joseph, 1991.
DeVane, William. *A Browning Handbook*. New York: Appletone-Century-Crofts-Bell, 1955.
DeVane, William, and Kenneth Leslie Knickerbocker. *New Letters of Robert Browning*. London: John Murray, 1951.
Diedrick, James. *Mathilde Blind: Late-Victorian Culture and the Woman of Letters*. Charlottesville: University of Virginia Press, 2016.
Dixon, Thomas. *The Invention of Altruism: Making Moral Meanings in Victorian Britain*. Oxford: Oxford University Press for the British Academy, 2008.
Dolan, Brian. *Josiah Wedgwood: Entrepreneur to the Enlightenment*. London: Harper Collins, 2004.
Dowling, Linda. 'Victorian Oxford and the Science of Language'. *Publication of the Modern Languages Association*, 97 (2), 1982.
Duprée, A. Hunter. *Asa Gray, 1810–1888*. Cambridge, MA: Harvard University Press, 1959.
———. 'Christianity and the Scientific Community in the Age of Darwin'. In *God and Nature Historical Essays on the Encounter between Christianity and Science*, edited by David C. Lindsay and Ronald L. Numbers. London: University of California Press, 1986.
Durant, John. 'Darwinism and Divinity: A Century of Debate'. In *Darwinism and Divinity: Essays on Evolution and Religious Belief*, edited by John Durant. Oxford: Blackwell, 1985.
Dzelzainis, Ella, and Cora Kaplan, ed. *Harriet Martineau: Authorship, Society and Empire*. Manchester: Manchester University Press, 2010.
Easley, Alexis. *First-Person Anonymous: Women Writers and Victorian Print Media, 1830–70*. Aldershot: Ashgate, 2016.
———. 'Gendered Observations: Harriet Martineau and the Woman Question'. In *Victorian Women Writers and the Woman Question*, edited by Nicola Diane Thompson. Cambridge: Cambridge University Press, 1999.
———. 'Authorship, Gender and Power in Victorian Culture: Harriet Martineau and the Periodical Press'. In *Nineteenth Century Media and the Construction of Identities*, edited by Laurel Brake, Bill Bell and David Finkelstein. Basingstoke: Palgrave, 2000.
Erskine, Fiona. 'The Origin of Species and the Science of Female Inferiority'. In *Charles Darwin's The Origin of Species: New Interdisciplinary Essays*, edited by David Amigoni and Jeff Wallace. Manchester: Manchester University Press, 1990.
Esmail, Jennifer. *Reading Victorian Deafness: Signs and Sounds in Victorian Literature and Culture*. Athens: Ohio University Press, 2013.
Evans, Samantha, ed. *Darwin and Women: A Selection of Letters*. Cambridge: Cambridge University Press, 2017.
Fiddes, Edward. *Chapters in the History of Owens College and of Manchester University, 1851–1914*. Manchester: Manchester University Press, 1937.
Finlayson, Iain. *Browning: A Private Life*. London: Harper and Collins, 2004.
Fiske, Shanyn. *Heretical Hellenism: Women Writers, Ancient Greece, and the Victorian Popular Imagination*. Athens: Ohio University Press, 2008.
Forster, E. M. *Marianne Thornton, 1797–1887*. London: Edward Arnold, 1956.
———. *The Journals and Diaries of E. M. Forster*, 3 vols, edited by Philip Gardner. London: Pickering & Chatto, 2011.
Fraser, Hilary. 'Periodicals and Reviewing'. In *The Cambridge History of Victorian Literature*, edited by Kate Flint. Cambridge: Cambridge University Press, 2012.
Fraser, Hilary, Stephanie Green and Judith Johnston. *Gender and the Victorian Periodical*. Cambridge: Cambridge University Press, 2003.
French, Richard. *Antivivisection and Medical Science in Victorian Society*. London: Princeton University Press, 1975.

Gamble, Robert C. G. *Mrs Gaskell's Personal Pantheon: Illuminating Mrs. Gaskell's Inner Circle.* Brighton: Edward Everett Root, 2020.
Gates, Barbara T. *Kindred Nature: Victorian and Edwardian Women Embrace the Living World.* Chicago: Chicago University Press, 1998.
Glynn, Jenifer. *The Pioneering Garretts: Breaking the Barriers for Women.* London: Hambledon Continuum, 2008.
Gouldstone, Timothy Maxwell. *The Rise and Decline of Anglican Idealism in the Nineteenth Century.* Basingstoke: Palgrave Macmillan, 2005.
Gray, F. Elizabeth, ed. *Women in Journalism at the Fin de Siècle: Making a Name for Herself.* Basingstoke: Palgrave Macmillan, 2012.
Gregory, Frederick. 'The Impact of Darwinism Evolution and Protestant Theology in the Nineteenth Century'. In *God and Nature Historical Essays on Encounters between Christianity and Science*, edited by David C. Lindberg and Ronald Numbers. London: California University Press, 1986.
Griffin, Ben. *The Politics of Gender in Victorian Britain.* Cambridge: Cambridge University Press, 2012.
Grosskurth, Phyllis. *Havelock Ellis: A Biography.* London: Quartet, 1981.
Guerin, Winifred. *Anne Thackeray Ritchie: A Biography.* Oxford: Oxford University Press, 1983.
Hall, Catherine. *White, Male and Middle Class Explorations in Feminism and History.* Cambridge: Polity Press, 1992.
Height, Gordon S. *George Eliot: A Biography.* Oxford: Clarendon Press, 1968.
Hall, Vance M. D. 'The Contribution of the Physiologist William Benjamin Carpenter (1813–1885) to the Development of the Principles of the Correlation of Forces and the Conservation of Energy'. *Medical History*, 23, 1979, 129–55.
Hamilton, Susan. *Frances Power Cobbe and Victorian Feminism.* Basingstoke: Palgrave Macmillan, 2006.
———. '"Her usual daring style": Feminist New Journalism, Pioneering Women, and Traces of Frances Power Cobbe'. In *Women in Journalism at the Fin de Siècle: Making a Name for Herself*, edited by F. Elizabeth Gray. Basingstoke: Palgrave Macmillan, 2012.
Hands, Timothy. *A George Eliot Chronology.* London: Macmillan, 1989.
Hardwick, Lorna. 'Women, Translators and Empowerment'. In *Women, Scholarship and Criticism: Gender and Knowledge, c.1790–1910*, edited by Joan Bellamy, Anne Lawrence and Gill Perry. Manchester: Manchester University Press, 2000.
Harris, José. *Private Lives, Public Spirit: A Social History of Britain, 1870–1914.* Oxford: Oxford University Press, 1993.
———. 'Frances Julia Wedgwood'. In *New Oxford Dictionary of National Biography*, edited by H. C. G. Matthew and Brian Harrison. Oxford: Oxford University Press, 2004.
Harris, Margaret, and Judith Johnston, eds. *The Journals of George Eliot.* Cambridge: Cambridge University Press, 1998.
Harrison, Anthony H. 'Christina Rossetti and the Sage Discourse of Feminist High Anglicanism'. In *Victorian Sages and Cultural Discourse*, edited by Thais E. Morgan. London: Rutgers University Press, 1990.
Harrison, Brian. *Separate Spheres: The Opposition to Women's Suffrage in Britain.* London: Croom Helm, 1978.
Harrison, J. F. C. *A History of the Working Men's College, 1854–1954.* London: Routledge & Kegan Paul, 1954.
Hart, Trevor A. *Thomas Erskine.* Edinburgh: Saint Andrew Press, 1993.
Hayter, Alethia. *Mrs Browning: A Poet's Work and Its Setting.* London: Faber and Faber, 1962.
Herstein, Sheila R. *A Mid-Victorian Feminist, Barbara Leigh Smith Bodichon.* London: Yale University Press, 1985.
Hesketh, Ian. *Victorian Jesus: J. R. Seeley, Religion, and the Cultural Significance of Anonymity.* Toronto: University of Toronto Press, 2017.
Heyck, T. W. *The Transformation of Intellectual Life in Victorian England.* London: Croom Helm, 1982.
Heimann, P. M. '*The Unseen Universe*: Physics and the Philosophy of Nature in Victorian Britain'. *British Journal for the History of Science*, vi (June 1972), 73–79.

Herbert, Sandra. *Charles Darwin, Geologist*. Ithaca: Cornell University Press, 2005.
Hilton, Boyd. *The Age of Atonement: The Influence of Evangelicanism on Social and Economic Thought, 1795–1865*. Oxford: Clarendon Press, 1988.
Hirsch, Pam. *Barbara Leigh Smith Bodichon, 1827–1891: Feminist, Artist and Rebel*. London: Chatto and Windus, 1998.
Hogben, John. *Richard Holt Hutton of 'The Spectator': A Monograph*. Edinburgh: Oliver & Boyd, 1899.
Holcombe, Lee. 'Victorian Wives and Property Reform of the Married Women's Property Law, 1857–1882'. In *A Widening Sphere: Changing Roles of Victorian Women*, edited by Martha Vicinus. London: Methuen, 1980.
Hollis, Patricia. *Ladies Elect: Women in English Local Government, 1865–1914*. Oxford: Clarendon Press, 1987.
———, ed. *Women in Public, 1850–1900 Documents of the Victorian Women's Movement*. London: George Allen & Unwin, 1979.
Holmes, Martha Stoddart. *Fictions of Affliction: Physical Disability on Victorian Culture*. Ann Arbor: University of Michigan Press, 2004.
Holmstrom, John, and Laurence Lerner. *George Eliot and Her Readers: A Selection of Cotemporary Reviews*. London: Bodley Head, 1966.
Horrocks, Don. *Laws of the Spiritual Order: Innovation and Reconstruction in the Soteriology of Thomas Erskine of Linlathen*. Carlisle: Paternoster Press, 2004.
Hudson, Derek. *Arthur Munby Man of Two Worlds: The Life and Diaries of Arthur J. Munby, 1828–1910*. London: John Murray, 1972.
Hudson, Gertrude Reese, ed. *Browning to His American Friends: Letters between the Brownings, the Storys and James Russell Lowell, 1841–1890*. London: Bowes & Bowes, 1965.
Hughes, Kathryn. *George Eliot: The Last Victorian*. London: Fourth Estate, 1998.
Hughes, Linda K. *Graham R.: Rosamund Marriott Watson, Woman of Letters*. Athens: Ohio University Press, 2005.
Hunt, Tristram. *The Radical Potter: Josiah Wedgwood and the Transformation of Britain*. London: Allen Lane, 2021.
Hurst, Isobel. *Victorian Women Writers and the Classics: The Feminine of Homer*. Oxford: Oxford University Press, 2006.
———. 'Ancient and Modern Women in the *Woman's World*', *Victorian Studies*, 52 (1), 42–51.
[Huxley, Leonard]. *The House of Smith Elder*. London: Privately printed, 1923.
Jack, Ian. *Browning's Major Poetry*. Oxford: Clarendon Press, 1993.
Jalland, Pat. *Death in the Victorian Family*. Oxford: Oxford University Press, 1996.
———. *Women, Marriage and Politics, 1860–1914*. Oxford: Clarendon Press, 1986.
James, Frank A. L. 'An Open Clash between Science and the Church? Wilberforce, Huxley and Hooker on Darwin at the British Association, Oxford 1860'. In *Science and Beliefs from Natural Philosophy to Natural Science, 1700–1900*, edited by David M. Knight and Matthew Eddy. Aldershot: Ashgate, 2005.
Jann, Rosemary. 'Revising the Descent of Woman: Eliza Burt Gamble'. In *Natural Eloquence: Women Reinscribe Science*, edited by Barbara Gates and Ann B. Shteir. London: Wisconsin University Press, 1997.
Jay, Elisabeth. *Mrs Oliphant: 'A Fiction to Herself', A Literary Life*. Oxford: Clarendon Press, 1995.
———. 'Women Writers and Religion: A Self Worth Saving, a Duty Worth Doing, and a Voice Worth Raising'. In *Women and Literature in Britain, 1800–1900*, edited by Joanne Shattock. Cambridge: Cambridge University Press, 2001.
Jenkyns, Richard. *The Victorians and Ancient Greece*. Oxford: Basil Blackwell, 1980.
Johnston, Judith, and Hilary Fraser. 'The Professionalization of Women's Writings: Extending the Canon'. In *Women and Literature in Britain, 1800–1900*, edited by Joanne Shattock. Cambridge: Cambridge University Press, 2001.
Karlin, Daniel. *Browning's Hatreds*. Oxford: Clarendon Press, 1993.

———. *The Courtship of Robert Browning and Elizabeth Barrett*. Oxford: Oxford University Press, 1985.
———, ed. *Robert Browning and Elizabeth Barrett: The Courtship Correspondence, 1845–1846*. Oxford: Clarendon Press, 1989.
———. 'The Brownings' Marriage Contemporary Representations'. *Studies in Browning and His Circle*, 21 (1997), 33–52.
Kaye, Elaine. *A History of Queen's College, London, 1848–1972*. London: Chatto & Windus, 1972.
Kenny, Anthony. *Arthur Hugh Clough: A Poet's Life*. London: Continuum, 2005.
Kent, Susan Kingsley. *Sex and Suffrage in Britain, 1860–1914*. London: Princeton University Press, 1987.
Keynes, Randall. *Annie's Box: Charles Darwin, His Daughter and Human Evolution*. London: Fourth Estate, 2001.
Knight, Mark, and Emma Mason. *Nineteenth-Century Religion and Literature: An Introduction*. Oxford: Oxford University Press, 2006.
Koven, Seth. *Slumming: Sexual and Social Politics in Victorian London*. Princeton, NJ: Princeton University Press, 2004.
Kragh, Helge S. *Entropic Creation: Religious Contexts of Thermodynamics and Cosmology*. Aldershot: Ashgate, 2008.
Lacey, Candida Ann, ed. *Barbara Leigh Smith and the Langham Place Group*. London: Routledge and Kegan Paul, 1986.
Levine, Philippa. *Feminist Lives in Victorian England Private Roles and Public Commitment*. Oxford: Basil Blackwell, 1990.
Lightman, Bernard. *The Origins of Agnosticism: Victorian Unbelief and the Limits of Knowledge*. Baltimore: Johns Hopkins University Press, 1987.
———. *Evolutionary Naturalism in Victorian Britain: The 'Darwinians' and Their Critics*. Farnham: Ashgate, 2009.
———. *Victorian Popularizers of Science*. Chicago: Chicago University Press, 2010.
———, ed. *Victorian Science in Context*. Chicago: Chicago University Press, 1997.
———. 'Creating a New Space for Debate: The Monthlies, Science and Religion'. In *Rethinking History, Science, and Religion*, edited by B. Lightman. Pittsburgh: Pittsburgh University Press, 2019.
———. 'The Theology of Victorian Scientific Naturalism'. In *Science Without God? Rethinking the History of Scientific Naturalism*, edited by Peter Harrison and Jon Roberts. Oxford: Oxford University Press, 2019.
Lindberg, David C., and Ronald L. Numbers, eds. *God and Nature: Historical Essays on the Encounter between Christianity and Science*. London: California University Press, 1986.
Litzinger, Boyd, and Donald Smalley, eds. *Robert Browning: The Critical Heritage*. London: Routledge, 1968.
Logan, Deborah Ann, ed. *The Collected Letters of Harriet Martineau*, 5 vols. London: Pickering & Chatto, 2007.
———. 'History Writing'. In *The Cambridge Companion to Victorian Women's Writing*, edited by Linda H. Peterson. Cambridge: Cambridge University Press, 2015.
Loy, James D., and Kent M. *Emma Darwin: A Victorian Life*. Gainesville: Florida University Press, 2010.
MacHale, Desmond. *George Boole: His life and Work*. Dun Laoghaire: Boole, 1985.
Mackinnon, Alison. 'Educated Doubt: Women, Religion and the Challenge of Higher Education c 1870–1920'. *Women's History Review*, 7 (2), 1988.
McClain, Frank, Richard Norris and John Owens. *F. D. Maurice: A Study*. Oxford: Cowley Publications, 1982.
Manier, Edward. *The Young Darwin and His Cultural Circle*. Dordrecht: D. Reidel, 1978.
Marshall, Gail. 'Adam Bede and "the Green Trash of the Railway Stall": George Eliot and the Lady Novelists of 1859'. In *British Women's Writing from Bronte to Bloomsbury*, vol. 1, edited by Adrienne E. Gavin and Carolyn Oulton. Basingstoke: Palgrave Macmillan, 2018.
Marshall, Catherine, Bernard Lightman and Richard England, eds. *The Papers of the Metaphysical Society, 1869–1880*. Oxford: Oxford University Press, 2015.

Martens, Britta. '"Hardly Shall I Tell My Joys and Sorrows": Robert Browning's Engagement with Elizabeth Barrett Browning's Poetics'. *Victorian Poetry*, 43 (1), Spring 2005.

Masterman, Charles F. G. *Frederick Denison Maurice*. London: A. R. Mowbray, 1907.

Mathers, Helen. 'Evangelicanism and Feminism: Josephine Butler 1828–1906'. In *Women, Religion and Feminism in Britain, 1750–1900*, edited by Sue Morgan. Basingstoke: Palgrave Macmillan, 2002.

Mayr, Ernst. *The Growth of Biological Thought Diversity, Evolution and Inheritance*. Cambridge, MA. Harvard University Press, 1982.

Marcus, Sharon. *Between Women: Friendship, Desire, and Marriage in Victorian England*. London: Princeton University Press, 2007.

McAleer, Edward C., ed. *Dearest Isa: Robert Browning's Letters to Isabella Blagden*. Austin: Texas University Press, 1951.

Melnyck, Julia, ed. *Women's Theology in Nineteenth Century Britain: Transfiguring the Faith of Their Fathers*. London: Garland, 1998.

Meredith, Michael, ed. *More than friend: The Letters of Robert Browning to Katherine de Kay Bronson*. Waco, TX: Armstrong Browning Library of Baylor University, 1985.

Miller, Betty. *Robert Browning: A Portrait*. London: John Murray, 1952.

Mitchell, Sally. *Frances Power Cobbe: Victorian, Feminist, Journalist, Reformer*. Charlottesville: Virginia University Press, 2004.

Moore, James. *The Post-Darwinian Controversies: A Study of the Protestant Struggle to Come to Terms with Darwin in Great Britain and America, 1870–1900*. Cambridge: Cambridge University Press, 1979.

———. 'Charles Darwin Lies in Westminster Abbey'. In *Charles Darwin: A Commemoration, 1882–1982*, edited by R. J. Berry. London: Published for the Linnean Society of London by Academic Press, 1982.

———. '"Of love and death": Why Darwin Gave Up Christianity'. In *History, Humanity and Evolution Essays for John C. Greene*, edited by James R. Moore. Cambridge: Cambridge University Press, 1989.

Morgan, Sue, ed. *Women, Religion and Feminism in Britain, 1750–1900*. Basingstoke: Palgrave Macmillan, 2002.

Morris, Ivan Rhys. 'Correlation and Control: William Robert Grove and the Construction of a New Philosophy of Scientific Reform'. *Studies in the History and Philosophy of Science*, 22 (4), December 1991, 589–621.

Morgan, Thais E., ed. *Victorian Sages and Cultural Discourse*. London: Rutgers University Press, 1990.

Murphy, Ann B., and Deidre Raftery, eds. *Emily Davies Collected Letters, 1861–1875*. Charlottesville: Virginia University Press, 2004.

Nestor, Pauline. *Female Friendships and Communities: Charlotte Bronte, George Eliot, Elizabeth Gaskell*. Oxford: Clarendon Press, 1985.

Neville-Sington, Pamela. *Robert Browning: Life after a Death*. London: Weidenfeld and Nicolson, 2004.

Newell, J. P. 'The Other Christian Socialist Alexander John Scott'. *The Heythrop Journal*, 24 (1983).

O'Leary, Patrick. *Sir James Mackintosh: The Whig Cicero*. Aberdeen: Aberdeen University Press, 1989.

Oliphant, Margaret. *The Autobiography of Margaret Oliphant: The Complete Text*, edited with an introduction by Elizabeth Jay. Oxford: Oxford University Press, 1990.

Oppenheim, Janet. *Shattered Nerves Doctors, Patients, and Depression in Victorian England*. Oxford: Oxford University Press, 1991.

———. *The Other World: Spiritualism and Psychical Research in England, 1850–1914*. Cambridge: Cambridge University Press, 1985.

Palmer, Beth. 'Assuming the Role of Editor'. In *The Cambridge Companion to Victorian Women's Writing*, edited by Linda H. Peterson. Cambridge: Cambridge University Press, 2015.

Parsons, Gerald. *Religion in Victorian Britain*, vol. 4, *Interpretations*. Manchester: Manchester University Press, 1988.

Peterson, Linda H. *Becoming a Woman of Letters: Myths of Authorship and Facts of the Victorian Market*. Princeton, NJ: Princeton University Press, 2009.

———, ed. *The Cambridge Companion to Victorian Women's Writing*. Cambridge: Cambridge University Press, 2015.
———. 'Harriet Martineau: Masculine Discourse, Female Sage'. In *Victorian Sages and Cultural Discourse*, edited by Thais E. Morgan. London: Rutgers University Press, 1990.
———. 'Harriet Martineau, Woman of Letters'. In *Harriet Martineau Authorship, Society and Empire*, edited by Ella Dzelzainis and Cora Kaplan. Manchester: Manchester University Press, 2010.
———. 'Women Writers and Self-Writing'. In *Women and Literature in Britain, 1800–1900*, edited by Joanne Shattock. Cambridge: Cambridge University Press, 2001.
Petrilli, Susan. 'Three Women in Semiotics: Welby, Boole, Langer'. *Semiotica*, 2010, 182 (1/4).
Purvis, June. *Hard Lessons: The Lives and Education of Working-Class Women in Nineteenth-Century England*. Cambridge: Polity Press, 1989.
Raddick, Gregory. *The Simian Tongue: The Long Debate about Animal Language*. Chicago: Chicago University Press, 2007.
Raia, Courtenay. *The New Prometheans Faith, Science, and the Supernatural Mind in the Victorian Fin de Siècle*. Chicago: University of Chicago Press, 2019.
Ramsay, A. M. *F. D. Maurice and the Conflicts of Modern Theology*. Cambridge: Cambridge University Press, 1951.
Reardon, Bernard M. G. *From Coleridge to Gore: A Century of Religious Thought in Britain*. London: Longman, 1971.
Reilly, Robert. *Josiah Wedgwood, 1730–1795*. London: Macmillan, 1992.
Rendall, Jane. *The Origins of Modern Feminism: Women in Britain, France and the United States, 1780–1860*. London: Macmillan, 1985.
———. 'John Stuart Mill, Liberal Politics, and the Movements for Women's Suffrage 1865–1873'. In *Women, Privilege, and Power in British Politics, 1750 to the Present*, edited by Amanda Vickery. Stanford, CA: Stanford University Press, 2001.
Richards, Robert J. *The Romantic Conception of Life: Science and Philosophy in the Age of Goethe*. Chicago: Chicago University Press, 2002.
Richards, Evelleen. *Darwin and the Making of Sexual Selection*. Chicago: University of Chicago Press, 2017.
———. 'Redrawing the Boundaries: Darwinian Science and Victorian Women Intellectuals'. In *Victorian Science in Context*, edited by Bernard Lightman. Chicago: Chicago University Press, 1997.
Rioux, Annie Boyd. *Constance Fenimore Woolson: Portrait of a Lady Novelist*. New York: W.W. Norton, 2016.
Robbins, William. *The Newman Brothers: An Essay in Comparative Intellectual Biography*. London: Heinemann, 1966.
Robson, Ann. 'A Bird's Eye View of Gladstone'. In *The Gladstonian Turn of Mind*, edited by Bruce Kinzer. Toronto: Toronto University Press, 1985.
Rogerson, John. *The Bible and Criticism in Victorian Britain: Profiles of F. D. Maurice and William Robertson Smith*. Sheffield: Sheffield Academic Press, 1995.
———. 'What Difference Did Darwin Make? The Interpretation of Genesis in the Nineteenth Century'. In *Reading Genesis after Darwin*, edited by Stephen C. Barton and David Wilkinson. Oxford: Oxford University Press, 2007.
Rover, Constance. *Women's Suffrage and Party Politics in Britain, 1866–1914*. London: Routledge & Kegan Paul, 1967.
Rowell, Geoffrey. *Hell and the Victorians: A Study of the Nineteenth Century Theological Controversies Concerning Eternal Punishment and the Future Life*. Oxford: Clarendon Press, 1974.
Sampson, Fiona. *Two Way Mirror: The Life of Elizabeth Barrett Browning*. London: Profile Books, 2021.
Sanders, Valerie. *Eve's Renegades: Victorian Anti-Feminist Women Novelists*. Basingstoke: Macmillan, 1994.
———. *The Brother-Sister Culture in Nineteenth Century Literature: From Austen to Woolf*. Basingstoke: Palgrave, 2002.
———. *The Private Lives of Victorian Women: Autobiography in Nineteenth-Century England*. New York: St Martin's Press, 1989.

———. *The Tragi-Comedy of Victorian Fatherhood*. Cambridge: Cambridge University Press, 2009.
———, ed. *Records of Girlhood: An Anthology of Nineteenth-Century Women's Childhoods*. Aldershot: Ashgate, 2000.
———, ed. *Harriet Martineau: Selected Letters*. Oxford: Clarendon Press, 1990.
Sanders, Valerie, and Gaby Weiner, eds. *Harriet Martineau and the Birth of Disciplines: Nineteenth-Century Intellectual Powerhouse*. London: Routledge, 2016.
Schaffer, Talia. *The Forgotten Female Aesthetes: Literary Culture in Late-Victorian England*. Charleston: Virginia University Press, 2000.
Secord, James A. *Victorian Sensation: The Extraordinary Publication, Reception, and Secret Authorship of Vestiges of the Natural History of Creation*. London: Chicago University Press, 2003.
———, ed. *Charles Darwin Evolutionary Writings*. Oxford: Oxford University Press, 2008.
Sell, Alan P. F. *Philosophical Idealism and Christian Belief*. Cardiff: University of Wales Press, 1995.
Shattock, Joanne. *The Oxford Guide to British Women Writers*. Oxford: Oxford University Press, 1993.
———, ed. *Journalism and the Periodical Press in Nineteenth-Century Britain*. Cambridge: Cambridge University Press, 2017.
———. *Women and Literature in Britain, 1800–1900*. Cambridge: Cambridge University Press, 2001.
———. 'Becoming a Professional Writer'. In *The Cambridge Companion to Victorian Women's Writing*, edited by Linda H. Peterson. Cambridge: Cambridge University Press, 2015.
———. 'Work for Women: Margaret Oliphant's Journalism'. In *Nineteenth Century Media and the Construction of Identities*, edited by Laurel Brake, Bill Bell and David Finkelstein. Basingstoke: Palgrave, 2000.
Showalter, Elaine. *A Literature of Their Own: British Women Writers from Bronte to Lessing*. London: Virago, 1984.
Smith, Barbara, ed. *Truth, Liberty, Religion: Essays Celebrating Two Hundred Years of Manchester College*. Oxford: Manchester College, 1986.
Smith, Crosbie. *The Science of Energy: A Cultural History of Energy Physics in Victorian Britain*. Chicago: Chicago University Press, 1998.
Spender, Dale, ed. *Feminist Theorists: Three Centuries of Women's Intellectual Traditions*. London: Women's Press, 1983.
Stabler, Jane. *The Artistry of Exile: Romantic and Victorian Writers in Italy*. Oxford: Oxford University Press, 2013.
Stephen, Barbara. *Emily Davies and Girton College*. London: Constable, 1927.
Strachey, Ray. *The Cause: A Short History of the Women's Movement in Great Britain*. London: Virago, 1978 (reprint).
Styler, Rebecca. *Literary Theology by Women Writers of the Nineteenth Century*. Farnham: Ashgate, 2010.
Sullivan, Alvin, ed. *British Literary Magazines: The Victorian and Edwardian Age, 1837–1913*. Westport, CT: Greenwood, 1984.
Summers, Ann. *Female Lives, Moral States*. Newbury, Berks: Threshold Press, 2000.
Surtees, Virginia. *Jane Welsh Carlyle*. Salisbury: Michael Russell, 1986.
———. *The Ludovisi Goddess: The Life of Louisa Lady Ashburton*. Salisbury: Michael Russell, 1986.
Sutherland, Gillian. *Faith, Duty and the Power of Mind: The Cloughs and Their Circle, 1820–1960*. Cambridge: Cambridge University Press, 2006.
———. *In Search of the New Woman: Middle-Class Women and Work in Britain, 1870–1914*. Cambridge: Cambridge University Press, 2015.
Symonds, Richard. *Inside the Citadel: Men and the Emancipation of Women, 1850–1920*. Basingstoke: Macmillan, 1999.
Taylor, David. *'Under the Cedar': The Lushingtons of Pyports: A Victorian Family in Cobham – and Elsewhere in Surrey*. Guildford: Grosvenor House, 2015.
Taylor, Marion Ann, and Heather E. Weir. *Let Her Speak for Herself: Nineteenth Century Women Writing on Women in Genesis*. Waco, TX: Baylor University Press, 2006.

Tener, Robert H. 'The Writings of Richard Holt Hutton: A Check-List of Identifications'. *Victorian Periodicals Newsletter*, 17 September 1972.
Tener, Robert H., and Malcolm Woodfield, eds. *A Victorian Spectator: Uncollected Writings of R. H. Hutton*. Bristol: Bristol Press, 1989.
Thompson, Ann, and Sasha Roberts, eds. *Women Reading Shakespeare, 1660–1900: An Anthology of Criticism*. Manchester: Manchester University Press, 1997.
Thompson, Nicola Diane. *Victorian Women Writers and the Woman Question*. Cambridge: Cambridge University Press, 1999.
Trevor, Meriel. *Newman's Journey*. London: Fontana, 1974.
Tuchman, Gaye, with Nina E. Fortin. *Edging Women Out: Victorian Novelists, Publishers, and Social Change*. London: Routledge, 1989.
Tuke, Margaret J. *A History of Bedford College for Women, 1849–1937*. London: Oxford University Press, 1939.
Tullberg, Rita McWilliams. *Women at Cambridge*. Cambridge: Cambridge University Press, 1998.
Turner, Frank M. *Between Science and Religion: The Reaction to Scientific Naturalism in Late Victorian England*. New Haven, CT: Yale University Press, 1974.
———. *Contesting Cultural Authority: Essays in Victorian Intellectual Life*. Cambridge: Cambridge University Press, 1993.
———. 'The Late Victorian Conflict of Science and Religion as an Event in Nineteenth Century Intellectual and Cultural History'. In *Science and Religion: New Historical Perspectives*, edited by Thomas Dixon, Geoffrey Cantor and Stephen Pumfey. Cambridge: Cambridge University Press, 2010.
Uglow, Jenny. *Elizabeth Gaskell: A Habit of Stories*. London: Faber and Faber, 1993.
———. *George Eliot*. London: Virago, 2008 (revised edition).
———. *The Lunar Men*. London: Faber and Faber, 2002.
———. 'Josephine Butler: From Sympathy to Theory'. In *Feminist Theorists: Three Centuries of Women's Intellectual Traditions*, edited by Dale Spender. London: Women's Press, 1983.
———. 'Manuscript Moments'. In *Lives for Sale: Biographer's Tales*, edited by Mark Bostridge. London: Continuum, 2004.
Valente, K. G. '"Giving Wings to Logic": Mary Everest Boole's Propagation and Fulfilment of a Legacy'. *British Journal for the History of Science*, March 2010.
Van Remoortel, Marianne. *Women, Work and the Victorian Periodical: Living by the Press*. London: Palgrave Macmillan, 2015.
Vanarsdel, Rosemary T. '*Macmillan's Magazine* and the Fair Sex: 1859–1874' (Part One). *Victorian Periodicals Review*, 33 (4), Winter 2000.
Vance, Norman. *The Victorians and Ancient Rome*. Oxford: Blackwell, 1997.
Vance, Norman, and Jennifer Wallace, eds. *The Oxford History of Classical Reception in English Literature, 4 (1790–1880)*. Oxford: Oxford University Press, 2015.
Vaughan Williams, Ursula. *R.V.W. A Biography of Ralph Vaughan Williams*. Oxford: Oxford University Press, 1964.
Vicinus, Martha. *A Widening Sphere: Changing Roles of Victorian Women*. Bloomington: Indiana University Press, 1987.
———. *Independent Women: Work and Community for Single Women, 1850–1920*. London: Virago, 1985.
———. *Intimate Friends: Women Who Loved Women, 1778–1928*. Chicago: Chicago University Press, 2004.
———, ed. *Suffer and Be Still: Women in the Victorian Age*. Bloomington: Indiana University Press, 1992.
———. '"The Gift of Love": Nineteenth Century Religion and Lesbian Passion'. In *Women, Religion and Feminism in Britain, 1750–1900*, edited by Sue Morgan. Basingstoke: Palgrave Macmillan, 2002.

Vickery, Amanda, ed. *Women, Privilege, and Power: British Politics 1750 to the Present*. Stanford, CA: Stanford University Press, 2001.
Vidler, Alec R. *F. D. Maurice and Company: Nineteenth Century Studies*. London: SCM Press, 1966.
Vincent, Andrew, and Reginald Plant. *Philosophy, Politics and Citizenship: The Life and Thought of the British Idealists*. Oxford: Basil Blackwell, 1984.
Von Arx, Jeffrey Paul. *Progress and Pessimism: Religion, Politics, and History in Late Nineteenth Century Britain*. Cambridge, MA: Harvard University Press, 1985.
Waldegrave, Katie. *The Poets' Daughters: Dora Wordsworth and Sara Coleridge*. London: Hutchison, 2013.
Wallace, Jennifer. '"Greek under the Trees": Classical Reception and Gender'. In *The Oxford History of Classical Reception in English Literature, vol. 4, 1790–1880*, edited by Norman Vance and Jennifer Wallace. Oxford: Oxford University Press, 2015.
Waller, Philip. *Writers, Readers and Reputations*. Oxford: Oxford University Press, 2006.
Waller, Ralph. 'James Martineau: The Development of His Religious Thought'. In *Truth, Liberty, Religion Essays Celebrating Two Hundred Years of Manchester College*, edited by Barbara Smith. Oxford: Manchester College, 1986.
Ward, Maisie. *Robert Browning and His World*, 2 vols. London: Cassell, 1968 and 1969.
Watts, Ruth. *Gender, Power and the Unitarians in England, 1760–1860*. London: Longman, 1998.
———. 'Rational Religion and Feminism: The Challenge of Unitarianism in the Nineteenth Century'. In *Women, Religion and Feminism, 1750–1900*, edited by Sue Morgan. Basingstoke: Palgrave Macmillan, 2002.
Webb, Clement C. J. *A Study of Religious Thought in England from 1850*. Oxford: Clarendon, 1933.
Webb, R. K. *Harriet Martineau: A Radical Victorian*. London: Heinemann, 1960.
———. 'The Unitarian Background'. In *Truth, Liberty, Religion: Essays Celebrating Two Hundred Years of Manchester College*, edited by Barbara Smith. Oxford: Manchester College, 1986.
Wedgwood, Barbara, and Hensleigh. *The Wedgwood Circle, 1730–1897: Four Generations of a Family and Their Friends*. London: Studio Vista, 1980.
Wedgwood, Barbara. 'Julia Wedgwood', unpublished PhD thesis, University of London, 1983.
Wedgwood, C. V. 'Out on a Limb'. *Listener*, LVI (1434), 20 September 1956, 416–18.
Wedgwood, Josiah C. *Memoirs of a Fighting Life*. London: Hutchinson, 1940.
Weiner, Gaby. 'Harriet Martineau: A Reassessment'. In *Feminist Theorists: Three Centuries of Women's Intellectual Traditions*, edited by Dale Spender. London: Women's Press, 1983.
Welch, Claude. *Protestant Thought in the Nineteenth Century, vol. 2, 1870–1914*. London: Yale University Press, 1985.
Wheal, Robert, ed. *Octavia Hill's Letters to Co-Workers, 1872–1911: Together with an Account of the Walmer Street Industrial Experiment*. London: Kyrle, 2005.
White, Cynthia L. *Women's Magazines, 1693–1968*. London: Michael Joseph, 1968.
Wilkes, Joanna. 'Reviewing'. In *The Cambridge Companion to Victorian Women's Writing*, edited by Linda H. Peterson. Cambridge: Cambridge University Press, 2015.
Willey, Basil. *More Nineteenth Century Studies: A Group of Honest Doubters*. London: Chatto & Windus, 1956.
———. *Nineteenth Century Studies: Coleridge to Matthew Arnold*. Cambridge: Cambridge University Press, 1949.
Wiltshire, Irene, ed. *Letters of Mrs Gaskell's Daughters, 1856–1914*. Penrith: Humanities Ebooks, 2012.
Wise, Thomas J., and T. L. Hood, eds. *Letters of Robert Browning*, collected by Thomas J. Wise; edited with an introduction and notes by Thurman L. Hood. London: Kennikat, 1973.
Witheridge, John. *The Excellent Dr Stanley: The Life of Dean Stanley of Westminster*. London: Michael Russell, 2013.
Woolford, John. *Browning the Revisionary*. Basingstoke: Macmillan, 1988.
———. 'Error and Erasure in Browning's *The Ring and the Book*'. *The Wordsworth Circle*, 2 & 3, Spring/Summer, 2016.

Woolford, John, and Daniel Karlin. *Robert Browning*. London: Longman, 1996.
Worth, George J. *Macmillan's Magazine, 1859–1907: 'No Flippancy or Abuse Allowed'*. Aldershot: Ashgate, 2003.
Young, David. *F. D. Maurice and Unitarianism*. Oxford: Clarendon Press, 1992.
Young, G. M. *Victorian England: Portrait of an Age*. London: Oxford University Press, 1953.
Zorn, Christa. *Vernon Lee: Aesthetics, History, and the Victorian Female Intellectual*. Athens: Ohio University Press, 2003.

INDEX

Abinger Hall, home of Effie and Thomas Farrer 213, 220, 224, 261, 283
Academy, The 268
Agnosticism 165, 184, 200, 236–37, 239, 271
Alderson, Lady 61
Alford, Dr 182
Allen, Fanny, J W's great aunt 12, 19, 52, 57, 74, 196–97, 316n56
Amberley, Lady 201
Anderson, Elizabeth Garrett 3, 81, 128, 173, 183, 192
    Campaign for election to London Education Board 1870 181–82
anti-vivisection 272, 280–82
Argyll, Duke of 209, 229–31, 334n19
Arnold, Matthew 49, 54, 268
Arnold, Thomas 18, 27
Ashburton, Lady 150
Athenaeum, The 35, 66, 70–71, 163, 268
Athenaeum Club, The 99, 105, 109, 219
Austen, Annie 187
Austen, Jane 66–67, 72
Aveling, Edward 239
Aylward, Mamie 2, 292

Bachofen, Johann Jacob 263
Backhouse, Juliet 144
Bacon, Francis 83, 86, 142, 195
Barbauld, Anna 17
Batten, Caroline, mother of Emily Gurney 126–28
Beale, Dorothea 28, 38, 44
Bedford College ('The College for Women in Bedford Square') 21, 22, 28, 30, 35, 38, 44, 52, 55, 90, 173, 183, 201, 213, 273
    College's establishment and early governance 40–45
Bedford College Magazine 234
Beethoven, Ludwig van 147, 151
Benn, Alfred 42, 179, 268–69, 275–76, 291, 298, 300–303

Bennett, Lucy 15
Bennett, William Sterndale 37, 41
Benslow House 183–84
Bentley, Thomas 297, 301
Bergson, Henri 287
Berry, Canon Alfred 235
Black, Clementia 288
Blackwood, John 170
Blagden, Isa 99, 139–40, 143, 146, 148
Blake, Sophia Jex 138, 175, 180
Blavatsky, Helena 272
Blind, Mathilde 138, 288–89, 306
Bodichon, Barbara 3, 44, 81, 128, 133, 153, 173, 174, 183, 187, 193, 201
Boer War 274
Bonham Carter, Alice 29–30, 41, 44, 47, 51, 67, 96, 160, 185, 286
Bonham Carter, Hilary 100, 102, 112
Bonham Carter, Hugh 68
Bookman, The 268
Boole, Lucy 286
Boole, Mary Ellen 285–86
Boole, Mary Everest 251, 253, 261, 272, 284, 297
Boucherett, Jessie 175, 180, 262
Bourne, Henry Fox 137
Bostock, Elizabeth 173, 183
Bright, Jacob 188
Bright, John 128
British Museum Reading Room 3, 138, 163, 272
Bronte, Charlotte 2, 59, 62–64, 65, 68, 70
    Villette 62–63
Bronte, Rev. Patrick 59, 62
Browne, Janet 228, 244
Browning, Elizabeth Barrett 1, 13, 70, 73, 99, 101–5, 109, 113–15, 118, 120–21, 140–52
    Last Poems 102, 110
Browning, Pen 99, 106, 113, 116, 140, 302
Browning, Reuben 101

Browning, Robert 1, 3–4, 25, 49, 54, 77, 97–98, 99–102, 107–8, 110–18, 122, 123, 128, 131–33, 151, 152, 157, 164, 166, 170, 177, 185, 187, 195, 201, 202, 205, 207, 216–17, 219, 251, 255, 257, 259, 274, 280, 293, 302–3, 305–6
  on the afterlife 104, 115
  Balaustion's Adventure 151
  The Inn Album 151
  last sighting of J W 152
  memories of his wife and claimed poetic inheritance from her 109, 114, 143, 145–46, 150, 151
  The Ring and the Book 112, 139–48, 150–53, 204, 209
  similarities between J W and Elizabeth Barrett Browning 70, 102–6, 110, 120–21, 146, 149
  varying interpretations of his friendship with J W 118–19, 147, 149–50
Browning, Sarianna 99, 140, 142
Bruce, Alexander Balmain 268
Bryce, James 174–75, 183, 191
Buckley, Arabella 81, 138, 247, 336 n93
Butler, Josephine 3, 173–75, 177–80, 189, 191, 282
Butler, Rev. George 174
Byerly sisters 17
Byerly, Tom 301

Caine, Barbara 4, 189
Caird, Mona 288
Campbell, Lady Archibald 279
Campbell, McLeod 123
Carlyle, Jane 13, 22, 25, 34, 164
Carlyle, Thomas 1, 4, 13, 35, 36, 48, 49, 52, 63, 123, 128, 148, 149, 164–66, 210, 251, 253, 260, 280, 296, 302
Carpenter, Lant 31
Carpenter, Mary 28, 263
Carpenter, William 88
Chamberlain, Joseph 192
Chambers, Robert
  Vestiges of the Natural History of Creation 82
Chapman Hall 101
Charity Organisation Society 272, 276
Chesterton, Gilbert Keith 272
Cheyne, Thomas 265
Christian Socialism 36, 50, 81, 96, 166, 184, 276
Church, Dean 287

Clarke, E. C. 184
Clough, Arthur Hugh 29, 54, 61, 172, 200, 219
Clough, Annie 191, 205
Clough, Blanche née Smith 29, 41, 205
Cobbe, Frances Power 3, 86, 135, 191, 219, 229, 251, 262–63, 306
  antivivisectionist 272, 280–81
  campaigner for female causes 128, 137, 170, 173–74, 192–93, 262–63
  domestic arrangements 133
  respect for J W 282
  upbringing 28, 90
  as a writer 81, 157–58, 175, 180, 188
Colenso, William 264
Coleridge, Samuel Taylor 31, 75, 160–62, 165–66, 196–97, 245, 253, 288, 300, 344n47
Coleridge, Sara 36
College for Working Women 187
Collins, Wilkie 167
Comte, Auguste and Comtism 93, 171–72, 203–5, 252–53, 260, 268, 276, 289
Contemporary Review 197, 207, 210, 261, 268, 274, 279
Conway, Mercure 146
Contagious Diseases Acts 173
Cook, Rachel 184–85, 187
Correlation of forces theory 233
Crum, May 274, 278, 297
Cumberland Place 103, 110, 115, 130, 139, 142–49, 213, 216–17

Darwin, Annie 14
Darwin, Bessie 285
Darwin, Caroline 7, 22, 234, 241, 310n17
Darwin, Catherine 7, 61
Darwin, Charles 2, 4, 7, 14, 18, 19–21, 49, 51, 81, 92, 95, 128, 167, 184, 190, 191, 195, 200, 202–3, 205, 209, 210, 216, 236–37, 253, 256, 261, 262–63, 280, 282, 285, 305–7
  death, funeral and posthumous evaluations 235–36, 239–41, 243–44, 246
  The Descent of Man 146, 171, 210, 227, 228–231, 234, 262
  The Expression of Emotions in Man and Animals 228, 232–33
  family row over presentation of Darwin's views on religion 237–39
  On the Origin of Species 81–89, 91, 138, 142, 165, 219, 228, 234, 239, 245, 304

'Recollections of the Development of my Mind and Character' 237–39, 241
relations with JW 12, 19, 21, 49, 74, 81, 86, 89, 92, 95, 159, 163, 166, 190, 203, 210, 227–34, 234, 237
The Variation of Animals and Plants under Domestication 228, 262
Darwin, Emma, née Wedgwood 7–9, 10–11, 19–21, 25, 82, 96, 195, 215, 216, 220–21, 231, 234, 239, 297, 300, 301
friendship with Fanny Wedgwood 19–20, 97, 234
marriage to Charles Darwin 19–20, 227, 235, 236, 243, 282
as a mother 14, 20, 21, 243
in old age 242–43
opinion of her brother, Hensleigh 17, 224, 262, 282–83
reactions to J W's publications 190, 241, 261, 269
views on religion 25, 228–29, 238, 240, 243
youth and education 17–18, 24, 34
Darwin, Erasmus, Charles Darwin's grandfather 301
Darwin, Erasmus ('Ras') Alvey, Charles Darwin's older brother 9–10, 19, 20, 23, 212, 218, 282
character and intellect 21, 235, 301
friendship with Hensleigh Wedgwood 21, 273
interest in and care for J W and her siblings 13, 17, 22, 26, 28, 35, 50, 52–54, 56, 61, 68, 73
involvement in women's higher education 40–42, 213
relationship with Fanny Wedgwood 21–22, 51, 68, 234
Darwin, Frank 227, 234, 235, 291, 293
composition of biography of Charles Darwin and family row over it 236–39, 241, 245
Darwin, George 227
Darwin, Horace 293
Darwin, Leonard 241
Darwin, Mary 21
Darwin, Robert, Charles Darwin's father 300
Darwin, Sukie née Wedgwood, Charles Darwin's mother 17
Darwin, Susan 51, 61, 76
Darwin, William 21, 190

Darwinism 140, 199, 209–10, 227, 231, 240–41, 244–47, 252, 259, 264, 271, 287, 289, 295, 304, 307
Davies, Emily 3, 128, 134, 135, 173, 174, 202–3, 219, 279
election to the London Education Board 181–82
establishment of Girton College Cambridge 182–87
Davies, Rev Llewelyn 50, 328n43
debate over the origins of speech 90–94
Dent, Edward 293
Dicey, Albert Venn 32, 128, 136, 191, 193, 271, 275, 286
Dicey, Eleanor née Bonham Carter 32, 41, 44, 136
Dickens, Katey 41
Dickinson, Goldsworthy Lowes 293
Dickinson, Lowes Cato 50, 206, 219, 275–6, 293
Disraeli, Benjamin 54, 191
Dobrée, Bonamy 110
Dodds, Marcus 268–69
Down House, the home of Charles and Emma Darwin 19, 20, 21, 86, 227, 239, 275, 280
Driver, Samuel Rolles 265, 268
Dutt, Romesh Chunder 294

Eastlake, Elizabeth, Lady 182
Eddy, Mary Baker 272
Edgeworth, Maria 8, 15, 16, 17, 28, 66, 72
Edgeworth, Richard 28
Eglinton, William 2
Eliot, George (Mary Ann Evans) 1, 2, 4, 20, 26, 27, 34, 42, 64, 72–73, 90, 138, 152, 157, 158, 164, 167, 170, 185, 207, 239, 251, 256, 262, 282, 288, 289, 302
Adam Bede 201
early career 41, 77, 201
the changing proprieties for calling on her 201–2, 205
friendship with JW 171, 195, 200–207, 207–8
her maxims 207
Middlemarch 144, 201–2, 204–5, 208
The Spanish Gypsy 152–53
Ellis, Havelock 285
The Englishwoman's Review 262
Epictetus 254, 261
Erskine, Annie 281

INDEX

Erskine, David 272, 340n6
Erskine, Fanny, J W's cousin and first wife of T. H. Farrer 47–48, 52, 56, 215–16
Erskine, Maitland, née Mackintosh 123
Erskine of Linlathen, Thomas 23–24, 30, 36, 63, 87, 123, 141, 195, 298
  as J W's mentor and spiritual counsellor 123–26, 164, 197–98
Erskine, William 123
Essays and Reviews 88
Euripides 112, 151, 278
Everett, Mrs and Mrs Turner, mediums 283–84
Ewald, Heinrich
  History of Israel 264

Faithfull, Emily 205, 278
Farrer, Ida 213, 215–17, 220
Farrer, Thomas Henry, Lord, husband of Effie Wedgwood 40, 52, 212–16, 274
Farrer, William 227
Fawcett, Millicent Garret 81, 191, 272, 279, 282
Fawcett, Philippa 272
Feuerbach, Ludwig 203–4
Flower, Euphrasia 144
Fordyce, John 239
Forster, Edwin Morgan 1–3, 4, 49, 52, 63, 73, 117, 213, 215–16, 251, 276, 291–92, 294, 296
  on J W 170, 221, 255, 274, 293, 296, 304, 306
  The Longest Journey 296–97
Forster, John 105
Forster, Laura 215, 292–93
Forster, William Edward 174
Fry, Roger 276
Furnival, Frederick 48, 50, 61, 63, 200

Galton, Francis 235, 282
Garrett, Agnes and Rhoda 272
Gaskell, Elizabeth 1, 2, 4, 17, 25, 28, 30, 42, 51, 55, 65, 69, 71, 128, 201, 212, 288, 302
  criticism of 75, 128
  friendship with Fanny Wedgwood 61
  as a mother 61, 74–75
  writing *Life of Charlotte Bronte* 57–59, 62–64
Gaskell, Flossy 61
Gaskell, Julia 61
Gaskell, Marianne 30, 61, 74, 332n5

Gaskell, Meta 30, 61–62, 64, 68, 71, 74–75, 128, 133, 212
Gaskell, Rev William 61–62, 83
Gibson, Emily 186–87
Geddes, Patrick 272, 274
Giraud-Teulon, Alexis 263
Girton College, Cambridge 44, 173, 182–83, 185
  at Hitchin 183–87
Gladstone, William Ewart 170, 190, 191–92, 256–57, 271, 282, 297
Goethe, Johann Wolfgang von 260, 263
Goldsmid, Lady 182
Gosse, Edmund and Philip 83
Gourlay, Jane 135, 195–96, 198, 220, 232
Governesses Benevolent Institution 36
Gower Street, Bloomsbury 20, 25, 49, 225, 269, 272, 273
Graham, William 236, 239
Gray, Asa 82–83, 87, 89, 92, 95, 230, 235, 239, 244, 246
Green, Thomas Hill 246, 253
Greg, William Rathbone 71, 264
Grote, George 149
Grove, George 50
Gurney, Edmund 282, 283
Gurney, Emily Russell 3, 74, 120, 121, 147, 149–152, 181, 188, 195, 202, 205, 208, 216, 220, 228, 232, 233, 241, 247, 282, 283, 284–86, 292
  as a campaigner for female causes 128, 134, 183–85
  friendship with J W 123, 126–30, 131–37, 141, 198, 276–77
  marriage to Russell Gurney 126–28, 134–36
Gurney, Russell 126–28, 130, 134–35, 288

Hardy, Thomas 271
Harding, Bessie 21
Hare, Julius 37, 95
Harris, José 2, 157, 271
Harrison, Frederic 287
Harrison, Jane 169, 272, 278
Hawkshaw Juliet 178–79
Hawkshaw, Mary, Godfrey Wedgwood's first wife 211
Hay, Matilda 133
Hearing aids 56, 76, 101, 151, 227, 303, 306
Hegel, Georg Wilhelm Friedrich 251, 253
Herford, Harold 3, 30, 269, 272, 276, 291, 293, 298, 304, 343n12

Herrmann, James 30
Herschel, Sir John 25, 86
Highgate Cemetery 199
Hill, Captain Charles 74–75
Hill, Octavia 17, 26, 50, 81, 153, 193, 201, 219, 221, 260–61, 276, 282
Hinton, Howard 284–86
Hinton, James 208, 272, 285–86, 287
Holland, Sir Henry 56, 315n3
Holland, Thurston 73, 332n5
Holland Park 225
Holmes, James, portrait painter 14
Homer 112, 251, 255–56
Hooker, Joseph Dalton 82, 84, 87, 230
Hopedene 216
Hort, Fenton 50, 183–84, 219
Hughes, Mary Ann ('Marian'), J W's companion 119, 211, 220–25, 274, 283–84, 286, 296
Hughes, Thomas 36, 77, 81, 128
Tom Brown's Schooldays 27, 66
Hunt, Thornton 201
Hurst & Blackett, publishers 64, 71
Hutton, Richard Holt 31, 34, 188, 191, 193, 254, 260, 280, 282, 285
  as J W's mentor 157–58, 162, 170, 172, 195, 197, 208–10, 251, 253, 256, 261, 287, 288, 296
Huxley, Thomas Henry 81–82, 84, 86, 88, 96, 182, 209, 219, 230, 232, 235, 236, 239, 241, 247, 280, 282–83, 287, 334n25

Idealism 86, 92, 94, 198, 245, 247, 253, 285, 296
Idlerocks, home of Hope and Godfrey Wedgwood 217, 223–25, 274–75, 293, 305
Ightham Mote 216
Ingall, Rosina, wife of Alfred Wedgwood 221, 224
Inglis, Mary ('MiLady') 51–52, 54, 108, 165, 196, 277
Inglis, Sir Robert 165, 196
International Journal of Ethics 296
Irish Home Rule 170, 271, 274, 279, 289
Irving, Edward 24, 123
Isbister and Company, publisher 267

James, Henry 143, 144, 168, 287
James, William 168, 282, 284, 287
Jervois, Kathleen 119, 277, 284

Jewsbury, Geraldine 71
Joachim, Joseph 205
Jones, Owen 201
Jowett, Benjamin 88, 92, 123, 126, 197, 213, 251, 253, 261, 265, 280, 285

Kant, Immanuel 33, 48, 86, 157, 198, 251, 253, 282
Karlin, Daniel 149
Keats, John 115–16
Kempis, Thomas à 207
The Kensington Society 128, 173, 183–84, 186
King's College, London 35, 38, 41
Kingsley, Charles 35–37, 48–50, 56, 81, 83–84, 88, 92, 123, 128, 165–66, 179, 181, 210, 219, 230, 261
Knatchbull-Hugessen, Edward 188

Ladies Education Association 28
Lamb, Charles 137, 235
Landor, Walter Savage 113, 302
Langham Place group 3, 173, 175
Langton, Rev. Charles 7, 119
Law, William 125, 233, 245
Leader 77
Lee, Vernon 167, 306
Lecky, William Hartpole 163
Leith Hill Place Surrey, home of John Wedgwood 26, 51, 216
Levy, Amy 278, 288
Lewes, George Henry 138, 201–4, 282
Lewes, Thornton 202
Lincoln, Abraham, President 134
Litchfield, Henrietta née Darwin 20, 135–6, 224, 229, 231–32, 238–39, 241, 243–44, 275, 291–92, 304
Litchfield, Richard 50, 136, 196, 200, 205, 219, 238, 276, 282, 297, 300
London Library 22, 138
London National Society for Women's Suffrage 189
London Quarterly 260
Linlathen 124–25, 129–30, 144
Linton, Eliza Lynn 70, 167, 206, 262, 288
Lloyd, Anna 184–85
Lodge, Oliver 282
Locker, Arthur 126
London Education Board 181–82
London Working Men's College 36, 49–50, 184, 293

London Working Women's College 36
London Quarterly Review 163, 268
Loyd, Mary 133
Lubbock, John 235
Lucretius 3, 239, 251, 256, 327n67
Ludlow, John 36, 63–65, 77, 81
Lumsden, Louisa 185–87
Lushington, Godfrey and Vernon 50, 200, 219, 269, 276
Lux Mundi 245
Lyell, Sir Charles 82, 90, 92–95, 128, 149, 227
  Principles of Geology 94–95, 227

Macaulay, Thomas Babbington 13, 25, 54
Mackintosh, Sir James, J W's maternal grandfather 7–9, 12, 13, 15, 23, 30, 38, 102, 119, 169, 326n54
  influence on J W's thought and writings 17, 190, 22–23, 259, 280, 288
  preference for his daughter, Fanny 8
  reputation as a "genius" 7
Mackintosh, Kitty, née Allen, J W's maternal grandmother 7, 56, 57, 280
Mackintosh, Robert 8, 26, 68
Macmillan, Alexander and Macmillan Publishers 81–82, 90, 95, 158–60, 163, 174, 298
Macmillan's Magazine 81, 84, 87, 90, 91–94, 179, 209
Maer Hall, Staffordshire, home of Jos Wedgwood 7–8, 12, 14, 17, 18, 19, 26, 82, 297, 300
  as Wedgwood family meeting place 7, 275
  the "Maer spirit" 241–42
Malthus, Thomas 3, 7, 9
Manning, Adelaide 128, 184
Manning, Charlotte 174, 183–85, 187, 202
Manning, Cardinal 209–10
Marcus Aurelius 252, 254, 256–57
Married Women's Property Act 188
Marsh, Anne 7, 12–13, 15, 64, 72, 315n3
Martin, Frances 187
Martineau, Harriet 1, 3, 24, 25, 28, 31, 34, 40, 68, 83, 166, 170, 302
  relations with her brother, James 13, 27
  friendship with Fanny Wedgwood 15, 17, 22, 29, 49, 51
  interest in and encouragement of J W 3, 9, 13–15, 28, 30, 75, 163
  as a writer 66, 158, 159, 288, 306
  ambivalent status as a role model 158, 163, 177, 193
  on deafness 56
Martineau, James 13, 18, 27, 35, 42, 61, 86, 166, 199, 209, 254, 280, 287
  as teacher 29–34, 38, 198, 307
  as religious thinker and leader 33–34, 40, 208, 253
Martineau, Rachel and her school in Liverpool 28–30, 34, 163
Masson, David 81, 90
Maudsley, Henry 285–86
Maurice, Edmond 65
Maurice, Frederick Denison 1, 4, 18, 30, 42, 48, 49–50, 56, 86–88, 119, 123–24, 128, 163, 165–66, 170, 184, 187, 195, 197–98, 208–10, 219, 221, 245, 258, 285, 302
  career 35–36, 38–40
  education for women 36–38, 40, 45, 182–83
  influence on J W 35, 38, 97, 104, 111, 198, 251–52, 254, 160, 267, 276, 288, 307
  J W's posthumous assessment of 165–66, 199–200
  promotes J W's writing career 76–77, 82, 87
Mayor, Joseph 297
Mazzini, Giuseppe 13
McCosh, James 171
Mendelssohn, Felix 207
Meredith, George 169
The Metaphysical Society 209, 285
Metcalfe, Fanny 183
Meteyard, Eliza 193, 297–300
Meynell, Alice 276, 288, 306
Mill, John Stuart 33, 91, 128, 174, 175, 181, 189, 207, 209, 262, 279, 289
  The Subjection of Women 177–79
Miller, Betty 106, 118, 143
Milsand, Joseph 139
Milton Bryan, home of Mary Inglis and Mary Rich 51–53, 108, 113, 196
Milton's *Paradise Lost* 24–25, 266
Modershall Church 293, 305
Mohl, Mary Elizabeth 101
Monckton Milnes, Richard, Lord Houghton 13, 100–101, 106, 302
Monthly Packet, The 260
Moore, Aubrey 227, 245–46
Moore, George 296
Moore, James 244, 246
More, Hannah 17

Morris, Emma, J W's maid 304
The Mortisection Society 286
Mount-Temple, Lady 282
Moxon, Edward 101
Mudie's Lending Library 64, 68
Müller, Max 91–94, 96, 228, 254, 287
Mullock, Dinah 138
Munby, Arthur 50, 187, 218–220, 224, 272, 274, 276
Munby, Hannah 219–20
Murray, John 159–60
Murray's Magazine 271
Myers, Frederic 203, 282, 284

National Observer 268
Neale, Edward 36
Neville-Sington, Pamela 118
Newman, Francis ('Frank') 35, 40–43, 49, 201, 245, 264, 280, 302, 307
Newman, John Henry 42, 54, 57, 112–13, 166, 172, 208, 209, 210
Newnham College, Cambridge 278
Nicholls, Rev Arthur 62
Nightingale, Florence 50, 55, 112, 177, 191, 193, 282, 306
Nightingale, Parthenope 55
Norris, W. W. 167
Norton, Charles Eliot 75, 201
Novikoff, Mme Olga 205
Nussey, Ellen 62

Oliphant, Lawrence 119
Oliphant, Margaret, writer 64, 157–58, 167, 170, 193, 206–7
Orr, Alexandra 101, 147, 205

Paley, William and Natural Theology 83, 86, 231, 245
Palgrave, Francis Turner 175
Pall Mall Gazette 163, 274
Parker, Robert 54, 212
Parkes, Bessie 133
Parslow, Joseph 21
Pater, Walter 251, 271
Pattison, Mrs Mark, née Emily Francis Strong 201
Penrose, Emily 272
Philo 253–54, 258
Plutarch 261
Podmore, Frank 282
Pollock, Sir Frederick 151

Ponsonby, Mary, wife of Sir Henry Ponsonby 205
Portes, Lucien de 137
Portsmouth, Eveline, Countess of 191, 279
Powell, Baden 88
Priestley, Joseph 18
Procter, Adelaide 116, 138

Queen Anne Street, 31, the Wedgwood family home in London 218, 283
Queen's College, London 28, 35, 45

Raverat, Gwen 221, 344n47
Reader 77
Reform Act of 1884 189–92
Reid, Elizabeth Jesser 28, 35, 40–42, 45
Rich, Claudius 23–24, 151
Rich, Mary, née Mackintosh, J W's step aunt 8–9, 12, 36, 40, 47, 56, 57, 68, 123, 160, 211, 220
  influence on J W 23, 34, 48, 51–52, 108, 121
  intervention in J W's friendship with Browning 108–9, 113
  in old age 195–96, 277
  views on religion 25, 126
  youth and early widowhood 23
Richardson, Anna 174
Ritchie, Anne Thackeray 164, 219, 278–79, 282
Robinson, Mary 272
Rogers, Samuel 13
Romilly, Lady, Elizabeth Amelia Jane 41
Roscoe, Ann Mary 208
Roscoe, Eliza 208
Roscoe, Edward Stanley 302
Rossetti, Christina 17, 81, 128, 138
Rossetti, Dante Gabriel 50, 219
Ruskin, John 1, 49–50, 63, 71, 128, 144, 164–66, 177, 209, 210, 269, 274, 276, 280, 282
Ruskin, Margaret née Cock, Ruskin's mother 63
Russell, Bertrand 287
Rutson, Albert 174

Salisbury, Robert Gascoyne-Cecil, Third Marquess of 191, 219
Sargent, John Singer 277
Saturday Review, The 70, 112, 137, 146, 157, 163, 170, 179–80, 182, 188, 252, 268
Schreiner, Olive 272, 278

Schwabe, Julie and Salis 54–55, 63, 100, 102, 272
Scott, Alexander 18, 24, 35, 36, 40, 41, 49, 52, 55, 63, 90, 95, 123, 158, 273
Scott, Ann 55–56, 63–64
Scott, Charles Prestwich 185
Scott, Sir Walter 164, 169
Seeley, John Robert 183, 184, 211, 257, 328n43
Sennett, Sophia 53, 71
Severn, Joseph 116
Shaen, Annie 63
Shakespeare, William 164, 169–70, 187
Shelley, Percy Byshe 145
Shirreff, Emily 3, 138, 185, 187, 282
Sidgwick, Henry and Eleanor 282
Simcox, Edith 191, 205, 208, 278
Sismondi, Jessie née Allen 19, 52, 57, 288
Smiles, Samuel 298
Smith, Bertha 29
Smith, Elder, publishers 68, 71, 140
Smith, Julia 29, 41
Smith, William Robertson 265, 268
Somerville, Mary 15
Southey, Robert
  The Life of Wesley 160–62
Spectator 170, 171, 188, 209, 227, 229, 234, 239, 244, 261, 272, 274, 281, 287, 288, 304
Spencer, Herbert 209, 246, 318n26
Spiritualism 271–72, 282–84
Spottiswoode family 56, 121
St Augustine 258–59, 260
Stanley, Arthur 123
Stanley Lady Augusta 124, 166, 197, 209
Stanley of Alderley, Lady 182
Stephen, Caroline 138, 276, 282, 293
Stephen, Fitzjames 165–66, 200, 302
Stephen, Leslie 39, 126, 128, 209, 238, 287
Sterling, John 35, 36, 38–39
Sterling, Hester 39, 51
Sterling, Julia 39, 51, 56, 71, 76, 110, 118, 201
Stevenson, Robert Louis 168, 271
Story, William 99
Strachey, Ray 193
Stewart, Balfour 233, 251
Stuart, Jessie née Crum 278
Swanwick, Anna 28, 31, 40–44, 128, 157, 173, 182, 191, 212, 255, 280
Swinburne, Algernon 101, 271
Synot, Henrietta 292

Tait, Peter 233
Taylor, Harriet 28
Temple, Frederick 88
Tennyson, Alfred, Lord 35, 37, 81, 91, 111–12, 128, 140, 163, 164, 209, 210, 256, 280, 282, 302
Thackeray, William Makepeace 35, 168
Thirlwall, Rev. Connop 99
Thornton, Henry 165
Thornton, Marianne 2, 9, 36, 48, 56, 68, 123, 193, 196, 292
The Times 180–81, 188, 229, 235, 304
Tollett, Ellen 25, 97, 158, 181, 197, 221, 234, 274
Townsend, Meredith 170
Trevelyan, George Otto 182
Trollope, Anthony 167
Trollope, Fanny 64
Trubner's, publisher 260
Turgenev, Ivan 207
Turnbull, Catherine 54, 73
Turner, Frank 253
Tyerman, Rev Luke
  The Life and Times of the Rev John Wesley M.A. Founder of the Methodists 160, 163
Tynan, Katherine 288
Tyndall, John 233, 287

Uglow, Jenny 2, 75
Unitarianism 18, 28–29, 31, 34, 83, 199

Vaughan Williams, Margaret and Ralph 235
Vicinus, Martha 132–33
Victoria Street Society, The (Society for the Protection of Animals Liable to Vivisection) 280
Virgil 254, 256–57, 260

Wallace, Alfred 82, 282
Ward, Mary, Mrs Humphrey 167–68, 191, 288
Ward, Maisie 118, 143
Waterhouse, Alfred 213
Watson, Rosamund 288, 306
Webb, Beatrice née Potter 54, 306
Webster, Augusta 157
Wedgwood, Alfred ("Tim"), J W's youngest brother 12, 26, 50, 52, 53, 221, 224, 273–74, 305
Wedgwood, Amy, J W's cousin 26
Wedgwood, Bertram ('Berry'), J W's nephew and ward 221, 224, 303, 305

Wedgwood, Bessie, née Allen, J W's grandmother 7, 9, 15
Wedgwood, Caroline, J W's cousin 74
Wedgwood, Cecil, J W's executor 224, 274, 285, 304–5
Wedgwood, Charlotte 7
Wedgwood, Cicely, J W's cousin 26
Wedgwood, Cicely Veronica
   on being a Wedgwood 25
Wedgwood, Claude 101
Wedgwood, Clement 136
Wedgwood, Eliza 224, 277, 302
Wedgwood, Elizabeth, J W's aunt 9, 12, 19, 20, 21, 51, 53, 181, 221, 227, 234
Wedgwood, Emily 212
Wedgwood, Ernest, J W's brother 12, 18, 20, 26, 27–28, 47, 50, 53, 67–68, 70, 221, 273–74
Wedgwood, Euphemia ('Effie'), Lady Farrer, J W's sister 12, 17, 26–28, 38, 44, 50, 52, 53, 62, 64, 68, 75–76, 96–97, 134, 173, 177, 185, 235, 261, 274, 277, 283, 297, 300
   at centre of her family 54–55, 118
   delayed marriage to T. H. Farrer 213–16
   JW changes will to include her 303–4
   in old age 305–6
   organises her sister's marriage to Godfrey 216–17
   relationship with JW 50–51, 55, 66, 71–72, 73, 102, 126, 128, 134, 211–15, 221, 261, 275, 305
   unsuccessfully courted by Godfrey Wedgwood 211–12
Wedgwood, Fanny (née Mackintosh), J W's mother 8, 18, 20–21, 26, 40, 44, 49, 52–54, 56, 73, 105, 123, 130, 151, 173, 178, 183, 196, 218–19, 220, 232–35, 264, 280
   close relationship with her father 7–9
   delayed marriage to Hensleigh Wedgwood 8–9
   encourages J W's literary career and her friendship with Browning 68, 76–77, 91, 99, 102, 105, 109, 160, 231
   as friend of Harriet Martineau and Mrs Gaskell 15–17, 22, 25, 29, 61
   ill health in last years and death 220, 283–84
   as a mother 9–15, 19, 21, 51, 55, 96–97
   pioneer in women's education 28, 35, 37–38, 41, 183
   tensions in relationship with J W 15, 76, 178, 264
   (*see also* Ras Darwin)
Wedgwood, Fanny, Emma Darwin's sister 17
Wedgwood, Frances Julia ('Snow')
Life
   birth and childhood 9–26
   schooling 27–34
   college education 37–45
   serious illness 56–57
   early career as a novelist 64–73
   paternal disapproval of her work 72, 90–91, 261–62
   switch to non-fiction 84–98, 157–58
   as a biographer 158–66
   periodical contributor 166–72
   tensions with her family 54–55, 75–76
   unconventional household 220–25
   deafness 56–7, 108, 303
   intense friendship with Browning 100–21, 139–53, 302–3
   sustaining relationship with Emily Gurney 126–36
   as a feminist 173–82, 188–94, 278–80, 294
   teaching at forerunner of Girton College 183–87
   religious doubts and depression 172, 195–200, 208
   changing attitudes towards Darwin and Darwinism 81, 86–90, 200, 209–10, 227–47, 252–3, 262–63, 295
   spiritualism and the afterlife 282–84
   productive final decade 291–302
   quiet death but contested will 303–4
Character
   awareness of evil 67–68, 88–89, 144, 151, 162, 166, 195–96, 199–200, 210, 224, 240, 254, 258, 261, 295, 303
   charm 110, 186, 202, 261, 268, 298, 302, 307
   concern with the afterlife 97, 104–5, 123, 158, 200, 235, 240, 243, 291
   critical acumen 93, 95, 120, 140, 150, 163–5, 197, 229, 266–7, 272
   depressions 52, 56–57, 76, 90, 102, 123–24, 130, 152, 195, 202, 295
   enjoyment of conversation 42, 54, 56, 62, 67, 76, 106, 126, 131–32, 204, 289, 303–4

Wedgwood, Frances Julia ('Snow') (*cont.*)
   extensive learning 3, 44–45, 57, 120, 251, 262, 269, 304, 307
   fondness for animals 220, 243, 280–81, 305
   impulsiveness 3, 105, 123, 277
   insecurity 72, 75, 106, 113, 121, 137, 204
   intellectualism 47, 120, 131, 153, 157, 163–4, 193, 210, 220, 228, 251, 307
   interest in the Wedgwood family and business 212, 217, 298
   liking for the company of older people 25, 51–52
   mentor to the young 277–78
   modesty 106, 221, 268–69, 307
   neediness and need to be needed 13, 26, 55, 74, 104, 119, 130, 131, 136, 198, 202, 221, 262–63, 277, 306
   sense of duty 22, 47, 57, 167, 241, 307
   sentimentality 143, 150, 224, 272, 288
   tendency to idolatry 97, 169, 195, 196, 200, 208, 210, 243
  Relationships
   Benn, A. W. 268–69, 275, 303
   Boole, Mary Everest 251, 253, 272, 284–8
   Browning, Robert 110–21, 139–153, 187, 205, 216–17, 255, 274, 302–3
   Cobbe, Frances Power 133, 157, 170, 188, 219, 272, 280, 282
   Charles and Emma Darwin 10–11, 19, 21, 74, 86, 89, 95, 159, 190, 195, 210, 220–21, 224, 227–34, 237, 239, 241–43, 244, 261, 269, 282
   Darwin, Erasmus ('Ras') 13, 17, 22–23, 26, 28, 52–54, 61, 73, 212, 235–36
   Davies, Emily 128, 174–75, 185–87, 204, 279
   Dickinson, Cato Lowes 50, 219, 275
   Eliot, George 153, 195, 200–208, 282
   Erskine, Thomas of Linlathen 123–26, 141, 143, 197–99, 201, 264
   Forster, E. M. 1–4, 170, 215, 221, 274, 292–93
   Gaskell, Elizabeth 51, 57–59, 61, 64, 75
   Gaskell, Meta 61–62, 64, 71, 74–75, 128
   Gurney, Emily 126–36, 195, 276–77, 284, 292
   Herford, Harold 272, 277, 293–96, 298, 303–4
   Hinton, Howard 284, 286
   Hill, Octavia 219, 260–61, 276
   Hughes, Mary Ann ('Marian') 220–25, 284, 296, 305
   Hutton, Richard Holt 157, 170, 172, 208–10, 256, 296
   Martineau, Harriet 3, 25, 30, 34, 158, 163–64, 193
   Martineau, James 30–34, 198, 307
   Maurice, F. D. 35–36, 38, 39, 49, 76–77, 97, 163, 198–200, 252, 254, 307
   Munby, Arthur 218–220, 274
   Newman, Francis (Frank) 41–43, 302, 307
   Rich, Mary 23–25, 51–52, 108–9, 196, 22
   Wedgwood, Effie Lady Farrer sister 50, 54–55, 66, 76, 102, 134, 211, 213–15, 303–5
   Wedgwood, Fanny mother 9–15, 18, 26, 28, 51–52, 54–6, 68, 73, 76–7, 96–7, 105, 109, 178, 220–21, 264, 283–84
   Wedgwood, Hensleigh father 9, 17–8, 34, 56, 62, 72–3, 90, 93, 105, 130, 224, 243, 261–2, 273, 302
   Wedgwood, Hope sister 50–51, 96, 130, 134, 160, 177, 211, 217, 220, 273–75, 278, 303, 305
   Wedgwood, Mackintosh eldest brother 12–13, 19, 27, 51, 53–54, 64, 70, 97, 110, 116, 195
  Writings
   articles on Darwin and Darwinism 82, 87–89, 227, 229–31, 239–41
   articles and letters in the *Spectator* 164, 170, 171, 188, 209–10, 234, 244, 272, 274, 280–81, 288
   articles on the origin of language 90–94, 318n47
   articles on Shakespeare, Virgil, Plutarch, Sir Walter Scott, William Law 169–70, 337n33, 261, 169, 125, 233
   Framleigh Hall 64–74
   Introduction to Alexander Scott's *Discourses* 90, 95–96, 158
   John Wesley and the Evangelical Reaction of the Eighteenth Century 158–64
   'Male and Female Created He Them' 229, 262–64, 279, 294
   The Message of Israel 157, 264–69
   The Moral Ideal 2, 34, 152, 157, 209, 251–62, 264, 274, 282, 291–97, 332n71
   new fiction reviews in *Contemporary Review* 164, 166–9

Nineteenth Century Teachers 174, 207, 210
An Old Debt 64–73, 106, 123
'The Old Order Changeth' 209–10, 246–47, 253, 276
The Personal Life of Josiah Wedgwood The Potter 280, 298–302
Wedgwood, Fanny ('Aunt Fanny Frank') 26
Wedgwood, Frank, J W's uncle 9, 26, 44, 71, 211, 297
Wedgwood, Godfrey, J W's cousin 9, 26, 27, 43, 51, 56, 71, 73, 96, 102, 119, 211–12, 223, 224, 274, 278
Wedgwood, Harry, J W's uncle 7, 26, 54, 63, 68, 74, 138
Wedgwood, Hensleigh, J W's father 13, 17, 24, 34, 36, 37, 41–42, 49, 51–52, 56, 62, 73, 82, 105, 123, 127, 130, 134, 184, 211, 213, 216, 218, 219, 231, 242–43, 261–62, 272–74, 284, 302
  credulity over Spiritualism 282–83
  On the Developement of Human Understanding 18
  Dictionary of Etymology 91
  disparagement of J W's abilities 28, 72, 91, 261
  early upbringing and rejection of career in the Potteries 7–8
  friendship with Ras Darwin 20, 22, 273
  interest in etymology 90–91, 93
  makes his home with J W as a widower 224
  marriage to Fanny Mackintosh 8–9, 61
  relationship with Charles Darwin 49, 82, 92, 227, 231–32
  stands on points of principle 18–19
Wedgwood, Hope, J W's youngest sister 12, 23, 28, 44, 51, 52, 53, 61, 96, 114, 173, 177, 211, 218, 223–24, 235, 273–74, 283–84, 293, 298, 303, 305
  closeness to sister Effie 26, 55, 130, 215–16, 306
  critic of J W's work 96, 160, 177
  marriage to Godfrey Wedgwood 216–7, 220, 275
  mixed feelings about J W in later years 274–5, 278, 303, 305
  tensions with J W 50–51, 68, 130, 134, 217, 220
Wedgwood, James Mackintosh ('Mack'), J W's oldest brother 12–14, 16, 19, 20, 26, 27, 50–51, 54–55, 64, 69–70, 96–98, 102–5, 110, 114, 116, 123, 195, 198

Wedgwood, James ('Jem'), J W's nephew and ward 224, 303, 305, 344n68
Wedgwood, Jessie, wife of Harry 7, 26
Wedgwood, John, J W's great uncle 301
Wedgwood, John, J W's uncle 7, 26
Wedgwood, John, J W's cousin 54
Wedgwood, Jos, J W's grandfather 7, 9, 15, 17–19, 166, 300–301, 344n47
  J W's memories of 25, 300, 301
Wedgwood, Josiah, the potter 298–302
Wedgwood, Josiah, J W's uncle 234
Wedgwood, Josiah C., M. P. 297
Wedgwood, Louisa, J W's cousin 26, 74
Wedgwood, Mary Euphrasia ('Bim') 277–78, 303, 305
Wedgwood, Richard 299
Wedgwood, Sarah Elizabeth, J W's great aunt 25, 300
Wedgwood, Tom 17, 297, 300
Welby, Victoria, Lady 272, 275–76, 286–87
Wellhausen, Julius 265–66
Wells, Gabriel 302–3
Wells, Herbert George 271, 287, 296
Wesley, John 158, 160–62, 185
Westcott, Rev. Brooke Foss 184, 245
Westminster Review 90–91, 93, 137, 163, 179
Whewell, William 83
Whitefield, George 162–63
Whitelands College 36–37
Wichelow, Lilly, mother of E. M. Forster 283, 292
Wilberforce, Samuel 84
Wilde, Oscar 271, 278–9
Williams, Charles 282
Wilson, Rev Thomas 41
Winkworth, Catherine 2, 31, 33, 42, 62–63, 74, 133, 158
Winkworth, Susanna 42, 63, 158, 174, 199
Wolstoneholme, Elizabeth 175
The Woman's World 278–79
Woodall, William 191
Woodhead, Sarah 186
Woolf, Virginia 90, 170, 278, 340n32
Wordsworth, Dorothy 17
Wordsworth, William 101, 234, 245, 256

Yonge Charlotte 25–26, 27, 167, 261, 288
Yorke, Harriet, Octavia Hill's companion 221

Zola, Emil 167

www.ingramcontent.com/pod-product-compliance
Lightning Source LLC
Chambersburg PA
CBHW050834230426
43667CB00012B/2000